Introduction to Philosophy

Introduction to Philosophy

James E. White
St. Cloud State University

West Publishing Company
Saint Paul   New York   Los Angeles   San Francisco

Copyeditor: Rosalie Maggio
Interior Design: David J. Farr, Imagesmythe, Inc.
Indexer: Hazel Blumberg-McKee

Library of Congress Cataloging-in-Publication Data

White, James E.
    Introduction to philosophy/James E. White
       p. cm.
    Includes bibliographies and index.
    ISBN 0-314-48150-8
    1. Philosophy—Introductions.   I. Title.
  BD21.W46 1989
    100—dc19

88-28265
CIP

Contents

Chapter 5
The Mind-Body Problem 171

Chapter 6
Personal Identity and Survival of Death 219

Chapter 7
The Basis for Morality 257

Chapter 8
What Should I Do? 295

Preface

This text is designed to introduce philosophy to students with little or no previous experience in the subject. It presents classical and contemporary readings on some of the main problems in philosophy: Does God exist? (chapter 1), Why does a good God allow evil to exist? (chapter 2), Can we know anything with absolute certainty or is every belief subject to doubt? (chapter 3), Is scientific determinism compatible with human freedom? (chapter 4), What is the mind, and how is it related to the body? (chapter 5), Is there any personal survival after death? (chapter 6), What is the basis of morality? (chapter 7), and What is the right thing to do? (chapter 8). Philosophers have been trying to find satisfactory answers to these questions for centuries. In fact, philosophy can be described as the attempt to answer such basic and important questions.

The readings contain many classics that are required reading for philosophy students, and as such are to be found in other introductory philosophy books. These classical readings include the selections by Plato, Aristotle, St. Anselm, St. Thomas Aquinas, St. Augustine, Hume, Pascal, Descartes, Locke, Mill, and Kant. To alleviate the difficulties students encounter in trying to read and understand these great classics of the past, the text offers commentaries by contemporary philosophers—for example, Wallace Matson restates and explains St. Anselm's ontological argument and O. K. Bouwsma critically examines Descartes' evil genius argument. The text also offers the following pedagogical aids:

Prologue. The prologue to the book explains the nature of philosophy, its traditional areas, and the value of studying philosophy. It also covers basic concepts and distinctions in logic.

Introductions. The chapter introductions explain the philosophical problem to be discussed in the chapter and the different philosophical solutions or positions on the problem. Thus the introduction for the first chapter presents five different positions that philosophers have taken on the existence of God.

Questions on the Readings. The questions following each reading not only test the student's understanding, but also pose difficulties, make comparisons with other readings, and so on. They are designed to stimulate thought and discussion. They could also be used for essay examinations.

Suggested Readings. These are not comprehensive bibliographies, but rather further readings that beginning students can usefully consult—the sort of readings that might have been included in the text.

Glossary. The glossary at the end of the text covers important technical terms in philosophy. Somewhat more detailed than usual, it is intended to go beyond what the student can learn by consulting the dictionary.

Besides the required classics, an attempt has been made to include up-to-date and important readings by contemporary authors. In this category is John Searle's "Can Computers Think?" Thomas Nagel's "What Is It Like to Be a Bat?" Daniel Dennett's "Where Am I?" and Onora O'Neill's "Kantian Approaches to Some Famine Problems."

Many authors in the text use masculine pronouns in a "neutral" sense to refer to both men and women and use "man" and "mankind" instead of "human being." Although these and other similar linguistic practices were accepted as standard English in the past, now many people consider such usages to be sexist and thus objectionable. I have avoided sexist, or exclusive, language in the prologue, chapter introductions, questions on the readings, suggested readings, and glossary.

In preparing the manuscript, I received help and support from a number of people. It is a pleasure to acknowledge them here. Elena White helped with the photocopying and proofreading. Barbara Seefeldt gave secretarial assistance. Professor Myron Anderson offered suggestions and lent books. Numerous anonymous reviewers gave extensive critiques of different versions of the book. It was a challenge to try to accommodate these reviewers. Nancy E. Crochiere, developmental editor at West Publishing Company, conducted a useful survey of philosophy teachers to see what sort of book was desired. Finally, Clark Baxter, my editor at West Publishing Company, was an unfailing source of encouragement and good advice.

Prologue

What is philosophy? The word "philosophy" is derived from two Greek words, *philos* meaning "love or pursuit" and *sophia* meaning "wisdom." In its original sense, then, "philosophy" means "the love or pursuit of wisdom," and a philosopher is someone who loves or pursues wisdom. The emphasis has usually been on the activity of pursuing wisdom rather than on the emotion that motivates the pursuit.

To better understand what the philosophical pursuit of wisdom involves, we can consider the life and teachings of Socrates (469–399 B.C.), one of the first great Greek philosophers. The historical Socrates left no writings of his own, but it is generally accepted that Socrates' life and teachings are more or less accurately presented in the early dialogues of his student Plato (427–347 B.C.), particularly in the *Apology,* the *Crito,* and the *Phaedo.* One of Socrates' most famous sayings is that "the unexamined life is not worth living." This examination of life in Greek philosophy involves the critical examination of ordinary concepts, beliefs, and assumptions, and the attempt to discover what makes life worthwhile. How is this done? Socrates thought that the rational questioning of common assumptions and beliefs (which has come to be called "Socratic questioning") could expose unthinking prejudices and produce more justifiable beliefs; this in turn would make life more worthwhile.

Following Socrates, we can regard philosophy as the critical examination of the basic assumptions of ordinary life and science, and the attempt to justify these assumptions or replace them with more justifiable beliefs. For example, many people believe that a life of wealth, fame, and power is the good life. Plato and his student Aristotle (384–322 B.C.) both discuss this belief and reject it as false. (See the reading by Aristotle in chapter 8.) In Judaism, Christianity, and Islam, it is believed that there exists a supreme personal God who created the universe. But how can this belief be justified? Another article of faith in religion is that people have an immortal soul that survives death. Can the truth of this belief be given a rational demonstration or not? In ordinary life we often make value judgments about right and wrong, good and bad. How can we correctly distinguish between what is right and what is wrong or between what is good and what is bad? In morality and the law, it is assumed that persons are free when they act, that they are morally responsible for what they do, and that punishment is morally acceptable. Are these beliefs really justified in view of the scientific assumption that all events, including human actions, are caused? All these questions are discussed in the text.

Although most philosophers will agree that assumptions should be critically examined and replaced with more justifiable beliefs, they do not agree about which beliefs are justifiable or about which assumptions are not justifiable. Unlike other disciplines, there is little consensus or agreement in philosophy about what is true or even reasonable. There are no final or definitive answers in philosophy; in a sense, it is still a young discipline even though it is about 2,500 years old.

The areas of philosophy. It is customary to describe a discipline in terms of its subject matter; for example, astronomy can be defined as the study of celestial bodies. In this section we will look at the main areas of philosophy: metaphysics, epistemology, ethics, aesthetics, social and political philosophy, and logic.

Metaphysics is the study of the nature of reality. One of the first philosophers to systematically deal with various questions about reality was Aristotle. According to a traditional story, when the works of Aristotle were being edited, a number of essays didn't seem to fit in any other books, so they were put together right after Aristotle's book on physics. Since the new book was after the physics book, it was called Metaphysics—"meta" means "after," so "metaphysics" means "after physics." The modern study of metaphysics consists largely of topics discussed by Aristotle in the book after physics. Following Aristotle, some of the main questions in metaphysics are: What sorts of things exist in the world? What is the difference between a substance and its attributes? What is the nature of space and time? What is causation? What is truth?

Epistemology, or the theory of knowledge, takes up questions about knowledge. Since Plato it has been thought that knowledge is justified true belief. Accordingly, epistemology includes the study of belief, truth, and justification. There are also issues about the origin and scope of knowledge. How do we get knowledge? Is all knowledge derived from sense-perception or not? In the history of philosophy we find a basic disagreement: empiricist philosophers like Aristotle believe that sense-perception is the foundation of knowledge, while rationalist philosophers like Plato hold that reason functions independently of sense-perception to produce knowledge. Another issue is about how much we can know. Are there some things beyond all possible knowledge, for example, the nature of God?

Ethics, or moral philosophy, is the study of moral values such as right and wrong, good and bad. It begins with the Platonic dialogues in which Socrates, the main protagonist of the dialogues, attempts to discover the meaning of his own life and the conditions that make life worth living. The Socratic question "How ought one to live?" is one of the main problems in ethics. As portrayed by Plato, Socrates was also interested in other question such as: What is justice? What actions are right? These are central questions in ethics. Modern ethics also discusses questions such as: What is intrinsically good? What are the fundamental human rights? What is the relation between law and morality? What is the relation between religion and morality?

Two areas of philosophical interest are related to ethics insofar as they are concerned with values. *Aesthetics* is the philosophical study of art; it includes an examination of the nature of beauty and an attempt to discover the nature of art. *Social and political philosophy* deals with such important questions about the nature and justification of the state as: How did the state arise? When do the needs of the state override the rights of an individual and when should the rights of the individual prevail?

Finally, *logic* is the formulation and application of the principles of right reasoning. As such, logic has a different relation to philosophy than the other branches. The other fields of study examine some object—reality, knowledge, values, etc. But traditionally logic has been a tool or method used by philosophers in their pursuit of truth. When Aristotle first formulated the principles of logic in a systematic way, the writings in which he did this came to be called the *Organon,* which means (in Greek) "instrument" or "tool." With the rise of mathematical and symbolic logic, logic itself has become an object of philosophical study. Hence even though logic is one of the tools used by philosophers, it has also become one of its fields of study.

The method of philosophy. When students begin a course in a discipline they usually have some idea about the methods that will be used. In geometry, one constructs proofs of theorems starting with axioms and postulates; in chemistry, one does experiments; in astronomy one looks at the stars. We might say that in the empirical sciences like physics and chemistry, one tests hypotheses by making observations and conducting experiments, using what can be called the method of the empirical sciences, while in exact sciences like geometry and mathematics, one constructs deductive proofs and makes calculations, using the method of the exact sciences.

Which method is used in philosophy? Philosophy does not use the method of the empirical sciences—there is no testing of hypotheses by making observations and conducting experiments. Some philosophers have explicitly claimed to be using the method of the exact sciences. For example, in his *Discourse on Method,* the French philosopher and mathematician René Descartes (1596–1650), who is considered the founder of modern philosophy, develops a plan for discovering truths in philosophy that bears some resemblance to the method used in geometry. First, he discards all his beliefs that are subject to doubt until nothing remains but absolutely certain truths. He says that this is like throwing all the apples out of a basket in order to find the apples that are not rotten. Second, he begins with the absolutely certain truths. As it turns out, he finds only one such truth, namely that the sentence "I exist" is true when I say it or think of it. Then he deduces other truths, for example, that God exists and is not a deceiver.

There is one feature of Descartes' method that is characteristic of almost all philosophy, and that is the use of arguments or what he called proofs. Thus we cannot go very far in philosophy without knowing something about arguments.

Some basic logical concepts and distinctions. The following brief review of the basic concepts and distinctions in logic is not intended to replace a course in logic; it merely presents some essentials for understanding the readings in the book.

To begin with, the authors of the readings often discuss arguments, for example, in the first chapter there is much discussion of arguments for and against the existence of God. An argument is a series of statements, one of which, the **conclusion**, is supposed to be established by the other statements, the **premises.** In our readings for chapter 1, St. Thomas Aquinas gives the following argument for saying that God does not exist: "If God existed, there would be no evil discoverable; but there is evil in the world. Therefore God does not exist." In this argument the conclusion, as indicated by the word "therefore," is "God does not exist." There are two premises. One is "If God existed, there would be no evil discoverable [in the world]." The other is "there is evil [discoverable] in the world."

In logic, arguments are classified as either deductive or inductive. A **deductive argument** claims to demonstrate that if the premises are true, then the conclusion must be true. St. Thomas' argument about the existence of evil is a deductive argument. It is also a **valid argument**, that is, if the premises are really true (and of course it is possible that they are not in fact true), then the conclusion must be true. It should be emphasized that a valid argument does not necessarily have true premises. St. Thomas would deny that the first premise of his argument, the one about the incompatibility of God's existence with the existence of evil, is true. But if it is true, which it may not be, then conclusion must be true. A valid argument that does have true premises is called a **sound argument.** Here is an example of a sound argument: "All human beings are mortal; Ronald Reagan is a human being; Therefore, Ronald Reagan is mortal." A deductive argument that is not valid is said to be invalid. In other words, an **invalid deductive argument** is one that can have true premises and a false conclusion. Another common way of putting it is to say that an invalid deductive argument is one in which the conclusion does not follow logically from the premises, while a valid deductive argument is one in which the conclusion does follow logically from the premises.

Now we can better understand the issue between Gaunilo and St. Anselm in the first reading for chapter 1. St. Anselm believes that his ontological argument is valid (and sound!) while Gaunilo insists that it is invalid, that the conclusion does not follow from the premises. This does not mean that Gaunilo denies that God exists; he is only denying that the conclusion "God exists" follows from Anselm's premises.

The other type of argument we encounter in the readings is inductive. An **inductive argument** does not claim that its conclusion must be true, but only that the conclusion has been established to be true with some degree of probability. These arguments are sometimes said to be "valid" or "invalid," but it seems better to reserve those terms for deductive arguments, and classify inductive arguments as, let us say, strong or weak. Roughly speaking, a strong inductive argument would establish the truth of its conclusion with a relatively high degree of probability, while a weak inductive argument would establish its conclusion with only a relatively low degree of probability.

There are various kinds of inductive arguments. One fairly common type is the argument from analogy, which goes more or less like this: Two things, A and B, have certain properties in common, a, b, and c. But A has a further property, d. So B (by analogy) also has this property d. In the readings for chapter 1, William Paley is usually interpreted as giving an argument from analogy that can be summarized as follows: A watch is designed for a certain purpose (telling time) and the eye is also designed for a certain purpose (vision), but the watch was made by a watchmaker, so the eye has the further property too—it was made by an Intelligent Creator.

The value of philosophy. Why should you study philosophy? First, the study of philosophy can have useful practical effects. Before you study philosophy your beliefs may include mere prejudices, unthinking assumptions, and irrational beliefs. The study of philosophy can free you from at least some of these. The more rational beliefs you acquire after studying philosophy may change your life. After studying ethics, for example, you may behave differently. In general, philosophy has had an enormous practical impact on the world: most of the ideas and theories that lie behind the political, legal, and educational institutions of the modern world were first formulated by philosophers. Second, some things are worth doing just for their own sake, and philosophy is one of them. As Aristotle said, philosophy begins with a sense of wonder. The study of philosophy helps satisfy this sense of wonder about human beings and their place in the universe.

The Existence of God

Chapter 1

Introduction

The problem. Many people in our society, perhaps even the majority of people, would say that they believe in the existence of God. Most believers would also agree that God, as they understand God, is a Supreme Being who created the universe and who is **omnipotent** (all-powerful), **omniscient** (all-wise), and **omnibenevolent** (all-good). There are disagreements about the other attributes of God. For instance, God is traditionally thought of as male, but some feminist theologians insist that God is female. Perhaps it is better to think of God as being neither male nor female, but as a Spirit that does not have any body or sex. Maybe God is a not a person at all, as pantheists believe. **Pantheism** is the view that God is identical with Nature or with the whole universe. Another alternative to the traditional conception of God is **deism.** According to this view, God created the universe and that is all; God does nothing further in the universe, such as working miracles or answering prayers.

In this chapter, we will not be concerned with seemingly unresolvable issues about God's attributes or about alternative conceptions of God. Instead we will concentrate on the traditional philosophical problem of whether God exists or not. To do this we need to decide upon some conception of God; otherwise, we will not know which God we are talking about. Let us agree for the sake of discussion that we are talking about God as usually conceived, that is, about God as the Supreme Creator who is omnipotent, omniscient, and omnibenevolent. This seems to be how God is understood in the main monotheistic religions of the world— Christianity, Judaism, and Islam.

Now our problem can be stated very simply: Does God exist or not?

Views of God's existence. It is standard to distinguish between five different responses to the problem about God's existence: theism, fideism, atheism, agnosticism, and noncognitivism. **Theism** is the view that God can be known to exist. In our readings, St. Anselm, St. Thomas Aquinas, Taylor, and Paley are theists. Even though he attacks Anselm's ontological argument, the monk Gaunilon believes that God exists on the basis of faith; his rejection of Anselm's argument does not conflict with his belief in God. Those who believe that God exists on the basis of faith rather than reason are said to be fideists, that is, their position is **fideism** rather than theism. To justify their belief, they appeal to faith alone rather than to reason. (For another example of fideism, see the reading by Kierkegaard in chapter 2.) **Atheism** is the view that God does not exist. Ernest Nagel is the only representative of this position in our readings.

A different position, held by Bertrand Russell and Thomas Huxley (see the suggested readings at the end of the chapter), is **agnosticism.** According to this view, neither God's existence nor God's nonexistence can be proved; we do not know if God exists or not. It may appear that agnosticism is compatible with fideism, but most agnostics would reject fideism because they hold that it is irrational and thus unacceptable to believe something without proof or evidence. Finally, **noncognitivism,** the view advocated by Flew, contends that it is not meaningful to talk about God. Thus, according to this view, the preceding positions on the existence of God are all meaningless.

A priori versus a posteriori. In the prologue to the book, we reviewed the basic logical concepts and distinctions essential to understanding the readings in this chapter. One more useful distinction—the one between a priori and a posteriori—should be mentioned. This is not a logical distinction, but one about how things are known to be true (or false). It is applied to both statements and arguments. A statement is **a priori** if it can be known to be true (or false) independently of experience. Thus the statement "God is omnipotent" is a priori because it is true by definition; it is true given the definition of the word "God" that we have adopted. A statement is **a posteriori** if we discover its truth or falsehood by appealing to experience or empirical evidence. For instance, St. Thomas' statement "There is evil in the universe" can be shown to be true by referring to various evils in the world—disease, disasters, pain, suffering, and so on.

The distinction between a priori and a posteriori is also applied, by extension, to arguments. An argument is a priori if its premises are a priori. In our readings, Anselm's ontological argument is classified as a priori because the premises are true as a matter of definition or logic and not because they refer to facts in the world. An argument is a posteriori if its premises are a posteriori. Paley's argument from design is a posteriori and so are St. Thomas' first three ways of proving God's existence.

St. Anselm and Gaunilon

A Debate on Anselm's Proof for the Existence of God

St. Anselm (1033–1109) was Abbot of Bec and later Archbishop of Canterbury. He is mainly known for

Reprinted with permission of The Free Press, A Division of Macmillan, Inc., from *Medieval Philosophy* by John F. Wippel and Allan B. Wolter. Copyright © 1969 by The Free Press.

the Proslogion, *in which his ontological argument occurs, and for other theological and philosophical works, including* Why God Became Man. *Not much is known about Gaunilon except that he was an eleventh-century Benedictine monk.*

St. Anselm's Ontological Argument

Some time ago at the pressing invitation of some brethren I did a small work as a sample of meditation based on faith. The work was written in the person of one seeking to throw light on an area of ignorance by silently reasoning with himself. Reflecting that what I had woven together was really a chain of many arguments, I began to ask myself whether one might not be able to find a single argument, needing no proof beyond itself, which would suffice by itself to link together such conclusions as that God truly exists, that he is the highest good—needing no other but needed for the existence and well-being of all else—and whatever else we believe to be true of the divine being. Diligently and often did I pursue this quest. Sometimes the solution seemed almost at hand; at other times it simply eluded the grasp of my mind. Finally I decided in despair to cease the search for something so impossible to find. But when I tried to put the matter out of mind lest I waste time that might profitably be spent on other matters in such a fruitless quest, it continued to importune me despite my unwillingness and efforts at resistance. And so it was that one day when I was weary of struggling against this obsession the solution I had despaired of finding suddenly appeared amidst the welter of my conflicting thoughts and I eagerly seized the idea I had been so strenuously fending off.

Thinking that, if I put down in writing what I was so happy to find, others too would find pleasure reading it, I did the following little tract which takes up this and some allied matters from the viewpoint of one who tries to bring his mind to contemplate God and seeks to understand what he believes. Neither this nor the earlier treatise seemed to deserve to be called a book or bear their author's name. Still I felt they should not be put out without some title to invite those in whose hands they fell to read them. To each I gave a name, calling the first *An Example of Meditation Based on Faith* and the second *Faith Seeking Understanding*. But when both had been copied frequently under these titles, I was urged to add my own name thereto, especially by Hugh, the reverend archbishop of Lyons and apostolic delegate to France, who commanded me by his apostolic authority to do so. That this might be more fittingly accomplished, I called the earlier work *Monologion* (i.e. a soliloquy) and the present work *Proslogion* (i.e. an allocution). . . .

O Lord, who grants understanding to faith, make me, so far as is good for me, to understand that you exist, as we believe, and that you are what we believe you to be. Now we believe you to be something greater than which we can conceive of nothing. Could it be then that there is no such nature, since "the fool says in his heart, 'There is no God' " [Ps. 13:1]? But surely this same fool, when he hears me say this, "something than which we can conceive of nothing greater," understands what he hears and what he understands is in his understanding even if he does not understand it to exist. For it is one thing for something to be in the understanding and quite another to understand that the thing in question exists. When a painter thinks of the work he will make beforehand, he has it in his understanding, but he does not think that what he has yet to make exists. But once he has painted it, he not only has it in his understanding but he understands that what he has made exists. Even the fool then must be convinced that in his understanding at least there is something than which nothing greater can be conceived, for when he hears this, he understands it and whatever is understood is in the understanding. But surely if the thing be such that we cannot conceive of something greater, it does not exist solely in the understanding. For if it were there only, one could also think of it as existing in reality and this is something greater. If the thing than which none greater can be thought were in the mind alone, then this same thing would both be and not be something than which nothing greater can be conceived. But surely this cannot be. Without doubt then there exists both in the understanding and in reality a being greater than which nothing can be conceived.

So truly does such a thing exist that it cannot be thought of as not existing. For we can think of something as existing which cannot be thought of as not existing, and such a thing is greater than what can be thought not to be. Wherefore, if the thing than which none greater can be thought could be conceived of as not existing, then this very thing than which none greater can be thought is not a thing than which none greater can be thought. But this is not possible. Hence, something greater than which nothing can be conceived so truly exists that it cannot be conceived not to be.

O Lord, our God, you are this being. So truly do you exist that you cannot even be thought of as nonexistent. And rightly so, for if some mind could think of something better than you, then the creature would rise above the Creator and would judge him, which is absurd. It is possible indeed to think of anything other than you as nonexistent. Of all beings then you alone have existence in the truest and highest sense, for nothing else so truly is or has existence in so great a measure. Why then does the fool "say in his heart, 'There is no God,' " when it is so evident to a reasoning mind that of all things you exist in a supreme degree? Why indeed save that he is stupid and a fool! . . .

Gaunilon's Reply

1. If one doubts or denies there is some such nature that nothing greater than it can be conceived, he is told that the existence of this being is proved, first, from the fact that in doubting or denying such he already has such a being in his understanding, for in hearing about it, he understands what is said. Next he is told that what he understands must needs exist not only in the intellect but in reality as well. And the proof of this is that a thing is greater if it also exists in reality than if it were in the understanding alone. Were it only in the intellect, even something that once existed would be greater that it. And so what is greater than all is less than something and thus not really greater than everything, which is clearly contradictory. It is necessary then that something greater than all, already proved to exist in the understanding, exists in reality as well, for otherwise it could not be greater than all. To this he might reply: . . .

They say that somewhere in the ocean there is an island, which because of the difficulty, or better, the impossibility of finding what does not exist, some call the lost island. And they say this island is inestimably wealthy, having all kinds of delights and riches in greater abundance even than the fabled "Fortunate Islands." And since it has no possessor or inhabitant, it excels all other inhabited countries in its possessions. Now should someone tell me that there is such an island, I could readily understand what he says, since there is no problem there. But suppose he adds, as though it were

already implied: "You can't doubt any more that this island, which is more excellent than any land, really exists somewhere, since you don't doubt that it is in your understanding and that it is more excellent not to be in the understanding only. Hence it is necessary that it really exists, for if it did not, any land which does would excel it and consequently the island which you already understand to be more excellent would not be such." If one were to try to prove to me that this island in truth exists and its existence should no longer be questioned, either I would think he was joking or I would not know whether to consider him or me the greater fool, me for conceding his argument or him for supposing he had established with any certainty such an island's existence without first showing such excellence to be real and its existence indubitable rather than just a figment of my understanding, whose existence is uncertain.

7. This then is an answer the fool could make to your arguments against him. When he is first assured that this being is so great that its nonexistence is inconceivable, and that this in turn is established for no other reason than that otherwise it would not excel all things, he could counter the same way and say: "When have I admitted there really is any such thing, i.e. something so much greater than everything else that one could prove to me it is so real, it could not even be conceived as unreal?" What we need at the outset is a very firm argument to show there is some superior being, bigger and better than all else that exists, so that we can go on from this to prove all the other attributes such a bigger and better being has to have. As for the statement that it is inconceivable that the highest thing of all should not exist, it might be better to say its nonexistence or even its possibility of nonexistence is unintelligible. For according to the true meaning of the word, unreal things are not intelligible, but their existence is conceivable in the way that the fool thinks that God does not exist. I most certainly know I exist, but for all that, I know my nonexistence is possible. As for that supreme being which God is, I understand without doubt both his existence and the impossibility of his nonexistence. But whether I can conceive of my nonexistence as

long as I most certainly know I exist, I don't know. But if I am able to, why can I not conceive of the nonexistence of whatever else I know with the same certainty? But if I cannot, then such an inability will not be something peculiar to God. . . .

Anselm's Reply to Gaunilon

But you claim our argument is on a par with the following. Someone imagines an island in the ocean which surpasses all lands in its fertility. Because of the difficulty, or rather impossibility, of finding what does not exist, he calls it "Lost Island." He might then say you cannot doubt that it really exists, because anyone can readily understand it from its verbal description. I assert confidently that if anyone finds something for me, besides that "than which none greater is conceivable," which exists either in reality or concept alone to which the logic of my argument can be applied, I will find and give him his "Lost Island," never to be lost again. But it now seems obvious that a thing such that none greater can be conceived cannot be thought of as nonexistent since it exists on such firm grounds of truth. For otherwise it would not exist at all. If anyone says he thinks it does not exist, then I declare that when he thinks this he either thinks of something than which a greater is inconceivable, or else he does not think at all. If he does not think, then neither does he think that what he is not thinking of is nonexistent. But if he does think, then he thinks of something which cannot be thought of as not existing. For if it could be conceived as nonexistent, it could be conceived as having a beginning and an end. Now this is impossible. Hence if anyone thinks of it, he thinks of something that cannot even be conceived to be nonexistent. Now whoever conceives it thus doesn't think of it as nonexistent, for if he did he would conceive what can't be conceived. Nonexistence is inconceivable, then, of something greater than which nothing can be conceived.

You claim moreover that when we say this supreme reality cannot be conceived of as nonexistent, it would be perhaps better to say that its nonexistence or even the possibility of its nonexistence is not understandable. But it is better to say it cannot be conceived. For had I said that the reality itself could not be understood not to exist, perhaps you, who insist that according to proper usage what is false cannot be understood, would object that nothing existing could be understood not to exist. For it is false to claim that what exists does not exist. Hence it would not be peculiar to God to be unable to be understood as nonexistent. If any one of the things that most certainly exist can be understood to be nonexistent, however, then other certain things can also be understood to be nonexistent. But this objection cannot be applied to "conceiving," if this is correctly understood. For though none of the things that exist can be understood not to exist, still they can all be conceived as nonexistent, except the greatest. For all—and only—those things can be conceived as nonexistent which have a beginning or end or consist of parts or do not exist in their entirety in any time or place, as I have said. Only that being which cannot be conceived to be nonexistent must be conceived as having no beginning or end or composition of parts but is whole and entire always and everywhere.

Consequently you must realize that you can conceive of yourself as nonexistent, though you most certainly know that you exist. You surprise me when you say you are not sure of this. For we conceive of many things as nonexistent which we know to exist and of many things as existent which we know do not exist. And we conceive them thus not by judging but by imagining them so. We can indeed conceive of something as existent even while we know it does not exist, because we are able to conceive the one at the same time that we know the other. But we cannot conceive nonexistence while knowing existence, because we cannot conceive existence and nonexistence at the same time. If anyone distinguishes between the two senses of the statement in this fashion, then, he will understand that nothing, as long as it is known to be, can be conceived not to be, and that whatever exists, with the exception of a thing such that no greater is conceivable, can be conceived of as nonexistent even when it is known to exist. This inability to be conceived of as nonexistent, then, is peculiar to God, even though there are many objects which cannot be conceived not to be while they are. As for the way in which God can still be said to be conceived as not existing, I believe this has been explained clearly enough in my little book itself.

Study Questions on St. Anselm and Gaunilon

1. How do you conceive of God? Compare your conception of God with Anselm's "something than which nothing greater can be conceived" (where "greater" means "more perfect"). Is your conception the same as Anselm's or different? Explain your answer.

2. Try to state Anselm's argument in your own words as clearly as you can. (Do this before reading Matson's formulation of the argument in the next reading. You should not expect your statement to match his. In fact, commentators typically give different reformulations of the argument; some of them even think that there is more than one argument.)

3. Critically evaluate the argument (or arguments) you have stated. Is it valid? If it is valid, is it also sound, that is, does it have true premises? Defend your answers. (Again, do this before reading Matson's critical analysis. Don't expect your evaluation to agree with his; in fact, commentators do not agree about the argument—many think that it is invalid, although some think it is sound.)

4. One way of putting Gaunilon's objection to Anselm is that Anselm's argument proves too much. Can you explain why this is a good way of describing Gaunilon's objection? How does Anselm reply? Is his reply adequate? Why or why not?

Wallace I. Matson

The Ontological Argument

Wallace I. Matson is Professor of Philosophy at the University of California, Berkeley.

Discussions of the traditional arguments for the existence of God usually begin with an account of the ontological argument (argument from the concept of being), as formulated by St. Anselm of Canterbury (1033–1109). The gist of it is this:

"God" means "the perfect Being." "Perfect Being" means "Being combining perfect power, perfect goodness, etc., *and perfect reality.*" Hence to say "God does not exist" amounts to uttering the contradiction "The Being which is (among other attributes) perfectly real is not

real." Therefore the statement "God exists" is necessarily true. Indeed, it is inconceivable that God should not exist, as it is inconceivable that there should be a round square or that there should not be a prime number greater than 29, though one might (mistakenly) think that he conceives it, entertains the possibility.

This argument has had a perennial fascination for philosophers. Some of the greatest, including Descartes and Leibniz, have defended it. At one time, even Bertrand Russell thought it valid:

I remember the precise moment, one day in 1894, as I was walking along Trinity Lane, when I saw in a flash (or thought I saw) that the ontological argument is valid. I had gone out to buy a tin of tobacco; on my way back, I suddenly threw it up in the air, and exclaimed as I caught it: "Great Scott, the ontological argument is sound."[1]

Philosophers—especially those, like the three just named, who are also mathematicians—are intrigued by the argument because it purports to bridge the gap between the realms of mathematical and factual truths. If it is valid, then there is at least one truth of fact, one true statement about what exists "out there," that is demonstrable by procedures like those used in

The reading is from Wallace I. Matson, *The Existence of God* (Ithaca, NY: Cornell University Press, 1965), pp. 44–55. Copyright ©1965 by Cornell University. Reprinted with permission of the publisher, Cornell University Press.

mathematical reasoning, and that shares moreover, in the absolute certainty (inconceivability of the opposite) that attaches to the theorems of logic and mathematics. Pure reason in an armchair can then tell us something—something of the last importance—about what there is. Mathematical statements do not have this character; though it is certain that two apples and two more apples make four apples, one cannot infer from this alone that there are any apples: cf. "two unicorns and two more unicorns make four unicorns."

One might suppose that theologians would be equally enthusiastic. For this argument, alone among the traditional three, is such that if it proves anything at all, it patently proves just what theologians are concerned to prove: the existence of God, the perfect Being, the Being than which a greater cannot be conceived—not perhaps merely a big bang or a limited universe-artificer. Yet very few theologians have espoused the argument. On its first appearance it was severely criticized by the monk Gaunilon, who pointed out that *something* must be wrong with it, for if not, then by similar reasoning one ought to be able to define into existence a perfect island. Subsequently, St. Thomas Aquinas rejected it; and thus the matter has stood to this day. Perhaps this bespeaks the greater skepticism of theologians as compared with philosophers.

St. Anselm's Formulation of the Argument

Anselm's writings are among the most charming to be found on the theological shelf. Particularly attractive is the passage in the *Proslogium* in which the ontological argument is set out. It is in the form of a commentary on the words of the Psalmist, "The fool hath said in his heart, There is no god." Anselm sets out to show that such a one in very truth is a fool, since what he utters is a contradiction.

In the following presentation, I preserve Anselm's words as far as possible, only abridging and altering the order slightly. (GCB = Being than which a greater cannot be conceived.)

1. Whatever is understood exists in the understanding.
2. When the fool hears of the GCB, he understands what he hears.
3. Therefore something exists in the understanding, at least, than which nothing greater can be conceived.
4. Suppose the GCB exists in the understanding alone: then it can be conceived to exist in reality;
5. which is greater.
6. Therefore if that than which nothing greater can be conceived exists in the understanding alone, the very Being than which nothing greater can be conceived is one than which a greater can be conceived.
7. Obviously this is impossible.
8. Assuredly that than which nothing greater can be conceived cannot exist in the understanding alone.
9. There is no doubt that there exists a Being than which nothing greater can be conceived, and it exists both in the understanding and in reality. (This is God.)

Criticism of the Argument

There are many ways of showing what is wrong with this reasoning. The most famous is Kant's doctrine that existence is not a predicate. When we say, "God is good," we predicate goodness of God, that is, we assert that God has the property of being good. Anselm assumes that in a similar way, when we say, "God is real," we ascribe a property, reality, to God. However (Kant objects), reality adds nothing to our conception of anything: "A hundred imaginary thalers have all the predicates of a hundred real thalers." If they did not, we should never be able to compare our conception with the object, to see whether our conception was *realized.* Before Kant, Hume had made the same point:

To reflect on any thing simply, and to reflect on it as existent, are nothing different from each other. That idea, when conjoin'd with the idea of any object, makes no addition to it. Whatever we conceive, we conceive to be existent. Any idea we please to form is the idea of a being; and the idea of a being is any idea we please to form.[2]

This refutation, however, is not definitive principally because the question "Is x a property?" has a precise and unambiguous answer only in the context of an ideal (completely formalized) language; and neither English, nor German, nor medieval Latin is such an ideal language. It is always open to a partisan of Anselm to reply: "Existence *is* a property—though admittedly of a unique kind; but every property is unique in some respect."

I shall try to criticize the argument in the spirit of Kant without invoking this somewhat dubious and controversial doctrine as self-evident. I shall take each premise of the argument, translate it into a synonymous expression not containing the word "exists," and see what happens then.

A minimum of apparatus must first be developed: the distinction between use and mention of a word, and the concept of denoting.

Suppose we overhear someone saying: "Schmidt understands horses," and we hear no more of the conversation. Then we cannot tell whether the speaker meant (*a*) Schmidt is knowledgeable about horses: easily senses their moods, knows what pleases them and what makes them nervous, can tell the skittish ones at a glance, and so on; or (*b*) Schmidt is making progress in English; he has just learned that the English for "Pferde" is "horses."

Context normally settles easily in which sense the sentence is to be taken. If it is *written* correctly, the ambiguity cannot arise in the first place, for sense (*b*) requires quotation marks around "horses." These marks serve to indicate that it is the *word* "horses" that is being talked about, not the animals to which the word refers. The word "horses" is being *mentioned* (talked about or written about), not *used* (to refer to nonlinguistic entities).

It is important to note that although in "Schmidt understands horses," the word "horses" is used to refer to animals that exist in the real world, a word can be used even when there is no actual object named by the word: e.g., "Unicorns are rare" contains a use-occurence of "unicorns."

Suppose, now, that we utter the true sentence: "Unicorns don't exist." Since it is clearly not the *word* "unicorn" the existence of which

we are denying, we must class this occurrence of the word as a use. This leads us to the question: What *is* the use of "unicorn" in this sentence? Some philosophers have supposed that the only kind of use a word has (at any rate, the only kind of use a noun has) is to refer; hence, since "unicorn" is not a meaningless noise, and is successfully used in the sentence, there must be some sort of thing—an idea, a **Subsistent Entity**—that is the referent.

Such metaphysics, however, can be avoided. First, the somewhat misleading term "use" should be nontendentiously defined as "successful linguistic employment other than mention." Second, we note that the meaning we convey in the sentence "Unicorns don't exist" can be just as well expressed by saying, "The word 'unicorn' doesn't denote anything." Here "denote" has this sense: "'W' denotes W's" means "The word 'W' is the name of objects of the W-kind." Then "W's don't exist," "W's aren't real," "There aren't any W's" are all expressions that come to the same as "'W' doesn't denote anything." Here we have erected a kind of bridge between use and mention: sentences asserting (or denying) existence, in which the word designating what is said (or denied) to exist is used, can be exactly rephrased as sentences asserting (or denying) that the same word, but now mentioned, has a **denotation**.

We can now return to the argument.

The first three premises constitute a subargument to show that the GCB "exists in the understanding." We can concede this, with the proviso that "exists in the understanding" means no more than "is understood." If anyone objects to this, it is incumbent on him to formulate a set of circumstances in which it could be truly said that some x existed in the understanding without being understood by anyone; or else, someone understood x, but x did not exist in the understanding.

The occurrences of "GCB" in the second and third premises are mentions. What the fool understands "when he hears of the GCB" is the *phrase;* it is clear at any rate that this is all that Anselm claims.

We can then paraphrase these premises as follows:

1′. Whatever is understood is understood.
2′. Someone understands "GCB."
3′. Therefore someone understands "GCB."

True, the paraphrase is trivial. But that is no serious objection, either to Anselm or to the translation. Anselm's purpose in these sentences was to elucidate his meaning of "exist in the understanding"; ours is better served by emphasizing the identity in meaning of this phrase with "be understood"; we accomplish this by reducing both terms to the same one.

The second premise, which is the same as the conclusion, is a factual statement to the effect that somebody (nearly everybody) understands the meaning of the phrase "Being than which a greater cannot be conceived." Some critics have objected that this premise is false, since the Being in question = God, and nobody understands (has adequate knowledge of) God. But this complaint seems to miss the point. We must grant that no one understands God, if to understand Him means to understand His motives, have His wisdom, etc. In this sense I do not understand the President of France, nor do I understand the phrase "richest man in the world" in the sense of knowing what it would feel like to be in that position. I certainly understand the words though, in the sense of knowing what the criteria are for identifying the occupants of these positions. Now it seems sufficient for Anselm's argument that the fool should understand "GCB" in this less grandiose sense: that the GCB should be the wisest, most powerful, best, etc., Being imaginable; and certainly one can understand what is intended by a phrase like "wisest possible" without being oneself as wise as possible. In fact, our own requirement is more stringent than is necessary. All that is needed for the argument is the concession that "GCB" should not be meaningless; and this condition may be met, even if one cannot specify criteria for applying the term to an object. "Most beautiful statue ever carved" is a meaningful phrase, though I do not know how to go about identifying its referent.

We come now to the meatier premises. The fourth consists of two clauses, the first being "Suppose the GCB exists in the understanding alone." In accordance with our rule for translating such expressions, the part of this not containing the word "alone" should be rendered "Suppose 'GCB' is understood," while the force of "alone" is to deny that the GCB "exists in reality." And since this comes to asserting that " 'GCB' does not denote anything," the whole "Suppose . . ." clause becomes: "Suppose 'GCB' is understood, but 'GCB' does not denote anything."

The second clause is "then it [the GCB] can be conceived to exist in reality." This is translated as "then 'GCB' can be conceived to denote something"; and the translation of the entire premise is:

4′. Suppose "GCB" is understood, but "GCB" does not denote anything: then "GCB" can be conceived to denote something;

This is the point at which Hume and Kant attack the argument, on the ground that there is no difference between conceiving and conceiving to denote; since, moreover, conceiving does not appear to differ from understanding, at least in the context of this argument, the premise reduces to the triviality:

4′. Suppose "GCB" is understood, but "GCB" does not denote anything: then "GCB" can be understood; and the argument collapses.

Anselm, however, clearly believed that there was a difference between conceiving merely, and conceiving to denote; and this is a prima facie reason to think there is some difference. But if we ask ourselves what the difference could be, we must conclude that it is one in attitude toward a conception, not in the conception itself; and this is to concede the Kant-Hume objection. Although just idly thinking about mermaids is not the same as believing that there are mermaids, the difference does not lie in the conception. "Mermaid" means "half-woman half-fish" for believer and unbeliever alike; the image conjured up when the word is pronounced is the same; the difference is that the believer believes this image to correspond to something of flesh and blood, whereas the unbeliever does not.

In any event, the argument can hardly survive scrutiny of its next premise:

5. which is greater.

The "which" refers to "existing in reality" (*sc.* the GCB), so that our paraphrase must be:

5′. "GCB" denoting something is greater than "GCB" not denoting anything.

The trouble with this rendering is that it does not appear to have any intelligible meaning. If the rephrasing is at fault, then there must be something wrong with our previous analysis of the equivalence between "X exists" and " 'X' denotes something." That may be; it is up to the objector to investigate the possibility.

Anselm's meaning is perhaps something like this: thinking of mermaids is different from not thinking at all; ergo, when one hears of mermaids, and understands what one hears, one is conceiving of *something*: to wit, something imaginary. But imaginary mermaids are poor thin things—just barely objects—as compared with (say) hippopotamuses of flesh and blood. Similarly, when one hears of the Greatest Conceivable Being, and understands what one hears, one is conceiving *something*—at worst, something imaginary, just barely an object. But it would be ludicrous to suppose that such a wraith could really be the Greatest Conceivable Being:

6. Therefore if that than which nothing greater can be conceived exists in the understanding alone, the very being than which nothing greater can be conceived is one than which a greater can be conceived.
7. Obviously this is impossible.

The if clause of premise 6 is easily put as "if 'GCB' is understood but does not denote anything"; but the remainder defies this treatment. At first sight it looks as if it should be rendered,

"then the GCB is not the GCB" (in which "GCB," for the first time in the argument, is *used*). If so, however, the whole premise would be a glaring **non sequitur**, and besides, the then clause and premise 7 would beg the question; for it is only "obviously impossible" for an *existent thing* not to be identical with itself. Let us suppose, then, that the two occurrences of "GCB" in the then clause are mentions: "then 'GCB' is not identical with 'GCB.' " This is an improvement, as it does not beg the question; but it is still a non sequitur. A concept cannot be self-contradictory just because it denotes nothing. Reality does not come in different grades, qualities, or concentrations.

Even if we grant Anselm his fundamental assumption of grades of reality, his argument is still invalid. Let us assume for the sake of argument that there are two species of existence, a higher and a lower, and that by the very nature of the concept, "GCB" must partake of the higher. We grant even that it is part of the concept that GCB must exist in reality, not merely in the understanding. It still does not follow that there exists in reality the Greatest Conceivable Being. All that can be concluded is that *if* there is a GCB it must be real—a trivial and harmless inference.

We show this in the following way. The ontological argument can be abbreviated thus:

1. "GCB" means, among other things, "perfectly Real Being."
2. Therefore the following statement is self-contradictory: "The GCB is not real."
3. Therefore the GCB *is* real.

Consider now the parallel argument:

1. "Myriagon" means "10,000-sided plane figure."
2. Therefore the following statement is self-contradictory: "The myriagon does not have 10,000 sides."
3. Therefore there is a myriagon with 10,000 sides.

This latter argument is easily seen to be fallacious. All that follows from the premises is that *if* anything is a myriagon, then necessarily it has 10,000 sides, neither more nor less. In exactly the same way, all that follows from the premises of the ontological argument is that *if* anything is the GCB, then necessarily that thing is real. There is no way of getting rid of the *if* by logic alone. If we grant that "unreal GCB" is a contradiction in terms, all we can infer is the Irish conclusion that "if it's unreal it can't be the GCB."

Consequences of the Failure of the Ontological Argument

If this short refutation (which is also to be found in Kant) is sufficient to dispose of the matter, then was not the long discussion of the existence-is-not-a-predicate business superfluous? No, because one point of great importance can be derived from the latter but not from the former: "logically necessary being" is a phrase without meaning. The shorter refutation suffices to show that the concept cannot guarantee the existence of its own referent; but it leaves open the possibility that God's essence entails His existence in the logical sense of entailment. In that case, the statement "God exists" would have not merely factual but logical certainty. If, however, denotation can, as a matter of logic, never be contained in a concept, then nothing—not even God—can have existence logically guaranteed it. There is not then, nor can there be, anything the nonexistence of which is inconceivable or involves contradiction.

Most philosophers have gone further and concluded that no meaning can be assigned to the phrase "necessary existence." They have then argued that the cosmological argument, which purposes to show that God necessarily exists, must in consequence be invalid; in other words (following Kant), the cosmological argument rests on the ontological and falls with it. As I shall point out in discussing the **cosmological argument**, however, it does not seem to me that one is obliged to interpret "God is the necessary Being" as meaning the same as "The sentence 'God exists' is necessarily true." "Necessary being" can mean, and I think does mean in most theological contexts, Being not subject to limitation by any other Being; unconditioned Being.

Notes

1. Bertrand Russell, "My Mental Development," in *The Philosophy of Bertrand Russell,* Paul A. Schilpp, ed. (Evanston, Ill,: Library of Living Philosophers, Inc., 1944), p. 10.
2. David Hume, *A Treatise of Human Nature* (1739), Bk. I, Pt. II, sec. 6.

Study Questions on Matson

1. What is Matson's account of the meaning of the word "God" (as Anselm uses the word)? Is this in accord with your understanding of God? Why or why not?

2. Compare Matson's formulation of the argument with your own. Are they in agreement or not?

3. What is Kant's objection to the argument? Why doesn't Matson consider it to be decisive?

4. Explain Matson's attack on the argument. Does he persuade you that the argument is invalid or not? Compare his view of the argument with your own.

St. Thomas Aquinas
Whether God Exists?

St. Thomas Aquinas (1225–1274), a member of the Dominican Order, was one of the greatest medieval philosophers. As an Angelic Doctor of the Roman Catholic Church, his teachings have a position of special authority, but this does not mean that all Catholic thinkers agree with him on every point of doctrine.

We proceed thus to the Third Article:—

Objection 1. It seems that God does not exist; because if one of two contraries be infinite, the other would be altogether destroyed. But the name *God* means that He is infinite goodness. If, therefore, God existed, there would be no evil discoverable; but there is evil in the world. Therefore God does not exist.

Obj. 2. Further, it is superfluous to suppose that what can be accounted for by a few principles has been produced by many. But it seems that everything we see in the world can be accounted for by other principles, supposing God did not exist. For all natural things can be reduced to one principle, which is nature; and all voluntary things can be reduced to one principle, which is human reason, or will. Therefore there is no need to suppose God's existence.

On the contrary, It is said in the person of God: *I am Who am* (*Exod.* iii, 14).

I answer that, The existence of God can be proved in five ways.

The first and more manifest way is the argument from motion. It is certain, and evident to our senses, that in the world some things are in motion. Now whatever is moved is moved by another, for nothing can be moved except it is in potentiality to that towards which it is moved; whereas a thing moves inasmuch as it is in act. For motion is nothing else than the reduction of

something from potentiality to actuality. But nothing can be reduced from potentiality to actuality, except by something in a state of actuality. Thus that which is actually hot, as fire, makes wood, which is potentially hot, to be actually hot, and thereby moves and changes it. Now it is not possible that the same thing should be at once in actuality and potentiality in the same respect, but only in different respects. For what is actually hot cannot simultaneously be potentially hot; but it is simultaneously potentially cold. It is therefore impossible that in the same respect and in the same way a thing should be both mover and moved, *i.e.,* that it should move itself. Therefore, whatever is moved must be moved by another. If that by which it is moved be itself moved, then this also must needs be moved by another, and that by another again. But this cannot go on to infinity, because then there would be no first mover, and, consequently, no other mover, seeing that subsequent movers move only inasmuch as they are moved by the first mover; as the staff moves only because it is moved by the hand. Therefore it is necessary to arrive at a first mover, moved by no other; and this everyone understands to be God.

The second way is from the nature of **efficient cause**. In the world of sensible things we find there is an order of efficient causes. There is no case known (neither is it, indeed, possible) in which a thing is found to be the efficient cause of itself; for so it would be prior to itself, which is impossible. Now in efficient causes it is not possible to go on to infinity, because in all efficient causes following in order, the first is the cause of the intermediate cause, and the intermediate is the cause of the ultimate cause, whether the intermediate cause be several, or one only. Now to take away the cause is to take away the effect. Therefore, if there be no first cause among efficient causes, there will be no ultimate, nor any intermediate, cause. But if in efficient causes it is possible to go on to infinity, there will be no first efficient cause, neither will there be an ultimate effect, nor any intermediate efficient causes; all of which is plainly false. Therefore it is necessary to admit a first efficient cause, to which everyone gives the name of God.

The reading is from Anton C. Pegis, ed., *Basic Writings of Saint Thomas Aquinas*, vol. 1 (New York: Random House, 1945), pp. 21–23. By permission of the A. C. Pegis Estate.

The third way is taken from possibility and necessity, and runs thus. We find in nature things that are possible to be and not to be, since they are found to be generated, and to be corrupted, and consequently, it is possible for them to be and not to be. But it is impossible for these always to exist, for that which can not-be at some time is not. Therefore, if everything can not-be, then at one time there was nothing in existence. Now if this were true, even now there would be nothing in existence, because that which does not exist begins to exist only through something already existing. Therefore, if at one time nothing was in existence, it would have been impossible for anything to have begun to exist; and thus even now nothing would be in existence—which is absurd. Therefore, not all beings are merely possible, but there must exist something the existence of which is necessary. But every necessary thing either has its necessity caused by another, or not. Now it is impossible to go on to infinity in necessary things which have their necessity caused by another, as has been already proved in regard to efficient causes. Therefore we cannot but admit the existence of some being having of itself its own necessity, and not receiving it from another, but rather causing in others their necessity. This all men speak of as God.

The fourth way is taken from the gradation to be found in things. Among beings there are some more and some less good, true, noble, and the like. But *more* and *less* are predicated of different things according as they resemble in their different ways something which is the maximum, as a thing is said to be hotter according as it more nearly resembles that which is hottest; so that there is something which is truest, something best, something noblest, and consequently, something which is most being, for those things that are greatest in truth are greatest in being, as it is written in *Metaph,* ii.[1] Now the maximum of heat, is the cause of all hot things, as is said in the same book.[2] Therefore there must also be something which is to all beings the cause of their being, goodness, and every other perfection; and this we call God.

The fifth way is taken from the governance of the world. We see that things which lack knowledge, such as natural bodies, act for an end, and this is evident from their acting always, or nearly always, in the same way, so as to obtain the best result. Hence it is plain that they achieve their end, not fortuitously, but designedly. Now whatever lacks knowledge cannot move towards an end, unless it be directed by some being endowed with knowledge and intelligence; as the arrow is directed by the archer. Therefore some intelligent being exists by whom all natural things are directed to their end; and this being we call God.

Reply Obj. 1. As Augustine says: *Since God is the highest good, He would not allow any evil to exist in His works, unless His omnipotence and goodness were such as to bring good even out of evil.*[3] This is part of the infinite goodness of God, that He should allow evil to exist, and out of it produce good.

Reply Obj. 2. Since nature works for a determinate end under the direction of a higher agent, whatever is done by nature must be traced back to God as to its first cause. So likewise whatever is done voluntarily must be traced back to some higher cause other than human reason and will, since these can change and fail; for all things that are changeable and capable of defect must be traced back to an immovable and self-necessary first principle, as has been shown.

Notes

1. *Metaph.* Ia, 1 (993b 30).
2. *Ibid.* (993b 25).
3. *Enchir.,* XI (PL 40, 236).

Questions on St. Thomas Aquinas

1. St. Thomas does not himself accept the argument about the existence of evil. Nevertheless many people (including Nagel in our readings) have found it convincing. Do you think it is a sound argument? Does St. Thomas give an acceptable reply at the end of the reading?

2. "But it seems that everything we see in the world can be accounted for by other principles, supposing God did not exist." Is this true? Can science, for example, explain everything without supposing the existence of God?

3. St. Thomas gives five ways of proving God's existence. Summarize each one of these arguments in your own words, and then critically evaluate them.

4. What if none of the arguments for God's existence is sound? What would be the consequence for belief in God?

Richard Taylor

The Argument from Contingency

Richard Taylor is Professor of Philosophy at the University of Rochester and adjunct Levitt-Spencer Professor of Philosophy at Union College.

An active, living, and religious belief in the gods has probably never arisen and been maintained on purely metaphysical grounds. Such beliefs are found in every civilized land and time, and are often virtually universal in a particular culture, yet relatively few men have much of a conception of metaphysics. There are in fact entire cultures, such as ancient Israel, to whom metaphysics is quite foreign, though these cultures may nevertheless be religious.

Belief in the gods seems to have its roots in human desires and fears, particularly those associated with self-preservation. Like all other creatures, men have a profound will to live, which is what mainly gives one's existence a meaning from one sunrise to the next. Unlike other creatures, however, men are capable of the full and terrible realization of their own inevitable decay. A man can bring before his mind the image of his own grave, and with it the complete certainty of its ultimate reality, and against this his will naturally recoils. It can hardly seem to him less than an absolute catastrophe, the very end, so far as he is concerned, of everything, though he has no difficulty viewing death, as it touches others more or less remote from

himself, as a perhaps puzzling, occasionally distressing, but nonetheless necessary aspect of nature. It is probably partly in response to this fear that he turns to the gods, as those beings of such power that they can overturn this verdict of nature.

The sources of religious belief are doubtless much more complex than this, but they seem to lie in man's will rather than in his speculative intelligence, nevertheless. Men who possess such a belief seldom permit any metaphysical considerations to wrest it from them, while those who lack it are seldom turned toward it by other metaphysical considerations. Still, in every land in which philosophy has flourished, there have been profound thinkers who have sought to discover some metaphysical basis for a rational belief in the existence of some supreme being or beings. Even though religion may properly be a matter of faith rather than reason, still, a philosophical person can hardly help wondering whether it might, at least in part, be also a matter of reason, and whether, in particular, the existence of God might be something that can be not merely believed but shown. It is this question that we want now to consider; that is, we want to see whether there are not strong metaphysical considerations from which the existence of some supreme being might reasonably be inferred.

The Principle of Sufficient Reason

Suppose you were strolling in the woods and, in addition to the sticks, stones, and other accustomed litter of the forest floor, you one day came upon some quite unaccustomed object, something not quite like what you had ever seen before and would never expect to find in such a place. Suppose, for example, that it is a large ball, about your own height, perfectly smooth

The reading is from Richard Taylor, *Metaphysics*, 3d ed., ©1983, pp. 103–112. Reprinted by permission of Prentice-Hall, Inc., Englewood Cliffs, NJ.

and translucent. You would deem this puzzling and mysterious, certainly, but if one considers the matter, it is no more inherently mysterious that such a thing should exist than that anything else should exist. If you were quite accustomed to finding such objects of various sizes around you most of the time, but had never seen an ordinary rock, then upon finding a large rock in the woods one day you would be just as puzzled and mystified. This illustrates the fact that something that is mysterious ceases to seem so simply by its accustomed presence. It is strange indeed, for example, that a world such as ours should exist; yet few men are very often struck by this strangeness, but simply take it for granted.

Suppose, then, that you have found this translucent ball and are mystified by it. Now whatever else you might wonder about it, there is one thing you would hardly question; namely, that it did not appear there all by itself, that it owes its existence to something. You might not have the remotest idea whence and how it came to be there, but you would hardly doubt that there was an explanation. The idea that it might have come from nothing at all, that it might exist without there being any explanation of its existence, is one that few people would consider worthy of entertaining.

This illustrates a metaphysical belief that seems to be almost a part of reason itself, even though few men ever think upon it; the belief, namely, that there is some explanation for the existence of anything whatever, some reason why it should exist rather than not. The sheer nonexistence of anything, which is not to be confused with the passing out of existence of something, never requires a reason; but existence does. That there should never have been any such ball in the forest does not require any explanation or reason, but that there should ever be such a ball does. If one were to look upon a barren plain and ask why there is not and never has been any large translucent ball there, the natural response would be to ask why there should be; but if one finds such a ball, and wonders why it is there, it is not quite so natural to ask why it should *not* be, as though existence should simply be taken for granted. That any-

thing should not exist, then, and that, for instance, no such ball should exist in the forest, or that there should be no forest for it to occupy, or no continent containing a forest, or no earth, nor any world at all, do not seem to be things for which there needs to be any explanation or reason; but that such things should be, does seem to require a reason.

The principle involved here has been called the **principle of sufficient reason.** Actually, it is a very general principle, and is best expressed by saying that , in the case of any positive truth, there is some sufficient reason for it, something which, in this sense, makes it true—in short, that there is some sort of explanation, known or unknown, for everything.

Now some truths depend on something else, and are accordingly called **contingent**, while others depend only upon themselves, that is, are true by their very natures and are accordingly called **necessary**. There is, for example, a reason why the stone on my window sill is warm; namely, that the sun is shining upon it. This happens to be true, but not by its very nature. Hence, it is contingent, and depends upon something other than itself. It is also true that all points of a circle are equidistant from the center, but this truth depends upon nothing but itself. No matter what happens, nothing can make it false. Similarly, it is a truth, and a necessary one, that if the stone on my window sill is a body, as it is, then it has a form, because this fact depends upon nothing but itself for its confirmation. Untruths are also, of course, either contingent or necessary, it being contingently false, for example, that the stone on my window sill is cold, and necessarily false that it is both a body and formless, because this is by its very nature impossible.

The principle of sufficient reason can be illustrated in various ways, as we have done, and if one thinks about it, he is apt to find that he presupposes it in his thinking about reality, but it cannot be proved. It does not appear to be itself a necessary truth, and at the same time it would be most odd to say it is contingent. If one were to try proving it, he would sooner or later have to appeal to considerations that are less plausible than the principle itself. Indeed, it is hard to see how one could even make an argument for it, without already assuming it. For this reason it might properly be called a presupposition of reason itself. One can deny that it is true, without embarrassment or fear of refutation, but one is then apt to find that what he is denying is not really what the principle asserts. We shall, then, treat it here as a datum—not something that is provably true, but as something which all men, whether they ever reflect upon it or not, seem more or less to presuppose.

The Existence of a World

It happens to be true that something exists, that there is, for example, a world, and although no one ever seriously supposes that this might not be so, that there might exist nothing at all, there still seems to be nothing the least necessary in this, considering it just by itself. That no world should ever exist at all is perfectly comprehensible and seems to express not the slightest absurdity. Considering any particular item in the world it seems not at all necessary in itself that it should ever have existed, nor does it appear any more necessary that the totality of these things, or any totality of things, should ever exist.

From the principle of sufficient reason it follows, of course, that there must be a reason, not only for the existence of everything in the world but for the world itself, meaning by "the world" simply everything that ever does exist, except God, in case there is a god. This principle does not imply that there must be some purpose or goal for everything, or for the totality of all things; for explanations need not, and in fact seldom are, teleological or purposeful. All the principle requires is that there be some sort of reason for everything. And it would certainly be odd to maintain that everything in the world owes its existence to something, that nothing in the world is either purely accidental, or such that it just bestows its own being upon itself, and then to deny this of the world itself. One can indeed *say* that the world is in some sense a pure accident, that there simply is no reason at all why this or any world should exist, and one

can equally say that the world exists by its very nature, or is an inherently necessary being. But it is at least very odd and arbitrary to deny of this existing world the need for any sufficient reason, whether independent of itself or not, while presupposing that there is a reason for every other thing that ever exists.

Consider again the strange ball that we imagine has been found in the forest. Now we can hardly doubt that there must be an explanation for the existence of such a thing, though we may have no notion what that explanation is. It is not, moreover, the fact of its having been found in the forest rather than elsewhere that renders an explanation necessary. It matters not in the least where it happens to be, for our question is not how it happens to be *there* but how it happens to exist at all. If we in our imagination annihilate the forest, leaving only this ball in an open field, our conviction that it is a contingent thing and owes its existence to something other than itself is not reduced in the least. If we now imagine the field to be annihilated, and in fact everything else as well to vanish into nothingness, leaving only this ball to constitute the entire physical universe, then we cannot for a moment suppose that its existence has thereby been explained, or the need of any explanation eliminated, or that its existence is suddenly rendered self-explanatory. If we now carry this thought one step further and suppose that no other reality ever has existed or ever will exist, that this ball forever constitutes the entire physical universe, then we must still insist on there being some reason independent of itself why it should exist rather than not. If there must be a reason for the existence of any particular thing, then the necessity of such a reason is not eliminated by the mere supposition that certain other things do *not* exist. And again, it matters not at all what the thing in question is, whether it be large and complex, such as the world we actually find ourselves in, or whether it be something small, simple and insignificant, such as a ball, a bacterium, or the merest grain of sand. We do not avoid the necessity of a reason for the existence of something merely by describing it in this way or that. And it would, in any event, seem quite plainly absurd to say that if the world were comprised entirely of a single ball about six feet in diameter, or of a single grain of sand, then it would be contingent and there would have to be some explanation other than itself why such a thing exists, but that, since the actual world is vastly more complex than this, there is no need for an explanation of its existence, independent of itself.

Beginningless Existence

It should now be noted that it is no answer to the question, why a thing exists, to state *how long* it has existed. A geologist does not suppose that he has explained why there should be rivers and mountains merely by pointing out that they are old. Similarly, if one were to ask, concerning the ball of which we have spoken, for some sufficient reason for its being, he would not receive any answer upon being told that it had been there since yesterday. Nor would it be any better answer to say that it had existed since before anyone could remember, or even that it had always existed; for the question was not one concerning its age but its existence. If, to be sure, one were to ask where a given thing came from, or how it came into being, then upon learning that it had always existed he would learn that it never really *came* into being at all; but he could still reasonably wonder why it should exist at all. If, accordingly, the world—that is, the totality of all things excepting God, in case there is a god—had really no beginning at all, but has always existed in some form or other, then there is clearly no answer to the question, where it came from and when; it did not, on this supposition, *come* from anything at all, at any time. But still, it can be asked why there is a world, why indeed there is a beginningless world, why there should have perhaps always been something rather than nothing. And, if the principle of sufficient reason is a good principle, there must be an answer to that question, an answer that is by no means supplied by giving the world an age, or even an infinite age.

Creation

This brings out an important point with respect to the concept of creation that is often misunderstood, particularly by those whose thinking has been influenced by Christian ideas. People tend to think that creation—for example, the creation of the world by God—*means* creation *in time,* from which it of course logically follows that if the world had no beginning in time, then it cannot be the creation of God. This, however, is erroneous, for creation means essentially *dependence,* even in Christian theology. If one thing is the creation of another, then it depends for its existence on that other, and this is perfectly consistent with saying that both are eternal, that neither ever came into being, and hence, that neither was ever created at any point of time. Perhaps an analogy will help convey this point. Consider, then, a flame that is casting beams of light. Now there seems to be a clear sense in which the beams of light are dependent for their existence upon the flame, which is their source, while the flame, on the other hand, is not similarly dependent for its existence upon them. The beams of light arise from the flame, but the flame does not arise from them. In this sense, they are the creation of the flame; they derive their existence from it. And none of this has any reference to time; the relationship of dependence in such a case would not be altered in the slightest if we supposed that the flame, and with it the beams of light, had always existed, that neither had ever *come* into being.

Now if the world is the creation of God, its relationship to God should be thought of in this fashion; namely, that the world depends for its existence upon God, and could not exist independently of God. If God is eternal, as those who believe in God generally assume, then the world may (though it need not) be eternal too, without that altering in the least its dependence upon God for its existence, and hence without altering its being the creation of God. The supposition of God's eternality, on the other hand, does not by itself imply that the world is eternal too; for there is not the least reason why something of finite duration might not depend for its existence upon something of infinite duration—though the reverse is, of course, impossible.

God

If we think of God as "the creator of heaven and earth," and if we consider heaven and earth to include everything that exists except God, then we appear to have, in the foregoing considerations, fairly strong reasons for asserting that God, as so conceived, exists. Now of course most people have much more in mind than this when they think of God, for religions have ascribed to God ever so many attributes that are not at all implied by describing him merely as the creator of the world; but that is not relevant here. Most religious persons do, in any case, think of God as being at least the creator, as that being upon which everything ultimately depends, no matter what else they may say about him in addition. It is, in fact, the first item in the creeds of Christianity that God is the "creator of heaven and earth." And, it seems, there are good metaphysical reasons, as distinguished from the persuasions of faith, for thinking that such a creative being exists.

If, as seems clearly implied by the principle of sufficient reason, there must be a reason for the existence of heaven and earth—i.e., for the world—then that reason must be found either in the world itself, or outside it, in something that is literally supranatural, or outside heaven and earth. Now if we suppose that the world—i.e., the totality of all things except God—contains within itself the reason for its existence, we are supposing that it exists by its very nature, that is, that it is a necessary being. In that case there would, of course, be no reason for saying that it must depend upon God or anything else for its existence; for if it exists by its very nature, then it depends upon nothing but itself, much as the sun depends upon nothing but itself for its heat. This, however, is implausible, for we find nothing about the world or anything in it to suggest that it exists by its own nature, and we do find, on the contrary, ever so many things to suggest that it does not. For in the first place, anything that exists by its very nature must necessarily be eternal and indestructible. It would be a self-contradiction to say of anything that it exists by its own nature, or is a necessarily existing thing, and at the same time to say that it comes into being or passes away, or that it ever could come into being or pass away. Nothing about the world seems at all like this, for concerning anything in the world, we can perfectly easily think of it as being annihilated, or as never having existed in the first place, without there being the slightest hint of any absurdity in such a supposition. Some of the things in the universe are, to be sure, very old; the moon, for example, or the stars and the planets. It is even possible to imagine that they have always existed. Yet it seems quite impossible to suppose that they owe their existence to nothing but themselves, that they bestow existence upon themselves by their very natures, or that they are in themselves things of such nature that it would be impossible for them not to exist. Even if we suppose that something, such as the sun, for instance, has existed forever, and will never cease, still we cannot conclude just from this that it exists by its own nature. If, as is of course very doubtful, the sun has existed forever and will never cease, then it is possible that its heat and light have also existed forever and will never cease; but that would not show that the heat and light of the sun exist by their own natures. They are obviously contingent and depend on the sun for their existence, whether they are beginningless and everlasting or not.

There seems to be nothing in the world, then, concerning which it is at all plausible to suppose that it exists by its own nature, or contains within itself the reason for its existence. In fact, everything in the world appears to be quite plainly the opposite, namely, something that not only need not exist, but at some time or other, past or future or both, does not in fact exist. Everything in the world seems to have a finite duration, whether long or short. Most things, such as ourselves, exist only for a short while; they come into being, then soon cease. Other things, like the heavenly bodies, last longer, but they are still corruptible, and from all that we can gather about them, they too seem destined eventually to perish. We arrive at the conclusion, then, that although the world may contain some things that have always existed and are destined never to perish, it is nevertheless doubtful that it contains any such thing and, in any case, everything in the world is capable of perishing, and nothing in it, however long it may already have existed and however long it may yet remain, exists by its own nature, but depends instead upon something else.

Although this might be true of everything in the world, is it necessarily true of the world itself? That is, if we grant, as we seem forced to, that nothing in the world exists by its own nature, that everything in the world is contingent and perishable, must we also say that the world itself, or the totality of all these perishable things, is also contingent and perishable? Logically, we are not forced to, for it is logically possible that the totality of all perishable things might itself be imperishable, and hence, that the world might exist by its own nature, even though it is comprised exclusively of things hat are contingent. It is not logically necessary that a totality should share the defects of its members. For example, even though every man is mortal, it does not follow from this that the human race, or the totality of all men, is also mortal; for it is possible that there will always be human beings, even though there are no human beings who will always exist. Similarly, it is possible that the world is in itself a necessary thing, even though it is comprised entirely of things that are contingent.

This is logically possible, but it is not plausible. For we find nothing whatever about the world, any more than in its parts, to suggest that it exists by its own nature. Concerning anything in the world, we have not the slightest difficulty in supposing that it should perish, or even that it should never have existed in the first place. We have almost as little difficulty in supposing this of the world itself. It might be somewhat hard to think of everything as utterly perishing and leaving no trace whatever of its ever having been, but there seems to be not the slightest difficulty in imagining that the world should never have existed in the first place. We can, for instance, perfectly easily suppose that nothing in the world had ever existed except, let us suppose, a single grain of sand, and we can thus suppose that this grain of sand has forever constituted the whole universe. Now if we consider just this grain of sand, it is quite impossible for us to suppose that it exists by its very nature, and could never have failed to exist. It clearly de-

pends for its existence upon something other than itself, if it depends on anything at all. The same will be true if we consider the world to consist, not of one grain of sand, but of two, or of a million, or, as we in fact find, of a vast number of stars and planets and all their minuter parts.

It would seem, then, that the world, in case it happens to exist at all—and this is quite beyond doubt—is contingent and thus dependent upon something other than itself for its existence, if it depends upon anything at all. And it must depend upon something, for otherwise there could be no reason why it exists in the first place. Now that upon which the world depends must be something that either exists by its own nature or does not. If it does not exist by its own nature, then it, in turn, depends for its existence upon something else, and so on. Now then, we can say either of two things; namely, (1) that the world depends for its existence upon something else, which in turn depends on still another thing, this depending upon still another, *ad infinitum;* or (2) that the world derives its existence from something that exists by its own nature and that is accordingly eternal and imperishable, and is the creator of heaven and earth. The first of these alternatives, however, is impossible, for it does not render a sufficient reason why anything should exist in the first place. Instead of supplying a reason why any world should exist, it repeatedly begs off giving a reason. It explains what is dependent and perishable in terms of what is itself dependent and perishable, leaving us still without a reason why perishable things should exist at all, which is what we are seeking. Ultimately, then, it would seem that the world, or the totality of contingent or perishable things, in case it exists at all, must depend upon something that is necessary and imperishable, and that accordingly exists, not in dependence upon something else, but by its own nature.

"Self-Caused"

What has been said thus far gives some intimation of what meaning should be attached to the concept of a self-caused being, a concept that is quite generally misunderstood, sometimes even by scholars. To say that something—God, for example—is self-caused, or is the cause of its own existence, does not mean that this being brings itself into existence, which is a perfectly absurd idea. Nothing can *bring* itself into existence. To say that something is self-caused (*causa sui*) means only that it exists, not contingently or in dependence upon something else, but by its own nature, which is only to say that it is a being which is such that it can neither come into being nor perish. Now whether such a being in fact exists or not, there is in any case no absurdity in the idea. We have found, in fact, that the principle of sufficient reason seems to point to the existence of such a being, as that upon which the world, with everything in it, must ultimately depend for its existence.

"Necessary Being"

A being that depends for its existence upon nothing but itself, and is in this sense self-caused, can equally be described as a necessary being; that is to say, a being that is not contingent, and hence not perishable. For in the case of anything that exists by its own nature and is dependent upon nothing else, it is impossible that it should not exist, which is equivalent to saying that it is necessary. Many persons have professed to find the gravest difficulties in this concept, too, but that is partly because it has been confused with other notions. If it makes sense to speak of anything as an *impossible* being, or something that by its very nature does not exist, then it is hard to see why the idea of a necessary being, or something that in its very nature exists, should not be just as comprehensible. And of course, we have not the slightest difficulty in speaking of something, such as a square circle or a formless body, as an impossible being. And if it makes sense to speak of something as being perishable, contingent, and dependent upon something other than itself for its existence, as it surely does, then there seems to be no difficulty in thinking of something as imperishable and dependent upon nothing other than itself for its existence.

"First Cause"

From these considerations we can see also what is properly meant by a first cause, an appellative that has often been applied to God by theologians, and that many persons have deemed an absurdity. It is a common criticism of this notion to say that there need not be any first cause, because the series of causes and effects that constitute the history of the universe might be infinite or beginningless and must, in fact, be infinite in case the universe itself had no beginning in time. This criticism, however, reflects a total misconception of what is meant by a first cause. *First* here does not mean first in time, and when God is spoken of as a first cause, he is not being described as a being which, at some time in the remote past, *started* everything. To describe God as a first cause is only to say that he is literally a *primary* rather than a secondary cause, an *ultimate* rather than a derived cause, or a being upon which all other things, heaven and earth, ultimately depend for their existence. It is, in short, only to say that God is the creator, in the sense of creation explained above. Now this, of course, is perfectly consistent with saying that the world is eternal or beginningless. As we have seen, one gives no reason for the existence of a world merely by giving it an age, even if it is supposed to have an infinite age. To use a helpful analogy, we can say that the sun is the first cause of daylight and, for that matter, of the moonlight of the night as well, which means only that daylight and moonlight ultimately depend upon the sun for their existence. The moon, on the other hand, is only a secondary or derivative cause of its light. This light would be no less dependent upon the sun if we affirmed that it had no beginning, for an ageless and beginningless light requires a source no less than an ephemeral one. If we supposed that the sun has always existed, and with it its light, then we would have to say that the sun has always been the first—i.e., the primary or ultimate—cause of its light. Such is precisely the manner in which God should be thought of, and is by theologians often thought of, as the first cause of heaven and earth.

Questions on Taylor

1. State and explain the principle of sufficent reason. Does this principle apply to God too? If it does, then God is not "self-caused," as Taylor says.

But if it does not, then the principle is not true; it has exceptions. How could Taylor respond to this problem?

2. How does Taylor explain creation? Is this how you understand creation? Why or why not?

3. What does Taylor mean when he says that God is a "necessary being?" Some commentators have thought that this concept does not make any sense. Do you agree or not? Explain your answer.

4. Try to state Taylor's argument as clearly as you can, in the same style as Matson stated the ontological argument in the last reading. Critically evaluate it. Is it valid? Is it sound?

William Paley

The Argument from Design

William Paley (1743–1805) taught philosophy before becoming a minister in the Church of England. His most important books are A View of the Evidence of Christianity, The Principles of Moral and Political Philosophy, *and* Natural Theology *(from which our reading is taken).*

Chapter One: State of the Argument

In crossing a heath, suppose I pitched my foot against a *stone* and were asked how the stone came to be there, I might possibly answer that for anything I knew to the contrary it had lain there forever; nor would it, perhaps, be very easy to show the absurdity of this answer. But suppose I had found a *watch* upon the ground, and it should be inquired how the watch happened to be in that place, I should hardly think of the answer which I had before given, that for anything I knew the watch might have always been there. Yet why should not this answer serve for the watch as well as for the stone; why is it not as admissible in the second case as in the first? For this reason, and for no other, namely, that when we come to inspect the watch, we perceive—what we could not discover in the stone—that its several parts are framed and put

together for a purpose, e.g., that they are so formed and adjusted as to produce motion, and that motion so regulated as to point out the hour of the day; that if the different parts had been differently shaped from what they are, or placed after any other manner or in any other order than that in which they are placed, either no motion at all would have been carried on in the machine, or none which would have answered the use that is now served by it. To reckon up a few of the plainest of these parts and of their offices, all tending to one result: we see a cylindrical box containing a coiled elastic spring, which, by its endeavor to relax itself, turns around the box. We next observe a flexible chain—artificially wrought for the sake of flexure—communicating the action of the spring from the box to the fusee. We then find a series of wheels, the teeth of which catch in and apply to each other, conducting the motion from the fusee to the balance and from the balance to the pointer, and at the same time, by the size and shape of those wheels, so regulating that motion as to terminate in causing an index, by an equable and measured progression, to pass over a given space in a given time. We take notice that the wheels are made of brass, in order to keep them from rust; the springs of steel, no other metal being so elastic; that over the face of the watch there is placed a glass, a material employed in no other part of the work, but in the room of which, if there had been any other than a transparent substance, the hour could not be seen without opening the case. This mechanism being observed—it requires indeed an examination of the instrument, and perhaps some previous knowledge of the subject, to perceive and understand it; but being

The reading is from William Paley, *Natural Theology*.

once, as we have said, observed and understood—the inference we think is inevitable, that the watch must have had a maker—that there must have existed, at some time and at some place or other, an artificer or artificers who formed it for the purpose which we find it actually to answer, who completely comprehended its construction and designed its use.

I. Nor would it, I apprehend, weaken the conclusion, that we had never seen a watch made—that we had never known an artist capable of making one—that we were altogether incapable of executing such a piece of workmanship ourselves, or of understanding in what manner it was performed; all this being no more than what is true of some exquisite remains of ancient art, of some lost arts, and, to the generality of mankind, of the more curious productions of modern manufacture. Does one man in a million know how oval frames are turned? Ignorance of this kind exalts our opinion of the unseen and unknown artist's skill, if he be unseen and unknown, but raises no doubt in our minds of the existence and agency of such an artist, at some former time and in some place or other. Nor can I perceive that it varies at all the inference, whether the question arise concerning a human agent or concerning an agent of a different species, or an agent possessing in some respects a different nature.

II. Neither, secondly, would it invalidate our conclusion, that the watch sometimes went wrong or that it seldom went exactly right. The purpose of the machinery, the design, and the designer might be evident, and in the case supposed, would be evident, in whatever way we accounted for the irregularity of the movement, or whether we could account for it or not. It is not necessary that a machine be perfect in order to show with what design it was made: still less necessary, where the only question is whether it were made with any design at all.

III. Nor, thirdly, would it bring any uncertainty into the argument, if there were a few parts of the watch, concerning which we could not discover or had not yet discovered in what manner they conduced to the general effect; or even some parts, concerning which we could not ascertain whether they conduced to that effect in any manner whatever. For, as to the first branch of the case, if by the loss, or disorder, or decay of the parts in question, the movement of the watch were found in fact to be stopped, or disturbed, or retarded, no doubt would remain in our minds as to the utility or intention of these parts, although we should be unable to investigate the manner according to which, or the connection by which, the ultimate effect depended upon their action or assistance; and the more complex the machine, the more likely is this obscurity to arise. Then, as to the second thing supposed, namely, that there were parts which might be spared without prejudice to the movement of the watch, and that we had proved this by experiment, these superfluous parts, even if we were completely assured that they were such, would not vacate the reasoning which we had instituted concerning other parts. The indication of contrivance remained, with respect to them, nearly as it was before.

IV. Nor, fourthly, would any man in his senses think the existence of the watch with its various machinery accounted for, by being told that it was one out of possible combinations of material forms; that whatever he had found in the place where he found the watch, must have contained some internal configuration or other; and that this configuration might be the structure now exhibited, namely, of the works of a watch, as well as a different structure.

V. Nor, fifthly, would it yield his inquiry more satisfaction, to be answered that there existed in things a principle of order, which had disposed the parts of the watch into their present form and situation. He never knew a watch made by the principle of order; nor can he even form to himself an idea of what is meant by a principle of order distinct from the intelligence of the watchmaker.

VI. Sixthly, he would be surprised to hear that the mechanism of the watch was no proof of contrivance, only a motive to induce the mind to think so:

VII. And not less surprised to be informed that the watch in his hand was nothing more than the result of the laws of *metallic* nature. It is a perversion of language to assign any law as the efficient, operative cause of any thing. A law presupposes an agent, for it is only the mode according to which an agent proceeds: it implies a power, for it is the order according to which that power acts. Without this agent, without this power, which are both distinct from itself, the *law* does nothing, is nothing. The expression, "the law of metallic nature," may sound strange and harsh to a philosophic ear; but it seems quite as justifiable as some others which are more familiar to him, such as "the law of vegetable nature," "the law of animal nature," or, indeed, as "the law of nature" in general, when assigned as the cause of phenomena, in exclusion of agency and power, or when it is substituted into the place of these.

VIII. Neither, lastly, would our observer be driven out of his conclusion or from his confidence in its truth by being told that he knew nothing at all about the matter. He knows enough for his argument; he knows the utility of the end; he knows the subserviency and adaptation of the means to the end. These points being known, his ignorance of other points, his doubts concerning other points affect not the certainty of his reasoning. The consciousness of knowing little need not beget a distrust of that which he does know.

Chapter Two:
State of the Argument Continued

Suppose, in the next place, that the person who found the watch should after some time discover that, in addition to all the properties which he had hitherto observed in it, it possessed the unexpected property of producing in the course of its movement another watch like itself—the thing is conceivable; that it contained within it a mechanism, a system of parts—a mold, for instance, or a complex adjustment of lathes, files, and other tools—evidently and separately calculated for this purpose; let us inquire what effect ought such a discovery to have upon his former conclusion.

I. The first effect would be to increase his admiration of the contrivance, and his conviction of the consummate skill of the contriver. Whether he regarded the object of the contrivance, the distinct apparatus, the intricate, yet in many parts intelligible mechanism by which it was carried on, he would perceive in this new

observation nothing but an additional reason for doing what he had already done—for referring the construction of the watch to design and to supreme art. If that construction *without* this property, or, which is the same thing, before this property had been noticed, proved intention and art to have been employed about it, still more strong would the proof appear when he came to the knowledge of this further property, the crown and perfection of all the rest.

II. He would reflect that, though the watch before him were *in some sense* the maker of the watch which was fabricated in the course of its movements, yet it was in a very different sense from that in which a carpenter, for instance, is the maker of a chair—the author of its contrivance, the cause of the relation of its parts to their use. With respect to these, the first watch was no cause at all to the second; in no such sense as this was it the author of the constitution and order, either of the parts which the new watch contained, or of the parts by the aid and instrumentality of which it was produced. We might possibly say, but with great latitude of expression, that a stream of water ground corn; but no latitude of expression would allow us to say, no stretch of conjecture could lead us to think that the stream of water built the mill, though it were too ancient for us to know who the builder was. What the stream of water does in the affair is neither more nor less than this: by the application of an unintelligent impulse to a mechanism previously arranged, arranged independently of it and arranged by intelligence, an effect is produced, namely, the corn is ground. But the effect results from the arrangement. The force of the stream cannot be said to be the cause or the author of the effect, still less of the arrangement. Understanding and plan in the formation of the mill were not the less necessary for any share which the water has in grinding the corn; yet is this share the same as that which the watch would have contributed to the production of the new watch, upon the supposition assumed in the last section. Therefore,

III. Though it be now no longer probable that the individual watch which our observer had found was made immediately by the hand of an artificer, yet this alteration does not in anywise affect the inference that an artificer had been originally employed and concerned in the production. The argument from design remains as it was. Marks of design and contrivance are no more accounted for now than they were before. In the same thing, we may ask for the cause of different properties. We may ask for the cause of the color of a body, of its hardness, of its heat; and these causes may be all different. We are now asking for the cause of that subserviency to a use, that relation to an end, which we have remarked in the watch before us. No answer is given to this question by telling us that a preceding watch produced it. There cannot be design without a designer; contrivance without a contriver; order without choice; arrangement without anything capable of arranging; subserviency and relation to a purpose without that which could intend a purpose; means suitable to an end, and executing their office in accomplishing that end, without the end ever having been contemplated or the means accommodated to it. Arrangement, disposition of parts, subserviency of means to an end, relation of instruments to a use imply the presence of intelligence and mind. No one, therefore, can rationally believe that the insensible, inanimate watch, from which the watch before us issued, was the proper cause of the mechanism we so much admire in it—could be truly said to have constructed the instrument, disposed its parts, assigned their office, determined their order, action, and mutual dependency, combined their several motions into one result, and that also a result connected with the utilities of other beings. All these properties, therefore, are as much unaccounted for as they were before.

IV. Nor is anything gained by running the difficulty farther back, that is, by supposing the watch before us to have been produced from another watch, that from a former, and so on indefinitely. Our going back ever so far brings us no nearer to the least degree of satisfaction upon the subject. Contrivance is still unaccounted for. We still want a contriver. A designing mind is neither supplied by this supposition nor dispensed with. If the difficulty were diminished the farther we went back, by going back indefinitely we might exhaust it. And this is the only case to which this sort of reasoning applies. Where there is a tendency, or, as we increase the number of terms, a continual approach toward a limit, *there,* by supposing the number of terms to be what is called infinite, we may conceive the limit to be attained; but where there is no such tendency or approach, nothing is effected by lengthening the series. There is no difference as to the point in question, whatever there may be as to many points, between one series and another—between a series which is finite and a series which is infinite. A chain composed of an infinite number of links can no more support itself than a chain composed of a finite number of links. And of this we are assured, though we never *can* have tried the experiment; because, by increasing the number of links, from ten, for instance, to a hundred, from a hundred to a thousand, etc., we make not the smallest approach, we observe not the smallest tendency toward self-support. There is no difference in this respect—yet there may be a great difference in several respects—between a chain of a greater or less length, between one chain and another, between one that is finite and one that is infinite. This very much resembles the case before us. The machine which we are inspecting demonstrates, by its construction, contrivance and design. Contrivance must have had a contriver, design a designer, whether the machine immediately proceeded from another machine or not. That circumstance alters not the case. That other machine may, in like manner, have proceeded from a former machine: nor does that alter the case; the contrivance must have had a contriver. That former one from one preceding it: no alteration still; a contriver is still necessary. No tendency is perceived, no approach toward a diminution of this necessity. It is the same with any and every succession of these machines—a succession of ten, of a hundred, of a thousand; with one series, as with another—a series which is finite, as with a series which is infinite. In whatever other respects they may differ, in this they do not. In all equally, contrivance and design are unaccounted for.

The question is not simply, how came the first watch into existence?—which question, it may be pretended, is done away by supposing the series of watches thus produced from one another to have been infinite, and consequently to have had no such *first* for which it was necessary to provide a cause. This, perhaps, would have been nearly the state of the question, if nothing had been before us but an unorganized, unmechanized substance, without mark or indication of contrivance. It might be difficult to show that such substance could not have existed from eternity, either in succession—if it were possible, which I think it is not, for unorganized bodies to spring from one another—or by individual perpetuity. But that is not the question now. To suppose it to be so is to suppose that it made no difference whether he had found a watch or a stone. As it is, the metaphysics of that question have no place; for, in the watch which we are examining are seen contrivance, design, an end, a purpose, means for the end, adaptation to the purpose. And the question which irresistibly presses upon our thoughts is, whence this contrivance and design? The thing required is the intending mind, the adapted hand, the intelligence by which that hand was directed. This question, this demand is not shaken off by increasing a number or succession of substances destitute of these properties; nor the more, by increasing that number to infinity. If it be said that, upon the supposition of one watch being produced from another in the course of that other's movements and by means of the mechanism within it, we have a cause for the watch in my hand, namely, the watch from which it proceeded; I deny that for the design, the contrivance, the suitableness of means to an end, the adaptation of instruments to a use, all of which we discover in the watch, we have any cause whatever. It is in vain, therefore, to assign a series of such causes or to allege that a series may be carried back to infinity; for I do not admit that we have yet any cause at all for the phenomena, still less any series of causes either finite or infinite. Here is contrivance but no contriver; proofs of design, but no designer.

V. Our observer would further also reflect that the maker of the watch before him was in truth and reality the maker of every watch produced from it: there being no difference, except that the latter manifests a more exquisite skill, between the making of another watch with his own hands, by the mediation of files, lathes, chisels, etc., and the disposing, fixing, and inserting of these instruments, or of others equivalent to them, in the body of the watch already made, in such a manner as to form a new watch in the course of the movements which he had given to the old one. It is only working by one set of tools instead of another.

The conclusion which the *first* examination of the watch, of its works, construction, and movement, suggested, was that it must have had, for cause and author of that construction, an artificer who understood its mechanism and designed its use. This conclusion is invincible. A *second* examination presents us with a new discovery. The watch is found, in the course of its movement, to produce another watch similar to itself; and not only so, but we perceive in it a system or organization separately calculated for that purpose. What effect would this discovery have or ought it to have upon our former inference? What, as has already been said, but to increase beyond measure our admiration of the skill which had been employed in the formation of such a machine? Or shall it, instead of this, all at once turn us round to an opposite conclusion, namely, that no art or skill whatever has been concerned in the business, although all other evidences of art and skill remain as they were, and this last and supreme piece of art be now added to the rest? Can this be maintained without absurdity? . . .

Chapter Five: Application of the Argument Continued

Every observation which was made in our first chapter concerning the watch may be repeated with strict propriety concerning the eye, concerning animals, concerning plants, concerning, indeed, all the organized parts of the works of nature. As,

I. When we are inquiring simply after the *existence* of an intelligent Creator, imperfection, inaccuracy, liability to disorder, occasional irregularities may subsist in a considerable degree without inducing any doubt into the question; just as a watch may frequently go wrong, seldom perhaps exactly right, may be faulty in some parts, defective in some, without the smallest ground of suspicion from thence arising that it was not a watch, not made, or not made for the purpose ascribed to it. When faults are pointed out, and when a question is started concerning the skill of the artist or the dexterity with which the work is executed, then, indeed, in order to defend these qualities from accusation, we must be able either to expose some intractableness and imperfection in the materials or point out some invincible difficulty in the execution, into which imperfection and difficulty the matter of complaint may be resolved; or, if we cannot do this, we must adduce such specimens of consummate art and contrivance proceeding from the same hand as may convince the inquirer of the existence, in the case before him, of impediments like those which we have mentioned, although, what from the nature of the case is very likely to happen, they be unknown and unperceived by him. This we must do in order to vindicate the artist's skill, or at least the perfection of it; as we must also judge of his intention and of the provisions employed in fulfilling that intention, not from an instance in which they fail but from the great plurality of instances in which they succeed. But, after all, these are different questions from the question of the artist's existence; or, which is the same, whether the thing before us be a work of art or not; and the questions ought al-ways to be kept separate in the mind. So likewise it is in the works of nature. Irregularities and imperfections are of little or no weight in the consideration when that consideration relates simply to the existence of a Creator. When the argument respects his attributes, they are of weight; but are then to be taken in conjunction—the attention is not to rest upon them, but they are to be taken in conjunction with the unexceptional evidences which we possess of skill, power, and benevolence displayed in other instances; which evidences may, in strength, number, and variety, be such and may so overpower apparent blemishes as to induce us, upon the most reasonable ground, to believe that these last ought to be referred to some cause, though we be ignorant of it, other than defect of knowledge or of benevolence in the author. . . .

Questions on Paley

1. Paley convincingly argues that the watch had a maker. But is it true that everything he says about the watch can be applied to the eye, animals, plants, and everything in nature? What is your position?

2. Is Paley's argument an a priori or a posteriori argument? Why?

3. In the next reading, Hume questions whether an intelligent Creator, assuming there is such a thing, is identical with God. Could Paley reply to this objection?

David Hume

Critique of the Argument from Design

The reading is from David Hume, *Dialogues Concerning Natural Religion,* ed. by Henry D. Aiken (New York: Hafner Publishing Co., 1948), pp. 17–23, p. 37, and pp. 38–41.

David Hume (1711–1776) was a Scottish philosopher and historian (he wrote a famous history of England). He is considered to be one of the most important modern philosophers.

Not to lose any time in circumlocutions, said Cleanthes, addressing himself to Demea, much less in replying to the pious declamations of Philo, I shall briefly explain how I conceive this matter. Look round the world, contemplate the whole and every part of it: you will find it to be nothing but one great machine, subdivided into an infinite number of lesser machines, which again admit of subdivisions to a degree beyond what human senses and faculties can trace and explain. All these various machines, and even their most minute parts, are adjusted to each other with an accuracy which ravishes into admiration all men who have ever contemplated them. The curious adapting of means to ends, throughout all nature, resembles exactly, though it much exceeds, the productions of human contrivance—of human design, thought, wisdom, and intelligence. Since therefore the effects resemble each other, we are led to infer, by all the rules of analogy, that the causes also resemble, and that the Author of nature is somewhat similar to the mind of man, though possessed of much larger faculties, proportioned to the grandeur of the work which he has executed. By this argument *a posteriori,* and by this argument alone, do we prove at once the existence of a Deity and his similarity to human mind and intelligence.

I shall be so free, Cleanthes, said Demea, as to tell you that from the beginning I could not approve of your conclusion concerning the similarity of the Deity to men, still less can I approve of the mediums by which you endeavour to establish it. What! No demonstration of the Being of God! No abstract arguments! No proofs *a priori!* Are these which have hitherto been so much insisted on by philosophers all fallacy, all sophism? Can we reach no farther in this subject than experience and probability? I will not say that this is betraying the cause of a Deity; but surely, by this affected candour, you give advantages to atheists which they never could obtain by the mere dint of argument and reasoning.

What I chiefly scruple in this subject, said Philo, is not so much that all religious arguments are by Cleanthes reduced to experience, as that they appear not to be even the most certain and irrefragable of that inferior kind. That a stone will fall, that fire will burn, that the earth has solidity, we have observed a thousand and a thousand times; and when any new instance of this nature is presented, we draw without hesitation the accustomed inference. The exact similarity of the cases gives us a perfect assur-

ance of a similar event, and a stronger evidence is never desired nor sought after. But wherever you depart, in the least, from the similarity of the cases, you diminish proportionably the evidence, and may at last bring it to a very weak *analogy,* which is confessedly liable to error and uncertainty. After having experienced the circulation of the blood in human creatures, we make no doubt that it takes place in Titius and Maevius; but from its circulation in frogs and fishes it is only a presumption, though a strong one, from analogy that it takes place in men and other animals. The analogical reasoning is much weaker when we infer the circulation of the sap in vegetables from our experience that the blood circulates in animals; and those who hastily followed that imperfect analogy are found, by more accurate experiments, to have been mistaken.

If we see a house, Cleanthes, we conclude, with the greatest certainty, that it had an architect or builder because this is precisely that species of effect which we have experienced to proceed from that species of cause. But surely you will not affirm that the universe bears such a resemblance to a house that we can with the same certainty infer a similar cause, or that the analogy is here entire and perfect. The dissimilitude is so striking that the utmost you can here pretend to is a guess, a conjecture, a presumption concerning a similar cause; and how that pretension will be received in the world, I leave you to consider.

It would surely be very ill received, replied Cleanthes; and I should be deservedly blamed and detested did I allow that the proofs of a Deity amounted to no more than a guess or conjecture. But is the whole adjustment of means to ends in a house and in the universe so slight a resemblance? the economy of final causes? the order, proportion, and arrangement of every part? Steps of a stair are plainly contrived that human legs may use them in mounting; and this inference is certain and infallible. Human legs are also contrived for walking and mounting; and this inference, I allow, is not altogether so certain because of the dissimilarity which you remark; but does it, therefore, deserve the name only of presumption or conjecture?

Good God! cried Demea, interrupting him,

where are we? Zealous defenders of religion allow that the proofs of a Deity fall short of perfect evidence! And you, Philo, on whose assistance I depended in proving the adorable mysteriousness of the Divine Nature, do you assent to all these extravagant opinions of Cleanthes? For what other name can I give them? or, why spare my censure when such principles are advanced, supported by such an authority, before so young a man as Pamphilus?

You seem not to apprehend, replied Philo, that I argue with Cleanthes in his own way, and, by showing him the dangerous consequences of his tenets, hope at last to reduce him to our opinion. But what sticks most with you, I observe, is the representation which Cleanthes has made of the argument *a posteriori;* and, finding that that argument is likely to escape your hold and vanish into air, you think it so disguised that you can scarcely believe it to be set in its true light. Now, however much I may dissent, in other respects, from the dangerous principle of Cleanthes, I must allow that he has fairly represented that argument, and I shall endeavour so to state the matter to you that you will entertain no further scruples with regard to it.

Were a man to abstract from everything which he knows or has seen, he would be altogether incapable, merely from his own ideas, to determine what kind of scene the universe must be, or to give the preference to one state or situation of things above another. For as nothing which he clearly conceives could be esteemed impossible or implying a contradiction, every chimera of his fancy would be upon an equal footing; nor could he assign any just reason why he adheres to one idea or system, and rejects the others which are equally possible.

Again, after he opens his eyes and contemplates the world as it really is, it would be impossible for him at first to assign the cause of any one event, much less of the whole of things, or of the universe. He might set his fancy a rambling, and she might bring him in an infinite variety of reports and representations. These would all be possible, but, being all equally possible, he would never of himself give a satisfactory account for his preferring one of them to the rest. Experience alone can point out to him the true cause of any phenomenon.

Now, according to this method of reasoning, Demea, it follows (and is, indeed, tacitly allowed by Cleanthes himself) that order, arrangement, or the adjustment of final causes, is not of itself any proof of design, but only so far as it has been experienced to proceed from that principle. For aught we can know *a priori*, matter may contain the source or spring of order originally within itself, as well as mind does; and there is no more difficulty in conceiving that the several elements, from an internal unknown cause, may fall into the most exquisite arrangement, than to conceive that their ideas, in the great universal mind, from a like internal unknown cause, fall into that arrangement. The equal possibility of both these suppositions is allowed. But, by experience, we find (according to Cleanthes) that there is a difference between them. Throw several pieces of steel together, without shape or form, they will never arrange themselves so as to compose a watch. Stone and mortar and wood, without an architect, never erect a house. But the ideas in a human mind, we see, by an unknown, inexplicable economy, arrange themselves so as to form the plan of a watch or house. Experience, therefore, proves that there is an original principle of order in mind, not in matter. From similar effects we infer similar causes. The adjustment of means to ends is alike in the universe, as in a machine of human contrivance. The causes, therefore, must be resembling.

I was from the beginning scandalized, I must own, with this resemblance which is asserted between the Deity and human creatures, and must conceive it to imply such a degradation of the Supreme Being as no sound theist could endure. With your assistance, therefore, Demea, I shall endeavour to defend what you justly call the adorable mysteriousness of the Divine Nature, and shall refute this reasoning of Cleanthes, provided he allows that I have made a fair representation of it.

When Cleanthes had assented, Philo, after a short pause, proceeded in the following manner.

That all inferences, Cleanthes, concerning fact are founded on experience, and that all experimental reasonings are founded on the supposition that similar causes prove similar effects, and similar effects similar causes, I shall not at present much dispute with you. But observe, I entreat you, with what extreme caution all just reasoners proceed in the transferring of experiments to similar cases. Unless the cases be exactly similar, they repose no perfect confidence in applying their past observation to any particular phenomenon. Every alteration of circumstances occasions a doubt concerning the event; and it requires new experiments to prove certainly that the new circumstances are of no moment or importance. A change in bulk, situation, arrangement, age, disposition of the air, or surrounding bodies—any of these particulars may be attended with the most unexpected consequences. And unless the objects be quite familiar to us, it is the highest temerity to expect with assurance, after any of these changes, an event similar to that which before fell under our observation. The slow and deliberate steps of philosophers here, if anywhere, are distinguished from the precipitate march of the vulgar, who, hurried on by the smallest similitude, are incapable of all discernment or consideration.

But can you think, Cleanthes, that your usual phlegm and philosophy have been preserved in so wide a step as you have taken when you compared to the universe houses, ships, furniture, machines, and, from their similarity in some circumstances, inferred a similarity in their causes? Thought, design, intelligence, such as we discover in men and other animals, is no more than one of the springs and principles of the universe, as well as heat or cold, attraction or repulsion, and a hundred others which fall under daily observation. It is an active cause by which some particular parts of nature, we find, produce alterations on other parts. But can a conclusion, with any propriety, be transferred from parts to the whole? Does not the great disproportion bar all comparison and inference? From observing the growth of a hair, can we learn anything concerning the generation of a man? Would the manner of a leaf's blowing, even though perfectly known, afford us any instruction concerning the vegetation of a tree?

But allowing that we were to take the *operations* of one part of nature upon another for the foundation of our judgment concerning the *ori-*gin of the whole (which never can be admitted), yet why select so minute, so weak, so bounded a principle as the reason and design of animals is found to be upon this planet? What peculiar privilege has this little agitation of the brain which we call *thought*, that we must thus make it the model of the whole universe? Our partiality in our own favour does indeed present it on all occasions, but sound philosophy ought carefully to guard against so natural an illusion.

So far from admitting, continued Philo, that the operations of a part can afford us any just conclusion concerning the origin of the whole, I will not allow any one part to form a rule for another part if the latter be very remote from the former. Is there any reasonable ground to conclude that the inhabitants of other planets possess thought, intelligence, reason, or anything similar to these faculties in men? When nature has so extremely diversified her manner of operation in this small globe, can we imagine that she incessantly copies herself throughout so immense a universe? And if thought, as we may well suppose, be confined merely to this narrow corner and has even there so limited a sphere of action, with what propriety can we assign it for the original cause of all things? The narrow views of a peasant who makes his domestic economy the rule for the government of kingdoms is in comparison a pardonable sophism.

But were we ever so much assured that a thought and reason resembling the human were to be found throughout the whole universe, and were its activity elsewhere vastly greater and more commanding than it appears in this globe, yet I cannot see why the operations of a world constituted, arranged, adjusted, can with any propriety be extended to a world which is in its embryo state, and is advancing towards that constitution and arrangement. By observation we know somewhat of the economy, action, and nourishment of a finished animal, but we must transfer with great caution that observation to the growth of a foetus in the womb, and still more to the formation of an animalcule in the loins of its male parent. Nature, we find, even from our limited experience, possesses an infinite number of springs and principles which incessantly discover themselves on every change of her position and situation. And what new and unknown principles would actuate her in so new and unknown a situation as that of the formation of a universe, we cannot, without the utmost temerity, pretend to determine.

A very small part of this great system, during a very short time, is very imperfectly discovered to us; and do we thence pronounce decisively concerning the origin of the whole?

Admirable conclusion! Stone, wood, brick, iron, brass, have not, at this time, in this minute globe of earth, an order or arrangement without human art and contrivance; therefore, the universe could not originally attain its order and arrangement without something similar to human art. But is a part of nature a rule for another part very wide of the former? Is it a rule for the whole? Is a very small part a rule for the universe? Is nature in one situation a certain rule for nature in another situation vastly different from the former?

And can you blame me, Cleanthes, if I here imitate the prudent reserve of Simonides, who, according to the noted story, being asked by Hiero, *What God was?* desired a day to think of it, and then two days more; and after that manner continually prolonged the term, without ever bringing in his definition or description? Could you even blame me if I had answered, at first, *that I did not know,* and was sensible that this subject lay vastly beyond the reach of my faculties? You might cry out sceptic and rallier, as much as you pleased; but, having found in so many other subjects much more familiar the imperfections and even contradictions of human reason, I never should expect any success from its feeble conjectures in a subject so sublime and so remote from the sphere of our observation. When two *species* of objects have always been observed to be conjoined together, I can *infer,* by custom, the existence of one wherever I *see* the existence of the other; and this I call an argument from experience. But how this argument can have place where the objects, as in the present case, are single, individual, without parallel or specific resemblance, may be difficult to explain. And will any man tell me with a serious countenance that an orderly universe must arise from some thought and art like the human be-

cause we have experience of it? To ascertain this reasoning it were requisite that we had experience of the origin of worlds; and it is not sufficient, surely, that we have seen ships and cities arise from human art and contrivance. . . .

But to show you still more inconveniences, continued Philo, in your anthropomorphism, please to take a new survey of your principles. *Like effects prove like causes.* This is the experimental argument; and this, you say too, is the sole theological argument. Now it is certain that the liker the effects are which are seen and the liker the causes which are inferred, the stronger is the argument. Every departure on either side diminishes the probability and renders the experiment less conclusive. You cannot doubt of the principle; neither ought you to reject its consequences.

All the new discoveries in astronomy which prove the immense grandeur and magnificence of the works of nature are so many additional arguments for a Deity, according to the true system of theism; but, according to your hypothesis of experimental theism, they become so many objections, by removing the effect still farther from all resemblance to the effects of human art and contrivance. . . .

Now, Cleanthes, said Philo, with an air of alacrity and triumph, mark the consequences. *First,* by this method of reasoning you renounce all claim to infinity in any of the attributes of the Deity. For, as the cause ought only to be proportioned to the effect, and the effect, so far as it falls under our cognizance, is not infinite, what pretensions have we, upon your suppositions, to ascribe that attribute to the Divine Being? You will still insist that, by removing him so much from all similarity to human creatures, we give in to the most arbitrary hypothesis, and at the same time weaken all proofs of his existence.

Secondly, you have no reason, on your theory, for ascribing perfection to the Deity, even in his finite capacity, or for supposing him free from every error, mistake, or incoherence, in his undertakings. There are many inexplicable difficulties in the works of nature which, if we allow a perfect author to be proved *a priori,* are easily solved, and become only seeming difficulties from the narrow capacity of man, who cannot trace infinite relations. But according to your method of reasoning, these difficulties become all real, and, perhaps, will be insisted on as new instances of likeness to human art and contrivance. At least, you must acknowledge that it is impossible for us to tell, from our limited views, whether this system contains any great faults or deserves any considerable praise if compared to other possible and even real systems. Could a peasant, if the *Æneid* were read to him, pronounce that poem to be absolutely faultless, or even assign to it its proper rank among the productions of human wit, he who had never seen any other production?

But were this world ever so perfect a production, it must still remain uncertain whether all the excellences of the work can justly be ascribed to the workman. If we survey a ship, what an exalted idea must we form of the ingenuity of the carpenter who framed so complicated, useful, and beautiful a machine? And what surprise must we feel when we find him a stupid mechanic who imitated others, and copied an art which, through a long succession of ages, after multiplied trials, mistakes, corrections, deliberations, and controversies, had been gradually improving? Many worlds might have been botched and bungled, throughout an eternity, ere this system was struck out; much labour lost, many fruitless trials made, and a slow but continued improvement carried on during infinite ages in the art of world-making. In such subjects, who can determine where the truth, nay, who can conjecture where the probability lies, amidst a great number of hypotheses which may be proposed, and a still greater which may be imagined?

And what shadow of an argument, continued Philo, can you produce from your hypothesis to prove the unity of the Deity? A great number of men join in building a house or ship, in rearing a city, in framing a commonwealth; why may not several deities combine in contriving and framing a world? This is only so much greater similarity to human affairs. By sharing the work among several, we may so much further limit the attributes of each, and get rid of that extensive power and knowledge which

must be supposed in one deity, and which, according to you, can only serve to weaken the proof of his existence. And if such foolish, such vicious creatures as man can yet often unite in framing and executing one plan, how much more those deities or demons, whom we may suppose several degrees more perfect!

To multiply causes without necessity is indeed contrary to true philosophy, but this principle applies not to the present case. Were one deity antecedently proved by your theory who were possessed of every attribute requisite to the production of the universe, it would be needless, I own, (though not absurd) to suppose any other deity existent. But while it is still a question whether all these attributes are united in one subject or dispersed among several independent beings, by what phenomena in nature can we pretend to decide the controversy? Where we see a body raised in a scale, we are sure that there is in the opposite scale, however concealed from sight, some counterpoising weight equal to it; but it is still allowed to doubt whether that weight be an aggregate of several distinct bodies or one uniform united mass. And if the weight requisite very much exceeds anything which we have ever seen conjoined in any single body, the former supposition becomes still more probable and natural. An intelligent being of such vast power and capacity as is necessary to produce the universe, or, to speak in the language of ancient philosophy, so prodigious an animal exceeds all analogy and even comprehension.

But further, Cleanthes: Men are mortal, and renew their species by generation; and this is common to all living creatures. The two great sexes of male and female, says Milton, animate the world. Why must this circumstance, so universal, so essential, be excluded from those numerous and limited deities? Behold, then, the theogeny of ancient times brought back upon us.

And why not become a perfect anthropomorphite? Why not assert the deity or deities to be corporeal, and to have eyes, a nose, mouth, ears, etc.? Epicurus maintained that no man had ever seen reason but in a human figure; therefore, the gods must have a human figure. And this argument, which is deservedly so much ridiculed by Cicero, becomes, according to you, solid and philosophical.

In a word, Cleanthes, a man who follows your hypothesis is able, perhaps, to assert or conjecture that the universe sometime arose from something like design; but beyond that position he cannot ascertain one single circumstance, and is left afterwards to fix every point of his theology by the utmost license of fancy and hypothesis. This world, for aught he knows, is very faulty and imperfect, compared to a superior standard, and was only the first rude essay of some infant deity who afterwards abandoned it, ashamed of his lame performance; it is the work only of some dependent, inferior deity, and is the object of derision to his superiors; it is the production of old age and dotage in some superannuated deity, and ever since his death has run on at adventures, from the first impulse and active force which it received from him. You justly give signs of horror, Demea, at these strange suppositions; but these, and a thousand more of the same kind, are Cleantes' suppositions, not mine. From the moment the attributes of the Diety are supposed finite, all these have place. And I cannot, for my part, think that so wild and unsettled a system of theology is, in any respect, preferable to none at all.

These suppositions I absolutely disown, cried Cleanthes: they strike me, however, with no horror, especially when proposed in that rambling way in which they drop from you. On the contrary, they give me pleasure when I see that, by the utmost indulgence of your imagination, you never get rid of the hypothesis of design in the universe, but are obliged at every turn to have recourse to it. To this concession I adhere steadily; and this I regard as a sufficient foundation for religion.

Questions on Hume

1. Philo (the skeptic many commentators think is speaking for Hume himself) claims that the argument from design is based on a very weak analogy. Do you agree? Why or why not?

2. Philo asserts that the argument cannot be used to show that God is infinite in any respect. Why is this? Is this a good criticism?

3. Philo also argues that the argument does not show that the Deity is perfect. On the contrary, Philo suggests that the world might be the imperfect work of some infant deity who has abandoned it, "ashamed of his lame performance." Does the defender of the argument have any reply to this or not? Explain your answer.

4. Philo also notes that it is very difficult to show the unity of the Creator. Do the various arguments, even if sound, prove that the same (identical) individual exists?

Ernest Nagel

Philosophical Concepts of Atheism

The reading is from Ernest Nagel, "Philosophical Concepts of Atheism," in J. E. Fairchild, ed., *Basic Beliefs* (New York: Sheridan House, Inc., 1959), pp. 167–186. Reprinted with permission.

Ernest Nagel (1901–1985) taught for many years at Columbia University. He was best known for his work in philosophy of science.

It is a natural expectation that this paper will show how atheism belongs to the great tradition of religious thought. Needless to say, this expectation is difficult to satisfy, and did anyone succeed in doing so he would indeed be performing the neatest conjuring trick of the week. But the expectation nevertheless does cause me some embarrassment, which is only slightly relieved by an anecdote Bertrand Russell reports in his recent book, *Portraits from Memory*. Russell was imprisoned during the First World War for pacifistic activities. On entering the prison he was asked a number of customary questions about himself for the prison records. One question was about his religion. Russell explained that he was an agnostic. "Never heard of it," the warden declared. "How do you spell it?" When Russell told him, the warden observed "Well, there are many religions, but I suppose they all worship the same God." Russell adds that this remark kept him cheerful for about a week. Perhaps philosophical atheism also is a religion.

1

I must begin by stating what sense I am attaching to the word "atheism," and how I am construing the theme of this paper. I shall understand by "atheism" a critique and a denial of the major claims of all varieties of theism. And by theism I shall mean the view which holds, as one writer has expressed it, "that the heavens and the earth and all that they contain owe their existence and continuance in existence to the wisdom and will of a supreme, self-consistent, omnipotent, omniscient, righteous, and benevolent being, who is distinct from, and independent of, what he has created." Several things immediately follow from these definitions.

In the first place, atheism is not necessarily an irreligious concept, for theism is just one among many views concerning the nature and origin of the world. The denial of theism is logically compatible with a religious outlook upon life, and is in fact characteristic of some of the great historical religions. For as readers of this volume will know, early **Buddhism** is a religion which does not subscribe to any doctrine about a god; and there are pantheistic religions and philosophies which, because they deny that God is a being separate from and independent of the world, are not theistic in the sense of the word explained above.

The second point to note is that atheism is not to be identified with sheer unbelief, or with disbelief in some particular creed of a religious group. Thus, a child who has received no religious instruction and has never heard about God, is not an atheist—for he is not denying any theistic claims. Similarly in the case of an adult who, if he has withdrawn from the faith of his fathers without reflection or because of frank indifference to any theological issue, is also not an atheist—for such an adult is not challenging theism and is not professing any views on the subject. Moreover, though the term "atheist" has been used historically as an abusive label for those who do not happen to subscribe to some regnant orthodoxy (for example, the ancient Romans called the early Christians atheists, because the latter denied the Roman divinities), or for those who engage in conduct regarded as immoral it is not in this sense that I am discussing atheism.

One final word of preliminary explanation. I propose to examine some *philosophic* concepts of atheism, and I am not interested in the slightest in the many considerations atheists have advanced against the evidences for some particular religious and theological doctrine—for example, against the truth of the Christian story. What I mean by "philosophical" in the present context is that the views I shall consider are directed against any form of theism, and have their origin and basis in a logical analysis of the theistic position, and in a comprehensive account of the world believed to be wholly intelligible without the adoption of a theistic hypothesis.

Theism as I conceive it is a theological proposition, not a statement of a position that belongs primarily to religion. On my view, religion as a historical and social phenomenon is primarily an institutionalized *cultus* or practice, which possesses identifiable social functions and which expresses certain attitudes men take toward their world. Although it is doubtful whether men ever engage in religious practices or assume religious attitudes without some more or less explicit interpretation of their ritual or some rationale for their attitude, it is still the case that it is possible to distinguish religion as a social and personal phenomenon from the theological doctrines which may be developed as justifications for religious practices. Indeed, in some of the great religions of the world the profession of a creed plays a relatively minor role. In short, religion is a form of social communion, a participation in certain kinds of ritual (whether it be a dance, worship, prayer, or the like), and a form of experience (sometimes, though not invariably, directed to a personal confrontation with divine and holy things). Theology is an articulated and, at its best, a rational attempt at understanding these feelings and practices, in the light of their relation to other parts of human experience, and in terms of some hypothesis concerning the nature of things entire.

2

As I see it, atheistic philosophies fall into two major groups: 1) those which hold that the theistic doctrine is meaningful, but reject it either on the ground that, (a) the positive evidence for it is insufficient, or (b) the negative evidence is quite overwhelming; and 2) those who hold that the theistic thesis is not even meaningful, and reject it (a) as just nonsense or (b) as literally meaningless but interpreting it as a symbolic rendering of human ideals, thus reading the theistic thesis in a sense that most believers in theism would disavow. It will not be possible in the limited space at my disposal to discuss the second category of atheistic critiques; and in any event, most of the traditional atheistic critiques of theism belong to the first group.

But before turning to the philosophical examination of the major classical arguments for theism, it is well to note that such philosophical critiques do not quite convey the passion with which atheists have often carried on their analyses of theistic views. For historically, atheism has been, and indeed continues to be, a form of social and political protest, directed as much against institutionalized religion as against theistic doctrine. Atheism has been, in effect, a moral revulsion against the undoubted abuses of the secular power exercised by religious leaders and religious institutions.

Religious authorities have opposed the correction of glaring injustices, and encouraged politically and socially reactionary policies. Religious institutions have been havens of obscurantist thought and centers for the dissemination of intolerance. Religious creeds have been used to set limits to free inquiry, to perpetuate inhumane treatment of the ill and the underprivileged, and to support moral doctrines insensitive to human suffering.

These indictments may not tell the whole story about the historical significance of religion; but they are at least an important part of the story. The refutation of theism has thus seemed to many as an indispensable step not only towards liberating men's minds from superstition, but also towards achieving a more equitable reordering of society. And no account of even the more philosophical aspects of atheistic thought is adequate, which does not give proper recognition to the powerful social motives that actuate many atheistic arguments.

But however this may be, I want now to discuss three classical arguments for the existence of God, arguments which have constituted at least a partial basis for theistic commitments. As long as theism is defended simply as a dogma, asserted as a matter of direct revelation or as the deliverance of authority, belief in the dogma is impregnable to rational argument. In fact, however, reasons are frequently advanced in support of the theistic creed, and these reasons have been the subject of acute philosophical critiques.

One of the oldest intellectual defenses of theism is the cosmological argument, also known as the argument from a first cause. Briefly put, the argument runs as follows. Every event must have a cause. Hence an event A must have as cause some event B, which in turn must have a cause C, and so on. But if there is no end to this backward progression of causes, the progression will be infinite; and in the opinion of those who use this argument, an infinite series of actual events is unintelligible and absurd. Hence there must be a first cause, and this first cause is God, the initiator of all change in the universe.

The argument is an ancient one, and is especially effective when stated within the framework of assumptions of Aristotelian physics; and it has impressed many generations of exceptionally keen minds. The argument is nonetheless a weak reed on which to rest the theistic thesis. Let us waive any question concerning the validity of the principle that every event has a cause, for though the question is important its discussion would lead us far afield. However, if the principle is assumed, it is surely incongruous to postulate a first cause as a way of escaping from the coils of an infinite series. For if everything must have a cause, why does not God require one for His own existence? The standard answer is that He does not need any, because He is self-caused. But if God can be self-caused, why cannot the world itself be self-caused? Why do we require a God transcending the world to bring the world into existence and to initiate changes in it? On the other hand, the supposed inconceivability and absurdity of an infinite series of regressive causes will be admitted by no one who has competent familiarity with modern mathematical analysis of infinity. The cosmological argument does not stand up under scrutiny.

The second "proof" of God's existence is usually called the ontological argument. It too has a long history going back to early Christian days, though it acquired great prominence only in medieval times. The argument can be stated in several ways, one of which is the following. Since God is conceived to be omnipotent, he is a perfect being. A perfect being is defined as one whose essence or nature lacks no attributes (or properties) whatsoever, one whose nature is complete in every respect. But it is evident that we have an idea of a perfect being, for we have just defined the idea; and since this is so, the argument continues, God who is the perfect being must exist. Why must he? Because his existence follows from his defined nature. For if God lacked the attribute of existence, he would be lacking at least one attribute, and would therefore not be perfect. To sum up, since we have an idea of God as a perfect being, God must exist.

There are several ways of approaching this argument, but I shall consider only one. The argument was exploded by the 18th century philosopher Immanuel Kant. The substance of Kant's criticism is that it is just a confusion to say that existence is an attribute, and that though the *word* "existence" may occur as the grammatical predicate in a sentence no attribute is being predicated of a thing when we say

that the thing exists or has existence. Thus, to use Kant's example, when we think of $100 we are thinking of the nature of this sum of money; but the nature of $100 remains the same whether we have $100 in our pockets or not. Accordingly, we are confounding grammar with logic if we suppose that some characteristic is being attributed to the nature of $100 when we say that a hundred dollar bill exists in someone's pocket.

To make the point clearer, consider another example. When we say that a lion has a tawny color, we are predicating a certain attribute of the animal, and similarly when we say that the lion is fierce or is hungry. But when we say the lion exists, all that we are saying is that something is (or has the nature of) a lion; we are not specifying an attribute which belongs to the nature of anything that is a lion. In short, the word "existence" does not signify any attribute, and in consequence no attribute that belongs to the nature of anything. Accordingly, it does not follow from the assumption that we have an idea of a perfect being that such a being exists. For the idea of a perfect being does not involve the attribute of existence as a constituent of that idea, since there is no such attribute. The ontological argument thus has a serious leak, and it can hold no water.

3

The two arguments discussed thus far are purely dialectical, and attempt to establish God's existence without any appeal to empirical data. The next argument, called the **argument from design**, is different in character, for it is based on what purports to be empirical evidence. I wish to examine two forms of this argument.

One variant of it calls attention to the remarkable way in which different things and processes in the world are integrated with each other, and concludes that this mutual "fitness" of things can be explained only by the assumption of a divine architect who planned the world and everything in it. For example, living organisms can maintain themselves in a variety of environments, and do so in virtue of their delicate mechanisms which adapt the organisms to all sorts of environmental changes. There is thus an intricate pattern of means and ends throughout the animate world. But the existence of this pattern is unintelligible, so the argument runs, except on the hypothesis that the pattern has been deliberately instituted by a Supreme Designer. If we find a watch in some deserted spot, we do not think it came into existence by chance, and we do not hesitate to conclude that an intelligent creature designed and made it. But the world and all its contents exhibit mechanisms and mutual adjustments that are far more complicated and subtle than are those of a watch. Must we not therefore conclude that these things too have a Creator?

The conclusion of this argument is based on an inference from analogy: the watch and the world are alike in possessing a congruence of parts and an adjustment of means to ends; the watch has a watch-maker; hence the world has a world-maker. But is the analogy a good one? Let us once more waive some important issues, in particular the issue whether the universe is the unified system such as the watch admittedly is. And let us concentrate on the question what is the ground for our assurance that watches do not come into existence except through the operations of intelligent manufacturers. The answer is plain. We have never run across a watch which has not been deliberately made by someone. But the situation is nothing like this in the case of the innumerable animate and inanimate systems with which we are familiar. Even in the case of living organisms, though they are generated by their parent organisms, the parents do not "make" their progeny in the same sense in which watch-makers make watches. And once this point is clear, the inference from the existence of living organisms to the existence of a supreme designer no longer appears credible.

Moreover, the argument loses all its force if the facts which the hypothesis of a divine designer is supposed to explain can be understood on the basis of a better supported assumption. And indeed, such an alternative explanation is one of the achievements of Darwinian biology. For Darwin showed that one can account for the variety of biological species, as well as for their adaptations to their environments, without invoking a divine creator and acts of special creation. The Darwinian theory explains the diversity of biological species in terms of chance variations in the structure of organisms, and of a mechanism of selection which retains those variant forms that possess some advantages for survival. The evidence for these assumptions is considerable; and developments subsequent to Darwin have only strenghthened the case for a thoroughly naturalistic explanation of the facts of biological adaptation. In any event, this version of the argument from design has nothing to recommend it.

A second form of this argument has been recently revived in the speculations of some modern physicists. No one who is familiar with the facts, can fail to be impressed by the success with which the use of mathematical methods has enabled us to obtain intellectual mastery of many parts of nature. But some thinkers have therefore concluded that since the book of nature is ostensibly written in mathematical language, nature must be the creation of a divine mathematician. However, the argument is most dubious. For it rests, among other things, on the assumption that mathematical tools can be successfully used only if the events of nature exhibit some *special* kind of order, and on the further assumption that if the structure of things were different from what they are mathematical language would be inadequate for describing such structure. But it can be shown that no matter what the world were like—even if it impressed us as being utterly chaotic—it would still possess some order, and would in principle be amenable to a mathematical description. In point of fact, it makes no sense to say that there is absolutely *no* pattern in any conceivable subject matter. To be sure, there are differences in complexities of structure, and if the patterns of events were sufficiently complex we might not be able to unravel them. But however that may be, the success of mathematical physics in giving us some understanding of the world around us does not yield the conclusion that only a mathematician could have devised the patterns of order we have discovered in nature.

4

The inconclusiveness of the three classical arguments for the existence of God was already made evident by Kant, in a manner substantially not different from the above discussion. There are, however, other types of arguments for theism that have been influential in the history of thought, two of which I wish to consider, even if only briefly.

Indeed, though Kant destroyed the classical intellectual foundations for theism, he himself invented a fresh argument for it. Kant's attempted proof is not intended to be a purely theoretical demonstration, and is based on the supposed facts of our moral nature. It has exerted an enormous influence on subsequent theological speculation. In barest outline, the argument is as follows. According to Kant, we are subject not only to physical laws like the rest of nature, but also to moral ones. These moral laws are **categorical imperatives**, which we must heed not because of their **utilitarian** consequences, but simply because as autonomous moral agents it is our duty to accept them as binding. However, Kant was keenly aware that though virtue may be its reward, the virtuous man (that is, the man who acts out of a sense of duty and in conformity with the moral law) does not always receive his just desserts in this world; nor did he shut his eyes to the fact that evil men frequently enjoy the best things this world has to offer. In short, virtue does not always reap happiness. Nevertheless, the highest human good is the realization of happiness commensurate with one's virtue; and Kant believed that it is a practical postulate of the moral life to promote this good. But what can guarantee that the highest good is realizable? Such a guarantee can be found only in God, who must therefore exist if the highest good is not to be a fatuous ideal. The existence of an omnipotent, omniscient, and omnibenevolent God is thus postulated as a **necessary condition** for the possibility of a moral life.

Despite the prestige this argument has acquired, it is difficult to grant it any force. It is easy enough to postulate God's existence. But as Bertrand Russell observed in another connection, postulation has all the advantages of theft over honest toil. NO postulation carries with it any assurance that what is postulated is actually the case. And though we may postulate God's existence as a means to guaranteeing the

possibility of realizing happiness together with virtue, the postulation establishes neither the actual realizability of this ideal nor the fact of his existence. Moreover, the argument is not made more cogent when we recognize that it is based squarely on the highly dubious conception that considerations of utility and human happiness must not enter into the determination of what is morally obligatory. Having built his moral theory on a radical separation of means from ends, Kant was driven to the desperate postulation of God's existence in order to relate them again. The argument is thus at best a *tour de force*, contrived to remedy a fatal flaw in Kant's initial moral assumptions. It carries no conviction to anyone who does not commit Kant's initial blunder.

One further type of argument, pervasive in much Protestant theological literature, deserves brief mention. Arguments of this type take their point of departure from the psychology of religious and mystical experience. Those who have undergone such experiences, often report that during the experience they feel themselves to be in the presence of the divine and holy, that they lose their sense of self-identity and become merged with some fundamental reality, or that they enjoy a feeling of total dependence upon some ultimate power. The overwhelming sense of transcending one's finitude which characterizes such vivid periods of life, and of coalescing with some ultimate source of all existence, is then taken to be compelling evidence for the existence of a surpreme being. In a variant form of this argument, other theologians have identified God as the object which satisfies the commonly experienced need for integrating one's scattered and conflicting impulses into a coherent unity, or as the subject which is of ultimate concern to us. In short, a proof of God's existence is found in the occurrence of certain distinctive experiences.

It would be flying in the face of well-attested facts were one to deny that such experiences frequently occur. But do these facts constitute evidence for the conclusion based on them? Does the fact, for example, that an individual experiences a profound sense of direct contact with an alleged transcendent ground of all reality, constitute competent evidence for the claim that there is such a ground and that it is the immediate cause of the experience? If well-established canons for evaluating evidence are accepted, the answer is surely negative. No one will dispute that many men do have vivid experiences in which such things as ghosts or pink elephants appear before them; but only the hopelessly credulous will without further ado count such experiences as establishing the existence of ghosts and pink elephants. To establish the existence of such things, evidence is required that is obtained under controlled conditions and that can be confirmed by independent inquirers. Again, though a man's report that he is suffering pain may be taken at face value, one cannot take at face value the claim, were he to make it, that it is the food he ate which is the cause (or a contributory cause) of his felt pain—not even if the man were to report a vivid feeling of abdominal disturbance. And similarly, an overwhelming feeling of being in the presence of the Divine is evidence enough for admitting the genuineness of such feeling; it is no evidence for the claim that a supreme being with a substantial existence independent of the experience is the cause of the experience.

5

Thus far the discussion has been concerned with noting inadequacies in various arguments widely used to support theism. However, much atheistic criticism is also directed toward exposing incoherencies in the very thesis of theism. I want therefore to consider this aspect of the atheistic critique, though I will restrict myself to the central difficulty in the theistic position which arises from the simultaneous attribution of omnipotence, omniscience, and omnibenevolence to the Deity. The difficulty is that of reconciling these attributes with the occurrence of evil in the world. Accordingly, the question to which I now turn is whether, despite the existence of evil, it is possible to construct a theodicy which will justify the ways of an infinitely powerful and just God to man.

Two main types of solutions have been proposed for this problem. One way that is frequently used is to maintain that what is commonly called evil is only an illusion, or at worst only the "privation" or absence of good. Accordingly, evil is not "really real," it is only the "negative" side of God's beneficence, it is only the product of our limited intelligence which fails to plumb the true character of God's creative bounty. A sufficient comment on this proposed solution is that facts are not altered or abolished by rebaptizing them. Evil may indeed be only an appearance and not genuine. But this does not eliminate from the realm of appearance the tragedies, the sufferings, and the iniquities which men so frequently endure. And it raises once more, though on another level, the problem of reconciling the fact that there is evil in the realm of appearance with God's alleged omnibenevolence. In any event, it is small comfort to anyone suffering a cruel misfortune for which he is in no way responsible, to be told that what he is undergoing is only the absence of good. It is a gratuitous insult to mankind, a symptom of insensitivity and indifference to human suffering, to be assured that all the miseries and agonies men experience are only illusory.

Another gambit often played in attempting to justify the ways of God to man is to argue that the things called evil are evil only because they are viewed in isolation; they are not evil when viewed in proper perspective and in relation to the rest of creation. Thus, if one attends to but a single instrument in an orchestra, the sounds issuing from it may indeed be harsh and discordant. But if one is placed at a proper distance from the whole orchestra, the sounds of that single instrument will mingle with the sounds issuing from the other players to produce a marvellous bit of symphonic music. Analogously, experiences we call painful undoubtedly occur and are real enough. But the pain is judged to be an evil only because it is experienced in a limited perspective—the pain is there for the sake of a more inclusive good, whose reality eludes us because our intelligences are too weak to apprehend things in their entirety.

It is an appropriate retort to this argument that of course we judge things to be evil in a human perspective, but that since we are not God this is the only proper perspective in which to judge them. It may indeed be the case that what is evil for us is not evil for some other part of creation. However, we are not this other part of creation, and it is irrelevant to argue that were we something other than what we are, our evaluations of what is good and bad would be different. Moreover, the worthlessness of the argument becomes even more evident if we remind ourselves that it is unsupported speculation to suppose that whatever is evil in a finite perspective is good from the purported perspective of the totality of things. For the argument can be turned around: what we judge to be a good is a good only because it is viewed in isolation; when it is viewed in proper perspective, and in relation to the entire scheme of things, it is an evil. This is in fact a standard form of the argument for a universal pessimism. Is it any worse than the similar argument for a universal optimism? The very raising of the question is a **reductio ad absurdum** of the proposed solution to the ancient problem of evil.

I do not believe it is possible to reconcile the alleged omnipotence and omnibenevolence of God with the unvarnished facts of human existence. In point of fact, many theologians have concurred in this conclusion; for in order to escape from the difficulty which the traditional attributes of God present, they have assumed that God is not all powerful, and that there are limits as to what He can do in his efforts to establish a righteous order in the universe. But whether such a modified theology is better off, is doubtful; and in any event, the question still remains whether the facts of human life support the claim that an omnibenevolent Deity, though limited in power, is revealed in the ordering of human history. It is pertinent to note in this connection that though there have been many historians who have made the effort, no historian has yet succeeded in showing to the satisfaction of his professional colleagues that the hypothesis of a Divine Providence is capable of explaining anything which cannot be explained just as well without this hypothesis.

6

This last remark naturally leads to the question whether, apart from their polemics against theism, philosophical atheists have not shared a common set of positive views, a common set of philosophical convictions which set them off from other groups of thinkers. In one very clear sense of this query the answer is indubitably negative. For there never has been what one might call a "school of atheism," in the way in which there has been a Platonic school or even a Kantian school. In point of fact, atheistic critics of theism can be found among many of the conventional groupings of philosophical thinkers—even, I venture to add, among professional theologians in recent years who in effect preach atheism in the guise of language taken bodily from the Christian tradition.

Nevertheless, despite the variety of philosophic positions to which at one time or another in the history of thought atheists have subscribed, it seems to me that atheism is not simply a negative standpoint. At any rate, there is a certain quality of intellectual temper that has characterized, and continues to characterize, many philosophical atheists. (I am excluding from consideration the so-called "village atheist," whose primary concern is to twit and ridicule those who accept some form of theism, or for that matter those who have any religious convictions.) Moreover, their rejection of theism is based not only on the inadequacies they have found in the arguments for theism, but often also on the positive ground that atheism is a corollary to a better supported general outlook upon the nature of things. I want therefore to conclude this discussion with a brief enumeration of some points of positive doctrine to which by and large philosophical atheists seem to me to subscribe. These points fall into three major groups.

In the first place, philosophical atheists reject the assumption that there are disembodied spirits, or that incorporeal entities of any sort can exercise a causal agency. On the contrary, atheists are generally agreed that if we wish to achieve any understanding of what takes place in the universe, we must look to the operations of organized bodies. Accordingly, the various processes taking place in nature, whether animate or inanimate, are to be explained in terms of the properties and structures of identifiable and spatio-temporally located objects. Moreover, the present variety of systems and activities found in the universe is to be accounted for on the basis of the transformations things undergo when they enter into different relations with one another—transformations which often result in the emergence of novel kinds of objects. On the other hand, though things are in flux and undergo alteration, there is no all-encompassing unitary pattern of change. Nature is ineradicably plural, both in respect to the individuals occurring in it as well as in respect to the processes in which things become involved. Accordingly, the human scene and the human perspective are not illusory; and man and his works are no less and no more "real" than are other parts or phases of the cosmos. At the risk of using a possibly misleading characterization, all of this can be summarized by saying that an atheistic view of things is a form of materialism.

In the second place, atheists generally manifest a marked empirical temper, and often take as their ideal the intellectual methods employed in the contemporaneous empirical sciences. Philosophical atheists differ considerably on important points of detail in their account of how responsible claims to knowledge are to be established. But there is substantial agreement among them that controlled sensory observation is the court of final appeal in issues concerning matters of fact. It is indeed this commitment to the use of an empirical method which is the final basis of the atheistic critique of theism. For at bottom this critique seeks to show that we can understand whatever a theistic assumption is alleged to explain, through the use of the proved methods of the positive sciences and without the introduction of empirically unsupported **ad hoc hypotheses** about a Deity. It is pertinent in this connection to recall a familiar legend about the French mathematical physicist Laplace. According to the story, Laplace made a personal presentation of a copy of his now famous book on celestial mechanics to Napoleon. Napoleon glanced through the volume, and finding no reference to the Deity asked Laplace whether God's existence played any role in the analysis. "Sire, I have no need for that hypothesis," Laplace is reported to have replied. The dismissal of sterile hypotheses characterizes not only the work of Laplace; it is

the uniform rule in scientific inquiry. The sterility of the theistic assumption is one of the main burdens of the literature of atheism both ancient and modern.

And finally, atheistic thinkers have generally accepted a utilitarian basis for judging moral issues, and they have exhibited a libertarian attitude toward human needs and impulses. The conceptions of the human good they have advocated are conceptions which are commensurate with the actual capacities of mortal men, so that it is the satisfaction of the complex needs of the human creature which is the final standard for evaluating the validity of a moral ideal or moral prescription.

In consequence, the emphasis of atheistic moral reflection has been this-worldly rather than other-worldly, individualistic rather than authoritarian. The stress upon a good life that must be consummated in this world, has made atheists vigorous opponents of moral codes which seek to repress human impulses in the name of some unrealizable other-worldly ideal. The individualism that is so pronounced a strain in many philosophical atheists has made them tolerant of human limitations and sensitive to the plurality of legitimate moral goals. On the other hand, this individualism has certainly not prevented many of them from recognizing the crucial role which institutional arrangements can play in achieving desirable patterns of human living. In consequence, atheists have made important contributions to the development of a climate of opinion favorable to pursuing the values of a liberal civilization and they have played effective roles in attempts to rectify social injustices.

Atheists cannot build their moral outlook on foundations upon which so many men conduct their lives. In particular, atheism cannot offer the incentives to conduct and the consolations for misfortune which theistic religions supply to their adherents. It can offer no hope of personal immortality, no threats of Divine chastisement, no promise of eventual recompense for injustices suffered, no blueprints to sure salvation. For on its view of the place of man in nature, human excellence and human dignity must be achieved within a finite life-span, or not at all, so that the rewards of moral endeavor must come from the quality of civilized living, and not from some source of disbursement that dwells outside of time. Accordingly, atheistic moral reflection at its best does not culminate in a quiescent ideal of human perfection, but is a vigorous call to intelligent activity—activity for the sake of realizing human potentialities and for eliminating whatever stands in the way of such realization. Nevertheless, though slavish resignation to remediable ills is not characteristic of atheistic thought, responsible atheists have never pretended that human effort can invariably achieve the heart's every legitimate desire. A tragic view of life is thus an uneliminable ingredient in atheistic thought. This ingredient does not invite or generally produce lugubrious lamentation. But it does touch the atheist's view of man and his place in nature with an emotion that makes the philosophical atheist a kindred spirit to those who, within the frameworks of various religious traditions, have developed a serenely resigned attitude toward the inevitable tragedies of the human estate.

Questions on Nagel

1. How does Nagel define atheism? According to Nagel, why is Buddhism an atheistic religion? Do you think it is possible for a Christian to be an atheist in Nagel's sense? Is it possible to be a theist and not accept any particular religion?

2. Why does Nagel attack religious authorities, institutions, and creeds? Do you agree with this attack or not? Defend your view.

3. Explain Nagel's criticisms of the standard proofs of God's existence (the cosmological argument, the ontological argument, the teleological argument, the moral argument, and the argument from religious experience). Are these criticisms convincing or not? Defend you answer.

4. According to Nagel, what is the central difficulty in the theistic position? How do theists try to solve the problem? Are their solutions satisfactory or not? Why or why not?

5. Nagel believes that atheists subscribe to at least three points of positive doctrine. What are they? Can one be an atheist and not subscribe to any of them? Are they acceptable to you? Why or why not?

Antony Flew, Basil Mitchell, and R. M. Hare

Theology and Falsification

Antony Flew is Professor of Philosophy at the University of Reading in England. R. M. Hare is currently Professor of Philosophy at the University of Florida, Gainesville. Basil Mitchell is Nolloth Professor of the Philosophy of the Christian Religion at Oxford University.

Reprinted with permission of Macmillan Publishing Company from *New Essays in Philosophical Theology* by A. Flew and A. MacIntyre. Copyright © 1955 by Flew and MacIntyre, renewed 1963.

A.   Antony Flew

Let us begin with a parable. It is a parable developed from a tale told by John Wisdom in his haunting and revelatory article 'Gods'.[1] Once upon a time two explorers came upon a clearing in the jungle. In the clearing were growing many flowers and many weeds. One explorer says, 'Some gardener must tend this plot'. The other disagrees, 'There is no gardener'. So they pitch their tents and set a watch. No gardener is ever seen. 'But perhaps he is an invisible gardener.' So they set up a barbed-wire fence. They electrify it. They patrol with bloodhounds. (For they remember how H. G. Well's *The Invisible Man* could be both smelt and touched though he could not be seen.) But no shrieks ever suggest that some intruder has received a shock. No movements of the wire ever betray an invisible climber. The bloodhounds never give cry. Yet still the Believer is not convinced. 'But there is a gardener, invisible, intangible, insensible to electric shocks, a gardener who has no scent and makes no sound, a gardener who comes secretly to look after the garden which he loves.' At last the Sceptic despairs, 'But what remains of your original assertion? Just how does what you call an invisible, intangible, eternally elusive gardener differ from an imaginary gardener or even from no gardener at all?'

In this parable we can see how what starts as an assertion, that something exists or that there is some analogy between certain complexes of phenomena, may be reduced step by step to an altogether different status, to an expression perhaps of a 'picture preference'.[2] The Sceptic says there is no gardener. The Believer says there is a gardener (but invisible, etc.). One man talks about sexual behavior. Another man prefers to talk of Aphrodite (but knows that there is not really a superhuman person additional to, and somehow responsible for, all sexual phenomena). The process of qualification may be checked at any point before the original assertion is completely withdrawn and something of that first assertion will remain (**Tautology**). Mr. Wells's invisible man could not, admittedly, be seen, but in all other respects he was a man like the rest of us. But though the process of qualification may be, and of course usually is, checked in time, it is not always judiciously so halted. Someone may dissipate his assertion completely without noticing that he has done so. A fine brash hypothesis may thus be killed by inches, the death by a thousand qualifications.

And in this, it seems to me, lies the peculiar danger, the endemic evil, of theological utterance. Take such utterances as 'God has a plan', 'God created the world', 'God loves us as a father loves his children'. They look at first sight very much like assertions, vast cosmological assertions. Of course, this is no sure sign that they either are, or are intended to be, assertions. But let us confine ourselves to the cases where those who utter such sentences intend them to express assertions. (Merely remarking parenthetically that those who intend or interpret such utterances as crypto-commands, expressions of wishes, disguised ejaculations, concealed ethics, or as anything else but assertions, are unlikely to succeed in making them either properly orthodox or practically effective.)

Now to assert that such and such is the case is necessarily equivalent to denying that such and such is not the case.[3] Suppose then that we are in doubt as to what someone who gives vent to an utterance is asserting, or suppose that, more radically, we are sceptical as to whether he is really asserting anything at all, one way of trying to understand (or perhaps it will be to expose) his utterance is to attempt to find what he would regard as counting against, or as being incompatible with, its truth. For if the utterance is indeed an assertion, it will necessarily be equivalent to a denial of the negation of that assertion. And anything which would count against the assertion, or which would induce the speaker to withdraw it and to admit that it had been mistaken, must be part of (or the whole of) the meaning of the negation of that assertion. And to know the meaning of the negation of an assertion, is as near as makes no matter, to know the meaning of that assertion.[4] And if there is nothing which a putative assertion denies then there is nothing which it asserts either: and so it is not really an assertion. When the Sceptic in the parable asked the Believer, 'Just how does what you call an invisible, intangible, eternally elusive gardener differ from an imaginary gardener or even from no gardener at all?' he was suggesting that the Believer's earlier statement had been so eroded by qualification that it was no longer an assertion at all.

Now it often seems to people who are not religious as if there was no conceivable event or series of events the occurrence of which would be admitted by sophisticated religious people to be a sufficient reason for conceding 'There wasn't a God after all' or 'God does not really love us then'. Someone tells us that God loves us as a father loves his children. We are reassured. But then we see a child dying of inoperable cancer of the throat. His earthly father is driven frantic in his efforts to help, but his Heavenly Father reveals no obvious sign of concern. Some qualification is made—God's love is 'not a merely human love' or it is 'an inscrutable love', perhaps—and we realize that such sufferings are quite compatible with the truth of the assertion that 'God loves us as a father (but, of course, . . .)'. We are reassured again. But then perhaps we ask: what is this assurance of God's (appropriately qualified) love worth, what is this apparent guarantee really a guarantee against? Just what would have to happen not merely (morally and wrongly) to tempt but also (logically and rightly) to entitle us to say 'God does not love us' or even 'God does not exist'? I therefore put to the succeeding symposiasts the simple central questions, 'What would have to occur or to have occurred to constitute for you a disproof of the love of, or of the existence of, God?'

B.   R. M. Hare

I wish to make it clear that I shall not try to defend Christianity in particular, but religion in general—not because I do not believe in Christianity, but because you cannot understand what Christianity is, until you have understood what religion is.

I must begin by confessing that, on the ground marked out by Flew, he seems to be completely victorious. I therefore shift my ground by relating another parable. A certain lunatic is convinced that all dons want to murder him. His friends introduce him to all the mildest and most respectable dons that they can find, and after each of them has retired, they say, 'You see, he doesn't really want to murder you; he spoke to you in a most cordial manner; surely you are convinced now?' But the lunatic replies 'Yes, but that was only his diabolical cunning; he's really plotting against me the whole time, like the rest of them; I know it I tell you'. However many kindly dons are produced, the reaction is still the same.

Now we say that such a person is deluded. But what is he deluded about? About the truth or falsity of an assertion? Let us apply Flew's test to him. There is no behaviour of dons that can be enacted which he will accept as counting against his theory; and therefore his theory, on this test, asserts nothing. But it does not follow that there is no difference between what he thinks about dons and what most of us think about them—otherwise we should not call him a lunatic and ourselves sane, and dons would

have no reason to feel uneasy about his presence in Oxford.

Let us call that in which we differ from this lunatic, our respective *bliks*. He has an insane *blik* about dons; we have a sane one. It is important to realize that we have a sane one, not no *blik* at all; for there must be two sides to any argument—if he has a wrong *blik*, then those who are right about dons must have a right one. Flew has shown that a *blik* does not consist in an assertion or system of them; but nevertheless it is very important to have the right *blik*.

Let us try to imagine what it would be like to have different *bliks* about other things than dons. When I am driving my car, it sometimes occurs to me to wonder whether my movements of the steering-wheel will always continue to be followed by corresponding alterations in the direction of the car. I have never had a steering failure, though I have had skids, which must be similar. Moreover, I know enough about how the steering of my car is made, to know the sort of thing that would have to go wrong for the steering to fail—steel joints would have to part, or steel rods break, or something—but how do I know that this won't happen? The truth is, I don't know; I just have a *blik* about steel and its properties, so that normally I trust the steering of my car; but I find it not at all difficult to imagine what it would be like to lose this *blik* and acquire the opposite one. People would say I was silly about steel; but there would be no mistaking the reality of the difference between our respective *bliks*—for example, I should never go in a motor-car. Yet I should hesitate to say that the difference between us was the difference between contradictory assertions. No amount of safe arrivals or bench-tests will remove my *blik* and restore the normal one; for my *blik* is compatible with any finite number of such tests.

It was Hume who taught us that our whole commerce with the world depends upon our *blik* about the world; and that differences between *bliks* about the world cannot be settled by observation of what happens in the world. That was why, having performed the interesting experiment of doubting the ordinary man's *blik* about the world, and showing that no proof could be given to make us adopt one *blik* rather than another, he turned to backgammon to take his mind off the problem. It seems, indeed, to be impossible even to formulate as an assertion the normal *blik* about the world which makes me put my confidence in the future reliability of steel joints, in the continued ability of the road to support my car, and not gape beneath it revealing nothing below; in the general non-homicidal tendencies of dons; in my own continued well-being (in some sense of that word that I may not now fully understand) if I continue to do what is right according to my lights; in the general likelihood of people like Hitler coming to a bad end. But perhaps a formulation less inadequate than most is to be found in the Psalms: 'The earth is weak and all the inhabiters thereof: I bear up the pillars of it'.

The mistake of the position which Flew selects for attack is to regard this kind of talk as some sort of *explanation,* as scientists are accustomed to use the word. As such, it would obviously be ludicrous. We no longer believe in God as an Atlas—*nous n'avons pas besoin de cette hypothèse.* But it is nevertheless true to say that, as Hume saw, without a *blik* there can be no explanation; for it is by our *bliks* that we decide what is and what is not an explanation. Suppose we believed that everything that happened, happened by pure chance. This would not of course be an assertion; for it is compatible with anything happening or not happening, and so, incidentally, is its contradictory. But if we had this belief, we should not be able to explain or predict or plan anything. Thus, although we should not be *asserting* anything different from those of a more normal belief, there would be a great difference between us; and this is the sort of difference that there is between those who really believe in God and those who really disbelieve in him.

The word 'really' is important, and may excite suspicion. I put it in, because when people have had a good Christian upbringing, as have most of those who now profess not to believe in any sort of religion, it is very hard to discover what they really believe. The reason why they find it so easy to think that they are not religious, is that they have never got into the frame of mind of one who suffers from the doubts to which religion is the answer. Not for them the terrors of the primitive jungle. Having abandoned some of the more picturesque fringes of religion, they think that they have abandoned the whole thing—whereas in fact they still have got, and could not live without, a religion of a comfortably substantial, albeit highly sophisticated, kind, which differs from that of many 're- ligious people' in little more than this, that 'religious people' like to sing Psalms about theirs —a very natural and proper thing to do. But nevertheless there may be a big difference lying behind—the difference between two people who, though side by side, are walking in different directions. I do not know in what direction Flew is walking; perhaps he does not know either. But we have had some examples recently of various ways in which one can walk away from Christianity, and there are any number of possibilities. After all, man has not changed biologically since primitive times; it is his religion that has changed, and it can easily change again. And if you do not think that such changes make a difference, get acquainted with some Sikhs and some Mussulmans of the same Punjabi stock; you will find them quite different sorts of people.

There is an important difference between Flew's parable and my own which we have not yet noticed. The explorers do not *mind* about their garden; they discuss it with interest, but not with concern. But my lunatic, poor fellow, minds about dons; and I mind about the steering of my car; it often has people in it that I care for. It is because I mind very much about what goes on in the garden in which I find myself, that I am unable to share the explorer's detachment.

C. Basil Mitchell

Flew's article is searching and perceptive, but there is, I think, something odd about his conduct of the theologian's case. The theologian surely would not deny that the fact of pain counts against the assertion that God loves

---

* *["we have no need for that hypothesis" – Ed.]*

men. This very incompatibility generates the most intractable of theological problems—the problem of evil. So the theologian *does* recognize the fact of pain as counting against Christian doctrine. But it is true that he will not allow it—or anything—to count decisively against it; for he is committed by his faith to trust in God. His attitude is not that of the detached observer, but of the believer.

Perhaps this can be brought out by yet another parable. In time of war in an occupied country, a member of the resistance meets one night a stranger who deeply impresses him. They spend that night together in conversation. The Stranger tells the partisan that he himself is on the side of the resistance—indeed that he is in command of it, and urges the partisan to have faith in him no matter what happens. The partisan is utterly convinced at that meeting of the Stranger's sincerity and constancy and undertakes to trust him.

They never meet in conditions of intimacy again. But sometimes the Stranger is seen helping members of the resistance, and the partisan is grateful and says to his friends, 'He is on our side'.

Sometimes he is seen in the uniform of the police handing over patriots to the occupying power. On these occasions his friends murmur against him: but the partisan still says, 'He is on our side'. He still believes that, in spite of appearances, the Stranger did not deceive him. Sometimes he asks the Stranger for help and receives it. He is then thankful. Sometimes he asks and does not receive it. Then he says, 'The Stranger knows best'. Sometimes his friends, in exasperation, say 'Well, what *would* he have to do for you to admit that you were wrong and that he is not on our side?' But the partisan refuses to answer. He will not consent to put the Stranger to the test. And sometimes his friends complain, 'Well, if *that's* what you mean by his being on our side, the sooner he goes over to the other side the better'.

The partisan of the parable does not allow anything to count decisively against the proposition 'The Stranger is on our side'. This is because he has committed himself to trust the Stranger. But he of course recognizes that the Stranger's ambiguous behaviour *does* count against what he believes about him. It is precisely this situation which constitutes the trial of his faith.

When the partisan asks for help and doesn't get it, what can he do? He can (*a*) conclude that the stranger is not on our side or; (*b*) maintain that he is on our side, but that he has reasons for withholding help.

The first he will refuse to do. How long can he uphold the second position without its becoming just silly?

I don't think one can say in advance. It will depend on the nature of the impression created by the Stranger in the first place. It will depend, too, on the manner in which he takes the Stranger's behaviour. If he blandly dismisses it as of no consequence, as having no bearing upon his belief, it will be assumed that he is thoughtless or insane. And it quite obviously won't do for him to say easily, 'Oh, when used of the Stranger the phrase "is on our side" *means* ambiguous behaviour of this sort.' In that case he would be like the religious man who says blandly of a terrible disaster 'It is God's will'. No, he will only be regarded as sane and reasonable in his belief, if he experiences in himself the full force of the conflict.

It is here that my parable differs from Hare's. The partisan admits that many things may and do count against his belief: whereas Hare's lunatic who has a *blik* about dons doesn't admit that anything counts against his *blik*. Nothing *can* count against *bliks*. Also the partisan has a reason for having in the first instance committed himself, viz. the character of the Stranger; whereas the lunatic has no reason for his *blik* about dons—because, of course, you can't have reasons for *bliks*.

This means that I agree with Flew that theological utterances must be assertions. The partisan is making an assertion when he says, 'The Stranger is on our side'.

Do I want to say that the partisan's belief about the Stranger is, in any sense, an explanation? I think I do. It explains and makes sense of the Stranger's behaviour: it helps to explain also the resistance movement in the context of which he appears. In each case it differs from the interpretation which the others put upon the same facts.

'God loves men' resembles 'the Stranger is on our side' (and many other significant statements, e.g. historical ones) in not being conclusively falsifiable. They can both be treated in at least three different ways: (1) As provisional hypotheses to be discarded if experience tells against them; (2) As significant articles of faith; (3) As vacuous formulae (expressing, perhaps, a desire for reassurance) to which experience makes no difference and which make no difference to life.

The Christian, once he has committed himself, is precluded by his faith from taking up the first attitude: 'Thou shalt not tempt the Lord thy God'. He is in constant danger, as Flew has observed, of slipping into the third. But he need not; and, if he does, it is a failure in faith as well as in logic.

D. Antony Flew

It has been a good discussion: and I am glad to have helped to provoke it. But now—at least in *University*—it must come to an end: and the Editors of *University* have asked me to make some concluding remarks. Since it is impossible to deal with all the issues raised or to comment separately upon each contribution, I will concentrate on Mitchell and Hare, as representative of two very different kinds of response to the challenge made in 'Theology and Falsification'.

The challenge, it will be remembered, ran like this. Some theological utterances seem to, and are intended to, provide explanations or express assertions. Now an assertion, to be an assertion at all, must claim that things stand thus and thus; *and not otherwise*. Similarly an explanation, to be an explanation at all, must explain why this particular thing occurs; *and not something else*. Those last clauses are crucial. And yet sophisticated religious people—or so it seemed to me—are apt to overlook this, and tend to refuse to allow, not merely that anything actually does occur, but that anything conceivably could occur, which would count against their theological assertions and explanations. But in so far as they do this their supposed explanations are actually bogus, and their seeming assertions are really vacuous.

Mitchell's response to this challenge is admirably direct, straightforward, and understanding. He agrees 'that theological utterances must be assertions'. He agrees that if they are to be assertions, there must be something that would count against their truth. He agrees, too, that believers are in constant danger of transforming their would-be assertions into 'vacuous formulae'. But he takes me to task for an oddity in my 'conduct of the theologian's case. The theologian surely would not deny that the fact of pain counts against the assertion that God loves men. This very incompatibility generates the most intractable of theological problems, the problem of evil'. I think he is right. I should have made a distinction between two very different ways of dealing with what looks like evidence against the love of God: the way I stressed was the expedient of qualifying the original assertion; the way the theologian usually takes, at first, is to admit that it looks bad but to insist that there is—there must be—some explanation which will show that, in spite of appearances, there really is a God who loves us. His difficulty, it seems to me, is that he has given God attributes which rule out all possible saving explanations. In Mitchell's parable of the Stranger it is easy for the believer to find plausible excuses for ambiguous behaviour: for the Stranger is a man. But suppose the Stranger is God. We cannot say that he would like to help but cannot: God is omnipotent. We cannot say that he would help if he only knew: God is omniscient. We cannot say that he is not responsible for the wickedness of others: God creates those others. Indeed an omnipotent, omniscient God must be an accessory before (and during) the fact to every human misdeed; as well as being responsible for every non-moral defect in the universe. So, though I entirely concede that Mitchell was absolutely right to insist against me that the theologian's first move is to look for an *explanation*, I still think that in the end, if relentlessly pursued, he will have to resort to the avoiding action of *qualification*. And there lies the danger of that death by a thousand qualifications, which would, I agree, constitute 'a failure in faith as well as in logic'.

Hare's approach is fresh and bold. He confesses that 'on the ground marked out by Flew, he seems to me to be completely victorious'. He therefore introduces the concept of *blik*. But while I think that there is room for some such concept in philosophy, and that philosophers should be grateful to Hare for his invention, I nevertheless want to insist that any attempt to analyse Christian religious utterances as expressions or affirmations of a *blik* rather than as (at least would-be) assertions about the cosmos is fundamentally misguided. *First,* because thus interpreted they would be entirely unorthodox. If Hare's religion really is a *blik,* involving no cosmological assertions about the nature and activities of a supposed personal creator, then surely he is not a Christian at all? *Second,* because thus interpreted, they could scarcely do the job they do. If they were not even intended as assertions then many religious activities would become fraudulent, or merely silly. If 'You ought *because* it is God's will' asserts no more than 'You ought', then the person who prefers the former phraseology is not really giving a reason, but a fraudulent substitute for one, a dialectical dud cheque. If 'My soul must be immortal *because* God loves his children, etc.' asserts no more than 'My soul must be immortal', then the man who reassures himself with theological arguments for immortality is being as silly as the man who tries to clear his overdraft by writing his bank a cheque on the same account. (Of course neither of these utterances would be distinctively Christian: but this discussion never pretended to be so confined.) Religious utterances may indeed express false or even bogus assertions: but I simply do not believe that they are not both intended and interpreted to be or at any rate to presuppose assertions, at least in the context of religious practice; whatever shifts may be demanded, in another context, by the exigencies of theological apologetic.

One final suggestion. The philosophers of religion might well draw upon George Orwell's last appalling nightmare *1984* for the concept of *doublethink*. '*Doublethink* means the power of holding two contradictory beliefs simultaneously, and accepting both of them. The party intellectual knows that he is playing tricks with reality, but by the exercise of *doublethink* he also satisfies himself that reality is not violated' (*1984*, p. 220). Perhaps religious intellectuals too are sometimes driven to doublethink in order to retain their faith in a loving God in face of the reality of a heartless and indifferent world. But of this more another time, perhaps.[5]

Notes

1. *P.A.S.,* 1944–5, reprinted as Ch. X of *Logic and Language,* Vol I (Blackwell, 1951), and in his *Philosophy and Psychoanalysis* (Blackwell, 1953).

2. Cf. J. Wisdom, 'Other Minds', *Mind,* 1940; reprinted in his *Other Minds* (Blackwell, 1952).

3. For those who prefer symbolism: $p \equiv \sim \sim p$.

4. For by simply negating $\sim p$ we get $p : \sim \sim p \equiv p$.

5. [Some footnotes have been eliminated, and the footnotes have been renumbered – Ed.]

Questions on Flew, Hare, and Mitchell

1. In their discussions, each philosopher gives us a parable or example that is supposed to illuminate something about religious belief in God. What is the point of each parable or example? How do they differ? Do they have common themes? Which story seems to you to best describe belief in God? Why?

2. Does Flew give an adequate reply to Mitchell and Hare or not? Explain your answer.

3. Is Flew an atheist? Explain your answer.

Suggested Readings

Frederick Sontag and M. Darrol Bryant, eds., *God: The Contemporary Discussion* (New York: The Rose of Sharon Press, 1982) is a collection of papers on the concept of God in Christianity, Islam, Hinduism, and other religions.

John Hick, ed., *The Existence of God* (New York: The Macmillan Co., 1964) is a collection of readings that includes classical statements of the ontological argument, the cosmological argument, the teleological argument, the moral argument, and the argument from religious experience. There are also articles about the meaning and verification of God.

The Ontological Argument, ed. Alvin Plantiga (New York: Doubleday Anchor Books, 1965) gives a comprehensive treatment of both classical and contemporary discussions of the argument.

An influential advocate of the ontological argument is Charles Hartshorne; see his book *Anselm's Discovery* (LaSalle, IL: Open Court, 1962).

Donald Burrill, ed., *The Cosmological Argument* (New York: Doubleday Anchor Books, 1967) has a good collection of critical papers on the first cause argument and other versions of the cosmological argument. Anthony Kenny, *Five Ways: St. Thomas Aquinas' Proofs of God's Existence* (London: Routledge & Kegan Paul, 1969) gives a careful and detailed exposition of each of Aquinas' five ways and then subjects them to critical evaluation.

Lecomte du Nouys, *Human Destiny* (New York: Longmans, Green & Co., 1947) is one of the best-known modern versions of the teleological argument. Richard Swineburne, *The Existence of God* (Oxford: Clarendon Press, 1979) argues in chapters 7 and 8 that the cosmological and teleological arguments are not deductively valid, but they do provide inductive evidence for the existence of God.

The classical statement of agnosticism (a word coined by Huxley) is T. H. Huxley's essay "Agnosticism" reprinted in his book *Science and the Christian Tradition* (New York: Appleton, 1894). Agnosticism is defended by Clarence Darrow in "Why I Am an Agnostic," reprinted in A. and L. Weinberg, eds., *Clarence Darrow—Verdicts Out of Court* (Chicago: Quadrangle Books, 1963). Bertrand Russell presents his controversial views on the existence of God, Jesus, and Christianity in *Why I Am Not a Christian* (New York: Simon and Schuster, 1957).

Peter Angeles, ed., *Critiques of God* (Buffalo, NY: Prometheus Books, 1976) contains essays representing atheistic and sceptical views of the problem of God's existence. George H. Smith, *Atheism: The Case Against God* (Buffalo, NY: Prometheus Books, 1979) presents an analysis and defense of atheism.

For discussions on the meaning of religious statements, verification, and falsification, see Flew and MacIntyre, ed., *New Essays in Philosophical Theology* (New York: Macmillan Press, 1955) and John Hick, ed., *Faith and the Philosophers* (New York: St. Martin's Press, 1964).

The Problem of Evil and Religious Faith

Chapter 2

Introduction

The problem of evil. In the last chapter, both St. Thomas and Ernest Nagel raised a serious problem for those who believe in the existence of God: God's omnipotence and omnibenevolence seem to be incompatible with the existence of evil. Why should this be? It seems undeniable that evil exists in the world, where evil includes both natural evil and moral evil. Natural evil is the evil found in the natural world that is not caused by human beings: diseases, injuries, and natural disasters such as earthquakes and hurricanes. Moral evil is evil produced by human beings: wars, murders, rapes, assaults, and so on. Both natural and moral evils cause a great deal of physical pain and mental suffering, and of course this pain and suffering is bad. So why does God allow natural and moral evil? If God is omnibenevolent, then surely God loves human beings enough to alleviate their pain and suffering; and if God is omnipotent, then God should be able to do this by abolishing all natural and moral evils from the world.

Another way of putting the problem that is perhaps more succinct is to argue that the following three statements cannot all be true: (1) Evil exists in the world. (2) God is omnipotent. (3) God is omnibenevolent. One of these statements must be false. As we have seen, the first statement about evil seems undeniable. So either (2) or (3) must be false—yet the theist believes that they are true. What can the theist say?

Attempted solutions to the problem of evil. The simplest way to solve the problem is to deny God's omnipotence or omnibenevolence, or to deny that God exists in the first place. But doing this amounts to accepting atheism in Nagel's sense of the term; it is a rejection of traditional theism in favor of some other belief, for instance, belief in the nonexistence of God, or belief in an evil god, or belief in a good god constantly struggling against an evil god.

The most implausible solution to the problem is to deny that evil exists. To say that no evil exists may seem a bit strange to those who have endured a great deal of pain and suffering, but there are those who have seriously advocated this view. Mary Baker Eddy, the founder of the Christian Science religion, maintained that evil is only an illusion of the mortal or human mind and that in reality there is no such thing as evil. But why is there even the illusion of evil? Why doesn't God eliminate this illusion too? Does it make sense to say that pain and suffering are illusions? Nothing seems more real than pain and suffering when you are experiencing it.

The standard theistic approach to the problem is not to deny the existence of evil, or to deny that God exists and is omnipotent and omnibenevolent, but rather to attempt to show how God's existence is compatible with the existence of evil in the world. One line of thought, briefly discussed by Nagel and represented by St. Augustine in our readings for this chapter, is to maintain that evil is not something positive but rather a "privation of good," or "good diminished." God's creation is good but not immutably so; it can be corrupted and thus made less good, and thus is evil. Only God is totally and immutably good.

The most popular solution to the problem, defended by John Hick in our readings, is what is often called the freewill solution. Moral evil is the result of the free will of humans; humans freely choose to do evil things, but this is not God's fault. God made humans free, and in order to be genuine, this freedom must allow humans the choice of acting wrongly.

The freewill solution has various difficulties. Some critics, for example J. L. Mackie in our readings, think that the notion of freedom of the will doesn't make any sense. Even if it does make sense to talk about human freedom, how is it possible for humans to be free if all human actions are caused or determined? This freedom-determinism problem will be discussed in chapter 4. Another objection made by Mackie is that an omnipotent God could have made humans who act freely, but who never do what is wrong. (Hick tries to reply to this objection in the readings.) Finally, the solution is incomplete; it explains the existence of moral evil but leaves out natural evil, which is surely not the result of human actions.

The freewill solution can be modified to explain natural evil by including Satan as one of the moral agents given freedom. Thus natural evil is not caused by humans, but by another moral agent with God-given freedom, namely Satan. This view can be found in the writings of St. Augustine, and has been endorsed by some contemporary Christian philosophers, for example, Steven T. Davis and Alvin Plantinga (see the suggested readings).

As John Hick notes in his article, St. Augustine offers another and different explanation of natural evil: it is God's punishment for sin. As St. Augustine says, "All evil is either sin or the punishment for sin." But what about those who do not sin, for example, innocent babies and children? The Augustinian answer is that they are still tainted with original sin, the sin of Adam and Eve, but they will be rewarded in heaven, and this will wipe out, or at least morally balance, the suffering they have endured in this life. But what about the suffering of nonhuman animals? Surely they are not tainted with original sin, and the orthodox view is that they do not go to heaven.

Another view traditionally attributed to St. Augustine and endorsed by St. Thomas (see the end of the reading in the last chapter) is that God allows evil to exist so that good may be produced from it. Hick calls this approach to the problem **Irenaean theodicy** (a rational explanation of why God allows evil to exist that is found in the writings of St. Irenaeus) and distinguishes it from Augustinian theodicy. As Hick explains this Irenaean theodicy, evil is part of God's plan of "soul-making" or making virtuous "heirs to eternal life." If God had made the world a hedonistic paradise, humans would not have the chance to develop virtues such as courage and fortitude. Furthermore, undesirable traits of character such as selfishness and fearfulness, which are produced by this unhappy world, can be removed in the next life.

Hick notes that the Irenaean solution to the problem of natural evil (which Hick has endorsed in other writings—see the suggested readings) assumes that humans not only survive death, but also that they will all eventually end up in heaven. The problem of survival of death, including Hick's views on the subject, is considered in chapter 6.

Religious faith.   Thus far the theist has been presented as one who defends belief in God using reason, someone who tries to demonstrate that God exists by means of arguments, and attempts to solve the problem of evil by giving a theodicy, a rational explanation of why God allows evil to exist. But suppose that it turns out to be impossible to prove that God exists, and that no adequate solution to the problem of evil can be found. Must the theist abandon belief in God? Certainly not. The theist can continue to believe on the basis of religious faith. In that case, the theist has abandoned theism in favor of fideism, the view that belief in God's existence can be based on faith alone.

One of the most famous defenses of religious faith is Pascal's wager. Pascal believes that it is impossible to know that God exists or to know the nature of God. Nevertheless, he thinks that we must wager that God exists or not. If you bet on God and win, your reward is eternal life in heaven. If you lose, and there is no God, you have lost nothing. On the other hand, if you bet against God (that is, you bet that God does not exist), and you win, you gain nothing, but if you lose, you lose an infinitely happy eternal life. Betting that God exists, therefore, is the best bet: you have everything to gain and nothing to lose.

Critics of Pascal's wager have pointed out that Pascal has overlooked some other possibilities. Stephen Stich (see the suggested readings) thinks that another alternative is belief in a jealous non-Christian God who will punish belief in the Christian God. William James in our readings points out that we might simply not bet at all, particularly if we have no tendency to choose either option.

James' own view is that if the choice between religion and agnosticism (or what James calls "skepticism") is a genuine option that is living (so that we have a tendency to choose), forced (we must make a choice), and momentous, then it is more reasonable to choose religion and risk being wrong than to choose agnosticism and risk losing the truth and the vital goods that religion gives us.

There is an ironic weakness in James' defense of faith, however, and that is that it can be used to defend anosticism instead of theistic faith. Instead of focusing on the good to be obtained from religion, why not concentrate on some of the bad effects? In the last chapter Nagel mentions several bad effects of religion as it has been practiced in the past—intolerance, obscurantist thought, and inhumane treatment of the ill and the underprivileged. Perhaps the various bad effects of religion outweigh the good effects. If so, it might be better from a practical point of view not to accept religious beliefs.

Both Pascal and James try to give a rational justification of faith in God. But what if these rational defenses fail too? There remains a last-ditch line of defense—an appeal to faith unsupported by reason. This appeal seems to involve a retreat from rationality to irrationality, an abandonment of reason in favor of faith. Our representative of this view in the readings is Soren Kierkegaard, who says the key to being a true Christian is feeling and commitment. It is not a question of simply believing some religious doctrine or proving God's existence or having some theological understanding of God. In fact, he admits that the doctrines of Christianity are paradoxical and absurd, and the nature of God is incomprehensible. But in the face of this we can make a leap of faith, and believe in God on the basis of "happy passion" or love.

St. Augustine

Evil Is the Absence of Good

St. Augustine (354–430) converted to Christianity in 386 and became one of the first Christian philosophers.

Chapter V

Questions Concerning the Origin of Evil in Regard to God, Who, Since He is the Chief Good, Cannot Be the Cause of Evil

And I sought "whence is evil?" And sought in an evil way; nor did I see the evil in my very search. And I set in order before the view of my spirit the whole creation, and whatever we can discern in it, such as earth, sea, air stars, trees, living creatures; and whatever in it we do not see, as the firmament of heaven, all the angels, too, and all the spiritual inhabitants thereof. But these very beings, as though they were bodies, my fancy disposed in such and such places, and I made one huge mass of all Thy creatures, distinguished according to the kinds of bodies—some of them being real bodies, some what I myself had feigned for spirits. And this mass I made huge—not as it was, which I could not know, but as large as I thought well, yet in every way finite. But Thee, O Lord, I imagined on every part environing and penetrating it, though in every way infinite; as if there were a sea everywhere, and on every side through immensity nothing but an infinite sea; and it contained within itself some sponge, huge, though finite, so that the sponge would in all its parts be filled from the immeasurable sea. So I conceived Thy creation to be itself finite, and filled by Thee, the Infinite. And I said, Behold God, and behold what God hath created; and God is good, most mightily and incomparably better than all these; but yet He, who is good, hath created them good, and behold how He encircleth and filleth them. Where, then, is evil, and whence,

The reading is from Whitney J. Oates, ed., *Basic Writings of Saint Augustine* (Grand Rapids, MI: Baker Book House, 1948), "Confessions," pp. 94–96, and "The Enchiridion," pp. 662–665. Reprinted by permission of Random House, Inc., and T & T Clark Ltd.

and how crept it in hither? What is its root, and what its seed? Or has it no being at all? Why, then, do we fear and shun that which has no being? Or if we fear it needlessly, then surely is that fear evil whereby the heart is unnecessarily pricked and tormented—and so much a greater evil, as we have naught to fear, and yet do fear. Therefore either that is evil which we fear, or the act of fearing is in itself evil. Whence, therefore, is it, seeing that God, who is good, has made all these things good? He, indeed, the greatest and chiefest Good, has created these lesser goods; but both Creator and created are all good. Whence is evil? Or was there some evil matter of which He made and formed and ordered it, but left something in it which He did not convert into good? But why was this? Was He powerless to change the whole lump, so that no evil should remain in it, seeing that He is omnipotent? Lastly, why would He make anything at all of it, and not rather by the same omnipotency cause it not to be at all? Or could it indeed exist contrary to His will? Or if it were from eternity, why did He permit it so to be for infinite spaces of times in the past, and was pleased so long after to make something out of it? Or if He wished now all of a sudden to do something, this rather should the Omnipotent have accomplished, that this evil matter should not be at all, and that He only should be the whole, true, chief, and infinite Good. Or if it were not good that He, who was good, should not also be the framer and creator of what was good, then that matter which was evil being removed, and brought to nothing, He might form good matter, whereof He might create all things. For He would not be omnipotent were He not able to create something good without being assisted by that matter which had not been created by Himself. Such things did I revolve in my miserable breast, overwhelmed with most gnawing cares lest I should die ere I discovered the truth; yet was the faith of Thy Christ, our Lord and Saviour, as held in the Catholic Church, fixed firmly in my heart, unformed, indeed, as yet upon many points, and diverging from doctrinal rules, but yet my mind did not utterly leave it, but every day rather drank in more and more of it. . . .

Chapter XI

What Is Called Evil in the Universe Is But the Absence of Good

And in the universe, even that which is called evil, when it is regulated and put in its own place, only enhances our admiration of the good; for we enjoy and value the good more when we compare it with the evil. For the Almighty God, who, as even the heathen acknowledge, has supreme power over all things, being Himself supremely good, would never permit the existence of anything evil among His works, if He were not so omnipotent and good that He can bring good even out of evil. For what is that which we call evil but the absence of good? In the bodies of animals, disease and wounds mean nothing but the absence of health; for when a cure is effected, that does not mean that the evils which were present—namely, the diseases and wounds—go away from the body and dwell elsewhere: they altogether cease to exist; for the wound or disease is not a substance, but a defect in the fleshy substance—the flesh itself being a substance, and therefore something good, of which those evils—that is, privations of the good which we call health—are accidents. Just in the same way, what are called vices in the soul are nothing but privations of natural good. And when they are cured, they are not transferred elsewhere: when they cease to exist in the healthy soul, they cannot exist anywhere else.

Chapter XII

All Beings Were Made Good, But Not Being Made Perfectly Good, Are Liable to Corruption

All things that exist, therefore, seeing that the Creator of them all is supremely good, are themselves good. But because they are not, like their Creator, supremely and unchangeably good, their good may be diminished and increased. But for good to be diminished is an evil, although, however much it may be diminished, it is necessary, if the being is to continue, that some good should remain to constitute the being. For however small or of whatever kind the being may be, the good which makes it a being cannot be destroyed without destroying the being itself. An uncorrupted nature is justly held in esteem. But if, still further, it be incorruptible, it is undoubtedly considered of still higher value. When it is corrupted, however, its corruption is an evil, because it is deprived of some sort of good. For if it be deprived of no good, it receives no injury; but it does receive injury, therefore it is deprived of good. Therefore, so long as a being is in process of corruption, there is in it some good of which it is being deprived; and if a part of the being should remain which cannot be corrupted, this will certainly be an incorruptible being, and accordingly the process of corruption will result in the manifestation of this great good. But if it do not cease to be corrupted, neither can it cease to possess good of which corruption may deprive it. But if it should be thoroughly and completely consumed by corruption, there will then be no good left, because there will be no being. Wherefore corruption can consume the good only by consuming the being. Every being, therefore, is a good; a great good, if it can not be corrupted; a little good, if it can: but in any case, only the foolish or ignorant will deny that it is a good. And if it be wholly consumed by corruption, then the corruption itself must cease to exist, as there is no being left in which it can dwell.

Chapter XIII

There Can Be No Evil Where There Is No Good; and an Evil Man Is an Evil Good

Accordingly, there is nothing of what we call evil, if there be nothing good. But a good which is wholly without evil is a perfect good. A good, on the other hand, which contains evil is a faulty or imperfect good; and there can be no evil where there is no good. From all this we arrive at the curious result: that since every being, so far as it is a being, is good, when we say that a faulty being is an evil being, we just seem to say that what is good is evil, and that nothing but what is good can be evil, seeing that every being is good, and that no evil can exist except in a being. Nothing, then, can be evil except some-

thing which is good. And although this, when stated, seems to be a contradiction, yet the strictness of reasoning leaves us no escape from the conclusion. We must, however, beware of incurring the prophetic condemnation: "Woe unto them that call evil good, and good evil: that put darkness for light, and light for darkness: that put bitter for sweet, and sweet for bitter."[1] And yet our Lord says: "An evil man out of the evil treasure of his heart bringeth forth that which is evil."[2] Now, what is an evil man but an evil being? for a man is a being. Now, if a man is a good thing because he is a being, what is an evil man but an evil good? Yet, when we accurately distinguish these two things, we find that it is not because he is a man that he is an evil, or because he is wicked that he is a good; but that he is a good because he is a man, and an evil because he is wicked. Whoever, then, says, "To be a man is an evil," or, "To be wicked is a good," falls under the prophetic denunciation: "Woe unto them that call evil good, and good evil!" For he condemns the work of God, which is the man, and praises the defect of man, which is the wickedness. Therefore every being, even if it be a defective one, in so far as it is a being is good, and in so far as it is defective is evil.

Chapter XIV

Good and Evil Are an Exception to the Rule That Contrary Attributes Cannot Be Predicated of the Same Subject. Evil Springs Up in What Is Good, and Cannot Exist Except in What Is Good

Accordingly, in the case of these contraries which we call good and evil, the rule of the logicians, that two contraries cannot be predicated at the same time of the same thing, does not hold. No weather is at the same time dark and bright: no food or drink is at the same time sweet and bitter: no body is at the same time and in the same place black and white: none is at the same time and in the same place deformed and beautiful. And this rule is found to hold in regard to many, indeed nearly all, contraries, that they cannot exist at the same time in any one thing. But although no one can doubt that good and evil are contraries, not only can they exist at the same time, but evil cannot exist without good, or in anything that is not good. Good, however, can exist without evil. For a man or an angel can exist without being wicked; but nothing can be wicked except a man or an angel: and so far as he is a man or an angel, he is good; so far as he is wicked, he is an evil. And these two contraries are so far co-existent, that if good did not exist in what is evil, neither could evil exist; because corruption could not have either a place to dwell in, or a source to spring from, if there were nothing that could be corrupted; and nothing can be corrupted except what is good, for corruption is nothing else but the destruction of good. From what is good, then, evils arose, and except in what is good they do not exist; nor was there any other source from which any evil nature could arise. For if there were, then, in so far as this was a being, it was certainly a good: and a being which was incorruptible would be a great good; and even one which was corruptible must be to some extent a good, for only by corrupting what was good in it could corruption do it harm.

Chapter XV

The Preceding Argument Is in No Wise Inconsistent With the Saying of Our Lord: "A Good Tree Cannot Bring Forth Evil Fruit"

But when we say that evil springs out of good, let it not be thought that this contradicts our Lord's saying: "A good tree cannot bring forth evil fruit."[3] For, as He who is the Truth says, you cannot gather grapes of thorns,[4] because grapes do not grow on thorns. But we see that on good soil both vines and thorns may be grown. And in the same way, just as an evil tree cannot bring forth good fruit, so an evil will cannot produce good works. But from the nature of man, which is good, may spring either a good or an evil will. And certainly there was at first no source from which an evil will could spring, except the nature of angel or of man, which was good. And our Lord Himself clearly shows this in the very same place where He speaks about the tree and its fruit. For He says: "Either make the tree good, and his fruit good; or else make the tree corrupt, and his fruit corrupt"[5]—clearly enough warning us that evil fruits do not grow on a good tree, nor good fruits on an evil tree; but that nevertheless the ground itself, by which He meant those whom He was then addressing, might grow either kind of trees.

Notes

1. Isa. v. 20
2. Luke vi. 45
3. Matt. vii. 18
4. Matt. vii. 16
5. Matt. vii. 33

Questions on St. Augustine

1. St. Augustine says that what we call evil is just the absence of good. Why does he believe this? Do you think this view is plausible? Why or why not?
2. St. Augustine believes that all things that exist are good. Can you think of any counter-examples, things that exist that are not good? What are they?
3. What does St. Augustine mean when he says that to be evil a thing must be good?

John Hick
The Problem of Evil

John Hick is currently Professor of Religion at Claremont Graduate School in California. Before beginning his teaching career, he was a Presbyterian minister in England.

The Problem

For many people it is, more than anything else, the appalling depth and extent of human suffering, together with the selfishness and greed which produce so much of this, that makes the idea of a loving Creator seem implausible and disposes them toward one of the various naturalistic theories of religion.

Rather than attempt to define "evil" in terms of some theological theory (for example, as "that which is contrary to God's will"), it seems better to define it ostensively, by indicating that to which the word refers. It refers to physical pain, mental suffering, and moral wickedness. The last is one of the causes of the first two, for an enormous amount of human pain arises from mankind's inhumanity. This pain includes such major scourges as poverty, oppression and persecution, war, and all the injustice, indignity, and inequity that occur in human societies. Even disease is fostered, to an extent that has not yet been precisely determined by psychosomatic medicine, by emotional and moral factors seated both in the individual and in his or her social environment. However, although a great deal of pain and suffering are caused by human action, there is much more that arises from such natural causes as bacteria and earthquakes, storm, fire, lightning, flood, and drought.

As a challenge to theism, the problem of evil has traditionally been posed in the form of a dilemma: if God is perfectly loving, God must wish to abolish all evil; and if God is all-powerful,

The reading is from John Hick, *Philosophy of Religion*, 3rd ed., ©1983, pp. 40–49. Reprinted by permission of Prentice-Hall, Inc., Englewood Cliffs, NJ.

God must be able to abolish all evil. But evil exists; therefore God cannot be both omnipotent and perfectly loving.

One possible solution (offered, for example, by contemporary Christian Science) can be ruled out immediately so far as the traditional Judaic-Christian faith is concerned. To say that evil is an illusion of the human mind is impossible within a religion based upon the stark realism of the Bible. Its pages faithfully reflect the characteristic mixture of good and evil in human experience. They record every kind of sorrow and suffering, every mode of "man's inhumanity to man" and of our painfully insecure existence in the world. There is no attempt to regard evil as anything but dark, menacingly ugly, heartrending, and crushing. There can be no doubt, then, that for biblical faith evil is entirely real and in no sense an illusion.

There are three main Christian responses to the problem of evil: the Augustinian response, hinging upon the concept of the fall of man from an original state of righteousness; the Irenaean response, hinging upon the idea of the gradual creation of a perfected humanity through life in a highly imperfect world; and the response of modern **process theology**, hinging upon the idea of a God who is not all-powerful and not in fact able to prevent the evils arising either in human beings or in the processes of nature.

Before examining each of these three responses, or theodicies,[1] we will discuss a position that is common to all of them.

The common ground is some form of what has come to be called the free-will defense, at least so far as the moral evil of human wickedness is concerned; for Christian thought has always seen moral evil as related to human freedom and responsibility. To be a person is to be a finite center of freedom, a (relatively) self-directing agent responsible for one's own decisions. This involves being free to act wrongly as well as rightly. There can therefore be no certainty in advance that a genuinely free moral agent will never choose amiss. Consequently, according to the strong form of free-will defense, the possibility of wrongdoing is logically inseparable from the creation of finite persons, and to say that God should not have created beings who might sin amounts to saying that God should not have created people.

This thesis has been challenged in some recent philosophical discussions of the problem of evil, in which it is claimed that no contradiction is involved in saying that God might have made people who would be genuinely free but who could at the same time be guaranteed always to act rightly. To quote from one of the these discussions:

If there is no **logical impossibility** *in a man's freely choosing the good on one, or on several occasions, there cannot be a logical impossibility in his freely choosing the good on every occasion. God was not, then, faced with a choice between making innocent automata and making beings who, in acting freely, would sometimes go wrong; there was open to him the obviously better possibility of making beings who would act freely but always go right. Clearly, his failure to avail himself of this possibility is inconsistent with his being both omnipotent and wholly good.* [2]

This argument has considerable power. A modified form of free-will defense has, however, been suggested in response to it. If by free actions we mean actions that are not externally compelled but flow from the nature of agents as they react to the circumstances in which they find themselves, then there is indeed no **contradiction** between our being free and our actions' being "caused" (by our own God-given nature) and thus being in principle predictable. However, it is suggested, there is a contradiction in saying that *God* is the cause of our acting as we do *and* that we are free beings specifically in relation to God. The contradiction is between holding that God has so made us that we shall of necessity act in a certain way, and that we are genuinely independent persons *in relation to God*. If all our thoughts and actions are divinely predestined, then however free and responsible we may seem to ourselves to be, we are not free and responsible in the sight of God but must instead be God's puppets. Such "freedom" would be comparable to that of patients acting out a series of posthypnotic suggestions: they appear to themselves to be free, but their volitions have actually been predetermined by the will of the hypnotist, in relation to whom the patients are

therefore not genuinely free agents. Thus, it is suggested, while God *could* have created such beings, there would have been no point in doing so—at least not if God is seeking to create sons and daughters rather than human puppets.

The Augustinian Theodicy

The main traditional Christian response to the problem of evil was first formulated by St. Augustine (354–430 A.D.) and has constituted the majority report of the Christian mind through the centuries, although it has been much criticized in recent times. It includes both philosophical and theological strands. The main philosophical position is the idea of the negative or privative nature of evil. Augustine holds firmly to the Hebrew-Christian conviction that the universe is good—that is to say, it is the creation of a good God for a good purpose. There are, according to Augustine, higher and lower, greater and lesser goods in immense abundance and variety; however, everything that has being is good in its own way and degree, except insofar as it has become spoiled or corrupted. Evil—whether it be an evil will, an instance of pain, or some disorder or decay in nature—has therefore not been set there by God but represents the going wrong of something that is inherently good. Augustine points to blindness as an example. Blindness is not a "thing." The only thing involved is the eye, which is in itself good; the evil of blindness consists of the lack of a proper functioning of the eye. Generalizing the principle, Augustine holds that evil always consists of the malfunctioning of something that is in itself good.

As it originally came forth from the hand of God, then, the universe was a perfect harmony expressing the creative divine intention. It was a graded hierarchy of higher and lower forms of being, each good in its own place. How, then, did evil come about? It came about initially in those levels of the universe that involve free will: the levels of the angels and of human beings. Some of the angels turned from the supreme Good, which is God, to lesser goods, thereby rebelling against their creator; they in turn tempted the first man and woman to fall. This fall of angelic and human beings was the origin of moral evil or sin. The natural evils of disease, of "nature red in tooth and claw," and of earthquake, storm, and so on are the penal consequences of sin, for humanity was intended to be lord of the earth, and this human defection has set all nature awry. Thus Augustine could say, "All evil is either sin or the punishment for sin."[3]

The Augustinian theodicy adds that at the end of history there will come the judgment, when many will enter into eternal life and many others (who in their freedom have rejected God's offer of salvation) into eternal torment. For Augustine, "since there is happiness for those who do not sin, the universe is perfect; and it is no less perfect because there is misery for sinners...the penalty of sin corrects the dishonour of sin."[4] He is invoking here a principle of moral balance according to which sin that is justly punished is thereby cancelled out and no longer mars the perfection of God's universe.

The Augustinian theodicy fulfills the intention lying behind it, which is to clear the creator of any responsibility for the existence of evil by loading that responsibility without remainder upon the creature. Evil stems from the culpable misuse of creaturely freedom in a tragic act, of cosmic significance, in the prehistory of the human race—an act that was prefigured in the heavenly realms by the incomprehensible fall of some of the angels, the chief of whom is now Satan, God's Enemy.

This theodicy has been criticized in the modern period, the first major critic being the great German Protestant theologian Friedrich Schleiermacher (1768–1834).[5]

The basic criticism is directed at the idea that a universe which God has created with absolute power, so as to be exactly as God wishes it to be, containing no evil of any kind, has nevertheless gone wrong. It is true that the free creatures who are part of it are free to fall. However, since they are finitely perfect, without any taint or trace of evil in them, and since they dwell in a finitely perfect environment, they will never in fact fall into sin. Thus, it is said, the very idea of a perfect creation's going wrong spontaneously and without cause is a self-contradiction. It amounts to the self-creation of evil out of nothing! It is significant that Augustine himself, when he asks why it is that some of the angels fell

while others remained steadfast, has to conclude that "These angels, therefore, either received less of the grace of the divine love than those who persevered in the same; or if both were created equally good, then, while the one fell by their evil will, the others were more abundantly assisted, and attained to the pitch of blessedness at which they have become certain that they should never fall from it."[6]

The basic criticism, then, is that a flawless creation would never go wrong and that if the creation does in fact go wrong the ultimate responsibility for this must be with its creator: for "This is where the buck stops"!

This criticism agrees with Mackie's contention...that it was logically possible for God to have created free beings who would never in fact fall. As we shall see in the next section, the alternative Irenaean theodicy takes up the further thought that although God *could* have created beings who were from the beginning finitely perfect, God has not in fact done so because such beings would never be able to become free and responsible sons and daughters of God.

A second criticism, made in the light of modern knowledge, is that we cannot today realistically think of the human species as having been once morally and spiritually perfect and then falling from that state into the chronic self-centeredness which is the human condition as we now know it. All the evidence suggests that humanity gradually emerged out of lower forms of life with a very limited moral awareness and with very crude religious conceptions. Again, it is no longer possible to regard the natural evils of disease, earthquakes, and the like as consequences of the fall of humanity, for we now know that they existed long before human beings came upon the scene. Life preyed upon life, and there were storms and earthquakes as well as disease (signs of arthritis have been found in the bones of some prehistoric animals) during the hundreds of millions of years before *homo sapiens* emerged.

A third criticism attacks the idea of the eternal torment of hell, which is affirmed to be the fate of a proportion of the human race. Since such punishment would never end, it could serve no constructive purpose. On the contrary, it is said, it would render impossible any solution to the problem of evil, for it would build both the sinfulness of the damned and the nonmoral evil of their pains and sufferings into the permanent structure of the universe.

The Irenaean Theodicy

Even from before the time of Augustine another response to the problem of evil had already been present within the developing Christian tradition. This has its basis in the thought of the early Greek-speaking Fathers of the Church, perhaps the most important of whom was St. Irenaeus (c. 130–c. 202 A.D.). He distinguished two stages of the creation of the human race.[7] In the first stage human beings were brought into existence as intelligent animals endowed with the capacity for immense moral and spiritual development. They were not the perfect pre-fallen Adam and Eve of the Augustinian tradition, but immature creatures, at the beginning of a long process of growth. In the second stage of their creation, which is now taking place, they are gradually being transformed through their own free responses from human animals into "children of God." (Irenaeus himself described the two stages as humanity being made first in the "image" and then into the "likeness" of God—referring to Genesis 1:26.)

If, going beyond Irenaeus himself, we ask why humans should have been initially created as immature and imperfect beings rather than as a race of perfect creatures, the answer centers upon the positive value of human freedom. Two mutually supporting considerations are suggested. One depends upon the intuitive judgment that a human goodness that has come about through the making of free and responsible moral choices, in situations of real difficulty and temptation, is intrinsically more valuable—perhaps even limitlessly more valuable—than a goodness that has been created ready-made, without the free participation of the human agent. This intuition points to the creation of the human race, not in a state of perfection, but in a state of imperfection from which it is nevertheless possible to move through moral struggle toward eventual completed humanization.

The other consideration is that if men and women had been initially created in the direct presence of God, who is infinite in life and power, goodness and knowledge, they would have had no genuine freedom in relation to their Maker. In order to be fully personal and therefore morally free beings, they have accordingly (it is suggested) been created at a distance from God—not a spatial but an epistemic distance, a distance in the dimension of knowledge. They are formed within and as part of an autonomous universe within which God is not overwhelmingly evident but in which God may become known by the free interpretative response of faith. . . . Thus the human situation is one of tension between the natural selfishness arising from our instinct for survival, and the calls of both morality and religion to transcend our self-centerdness. Whereas the Augustinian theology sees our perfection as lying in the distant past, in an original state long since forfeited by the primordial calamity of the fall, the Irenaean type of theology sees our perfection as lying before us in the future, at the end of a lengthy and arduous process of further creation through time.

Thus the answer of the Irenaean theodicy to the question of the origin of moral evil is that it is a necessary condition of the creation of humanity at an epistemic distance from God, in a state in which one has a genuine freedom in relation to one's Maker and can freely develop, in response to God's noncoercive presence, toward one's own fulfillment as a child of God.

We may now turn to the problem of pain and suffering. Even though the bulk of actual human pain is traceable, as a sole or part cause, to misused human freedom, there remain other sources of pain that are entirely independent of the human will—for example, bacteria, earthquake, hurricane, storm, flood, drought, and blight. In practice it is often impossible to trace a boundary between the suffering that results from human wickedness and folly and that which befalls humanity from without; both are inextricably mingled in human experience. For our present purpose, however, it is important to note that the latter category does exist and that it seems to be built into the very structure of our world. In response to it, theodicy, if it is wisely conducted, follows a negative path. It is not possible to show positively that each item of human pain serves God's purpose of good; on the other hand, it does seem possible to show that the divine purpose, at least as it is understood in the Irenaean theology, could not be forwarded in a world that was designed as a permanent hedonistic paradise.[8]

An essential premise of this argument concerns the nature of the divine purpose in creating the world. The skeptic's normal assumption is that humanity is to be viewed as a completed creation and that God's purpose in making the world was to provide a suitable dwelling place for this fully formed creature. Since God is good and loving, the environment that God creates for human life will naturally be as pleasant and as comfortable as possible. The problem is essentially similar to that of someone who builds a cage for a pet animal. Since our world in fact contains sources of pain, hardship, and danger of innumerable kinds, the conclusion follows that this world cannot have been created by a perfectly benevolent and all-powerful deity.[9]

According to the Irenaean theodicy, however, God's purpose was not to construct a paradise whose inhabitants would experience a maximum of pleasure and a minimum of pain. The world is seen, instead, as a place of "soul-making" or person-making in which free beings, grappling with the tasks and challenges of their existence in a common environment, may become "children of God" and "heirs of eternal life." Our world, with all its rough edges, is the sphere in which this second and harder state of the creative process is taking place.

This conception of the world (whether or not set in Irenaeus's theological framework) can be supported by the method of "counterfactual hypothesis." Suppose that, contrary to fact, this world were a paradise from which all possibility of pain and suffering were excluded. The consequences would be very far-reaching. For example, no one could ever injure anyone else: the murderer's knife would turn to paper or the bullets to thin air; the bank safe, robbed of a million dollars, would miraculously become filled with another million dollars; fraud, deceit, conspiracy, and treason would somehow leave the fabric of society undamaged. No one would

ever be injured by accident: the mountain climber, steeplejack, or playing child falling from a height would float unharmed to the ground; the reckless driver would never meet with disaster. There would be no need to work since no harm could result from avoiding work; there would be no call to be concerned for others in time of need or danger, for in such a world there could be no real needs or dangers.

To make possible this continual series of individual adjustments, nature would have to work by "special providences" instead of running according to general laws that we must learn to respect on penalty of pain or death. The laws of nature would have to be extremely flexible: sometimes gravity would operate, sometimes not; sometimes an object would be hard and solid, sometimes soft. There could be no sciences, for there would be no enduring world structure to investigate. In eliminating the problems and hardships of an objective environment with its own laws, life would become like a dream in which, delightfully but aimlessly, we would float and drift at ease.[10]

One can at least begin to imagine such a world—and it is evident that in it our present ethical concepts would have no meaning. If, for example, the notion of harming someone is an essential element in the concept of a wrong action, in a hedonistic paradise there could be no wrong actions—nor therefore any right actions in distinction from wrong. Courage and fortitude would have no point in an environment in which there is, by definition, no danger or difficulty. Generosity, kindness, the *agape* aspect of love, prudence, unselfishness, and other ethical notions that presuppose life in an objective environment could not even be formed. Consequently, such a world, however well it might promote pleasure, would be very ill adapted for the development of the moral qualities of human personality. In relation to this purpose it might well be the worst of all possible worlds!

It would seem, then, that an environment intended to make possible the growth in free beings of the finest characteristics of personal life must have a good deal in common with our present world. It must operate according to general and dependable laws, and it must present real dangers, difficulties, problems, obstacles, and possibilities of pain, failure, sorrow, frustration, and defeat. If it did not contain the particular trials and perils that—subtracting the considerable human contribution—our world contains, it would have to contain others instead.

To realize this fact is not, by any means, to be in possession of a detailed theodicy. However, it is to understand that this world, with all its "heartaches and the thousand natural shocks that flesh is heir to," an environment so manifestly not designed for the maximization of human pleasure and the minimization of human pain, may nevertheless be rather well adapted to the quite different purpose of "soul making."[11]

And so the Irenaean answer to the question, Why natural evil? is that only a world that has this general character could constitute an effective environment for the second stage (or the beginning of the second stage) of God's creative work, whereby human animals are being gradually transformed through their own free responses into "children of God."

At this point, the Irenaean theodicy points forward in three ways to the subject of life after death. . . .

First, although there are many striking instances of good being triumphantly brought out of evil through a person's reaction to it, there are many other cases in which the opposite has happened. Sometimes obstacles breed strength of character, dangers evoke courage and unselfishness, and calamities produce patience and moral steadfastness. On the other hand, sometimes they lead to resentment, fear, grasping selfishness, and disintegration of character. Therefore, it would seem that any divine purpose of soul making that is at work in earthly history must continue beyond this life if it is ever to achieve more than a partial and fragmentary success.

Second, if we ask the ultimate question—whether the business of person making is worth all the toil and sorrow of human life—the answer must be in terms of a future good great enough to justify all that has happened on the way to it. Its claim is that the endless enjoyment of that fullness of life and joy, beyond our present imaginations, which is the eventual fulfillment of God's love toward us, will render manifestly worthwhile all the pain and travail of the long journey of human life toward it, both in this world and perhaps in other worlds as well.

Third, not only does a theodicy of the Irenaean type require a positive doctrine of life after death but, insofar as the theodicy is to be complete, it also requires that *all* human beings shall in the end attain the heavenly state.

This Irenaean type of theodicy has been criticized from a variety of points of view. Some Christian theologians have protested against its rejection of the traditional doctrines both of the fall of humanity and of the final damnation of many. Philosophical critics have argued that, while it shows with some plausibility that a person-making world cannot be a paradise, it does not thereby justify the *actual extent* of human suffering, including such gigantic evils as the Jewish Holocaust.[12] Others, however, claim that this theodicy does succeed in showing why God's world, as a sphere involving contingency and freedom, is such that even these things can, alas, happen—even though human history would have been much better without such conspicuous crimes and horrors. There is also unresolvable disagreement as to whether so painful a creative process, even though leading to an infinite good, can be said to be the expression of divine goodness.

Notes

1. "Theodicy," formed (by Leibniz) from the Greek *theos,* god, and *dike,* righteous, is a technical term for attempts to solve the theological problem of evil.

2. J. L. Mackie, "Evil and Omnipotence," *Mind* (April 1955), p. 209. A similar point is made by Antony Flew in "Divine Omnipotence and Human Freedom," *New Essays in Philosophical Theology.* An important critical comment on these arguments is offered by Ninian Smart in "Omnipotence, Evil and Supermen," *Philosophy* (April 1961), with replies by Flew (January 1962) and Mackie (April 1962).

3. *De Genesi Ad Litteram,* Imperfectus liber, 1.3.

4. *On Free Will,* III, ix. 26.

5. See Schleiermacher's *The Christian Faith.*

6. *City of God,* Bk. 12, Chap. 9

7. See Irenaeus, *Against Heresies,* Bk. IV, Chaps. 37 and 38.

8. From The Greek *hedone,* pleasure.

9. This is essentially David Hume's argument in his discussion of the problem of evil in his *Dialogues,* Part XI.

10. Tennyson's poem, "The Lotus-Eaters," well expresses the desire (analyzed by Freud as a wish to return to the peace of the womb) for such "dreamful ease."

11. This discussion has been confined to the problem of human suffering. The large and intractable problem of animal pain is not taken up here. For a discussion of it see, for example, Austin Farrer, *Love Almighty and Ills Unlimited* (Garden City, N.Y.: Doubleday & Company, Inc., 1961), Chap. 5; and John Hick, *Evil and the God of Love*, 2nd ed. (London: Macmillan, and New York: Harper & Row, 1977; paperback version in Collins' Fount series.), pp. 309–17. The latter book includes a comprehensive presentation of a theodicy of the Irenaean type.

12. See, for example, Edward H. Madden and Peter H. Hare, *Evil and the Concept of God* (Springfield, Ill.: Charles C. Thomas, 1968), Chap. 5.

Questions on Hick

1. Why does Hick reject the Christian Science solution to the problem of evil? Do you agree with his criticism? Why or why not?

2. How does Hick respond to Mackie's objection to the freewill defense? (This is only one of Mackie's objections. See the next reading.) Is Hick's reply convincing? Explain.

3. How does Hick explain Augustinian theodicy? What is the "basic criticism" of this solution according to Hick? Is this a decisive criticism?

4. What are the other two criticisms of Augustinian theodicy? Is there a good reply to them or not? Defend your answer.

5. Explain Irenaean theodicy. How has it been criticized? Can you think of any replies to these criticisms? What are they?

J. L. Mackie
Evil and Omnipotence

John L. Mackie (1917–1981) was a Fellow of University College, Oxford University.

The traditional arguments for the existence of God have been fairly thoroughly criticized by philosophers. But the theologian can, if he wishes, accept this criticism. He can admit that no rational proof of God's existence is possible. And he can still retain all that is essential to his position, by holding that God's existence is known in some other, non-rational way. I think, however, that a more telling criticism can be made by way of the traditional problem of evil. Here it can be shown, not that religious beliefs lack rational support, but that they are positively irrational, that the several parts of the essential theological doctrine are inconsistent

The reading is from J. L. Mackie, "Evil and Omnipotence," *Mind*, Vol. LXIV, No. 254 (1955), pp. 200–212. Reprinted by permission of Oxford University Press.

with one another, so that the theologian can maintain his position as a whole only by a much more extreme rejection of reason than in the former case. He must now be prepared to believe, not merely what cannot be proved, but what can be *disproved* from other beliefs that he also holds.

The problem of evil, in the sense in which I shall be using the phrase, is a problem only for someone who believes that there is a God who is both omnipotent and wholly good. And it is a logical problem, the problem of clarifying and reconciling a number of beliefs: it is not a scientific problem that might be solved by further observations, or a practical problem that might be solved by a decision or an action. These points are obvious; I mention them only because they are sometimes ignored by theologians, who sometimes parry a statement of the problem with such remarks as "Well, can you solve the problem yourself?" or "This is a mystery which may be revealed to us later" or "Evil is something to be faced and overcome, not to be merely discussed."

In its simplest form the problem is this: God is omnipotent; God is wholly good; and yet evil exists. There seems to be some contradiction between these three propositions, so that if any two of them were true the third would be false. But at the same time all three are essential parts of most theological positions: the theologian, it seems, at once *must* adhere and *cannot consistently* adhere to all three. (The problem does not arise only for theists, but I shall discuss it in the form in which it presents itself for ordinary theism.)

However, the contradiction does not arise immediately; to show it we need some additional premises, or perhaps some quasi-logical rules connecting the terms "good", "evil", and "omnipotent". These additional principles are that good is opposed to evil, in such a way that a good thing always eliminates evil as far as it can, and that there are no limits to what an omnipotent thing can do. From these it follows that a good omnipotent thing eliminates evil completely, and then the propositions that a good omnipotent thing exists, and that evil exists, are incompatible.

A. Adequate Solutions

Now once the problem is fully stated it is clear that it can be solved, in the sense that the problem will not arise if one gives up at least one of the propositions that constitute it. If you are prepared to say that God is not wholly good, or not quite omnipotent, or that evil does not exist, or that good is not opposed to the kind of evil that exists, or that there are limits to what an omnipotent thing can do, then the problem of evil will not arise for you.

There are, then, quite a number of adequate solutions of the problem of evil, and some of these have been adopted, or almost adopted, by various thinkers. For example, a few have been prepared to deny God's omnipotence, and rather more have been prepared to keep the term "omnipotence" but severely to restrict its meaning, recording quite a number of things that an omnipotent being cannot do. Some have said that evil is an illusion, perhaps because they held that the whole world of temporal, changing things is an illusion, and that what we call evil belongs only to this world, or perhaps because they held that although temporal things *are* much as we see them, those that we call evil are not really evil. Some have said that what we call evil is merely the privation of good, that evil in

a positive sense, evil that would really be opposed to good, does not exist. Many have agreed with Pope that disorder is harmony not understood, and that partial evil is universal good. Whether any of these views is *true* is, of course, another question. But each of them gives an adequate solution of the problem of evil in the sense that if you accept it this problem does not arise for you, though you may of course, have *other* problems to face.

But often enough these adequate solutions are only *almost* adopted. The thinkers who restrict God's power, but keep the term 'omnipotence', may reasonably be suspected of thinking, in other contexts, that his power is really unlimited. Those who say that evil is an illusion may also be thinking, inconsistently, that this illusion is itself an evil. Those who say that "evil" is merely privation of good may also be thinking, inconsistently, that privation of good is an evil. (The fallacy here is akin to some forms of the "naturalistic fallacy" in ethics, where some think, for example, that "good" is just what contributes to evolutionary progress, and that evolutionary progress is itself good.) If Pope meant what he said in the first line of his couplet, that "disorder" is only harmony not understood, the "partial evil" of the second line must, for consistency, mean "that which, taken in isolation, falsely appears to be evil", but it would more naturally mean "that which, in isolation, really is evil". The second line, in fact, hesitates between two views, that "partial evil" isn't really evil, since only the universal quality is real, and that "partial evil" is really an evil, but only a little one.

In addition, therefore, to adequate solutions, we must recognize unsatisfactory inconsistent solutions, in which there is only a half-hearted or temporary rejection of one of the propositions which together constitute the problem. In these, one of the constituent propositions is explicitly rejected, but it is covertly reasserted or assumed elsewhere in the system.

B. Fallacious Solutions

Besides these half-hearted solutions, which explicitly reject but implicitly assert one of the constituent propositions, there are definitely fallacious solutions which explicitly maintain all the constituent propositions, but implicitly reject at least one them in the course of the argument that explains away the problem of evil.

There are, in fact, many so-called solutions which purport to remove the contradiction without abandoning any of its constituent propositions. These must be fallacious, as we can see from the very statement of the problem, but it is not so easy to see in each case precisely where the fallacy lies. I suggest that in all cases the fallacy has the general form suggested above: in order to solve the problem one (or perhaps more) of its constituent propositions is given up, but in such a way that it appears to have been retained, and can therefore be asserted without qualification in other contexts. Sometimes there is a further complication: the supposed solution moves to and fro between, say, two of the constituent propositions, at one point asserting the first of these but covertly abandoning the second, at another point asserting the second but covertly abandoning the first. These fallacious solutions often turn upon some **equivocation** with the words "good" and "evil", or upon some vagueness about the way in which good and evil are opposed to one another, or about how much is meant by "omnipotence". I propose to examine some of these so-called solutions, and to exhibit their fallacies in detail. Incidentally, I shall also be considering whether an adequate solution could be reached by a minor modification of one or more of the constituent propositions, which would, however, still satisfy all the essential requirements of ordinary theism.

1. "Good Cannot Exist Without Evil" or "Evil Is Necessary as a Counterpart to Good"

It is sometimes suggested that evil is necessary as a counterpart to good, that if there were no evil there could be no good either, and that this solves the problem of evil. It is true that it points to an answer to the question "Why should there be evil?" But it does so only by qualifying some of the propositions that constitute the problem.

First, it sets a limit to what God can do, saying that God *cannot* create good without simultaneously creating evil, and this means either that God is not omnipotent or that there are *some* limits to what an omnipotent thing can do. It may be replied that these limits are always presupposed, that omnipotence has never meant the power to do what is logically impossible, and on the present view the existence of good without evil would be a logical impossibility. This interpretation of omnipotence may, indeed, be accepted as a modification of our original account which does not reject anything that is essential to theism, and I shall in general assume it in the subsequent discussion. It is, perhaps, the most common theistic view, but I think that some theists at least have maintained that God can do what is logically impossible. Many theists, at any rate, have held that logic itself is created or laid down by God, that logic is the way in which God arbitrarily chooses to think. (This is, of course, parallel to the ethical view that morally right actions are those which God arbitrarily chooses to command, and the two views encounter similar difficulties.) And *this* account of logic is clearly inconsistent with the view that God is bound by **logical necessities**—unless it is possible for an omnipotent being to bind himself, an issue which we shall consider later, when we come to the Paradox of Omnipotence. This solution of the problem of evil cannot, therefore, be consistently adopted along with the view that logic is itself created by God.

But, secondly, this solution denies that evil is opposed to good in our original sense. If good and evil are counterparts, a good thing will not "eliminate evil as far as it can." Indeed, this view suggests that good and evil are not strictly qualities of things at all. Perhaps the suggestion is that good and evil are related in much the same way as great and small. Certainly, when the term "great" is used relatively as a condensation of "greater than so-and-so", and "small" is used correspondingly, greatness and smallness are counterparts and cannot exist without each other. But in this sense greatness is not a quality, not an intrinsic feature of anything; and it would be absurd to think of a movement in favour of greatness and against smallness in this sense. Such a movement would be self-defeating, since relative greatness can be promoted only by a simultaneous promotion of relative smallness. I feel sure that no theists would be content to regard God's goodness as analogous to this—as if what he supports were not the *good* but the *better*, and as if he had the paradoxical aim that all things should be better than other things.

This point is obscured by the fact that "great" and "small" seem to have an absolute as well as a relative sense. I cannot discuss here whether there is absolute magnitude or not, but if there is, there could be an absolute sense for "great", it could mean of at least a certain size, and it would make sense to speak of all things getting bigger, of a universe that was expanding all over, and therefore it would make sense to speak of promoting greatness. But in *this* sense great and small are not logically necessary counterparts: either quality could exist without the other. There would be no logical impossibility in everything's being small or in everything's being great.

Neither in the absolute nor in the relative sense, then, of "great" and "small" do these terms provide an analogy of the sort that would be needed to support this solution of the problem of evil. In neither case are greatness and smallness *both* necessary counterparts *and* mutually opposed forces or possible objects for support and attack.

It may be replied that good and evil are necessary counterparts in the same way as any quality and its logical opposite: redness can occur, it is suggested, only if non-redness also occurs. But unless evil is merely the privation of good, they are not logical opposites, and some further argument would be needed to show that they are counterparts in the same way as genuine logical opposites. Let us assume that this could be given. There is still doubt of the correctness of the metaphysical principle that a quality must have a real opposite: I suggest that it is not really impossible that everything should be, say, red, that the truth is merely that if everything were red we should not notice redness, and so we should have no word "red"; we observe and give names to qualities only if they have real opposites. If so, the principle that a term must have an opposite would belong only to our language or to our thought, and would not be an ontolog-

ical principle, and, correspondingly, the rule that good cannot exist without evil would not state a logical necessity of a sort that God would just have to put up with. God might have made everything good, though *we* should not have noticed it if he had.

But, finally, even if we concede that this *is* an ontological principle, it will provide a solution for the problem of evil only if one is prepared to say, "Evil exists, but only just enough evil to serve as the counterpart of good." I doubt whether any theist will accept this. After all, the *ontological* requirement that non-redness should occur would be satisfied even if all the universe, except for a minute speck, were red, and, if there were a corresponding requirement for evil as a counterpart to good, a minute dose of evil would presumably do. But theists are not usually willing to say, in all contexts, that all the evil that occurs is a minute and necessary dose.

2. *"Evil Is Necessary as a Means to Good"*

It is sometimes suggested that evil is necessary for good not as a counterpart but as a means. In its simple form this has little plausibility as a solution of the problem of evil, since it obviously implies a severe restriction of God's power. It would be a *causal* law that you cannot have a certain end without a certain means, so that if God has to introduce evil as a means to good, he must be subject to at least some causal laws. This certainly conflicts with what a theist normally means by omnipotence. This view of God as limited by causal laws also conflicts with the view that causal laws are themselves made by God, which is more widely held than the corresponding view about the laws of logic. This conflict would, indeed, be resolved if it were possible for an omnipotent being to bind himself, and this possibility has still to be considered. Unless a favourable answer can be given to this question, the suggestion that evil is necessary as a means to good solves the problem of evil only by denying one of its constituent propositions, either that God is omnipotent or that "omnipotent" means what it says.

3. "The Universe Is Better With Some Evil in It Than It Could Be If There Were No Evil"

Much more important is a solution which at first seems to be a mere variant of the previous one, that evil may contribute to the goodness of a whole in which it is found, so that the universe as a whole is better as it is, with some evil in it, than it would be if there were no evil. This solution may be developed in either of two ways. It may be supported by an aesthetic analogy, by the fact that contrasts heighten beauty, that in a musical work, for example, there may occur discords which somehow add to the beauty of the work as a whole. Alternatively, it may be worked out in connexion with the notion of progress, that the best possible organization of the universe will not be static, but progressive, that the gradual overcoming of evil by good is really a finer thing than would be the eternal unchallenged supremacy of good.

In either case, this solution usually starts from the assumption that the evil whose existence gives rise to the problem of evil is primarily what is called physical evil, that is to say, pain. In Hume's rather half-hearted presentation of the problem of evil, the evils that he stresses are pain and disease, and those who reply to him argue that the existence of pain and disease makes possible the existence of sympathy, benevolence, heroism, and the gradually successful struggle of doctors and reformers to overcome these evils. In fact, theists often seize the opportunity to accuse those who stress the problem of evil of taking a low, materialistic view of good and evil, equating these with pleasure and pain, and of ignoring the more spiritual goods which can arise in the struggle against evils.

But let us see exactly what is being done here. Let us call pain and misery "first order evil" or "evil (1)". What contrasts with this, namely, pleasure and happiness, will be called "first order good" or "good (1)". Distinct from this is "second order good" or "good (2)" which somehow emerges in a complex situation in which evil (1) is a necessary component—logically, not merely causally, necessary. (Exactly *how* it emerges does not matter: in the crudest version of this solution good (2) is simply the heightening of happiness by the contrast with misery, in other versions it includes sympathy with suffering, heroism in facing danger, and the gradual decrease of first order evil and increase of first order good.) It is also being assumed that second order good is more important than first order good or evil, in particular that it more than outweighs the first order evil it involves.

Now this is a particularly subtle attempt to solve the problem of evil. It defends God's goodness and omnipotence on the ground that (on a sufficiently long view) this is the best of all logically possible worlds, because it includes the important second order goods, and yet it admits that real evils, namely first order evils, exist. But does it still hold that good and evil are opposed? Not clearly, in the sense that we set out originally: good does not tend to eliminate evil in general. Instead, we have a modified, a more complex pattern. First order good (*e.g.* happiness) *contrasts with* first order evil (*e.g.* misery): these two are opposed in a fairly mechanical way; some second order goods (*e.g.* benevolence) try to maximize first order good and minimize first order evil; but God's goodness is not this, it is rather the will to maximize *second* order good. We might, therefore, call God's goodness an example of a third order goodness, or good (3). While this account is different from our original one, it might well be held to be an improvement on it, to give a more accurate description of the way in which good is opposed to evil, and to be consistent with the essential theist position.

There might, however, be several objections to this solution.

First, some might argue that such qualities as benevolence—and *a fortiori* the third order goodness which promotes benevolence—have a merely derivative value, that they are not higher sorts of good, but merely means to good (1), that is, to happiness, so that it would be absurd for God to keep misery in existence in order to make possible the virtues of benevolence, heroism, etc. The theist who adopts the present solution must, of course, deny this, but he can do so with some plausibility, so I should not press this objection.

Secondly, it follows from this solution that God is not in our sense benevolent or sympathetic: he is not concerned to minimize evil (1), but only to promote good (2); and this might be a disturbing conclusion for some theists.

But, thirdly, the fatal objection is this. Our analysis shows clearly the possibilty of the existence of a *second* order evil, an evil (2) contrasting with good (2) as evil (1) contrasts with good (1). This would include malevolence, cruelty, callousness, cowardice, and states in which good (1) is decreasing and evil (1) increasing. And just as good (2) is held to be the important kind of good, the kind that God is concerned to promote, so evil (2) will, by analogy, be the important kind of evil, the kind which God, if he were wholly good and omnipotent, would eliminate. And yet evil (2) plainly exists, and indeed most theists (in other contexts) stress its existence more than that of evil (1). We should, therefore, state the problem of evil in terms of second order evil, and against this form of the problem the present solution is useless.

An attempt might be made to use this solution again, at a higher level, to explain the occurrence of evil (2): indeed the next main solution that we shall examine does just this, with the help of some new notions. Without any fresh notions, such a solution would have little plausibility: for example, we could hardly say that the really important good was a good (3), such as the increase of benevolence in proportion to cruelty, which logically required for its occurrence the occurrence of some second order evil. But even if evil (2) could be explained in this way, it is fairly clear that there would be third order evils contrasting with this third order good: and we should be well on the way to an infinite regress, where the solution of a problem of evil, stated in terms of evil (n), indicated the existence of an evil ($n + 1$), and a further problem to be solved.

4. *"Evil Is Due to Human Freewill"*

Perhaps the most important proposed solution of the problem of evil is that evil is not to be ascribed to God at all, but to the independent actions of human beings, supposed to have been endowed by God with freedom of the will. This solution may be combined with the preceding one: first order evil (*e.g.* pain) may be justified as a logically necessary component in second order good (*e.g.* sympathy) while second order evil (*e.g. cruelty*) is not *justified,* but is so ascribed to human beings that God cannot be held responsible for it. This combination evades my third criticism of the preceding solution.

The freewill solution also involves the preceding solution at a higher level. To explain why a wholly good God gave men freewill although it would lead to some important evils, it must be argued that it is better on the whole that men should act freely, and sometimes err, than that they should be innocent automata, acting rightly in a wholly determined way. Freedom, that is to say, is now treated as a third order good, and as being more valuable than second order goods (such as sympathy and heroism) would be if they were deterministically produced, and it is being assumed that second order evils, such as cruelty, are logically necessary accompaniments of freedom, just as pain is a logically necessary precondition of sympathy.

I think that this solution is unsatisfactory primarily because of the incoherence of the notion of freedom of the will: but I cannot discuss this topic adequately here, although some of my criticisms will touch upon it.

First, I should query the assumption that second order evils are logically necessary accompaniments of freedom. I should ask this: if God has made men such that in their free choices they sometimes prefer what is good and sometimes what is evil, why could he not have made men such that they always freely choose the good? If there is no logical impossibility in a man's freely choosing the good on one, or on several, occasions, there cannot be a logical impossibility in his freely choosing the good on every occasion. God was not, then, faced with a choice between making innocent automata and making beings who, in acting freely, would sometimes go wrong: there was open to him the obviously better possibility of making beings who would act freely but always go right. Clearly, his failure to avail himself of this possibility is inconsistent with his being both omnipotent and wholly good.

If it is replied that this objection is absurd, that the making of some wrong choices is logically necessary for freedom, it would seem that "freedom" must here mean complete randomness or indeterminacy, including randomness with regard to the alternatives good and evil, in other words that men's choices and consequent actions can be "free" only if they are not determined by their characters. Only on this assumption can God escape the responsibility for men's actions; for if he made them as they are, but did not determine their wrong choices, this can only be because the wrong choices are not determined by men as they are. But then if freedom is randomness, how can it be a characteristic of *will*? And, still more, how can it be the most important good? What value or merit would there be in free choices if these were random actions which were not determined by the nature of the agent?

I conclude that to make this solution plausible two different senses of "freedom" must be confused, one sense which will justify the view that freedom is a third order good, more valuable than other goods would be without it, and another sense, sheer randomness, to prevent us from ascribing to God a decision to make men such that they sometimes go wrong when he might have made them such that they would always freely go right.

This criticism is sufficient to dispose of this solution. But besides this there is a fundamental difficulty in the notion of an omnipotent God creating men with free will, for if men's wills are really free this must mean that even God cannot control them, that is, that God is no longer omnipotent. It may be objected that God's gift of freedom to men does not mean that he *cannot* control their wills, but that he always *refrains* from controlling their wills. But why, we may ask, should God refrain from controlling evil wills? Why should he not leave men free to will rightly, but intervene when he sees them beginning to will wrongly? If God could do this, but does not, and if he is wholly good, the only explanation could be that even a wrong free act of will is not really evil, that its freedom is a value which outweighs its wrongness, so that there

would be a loss of value if God took away the wrongness and the freedom together. But this is utterly opposed to what theists say about sin in other contexts. The present solution of the problem of evil, then, can be maintained only in the form that God has made men so free that he *cannot* control their wills.

This leads us to what I call the Paradox of Omnipotence: can an omnipotent being make things which he cannot subsequently control? Or, what is practically equivalent to this, can an omnipotent being make rules which then bind himself? (These are practically equivalent because any such rules could be regarded as setting certain things beyond his control, and *vice versa*.) The second of these formulations is relevant to the suggestions that we have already met, that an omnipotent God creates the rules of logic or causal laws, and is then bound by them.

It is clear that this is a paradox: the questions cannot be answered satisfactorily either in the affirmative or in the negative. If we answer "Yes", it follows that if God actually makes things which he cannot control, or makes rules which bind himself, he is not omnipotent once he has made them: there are *then* things which he cannot do. But if we answer "No", we are immediately asserting that there are things which he cannot do, that is to say that he is already not omnipotent.

It cannot be replied that the question which sets this paradox is not a proper question. It would make perfectly good sense to say that a human mechanic has made a machine which he cannot control: if there is any difficulty about the question it lies in the notion of omnipotence itself.

This, incidentally, shows that although we have approached this paradox from the free will theory, it is equally a problem for a theological determinist. No one thinks that machines have free will, yet they may well be beyond the control of their makers. The determinist might reply that anyone who makes anything determines its ways of acting, and so determines its subsequent behaviour: even the human mechanic does this by his *choice* of materials and structure for his machine, though he does not know all about either of these: the mechanic thus determines, though he may not foresee, his machine's actions. And since God is omniscient, and since his creation of things is total, he both determines and foresees the ways in which his creatures will act. We may grant this, but it is beside the point. The question is not whether God *originally* determined the future actions of his creatures, but whether he can *subsequently* control their actions, or whether he was able in his original creation to put things beyond his subsequent control. Even on determinist principles the answers "Yes" and "No" are equally irreconcilable with God's omnipotence.

Before suggesting a solution of this paradox, I would point out that there is a parallel Paradox of Sovereignty. Can a legal sovereign make a law restricting its own future legislative power? For example, could the British parliament make a law forbidding any future parliament to socialize banking, and also forbidding the future repeal of this law itself? Or could the British parliament, which was legally sovereign in Australia in, say, 1899, pass a valid law, or series of laws, which made it no longer sovereign in 1933? Again, neither the affirmative nor the negative answer is really satisfactory. If we were to answer "Yes", we should be admitting the validity of a law which, if it were actually made, would mean that parliament was no longer sovereign. If we were to answer "No", we should be admitting that there is a law, not logically absurd, which parliament cannot validly make, that is, that parliament is not now a legal sovereign. This paradox can be solved in the following way. We should distinguish between first order laws, that is laws governing the actions of individuals and bodies other than the legislature, and second order laws, that is laws about laws, laws governing the actions of the legislature itself. Correspondingly, we should distinguish two orders of sovereignty, first order sovereignty (sovereignty (1)) which is unlimited authority to make first order laws, and second order sovereignty (sovereignty (2)) which is unlimited authority to make second order laws. If we say that parliament is sovereign we might mean that any parliament at any time has sovereignty (1), or we might mean that parliament has both sovereignty (1) and sovereignty (2) at present, but we cannot without contradiction

mean both that the present parliament has sovereignty (2) and that every parliament at every time has sovereignty (1), for if the present parliament has sovereignty (2) it may use it to take away the sovereignty (1) of later parliaments. What the paradox shows is that we cannot ascribe to any continuing institution legal sovereignty in an inclusive sense.

The analogy between omnipotence and sovereignty shows that the paradox of omnipotence can be solved in a similar way. We must distinguish between first order omnipotence (omnipotence (1)), that is unlimited power to act, and second order omnipotence (omnipotence (2)), that is unlimited power to determine what powers to act things shall have. Then we could consistently say that God all the time has omnipotence (1), but if so no beings at any time have powers to act independently of God. Or we could say that God at one time had omnipotence (2), and used it to assign independent powers to act to certain things, so that God thereafter did not have omnipotence (1). But what the paradox shows is that we cannot consistently ascribe to any continuing being omnipotence in an inclusive sense.

An alternative solution of this paradox would be simply to deny that God is a continuing being, that any times can be assigned to his actions at all. But on this assumption (which also has difficulties of its own) no meaning can be give to the assertion that God made men with wills so free that he could not control them. The paradox of omnipotence can be avoided by putting God outside time, but the freewill solution of the problem of evil cannot be saved in this way, and equally it remains impossible to hold that an omnipotent God *binds himself* by causal or logical laws.

Conclusion

Of the proposed solutions of the problem of evil which we have examined, none has stood up to criticism. There may be other solutions which require examination, but this study strongly suggests that there is no valid solution of the problem which does not modify at least one of the constituent propositions in a way which would seriously affect the essential core of the ·theistic position.

Quite apart from the problem of evil, the paradox of omnipotence has shown that God's omnipotence must in any case be restricted in one way or another, that unqualified omnipotence cannot be ascribed to any being that continues through time. And if God and his actions are not in time, can omnipotence, or power of any sort, be meaningfully ascribed to him?

Questions on Mackie

1. What are the "adequate solutions" to the problem of evil in Mackie's sense of the term? Are these solutions really adequate or not?

2. How does Mackie attack St. Augustine's view of evil as the privation of good? Is this attack convincing?

3. Carefully state and explain the first three so-called fallacious solutions to the problem of evil. Then clearly explain Mackie's criticisms. Are these criticisms decisive or not? Is there any way to reply to them? If so, how?

4. How does Mackie explain the freewill solution? Does he succeed in refuting it or not? Explain your answer. Take into account Hick's reply to Mackie in the previous reading.)

Blaise Pascal
The Wager

Blaise Pascal (1623–1662), the French mathematician, made important contributions in probability theory; he was also an inventor, physicist, and philosopher.

This is what I see and what troubles me. I look on all sides, and I see only darkness everywhere. Nature presents to me nothing which is not matter of doubt and concern. If I saw nothing there which revealed a Divinity, I would come to a negative conclusion; if I saw everywhere the signs of a Creator, I would remain peacefully in faith. But, seeing too much to deny and too little to be sure, I am in a state to be pitied; wherefore I have a hundred times wished that if a God maintains nature, she should testify to Him unequivocally, and that, if the signs she gives are deceptive, she should suppress them altogether;

The reading is from Blaise Pascal, *Thoughts*, trans. W. F. Trotter (New York: Collier and Sons, 1938), pp. 82–87. Reprinted with permission of *The Harvard Classics*, 1965 edition, © Grolier Inc.

that she should say everything or nothing, that I might see which cause I ought to follow. Whereas in my present state, ignorant of what I am or of what I ought to do, I know neither my condition nor my duty. My heart inclines wholly to know, where is the true good, in order to follow it; nothing would be too dear to me for eternity.

I envy those whom I see living in the faith with such carelessness, and who make such a bad use of a gift of which it seems to me I would make such a different use.

It is incomprehensible that God should exist, and it is incomprehensible that He should not exist, that the soul should be joined to the body, and that we should have no soul; that the world should be created, and that it should not be created, &c.; that original sin should be, and that it should not be.

Do you believe it to be impossible that God is infinite, without parts?—Yes. I wish therefore to show you an infinite and indivisible thing. It is a point moving everywhere with an infinite velocity; for it is one in all places, and is all totality in every place.

Let this effect of nature, which previously seemed to you impossible, make you know that there may be others of which you are still ignorant. Do not draw this conclusion from your experiment, that there remains nothing for you to know; but rather that there remains an infinity for you to know.

Infinite movement, the point which fills everything, the moment of rest; infinite without quantity, indivisible and infinite.

Infinite—nothing.—Our soul is cast into a body, where it finds number, time, dimension. Thereupon it reasons, and calls this nature, necessity, and can believe nothing else.

Unity joined to infinity adds nothing to it, no more than one foot to an infinite measure. The finite is annihilated in the presence of the infinite, and becomes a pure nothing. So our spirit before God, so our justice before divine justice. There is not so great a disproportion between our justice and that of God, as between unity and infinity.

The justice of God must be vast like His compassion. Now justice to the outcast is less vast, and ought less to offend our feelings than mercy towards the elect.

We know that there is an infinite, and are ignorant of its nature. As we know it to be false that numbers are finite, it is therefore true that there is an infinity in number. But we do not know what it is. It is false that it is even, it is false that it is odd; for the addition of a unit can make no change in its nature. Yet it is a number, and every number is odd or even (this is certainly true of every finite number). So we may well know that there is a God without knowing what He is. Is there not one substantial truth, seeing there are so many things which are not the truth itself?

We know then the existence and nature of the finite, because we also are finite and have extension. We know the existence of the infinite, and are ignorant of its nature, because it has extension like us, but not limits like us. But we know neither the existence nor the nature of God, because He has neither extension nor limits.

But by faith we know His existence; in glory we shall know His nature. Now, I have already shown that we may well know the existence of a thing, without knowing its nature.

Let us now speak according to natural lights.

If there is a God, He is infinitely incomprehensible, since, having neither parts nor limits, He has no affinity to us. We are then incapable of knowing either what He is or if He is. This being so, who will dare to undertake the decision of the question? Not we, who have no affinity to Him.

Who then will blame Christians for not being able to give a reason for their belief, since they profess a religion for which they cannot give a reason? They declare, in expounding it to the world, that it is a foolishness **stultitiam;** and then you complain that they do not prove it! If they proved it, they would not keep their word; it is in lacking proofs, that they are not lacking in sense. "Yes, but although this excuses those who offer it as such, and take away from them the blame of putting it forward without reason, it does not excuse those who receive it." Let us then examine this point, and say, "God is, or He is not." But to which side shall we incline? Reason can decide nothing here. There is an infinite chaos which separates us. A game is being played at the extremity of this infinite distance where heads or tails will turn up. What will you wager? According to reason, you can do neither the one thing nor the other; according to reason, you can defend neither of the propositions.

Do not then reprove for error those who have made a choice; for you know nothing about it. "No, but I blame them for having made, not this choice, but a choice; for again both he who chooses heads and he who chooses tails are equally at fault, they are both in the wrong. The true course is not to wager at all."

—Yes; but you must wager. It is not optional. You are embarked. Which will you choose then? Let us see. Since you must choose, let us see which interests you least. You have two things to lose, the true and the good; and two things to stake, your reason and your will, your knowledge and your happiness; and your nature has two things to shun, error and misery. Your reason is no more shocked in choosing one rather that the other, since you must of necessity choose. This is one point settled. But your happiness? Let us weigh the gain and the loss in wagering that God is. Let us estimate these two chances. If you gain, you gain all; if you lose, you lose nothing. Wager then without hesitation that He is.—"That is very fine. Yes, I must wager; but I may perhaps wager too much."—Let us see. Since there is an equal risk of gain and of loss, if you had only to gain two lives, instead of one, you might still wager. But if there were three lives to gain, you would have to play (since you are under the necessity of playing), and you would be imprudent, when you are forced to play, not to chance your life to gain three at a game where there is an equal risk of loss and gain. But there is an eternity of life and happiness. And this being so, if there were an infinity of chances, of which one only would be for you, you would still be right in wagering one to win two, and you would act stupidly, being obliged to play, by refusing to stake one life against three at a game in which out of an infinity of chances there is one for you, if there were an infinity of an infinitely happy life to gain. But there is here an infinity of an infinitely happy life to gain, a chance of gain against a finite number of chances of loss, and what you stake is finite. It is all divided; wherever the infinite is and there is not an infinity of chances of loss against that of gain, there is no time to hesitate, you must give all. And thus, when one is forced to play, he must renounce reason to preserve his life, rather than risk it for infinite gain, as likely to happen as the loss of nothingness.

For it is no use to say it is uncertain if we will gain, and it is certain that we risk, and that the infinite distance between the *certainty* of what is staked and the *uncertainty* of what will be gained, equals the finite good which is certainly staked against the uncertain infinite. It is not so, as every player stakes a certainty to gain an uncertainty, and yet he stakes a finite certainty to gain a finite uncertainty, without transgressing against reason. There is not an infinite distance between the certainty staked and the uncertainty of the gain; that is untrue. In truth, there is an infinity between the certainty of gain and the certainty of loss. But the uncertainty of the gain is proportioned to the certainty of the stake according to the proportion of the chances of gain and loss. Hence it comes that, if there are as many risks on one side as on the other, the course is to play even; and then the certainty of the stake is equal to the uncertainty of the gain,

so far is it from fact that there is an infinite distance between them. And so our proposition is of infinite force, when there is the finite to stake in a game where there are equal risks of gain and of loss, and the infinite to gain. This is demonstrable; and if men are capable of any truths, this is one.

"I confess it, I admit it. But still is there no means of seeing the faces of the cards?"—Yes, Scripture and the rest, &c.—"Yes, but I have my hands tied and my mouth closed; I am forced to wager, and am not free. I am not released, and am so made that I cannot believe. What then would you have me do?"

True. But at least learn your inability to believe, since reason brings you to this, and yet you cannot believe. Endeavour then to convince yourself, not by increase of proofs of God, but by the abatement of your passions. You would like to attain faith, and do not know the way; you would like to cure yourself of unbelief, and ask the remedy for it. Learn of those who have been bound like you, and who now stake all their possessions. These are people who know the way which you would follow, and who are cured of an ill of which you would be cured. Follow the way by which they began; by acting as if they believe, taking the holy water, having masses said, &c. Even this will naturally make you believe, and deaden your acuteness.—"But this is what I am afraid of."—And why? What have you to lose?

But to show you that this leads you there, it is this which will lessen the passions, which are your stumbling-blocks.

The end of this discourse.—Now what harm will befall you in taking this side? You will be faithful, honest, humble, grateful, generous, a sincere friend, truthful. Certainly you will not have those poisonous pleasures, glory and luxury; but will you not have others? I will tell you that you will thereby gain in this life, and that, at each step you take on this road, you will see so great certainty of gain, so much nothingness in what you risk, that you will at last recognize that you have wagered for something certain and infinite for which you have given nothing.

"Ah! This discourse transports me, charms me," &c.

If this discourse pleases you and seems impressive, know that it is made by a man who has knelt, both before and after it, in prayer to that Being, infinite and without parts, before whom he lays all he has, for you also to lay before Him all you have for your own good and for His glory, that so strength may be given to lowliness.

William James
The Will to Believe

William James (1842–1910), the American philosopher and psychologist, taught at Harvard University.

In the recently published *Life* by Leslie Stephen of his brother, Fitzjames, there is an account of a school to which the latter went when he was a boy. The teacher, a certain Mr. Guest, used to converse with his pupils in this wise: "Gurney, what's the difference between justification and sanctification?—Stephen, prove the Omnipotence of God!" etc. In the midst of our Harvard freethinking and indifference we are prone to imagine that here at your good old orthodox College conversation continues to be somewhat upon this order; and to show you that we at Harvard have not lost all interest in these vital subjects, I have brought with me tonight something like a sermon on justification by faith to read to you—I mean an essay in justification *of* faith, a defence of our right to adopt a believing attitude in religious matters, in spite of the fact that our merely logical intellect may not have been

Reprinted by permission of the publishers from *The Will to Believe and Other Essays in Popular Philosophy* by William James, Frederick H. Burkhardt, et al., eds., Cambridge, Mass.: Harvard University Press, Copyright © 1979 by The President and Fellows of Harvard College.

coerced. "The Will to Believe," accordingly, is the title of my paper.[1]

I have long defended to my own students the lawfulness of voluntarily adopted faith; but as soon as they have got well imbued with the logical spirit, they have as a rule refused to admit my contention to be lawful philosophically, even though in point of fact they were personally all the time chock-full of some faith or other themselves. I am all the while, however, so profoundly convinced that my own position is correct, that your invitation has seemed to me a good occasion to make my statements more clear. Perhaps your minds will be more open than those with which I have hitherto had to deal. I will be as little technical as I can, though I must begin by setting up some technical distinctions that will help us in the end.

I

Let us give the name of *hypothesis* to anything that may be proposed to our belief; and just as the electricians speak of live and dead wires, let us speak of any hypothesis as either live or dead. A live hypothesis is one which appeals as a real possibility to him to whom it is proposed. If I ask you to believe in the Mahdi, the notion makes no electric connection with your nature—it refuses to scintillate with any credibility at all. As an hypothesis it is completely dead. To an Arab, however (even if he be not one of the Mahdi's followers), the hypothesis is among the mind's possibilities: it is alive. This shows that deadness and liveness in an hypothesis are not intrinsic properties, but relations to the individual thinker. They are measured by his willingness to act. The maximum of liveness in an hypothesis means willingness to act irrevocably. Practically, that means belief; but there is some believing tendency wherever there is willingness to act at all.

Next, let us call the decision between two hypotheses an *option*. Options may be of several kinds. They may be—1, *living* or *dead*; 2, *forced* or *avoidable*; 3, *momentous* or *trivial*; and for our purposes we may call an option a *genuine* option when it is of the forced, living and momentous kind.

1. A living option is one in which both hypotheses are live ones. If I say to you: "Be a theosophist or be a mahomedan," it is probably a dead option, because for you neither hypothesis is likely to be alive. But if I say "Be an agnostic or be a Christian," it is otherwise: trained as you are, each hypothesis makes some appeal, however small, to your belief.
2. Next, if I say to you: "Choose between going out with your umbrella or without it," I do not offer you a genuine option, for it is not forced. You can easily avoid it by not going out at all. Similarly, if I say "Either love me or hate me," "Either call my theory true or call it false," your option is avoidable. You may remain indifferent to me, neither loving nor hating, and you may decline to offer any judgement as to my theory. But if I say "Either accept this truth or go without it," I put on you a forced option, for there is no standing place outside of the alternative. Every dilemma based on a complete logical disjunction, with no possibility of not choosing, is an option of this forced kind.
3. Finally, if I were Dr. Nansen and proposed to you to join my North Pole expedition, your option would be momentous; for this would probably be your only similar opportunity, and your choice now would either exclude you from the North Pole sort of immortality altogether or put at least the chance of it into your hands. He who refuses to embrace a unique opportunity loses the prize as surely as if he tried and failed. *Per contra*, the option

is trivial when the opportunity is not unique, when the stake is insignificant, or when the decision is reversible if it later prove unwise. Such trivial options abound in the scientific life. A chemist finds an hypothesis live enough to spend a year in its verification: he believes in it to that extent. But if his experiments prove inconclusive either way, he is quit for his loss of time, no vital harm being done.

It will facilitate our discussion if we keep all these distinctions well in mind.

II

The next matter to consider is the actual psychology of human opinion. When we look at certain facts, it seems as if our passional and volitional nature lay at the root of all our convictions. When we look at others, it seems as if they could do nothing when the intellect had once said its say. Let us take the latter facts up first.

Does it not seem preposterous on the very face of it to talk of our opinions being modifiable at will? Can our will either help or hinder our intellect in its perceptions of truth? Can we, by just willing it, believe that Abraham Lincoln's existence is a myth and that the portraits of him in *McClure's Magazine* are all of someone else? Can we, by any effort of our will, or by any strength of wish that it were true, believe ourselves well and about when we are roaring with rheumatism in bed, or feel certain that the sum of the two one-dollar bills in our pocket must be a hundred dollars? We can *say* any of these things, but we are absolutely impotent to believe them; and of just such things is the whole fabric of the truths that we do believe in made up—matters of fact, immediate or remote, as Hume said, and relations between ideas, which are either there or not there for us if we see them so, and which if not there cannot be put there by any action of our own.

In Pascal's *Thoughts* there is a celebrated passage known in literature as Pascal's wager. In it he tries to force us into Christianity by reasoning as if our concern with truth resembled our concern with the stakes in a game of chance.

Translated freely his words are these: You must either believe or not believe that God is—which will you do? Your human reason cannot say. A game is going on between you and the nature of things which at the day of judgment will bring out either heads or tails. Weigh what your gains and your losses would be if you should stake all you have on heads, or God's existence: If you win in such case, you gain eternal beatitude; if you lose, you lose nothing at all. If there were an infinity of chances, and only one for God in this wager, still you ought to stake your all on God; for though you surely risk a finite loss by this procedure, any finite loss is reasonable, even a certain one is reasonable, if there is but the possibility of infinite gain. Go, then, and take holy water, and have masses said; belief will come and stupefy your scruples . . . Why should you not? At bottom, what have you to lose?

You probably feel that when religious faith expresses itself thus, in the language of the gaming-table, it is put to its last trumps. Surely Pascal's own personal belief in masses and holy water had far other springs; and this celebrated page of his is but an argument for others, a last desperate snatch at a weapon against the hardness of the unbelieving heart. We feel that a faith in masses and holy water adopted willfully after such a mechanical calculation would lack the inner soul of faith's reality; and if we were ourselves in the place of the Deity, we should probably take particular pleasure in cutting off believers of this pattern from their infinite reward. It is evident that unless there be some pre-existing tendency to believe in masses and holy water, the option offered to the will by Pascal is not a living option. Certainly no Turk ever took to masses and holy water on its account; and even to us Protestants these means of salvation seem such foregone impossibilities that Pascal's logic, invoked for them specifically, leaves us unmoved. As well might the Mahdi write to us, saying "I am the Expected One whom God has created in his effulgence. You shall be infinitely happy if you confess me; otherwise you shall be cut off from the light of the sun. Weigh, then, your infinite gain if I am genuine against your finite sacrifice if I am not!" His logic would be that of Pascal; but he would vainly use it on us,

for the hypothesis he offers us is dead. No tendency to act on it exists in us to any degree.

The talk of believing by our volition seems, then, from one point of view, simply silly. From another point of view it is worse than silly, it is vile. When one turns to the magnificent edifice of the physical sciences, and sees how it was reared; what thousands of disinterested moral lives of men lie buried in its mere foundations; what patience and postponement, what choking down of preference, what submission to the icy laws of outer fact are wrought into its very stones and mortar; how absolutely impersonal it stands in its vast augustness—then how besotted and contemptible seems every little sentimentalist who comes blowing his voluntary smoke-wreaths, and pretending to decide things from out of his private dream! Can we wonder if those bred in the rugged and manly school of science should feel like spewing such subjectivism out of their mouths? The whole system of loyalties which grow up in the schools of science go dead against its toleration; so that it is only natural that those who have caught the scientific fever should pass over to the opposite extreme, and write sometimes as if the incorruptibly truthful intellect ought positively to prefer bitterness and unacceptableness to the heart in its cup.

> *"It fortifies my soul to know*
> *That, though I perish, Truth is so—"*

sings Clough, whilst Huxley exclaims: "My only consolation lies in the reflection that, however bad our posterity may become, so long as they hold by the plain rule of not pretending to believe what they have no reason to believe because it may be to their advantage so to pretend [the word 'pretend' is surely here redundant], they will not have reached the lowest depths of immorality." And that delicious *enfant terrible* Clifford writes: "Belief is desecrated when given to unproved and unquestioned statements, for the solace and private pleasure of the believer....Whoso would deserve well of his fellows in this matter will guard the purity of his belief with a very fanaticism of jealous care, lest at any time it should rest on an unworthy object, and catch a stain which can never be wiped away....If [a] belief has been accepted on insufficient evidence [even though the belief be true, as Clifford on the same page explains], the pleasure is a stolen one....It is sinful, because it is stolen in defiance of our duty to mankind. That duty is to guard ourselves from such beliefs as from a pestilence, which may shortly master our own body and then spread to the rest of the town....It is wrong always, everywhere, and for anyone, to believe anything upon insufficient evidence."

III

All this strikes one as healthy, even when expressed, as by Clifford, with somewhat too much of robustious pathos in the voice. Freewill and simple wishing do seem, in the matter of our credences, to be only fifth wheels to the coach. Yet if anyone should thereupon assume that intellectual insight is what remains after wish and will and sentimental preference have taken wing, or that pure reason is what then settles our opinions, he would fly quite as directly in the teeth of the facts.

It is only our already dead hypotheses that our willing nature is unable to bring to life again. But what has made them dead for us is for the most part a previous action of our willing nature of an antagonistic kind. When I say "willing nature," I do not mean only such deliberate volitions as may have set up habits of belief that we cannot now escape from—I mean all such factors of belief as fear and hope, prejudice and passion, imitation and partisanship, the circumpressure of our caste and set. As a matter of fact we find ourselves believing, we hardly know how or why. Mr. Balfour gives the name of "authority" to all those influences, born of the intellectual climate, that make hypotheses possible or impossible for us, alive or dead. Here in this room, we all of us believe in molecules and the conservation of energy, in democracy and necessary progress, in Protestant Christianity and the duty of fighting for "the doctrine of the immortal Monroe," all for no reasons worthy of the name. We see into these matters with no more inner clearness, and probably with much

less, than any disbeliever in them might possess. His unconventionality would probably have some grounds to show for its conclusions; but for us, not insight, but the *prestige* of the opinions, is what makes the spark shoot from them and light up our sleeping magazines of faith. Our reason is quite satisfied, in nine hundred and ninety-nine cases out of every thousand of us, if it can find a few arguments that will do to recite in case our credulity is criticized by someone else. Our faith is faith in someone else's faith, and in the greatest matters this is most the case. Our belief in truth itself, for instance, that there is a truth, and that our minds and it are made for each other—what is it but a passionate affirmation of desire, in which our social system backs us up? We want to have a truth; we want to believe that our experiments and studies and discussions must put us in a continually better and better position towards it; and on this line we agree to fight out our thinking lives. But if a pyrrhonistic sceptic asks us *how we know* all this, can our logic find a reply? No! Certainly it cannot. It is just one volition against another—we willing to go in for life upon a trust or assumption which he, for his part, does not care to make.[2]

As a rule we disbelieve all facts and theories for which we have no use. Clifford's cosmic emotions find no use for Christian feelings. Huxley belabors the bishops because there is no use for sacerdotalism in his scheme of life. Newman, on the contrary, goes over to Romanism, and finds all sorts of reasons good for staying there, because a priestly system is for him an organic need and delight. Why do so few "scientists" even look at the evidence for telepathy, so called? Because they think, as a leading biologist, now dead, once said to me, that even if such a thing were true, scientists ought to band together to keep it suppressed and concealed. It would undo the uniformity of Nature and all sorts of other things without which scientists cannot carry on their pursuits. But if this very man had been shown something which as a scientist he might *do* with telepathy, he might not only have examined the evidence, but even have found it good enough. This very law which the logicians would impose upon us—if I may give the name of logicians to those who would rule out our willing nature here—is based on nothing but their own natural wish to exclude all elements for which they, in their professional quality of logicians, can find no use.

Evidently, then, our non-intellectual nature does influence our convictions. There are passional tendencies and volitions which run before and others which come after belief, and it is only the latter that are too late for the fair; and they are not too late when the previous passional work has been already in their own direction. Pascal's argument, instead of being powerless, then seems a regular clincher, and is the last stroke needed to make our faith in masses and holy water complete. The state of things is evidently far from simple; and pure insight and logic, whatever they might do ideally, are not the only things that really do produce our creeds.

IV

Our next duty, having recognized this mixed-up state of affairs, is to ask whether it be simply reprehensible and pathological, or whether, on the contrary, we must treat it as a normal element in making up our minds. The thesis I defend is, briefly stated, this: *Our passional nature not only lawfully may, but must, decide an option between propositions, whenever it is a genuine option that cannot by its nature be decided on intellectual grounds; for to say, under such circumstances, "Do not decide, but leave the question open," is itself a passional decision—just like deciding yes or no— and is attended with the same risk of losing the truth.*

VII

One more point, small but important, and our preliminaries are done. There are two ways of looking at our duty in the matter of opinion— ways entirely different, and yet ways about whose difference the theory of knowledge seems hitherto to have shown very little concern. *We must know the truth;* and *we must avoid error*—these are our first and great commandments as would-be knowers; but they are not two ways of stating an identical commandment,

they are two separable laws. Although it may indeed happen that when we believe the truth A, we escape as an incidental consequence from believing the falsehood B, it hardly ever happens that by merely disbelieving B, we necessarily believe A. We may in escaping B fall into believing other falsehoods, C or D, just as bad as B; or we may escape B by not believing anything at all, not even A.

Believe truth! Shun error!—these, we see, are two materially different laws; and by choosing between them we may end by colouring differently our whole intellectual life. We may regard the chase for truth as paramount, and the avoidance of error as secondary; or we may, on the other hand, treat the avoidance of error as more imperative, and let truth take its chance. Clifford, in the instructive passage which I have quoted, exhorts us to the latter course. Believe nothing, he tells us, keep your mind in suspense forever, rather than by closing it on insufficient evidence incur the awful risk of believing lies. You, on the other hand, may think that the risk of being in error is a very small matter when compared with the blessings of real knowledge, and be ready to be duped many times in your investigation rather than postpone indefinitely the chance of guessing true. I myself find it impossible to go with Clifford. We must remember that these feelings of our duty about either truth or error are in any case only expressions of our passional life. Biologically considered, our minds are as ready to grind out falsehood as veracity, and he who says "Better go without belief forever than believe a lie!" merely shows his own preponderant private horror of becoming a dupe. He may be critical of many of his desires and fears, but this fear he slavishly obeys. He cannot imagine anyone questioning its binding force. For my own part, I have also a horror of being duped; but I can believe that worse things than being duped may happen to a man in this world: so Clifford's exhortation has to my ears a thoroughly fantastic sound. It is like a general informing his soldiers that it is better to keep out of battle forever than to risk a single wound. Not so are victories either over enemies or over nature gained. Our errors are surely not such awfully solemn things. In a world where we are so certain to incur them in spite of all our caution, a certain lightness of heart seems healthier than this excessive nervousness on their behalf. At any rate, it seems the fittest thing for the empiricist philosopher.

VIII

And now, after all this introduction, let us go straight at our question. I have said, and now repeat it, that not only as a matter of fact do we find our passional nature influencing us in our opinions, but that there are some options between opinions in which this influence must be regarded both as an inevitable and as a lawful determinant of our choice.

I fear here that some of you my hearers will begin to scent danger, and lend an inhospitable ear. Two first steps of passion you have indeed had to admit as necessary—we must think so as to avoid dupery, and we must think so as to gain truth; but the surest path to those ideal consummations, you will probably consider, is from now onwards to take no farther passional step.

Well, of course I agree as far as the facts will allow. Wherever the option between losing truth and gaining it is not momentous, we can throw the chance of *gaining truth* away, and at any rate save ourselves from any chance of *believing falsehood,* by not making up our minds at all till objective evidence has come. In scientific questions, this is almost always the case; and even in human affairs in general, the need of acting is seldom so urgent that a false belief to act on is better than no belief at all. Law courts, indeed, have to decide on the best evidence attainable for the moment, because a judge's duty is to make law as well as to ascertain it, and (as a learned judge once said to me) few cases are worth spending much time over: the great thing is to have them decided on *any* acceptable principle, and got out of the way. But in our dealings with objective nature we obviously are recorders, not makers, of the truth; and decisions for the mere sake of deciding promptly and getting on to the next business would be wholly out of place. Throughout the breadth of physical nature facts are what they are quite independently of us, and seldom is there any such hurry about them that the risks of being duped by believing a premature theory need be faced. The questions here are always trivial options, the hypotheses are hardly living (at any rate not living for us spectators), the choice between believing truth or falsehood is seldom forced. The attitude of sceptical balance is therefore the absolutely wise one if we would escape mistakes. What difference, indeed, does it make to most of us whether we have or have not a theory of the Röntgen rays, whether we believe or not in mind-stuff, or have a conviction about the causality of conscious states? It makes no difference. Such options are not forced on us. On every account it is better not to make them, but still keep weighing reasons *pro et contra* with an indifferent hand.

I speak, of course, here of the purely judging mind. For purposes of discovery such indifference is to be less highly recommended, and science would be far less advanced than she is if the passionate desires of individuals to get their own faiths confirmed had been kept out of the game. See for example the sagacity which Spencer and Weismann now display. On the other hand, if you want an absolute duffer in an investigation, you must, after all, take the man who has no interest whatever in its results: he is the warranted incapable, the positive fool. The most useful investigator, because the most sensitive observer, is always he whose eager interest in one side of the question is balanced by an equally keen nervousness lest he become deceived.[3] Science has organized this nervousness into a regular *technique*, her so-called method of verification; and she has fallen so deeply in love with the method that one may even say she has ceased to care for truth by itself at all. It is only truth as technically verified that interests her. The truth of truths might come in merely affirmative form, and she would decline to touch it. Such truth as that, she might repeat with Clifford, would be stolen in defiance of her duty to mankind. Human passions, however, are stronger than technical rules. "Le coeur a ses raisons," as Pascal says "que la raison ne connaît point";* and however indifferent to all but the bare rules of the game the umpire, the

_____

[* "The heart has its reasons which reason cannot know." Ed.]

abstract intellect, may be, the concrete players who furnish him the materials to judge of are usually, each one of them, in love with some pet "live hypothesis" of his own. Let us agree, however, that wherever there is no forced option, the dispassionately judicial intellect with no pet hypothesis, saving us, as it does, from dupery at any rate, ought to be our ideal.

The question next arises: Are there not somewhere forced options in our speculative questions, and can we (as men who may be interested at least as much in positively gaining truth is in merely escaping dupery) always wait with impunity till the coercive evidence shall have arrived? It seems *a priori* improbable that the truth should be so nicely adjusted to our needs and powers as that. In the great boarding-house of nature, the cakes and the butter and the syrup seldom come out so even and leave the plates so clean. Indeed, we should view them with scientific suspicion if they did.

IX

Moral questions immediately present themselves as questions whose solution cannot wait for sensible proof. A moral question is a question not of what sensibly exists, but of what is good, or would be good if it did exist. Science can tell us what exists; but to compare the *worths*, both of what exists and of what does not exist, we must consult not science, but what Pascal calls our heart. Science herself consults her heart when she lays it down that the infinite ascertainment of fact and correction of false belief are the supreme goods for man. Challenge the statement and science can only repeat it oracularly, or else prove it by showing that such ascertainment and correction bring man all sorts of other goods which man's heart in turn declares. The question of having moral beliefs at all or not having them is decided by our will. Are our moral preferences true or false, or are they only odd biological phenomena, making things good or bad for *us*, but in themselves indifferent? How can your pure intellect decide? If your heart does not *want* a world of moral reality, your head will assuredly never make you believe in one. Mephistophelian scepticism, indeed, will satisfy the head's play-instincts much better than any rig-

orous idealism can. Some men (even at the student age) are so naturally cool-hearted that the moralistic hypothesis never has for them any pungent life, and in their supercilious presence the hot young moralist always feels strangely ill at ease. The appearance of knowingness is on their side, of *naiveté* and gullibility on his. Yet, in the inarticulate heart of him, he clings to it that he is not a dupe, and that there is a realm in which (as Emerson says) all their wit and intellectual superiority is no better than the cunning of a fox. Moral scepticism can no more be refuted or proved by logic than intellectual scepticism can. When we stick to it that there *is* truth (be it of either kind), we do so with our whole nature, and resolve to stand or fall by the results. The sceptic with his whole nature adopts the doubting attitude; but which of us is the wiser, Omniscience only knows.

Turn now from these wide questions of good to a certain class of questions of fact, questions concerning personal relations, states of mind between one man and another. *Do you like me or not?*—for example. Whether you do or not depends, in countless instances, on whether I meet you halfway, am willing to assume that you must like me, and show you trust and expectation. The previous faith on my part in your liking's existence is in such cases what makes your liking come. But if I stand aloof, and refuse to budge an inch until I have objective evidence, until you shall have done something apt, as the absolutists say, *ad extorquendum assensum meum,** ten to one your liking never comes. How many women's hearts are vanquished by the mere sanguine insistence of some man that they *must* love him! he will not consent to the hypothesis that they cannot. The desire for a certain kind of truth here brings about that special truth's existence; and so it is in innumerable cases of other sorts. Who gains promotions, boons, appointments, but the man in whose life they are seen to play the part of live hypotheses, who discounts them, sacrifices other things for their sake before they have come, and takes risks for them in advance? His faith acts on the powers above him as a claim, and creates its own verification.

—————

[* *"until my assent has been compelled." Ed.*]

A social organism of any sort whatever, large or small, is what it is because each member proceeds to his own duty with a trust that the other members will simultaneously do theirs. Wherever a desired result is achieved by the co-operation of many independent persons, its existence as a fact is a pure consequence of the precursive faith in one another of those immediately concerned. A government, an army, a commercial system, a ship, a college, an athletic team, all exist on this condition, without which not only is nothing achieved, but nothing is even attempted. A whole train of passengers (individually brave enough) will be looted by a few highwaymen, simply because the latter can count on one another, while each passenger fears that if he makes a movement of resistance, he will be shot before anyone else backs him up. If we believed that the whole car-full would rise at once with us, we should each severally rise, and train-robbing would never even be attempted. There are, then, cases where a fact cannot come at all unless a preliminary faith exists in its coming. *And where faith in a fact can help create the fact,* that would be an insane logic which should say that faith running ahead of scientific evidence is the "lowest kind of immorality" into which a thinking being can fall. Yet such is the logic by which our scientific absolutists pretend to regulate our lives!

X

In truths dependent on our personal action, then, faith based on desire is certainly a lawful and possibly an indispensable thing.

But now, it will be said, these are all childish human cases, and have nothing to do with great cosmical matters, like the question of religious faith. Let us then pass on to that. Religions differ so much in their accidents that in discussing the religious question we must make it very generic and broad. What then do we now mean by the religious hypothesis? Science says things are; morality says some things are better than other things; and religion says essentially two things.

First, she says that the best things are the more eternal things, the overlapping things, the things in the universe that throw the last stone, so to speak, and say the final word. "Perfection is eternal"—this phrase of Charles Secrétan seems a good way of putting this affirmation of religion, an affirmation which obviously cannot yet be verified scientifically at all.

The second affirmation of religion is that we are better off even now if we believe her first affirmation to be true.

Now let us consider what the logical elements of this situation are *in case the religious hypothesis in both its branches be really true.* (Of course, we must admit that possibility at the outset. If we are to discuss the question at all, it must involve a living option. If for any of you religion be a hypothesis that cannot, by any living possibility be true, then you need go no farther. I speak to the "saving remnant" alone.) So proceeding, we see, first, that religion offers itself as a *momentous* option. We are supposed to gain, even now, by our belief, and to lose by our non-belief, a certain vital good. Secondly, religion is a *forced* option, so far as that good goes. We cannot escape the issue by remaining sceptical and waiting for more light, because, although we do avoid error in that way *if religion be untrue,* we lose the good, *if it be true,* just as certainly as if we positively chose to disbelieve. It is as if a man should hesitate indefinitely to ask a certain woman to marry him because he was not perfectly sure that she would prove an angel after he brought her home. Would he not cut himself off from that particular angel-possibility as decisively as if he went and married someone else? Scepticism, then, is not avoidance of option; it is option of a certain particular kind of risk. *Better risk loss of truth than chance of error*—that is your faith-vetoer's exact position. He is actively playing his stake as much as the believer is; he is backing the field against the religious hypothesis, just as the believer is backing the religious hypothesis, against the field. To preach scepticism to us as a duty until "sufficient evidence" for religion be found, is tantamount therefore to telling us, when in presence of the religious hypothesis, that to yield to our fear of its being error is wiser and better than to yield to our hope that it may be true. It is not intellect against all passions, then; it is only intellect with one passion laying down its law. And by what, forsooth, is the supreme wisdom of this passion warranted? Dupery for dupery, what proof is there that dupery through hope is so much worse than dupery through fear? I, for one, can see no proof; and I simply refuse obedience to the scientist's command to imitate his kind of option, in a case where my own stake is important enough to give me the right to choose my own form of risk. If religion be true and the evidence for it be still insufficient, I do not wish, by putting your extinguisher upon my nature (which feels to me as if it had after all some business in this matter), to forfeit my sole chance in life of getting upon the winning side—that chance depending, of course, on my willingness to run the risk of acting as if my passional need of taking the world religiously might be prophetic and right.

All this is on the supposition that it really may be prophetic and right, and that, even to us who are discussing the matter, religion is a live hypothesis which may be true. Now to most of us religion comes in a still farther way that makes a veto on our active faith even more illogical. The more perfect and more eternal aspect of the universe is represented in our religions as having personal form. The universe is no longer a mere *It* to us, but a *Thou,* if we are religious; and any relation that may be possible from person to person might be possible here. For instance, although in one sense we are passive portions of the universe, in another we show a curious autonomy, as if we were small active centres on our own account. We feel, too, as if the appeal of religion to us were made to our own active goodwill, as if evidence might be forever withheld from us unless we met the hypothesis half-way. To take a trivial illustration: just as a man who in a company of gentlemen made no advances, asked a warrant for every concession, and believed no one's word without proof, would cut himself off by such churlishness from all the social rewards that a more trusting spirit would earn—so here, one who should shut himself up in snarling logicality and try to make the gods extort his recognition willy-nilly, or not get it at all, might cut himself off forever from his only opportunity of making the gods' acquaintance. This feeling, forced on us we know not whence, that by obstinately believing that there are gods (although not to do so would be so easy

both for our logic and our life) we are doing the universe the deepest service we can, seems part of the living essence of the religious hypothesis. If the hypothesis *were* true in all its parts, including this one, then pure intellectualism, with its veto on our making willing advances, would be an absurdity; and some participation of our sympathetic nature would be logically required. I, therefore, for one, cannot see my way to accepting the agnostic rules for truth-seeking, or wilfully agree to keep my willing nature out of the game. I cannot do so for this plain reason, that *a rule of thinking which would absolutely prevent me from acknowledging certain kinds of truth if those kinds of truth were really there, would be an irrational rule.* That for me is the long and short of the formal logic of the situation, no matter what the kinds of truth might materially be.

I confess I do not see how this logic can be escaped. But sad experience makes me fear that some of you may still shrink from radically saying with me, in *abstracto,* that we have the right to believe at our own risk any hypothesis that is live enough to tempt our will. I suspect, however, that if this is so, it is because you have got away from the abstract logical point of view altogether, and are thinking (perhaps without realizing it) of some particular religious hypothesis which for you is dead. The freedom to "believe what we will" you apply to the case of some patent superstition; and the faith you think of is the faith defined by the schoolboy when he said, "Faith is when you believe something that you know ain't true." I can only repeat that this is misapprehension. *In concreto,* the freedom to believe can only cover living options which the intellect of the individual cannot by itself resolve; and living options never seem absurdities to him who has them to consider. When I look at the religious question as it really puts itself to concrete men, and when I think of all the possibilities which both practically and theoretically it involves, then this command that we shall put a stopper on our heart, instincts and courage, and *wait*—acting of course meanwhile more or less as if religion were *not* true[4]—till doomsday, or till such time as our intellect and senses working together may have raked in evidence enough—this command, I say, seems to me the queerest idol ever manufactured in the philosophic cave. Were we scholastic absolutists, there might be more excuse. If we had an infallible intellect with its objective certitudes, we might feel ourselves disloyal to such a perfect organ of knowledge in not trusting to it exclusively, in not waiting for its releasing word. But if we are empiricists, if we believe that no bell in us tolls to let us know for certain when truth is in our grasp, then it seems a piece of idle fantasticality to preach so solemnly our duty of waiting for the bell. Indeed we *may* wait if we will—I hope you do not think that I am denying that—but if we do so, we do so at our peril as much as if we believed. In either case we *act*, taking our life in our hands. No one of us ought to issue vetoes to the other, nor should we bandy words of abuse. We ought, on the contrary, delicately and profoundly to respect one another's mental freedom—then only shall we bring about the intellectual republic; then only shall we have that spirit of inner tolerance without which all our outer tolerance is soulless, and which is empiricism's glory; then only shall we live and let live, in speculative as well as in practical things.

I began by a reference to Fitzjames Stephen; let me end by a quotation from him. "What do you think of yourself? What do you think of the world?. . . These are questions with which all must deal as it seems good to them. They are riddles of the Sphinx, and in some way or other we must deal with them. . . . In all important transactions of life we have to take a leap in the dark. . . . If we decide to leave the riddles unanswered, that is a choice. If we waver in our answer, that too is a choice; but whatever choice we make, we make it at our peril. If a man chooses to turn his back altogether on God and the future, no one can prevent him. No one can show beyond reasonable doubt that he is mistaken. If a man thinks otherwise, and acts as he thinks, I do not see how any one can prove that *he* is mistaken. Each must act as he thinks best, and if he is wrong so much the worse for him. We stand on a mountain pass in the midst of whirling snow and blinding mist, through which we get glimpses now and then of paths which may be deceptive. If we stand still, we shall be frozen to death. If we take the wrong road, we shall be dashed to pieces. We do not certainly know whether there is any right one. What must we do? 'Be strong and of a good courage.' Act for the best, hope for the best, and take what comes. . . . If death ends all, we cannot meet death better."[5]

Notes

1. An Address to the Philosophical Clubs of Yale and Brown Universities. Published in the *New World*, June 1896.

2. Compare the admirable page 310 in S. H. Hodgson's *Time and Space*, London, 1865.

3. Compare Wilfrid Ward's Essay, "The Wish to Believe," in his *Witnesses to the Unseen*, Macmillan & Co., 1893.

4. Since belief is measured by action, he who forbids us to believe religion to be true, necessarily also forbids us to act as we should if we did believe it to be true. The whole defence of religious faith hinges upon action. If the action required or inspired by the religious hypothesis is in no way different from that dictated by the naturalistic hypothesis, then religious faith is a pure superfluity, better pruned away, and controversy about its legitimacy is a piece of idle trifling, unworthy of serious minds. I myself believe, of course, that the religious hypothesis gives to the world an expression which specifically determines our reactions, and makes them in a large part unlike what they might be on a purely naturalistic scheme of belief.

5. *Liberty, Equality, Fraternity*, p. 353, 2nd edition. London, 1874.

Questions on James

1. What thesis about options does James wish to defend? How does he go about defending it?

2. James claims that religion says essentially two things. What are they? Do you agree? Why or why not?

3. According to James, why should we choose the religious hypothesis rather than scepticism? Are you convinced or not? Explain your position.

Soren Kierkegaard

The Leap of Faith

Soren Kierkegaard (1813–1855), a Danish philosopher, was ordained a Lutheran minister but often attacked institutional religion.

But what is this unknown something with which the Reason collides when inspired by its paradoxical passion, with the result of unsettling even man's knowledge of himself? It is the Unknown. It is not a human being, in so far as we know what man is; nor is it any other known thing. So let us call this unknown something: *the God.* It is nothing more than a name we assign to it. The idea of demonstrating that this unknown something (the God) exists, could scarcely suggest itself to the Reason. For if the God does not exist it would of course be impossible to prove it; and if he does exist it would be folly to attempt it. For at the very outset, in beginning my proof, I would have presupposed it, not as doubtful but as certain (a presupposition is never doubtful, for the very reason that it is a presupposition), since otherwise I would not begin, readily understanding that the whole would be impossible if he did not exist. But if when I speak of proving the God's existence I mean that I propose to prove that the Unknown, which exists, is the God, then I express myself unfortunately. For in that case I do not prove anything, least of all an existence, but merely develop the content of a conception. Generally speaking, it is a difficult matter to prove that anything exists; and what is still worse for the intrepid souls who undertake the venture, the difficulty is such that fame scarcely awaits those who concern themselves with it. The entire demonstration always turns into something very different and becomes an additional development of the consequences that flow from my having assumed that the object in

The reading is from Soren Kierkegaard, *Philosophical Fragments*, trans. David F. Swenson. Copyright 1936, © 1962 by Princeton University Press. Excerpts, pp. 49–57 and 72–73 reprinted with permission of Princeton University Press.

question exists. Thus I always reason from existence, not toward existence, whether I move in the sphere of palpable sensible fact or in the realm of thought. I do not for example prove that a stone exists, but that some existing thing is a stone. The procedure in a court of justice does not prove that a criminal exists, but that the accused, whose existence is given, is a criminal. . . . Existence . . . is never subject to demonstration. Let us take ample time for consideration. We have no such reason for haste as have those who from concern for themselves or for the God or for some other thing, must make haste to get existence demonstrated. Under such circumstances there may indeed be need for haste, especially if the prover sincerely seeks to appreciate the danger that he himself, or the thing in question, may be non-existent unless the proof is finished and does not surreptitiously entertain the thought that it exists whether he succeeds in proving it or not.

If it were proposed to prove Napoleon's existence from Napoleon's deeds, would it not be a most curious proceeding? His existence does indeed explain his deeds, but the deeds do not prove *his* existence, unless I have already understood the word "his" so as thereby to have assumed his existence. But Napoleon is only an individual, and in so far there exists no absolute relationship between him and his deeds; some other person might have performed the same deeds. Perhaps this is the reason why I cannot pass from the deeds to existence. If I call these deeds the deeds of Napoleon the proof becomes superfluous, since I have already named him; if I ignore this, I can never prove from the deeds that they are Napoleon's, but only in a purely ideal manner that such deeds are the deeds of a great general, and so forth. But between the God and his works there is an absolute relationship; God is not a name but a concept. Is this perhaps the reason that his *essentia involvit existentiam*?[1] The works of the God are such that only the God can perform them. Just so, but where then are the works of the God? The works from which I would deduce his existence are not directly and immediately given. The wisdom in nature, the goodness, the wisdom in the governance of the world—are all these manifest, perhaps, upon the very face of things? Are we not here confronted with the most terrible temptations to doubt, and is it not impossible finally to dispose of all these doubts? But from such an order of things I will surely not attempt to prove God's existence; and even if I began I would never finish, and would in addition have to live constantly in suspense, lest something so terrible should suddenly happen that my bit of proof would be demolished. From what works then do I propose to derive the proof? From the works as apprehended through an ideal interpretation, i.e., such as they do not immediately reveal themselves. But in that case it is not from the works that I make the proof; I merely develop the ideality I have presupposed, and because of my confidence in *this* I make so bold as to defy all objections, even those that have not yet been made. In beginning my proof I presuppose the ideal interpretation, and also that I will be successful in carrying it through; but what else is this but to presuppose that the God exists, so that I really begin by virtue of confidence in him?

And how does the God's existence emerge from the proof? Does it follow straightway, without any breach of continuity? Or have we not here an analogy to the behaviour of the little Cartesian dolls? As soon as I let go of the doll it stands on its head. As soon as I let it go—I must therefore let it go. So also with the proof. As long as I keep my hold on the proof, i.e., continue to demonstrate, the existence does not come out, if for no other reason than that I am engaged in proving it; but when I let the proof go, the existence is there. But this act of letting go is surely also something; it is indeed a contribution of mine. Must not this also be taken into the account, this little moment, brief as it may be—it need not be long, for it is a *leap*. However brief this moment, if only an instantaneous now, this "now" must be included in the reckoning. If anyone wishes to have it ignored, I will use it to tell a little anecdote, in order to show that it nevertheless does exist. Chrysippus was experimenting with a sorties to see if he could not bring about a break in its quality, either progressively or retrogressively. But Carneades could not get it in his head when the new quality actually emerged. Then Chrysippus told him to try making a little pause in the reckoning, and

so—so it would be easier to understand. Carneades replied: With the greatest pleasure, please do not hesitate on my account; you may not only pause, but even lie down to sleep, and it will help you just as little; for when you awake we will begin again where you left off. Just so; it boots as little to try to get rid of something by sleeping as to try to come into the possession of something in the same manner.

Whoever therefore attempts to demonstrate the existence of God (except in the sense of clarifying the concept...) proves in lieu thereof something else, something which at times perhaps does not need a proof, and in any case needs none better; for the fool says in his heart that there is no God, but whoever says in his heart or to men: Wait just a little and I will prove it—what a rare man of wisdom is he![2] If in the moment of beginning his proof it is not absolutely undetermined whether the God exists or not, he does not prove it; and if it is thus undetermined in the beginning he will never come to begin, partly from fear of failure, since the God perhaps does not exist, and partly because he has nothing with which to begin.—A project of this kind would scarcely have been undertaken by the ancients. Socrates at least, who is credited with having put forth the physico-teleological proof for God's existence, did not go about it in any such manner. He always presupposes the God's existence, and under this presuppositon seeks to interpenetrate nature with the idea of purpose. Had he been asked why he pursued this method, he would doubtless have explained that he lacked the courage to venture out upon so perilous a voyage of discovery without having made sure of the God's existence behind him. At the word of the God he casts his net as if to catch the idea of purpose; for nature herself finds many means of frightening the inquirer, and distracts him by many a digression.

The paradoxical passion of the Reason thus comes repeatedly into collision with this Unknown, which does indeed exist, but is unknown, and in so far does not exist. The Reason cannot advance beyond this point, and yet it cannot refrain in its paradoxicalness from arriving at this limit and occupying itself therewith. It will not serve to dismiss its relation to it simply by asserting that the Unknown does not exist, since this itself involves a relationship. But what then is the Unknown, since the designation of it as the God merely signifies for us that it is unknown? To say that it is the Unknown because it cannot be known, and even if it were capable of being known, it could not be expressed, does not satisfy the demands of passion, though it correctly interprets the Unknown as a limit; but a limit is precisely a torment for passion, though it also serves as an incitement. And yet the Reason can come no further. . . .

What then is the Unknown? It is the limit to which the Reason repeatedly comes, and in so far, substituting a static form of conception for the dynamic, it is the different, the absolutely different. But because it is absolutely different, there is no mark by which it could be distinguished. When qualified as absolutely different it seems on the verge of disclosure, but this is not the case; for the Reason cannot even conceive an absolute unlikeness. The Reason cannot negate itself absolutely, but uses itself for the purpose, and thus conceives only such an unlikeness within itself as it can conceive by means of itself; it cannot absolutely transcend itself, and hence conceives only such a superiority over itself as it can conceive by means of itself. Unless the Unknown (the God) remains a mere limiting conception, the single idea of difference will be thrown into a state of confusion, and become many ideas of many differences. The Unknown is then in a condition of dispersion . . . , and the Reason may choose at pleasure from what is at hand and the imagination may suggest (the monstrous, the ludicrous, etc.)

But it is impossible to hold fast to a difference of this nature. Every time this is done it is essentially an arbitrary act, and deepest down in the heart of piety lurks the mad caprice which knows that it has itself produced the God. If no specific determination of difference can be held fast, because there is no distinguishing mark, like and unlike finally become identified with one another, thus sharing the fate of all such dialectical opposites. The unlikeness clings to the Reason and confounds it, so that the Reason no longer knows itself and quite consistently confuses itself with the unlikeness. On this point paganism has been sufficiently prolific in fantastic inventions. As for the last named supposition,

the self-irony of the Reason, I shall attempt to delineate it merely by a stroke or two, without raising any question of its being historical. There exists an individual whose appearance is precisely like that of other men; he grows up to manhood like others, he marries, he has an occupation by which he earns a livelihood, and he makes provisions for the future as befits a man. For though it may be beautiful to live like the birds of the air, it is not lawful, and may lead to the sorriest of consequences: either starvation if one has enough persistence, or dependence on the bounty of others. This man is also the God. How do I know? I cannot know it, for in order to know it I would have to know the God, and the nature of the difference between the God and man; and this I cannot know, because the Reason has reduced it to likeness with that from which it was unlike. Thus the God becomes the most terrible of decievers, because the Reason has decieved itself. The Reason has brought the God as near as possible, and yet he is as far away as ever. . . .

But how does the learner come to realize an understanding with this Paradox? We do not ask that he understand the Paradox but only understand that this is the paradox. How this takes place we have already shown. It comes to pass when the Reason and the Paradox encounter one another happily in the Moment, when the Reason sets itself aside and the Paradox bestows itself. The third entity in which this union is realized (for it is not realized in the Reason, since it is set aside: nor in the Paradox, which bestows itself—hence it is realized in something) is that happy passion to which we will now assign a name, though it is not the name that so much matters. We shall call this passion: *Faith.* This then must be the condition of which we have spoken, which the Paradox contributes. Let us not forget that if the Paradox does not grant this condition the learner must be in possession of it.

Notes

1. ["essence involves existence." Kierkegaard's footnote at this place has been eliminated.—Ed.]
2. What an excellent subject for a comedy of the higher lunacy!

1. Why does Kierkegaard think that trying to prove God's existence is pointless? Do you agree?

2. What do you think Kierkegaard means by "faith"?

3. How do you understand faith?

Suggested Readings

Stephen T. Davis, "Free Will and Evil," in Stephen T. Davis, ed., *Encountering Evil* (Atlanta: John Knox Press, 1981), pp. 69–79, defends the view that the Devil is the cause of natural evils like disease and earthquakes.

Brian Davies, *An Introduction to the Philosophy of Religion* (New York: Oxford University Press, 1982), chapter 3, covers issues raised by the problem of evil, and argues that evil does not count decisively against God's existence.

John Hick, *Evil and the God of Love,* rev. ed. (San Francisco: Harper & Row, 1978), explains and defends what he calls the Irenaean solution to the problem of evil for natural evil, and the freewill solution for moral evil.

In *The Problem of Pain* (New York: Macmillan Press, 1962), C.S. Lewis, the popular Christian apologist, tries to deal with the problem of suffering, including animal suffering.

Nelson Pike, ed., *God and Evil: Readings on the Theological Problem of Evil* (Englewood Cliffs, NJ: Prentice-Hall, Inc., 1964) is a standard collection of articles with a complete bibliography.

Alvin Plantiga, *God and Other Minds: A Study of the Rational Justification of Belief in God* (Ithaca, NY: Cornell University Press, 1967), chapters 5–7, part II, discusses the problem of evil, the freewill defense, and problems with divine omnipotence. In his book *God, Freedom, and Evil* (New York: Harper & Row, 1974), p. 25, Plantiga discusses Satan or Lucifer as the cause of natural evil.

Michael Peterson, *Evil and the Christian God* (Grand Rapids, MI: Baker, 1982) is an evangelical Christian who wants to reconcile evil with the God of the Bible.

Richard Swineburne, *The Existence of God* (Oxford: Clarendon Press, 1979), chapter II, treats the traditional approaches to the problem of evil and holds that evil doesn't count as evidence against God's existence.

Stephen P. Stich, "The Recombinant DNA Debate," *Philosophy and Public Affairs,* vol. 7 (1978) compares Pascal's wager with "doomsday scenario" arguments used in the debate about DNA research, and claims that both arguments are defective.

James Cargile, "Pascal's Wager," *Philosophy* 41 (1966): 229–236 gives a careful reformulation of Pascal's wager, discusses James' criticisms, and then critically evaluates the wager.

Williams James' essay in the readings is a reply to William Clifford, "The Ethics of Belief," in his *Lectures and Essays,* vol. II (London: Macmillan, 1879), which gives a moral argument for agnosticism. In contrast to James, Clifford thinks that no hypothesis is worthy of belief unless there is sufficient evidence for it.

Basil Mitchell, ed., *Faith and Logic* (London: Allen & Unwin, 1957) is a collection of papers on religious faith and related topics.

John Hick, *Faith and Knowledge,* 2d ed. (Ithaca, NY: Cornell University Press, 1960) defends religious faith.

Walter Kaufman, *The Faith of a Heretic* (Garden City, NY: Doubleday, 1961) attacks religious faith.

Scepticism and Knowledge

Chapter 3

Introduction

Chapter 3

Scepticism. In the last chapter, Kierkegaard argued that it is impossible to prove that God exists, and that the only basis for belief was faith. However, a sceptic will say that such a belief is not certain; it does not amount to knowledge. In general, **scepticism** can be defined as the view that knowledge is not possible where knowledge implies certainty.

In the history of philosophy, we find that philosophers have adopted scepticism about a number of things in addition to God's existence. In the first reading for this chapter, for example, we find Descartes in his Meditations raising sceptical doubts about knowledge based on the senses, the sort of knowledge we find in physics and astronomy, and knowledge based on reasoning, the sort of knowledge we have in mathematics and geometry. If we suppose that God is deceiving us, then all our perceptions could be mistaken; we couldn't even be sure that we are correct when we count the sides of a square, or add two and three. Perhaps the most famous of Descartes' sceptical arguments is the one about the evil demon (or genius) who uses all its vast powers to deceive us. This argument is examined and rejected by O. K. Bouwsma in the second reading for the chapter. Bouwsma contends that the sort of total deception Descartes imagines is not really possible. A variation of this argument is given by Keith Lehrer (see the suggested readings). Instead of an evil demon, Lehrer imagines that there are intellectually superior alien beings in another galaxy called Googols who deceive us by sending out peculiar waves that affect our brains. Another variation of this argument is to imagine that you are a brain in a vat being stimulated in such a way that you seem to have a body when you really don't.

What is the point of these arguments? Lehrer wants to defend scepticism as a tenable view. If we cannot disprove his sceptical hypothesis about the Googols (and this is indeed hard to do), then it seems that we cannot be sure about any of our ordinary beliefs; we must doubt them or adopt scepticism. In other words, if we do not know that the sceptical hypothesis is false, then scepticism is true.

Descartes, however, does not want to defend scepticism. The doubts he raises are only "methodological doubts," that is, they are part of his program of subjecting all his beliefs to doubt in order to find a belief that cannot be doubted. He compares this to throwing out all the apples in a basket in order to eliminate the rotten apples and find a good apple. Once he has found an indubitable belief, he can use it to establish other truths by means of arguments. One of the first things that Descartes tries to prove is what kind of being he is, and then, in the Third Meditation, that God exists and is not a deceiver.

Rationalism. Because he tries to use arguments to gain knowledge of God's existence, the nature of a person, and the existence of external objects, Descartes is said to be a rationalist. **Rationalism** is the view that knowledge can be gained by the use of reason, particularly a priori reasoning as distinguished from a posteriori reasoning. The method used by a rationalist such as Descartes is like the method used in geometry. One starts with axioms and postulates that are certain, and then deduces other theorems from them. In Descartes' case, he begins with the truth "I exist," and then tries to deduce from this what kind of being he is, the existence of God, and the existence of external objects. Finding knowledge for the rationalist like Descartes is like building a house: you start with a firm foundation, and then build up from the foundation, brick by brick, until the house is complete. The house cannot stand unless it has a good foundation.

But how does Descartes know that "I exist" is absolutely certain? Why does this belief survive the test of methodological doubt? To answer this question, a close examination of the Meditations is required. In the Meditations, Descartes expresses his important discovery as follows: "The proposition 'I am, I exist,' is necessarily true each time that I pronounce it, or that I mentally conceive it." How is this truth to be understood? The most popular interpretation is that Descartes is using an argument, the "cogito argument," to prove that "I exist" is true. The argument goes like this: "I think; whatever thinks exists; therefore, I exist." But this interpretation is open to criticism. The proposition "I exist" cannot be the first thing that is certain if two other propositions, the two premises of the argument, have to be known to be true first. Furthermore, Descartes cannot be certain of the truth of the premise "I think"; he could only be certain that there is a thought. Another interpretation is the intuitional one, that Descartes has had a mental intuition that his existence is certain, just as he can intuit that a triangle has three sides only. The trouble with this is that the evil demon or God could deceive Descartes into thinking he was intuiting something when the thing was in fact false. Fred Feldman's interpretation (see the suggested readings) is that Descartes has simply discovered a belief that is **metaphysically certain** because there is no reason to doubt it.

Knowledge of the External World. At the end of the Second Meditation, we find a rather puzzling argument about a piece of wax. The conclusion of the argument seems to be that it is easier for a person to know that he or she exists than to know that an external object such as a piece of wax exists. How then do we know that external objects exist? This is a famous problem in epistemology, or theory of knowledge. Descartes' own solution requires that God exists and is not a deceiver. In our readings, John Locke tries to solve the problem in a different way, by appealing to our experiences. This means that Locke is an **empiricist,** one who believes that knowledge comes from experience. Suppose we look at a sheet of paper. It is as certain as anything can be that we see something white, or at least that we have an "idea," that is, a visual sense-impression (or what Russell calls a "sense-datum"), of whiteness. But this idea must be caused by something, namely an external object, an object that exists apart from our perceptions. Locke assumes that this thing is a material substance, that is, something having spatial location and dimension that does not think. Locke grants, however, that our knowledge of the existence of external objects does not go beyond objects present to the senses. Our memories of past objects might be mistaken.

In the next reading, Bertrand Russell discusses a problem with Locke's view, namely his assumption that external objects are material substances. How can he possibly know that if he cannot directly perceive them, but is aware only of the sensory ideas caused by them? Perhaps as the philosopher Berkeley says, there is no such thing as matter, something nonmental existing apart from minds and consciousness. According to Berkeley's view, called **idealism** (as opposed to Locke's realism), only minds and their ideas exist. The cause of our sensory ideas is not matter, but another Mind, namely God. The real piece of paper is not a material substance, but an idea, or collection of ideas, in God's mind. The problem, then, is that even if we grant that external objects exist, we have no way of knowing what sort of objects they are. In Russell's terms, we are confined to a world of appearances with no way of finding out about the reality behind the appearances.

Scepticism about Causation.　　Another famous sceptical problem is raised by Hume in the readings. According to Hume's analysis, all knowledge can be divided into one of two categories, knowledge concerning "relations of ideas," or the sort of knowledge we have in geometry and algebra, and knowledge concerning "matters of fact," or knowledge about the world, for example, that the sun will rise tomorrow. The first sort of knowledge is based solely on reasoning; the second requires experience.

All knowledge concerning matters of fact, Hume claims, is based on knowledge of cause and effect. How do we find out about causal relations? By experience—but this is knowledge of matters of fact again, and we have gone in a circle. It seems that we can't independently establish knowledge of either causal relations or matters of fact because knowledge of one requires knowledge of the other. We are left with a sceptical conclusion that we don't really have knowledge of either causal relations or matters of fact.

Let us illustrate the problem with one of Hume's examples. We believe that when one billiard ball hits a second, the second ball will move. We believe that the first ball will cause the second ball to move. But we don't know this by reasoning alone. We can easily imagine that the second ball might *not* move when hit. No, our belief in the causal relation is based on past experiences with one billiard ball hitting another or objects in general colliding with each other. But those past experiences establish a causal relation only if we assume future experiences will be like past experiences. But how do we justify the assumption that future experiences will be like past experiences? We cannot do this by reasoning, for we can easily imagine that the future might be different from the past. We can only appeal to experience, to the fact that we have had experiences—in the past—of the future being like the past. But these past experiences justify the assumption only if it is presupposed that future experiences will be like these past experiences, and of course that is the very thing we are trying to justify. We have gone in a circle or **begged the question**. The upshot is that we have no way of knowing that in the future a billiard ball will move when it is hit, or that there is a causal relation.

Hume's own "sceptical solution" to the problem does not attempt to justify knowledge of causal relations—we are left with scepticism about them. Instead he gives a psychological explanation of the matter. Events that are conjoined in the past are connected by us because of habit, and this habit makes us believe that they will be conjoined in the future. Thus, according to Hume, we have no rational justification of the belief in causation; it is merely the product of habit or custom.

The Problem of Induction. Hume does not use the word "induction," but the problem he raises has come to be called the problem of induction. As Max Black explains it in the readings, the problem is one of justifying inductive reasoning. Inductive reasoning comes in different forms, but according to Black, the basic form is reasoning from "some A's are B," to "all A's are B." (For example, "sometimes water has boiled at 100 degrees Centigrade, so all water will boil at 100 degrees Centigrade.") But going from "some" to "all," the so-called inductive leap, is deductively invalid. Hume's point is well-taken—just because some water has boiled at a certain temperature does not prove that all water will do this. It is logically possible that the next water we boil will not do this.

One solution to the problem is to try to turn the inductive argument into a deductive one by simply adding another premise, for instance, the principle of the uniformity of nature (that the future will resemble the past). Then we have a deductive argument: "In the past some A's have been B; future A's will be like past A's (the uniformity of nature principle); so in the future A's will be B." But how do we know that the uniformity of nature principle is true? Hume says we do not know that it is true a priori, and if we appeal to past experience we are begging the question. We are left with an unjustifiable principle.

Black reviews four other attempts to solve the problem and argues that they all fail. His own solution, or rather linguistic dissolution, of the problem is to insist that inductive reasoning is what we mean by "justification," and thus no general justification of induction is possible or even needed.

René Descartes

Meditations (I and II)

René Descartes (1596–1650), French philosopher and mathematician, is often regarded as the founder of modern philosophy.

Meditation I

Of the Things Which May Be Brought within the Sphere of the Doubtful.

It is now some years since I detected how many were the false beliefs that I had from my earliest youth admitted as true, and how doubtful was everything I had since constructed on this basis; and from that time I was convinced that I must once for all seriously undertake to rid myself of all the opinions which I had formerly accepted, and commence to build anew from the foundation, if I wanted to establish any firm and permanent structure in the sciences. But as this enterprise appeared to be a very great one, I waited until I had attained an age so mature that I could not hope that at any later date I should be better fitted to execute my design. This reason caused me to delay so long that I should feel that I was doing wrong were I to occupy in deliberation the time that yet remains to me for action. Today, then, since very opportunely for the plan I have in view I have delivered my mind from every care [and am happily agitated by no passions] and since I have procured for myself an assured leisure in a peaceable retirement, I shall at last seriously and freely address myself to the general upheaval of all my former opinions.

Now for this object it is not necessary that I should show that all of these are false—I shall perhaps never arrive at this end. But inasmuch as reason already persuades me that I ought no less carefully to withhold my assent from matters which are not entirely certain and indubitable than from those which appear to me mani-

The reading is from *The Philosophical Works of Descartes*, trans. Elizabeth S. Haldane and G. R. T. Ross, vol. I (New York: Dover Publications, 1931), pp. 144–156. ©Cambridge University Press. Reprinted with the permission of Cambridge University Press.

festly to be false, if I am able to find in each one some reason to doubt, this will suffice to justify my rejecting the whole. And for that end it will not be requisite that I should examine each in particular, which would be an endless undertaking; for owing to the fact that the destruction of the foundations of necessity brings with it the downfall of the rest of the edifice, I shall only in the first place attack those principles upon which all my former opinions rested.

All that up to the present time I have accepted as most true and certain I have learned either from the senses or through the senses; but it is sometimes proved to me that these senses are deceptive, and it is wiser not to trust entirely to any thing by which we have once been deceived.

But it may be that although the senses sometimes deceive us concerning things which are hardly perceptible, or very far away, there are yet many others to be met with as to which we cannot reasonably have any doubt, although we recognize them by their means. For example, there is the fact that I am here, seated by the fire, attired in a dressing gown, having this paper in my hands and other similar matters. And how could I deny that these hands and this body are mine, were it not perhaps that I compare myself to certain persons, devoid of sense, whose cerebella are so troubled and clouded by the violent vapours of black bile, that they constantly assure us that they think they are kings when they are really quite poor, or that they are clothed in purple when they are really without covering, or who imagine that they have an earthenware head or are nothing but pumpkins or are made of glass. But they are mad, and I should not be any the less insane were I to follow examples so extravagant.

At the same time I must remember that I am a man, and that consequently I am in the habit of sleeping, and in my dreams representing to myself the same things or sometimes even less probable things, than do those who are insane in their waking moments. How often has it happened to me that in the night I dreamt that I found myself in this particular place, that I was dressed and seated near the fire, whilst in reality I was lying undressed in bed! At this moment it does indeed seem to me that it is with eyes awake that I am looking at this paper; that this head which I move is not asleep, that it is deliberately and of set purpose that I extend my hand and perceive it: what happens in sleep does not appear so clear nor so distinct as does all this. But in thinking over this I remind myself that on many occasions I have in sleep been deceived by similar illusions, and in dwelling carefully on this reflection I see so manifestly that there are no certain indications by which we may clearly distinguish wakefulness from sleep that I am lost in astonishment. And my astonishment is such that it is almost capable of persuading me that I now dream.

Now let us assume that we are asleep and that all these particulars, e.g. that we open our eyes, shake our head, extend our hands, and so on, are but false delusions; and let us reflect that possibly neither our hands nor our whole body are such as they appear to us to be. At the same time we must at least confess that the things which are represented to us in sleep are like painted representations which can only have been formed as the counterparts of something real and true, and that in this way those general things at least, i.e. eyes, a head, hands, and a whole body, are not imaginary things, but things really existent. For, as a matter of fact, painters, even when they study with the greatest skill to represent sirens and satyrs by forms the most strange and extraordinary, cannot give them natures which are entirely new, but merely make a certain medley of the members of different animals; or if their imagination is extravagant enough to invent something so novel that nothing similar has ever before been seen, and that then their work represents a thing purely fictitious and absolutely false, it is certain all the same that the colours of which this is composed are necessarily real. And for the same reason, although these general things, to wit, [a body], eyes, a head, hands, and such like, may be imaginary, we are bound at the same time to confess that there are at least some other objects yet more simple and more universal, which are real and true; and of these just in the same way as with certain real colours, all these images of things which dwell in our thoughts, whether true and real or false and fantastic, are formed.

To such a class of things pertains corporeal nature in general, and its extension, the figure of extended things, their quantity or magnitude and number, as also the place in which they are, the time which measures their duration, and so on.

That is possibly why our reasoning is not unjust when we conclude from this that Physics, Astronomy, Medicine and all other sciences which have as their end the consideration of composite things, are very dubious and uncertain; but that Arithmetic, Geometry and other sciences of that kind which only treat of things that are very simple and very general, without taking great trouble to ascertain whether they are actually existent or not, contain some measure of certainty and an element of the indubitable. For whether I am awake or asleep, two and three together always form five, and the square can never have more than four sides, and it does not seem possible that truths so clear and apparent can be suspected of any falsity [or uncertainty].

Nevertheless I have long had fixed in my mind the belief that an all-powerful God existed by whom I have been created such as I am. But how do I know that He has not brought it to pass that there is no earth, no heaven, no extended body, no magnitude, no place, and that nevertheless [I possess the perceptions of of all these things and that] they seem to me to exist just exactly as I now see them? And, besides, as I sometimes imagine that others deceive themselves in the things which they think they know best, how do I know that I am not deceived every time that I add two and three, or count the sides of a square, or judge of things yet simpler, if anything simpler can be imagined? But possibly God has not desired that I should be thus deceived, for He is said to be supremely good. If, however, it is contrary to His goodness to have made me such that I constantly deceive myself, it would also appear to be contrary to His goodness to permit me to be sometimes deceived, and nevertheless I cannot doubt that He does permit this.

There may indeed be those who would prefer to deny the existence of a God so powerful, rather than believe that all other things are uncertain. But let us not oppose them for the present, and grant that all that is here said of a God is a fable; nevertheless in whatever way they suppose that I have arrived at the state of being that I have reached—whether they attribute it to fate or to accident, or make out that it is by a continual succession of antecedents, or by some other method—since to err and deceive oneself is a defect, it is clear that the greater will be the probability of my being so imperfect as to deceive myself ever, as is the Author to whom they assign my origin the less powerful. To these reasons I have certainly nothing to reply, but at the end I feel constrained to confess that there is nothing in all that I formerly believed to be true, of which I cannot in some measure doubt, and that not merely through want of thought or through levity, but for reasons which are very powerful and maturely considered; so that henceforth I ought not the less carefully refrain from giving credence to these opinions than to that which is manifestly false, if I desire to arrive at any certainty [in the sciences].

But it is not sufficient to have made these remarks, we must also be careful to keep them in mind. For these ancient and commonly held opinions still revert frequently to my mind, long and familiar custom having given them the right to occupy my mind against my inclination and rendered them almost masters of my belief; nor will I ever lose the habit of deferring to them or of placing my confidence in them, so long as I consider them as they really are, i.e. opinions in some measure, doubtful, as I have just shown, and at the same time highly probable, so that there is much more reason to believe in than to deny them. That is why I consider that I shall not be acting amiss, if, taking of set purpose a contrary belief, I allow myself to be deceived, and for a certain time pretend that all these opinions are entirely false and imaginary, until at last, having thus balanced my former prejudices with my latter [so that they cannot divert my opinions more to one side than to the other], my judgment will no longer be dominated by bad usage or turned away from the right knowledge of the truth. For I am assured that there can be neither peril nor error in this course, and that I cannot at present yield too much to distrust, since I am not considering the question of action, but only of knowledge.

I shall then suppose, not that God who is supremely good and the fountain of truth, but some evil genius not less powerful than deceitful, has employed his whole energies in deceiving me; I shall consider that the heavens, the earth, colours, figures, sound, and all other external things are nought but the illusions and dreams of which this genius has availed himself in order to lay traps for my credulity; I shall consider myself as having no hands, no eyes, no flesh, no blood, nor any senses, yet falsely believing myself to possess all these things; I shall remain obstinately attached to this idea, and if by this means it is not in my power to arrive at the knowledge of any truth, I may at least do what is in my power [i.e. suspend my judgement], and with firm purpose avoid giving credence to any false thing, or being imposed upon by this arch deceiver, however powerful and deceptive he may be. But this task is a laborious one, and insensibly a certain lassitude leads me into the course of my ordinary life. And just as a captive who in sleep enjoys an imaginary liberty, when he begins to suspect that his liberty is but a dream, fears to awaken, and conspires with these agreeable illusions that the deception may be prolonged, so insensibly of my own accord I fall back into my former opinions, and I dread awakening from this slumber, lest the laborious wakefulness which would follow the tranquility of this repose should have to be spent not in daylight, but in the excessive darkness of the difficulties which have just been discussed.

Meditation II

Of the Nature of the Human Mind; and that It Is More Easily Known Than the Body.

The Meditation of yesterday filled my mind with so many doubts that it is no longer in my power to forget them. And yet I do not see in what manner I can resolve them; and, just as if I had all of a sudden fallen into very deep water, I am so disconcerted that I can neither make certain of setting my feet on the bottom, nor can I swim and so support myself on the surface. I shall nevertheless make an effort and follow anew the same path as that on which I yesterday entered, i.e. I shall proceed by setting aside all that in which the least doubt could be supposed to exist, just as if I had discovered that it was absolutely false; and I shall ever follow in this road until I have met with something which is certain, or at least, if I can do nothing else, until I have learned for certain that there is nothing in the world that is certain. Archimedes, in order that he might draw the terrestrial globe out of its place, and transport it elsewhere, demanded only that one point should be fixed and immovable; in the same way I shall have the right to conceive high hopes if I am happy enough to discover one thing only which is certain and indubitable.

I suppose, then, that all the things that I see are false; I persuade myself that nothing has ever existed of all that my fallacious memory represents to me. I consider that I possess no senses; I imagine that body, figure, extension, movement and place are but the fictions of my mind. What, then, can be esteemed as true? Perhaps nothing at all, unless that there is nothing in the world that is certain.

But how can I know there is not something different from those things that I have just considered, of which one cannot have the slightest doubt? Is there not some God, or some other being by whatever name we call it, who puts these reflections into my mind? That is not necessary, for is it not possible that I am capable of producing them myself? I myself, am I not at least something? But I have already denied that I had senses and body. Yet I hesitate, for what follows from that? Am I so dependent on body and senses that I cannot exist without these? But I was persuaded that there was nothing in all the world, that there was no heaven, no earth, that there were no minds, nor any bodies: was I not then likewise persuaded that I did not exist? Not at all; of a surety I myself did exist since I persuaded myself of something [or merely because I thought of something.] But there is some deceiver or other, very powerful and very cunning, who ever employs his ingenuity in deceiving me. Then without doubt I exist also if he deceives me, and let him deceive me as much as he will, he can never cause me to be nothing so long as I think that I am something. So that after having reflected well and carefully examined all things, we must come to the definite conclusion that this proposition: I am, I exist, is necessarily true each time that I pronounce it, or that I mentally conceive it.

But I do not yet know clearly enough what I am, I who am certain that I am; and hence I must be careful to see that I do not imprudently take some other object in place of myself, and thus that I do not go astray in respect of this knowledge that I hold to be the most certain and most evident of all that I have formerly learned. That is why I shall now consider anew what I believed myself to be before I embarked upon these last reflections; and of my former opinions I shall withdraw all that might even in a small degree be invalidated by the reasons which I have just brought forward, in order that there may be nothing at all left beyond what is absolutely certain and indubitable.

What then did I formerly believe myself to be? Undoubtedly I believed myself to be a man. But what is a man? Shall I say a reasonable animal? Certainly not; for then I should have to inquire what an animal is, and what is reasonable; and thus from a single question I should insensibly fall into an infinitude of others more difficult; and I should not wish to waste the little time and leisure remaining to me in trying to unravel subtleties like these. But I shall rather stop here to consider the thoughts which of themselves spring up in my mind, and which were not inspired by anything beyond my own nature alone when I applied myself to the consideration of my being. In the first place, then, I considered myself as having a face, hands, arms, and all that system of members composed of bones and flesh as seen in a corpse which I designated by the name of body. In addition to this I considered that I was nourished, that I walked, that I felt, and that I thought, and I referred all these actions to the soul: but I did not stop to consider what the soul was, or if I did stop, I imagined that it was something extremely rare and subtle like a wind, a flame, or an ether, which was spread throughout my grosser parts. As to body I had no manner of doubt about its nature, but thought I had a very clear knowledge of it; and if I had desired to explain it according to the notions that I had then formed of it, I should have described it thus: By the body I understand all that which can be defined by a certain figure: something which can be confined in a certain place, and which can fill a given space in such a way that every other body will be excluded from it; which can be perceived either by touch, or by sight, or by hearing, or by taste, or by smell: which can be moved in many ways not, in truth, by itself, but by something which is foreign to it, by which it is touched [and from which it receives impressions]: for to have the power of self-movement, as also of feeling or of thinking, I did not consider to appertain to the nature of body: on the contrary, I was rather astonished to find that faculties similar to them existed in some bodies.

But what am I, now that I suppose that there is a certain genius which is extremely powerful, and, if I may say so, malicious, who employs all his powers in deceiving me? Can I affirm that I possess the least of all those things which I have just said pertain to the nature of body? I pause to consider, I revolve all these things in my mind, and I find none of which I can say that it pertains to me. It would be tedious to stop to enumerate them. Let us pass to the attributes of soul and see if there is any one which is in me? What of nutrition or walking [the first mentioned]? But if it is so that I have no body it is also true that I can neither walk nor take nourishment. Another attribute is sensation. But one cannot feel without body, and besides I have thought I perceived many things during sleep that I recognised in my waking moments as not having been experienced at all. What of thinking? I find here that thought is an attribute that belongs to me; it alone cannot be separated from me. I am, I exist, that is certain. But how often? Just when I think; for it might possibly be the case if I ceased entirely to think, that I should likewise cease altogether to exist. I do not now admit anything which is not necessarily true: to speak accurately I am not more than a thing which thinks, that is to say a mind or a soul, or an understanding, or a reason, which are terms whose significance was formerly unknown to me. I am, however, a real thing and really exist; but what thing? I have answered: a thing which thinks.

And what more? I shall exercise my imagination [in order to see if I am not something more]. I am not a collection of members which we call the human body: I am not a subtle air distributed through these members, I am not a wind, a fire, a vapour, a breath, or anything at all which I can imagine or conceive: because I have assumed that all these were nothing. Without changing that supposition I find that I only leave myself certain of the fact that I am somewhat. But perhaps it is true that these same things which I supposed were nonexistent because they are unknown to me, are really not different from the self which I know. I am not sure about this, I shall not dispute about it now; I can only give judgement on things that are known to me. I know that I exist, and I inquire what I am, I whom I know to exist. But it is very certain that the knowledge of my existence taken in its precise significance does not depend on things whose existence is not yet known to me; consequently it does not depend on those which I can feign in imagination. And indeed the very term *feign* in imagination proves to me my error, for I really do this if I image myself a something, since to imagine is nothing else than to contemplate the figure or image of a corporeal thing. But I already know for certain that I am, and that it may be that all these images, and, speaking generally, all things that relate to the nature of body are nothing but dreams [and chimeras]. For this reason I see clearly that I have as little reason to say, 'I shall stimulate my imagination in order to know more distinctly what I am,' than if I were to say, 'I am now awake, and I perceive somewhat that is real and true: but because I do not yet perceive it distinctly enough, I shall go to sleep of express purpose, so that my dreams may represent the perception with greatest truth and evidence.' And, thus, I know for certain that nothing of all that I can understand by means of my imagination belongs to this knowledge which I have of myself, and that it is necessary to recall the mind from this mode of thought with the utmost diligence in order that it may be able to know its own nature with perfect distinctness.

But what then am I? A thing which thinks. What is a thing which thinks? It is a thing which doubts, understands, [conceives], affirms, denies, wills, refuses, which also imagines and feels.

Certainly it is no small matter if all these

things pertain to my nature. But why should they not so pertain? Am I not that being who now doubts nearly everything, who nevertheless understands certain things, who affirms that one only is true, who denies all the others, who desires to know more, is averse from being deceived, who imagines many things, sometimes indeed despite his will, and who perceives many likewise, as by the intervention of the bodily organs? Is there nothing in all this which is as true as it is certain that I exist, even though I should always sleep and though he who has given me being employed all his ingenuity in deceiving me? Is there likewise any one of these attributes which can be distinguished from my thought, or which might be said to be separated from myself? For it is so evident of itself that it is I who doubt, who understand, and who desire, that there is no reason here to add anything to explain it. And I have certainly the power of imagining likewise; for although it may happen (as I formerly supposed) that none of the things which I imagine are true, nevertheless this power of imagining does not cease to be really in use, and it forms part of my thought. Finally, I am the same who feels, that is to say, who perceives certain things, as by the organs of sense, since in truth I see light, I hear noise, I feel heat. But it will be said that these phenomena are false and that I am dreaming. Let it be so; still it is at least quite certain that it seems to me that I see light, that I hear noise and that I feel heat. That cannot be false; properly speaking it is what is in me called feeling; and used in this precise sense that is no other thing than thinking.

From this time I begin to know what I am with a little more clearness and distinction than before; but nevertheless it still seems to me, and I cannot prevent myself from thinking, that corporeal things, whose images are framed by thought, which are tested by the senses, are much more distinctly known than that obscure part of me which does not come under the imagination. Although really it is very strange to say that I know and understand more distinctly these things whose existence seems to me dubious, which are unknown to me, and which do not belong to me, than others of the truth of which I am convinced, which are known to me and which pertain to my real nature, in a word,

than myself. But I see clearly how the case stands: my mind loves to wander, and cannot yet suffer itself to be retained with the just limits of truth. Very good, let us once more give it the freest rein, so that, when afterwards we seize the proper occasion for pulling up, it may the more easily be regulated and controlled.

Let us begin by considering the commonest matters, those which we believe to be the most distinctly comprehended, to wit, the bodies which we touch and see; not indeed bodies in general, for these general ideas are usually a little more confused, but let us consider one body in particular. Let us take, for example, this piece of wax: it has been taken quite freshly from the hive, and it has not yet lost the sweetness of the honey which it contains; it still retains somewhat of the odour of the flowers from which it has been culled; its colour, its figure, its size are apparent; it is hard, cold, easily handled, and if you strike it with the finger, it will emit a sound. Finally all the things which are requisite to cause us distinctly to recognise a body, are met with in it. But notice that while I speak and approach the fire what remained of the taste is exhaled, the smell evaporates, the colour alters, the figure is destroyed, the size increases, it becomes liquid, it heats, scarcely can one handle it, and when one strikes it, no sound is emitted. Does the same wax remain after this change? We must confess that it remains; none would judge otherwise. What then did I know so distinctly in this piece of wax? It could certainly be nothing of all that the senses brought to my notice, since all these things which fall under taste, smell, sight, touch, and hearing, are found to be changed, and yet the same wax remains.

Perhaps it was what I now think, viz, that this wax was not that sweetness of honey, nor that agreeable scent of flowers, nor that particular whiteness, nor that figure, nor that sound, but simply a body which a little while before appeared to me as perceptible under these forms, and which is now perceptible under others. But what, precisely, is it that I imagine when I form such conceptions? Let us attentively consider this, and, abstracting from all that does not belong to the wax, let us see what remains. Certainly nothing remains excepting a certain extended thing which is flexible and movable. But what is the meaning of flexible and movable? Is it not that I imagine that this piece of wax being round is capable of becoming square and of passing from a square to a triangular figure? No, certainly it is not that, since I imagine it admits of an infinitude of similar changes, and I nevertheless do not know how to compass the infinitude by my imagination, and consequently this conception which I have of the wax is not brought about by the faculty of imagination. What now is this extension? Is it not also unknown? For it becomes greater when the wax is melted, greater when it is boiled, and greater still when the heat increases; and I should not conceive [clearly] according to truth what wax is, if I did not think that even this piece that we are considering is capable of receiving more variations in extension than I have ever imagined. We must then grant that I could not even understand through the imagination what this piece of wax is, and that it is my mind alone which perceives it. I say this piece of wax in particular, for as to wax in general it is yet clearer. But what is this piece of wax which cannot be understood excepting by the [understanding or] mind? It is certainly the same that I see, touch, imagine, and finally it is the same which I have always believed it to be from the beginning. But what must particularly be observed is that its perception is neither an act of vision, nor of touch, nor of imagination, and has never been such although it may have appeared formerly to be so, but only an intuition of the mind, which may be imperfect and confused as it was formerly, or clear and distinct as it is at present, according as my attention is more or less directed to the elements which are found in it, and of which it is composed.

Yet in the meantime I am greatly astonished when I consider [the great feebleness of mind] and its proneness to fall [insensibly] into error; for although without giving expression to my thoughts I consider all this in my own mind, words often impede me and I am almost deceived by the terms of ordinary language. For we say that we see the same wax, if it is present, and not that we simply judge that it is the same from its having the same colour and figure. From this I should conclude that I knew the wax by means of vision and not simply by the intui-

tion of the mind; unless by chance I remember that, when looking from a window and saying I see men who pass in the street, I really do not see them, but infer that what I see is men, just as I say that I see wax. And yet what do I see from the window but hats and coats which may cover automatic machines? Yet I judge these to be men. And similarly solely by the faculty of judgment which rests in my mind, I comprehend that which I believed I saw with my eyes.

A man who makes it his aim to raise his knowledge above the common should be ashamed to derive the occasion for doubting from the forms of speech invented by the vulgar; I prefer to pass on and consider whether I had a more evident and perfect conception of what the wax was when I first perceived it, and when I believed I knew it by means of the external senses or at least by the common sense as it is called, that is to say by the imaginative faculty, or whether my present conception is clearer now that I have most carefully examined what it is, and in what way it can be known. It would certainly be absurd to doubt as to this. For what was there in this first perception which was distinct? What was there which might not as well have been perceived by any of the animals? But when I distinguish the wax from its external forms, and when, just as if I had taken from it its vestments, I consider it quite naked, it is certain that although some error may still be found in my judgement, I can nevertheless not perceive it thus without a human mind.

But finally what shall I say of this mind, that is, of myself, for up to this point I do not admit in myself anything but mind? What then, I who seem to perceive this piece of wax so distinctly, do I not know myself, not only with much more truth and certainty, but also with much more distinctness and clearness? For if I judge that the wax is or exists from the fact that I see it, it certainly follows much more clearly that I am or that I exist myself from the fact that I see it. For it may be that what I see is not really wax, it may also be that I do not possess eyes with which to see anything; but it cannot be that when I see, or (for I no longer take account of the distinction) when I think I see, that I myself who think am nought. So if I judge that the wax exists from the fact that I touch it, the same thing will follow, to wit, that I am; and if I judge that my imagination, or some other cause, whatever it is, persuades me that wax exists, I shall still conclude the same. And what I have here remarked of wax may be applied to all other things which are external to me [and which are met with outside of me]. And further, if the [notion or] perception of wax has seemed to me clearer and more distinct, not only after the sight or the touch, but also after many other causes have rendered it quite manifest to me, with how much more [evidence] and distinctness must it be said that I now know myself, since all the reasons which contribute to the knowledge of wax, or any other body whatever, are yet better proofs of the nature of my mind! And there are so many other things in the mind itself which may contribute to the elucidation of its nature, that those which depend on body such as these just mentioned, hardly merit being taken into account.

But finally here I am, having insensibly reverted to the point I desired, for, since it is now manifest to me that even bodies are not properly speaking known by the senses or by the faculty of imagination, but by the understanding only, and since they are not known from the fact that they are seen or touched, but only because they are understood, I see clearly that there is nothing which is easier for me to know than my mind. But because it is difficult to rid oneself so promptly of an opinion to which one was accustomed for so long, it will be well that I should halt a little at this point, so that by the length of my meditation I may more deeply imprint on my memory this new knowledge.

Questions on Descartes

1. Descartes begins by raising doubts about knowledge gained from the senses. State his arguments beginning with illusion and hallucination and critically evaluate them.

2. Descartes next turns to knowledge in arithmetic and geometry. Why does he think that he could be mistaken about adding two and three, or about the sides of a triangle? Do you agree? Why or why not?

3. In the Second Meditation, Descartes thinks that he has found a certain truth. What is it exactly? Why is it supposed to be certain?

4. Why does Descartes think that he is a mind or soul rather than a body? What is a mind or soul? (These questions are taken up in chapter 5, but see if you can follow his argument in the Second Meditation.)

5. At the end of the Second Meditation, you will find a complicated argument about a piece of wax. Try to reconstruct this argument. What is the conclusion? What are the premises? Is it valid? Is it sound? (Descartes may be trying to prove a number of different things with the same argument.)

O. K. Bouwsma
Descartes' Evil Genius

O. K. Bouwsma (1898–1978) taught for 50 years at the University of Nebraska and the University of Texas at Austin. The reading is from his book Philosophical Essays.

There was once an evil genius who promised the mother of us all that if she ate of the fruit of the tree, she would be like God, knowing good and evil. He promised knowledge. She did eat and she learned, but she was disappointed, for to know good and evil and not to be God is awful. Many an Eve later, there was rumor of another evil genius. This evil genius promised no good, promised no knowledge. He made a boast, a boast so wild and so deep and so dark that those who heard it cringed in hearing it. And what was that boast? Well, that apart from a few, four or five, clear and distinct ideas, he could deceive any son of Adam about anything. So he boasted.

And with some result? Some indeed! Men going about in the brightest noonday would look and exclaim: "How obscure!" and if some careless merchant counting his apples was heard to say: "Two and three are five," a hearer of the boast would rub his eyes and run away. This evil genius still whispers, thundering, among the leaves of books, frightening people, whispering: "I can. Maybe I will. Maybe so, maybe not." The tantalizer! In what follows I should like to examine the boast of this evil genius.

I am referring, of course, to that evil genius of whom Descartes writes:

I shall then suppose, not that God who is supremely good and the fountain of truth, but some evil genius not less powerful than deceitful, has employed his whole energies in deceiving me; I shall consider that the heavens, the earth, the colors, figures, sound, and all other external things are nought but illusions and dreams of which this evil genius has availed himself, in order to lay traps for my credulity; I shall consider myself as having no hands, no eyes, no flesh, no blood, nor any senses, yet falsely believing myself to possess all these things.[1]

This then is the evil genius whom I have represented as boasting that he can deceive us about all these things. I intend now to examine this boast, and to understand how this deceiving and being deceived are to take place. I expect to discover that the evil genius may very well deceive us, but that if we are wary, we need not be deceived. He will deceive us, if he does, by bathing the word "illusion" in a fog. This then will be the word to keep our minds on. In order to accomplish all this, I intend to describe the evil genius carrying out his boast in two adventures. The first of these I shall consider a thoroughly transparent case of deception. The word "illusion" will find a clear and familiar application. Nevertheless in this instance the evil genius will not have exhausted "his whole energies in deceiving us." Hence we must aim to imagine a further trial of the boast, in which the "whole energies" of the evil genius are exhausted. In this instance I intend to show that the evil genius is himself befuddled, and that if we too exhaust some of our energies in sleuthing after the peculiarities in his diction, then we need not be deceived either.

Let us imagine the evil genius then at his ease meditating that very bad is good enough for him, and that he would let bad enough alone. All the old pseudos, pseudo names and pseudo statements, are doing very well. But today it was different. He took no delight in common lies, everyday fibs, little ones, old ones. He wanted something new and something big. He scratched his genius; he uncovered an idea. And he scribbled on the inside of his tattered halo, "Tomorrow, I will deceive," and he smiled, and his words were thin and like fine wire. "Tomorrow I will change everything, everything, everything. I will change flowers, human beings, trees, hills, sky, the sun, and everything else into paper. Paper alone I will not change. There will be paper flowers, paper human beings, paper trees. And human beings will be deceived. They will think that there are flowers, human beings, and trees, and there will be nothing but paper. It will be gigantic. And it ought to work. After all men have been deceived with much less trouble. There was a sailor, a Baptist I believe, who said that all was water. And there was no more water then than there is now. And there was a pool-hall keeper who said that all was billiard balls. That's a long time ago of course, a long time before they opened one, and listening, heard that it was full of the sound of a trumpet. My prospects are good. I'll try it."

And the evil genius followed his own directions and did according to his words. And this is what happened.

Imagine a young man, Tom, bright today as he was yesterday, approaching a table where yesterday he had seen a bowl of flowers. Today it suddenly strikes him that they are not flowers. He stares at them troubled, looks away, and looks again. Are they flowers? He shakes his head. He chuckles to himself. "Huh! that's funny. Is this a trick? Yesterday there certainly were flowers in that bowl." He sniffs suspiciously, hopefully, but smells nothing. His nose gives no assurance. He thinks of the birds that flew down to peck at the grapes in the picture and of the mare that whinnied at the likeness of Alexander's horse. Illusions! The picture oozed no juice, and the likeness was still. He walked slowly to the bowl of flowers. He looked, and he sniffed, and he raised his hand. He stroked a petal lightly, lover of flowers, and he drew back. He could scarcely believe his fingers. They were not flowers. They were paper.

As he stands, perplexed, Milly, friend and dear, enters the room. Seeing him occupied with the flowers, she is about to take up the bowl and offer them to him, when once again he is overcome with feelings of strangeness. She looks just like a great big doll. He looks more closely, closely as he dares, seeing this may be Milly after all. Milly, are you Milly?—that wouldn't do. Her mouth clicks as she opens it, speaking, and it shuts precisely. Her forehead shines, and he shudders at the thought of Mme Tussaud's. Her hair is plaited, evenly, perfectly, like Milly's but as she raises one hand to guard its order, touching it, preening, it whispers like a newspaper. Her teeth are white as a genteel monthly. Her gums are pink, and there is a clapper in her mouth. He thinks of mama dolls, and of the rubber doll he used to pinch; it had a misplaced navel right in the pit of the back, that whistled. Galatea in paper! Illusions!

He noted all these details, flash by flash by flash. He reaches for a chair to steady himself and just in time. She approaches with the bowl of flowers, and, as the bowl is extended towards him, her arms jerk. The suppleness, the smoothness, the roundness of life is gone. Twitches of a smile mislight up her face. He extends his hand to take up the bowl and his own arms jerk as hers did before. He takes the bowl, and as he does so sees his hand. It is pale, fresh, snowy. Trembling, he drops the bowl, but it does not break, and the water does not run. What a mockery!

He rushes to the window, hoping to see the real world. The scene is like a theatre-set. Even the pane in the window is drawn very thin, like cellophane. In the distance are the forms of men walking about and tossing trees and houses and boulders and hills upon the thin cross section of a truck that echoes only echoes of chugs as it moves. He looks into the sky upward, and it is low. There is a patch straight above him, and one seam is loose. The sun shines out of the blue like a drop of German silver. He reaches out with his pale hand, crackling the cellophane, and his hand touches the sky. The sky shakes and tiny bits of it fall, flaking his white hand with confetti.

Make-believe!

He retreats, crinkling, creaking, hiding his sight. As he moves he misquotes a line of poetry: "Those are perils that were his eyes," and he mutters, "Hypocritical pulp!" He goes on: "I see that the heavens, the earth, colors, figures, sound, and all other external things, flowers, Milly, trees and rocks and hills are paper, paper laid as traps for my credulity. Paper flowers, paper Milly, paper sky!" Then he paused, and in sudden fright he asked "And what about me?" He reaches to his lip and with two fingers tears the skin and peels off a strip of newsprint. He looks at it closely, grim. "I shall consider myself as having no hands, no eyes, no flesh, no blood, or any senses." He lids his paper eyes and stands dejected. Suddenly he is cheered. He exclaims: *Cogito me papyrum esse, ergo sum.*" He has triumphed over paperdom.

I have indulged in this phantasy in order to illustrate the sort of situation which Descartes' words might be expected to describe. The evil genius attempts to deceive. He tries to mislead Tom into thinking what is not. Tom is to think that these are flowers, that this is the Milly that was, that those are trees, hills, the heavens, etc. And he does this by creating illusions, that is, by making something that looks like flowers, artificial flowers; by making something that looks like and sounds like and moves like Milly, an artificial Milly. An illusion is something that looks like or sounds like, so much like, something else that you either mistake it for something else, or you can easily understand how someone might come to do this. So when the evil genius creates illusions intending to deceive he makes things which might quite easily be mistaken for what they are not. Now in the phantasy as I discovered it Tom is not deceived. He does experience the illusion, however. The intention of this is not to cast any reflection upon the deceptive powers of the evil genius. With such refinements in the paper art as we now know, the evil genius might very well have been less unsuccessful. And that in spite of his rumored lament: "And I made her of the best paper!" No, that Tom is not deceived, that he detects the illusion, is introduced in order to remind ourselves how illusions are detected. That the paper flowers are illusory is revealed by the recognition that they are paper. As soon as Tom realizes that though they look like flowers but are paper, he is acquainted with, sees through the illusion, and is not deceived. What is required, of course, is that he know the difference between flowers and paper, and that when presented with one or the other he can tell the difference. The attempt of the evil genius also presupposes this. What he intends is that though Tom knows this difference, the paper will look so much like flowers that Tom will not notice the respect in which the paper is different from the flowers. And even though Tom had actually been deceived and had not recognized the illusion, the evil genius himself must have been aware of the difference, for this is involved in his design. This is crucial, as we shall see when we come to consider the second adventure of the evil genius.

As you will remember I have represented the foregoing as an illustration of the sort of situation which Descartes' words might be expected to describe. Now, however, I think that this is misleading. For though I have described a situation in which there are many things, nearly all of which are calculated to serve as illusions, this question may still arise. Would this paper world still be properly described as a world of illusions? If Tom says: "These are flowers," or "These look like flowers" (uncertainly), then the illusion is operative. But if Tom says: "These are paper," then the illusion has been destroyed. Descartes uses the words: "And all other external things are nought but illusions." This means that the situation which Descartes has in mind is such that if Tom says: "These are flowers," he will be wrong, but he will be wrong also if he says: "These are paper," and it won't matter what sentence of that type he uses. If he says: "These are rock"—or cotton or cloud or wood—he is wrong by the plan. He will be right only if he says: "These are illusions." But the project is to keep him from recognizing the illusions. This means that the illusions are to be brought about not by anything so crude as paper or even cloud. They must be made of the stuff that dreams are made of.

Now let us consider this second adventure.

The design then is this. The evil genius is to create a world of illusions. There are to be no flowers, no Milly, no paper. There is to be nothing at all, but Tom is every moment to go on mistaking nothing for something, nothing at all for flowers, nothing at all for Milly, etc. This is, of course, quite different from mistaking paper for flowers, paper for Milly. And yet all is to be arranged in such a way that Tom will go on just as we now do, and just as Tom did before the paper age, to see, hear, smell the world. He will love the flowers, he will kiss Milly, he will blink at the sun. So he thinks. And in thinking about these things he will talk and argue just as we do. But all the time he will be mistaken. There are no flowers, there is no kiss, there is no sun. Illusions all. This then is the end at which the evil genius aims.

How now is the evil genius to attain this end? Well, it is clear that a part of what he aims at will be realized if he destroys everything. Then there will be no flowers, and if Tom thinks that there are flowers he will be wrong. There will be no face that is Milly's and no tumbled beauty on her head, and if Tom thinks that there is Milly's face and Milly's hair, he will be wrong. It is necessary then to see to it that there are none of these things. So the evil genius, having failed with paper, destroys even all paper. Now there is nothing to see, nothing to hear, nothing to smell, etc. But this is not enough to deceive. For though Tom sees nothing, and neither hears nor smells anything, he may also think that he sees nothing. He must also be misled into thinking that he does see something, that there are flowers and Milly, and hands, eyes, flesh, blood, and all other senses. Accordingly the evil genius restores to Tom his old life. Even the memory of that paper day is blotted out, not a scrap remains. Witless Tom lives on, thinking, hoping, loving as he used to, unwitted by the great destroyer. All that seems so solid, so touchable to seeming hands, so biteable to apparent teeth, is so flimsy that were the evil genius to poke his index at it, it would curl away save for one tiny trace, the smirch of that index. So once more the evil genius has done according to his word.

And now let us examine the result.

I should like first of all to describe a passage of Tom's life. Tom is all alone, but he doesn't know it. What an opportunity for methodologico-metaphysico-solipsimo! I intend, in any case, to disregard the niceties of his being so alone and to borrow his own words, with the warning that the evil genius smiles as he reads them. Tom writes:

Today, as usual, I came into the room and there was the bowl of flowers on the table. I went up to them, caressed them, and smelled over them. I thank God for flowers! There's nothing so real to me as flowers. Here the genuine essence of the world's substance, as its gayest and most hilarious speaks to me. It seems unworthy even to think of them as erect, and waving on pillars of sap. Sap! Sap!

There was more in the same vein, which we need not bother to record. I might say that the evil genius was a bit amused, snickered in fact, as he read the words "so real," "essence," "substance," etc., but later he frowned and seemed puzzled. Tom went on to describe how Milly came into the rom, and how glad he was to see her. They talked about the flowers. Later he walked to the window and watched the gardener clearing a space a short distance away. The sun was shining, but there were a few heavy clouds. He raised the window, extended his hand and four large drops of rain wetted his hand. He returned to the room and quoted to Milly a song from *The Tempest*. He got all the words right, and was well pleased with himself. There was more he wrote, but this was enough to show how quite normal everything seems. And, too, how successful the evil genius is.

And the evil genius said to himself, not quite in solipsimo, "Not so, not so, not at all so."

The evil genius was, however, all too human. Admiring himself but unadmired, he yearned for admiration. To deceive but to be unsuspected is too little glory. The evil genius set about then to plant the seeds of suspicion. But how to do this? Clearly there was no suggestive paper to tempt Tom's confidence. There was nothing but Tom's mind, a stream of seemings and of words to make the seemings seem no seemings. The evil genius must have words with

Tom and must engage the same seemings with him. To have words with Tom is to have the words together, to use them in the same way, and to engage the same seemings is to see and to hear and to point to the same. And so the evil genius, free spirit, entered in at the door of Tom's pineal gland and lodged there. He floated in the humors that flow, glandwise and sensewise, everywhere being as much one with Tom as difference will allow. He looked out of the same eyes, and when Tom pointed with his finger, the evil genius said "This" and meant what Tom, hearing, also meant, seeing. Each heard with the same ear what the other heard. For every sniffing of the one nose there were two identical smells, and there were two tactualities for every touch. If Tom had had a toothache, together they would have pulled the same face. The twinsomeness of two monads finds here the limit of identity. Nevertheless there was otherness looking out of those eyes as we shall see.

It seems then that on the next day, the evil genius "going to and fro" in Tom's mind and "walking up and down in it," Tom once again, as his custom was, entered the room where the flowers stood on the table. He stopped, looked admiringly, and in a caressing voice said: "Flowers! Flowers!" And he lingered. The evil genius, more subtle "than all the beasts of the field," whispered "Flowers? Flowers?" For the first time Tom has an intimation of company, of some intimate partner in perception. Momentarily he is checked. He looks again at the flowers. "Flowers? Why, of course, flowers." Together they look out of the same eyes. Again the evil genius whispers, "Flowers?" The seed of suspicion is to be the question. But Tom now raises the flowers nearer to his eyes almost violently as though his eyes were not his own. He is, however, not perturbed. The evil genius only shakes their head. "Did you every hear of illusions?" says he.

Tom, still surprisingly good-natured, responds: "But you saw them, didn't you? Surely you can see through my eyes. Come, let us bury my nose deep in these blossoms, and take one long breath together. Then tell whether you can recognize these as flowers."

So they dunked the one nose. But the evil genius said "Huh!" as much as to say: What has all this seeming and smelling to do with it? Still he explained nothing. And Tom remained as confident of the flowers as he had been at the first. The little seeds of doubt, "Flowers? Flowers?" and again "Flowers?" and "Illusions?" and now this stick in the spokes, "Huh!" made Tom uneasy. He went on: "Oh, so you are one of these seers that has to touch everything. You're a tangibilite. Very well, here's my hand, let's finger these flowers. Careful! They're tender."

The evil genius was amused. He smiled inwardly and rippled in a shallow humor. To be taken for a materialist! As though the grand illusionist was not a spirit! Nevertheless, he realized that though deception is easy where the lies are big enough (where had he heard that before?), a few scattered, questioning words are not enough to make guile grow. He was tempted to make a statement, and he did. He said, "Your flowers are nothing but illusions."

"My flowers illusions?" exclaimed Tom, and he took up the bowl and placed it before a mirror. "See," said he, "here are the flowers and here, in the mirror, is an illusion. There's a difference surely. And you with my eyes, my nose, and my fingers can tell what that difference is. Pollen on your fingers touching the illusion? send Milly the flowers in the mirror? Set a bee to suck honey out of this glass? You know all this as well as I do. I can tell flowers from illusions, and my flowers, as you now plainly see, are not illusions."

The evil genius was now sorely tried. He had his make-believe, but he also had his pride. Would he now risk the make-believe to save his pride? Would he explain? He explained.

"Tom," he said, "notice. The flowers in the mirror look like flowers, but they only look like flowers. We agree about that. The flowers before the mirror also look like flowers. But they, you say, are flowers because they also smell like flowers and they feel like flowers, as though they would be any more flowers because they also like flowers multiply. Imagine a mirror such that it reflected not only the looks of flowers, but also their fragrance and their petal surfaces, and then you smelled and touched, and the flowers before the mirror would be just like the flowers in the mirror. Then you could see immediately that the flowers before the mirror are illusions just as those in the mirror are illusions. As it is now, it is clear that the flowers in the mirror are thin illusions, and the flowers before the mirror are thick. Thick illusions are the best for deception. And they may be as thick as you like. From them you may gather pollen, send them to Milly, and foolish bees may sleep in them."

But Tom was not asleep. "I see that what you mean by thin illusions is what I mean by illusions, and what you mean by thick illusions is what I mean by flowers. So when you say that my flowers are your thick illusions this doesn't bother me. And as for your mirror that mirrors all layers of your thick illusions, I shouldn't call that a mirror at all. It's a duplicator, and much more useful than a mirror, provided you can control it. But I do suppose that when you speak of thick illusions you do mean that thick illusions are related to something you call flowers in much the same way that the thin illusions are related to the thick ones. Is that true?"

The evil genius was now diction-deep in explanations and went on. "In the first place let me assure you that these are not flowers. I destroyed all flowers. There are no flowers at all. There are only thin and thick illusions of flowers. I can see your flowers in the mirror, and I can smell and touch the flowers before the mirror. What I cannot smell and touch, having seen as in the mirror, is not even thick illusion. But if I cannot also *cerpicio* what I see, smell, touch, etc., what I have then seen is not anything real. *Esse est cerpici.* I just now tried to *cerpicio* your flowers, but there was nothing there. Man is after all a four- or five- or six-sense creature and you cannot expect much from so little."

Tom rubbed his eyes and his ears tingled with an eighteenth-century disturbance. Then he stared at the flowers. "I see," he said, "that this added sense of yours has done wickedly with our language. You do not mean by illusion what we mean, and neither do you mean by flowers what we mean. As for *cerpicio* I wouldn't be surprised if you'd made up that word just to puzzle us. In any case what you destroyed is what, according to you, you used to *cerpicio*. So there is nothing for you to *cerpicio* any more. But there still are what we mean by flowers. If your intention was to deceive, you must learn the language of those you are to deceive. I should say that you are like the doctor who prescribes for his patients what is so bad for himself and is then surprised at the health of his patients." And he pinned a flower near their nose.

The evil genius, discomfited, rode off on a corpuscle. He had failed. He took to an artery, made haste to the pineal exit, and was gone. Then "sun by sun" he fell. And he regretted his mischief.

I have tried in this essay to understand the boast of the evil genius. His boast was that he could deceive, deceive about "the heavens, the earth, the colors, figures, sound, and all other external things." In order to do this I have tried to bring clearly to mind what deception and such deceiving would be like. Such deception involves illusions and such deceiving involves the creation of illusions. Accordingly I have tried to imagine the evil genius engaged in the practice of deception, busy in the creation of illusions. In the first adventure everything is plain. The evil genius employs paper, paper making believe it's many other things. The effort to deceive, ingenuity in deception, being deceived by paper, detecting the illusion—all these are clearly understood. It is the second adventure, however, which is more crucial. For in this instance it is assumed that the illusion is of such a kind that no seeing, no touching, no smelling, are relevant to detecting the illusion. Nevertheless the evil genius sees, touches, smells, and does detect the illusion. He made the illusion; so, of course, he must know it. How then does he know it? The evil genius has a sense denied to men. He senses the flower-in-itself, Milly-in-her-self, etc. So he creates illusions made up of what can be seen, heard, smelled, etc., illusions all because when seeing, hearing, and smelling have seen, heard, and smelled all, the special sense senses nothing. So what poor human beings sense is the illusion of what only the evil genius can sense. This is formidable. Nevertheless, once again everything is clear. If we admit the special sense, then we can readily see how it is that the evil genius should have been so confident. He has certainly created his own illusions, though he has not himself been deceived. But neither has anyone else been deceived. For human beings do not use the word "illusion" by relation to a sense with which only the evil genius is blessed.

I said that the evil genius had not been deceived, and it is true that he has not been deceived by his own illusions. Nevertheless he was deceived in boasting that he could deceive, for his confidence in this is based upon an ignorance of the difference between our uses of the words, "heavens," "earth," "flowers," "Milly," and "illusions" of these things, and his own uses of these words. For though there certainly is an analogy between our own uses and his, the difference is quite sufficient to explain his failure at grand deception. We can also understand how easily Tom might have been taken in. The dog over the water dropped his meaty bone for a picture on the water. Tom, however, dropped nothing at all. But the word "illusion" is a trap.

I began this essay uneasily, looking at my hands and saying "no hands," blinking my eyes and saying "no eyes." Everything I saw seemed to me like something Cheshire, a piece of cheese, for instance, appearing and disappearing in the leaves of the tree. Poor kitty! And now? Well. . . .

Notes

1. *Philosophical Works of Descartes*, trans. E. S. Haldane and G. R. T. Ross (2 vols.; Cambridge: Cambridge University Press, 1912), I, 147.

Questions on Bouwsma

1. Bouwsma argues that the deception of the evil genius involves some confusion about the word "illusion" (between "thick" and "thin" illusions). Explain this alleged confusion and how it can be avoided.

2. The evil genius says, "I just now tried to *cerpicio* your flowers, but there was nothing there." Explain the meaning (if any) of this sentence.

3. Has Bouwsma convinced you that the evil genius could not possibly deceive you without your knowing it? Why or why not?

John Locke

Perception and Knowledge

John Locke (1632–1704) is one of the most important English philosophers. He is best known for his empiricist theory of knowledge and his natural rights political theory.

1. The knowledge of our own being we have by intuition. The existence of a God, reason clearly makes known to us, as has been shown.

The knowledge of the existence of *any other thing* we can have only by *sensation*: for there being no necessary connexion of real existence with any *idea* a man hath in his memory; nor of any other existence but that of God with the existence of any particular man: no particular man can know the existence of any other being, but only when, by actual operating upon him, it makes itself perceived by him. For, the having the idea of anything in our mind, no more proves the existence of that thing, than the picture of a man evidences his being in the world, or the visions of a dream make thereby a true history.

2. It is therefore the *actual receiving* of ideas from without that gives us notice of the existence of other things, and makes us know, that something doth exist at that time without us, which causes that idea in us; though perhaps we neither know nor consider how it does it. For it takes not from the certainty of our senses, and the ideas we receive by them, that we know not the manner wherein they are produced: v.g. whilst I write this, I have, by the paper affecting my eyes, that idea produced in my mind, which, whatever object causes, I call *white*; by which I know that that quality or accident (i.e. whose appearance before my eyes always causes that idea) doth really exist, and hath a being without me. And of this, the greatest assurance I can

The reading is from John Locke, *An Essay Concerning Human Understanding*, vol. 2, ed. Alexander Campbell Fraser (New York: Dover Publications, 1959), pp. 325–336.

possibly have, and to which my faculties can attain, is the testimony of my eyes, which are the proper and sole judges of this thing; whose testimony I have reason to rely on as so certain, that I can no more doubt, whilst I write this, that I see white and black, and that something really exists that causes that sensation in me, than that I write or move my hand; which is a certainty as great as human nature is capable of, concerning the existence of anything, but a man's self alone, and of God.

3. The notice we have by our senses of the existing of things without us, though it be not altogether so certain as our intuitive knowledge, or the deductions of our reason employed about the clear abstract ideas of our own minds; yet it is an assurance that deserves the name of *knowledge*. If we persuade ourselves that our faculties act and inform us right concerning the existence of those objects that affect them, it cannot pass for an ill-grounded confidence: for I think nobody can, in earnest, be so sceptical as to be uncertain of the existence of those things which he sees and feels. At least, he that can doubt so far, (whatever he may have with his own thoughts,) will never have any controversy with me; since he can never be sure I say anything contrary to his own opinion. As to myself, I think God has given me assurance enough of the existence of things without me: since, by their different application, I can produce in myself both pleasure and pain, which is one great concernment of my present state. This is certain: the confidence that our faculties do not herein deceive us, is the greatest assurance we are capable of concerning the existence of material beings. For we cannot act anything but by our faculties; nor talk of knowledge itself, but by the help of those faculties which are fitted to apprehend even what knowledge is.

But besides the assurance we have from our senses themselves, that they do not err in the information they give us of the existence of things without us, when they are affected by them, we are further confirmed in this assurance by other concurrent reasons:—

4. I. It is plain those perceptions are produced in us by exterior causes affecting our senses: because those that want the *organs* of any sense, never can have the ideas belonging to

that sense produced in their minds. This is too evident to be doubted: and therefore we cannot but be assured that they come in by the organs of that sense, and no other way. The organs themselves, it is plain, do not produce them: for then the eyes of a man in the dark would produce colours, and his nose smell roses in the winter: but we see nobody gets the relish of a pineapple, till he goes to the Indies, where it is, and tastes it.

5. II. Because sometimes I find that *I cannot avoid the having those ideas produced in my mind.* For though, when my eyes are shut, or windows fast, I can at pleasure recall to my mind the ideas of light, or the sun, which former sensations had lodged in my memory; so I can at pleasure lay by *that* idea, and take into my view that of the smell of a rose, or taste of sugar. But, if I turn my eyes at noon towards the sun, I cannot avoid the ideas which the light or sun then produces in me. So that there is a manifest difference between the ideas laid up in my memory, (over which, if they were there only, I should have constantly the same power to dispose of them, and lay them by at pleasure,) and those which force themselves upon me, and I cannot avoid having. And therefore it must needs be some exterior cause, and the brisk acting of some objects without me, whose efficacy I cannot resist, that produces those ideas in my mind, whether I will or no. Besides, there is nobody who doth not perceive the difference in himself between contemplating the sun, as he hath the idea of it in his memory, and actually looking upon it: of which two, his perception is so distinct, that few of his ideas are more distinguishable one from another. And therefore he hath certain knowledge that they are not *both* memory, or the actions of his mind, and fancies only within him; but that actual seeing hath a cause without.

6. III. Add to this, that many of those ideas are *produced in us with pain,* which afterwards we remember without the least offence. Thus, the pain of heat or cold, when the idea of it is revived in our minds, gives us no disturbance; which, when felt, was very troublesome; and is again, when actually repeated: which is occasioned by the disorder the external object causes in our bodies when applied to them: and we remember the pains of hunger, thirst, or the

headache, without any pain at all; which would either never disturb us, or else constantly do it, as often as we thought of it, were there nothing more but ideas floating in our minds, and appearances entertaining our fancies, without the real existence of things affecting us from abroad. The same may be said of *pleasure,* accompanying several actual sensations. And though mathematical demonstration depends not upon sense, yet the examining them by diagrams gives great credit to the evidence of our sight, and seems to give it a certainty approaching to that of demonstration itself. For, it would be very strange, that a man should allow it for an undeniable truth, that two angles of a figure, which he measures by lines and angles of a diagram, should be bigger one than the other, and yet doubt of the existence of those lines and angles, which by looking on he makes use of to measure that by.

7. IV. Our *senses* in many cases *bear witness to the truth of each other's report,* concerning the existence of sensible things without us. He that *sees* a fire, may, if he doubt whether it be anything more than a bare fancy, *feel* it too; and be convinced, by putting his hand in it. Which certainly could never be put into such exquisite pain by a bare idea or phantom, unless that the pain be a fancy too: which yet he cannot, when the burn is well, by raising the idea of it, bring upon himself again.

Thus I see, whilst I write this, I can change the appearance of the paper; and by designing the letters, tell *beforehand* what new idea it shall exhibit the very next moment, by barely drawing my pen over it: which will neither appear (let me fancy as much as I will) if my hands stand still; or though I move my pen, if my eyes be shut: nor, when those characters are once made on the paper, can I choose afterwards but see them as they are; that is, have the ideas of such letters as I have made. Whence it is manifest, that they are not barely the sport and play of my own imagination when I find that the characters that were made at the pleasure of my own thoughts, do not obey them; nor yet cease to be, whenever I shall fancy it, but continue to affect my senses constantly and regularly, according to the figures I made them. To which if we will add, that the sight of those shall, from another man, draw such sounds as I beforehand design they shall stand for, there will be little reason left to doubt that those words I write do really exist without me, when they cause a long series of regular sounds to affect my ears, which could not be the effect of my imagination, nor could my memory retain them in that order.

8. But yet, if after all this any one will be so sceptical as to distrust his senses, and to affirm that all we see and hear, feel and taste, think and do, during our whole being, is but the series and deluding appearances of a long dream, whereof there is no reality; and therefore will question the existence of all things, or our knowledge of anything: I must desire him to consider, that, if all be a dream, then he doth but dream that he makes the question, and so it is not much matter that a waking man should answer him. But yet, if he pleases, he may dream that I make him this answer, That the certainty of things existing in *rerum natura* when we have the testimony of our senses for it is not only as great as our frame can attain to, but as our condition needs. For, our faculties being suited not to the full extent of being, nor to a perfect, clear, comprehensive knowledge of things free from all doubt and scruple; but to the preservation of us, in whom they are; and accommodated to the use of life: they serve to our purpose well enough, if they will but give us certain notice of those things, which are convenient or inconvenient to us. For he that sees a candle burning, and hath experimented the force of its flame by putting his finger in it, will little doubt that this is something existing without him, which does him harm, and puts him to great pain: which is assurance enough, when no man requires greater certainty to govern his actions by than what is as certain as his actions themselves. And if our dreamer pleases to try whether the glowing heat of a glass furnace be barely a wandering imagination in a drowsy man's fancy, by putting his hand into it, he may perhaps be wakened into a certainty greater than he could wish, that it is something more than bare imagination. So that this evidence is as great as we can desire, being as certain to us as our pleasure or pain, i.e. happiness or misery; beyond which we have no concernment, either of knowing or being. Such an assurance of the existence of things without us is sufficient to direct us in the attaining the good and avoiding the evil which is caused by them, which is the important concernment we have of being made acquainted with them.

9. In fine, then, when our senses do actually convey into our understandings any idea, we cannot but be satisfied that there doth something *at that time* really exist without us, which doth affect our senses, and by them give notice of itself to our apprehensive faculties, and actually produce that idea which we then perceive: and we cannot so far distrust their testimony, as to doubt that such *collections* of simple ideas as we have observed by our senses to be united together, do really exist together. But this knowledge extends as far as the present testimony of our senses, employed about particular objects that do then affect them, and no further. For if I saw such a collection of simple ideas as is wont to be called *man*, existing together one minute since, and am now alone, I cannot be certain that the same man exists now, since there is no *necessary connexion* of his existence a minute since with his existence now: by a thousand ways he may cease to be, since I had the testimony of my senses for his existence. And if I cannot be certain that the man I saw last to-day is now in being, I can less be certain that he is so who hath been longer removed from my senses, and I have not seen since yesterday, or since the last year: and much less can I be certain of the existence of men that I never saw. And, therefore, though it be highly probable that millions of men do now exist, yet, whilst I am alone, writing this, I have not that certainty of it which we strictly call knowledge; though the great likelihood of it puts me past doubt, and it be reasonable for me to do several things upon the confidence that there are men (and men also of my acquaintance, with whom I have to do) now in the world: but this is but probability, not knowledge.

10. Whereby yet we may observe how foolish and vain a thing it is for a man of a narrow knowledge, who having reason given him to judge of the different evidence and probability of things, and to be swayed accordingly; how vain, I say, it is to expect demonstration and cer-

tainty in things not capable of it; and refuse assent to very rational propositions, and act contrary to very plain and clear truths, because they cannot be made out so evident, as to surmount every the least (I will not say reason, but) pretence of doubting. He that, in the ordinary affairs of life, would admit of nothing but direct plain demonstration, would be sure of nothing in this world, but of perishing quickly. The wholesomeness of his meat or drink would not give him reason to venture on it: and I would fain know what it is he could do upon such grounds as are capable of no doubt, no objection.

Questions on Locke

1. According to Locke, how do we know that something, say a piece of white paper, exists? What objections would Descartes make? (Hint: Remember the "wax" argument.) In your opinion, who is right, Locke or Descartes?

2. "Nobody can, in earnest, be so sceptical as to be uncertain of those things which he sees and feels." Is this true? Why or why not?

3. Here is a sceptical argument: "It takes millions of years for the light from a star to reach us. The star might have ceased to exist millions of years ago, and yet the light is still reaching us. So when we see a star, it might not exist. Thus we cannot even trust our visual perception." Can you think of a good reply to this? What is it?

Bertrand Russell

Appearance and Reality

Bertrand Russell (1872–1970), one of the greatest philosophers of the twentieth century, wrote dozens of books in philosophy. Because of his pacifism and unconventional views about moral issues, he was imprisoned, dismissed from a teaching position in England, and barred from accepting a position in the United States.

Is there any knowledge in the world which is so certain that no reasonable man could doubt it? This question, which at first sight might not seem difficult, is really one of the most difficult that can be asked. When we have realized the obstacles in the way of a straightforward and confident answer, we shall be well launched on the study of philosophy—for philosophy is merely the attempt to answer such ultimate questions, not carelessly and dogmatically, as we

The reading is from Bertrand Russell, *The Problem of Philosophy* (New York: Oxford University Press, 1959), ch. 1, pp. 7–16. Reprinted by permission of Oxford University Press.

do in ordinary life and even in the sciences, but critically, after exploring all that makes such questions puzzling, and after realizing all the vagueness and confusion that underlie our ordinary ideas.

In daily life, we assume as certain many things which, on a closer scrutiny, are found to be so full of apparent contradictions that only a great amount of thought enables us to know what it is that we really may believe. In the search for certainty, it is natural to begin with our present experiences, and in some sense, no doubt, knowledge is to be derived from them. But any statement as to what it is that our immediate experiences make us know is very likely to be wrong. It seems to me that I am now sitting in a chair, at a table of a certain shape, on which I see sheets of paper with writing or print. By turning my head I see out of the window buildings and clouds and the sun. I believe that the sun is about ninety-three million miles from the earth; that it is a hot globe many times bigger than the earth; that, owing to the earth's rotation, it rises every morning, and will continue to do so for an indefinite time in the future. I believe that, if any other normal person comes into my room, he will see the same chairs and tables and books and papers as I see, and that the table which I see is the same as the table which I feel pressing against my arm. All this seems to be so evident as to be hardly worth stating, except in answer to a man who doubts whether I know anything. Yet all this may be reasonably doubted, and all of it requires much careful discussion before we can be sure that we have stated it in a form that is wholly true.

To make our difficulties plain, let us concentrate attention on the table. To the eye it is oblong, brown and shiny, to the touch it is smooth and cool and hard; when I tap it, it gives out a wooden sound. Any one else who sees and feels and hears the table will agree with this description, so that it might seem as if no difficulty would arise; but as soon as we try to be more precise our troubles begin. Although I believe that the table is 'really' of the same colour all over, the parts that reflect the light look much brighter than the other parts, and some parts look white because of reflected light. I know that, if I move, the parts that reflect the light will be different, so that the apparent distribution of colours on the table will change. It follows that if several people are looking at the table at the same moment, no two of them will see exactly the same distribution of colours, because no two can see it from exactly the same point of view, and any change in the point of view makes some change in the way the light is reflected.

For most practical purposes these differences are unimportant, but to the painter they are all-important: the painter has to unlearn the habit of thinking that things seem to have the colour which common sense says they 'really' have, and to learn the habit of seeing things as they appear. Here we have already the beginning of one of the distinctions that cause most trouble in philosophy—the distinction between 'appearance' and 'reality', between what things seem to be and what they are. The painter wants to know what things seem to be, the practical man and the philosopher want to know what they are; but the philosopher's wish to know this is stronger than the practical man's, and is more troubled by knowledge as to the difficulties of answering the question.

To return to the table. It is evident from what we have found, that there is no colour which preeminently appears to be *the* colour of the table, or even of any one particular part of the table—it appears to be of different colours from different points of view, and there is no reason for regarding some of these as more really its colour than others. And we know that even from a given point of view the colour will seem different by artificial light, or to a colour-blind man, or to a man wearing blue spectacles, while in the dark there will be no colour at all, though to touch and hearing the table will be unchanged. This colour is not something which is inherent in the table, but something depending upon the table and the spectator and the way the light falls on the table. When, in ordinary life, we speak of *the* colour of the table, we only mean the sort of colour which it will seem to have to a normal spectator from an ordinary point of view under usual conditions of light. But the other colours which appear under other conditions have just as good a right to be considered real; and therefore, to avoid favouritism, we are compelled to deny that, in itself, the table has any one particular colour.

The same thing applies to the texture. With the naked eye one can see the grain, but otherwise the table looks smooth and even. If we looked at it through a microscope, we should see roughnesses and hills and valleys, and all sorts of differences that are imperceptible to the naked eye. Which of these is the 'real' table? We are naturally tempted to say that what we see through the microscope is more real, but that in turn would be changed by a still more powerful microscope. If, then, we cannot trust what we see with the naked eye, why should we trust what we see through a microscope? Thus, again, the confidence in our senses with which we began deserts us.

The *shape* of the table is no better. We are all in the habit of judging as to the 'real' shapes of things, and we do this so unreflectingly that we come to think we actually see the real shapes. But, in fact, as we all have to learn if we try to draw, a given thing looks different in shape from every different point of view. If our table is 'really' rectangular, it will look, from almost all points of view, as if it had two acute angles and two obtuse angles. If opposite sides are parallel, they will look as if they converged to a point away from the spectator; if they are of equal length, they will look as if the nearer side were longer. All these things are not commonly noticed in looking at a table, because experience has taught us to construct the 'real' shape from the apparent shape, and the 'real' shape is what interests us as practical men. But the 'real' shape is not what we see; it is something inferred from what we see. And what we see is constantly changing in shape as we move about the room; so that here again the senses seem not to give us the truth about the table itself, but only about the appearance of the table.

Similar difficulties arise when we consider the sense of touch. It is true that the table always gives us a sensation of hardness, and we feel that it resists pressure. But the sensation we obtain depends upon how hard we press the table and also upon what part of the body we press with; thus the various sensations due to various pressures or various parts of the body cannot be supposed to reveal *directly* any definite property of the table, but at most to be *signs* of some property which perhaps *causes* all the sensations, but is not actually apparent in any of them. And the same applies still more obviously to the sounds which can be elicited by rapping the table.

Thus, it becomes evident that the real table, if there is one, is not the same as what we immediately experience by sight or touch or hearing. The real table, if there is one, is not *immediately* known to us at all, but must be an inference from what is immediately known. Hence, two very difficult questions at once arise; namely, (1) Is there a real table at all? (2) If so, what sort of object can it be?

It will help us in considering these questions to have a few simple terms of which the meaning is definite and clear. Let us give the name of **'sense-data'** to the things that are immediately known in sensation: such things as colours, sounds, smells, hardnesses, roughnesses, and so on. We shall give the name 'sensation' to the experience of being immediately aware of these things. Thus, whenever we see a colour, we have a sensation *of* the colour, but the colour itself is a sense-datum, not a sensation. The colour is that *of* which we are immediately aware, and the awareness itself is the sensation. It is plain that if we are to know anything about the table, it must be by means of the sense-data—brown colour, oblong shape, smoothness, etc.—which we associate with the table; but, for the reasons which have been given, we cannot say that the table *is* the sense-data, or even that the sense-data are directly properties of the table. Thus a problem arises as to the relation of the sense-data to the real table, supposing there is such a thing.

The real table, if it exists, we will call a 'physical object'. Thus we have to consider the relation of sense-data to physical objects. The collection of all physical objects is called 'matter'. Thus our two questions may be re-stated as follows: (1) Is there any such thing as matter? (2) If so, what is its nature?

The philosopher who first brought prominently forward the reasons for regarding the immediate objects of our senses as not existing independently of us was Bishop Berkeley (1685–1753). His *Three Dialogues between Hylas and Philonous, in Opposition to Sceptics and Atheists,* undertake to prove that there is no such thing as matter at all, and that the world consists of nothing but minds and their ideas. Hylas has hitherto believed in matter, but he is no match for Philonous, who mercilessly drives him into contradictions and paradoxes, and makes his own denial of matter seem, in the end, as if it were almost common sense. The arguments employed are of very different value: some are important and sound, others are confused or quibbling. But Berkeley retains the merit of having shown that the existence of matter is capable of being denied without absurdity, and that if there are any things that exist independently of us they cannot be the immediate objects of our sensations.

There are two different questions involved when we ask whether matter exists, and it is important to keep them clear. We commonly mean by 'matter' something which is opposed to 'mind', something which we think of as occupying space and as radically incapable of any sort of thought or consciousness. It is chiefly in this sense that Berkeley denies matter; that is to say, he does not deny that the sense-data which we commonly take as signs of the existence of the table are really signs of the existence of *something* independent of us, but he does deny that this something is non-mental, that it is neither mind nor ideas entertained by some mind. He admits that there must be something which continues to exist when we go out of the room or shut our eyes, and that what we call seeing the table does really give us reason for believing in something which persists even when we are not seeing it. But he thinks that this something cannot be radically different in nature from what we see, and cannot be independent of seeing altogether, though it must be independent of *our* seeing. He is thus led to regard the 'real' table as an idea in the mind of God. Such an idea has the required permanence and independence of ourselves, without being—as matter would otherwise be—something quite unknowable, in the sense that we can only infer it, and can never be directly and immediately aware of it.

Other philosophers since Berkeley have also held that, although the table does not depend for its existence upon being seen by me, it does depend upon being seen (or otherwise apprehended in sensation) by *some* mind—not necessarily the mind of God, but more often the whole collective mind of the universe. This they hold, as Berkeley does, chiefly because they think there can be nothing real—or at any rate nothing known to be real—except minds and their thoughts and feelings. We might state the argument by which they support their view in some such way as this: 'Whatever can be thought of is an idea in the mind of the person thinking of it; therefore nothing can be thought of except ideas in minds; therefore anything else is inconceivable, and what is inconceivable cannot exist.'

Such an argument, in my opinion, is fallacious; and of course those who advance it do not put it so shortly or so crudely. But whether valid or not, the argument has been very widely advanced in one form or another; and very many philosophers, perhaps a majority, have held that there is nothing real except minds and their ideas. Such philosophers are called 'idealists'. When they come to explaining matter, they either say, like Berkeley, that matter is really nothing but a collection of ideas, or they say, like Leibniz (1646–1716), that what appears as matter is really a collection of more or less rudimentary minds.

But these philosophers, though they deny matter as opposed to mind, nevertheless, in another sense, admit matter. It will be remembered that we asked two questions; namely, (1) Is there a real table at all? (2) If so, what sort of object can it be? Now both Berkeley and Leibniz admit that there is a real table, but Berkeley says it is certain ideas in the mind of God, and Leibniz says it is a colony of souls. Thus both of them answer our first question in the affirmative, and only diverge from the views of ordinary mortals in their answer to our second question. In fact, almost all philosophers seem to be agreed that there is a real table: they almost all agree that, however much our sense-data—colour, shape, smoothness, etc.—may depend upon us, yet their occurrence is a sign of something existing independently of us, something differing, perhaps, completely from our sense-data, and yet to be regarded as causing those sense-data whenever we are in a suitable relation to the real table.

Now obviously this point in which the philosophers are agreed—the view that there *is* a real table, whatever its nature may be—is vitally important, and it will be worth while to consider what reasons there are for accepting this view before we go on to the further question as to the nature of the real table. . . .

Before we go farther it will be well to consider for a moment what it is that we have discovered so far. It has appeared that, if we take any common object of the sort that is supposed to be known by the senses, what the senses *immediately* tell us is not the truth about the object as it is apart from us, but only the truth about certain sense-data which, so far as we can see, depend upon the relations between us and the object. Thus what we directly see and feel is merely 'appearance', which we believe to be a sign of some 'reality' behind. But if the reality is not what appears, have we any means of knowing whether there is any reality at all? And if so, have we any means of finding out what it is like?

Such questions are bewildering, and it is difficult to know that even the strangest hypotheses may not be true. Thus our familiar table, which has roused but the slightest thoughts in us hitherto, has become a problem full of surprising possibilities. The one thing we know about it is that it is not what it seems. Beyond this modest result, so far, we have the most complete liberty of conjecture. Leibniz tells us it is a community of souls; Berkeley tells us it is an idea in the mind of God; sober science, scarcely less wonderful, tells us it is a vast collection of electric charges in violent motion.

Among these surprising possibilities, doubt suggests that perhaps there is no table at all. Philosophy, if it cannot *answer* so many questions as we could wish, has at least the power of *asking* questions which increase the interest of the world, and show the strangeness and wonder lying just below the surface even in the commonest things of daily life.

Questions on Russell

1. "The real table, if there is one, is not *immediately* known to us at all, but must be an inference from what is immediately known." How does Russell reach this conclusion? Does he have a sound argument or not? Explain your answer.

2. What is matter? Why does Berkeley deny its existence? Russell says that Berkeley's argument (or the argument he attributes to Berkeley) is fallacious. But where is the fallacy? See if you can find it.

3. Explain the distinction between appearance and reality. Why can't we find out what reality is like, according to Russell? Can you think of any way of discovering the nature of reality? What is it?

David Hume

Scepticism about Causation

For biographical information, see the reading by Hume in chapter 1.

Sceptical Doubts Concerning the Operations of the Understanding

Part I

All the objects of human reason or enquiry may naturally be divided into two kinds, to wit, *Relations of Ideas,* and *Matters of Fact.* Of the first kind are the sciences of Geometry, Algebra, and Arithmetic; and in short, every affirmation which is either intuitively or demonstratively certain. *That the square of the hypotenuse is equal to the square of the two sides,* is a proposition which ex-

The reading is from David Hume, *Enquiries Concerning the Human Understanding and Concerning the Principles of Morals,* ed. L. A. Selby-Bigge (Oxford: Clarendon Press, 1961), pp. 25–47.

presses a relation between these figures. *That three times five is equal to half of thirty,* expresses a relation between these numbers. Propositions of this kind are discoverable by the mere operation of thought, without dependence on what is anywhere existent in the universe. Though there never were a circle or triangle in nature, the truths demonstrated by Euclid would for ever retain their certainty and evidence.

Matters of fact, which are the second objects of human reason, are not ascertained in the same manner; nor is our evidence of their truth, however great, of a like nature with the foregoing. The contrary of every matter of fact is still possible; because it can never imply a contradiction, and is conceived by the mind with the same facility and distinctness, as if ever so conformable to reality. *That the sun will not rise to-morrow* is no less intelligible a proposition, and implies no more contradiction than the affirmation, *that it will rise.* We should in vain, therefore, attempt to demonstrate its falsehood. Were it demonstratively false, it would imply a contradiction, and could never be distinctly conceived by the mind.

It may, therefore, be a subject worthy of curiosity, to enquire what is the nature of that evidence which assures us of any real existence and matter of fact, beyond the present testimony of our senses, or the records of our memory. This part of philosophy, it is observable, has been little cultivated, either by the ancients or moderns; and therefore our doubts and errors, in the prosecution of so important an enquiry, may be the more excusable; while we march through such difficult paths without any guide or direction. They may even prove useful, by exciting curiosity, and destroying that implicit faith and security, which is the bane of all reasoning and free enquiry. The discovery of defects in the common philosophy, if any such there be, will not, I presume, be a discouragement, but rather an incitement, as is usual, to attempt something more full and satisfactory that has yet been proposed to the public.

All reasonings concerning matter of fact seem to be founded on the relation of *Cause and Effect*. By means of that relation alone we can go beyond the evidence of our memory and senses. If you were to ask a man, why he believes any matter of fact, which is absent; for instance, that his friend is in the country, or in France; he would give you a reason; and this reason would be some other fact; as a letter received from him, or the knowledge of his former resolutions and promises. A man finding a watch or any other machine in a desert island, would conclude that there had once been men in that island. All our reasonings concerning fact are of the same nature. And here it is constantly supposed that there is a connexion between the present fact and that which is inferred from it. Were there nothing to bind them together, the inference would be entirely precarious. The hearing of an articulate voice and rational discourse in the dark assures us of the presence of some person: Why? because these are the effects of the human make and fabric, and closely connected with it. If we anatomize all the other reasonings of this nature, we shall find that they are founded on the relation of cause and effect, and that this relation is either near or remote, direct or collateral. Heat and light are collateral effects of fire, and the one effect may justly be inferred from the other.

If we would satisfy ourselves, therefore, concerning the nature of that evidence, which assures us of matters of fact, we must enquire how we arrive at the knowledge of cause and effect. . . .

This proposition, *that causes and effect are discoverable, not by reason but by experience,* will readily be admitted with regard to such objects, as we remember to have once been altogether unknown to us; since we must be conscious of the utter inability, which we then lay under, of foretelling what would arise from them. Present two smooth pieces of marble to a man who has no tincture of natural philosophy; he will never discover that they will adhere together in such a manner as to require great force to separate them in a direct line, while they make so small a resistance to a lateral pressure. Such events, as bear little analogy to the common course of nature, are also readily confessed to be known only by experience; nor does any man imagine that the explosion of gunpowder, or the attraction of a loadstone, could ever be discovered by arguments *a priori*. In like manner, when an effect is supposed to depend upon an intricate machinery or secret structure of parts, we make no difficulty in attributing all our knowledge of it to experience. Who will assert that he can give the ultimate reason, why milk or bread is proper nourishment for a man, not for a lion or a tiger?

But the same truth may not appear, at first sight, to have the same evidence with regard to events, which have become familiar to us from our first appearance in the world, which bear a close analogy to the whole course of nature, and which are supposed to depend on the simple qualities of objects, without any secret structure of parts. We are apt to imagine that we could discover these effects by the mere operation of our reason, without experience. We fancy, that were we brought on a sudden into this world, we could at first have inferred that one Billiard-ball would communicate motion to another upon impulse; and that we needed not to have waited for the event, in order to pronounce with certainty concerning it. Such is the influence of custom, that, where it is strongest, it not only covers our natural ignorance, but even conceals itself, and seems not to take place, merely because it is found in the highest degree.

But to convince us that all the laws of nature, and all the operations of bodies without exception, are known only by experience, the following reflections may, perhaps, suffice. Were any object presented to us, and were we required to pronounce concerning the effect, which will result from it, without consulting past observation; after what manner, I beseech you, must the mind proceed in this operation? It must invent or imagine some event, which it ascribes to the object as its effect; and it is plain that this invention must be entirely arbitrary. The mind can never possibly find the effect in the supposed cause, by the most accurate scrutiny and examination. For the effect is totally different from the cause, and consequently can never be discovered in it. Motion in the second Billiard-ball is a quite distinct event from motion in the first; nor is there anything in the one to suggest the smallest hint of the other. A stone or piece of metal raised into the air, and left without any support, immediately falls: but to consider the matter *a priori*, is there anything we discover in this situation which can beget the idea of a downward, rather that an upward, or any other motion, in the stone or metal?

And as the first imagination or invention of a particular effect, in all natural operations, is arbitrary, where we consult not experience; so must we also esteem the supposed tie or connexion between the cause and effect, which binds them together, and renders it impossible that any other effect could result from the operation of that cause. When I see, for instance, a Billiard-ball moving in a straight line towards another; even suppose motion in the second ball should by accident be suggested to me, as the result of their contact or impulse; may I not conceive, that a hundred different events might as well follow from that cause? May not both these balls remain at absolute rest? May not the first ball return in a straight line, or leap off from the second in any line or direction? All these suppositions are consistent and conceivable. Why then should we give the preference to one, which is no more consistent or conceivable than the rest? All our reasonings *a priori* will never be able to show us any foundation for this preference.

In a word, then, every effect is a distinct event from its cause. It could not, therefore, be discovered in the cause, and the first invention or conception of it, *a priori*, must be entirely ar-

bitrary. And even after it is suggested, the conjunction of it with the cause must appear equally arbitrary; since there are always many other effects, which, to reason, must seem fully as consistent and natural. In vain, therefore, should we pretend to determine any single event, or infer any cause or effect, without the assistance of observation and experience. . . .

Part II

But we have not yet attained any tolerable satisfaction with regard to the question first proposed. Each solution still gives rise to a new question as difficult as the foregoing, and leads us on to farther enquiries. When it is asked, *What is the nature of all our reasonings concerning matter of fact?* the proper answer seems to be, that they are founded on the relation of cause and effect. When again it is asked, *What is the foundation of all our reasonings and conclusions concerning that relation?* it may be replied in one work, Experience. But if we still carry on our sifting humour, and ask, *What is the foundation of all conclusions from experience?* this implies a new question, which may be of more difficult solution and explication. Philosophers, that give themselves airs of superior wisdom and sufficiency, have a hard task when they encounter persons of inquisitive dispositions, who push them from every corner to which they retreat, and who are sure at last to bring them to some dangerous dilemma. The best expedient to prevent this confusion, is to be modest in our pretensions; and even to discover the difficulty ourselves before it is objected to us. By this means, we may make a kind of merit of our very ignorance.

I shall content myself, in this section, with an easy task, and shall pretend only to give a negative answer to the question here proposed. I say then, that, even after we have experience of the operations of cause and effect, our conclusions from that experience are *not* founded on reasoning, or any process of the understanding. This answer we must endeavor both to explain and to defend. . . .

In reality, all arguments from experience are founded on the similarity which we discover among natural objects, and by which we are induced to expect effects similar to those which we have found to follow from such objects. And though none but a fool or madman will ever pretend to dispute the authority of experience, or to reject that great guide of human life, it may surely be allowed a philosopher to have so much curiosity at least as to examine the principle of human nature, which gives this mighty authority to experience, and makes us draw advantage from that similarity which nature has placed among different objects. From causes which appear *similar* we expect similar effects. This is the sum of all our experimental conclusions. Now it seems evident that, if this conclusion were formed by reason, it would be as perfect at first, and upon one instance, as after ever so long a course of experience. But the case is far otherwise. Nothing so like as eggs; yet no one, on account of this appearing similarity, expects the same taste and relish in all of them. It is only after a long course of uniform experiments in any kind, that we attain a firm reliance and security with regard to a particular event. Now where is that process of reasoning which, from one instance, draws a conclusion, so different from that which it infers from a hundred instances that are nowise different from that single one? This question I propose as much for the sake of information, as with an intention of raising difficulties. I cannot find, I cannot imagine any such reasoning. But I keep my mind still open to instruction, if any one will vouchsafe to bestow it on me.

Should it be said that, from a number of uniform experiments, we *infer* a connexion between the sensible qualities and the secret powers; this, I must confess, seems the same difficulty, couched in different terms. The question still recurs, on what process of argument this *inference* is founded? Where is the medium, the interposing ideas, which join propositions so very wide of each other? It is confessed that the colour, consistence, and other sensible qualities of bread appear not, of themselves, to have any connexion with the secret powers of nourishment and support. For otherwise we could infer these secret powers from the first appearance of these sensible qualities, without the aid of experience; contrary to the sentiment of all philosophers, and contrary to plain matter of fact. Here, then, is our natural state of ignorance

with regard to the powers and influence of all objects. How is this remedied by experience? It only shows us a number of uniform effects, resulting from certain objects, and teaches us that those particular objects, at that particular time, were endowed with such powers and forces. When a new object, endowed with similar sensible qualities, is produced, we expect similar powers and forces, and look for a like effect. From a body of like colour and consistence with bread we expect like nourishment and support. But this surely is a step or progress of the mind, which wants to be explained. When a man says, *I have found, in all past instances, such sensible qualities conjoined with such secret powers:* And when he says, *Similar sensible qualities will always be conjoined with similar secret powers,* he is not guilty of a tautology, nor are these propositions in any respect the same. You say that the one proposition is an inference from the other. But you must confess that the inference is not intuitive; neither is it demonstrative: Of what nature is it, then? To say it is experimental, is begging the question. For all inferences from experience suppose, as their foundation, that the future will resemble the past, and that similar powers will be conjoined with similar sensible qualities. If there be any suspicion that the course of nature may change, and that the past may be no rule for the future, all experience becomes useless, and can give rise to no inference or conclusion. It is impossible, therefore, that any arguments from experience can prove this resemblance of the past to the future; since all these arguments are founded on the supposition of that resemblance. Let the course of things be allowed hitherto ever so regular; that alone, without some new argument or inference, proves not that, for the future, it will continue so. In vain do you pretend to have learned the nature of bodies from your past experience. Their secret nature, and consequently all their effects and influence, may change, without any change in their sensible qualities. This happens sometimes, and with regard to some objects: Why may it not happen always, and with regard to all objects? What logic, what process of argument secures you against this supposition? My practice, you say, refutes my doubts. But you mistake the purport of my question. As an agent, I am quite satisfied in the point; but as a philosopher, who has some share of curiosity, I will not say scepticism, I want to learn the foundation of this inference. No reading, no enquiry has yet been able to remove my difficulty, or give me satisfaction in a matter of such importance. Can I do better than propose the difficulty to the public, even though, perhaps, I have small hopes of obtaining a solution? We shall at least, by this means, be sensible of our ignorance, if we do not augment our knowledge.

I must confess that a man is guilty of unpardonable arrogance who concludes, because an argument has escaped his own investigation, that therefore it does not really exist. I must also confess that, though all the learned, for several ages, should have employed themselves in fruitless search upon any subject, it may still, perhaps, be rash to conclude positively that the subject must, therefore, pass all human comprehension. Even though we examine all the sources of our knowledge, and conclude them unfit for such a subject, there may still remain a suspicion, that the enumeration is not complete, or the examination not accurate. But with regard to the present subject, there are some considerations which seem to remove all this accusation of arrogance or suspicion of mistake.

It is certain that the most ignorant and stupid peasants—nay infants, nay even brute beasts—improve by experience, and learn the qualities of natural objects, by observing the effects which result from them. When a child has felt the sensation of pain from touching the flame of a candle, he will be careful not to put his hand near any candle; but will expect a similar effect from a cause which is similar in its sensible qualities and appearance. If you assert, therefore, that the understanding of the child is led into this conclusion by any process of argument or ratiocination, I may justly require you to produce that argument; nor have you any pretence to refuse so equitable a demand. You cannot say that the argument is abstruse, and may possibly escape your enquiry; since you confess that it is obvious to the capacity of a mere infant. If you hesitate, therefore, a moment, or if, after reflection, you produce any intricate or profound argument, you, in a man-

ner, give up the question, and confess that it is not reasoning which engages us to suppose the past resembling the future, and to expect similar effects from causes which are, to appearance, similar. This is the proposition which I intended to enforce in the present section. If I be right, I pretend not to have made any mighty discovery. And if I be wrong, I must acknowledge myself to be indeed a very backward scholar; since I cannot now discover an argument which, it seems, was perfectly familiar to me long before I was out of my cradle.

Sceptical Solution of These Doubts
Part I

. . . Nature will always maintain her rights, and prevail in the end over any abstract reasoning whatsoever. Though we should conclude, for instance, as in the foregoing section, that, in all reasonings from experience, there is a step taken by the mind which is not supported by any argument or process of the understanding; there is no danger that these reasonings, on which almost all knowledge depends, will ever be affected by such a discovery. If the mind be not engaged by argument to make this step, it must be induced by some other principle of equal weight and authority; and that principle will preserve its influence as long as human nature remains the same. What that principle is may well be worth the pains of enquiry.

Suppose a person, though endowed with the strongest faculties of reason and reflection, to be brought on a sudden into this world; he would, indeed, immediately observe a continual succession of objects, and one event following another; but he would not be able to discover anything farther. He would not, at first, by any reasoning, be able to reach the idea of cause and effect; since the particular powers, by which all natural operations are performed, never appear to the senses; nor is it reasonable to conclude, merely because one event, in one instance, precedes another, that therefore the one is the cause, the other the effect. Their conjunction may be arbitrary and casual. There may be no reason to infer the existence of one from the appearance of the other. And in a word, such a person, without more experience, could never employ his conjecture of reasoning concerning any matter of fact, or be assured of anything beyond what was immediately present to his memory and senses.

Suppose, again, that he has acquired more experience, and has lived so long in the world as to have observed familiar objects or events to be constantly conjoined together; what is the consequence of this experience? He immediately infers the existence of one object from the appearance of the other. Yet he has not, by all his experience, acquired any idea or knowledge of the secret power by which the one object produces the other; nor is it, by any process of reasoning, he is engaged to draw this inference. But still he finds himself determined to draw it: And though he should be convinced that his understanding has no part in the operation, he would nevertheless continue in the same course of thinking. There is some other principle which determines him to form such a conclusion.

This principle is Custom or Habit. For wherever the repetition of any particular act or operation produces a propensity to renew the same act or operation, without being impelled by any reasoning or process of the understanding, we always say, that this propensity is the effect of *Custom*. By employing that word, we pretend not to have given the ultimate reason of such a propensity. We only point out a principle of human nature, which is universally acknowledged, and which is well known by its effects. Perhaps we can push our enquiries no farther, or pretend to give the cause of this cause; but must rest contented with it as the ultimate principle, which we can assign, of all our conclusions from experience. It is sufficient satisfaction, that we can go so far, without repining at the narrowness of our faculties because they will carry us no farther. And it is certain we here advance a very intelligible proposition at least, if not a true one, when we assert that, after the constant conjunction of two objects—heat and flame, for instance, weight and solidity—we are determined by custom alone to expect the one from the appearance of the other. This hypothesis seems even the only one which explains the difficulty, why we draw, from a thousand instances, an inference which we are not able to draw from one instance, that is, in no respect, different from them. Reason is incapable of any such variation. The conclusions which it draws from considering one circle are the same which it would form upon surveying all the circles in the universe. But no man, having seen only one body move after being impelled by another, could infer that every other body will move after a like impulse. All inferences from experience, therefore, are effects of custom, not of reasoning.

Custom, then, is the great guide of human life. It is that principle alone which renders our experience useful to us, and makes us expect, for the future, a similar train of events with those which have appeared in the past. Without the influence of custom, we should be entirely ignorant of every matter of fact beyond what is immediately present to the memory and senses. We should never know how to adjust means to ends, or to employ our natural powers in the production of any effect. There would be an end at once of all action, as well as of the chief part of speculation.

But here it may be proper to remark, that though our conclusions from experience carry us beyond our memory and senses, and assure us of matters of fact which happened in the most distant places and most remote ages, yet some fact must always be present to the senses or memory, from which we may first proceed in drawing these conclusions. A man, who should find in a desert country the remains of pompous buildings, would conclude that the country had, in ancient times, been cultivated by civilized inhabitants; but did nothing of this nature occur to him, he could never form such an inference. We learn the events of former ages from history; but then we must peruse the volumes in which this instruction is contained, and thence carry up our inferences from one testimony to another, till we arrive at the eyewitnesses and spectators of these distant events. In a word, if we proceed not upon some fact, present to the memory or senses, our reasonings would be merely hypothetical; and however the particular links might be connected with each other, the whole chain of inferences would have nothing to support it, nor could we ever, by its means, arrive at the knowledge of any real existence. If I ask why you believe any particular matter of fact, which you relate, you must tell me some reason; and this reason will be some other fact, connected with it. But as you cannot proceed after this manner, *in infinitum,* you must at last terminate in some fact, which is present to your memory or senses; or must allow that your belief is entirely without foundation.

What, then, is the conclusion of the whole matter? A simple one; though, it must be confessed, pretty remote from the common theories of philosophy. All belief of matter of fact or real existence is derived merely from some object, present to the memory or senses, and a customary conjunction between that and some other object. Or in other words; having found, in many instances, that any two kinds of objects—flame and heat, snow and cold—have always been conjoined together; if flame or snow be presented anew to the senses, the mind is carried by custom to expect heat or cold, and to *believe* that such a quality does exist, and will discover itself upon a nearer approach. This be-

lief is the necessary result of placing the mind in such circumstances. It is an operation of the soul, when we are so situated, as unavoidable as to feel the passion of love, when we receive benefits; or hatred, when we meet with injuries. All these operations are a species of natural instincts, which no reasoning or process of the thought and understanding is able either to produce or to prevent.

Questions on Hume

1. Distinguish between "relations of ideas" and "matters of fact." How do we obtain knowledge of matters of fact according to Hume?
2. Why does Hume think that we cannot be certain about matters of fact or causal relations? Try to reconstruct Hume's argument. Has he convinced you? Explain your answer.
3. Explain Hume's "sceptical solution." Is it acceptable or not? What is your view?

Max Black
The Justification of Induction

Max Black is Professor Emeritus of Philosophy at Cornell University.

The Importance of Induction

If a dog barks at me each time I pass by, I naturally expect him to bark again the next time he sees me. This is an example of *inductive reasoning* in its most primitive form. From knowledge about a *sample* of cases, those in which the dog has already barked, I draw a conclusion about a

From *Philosophy of Science Today,* edited by Sidney Morgenbesser. © 1967 by Basic Books, Inc. Reprinted by permission of Basic Books, Inc., Publishers.

case not included in that sample—I anticipate what will happen the next time.

Let us now take a more sophisticated example: On applying a lighted match to a scrap of cellophane, I find that it catches fire; I conclude that any similar piece of cellophane would also burn in a similar situation. Here we have an inference from what happened in *one case* to what would happen in *any* similar case. One last example: An entomologist finds that each examined beetle of a certain species has a green spot on its back and concludes that *all* beetles of that species will have the same marking.

Such familiar examples of inductive reasoning involve a transition from information about a given set of objects or situations to a conclusion about some wider, more inclusive, set. We might say that all of them consist of reasoning from *samples.* Let us therefore agree to understand by an inductive argument one in which the conclusion refers to at least one thing that is not referred to by the premises.

The simplest forms of inductive arguments, on whose correctness the more sophisticated ones ultimately depend, can be represented as follows: "Such and such A's are B; therefore another A is B" or again, "*Some A's* (selected in such and such a fashion) are B; therefore all A's are B." We need not consider ways of improving these formulas, since the problem of justifying induction remains essentially the same in all forms of inductive reasoning, whether primitive or sophisticated.

It has been held, very widely though not universally, that the use of inductive reasoning is a distinctive feature of scientific method, integrally connected with the discovery of scientific laws and generalizations. In strict *deductive* reasoning, we are limited to rearranging information about the data referred to in the premises, and never advance to knowledge about the hitherto unobserved; by means of inductive reasoning, however, we make the leap from "some" to "all"; from the known present to the predicted future; from the finite data of observation to laws covering all that will be and could be. The so-called "inductive leap" (from "some" to "any" and "all") seems indispensable in science no less than in ordinary life.

Indeed, the very language we use to refer to persons and material objects implies a belief in the permanence of objects and the continuity of their properties that can be grounded only in inductive reasoning from experience. There can be no serious question of human beings rejecting inductive reasoning as unsound: to do so would be tantamount to destroying the very language we use to talk about the universe and about ourselves and would lead to the kind of last-ditch scepticism that lacks even the words to express itself.

Doubts About Induction

It is altogether reasonable to wonder how the use of this powerful method of reasoning can be justified. Indeed, certain features of inductive argument, as we have defined it, can easily awaken serious disquiet. In logic, we have all been taught that the transition from a "some" in the premises to an "all" in the conclusion is a transparent fallacy: if some men are white-skinned, it by no means follows that *all* men are; how, then, can we be justified in wholesale violation of this plain and simple rule? Again, induc-

tions are notoriously fallible; the gambler who expects a sequence of reds on the roulette wheel to continue indefinitely will soon be undeceived. In our dealings with nature, are we in any stronger position than the gambler who has had a luck sequence of throws? Are we perhaps about to come to the end of our lucky guesses about nature? How can we possibly *know* that the sun will rise tomorrow?

For the sake of clarity, it is essential to distinguish such sweeping sceptical doubts from practical questions about the reliability of inductive procedures. It is one thing to ask whether a given inductive procedure is sufficiently reliable for a given purpose; different and more basic questions are at issue when we ask how *any* inductive argument can be justified. We have well-tested methods for discriminating random events, such as those that occur on a roulette table, from lawful ones: where practical decision is in question, it would be foolish to consider the contingency that the sun might *not* rise the next day. On the other hand, in cases where inductive conclusions based upon sampling are relatively unreliable, we know in principle how to improve the reliability of the sampling process. There is no difficulty in principle about meeting any practical criticism of a given inductive procedure.

By contrast, the question of justification raised by the philosopher is one of the utmost generality. He is perplexed to understand how *any* inductive reasoning, no matter how satisfactory by the standards of common sense or of good statistical practice, can really count as acceptable. He finds it hard to understand how the "inductive leap," which seems to involve a plain logical fallacy, could *ever* be justified. The problem has no immediate bearing upon scientific practice, but is of the first importance for evaluating the claims of science to be a vehicle of truth about the universe. It seems that unless induction can be justified, our claims to have scientific *knowledge* must be rejected as unfounded and science will have to count as no better than any other unsubstantiated *faith*. However appealing such a sceptical conclusion might be to those who welcome any proof of man's impotence, it is one to be accepted only after the most careful investigation.

Five Attempted Solutions

In the course of the intensive consideration that philosophers of science have given to this problem, almost every conceivable answer has been defended.

1. Perhaps the most drastic solution available consists of a denial that induction plays, or ought to play, any part in scientific method. This view has been most eloquently defended in recent times by Professor Karl Popper, who has argued in numerous writings that the proper business of science is the *deductive testing* of empirical hypotheses. According to him, there is no rational way of arriving at generalizations from the examination of sampled cases—no rational way of making the inductive leap—but once such a generalization has been produced, by whatever means, there *is* a rational way of discovering whether it meets the tests of observation and experiment. Such generalizations or hypotheses can be conclusively *falsified*, but never verified, never shown to be true. The task of empirical science is falsification, putting to the trial of experience bold "conjectures" about the world, and not the impossible task of discovering truth.

For all the ingenuity with which this provocative view has been argued (to which I cannot do justice in this brief essay), the "no induction" view, as it might be called, has not received wide acceptance. It seems too paradoxical a conception of science that it should consist only of the elimination of error, rather than the progressive discovery of approximations to the truth. And induction seems to creep in by the back door in Popper's theory of "corroboration," that is, of the criteria by which we discriminate between the relative strengths of hypotheses, none of which are falsified by the known observational facts.

2. One might think that common sense can provide a simple and satisfactory answer to the problem of induction. If a layman is asked why he trusts an inductive argument from "some" to "all," the chances are he will say that this kind of argument has "always worked in the past." (One might have some doubts about that "always," but no matter.) How foolish it would be, we can imagine the plain man saying, to abandon techniques that have worked so well and have pro-

duced such spectacular successes in technology and in pure science. Well, let it be granted that induction *has* "worked" in the past; what grounds does this give us for expecting it to work in the future? If we conclude that induction *will* work because it *has* worked we are arguing—inductively!

As the philosopher David Hume pointed out long ago in a famous discussion of the problem, we seem here to be begging the question. The best method we have for settling specific empirical questions—arguing from the known character of observed instances—leaves us in the lurch when we try to find a *general* justification of induction. To offer an inductive justification to anybody who doubts that induction is *ever* justified is obviously futile. (On the other hand, some modern writers have argued, with some success, that inductive arguments can be applied to themselves, in order to improve their own reliability. It is at any rate not obvious that any objectionable circularity is here involved. The status of such so-called "self-supporting" inductive arguments is still controversial. In any case, self-supporting arguments, even if allowed to be sound, have no direct bearing on the general problem of justification.)

3. A favorite approach to the problem of justification begins by asserting that inductive arguments, in the form considered in this essay, are basically *incomplete*. Transition from "some" to "all," from a premise about a sample to a conclusion about the population from which that sample was drawn, is held to rely upon unstated *assumptions*. Until such assumptions are made explicit, the inductive inference is unsound—the inductive *leap* is never justified by itself: an inductive argument needs an extra premise in order to become valid. There needs to be supplied some principle that "the future will resemble the past" or some more general principle of "the Uniformity of Nature." Once such a principle has been introduced into the argument, and only then, that argument will become logically respectable. (It will be noticed that this line of attack on the problem tacitly assumes that only *deductive* argument is irreproachable. By implicity denying the possibility of distinctive inductive arguments, this position resembles the "no induction" view previously mentioned.)

The formulation of general principles that might plausibly play the part of missing premises in inductive arguments is a matter of great difficulty. Since nature obviously exhibits variety as well as uniformity, irregularity as well as order, it is hard to state a principle of uniformity without producing something that is plainly false. For example, the principle that *whenever* some A's are B, all A's are B is a grotesque overstatement. And even such a sophisticated version as John Maynard Keynes's famous principle of the "Limitation of Independent Variety" has been subjected to damaging criticism. It seems fair to say that nobody has yet produced a suitably qualified candidate for the title of the "Basic Principle of Inductive Inference"—although many have tried.

We need not enter into the technicalities of this attempt to bolster induction by supplying an additional grand premise. There is in my opinion a conclusive objection against this whole line of approach. Imagine the desired general principle produced: then it will be either *a priori* true or contingently true. If the first, it is a necessary truth, holding independently of the facts, like a logical or mathematical principle. But then it cannot support the transition from "some" to "all." It is easy to see that if the conclusion of an inductive argument does not *follow* deductively from the premises, the case is not altered when a necessary truth is added to the premises. But if the proposed principle is contingently true, it would not hold in all possible worlds, but must formulate something true of *our* universe.

How then is its truth to be known? Only, it seems, by the familiar methods, the best we know, of observation and inductive reasoning. Indeed, we may go further: our confidence in particular laws of nature, the conclusions of inductive inferences, is *better* grounded than our confidence in the truth of any alleged principle about the general uniformity of nature. Such evidence as we have for the orderliness of the universe is derived from our knowledge of particular regularities and not vice versa. The search for grand principles of induction therefore merely shifts the problem without solving it: the problem of establishing such principles is

just the old one of justifying induction—in another and even less tractable form.

4. So far, I have made no reference to probability, in order to avoid complicating what is already a sufficiently complicated subject. Yet problems of induction and of probability are intertwined. It is important to notice, for instance, that the conclusion of a sound inductive argument follows from its premises only with a certain probability. Given a good inductive argument for some conclusion, we can always conceive of *stronger* evidence: inductive inferences can sometimes be compared with respect to their relative strengths in a way that would be quite inappropriate for deductive inferences. Some students of the theory of induction have therefore held that a reference to probability should be part of the conclusion of a properly expressed inductive argument. For instance, the correct conclusion from the premise "All examined A's have been B," they say, is not "All A's are B," but perhaps, "It is more probable than not that all A's are B" or something similar. And the suggestion has often been made that neglect of such reference to probability is responsible for the inadequacy of the attempts to justify induction that we have so far considered.

Replacing a conclusion of the form "All A's are B" by a conclusion of the form "It is more probable than not that all A's are B" amounts to weakening the conclusion. (We may recall here that those who hoped to add an extra premise concerning the uniformity of nature were engaged in strengthening the premises. So both lines of attack aim at bringing inductive arguments closer to satisfying the standards of valid deductive argument.)

Our verdict on this attempt to make induction respectable by introducing probability must depend upon the meaning we attach to the relevant probability statement. According to one conception of the meaning of probability, the conclusion "It is more probable than not that all A's are B" follows *strictly* from the premise "All examined A's have been B": it is logically impossible that the premise should be true while the probability conclusion is false. On this interpretation, we would have a valid deductive argument, with no "inductive leap," if we introduced reference to probability into the conclusion. But this reading of inductive arguments is useless: our whole attempt has been to understand how it is possible to end in a conclusion that goes beyond the premises, by referring to things or situations that are not covered by those premises. Replacing the original inductive argument by some deductive substitute, however ingeniously constructed, will not be a solution.

There is another way of understanding probability, according to which the probability conclusion makes a genuinely empirical claim about what would be found true in a large number of similar cases. To say that the conclusion is "It is more probable than not that all A's are B" would be tantamount to saying something like "In most cases in which the examined A's have been B, it will be found subsequently that all A's are B." On this view, the argument, as amended by explicit references to probability, remains genuinely inductive. But by the same token we are confronted once again with the inductive leap. The new conclusion does not follow strictly from the premises, and we are still faced with the troublesome problem of how it can be rational to go beyond the evidence, in the manner that is characteristic of genuinely inductive arguments.

Those who insist that the conclusions of inductive arguments should be probability statements are faced with the same dilemma that bedevils all previous attempts to justify induction: either the argument is left in its original form, and then it seems to be invalid; or else it is replaced by some valid deductive argument (either by strengthening the premises or by weakening the conclusion), and then it is not an inductive argument at all.

5. I turn, finally, to the so-called "pragmatic" justifications of induction, which have seemed to many modern students of the problem to provide a satisfactory answer to this ancient puzzle. The basic ideas underlying this approach were independently formulated by Charles Sanders Peirce and by Hans Reichenbach, the latter of whom argued the position with great ingenuity and pertinacity.

Consider the following familiar position in ordinary life. A doctor, who is treating a patient suffering from some serious disease, has reason to believe that the only chance of saving the patient's life is to perform a certain operation; suppose also that there is no guarantee of the operation's proving successful: if the doctor is right in thinking that the patient will die in any case if the operation is not performed, he is justified in operating. To put the matter in another way: If a *necessary condition* for saving the patient's life is performing the operation, then that operation is justified, even though the outcome is unknown and the risks are great. This might be called a case of "nothing to lose by trying"—resort to the dangerous operation may be a "forlorn hope," but it is a justifiable one.

Those who apply this idea to the justification of induction argue as follows: Hume was right when he said that it was impossible to argue from the present to the future, from the known to the unknown. The "inductive leap" cannot be justified in the way that philosophers and scientists have hoped. Nevertheless, we badly need knowledge ranging beyond our observations and nothing can prevent us from trying to obtain it. Suppose it could be shown that the *only way* to reach such knowledge is by following inductive procedures. Then we should be in the position of the doctor or the patient in the original example, with nothing to lose by trying. If following inductive procedures is a *necessary condition* for anticipating the unknown, we shall be practically or—as people say, "pragmatically"—justified in following that procedure.

We may agree that the general line of argument is plausible; its contribution to the problem of justifying induction will depend upon how successful its defenders are in showing that some kind of inductive procedure is a necessary condition for making correct generalizations about the unknown or the unobserved.

The model usually employed has approximately the following character: Suppose we are performing a series of observations and are interested in some property P. If in the first 100 trials we find that P has appeared in 65 cases, we assume provisionally that in the *long run* the proportion of favorable cases will be close to $65/100$. As we continue our trials, we may find, say, 87 favorable cases in the first 150 observation: we therefore correct our estimate and now expect the proportion of favorable cases to be near 85/150. We proceed in this same way: whenever we find that k out of l trials exhibit the property P, we provisionally assume that the proportion in the long run will be close to k/l.

Since there is no guarantee that the fractions we progressively find in this way will ultimately converge to a limit, our attempt to anticipate the overall character of the entire series of observations may be defeated after all. But *if* there is a limit (which we cannot know) this procedure of successive correction will eventually bring us close to the true value of that limit. We are justified in following the procedure, because we have nothing to lose. If the series of successive fractions is sufficiently irregular, *no* method of forecasting its ultimate character will be possible; while if it has the regularity of a convergent series, our method will bring us close to the desired answer sooner or later.

This idea is too ingenious and too complicated to be criticized in a few words. I have argued at length elsewhere that it fails. Some of the strongest objections that I and other critics have brought to light are technical ones, having to do with the impossibility, according to the pragmatic view, of preferring one method of estimation to another. But the basic objection is that the whole approach concedes too much to the sceptical critics of induction. Those who agree with Hume that *knowledge* of the unobserved is, strictly speaking, impossible, will always find themselves with empty hands at the conclusion of an inductive procedure, no matter how ingeniously they try to wriggle out of their predicament.

The Disappearance of the Problem

We seem now to have arrived at a stalemate. None of the ways of justifying induction that have been explored by a long line of able and acute thinkers seem to offer any prospects of success. Attempts to justify induction by using inductive procedures seem hopelessly circular; attempts to find principles expressing the alleged uniformity of nature simply raise the old questions in a new form; introducing probability statements does not help; and the fashionable "pragmatic" justifications really leave us helpless against sceptical objections to induction. Considering the intensity with which the problem has been studied, there is no hope that we shall do better where so many powerful intellects have labored in vain.

Now when we meet with a situation like this, there is usually reason to suppose that the nature of the problem has been misconceived, and that the apparently insurmountable difficulties arise from misunderstanding. The view is steadily gaining ground that this is the situation with regard to the celebrated problem of justifying induction.

The very notion of justification implies some *standard* of justification: to justify induction must be to show that that kind of reasoning satisfies some relevant criterion of what is regarded as reasonable. Now the long history of the subject shows that nearly everybody who has grappled with the problem has really had before his mind the standards of *deductive* reasoning: however widely the various attempts to justify induction differ, they all assume that the only really reputable mode of reasoning, the only "strict" method, is that in which the conclusion follows by logical necessity from the premises.

But induction, *by definition,* is not deduction: the idea of the so-called "inductive leap" is built into our conception of an inductive argument. To try to convert inductive arguments into deductive ones is as futile an attempt as that of the child who argued that a horse was really a cow— only without horns. The beginning of wisdom in this extremely complicated and controversial domain is therefore the recognition that no *general* justification of induction, of the sort that philosophers of science have hoped to uncover, is either possible or needed. What we *mean* by justifying a specific empirical generalization is an inductive demonstration, using principles that have been found to work in the kind of case in question, that the generalization is true or at least probable. When we try to apply this relatively definite notion of justification to induction itself, the very notion of justification becomes unclear.

It is not so much that we do not know how to justify induction as that we do not know and cannot imagine what we would *accept* as such a justification. Clarity, here—which cannot, of course, be achieved without the hardest intellectual labor—ought to result in the disappearance of the alleged "problem of induction." If this view is correct, as I hold it to be, the problem of induction will eventually be classified with such famous "insoluble" problems as that of squaring the circle or that of inventing perpetual-motion machines. And as in those famous cases, the quest for the impossible does not seem, from the long perspective of history, to have been futile. For the byproducts of serious investigation may be even more important that its ostensible goal. If our knowledge of the character of inductive procedures is as rich and

as sophisticated as it is today, no little of the credit must be assigned to those who have labored so long and so unsuccessfully at trying to justify induction.

Questions on Black

1. What is the problem with inductive reasoning as Black explains it?

2. Black reviews and rejects five different attempts to solve the problem. What is each solution and what is wrong with it according to Black?

3. How does Black propose to dissolve the problem or make it disappear? Is this approach satisfactory? Why or why not?

Suggested Readings

Many introductions to the theory of knowledge are available. A good place to start is A. J. Ayer, *The Problem of Knowledge* (Baltimore: Penguin Books, 1956). Another introductory book that is more difficult than Ayer is R. M. Chisholm, *Theory of Knowledge,* 2d ed. (Englewood Cliffs, NJ: Prentice-Hall, 1977).

There are also numerous anthologies covering the field. Recommended are Robert Ammerman and Marcus Singer, eds., *Belief, Knowledge, and Truth: Readings in the Theory of Knowledge* (New York: Scribners, 1970); Roderick M. Chisholm and Robert J. Swartz, eds., *Empirical Knowledge: Readings from Contemporary Sources* (Englewood Cliffs, NJ: Prentice-Hall, 1973); and Michael D. Roth and Leon Galis, eds., *Knowing* (New York: Random House, 1970).

For more commentary on Descartes see Willis Doney, ed., *Descartes: A Collection of Critical Essays* (Garden City, NY: Anchor Books, 1967) and Anthony Kenny, *Descartes: A Study of His Philosophy* (New York: Random House, 1968). Fred Feldman, *A Cartesian Introduction to Philosophy* (New York: McGraw-Hill, 1986) gives a very careful exposition and interpretation of Descartes' *Meditations.*

An introductory textbook that has a good discussion of the problems of perceptual knowledge is James Cornman and Keith Lehrer, *Philosophical Problems and Arguments: An Introduction* (New York: Macmillan, 1968).

Keith Lehrer's views on scepticism and knowledge can be found in his *Knowledge* (Oxford: Clarendon Press, 1974). Peter Unger defends scepticism in *Ignorance* (Oxford: Oxford University Press, 1975).

The classic critique of Locke's view (as Bertrand Russell says in the reading) is given by George Berkeley in his *Three Dialogues between Hylas and Philonous*, ed. Colin M. Turbayne (Indianapolis: Bobbs-Merrill, 1954). For more discussion on Berkeley see A. J. Ayer, *The Foundations of Empirical Knowledge* (London: Macmillan, 1940).

An anthology on attempts to solve Hume's problem is Richard Swinburne, ed., *The Justification of Induction* (Oxford: Oxford University Press, 1974). Wesley C. Salmon, "Unfinished Business: The Problem of Induction," *Philosophical Studies,* vol. 33 (1978) reviews different attempts to solve the problem of induction and claims that they all fail.

A recent discussion of the topics in this chapter is found in Robert Audi, *Belief, Justification and Knowledge* (Belmont, CA: Wadsworth, 1988).

The Freedom-Determinism Problem

Chapter 4

Introduction

The Freedom-Determinism Problem.   In the discussion on the freewill solution to the problem of evil in chapter 2, we noted that one objection is that human freedom seems to be incompatible with **determinism,** the view that every event is caused. This is the traditional freedom-determinism problem. But why is there an incompatibility, or least the appearance of one?

Determinism. To get the problem in focus, we need a better understanding of determinism. In science and everyday life, it is assumed that natural events are caused by physical conditions or events that occur before the event. For example, if the water in a car radiator freezes, most people would agree that this event is caused by the temperature in the radiator dropping below 32 degrees Fahrenheit. The assumption that every event is caused implies that there are causal laws covering every event. These laws would have the general form "If physical conditions or events C obtain, then event E will occur." Most scientists will agree that they know some laws of this form, for example, "If ice is put in water, it will float," and even if they have not yet discovered the most general basic laws that cover all events, they still assume that such laws can be discovered, at least in principle.

Besides assuming that events are caused, scientists also assume that events can be predicted in principle before they occur. If one knows the causal laws applying to an event, and the relevant causal events and conditions, the event can be predicted. To return to the uncontroversial example about the ice on the water, we know that if ice is put into water, it will float (that is one of the causal laws covering the event), and so if we put ice in water now, we can deduce that the ice will float.

Scientists do not think that they can in fact predict the occurrence of any given event. At the present stage of development in science, the causal laws covering all events are not known, nor is there a complete knowledge of all the antecedent physical events in the universe. But most scientists have believed that it is possible in principle to do this for any given event. (Many nuclear scientists would say that predictability is not possible at the subatomic level, but as B. F. Skinner points out in the readings, this does not mean that subatomic events are not caused.) To explain the possibility of predicting any event, the eighteenth-century astronomer Pierre Laplace imagined that there is an omniscient being, a Demon, who knows all the antecedent conditions for any given event, and all the causal laws for any such event. Given this knowledge the Laplacean Demon could predict the occurrence of any event before it occurs, even human events, for example, the candidate you will vote for in the next election. Or, if you prefer, you could imagine God predicting everything you will do before you do it. In fact, God's omniscience would allow God to know everything you will do for your whole life.

Hard Determinism.   Many behaviorial scientists believe that determinism applies to human behavior. After all, if every event can be causally explained and predicted, then human behavior must be included. In our first reading for this chapter, B. F. Skinner assumes human behavior is covered by causal laws just like any other event, and that human behavior can be predicted and controlled like other natural events. Skinner believes that determinism is incompatible with freedom, and specifically with the belief that humans have a free will, a will that operates without being caused to do so by any physical events or conditions.

The view that Skinner adopts is usually called **hard determinism.** This view asserts that (1) determinism is true and (2) determinism is incompatible with human freedom (the **incompatibility thesis**). It should be emphasized that it is possible to accept one of these assertions without the other. Some philosophers accept determinism and deny the incompatibility thesis (this is called **soft determinism**), and others reject determinism and accept the incompatibility thesis (this is part of the nondeterministic position.)

Hard determinists typically go on to argue that no one is morally responsible for his or her actions, and that no one deserves to be punished. This line of argument was used by Clarence Darrow, the famous trial lawyer, in the case of Loeb and Leopold. These two Chicago boys brutally murdered fourteen-year-old Bobbie Franks, a cousin of Loeb's. They both confessed before their trial, so the issue was not legal guilt, but how they should be punished—the death sentence or life imprisonment? In his defense, Darrow argued that the boys were helpless victims of their environment and heredity, that they were not morally responsible for what they did, and that they should not receive the death penalty. Darrow's plea was successful. The boys each received a life sentence; one died in prison, and the other was later paroled.

Soft Determinism.   Many philosophers have accepted the truth of determinism, but denied that it is incompatible with human freedom. They distinguish between freedom and freewill, and argue that even if determinism is incompatible with freewill, as B. F. Skinner says, this does not mean that it is incompatible with freedom. This position, called soft determinism, is defended in our readings by Kai Nielsen. As he explains it, soft determinists maintain that determinism and human freedom are logically compatible, and they agree with hard determinists that every human action has a cause in the sense of there being sufficient conditions for its occurrence. But the fact that an action is caused does not mean that it cannot be free. An action of a given agent A is free, according to Nielsen, if (1) A could have done otherwise if A had chosen to, (2) A's actions are voluntary in the sense that the kleptomaniac's stealing is not, and (3) nobody compelled A to choose.

Soft determinism has been attacked in several different ways. One line of criticism, based on **psychoanalytic theory**, is presented by John Hospers in our readings. Nielsen thinks that we can make a clear distinction between neurotic behavior that is not free, such as the kleptomaniac's stealing, and so-called voluntary behavior, such as a woman choosing to marry a man. But is such a distinction defensible? According to Hospers, even normal behavior is unconsciously motivated; thus the woman who keeps "choosing" to marry an abusive man is doing this because she is masochistic—she has an unconscious super-ego desire to punish herself—and her conscious reasons for her choices are merely rationalizations covering up the real unconscious causes. In Hosper's hard deterministic view, everyone's behavior is unconsciously motivated, and thus none of us have control over what we do or are morally responsible for our actions.

Another powerful criticism of soft determinism is developed by Richard Taylor in the last reading. The soft determinist like Nielsen assumes that volitions are something that people can control, that people can always choose differently, and thus that people can act otherwise than they did act. But a consistent soft determinist will have to admit that volitions are caused like anything else, and these causes may well be something over which the person has no control. Taylor imagines that a clever physiologist causes a person to have volitions simply by pushing various buttons on an instrument. In that case, we would hardly say that the person is free; this person is just a puppet of the physiologist, being moved about by volitions. Taylor thinks that this example refutes the soft determinist's position.

Nondeterminism.   A third position found in our readings is **nondeterminism.** This is the view that human beings are sometimes free when they act, that this freedom is incompatible with determinism, and consequently that determinism is false. There are two representatives of this position in our readings, C. A. Campbell and Richard Taylor. According to Campbell, the sort of freedom required for moral responsibility is what he calls **contra-causal freedom.** This freedom involves a break in the causal chain of events not allowed by determinism, and exists when a person "could have acted otherwise." But what does it mean to say that a person "could have acted otherwise"? Campbell rejects the hypothetical interpretation (adopted by Nielsen) that a person could have acted otherwise *if* she or he had chosen to. This amounts to saying that the person is merely free from external constraint. Instead Campbell defends what he calls the "categorical" interpretation of "could have acted otherwise," which posits an act of the will that is not caused by any other event. Campbell admits, however, that this contra-causal freedom is not always available, but can be found only in cases where there is a moral conflict between desire and duty.

Taylor's theory requires a special sort of causation, agent causation, in which the self or person is a substance that can cause events independent of external causes. According to this view, people are free agents when they cause their actions themselves without there being any other causes. This conflicts with determinism because it posits events—the person's free actions—that are not caused by antecedent events or conditions.

B. F. Skinner

Science and Human Behavior

B. F. Skinner is a contemporary psychologist who is one of the leading advocates of the movement in psychology known as behaviorism. He has written many books about behaviorism including Beyond Freedom and Dignity, About Behaviorism, *and* The Shaping of a Behaviorist.

Science as a Corrective

. . . The methods of science have been enormously successful wherever they have been tried. Let us then apply them to human affairs. We need not retreat in those sectors where science has already advanced. It is necessary only to bring our understanding of human nature up to the same point. Indeed, this may well be our only hope. If we can observe human behavior carefully from an objective point of view and come to understand it for what it is, we may be able to adopt a more sensible course of action. The need for establishing some such balance is now widely felt, and those who are able to control the direction of science are acting accordingly. It is understood that there is no point in

furthering a science of nature unless it includes a sizable science of human nature, because only in that case will the results be wisely used. It is possible that science has come to the rescue and that order will eventually be achieved in the field of human affairs.

The Threat to Freedom

There is one difficulty, however. The application of science to human behavior is not so simple as it seems. Most of those who advocate it are simply looking for "the facts." To them science is little more than careful observation. They want to evaluate human behavior as it really is rather than as it appears to be through ignorance or prejudice, and then to make effective decisions and move on rapidly to a happier world. But the way in which science has been applied in other fields shows that something more is involved. Science is not concerned just with "getting the facts," after which one may act with greater wisdom in an unscientific fashion. Science supplies its own wisdom. It leads to a new conception of a subject matter, a new way of thinking about that part of the world to which it has addressed itself. If we are to enjoy the advantages of science in the field of human affairs, we must be prepared to adopt the working model of behavior to which a science will inevitably lead. But very few of those who advocate the application of scientific method to current problems are willing to go that far.

Science is more than the mere description of events as they occur. It is an attempt to discover order, to show that certain events stand in lawful relations to other events. No practical technology can be based upon science until such relations have been discovered. But order is not only a possible end product; it is a working assumption which must be adopted at the very start. We cannot apply the methods of science to a subject matter which is assumed to move about capriciously. Science not only describes, it predicts. It deals not only with the past but with the future. Nor is prediction the last word: to the extent that relevant conditions can be altered, or otherwise controlled, the future can be controlled. If we are to use the methods of science in the field of human affairs, we must assume that behavior is lawful and determined. We must expect to discover that what a man does is the result of specifiable conditions and that once these conditions have been discovered, we can anticipate and to some extent determine his actions.

This possibility is offensive to many people. It is opposed to a tradition of long standing which regards man as a free agent, whose behavior is the product, not of specifiable antecedent conditions, but of spontaneous inner changes of course. Prevailing philosophies of human nature recognize an internal "will" which has the power of interfering with causal relationships and which makes the prediction and control of behavior impossible. To suggest that we abandon this view is to threaten many cherished beliefs—to undermine what appears to be a stimulating and productive conception of human nature. The alternative point of view insists upon recognizing coercive forces in human conduct which we may prefer to disregard. It challenges our aspirations, either worldly or otherworldly. Regardless of how much we stand to gain from supposing that human behavior is the proper subject matter of a science, no one who is a product of Western civilization can do so without a struggle. We simply do not want such a science.

Conflicts of this sort are not unknown in the history of science. When Aesop's lion was shown a painting in which a man was depicted killing a lion, he commented contemptuously, "The artist was obviously a man." Primitive beliefs about man and his place in nature are usually flattering. It has been the unfortunate responsibility of science to paint more realistic pictures. The **Copernican theory of the solar system** displaced man from his pre-eminent position at the center of things. Today we accept this theory without emotion, but originally it met with enormous resistance. Darwin challenged a practice of segregation in which man set himself firmly apart from the animals, and the bitter struggle which arose is not yet ended. But though Darwin put man in his biological place, he did not deny him a possible position as master. Special faculties or a special capacity for spontaneous, creative action might have emerged in the process of evolution. When that distinction is now questioned, a new threat arises.

There are many ways of hedging on the theoretical issue. It may be insisted that a science of human behavior is impossible, that behavior has certain essential features which forever keep it beyond the pale of science. But although this argument may dissuade many people from further inquiry, it is not likely to have any effect upon those who are willing to try and see. Another objection frequently offered is that science is appropriate up to a certain point, but that there must always remain an area in which one can act only on faith or with respect to a "value judgment": science may tell us *how* to deal with human behavior, but just *what* is to be done must be decided in an essentially nonscientific way. Or it may be argued that there is another kind of science which is compatible with doctrines of personal freedom. For example, the social sciences are sometimes said to be fundamentally different from the natural sciences and not concerned with the same kinds of lawfulness. Prediction and control may be forsworn in favor of "interpretation" or some other species of understanding. But the kinds of intellectual activities exemplified by value judgments or by intuition or interpretation have never been set forth clearly, nor have they yet shown any capacity to work a change in our present predicament.

The Practical Issue

Our current practices do not represent any well-defined theoretical position. They are, in fact, thoroughly confused. At times we appear to regard a man's behavior as spontaneous and responsible. At other times we recognize that inner determination is at least not complete, that the individual is not always to be held to account. We have not been able to reject the slowly accumulating evidence that circumstances beyond the individual are relevant. We sometimes exonerate a man by pointing to "extenuating circumstances." We no longer blame the uneducated for their ignorance or call the unemployed lazy. We no longer hold children wholly accountable for their delinquencies. "Ignorance of the law" is no longer wholly inexcusable: "Father, forgive them; for they know not what they do." The insane have long since been cleared of responsibility for their condition, and the kinds of neurotic or psychotic behavior to which we now apply this extenuation are multiplying.

But we have not gone all the way. We regard the common man as the product of his environment; yet we reserve the right to give personal credit to great men for their achievements. (At the same time we take a certain delight in proving that part of the output of even such men is due to the "influence" of other men or to some trivial circumstance in their personal history.) We want to believe that right-minded men are moved by valid principles even though we are willing to regard wrong-minded men as victims of erroneous propaganda. Backward peoples may be the fault of a poor culture, but we want to regard the elite as something more than the product of a good culture. Though we observe that Moslem children in general become Moslems while Christian children in general become Christians, we are not willing to accept an accident of birth as a basis for belief. We dismiss those who disagree with us as victims of ignorance, but we regard the promotion of our own religious beliefs as something more than the arrangement of a particular environment.

All of this suggests that we are in transition. We have not wholly abandoned the traditional philosophy of human nature; at the same time we are far from adopting a scientific point of view without reservation. We have accepted the assumption of determinism in part; yet we allow our sympathies, our first allegiances, and our personal aspirations to rise to the defense of the traditional view. We are currently engaged in a sort of patchwork in which new facts and methods are assembled in accordance with traditional theories.

If this were a theoretical issue only, we would have no cause for alarm; but theories affect practices. A scientific conception of human behavior dictates one practice, a philosophy of personal freedom another. Confusion in theory means confusion in practice. The present unhappy condition of the world may in large measure be traced to our vacillation. The principal issues in dispute between nations, both in peaceful assembly and on the battlefield, are intimately concerned with the problem of human freedom and control. Totalitarianism or democracy, the state or the individual, planned society or laissez-faire, the impression of cultures upon alien peoples, economic determinism, individual initiative, propaganda, education, ideological warfare—all concern the fundamental nature of human behavior. We shall almost certainly remain ineffective in solving these problems until we adopt a consistent point of view.

We cannot really evaluate the issue until we understand the alternatives. The traditional view of human nature in Western culture is well known. The conception of a free, responsible individual is embedded in our language and pervades our practices, codes, and beliefs. Given an example of human behavior, most people can describe it immediately in terms of such a conception. The practice is so natural that it is seldom examined. A scientific formulation, on the other hand, is new and strange. Very few people have any notion of the extent to which a science of human behavior is indeed possible. In what way can the behavior of the individual or of groups of individuals be predicted and controlled? What are laws of behavior like? What over-all conception of the human organism as a behaving system emerges? It is only when we have answered these questions, at least in a preliminary fashion, that we may consider the implications of a science of human behavior with respect to either a theory of human nature or the management of human affairs. . . .

Some Objections to a Science of Behavior

The report of a single event raises no theoretical problems and comes into no conflict with philosophies of human behavior. The scientific laws or systems which express uniformities are likely to conflict with theory because they claim the same territory. When a science of behavior reaches the point of dealing with lawful relationships, it meets the resistance of those who give their allegiance to prescientific or extrascientific conceptions. The resistance does not always take the form of an overt rejection of science. It may be transmuted into claims of limitations, often expressed in highly scientific terms.

It has sometimes been pointed out, for example, that physical science has been unable to maintain its philosophy of determinism, particularly at the subatomic level. The **Principle of Indeterminacy** states that there are circumstances under which the physicist cannot put himself in possession of all relevant information: if he chooses to observe one event, he must relinquish the possibility of observing another. In our present state of knowledge, certain events therefore appear to be unpredictable. It does not follow that these events are free or capricious. Since human behavior is enormously complex and the human organism is of limited dimensions, many acts may involve processes to which the Principle of Indeterminacy applies. It does not follow that behavior is free, but only that it may be beyond the range of a predictive or controlling science. Most students of behavior, however, would be willing to settle for the degree of prediction and control achieved by the physical sciences in spite of this limitation. A final answer to the problem of lawfulness is to be sought, not in the limits of any hypothetical mechanism within the organism, but in our ability to demonstrate lawfulness in the behavior of the organism as a whole.

A similar objection has a logical flavor. It is contended that reason cannot comprehend itself or—in somewhat more substantial terms—that the behavior required in understanding one's own behavior must be something beyond the behavior which is understood. It is true that knowledge is limited by the limitations of the knowing organism. The number of things in the world which might be known certainly exceeds the number of possible different states in all possible knowers. But the laws and systems of science are designed to make a knowledge of particular events unimportant. It is by no means necessary that one man should understand all the facts in a given field, but only that he should understand all the *kinds* of facts. We have no reason to suppose that the human intellect is incapable of formulating or comprehending the basic principles of human behavior—certainly not until we have a clearer notion of what those principles are.

The assumption that behavior is a lawful scientific datum sometimes meets with another objection. Science is concerned with the general, but the behavior of the individual is necessarily unique. The "case history" has a richness and flavor which are in decided contrast with general principles. It is easy to convince oneself that there are two distinct worlds and that one is beyond the reach of science. This distinction is not peculiar to the study of behavior. It can always be made in the early stages of any science, when it is not clear what we may deduce from a general principle with respect to a particular case. What the science of physics has to say about the world is dull and colorless to the beginning student when compared with his daily experience, but he later discovers that it is actually a more incisive account of even the single instance. When we wish to deal effectively with the single instance, we turn to science for help. The argument will lose cogency as a science of behavior progresses and as the implications of its general laws become clear. A comparable argument against the possibility of a science of medicine has already lost its significance. In *War and Peace*, Tolstoy wrote of the illness of a favorite character as follows:

Doctors came to see Natasha, both separately and in consultation. They said a great deal in French, in German, and in Latin. They criticised one another, and prescribed the most diverse remedies for all the diseases they were familiar with. But it never occurred to one of them to make the simple reflection that they could not understand the disease from which Natasha was suffering, as no single disease can be fully understood in a living person; for every living person has his

individual peculiarities and always has his own
peculiar, new, complex complaints unknown to
medicine—not a disease of the lungs, of the kidneys, of
the skin, of the heart, and so on, as described in medical
books, but a disease that consists of one out of the
innumerable combinations of ailments of those organs.

Tolstoy was justified in calling every sickness a unique event. Every action of the individual is unique, as well as every event in physics and chemistry. But his objection to a science of medicine in terms of uniqueness was unwarranted. The argument was plausible enough at the time; no one could then contradict him by supplying the necessary general principles. But a great deal has happened in medical science since then, and today few people would care to argue that a disease cannot be described in general terms or that a single case cannot be discussed by referring to factors common to many cases. The intuitive wisdom of the old-style diagnostician has been largely replaced by the analytical procedures of the clinic, just as a scientific analysis of behavior will eventually replace the personal interpretation of unique instances.

A similar argument is leveled at the use of statistics in a science of behavior. A prediction of what the *average* individual will do is often of little or no value in dealing with a particular individual. The actuarial tables of life-insurance companies are of no value to a physician in predicting the death or survival of a particular patient. This issue is still alive in the physical sciences, where it is associated with the concepts of causality and probability. It is seldom that the science of physics deals with the behavior of individual molecules, atoms, or subatomic particles. When it is occasionally called upon to do so, all the problems of the particular event arise. In general a science is helpful in dealing with the individual only insofar as its laws refer to individuals. A science of behavior which concerns only the behavior of groups is not likely to be of help in our understanding of the particular case. But a science may also deal with the behavior of the individual, and its success in doing so must be evaluated in terms of its achievements rather than any a priori contentions.

The extraordinary complexity of behavior is sometimes held to be an added source of difficulty. Even though behavior may be lawful, it may be too complex to be dealt with in terms of law. Sir Oliver Lodge once asserted that "though an astronomer can calculate the orbit of a planet or comet or even a meteor, although a physicist can deal with the structure of atoms, and a chemist with their possible combinations, neither a biologist nor any scientific man can calculate the orbit of a common fly." This is a statement about the limitations of scientists or about their aspirations, not about the suitability of a subject matter. Even so, it is wrong. It may be said with some assurance that if no one has calculated the orbit of a fly, it is only because no one has been sufficiently interested in doing so. The tropistic movements of many insects are now fairly well understood, but the instrumentation needed to record the flight of a fly and to give an account of all the conditions affecting it would cost more than the importance of the subject justifies. There is, therefore, no reason to conclude, as the author does, that "an incalculable element of self-determination thus makes its appearance quite low down the animal scale." Self-determination does not follow from complexity. Difficulty in calculating the orbit of the fly does not prove capriciousness, though it may make it impossible to prove anything else. The problems imposed by the complexity of a subject matter must be dealt with as they arise. Apparently hopeless cases often become manageable in time. It is only recently that any sort of lawful account of the weather has been possible. We often succeed in reducing complexity to a reasonable degree by simplifying conditions in the laboratory; but where this is impossible, a statistical analysis may be used to achieve an inferior, but in many ways acceptable, prediction. Certainly no one is prepared to say now what a science of behavior can or cannot accomplish eventually. Advance estimates of the limits of science have generally proved inaccurate. The issue is in the long run pragmatic: we cannot tell until we have tried.

Still another objection to the use of scientific method in the study of human behavior is that behavior is an anomalous subject matter because a prediction made about it may alter it. If we tell a friend that he is going to buy a particular kind of car, he may react to our prediction by buying a different kind. The same effect has been used to explain the failures of public opinion polls. In the presidential election of 1948 it was confidently predicted that a majority of the voters would vote for a candidate who, as it turned out, lost the election. It has been asserted that the electorate reacted to the prediction in a contrary way and that the published prediction therefore had an effect upon the predicted event. But it is by no means necessary that a prediction of behavior be permitted to affect the behaving individual. There may have been practical reasons why the results of the poll in question could not be withheld until after the election, but this would not be the case in a purely scientific endeavor.

There are other ways in which observer and observed interact. Study distorts the thing studied. But there is no special problem here peculiar to human behavior. It is now accepted as a general principle in scientific method that it is necessary to interfere in some degree with any phenomenon in the act of observing it. A scientist may have an effect upon behavior in the act of observing or analyzing it, and he must certainly take this effect into account. But behavior may also be observed with a minimum of interaction between subject and scientist, and this is the case with which one naturally tries to begin.

A final objection deals with the practical application of a scientific analysis. Even if we assume that behavior is lawful and that the methods of science will reveal the rules which govern it, we may be unable to make any technological use of these rules unless certain conditions can be brought under control. In the laboratory many conditions are simplified and irrelevant conditions often eliminated. But of what value are laboratory studies if we must predict and control behavior where a comparable simplification is impossible? It is true that we can gain control over behavior only insofar as we can control the factors responsible for it. What a scientific study does is to enable us to make optimal use of the control we possess. The labora-

tory simplification reveals the relevance of factors which we might otherwise overlook.

We cannot avoid the problems raised by a science of behavior by simply denying that the necessary conditions can be controlled. In actual fact there is a considerable degree of control over many relevant conditions. In penal institutions and military organizations the control is extensive. We control the environment of the human organism in the nursery and in institutions which care for those to whom the conditions of the nursery remain necessary in later life. Fairly extensive control of conditions relevant to human behavior is maintained in industry in the form of wages and conditions of work, in schools in the form of grades and conditions of work, in commerce by anyone in possession of goods or money, by governmental agencies through the police and military, in the psychological clinic through the consent of the controllee, and so on. A degree of effective control, not so easily identified, rests in the hands of entertainers, writers, advertisers, and propagandists. These controls, which are often all too evident in their practical application, are more than sufficient to permit us to extend the results of a laboratory science to the interpretation of human behavior in daily affairs—for either theoretical or practical purposes. Since a science of behavior will continue to increase the effective use of this control, it is now more important than ever to understand the processes involved and to prepare ourselves for the problems which will certainly arise.

Questions on Skinner

1. How does Skinner characterize science? How can science be applied to human behavior?

2. Skinner replies to a number of objections to the science of human behavior. Has he persuaded you that a science of human behavior is possible? Explain your answer.

3. If Skinner is right, what does this imply for moral responsibility and punishment?

Kai Nielsen
The Compatibility of Freedom and Determinism

Kai Nielsen is Professor of Philosophy at the University of Calgary.

I

. . . What I now wish to consider is what I take to be the most significant question we can ask about determinism and human conduct: Is determinism compatible with our central beliefs concerning the freedom of conduct and moral responsibility? It was because they thought that such beliefs were plainly incompatible that Dostoyevski and James were so nagged by determinism. With such philosophers as Thomas Hobbes, David Hume, John Stuart Mill, Moritz Schlick, and A. J. Ayer—all staunch defenders of the **compatibility thesis**—there is a vast shift not only in argument but also in attitude. There is no *Angst* over the ubiquitousness of causal laws. There is no feeling that life would be meaningless and man would be a prisoner of his past if determinism were true. Holbach is wrong. Even if determinism is true, freedom is not an illusion. The belief that it is an illusion is a philosophical confusion resting on a failure to pay sufficiently close attention either to the actual role of our concept of freedom in our lives or to the actual nature of determinism. It is such a twin failure that generates the conflicts we have been investigating.

The crucial point to note initially is that Mill and Schlick, as much as Holbach and Darrow, are thoroughgoing determinists. But they are determinists who do not believe that freedom and determinism are incompatible. James dismissed this position contemptuously with the label 'soft determinism'. For him 'soft deter-

minism' had an emotive force similar to 'soft on Communism'. But while a summer bachelor is no bachelor at all, a soft determinist is just as much a determinist as a hard determinist. I shall continue to use the label 'soft determinism'— although I shall not use it in any derogatory sense—to refer to the view that maintains that determinism and human freedom are logically compatible. (Sometimes in the literature they are called "compatibilists'.) A view such as Holbach's or Darrow's, which Schlick says rests on "a whole series of confusions," I shall call 'hard determinism'. (Sometimes in the literature 'hard determinists' are called 'incompatibilists', for they believe freedom and determinism are incompatible.) But both hard and soft determinists agree that every event or state, including every human action or attitude, has a cause; that is, for anything whatsoever there are sufficient conditions for its occurrence.

The at least *prima facie* surprising thing is that these soft-determinists still believe in the freedom of conduct and believe that human beings are—at least sometimes, anyway— responsible moral agents capable of acting in specific situations in ways other than those in which they in fact acted. Let us see how the soft determinist argument unfolds.

II

Morality, soft determinists argue, has or should have no interest in the determinism/indeterminism controversy. Morality is indeed vitally interested in the freedom of conduct, for it only makes sense to say that men ought to do one thing rather than another on the assumption that sometimes they can do other than what they in fact do. If no man can do other than what he does in fact do, then all talk of what men ought to do or what is right and wrong is indeed senseless.[1] But to be interested in the freedom of conduct, as morality properly is, is not at all to be interested in some mysterious and no doubt illusory 'freedom of the will'. 'Freedom' has its opposite, 'compulsion' or 'coercion.' A man is free if he does not act under compulsion. He is free when he is able to do what he wants to do or when his acts and actions are in accordance with his own choices and decisions, and when what he wants to do or what he chooses is not determined by some person, force, or some disposition, such as kleptomania, which has gained ascendency over him. He is, by contrast, unfree to the extent that he is unable to achieve what he wants to achieve and to act in accordance with choices based on his own rational deliberation because of either outside influence or psychological malaise. 'Freedom' does not mean some scarcely intelligible state of affairs, 'exemption or partial exemption from causal law' or 'breach of causal continuity'. To be free is to have the ability and opportunity to do what one wants to do and to act in accordance with one's own rational deliberations, without constraint and compulsion. It is something which, of course, admits of degrees.

Mill, Schlick, and Ayer argue that an anthropomorphic view of our language tricks us into thinking that man cannot be free if determinism is true. People tend to think that if determinism is true, events are in the power of other events and a person's acts or actions cannot alter the course of events. What will happen in the future is already fixed by immutable causal laws. But such views rest on unrealistic, anthropomorphic thinking. They are scarcely a part of a tough-minded deterministic world perspective.

Similar anthropomorphic transformations are made with 'necessity' and the little word 'cause'. And this, too, leads to needless befuddlement by causing us to misunderstand the actual workings of our language. It is, for example, terribly easy for the unwary to confuse causal and logical necessitation. But there is a very considerable difference in the meaning of 'must' in 'If you cut off his head, he must die' and 'If it is a square, it must have four sides'. In the latter case—an example of logical necessitation—'having four sides' follows by virtue of the meaning of the term 'square'. The 'must' refers to this logical relationship. In the former case, it holds in virtue of something in the world. People also infer mistakenly that the event or effect is somehow contained in the cause. But this mystification is hardly intelligible.

There is also, as Schlick points out, a persistent confusion between laws of nature and legal laws.[2] The word 'law' has very different meanings in such cases. Legal laws *prescribe* a certain course of action. Many of them are intended to constrain or coerce you into acting in a certain way. But laws of nature are not prescriptions to act in a certain way. They do not constrain you; rather, they are statements of regularities, of *de facto* invariable sequences that are parts of the world. In talking of such natural laws, we often bring in an uncritical use of 'force', as if the earth were being pushed and pulled around by the sun. Putting the matter this way makes one feel as if one is always being compelled or constrained, when in reality one is not. Without the anthropomorphic embellishment, it becomes evident that a determinist commits himself, when he asserts that *A* causes *B*, to the view that *whenever* an event or act of type *A* occurs, an event or act of type *B* will occur. The part about compulsion or constraint is metaphorical. It is because of the metaphor, and not because of the fact, that we come to think that there is an antithesis between causality and freedom. It is the *manner* here and not the *matter* that causes the trouble.

Demythologized and correctly conceived, causal necessity as applied to human actions is, Mill argues, simply this: Given the motives that are present to an individual's mind, and given the character and disposition of the individual, the manner in which he will act can be "unerringly inferred." That is to say, if we knew the person thoroughly, and knew all the inducements acting upon him, we could predict or retrodict his conduct with as much certainty as we can predict any physical event. This, Mill argues, is a bit of common sense and is in reality not in conflict with our operative concept of human freedom, for even if we say that all human acts are in principle predictable, this is not to say that people are acting under compulsion or constraint, for to say that their actions are predictable is not to say or even to give one to understand that they are being manipulated by anything or anybody. Being under some sort of compulsion or constraint is what limits our freedom.

III

The natural reaction to such a belief is this: If 'causal necessity' means anything, it means that no human being could, *categorically* could, do anything other in exactly similar circumstances than what he in fact does. If determinism is true, we must believe that for every event and for every action there are sufficient conditions, and when these conditions obtain, the action must occur. Since this is so, aren't all our actions in reality under constraint and thus, after all, not really free?

Soft determinists try to show that such an objection is a snarl of conceptual confusions, and that once we untangle them we will not take this incompatibilist line. A. J. Ayer makes one of the clearest and most forceful defenses of this view. His argument will be followed here, with a few supplementations from Mill.[3]

The conceptual facts we need to clarify are these: If the word 'freedom' is to have a meaning, it must be contrasted with something, for otherwise it is quite unintelligible. If I tell you I have just bought a wok, but I cannot contrast a wok with any *conceivable* thing that I would *deny* is a wok or not assert is a wok, then I have not been able to convey to you the meaning of 'wok'. In fact, if it is not so contrastable, it is indeed meaningless. The same thing obtains for any descriptive term. Thus, 'freedom', if it is to be intelligible, must be contrastable with something. There must at least be some *conceivable* situations in which it is correct to use the word and some *conceivable* situations in which it would not be correct. Yet it is plainly not an unintelligible sound, but a word with a use in our discourse. So we must look for its nonvacuous contrast. It is here where the soft determinists' initial point is critical. 'Freedom' is to be contrasted with 'constraint' or 'compulsion' rather than with 'determinism', for if we try to contrast it with 'determinism', it is far from clear that we get an intelligible contrast. It is not clear what sort of an action we would count as a 'causeless action'. But if we contrast 'freedom' and 'constraint', the contrast is clear. So we should say that a man's action is not free when it is constrained or when he is compelled to do what he does.

Suppose I say, "There is to be no smoking in the classroom." By this act I put the people in the room under constraint. I limit their freedom. But suppose Fearless Fosdick lights up anyway and I say, "Put it out, Mister, if you want to stay in the class." I in effect compel him, or at least attempt to compel him, to put it out. Being compelled or constrained to do something may very well entail that the act has a cause. But plainly the *converse* does not hold. As Ayer puts it, "From the fact that my action is causally determined it does not necessarily follow that I am constrained to do it." This is an important point to make, for to say this is in effect to claim that it does not necessarily follow from the fact that my actions are determined that I am not free. But, as I have said, if instead we take 'freedom' and 'being causally determined' as our contrastible terms, we get no clear contrast. On the other hand, even in a deterministic world we have with our above distinction between 'freedom' and 'compulsion' or 'constraint' preserved the needed contrast.

In setting out this contrast between when a man is or is not free, it is important to ask in what circumstances I can legitimately be said to be constrained and so *not* to be free.

1. *When I am compelled by another person to do what he wants.* Such a compulsion need not altogether deprive me of my power of choice. The man who compels me in a certain way need not hypnotize me or make it physically impossible for me to go against his will. It is sufficient that he should induce me to do what he wants by making it plain to me that if I do not, he will bring about some situation that I regard as having even more undesirable consequences than the consequences of acting as he desires. In such a circumstance I am acting under constraint and involuntarily, although it is not true that my freedom to act here is utterly circumscribed.

2. *Where a man has attained a habitual ascendency over me.* Indeed, in such a circumstance I can come to want to do what Big Brother wishes. Nevertheless, I still do not act freely because I am in reality deprived of the power of choice. And in this context this means I have acquired so strong a habit of obedience that I no

longer go through the process of deciding whether or not to do what the other person wants. About other matters I may still deliberate, but as regards the fulfillment of this other person's desires, my own deliberations have ceased to be an effective causal factor in my behavior. For this reason I may properly be said to be constrained since I have lost my power of choice in these matters.

3. *In order for me to be unfree in certain respects, it need not be a man or group of men that have gained ascendency over me.* A kleptomaniac cannot correctly be said to be a free agent, in respect to his stealing, because even if he does go through what appears to be deliberations about whether to steal or not to steal, such deliberations are irrelevant to his actual behavior in the respect of whether he will or will not steal. Whatever he resolved to do, he would steal all the same.[4]

This case is important because it clearly shows the difference between the man—the kleptomaniac—who is not free with respect to his stealing and an ordinary thief who is. The ordinary thief goes through a process of deciding whether or not to steal, and his decision decisively effects his behavior. If he actually resolved to refrain from stealing, he could carry out his resolution. But this is not so with the kleptomaniac. Thus, this observable difference between the ordinary thief and the kleptomaniac, quite independently of the issue of determinism, enables us to ascertain that the former is freer than the latter.

Note that in both cases, if determinism is true, then what either individual decides to do is causally determined. When we reflect on this, we are inclined to say that although it may be true that, unlike the kleptomaniac, the ordinary thief could refrain from stealing *if he chose*, yet since there is a cause, or set of causes, which causally necessitates his choosing as he does, how can he properly be said to have the power of choice? He indeed may not *feel* compelled the way the kleptomaniac does, but neither in some circumstances does the person over whom someone else has gained an ascendency. But the chains of causation by which the thief is bound are no less effective or coercive for being invisible.

Cases are being run together in this last remark that ought not to be run together. If we keep them distinct, in each instance we have a clearer contrast between actions that are free and actions that are not free. There remains a crucial difference between the thief and the kleptomaniac, namely that *the thief can choose not to steal and his choice can be effective.* The kleptomaniac cannot do that. Again, even in a deterministic world, there is a difference between the neophyte over whom someone has gained ascendency and someone who is not afflicted with kleptomania. For the latter there is no one whose very word is law, that is, who compels action. The thief, but not the kleptomaniac, feels no overwhelming compulsion to steal; and the person who must do what Big Brother dictates will feel an irresistible compulsion to do what he dictates as soon as it goes against something he would *otherwise* very much want to do, or if his rationale for doing it is effectively challenged by someone else.

A simpler case will make even clearer how it is that the notions of compulsion and constraint give the necessary contrast with our concept of freedom and not the concept of determinism or causal necessitation. There is indeed a difference between the man who suffers from a compulsion neurosis to wash his hands and the man who gets up and washes his hands because they are in fact dirty. Both actions have causes, but not all causes are constraining or compelling causes—they are not like a compulsion to wash our hands—and it is only the latter sort of causes that makes men unfree.

IV

Yet, in spite of these evident contrasts, we are still haunted, when we are in the grip of a philosophical perplexity about freedom and determinism, by the question, or muddle felt as a question: Do not all causes equally necessitate? It is not arbitrary "to say that a person is free when he is necessitated in one fashion but not when he is necessitated in another"?

Soft determinists reply that if 'necessitate' merely means 'cause', then of course 'All causes equally necessitate' is equivalent to 'All causes equally cause'—and that is hardly news. But

'All causes equally constrain or compel' is not true. If one event is the cause of another, we are stating that the event said to be the effect would not have occurred if it had not been for the occurrence of the event said to be the cause. But this states nothing about compulsion or constraint. There is indeed an invariable concomitance between the two classes of events; but there is no compulsion in any but a metaphorical sense. Such invariable concomitance gives a necessary but not sufficient condition for causation. It is difficult and perhaps even impossible to say what constitutes a sufficient condition. But given the frequent situations in which we speak of one thing causing another without asserting or implying a compulsion or constraint, they plainly are not further necessary conditions. (When I watch a wren in the park my behavior has causes sufficient for its occurrence, but I was neither compelled, constrained, nor forced to watch the wren.) Whatever more we need beyond invariable concomitance for causation, compulsion isn't one of the elements.

Even in a deterministic world we can do other than what we in fact do, since all 'cans' are constitutionally iffy.[5] That is to say, they are all hypothetical. This dark saying needs explanation. Consider what we actually mean by saying, 'I could have done otherwise.' It means, soft determinists argue, 'I should have acted otherwise if I had chosen' or 'I would have done otherwise if I had wanted to'. And "I can do X" means 'If I want to I shall do X' or 'If I choose to do X I will do X".

In general, soft determinists argue, we say a man is free rather than unfree when the following conditions hold:

1. He could have done otherwise if he had chosen to.
2. His actions are voluntary in the sense that the kleptomaniac's stealing is not.
3. Nobody compelled him to choose as he did.

Now it should be noted that these conditions are frequently fulfilled or satisfied. Thus, 'freedom' has a definite contrast and application. Basically it contrasts with constraint. Since this is so, we can say when it is true or probably

true to assert that a man is free, and when it is false or probably false to say that he is free. Given the truth of this, it is evident that a man can act as a free and responsible moral agent even though his actions are determined. If we are not talking about some obscure notion of 'free will' but about what Schlick calls the 'freedom of conduct', freedom is after all compatible with determinism.

V

Hard determinists characteristically respond to such arguments by claiming that such an analysis does not dig deep enough. It neglects the fact that while we are frequently able to do what we will or choose, or to do what we want or dislike doing least, in no instance in our lives are we able to will other than what we will, choose other than what we choose, want other than what we in fact want, or dislike other than what we in fact dislike. This is what Holbach was driving at when he claimed that freedom is an illusion. We indeed may sometimes have freedom of *action*, but we do not have what is really crucial, namely freedom of *will* or freedom of *choice*. A man's choices and strivings characteristically flow from his character, but, as Mill puts the argument against his own position, "his character is formed *for* him, and not by him; therefore his wishing that it had been formed differently is of no use; he has no power to alter it."[6]

Mill's response here is very instructive. Because in the ultimate resort a man's character is formed for him, it does not follow that it cannot *in part* be formed by him. We may in fact desire in one way or another to alter our personalities. We indeed may not be satisfied with our lives. And sometimes when we feel this way we are in a position to alter in some measure the course of our lives. These things are sometimes in our power. Furthermore, no one willed us to be anything in particular. That we have a certain sort of character is not the result, in most instances at any rate, of a deliberate design on anyone's part. Moreover, "we are exactly as capable of making our character, if we will, as others are of making it for us." Our personalities are alterable and in fact do change in many instances. Although we have no control over the *initial formation* of our character, we, within limits, can alter it if we want to do so.

To this the hard determinist still replies that the rub is '*If* we will or *if* we want to'. To admit this, he contends, is in effect to surrender the whole point, "since the will to alter our own character is given us, not by any efforts of ours, but by circumstances which we cannot help. . . ."

Mill agrees this is "most true," and if the hard determinist sticks here we cannot dislodge him. But, Mill goes on to say, "to think that we have no power of altering our character, and to think that we shall not use our power unless we desire to use it, are very different things, and have a very different effect on the mind." A person who does not wish to alter his character cannot *feel the depressing effect* of the hard-determinist doctrine. Mill then goes on to make the crucial observation that "a person feels morally free who feels that his habits or his temptations are not his masters but he theirs. . . ." And such a man, according to Mill, is a free agent even though he is a determined part in a deterministic universe.

I believe the general drift of Mill's remarks here are a step in the right direction, but they are not without their difficulties. And these difficulties are sufficient to require a modification of Mill's views. A man can certainly very well *feel* free and still not *be* free, *feel* that he is the master of his actions when he is not. Certain neurotic and psychotic types feel that certain things are in their power when in reality they are not. But it is here that the conditions I set forth earlier, largely following Ayer, are crucial. If a man is not being compelled or constrained by another person or institution or cataclysmic occurrence (for example, an earthquake or something of that order) and if no person, force, or disposition (for example, kleptomania) has gained as-

cendency over him so that he cannot think and act rationally, then when he *feels* his habits or temptations are not his masters but he theirs, in those circumstances he is indeed a free moral agent. If he is a rational agent he is responsible for what it is in his power to do; and to the degree that it is in his power to do one thing rather than another, he is correctly said to be free.

Notes

1. The point I make here is somewhat more controversial than my exposition would give one to understand. See here W. K. Frankena, "Obligation and Ability," in Max Black (ed.), *Philosophical Analysis* (Ithaca, N.Y.: 1950).

2. Moritz Schlick, *Problems of Ethics* (New York: 1939), pp. 146–148.

3. See A. J. Ayer, "Freedom and Necessity," in his *Philosophical Essays* (New York: 1963).

4. Some criminologists and psychologists have doubts about the viability of the very concept of kleptomania. And given the complexity of the phenomena referred to when we speak of 'kleptomania', it might be alleged that we should probe deeper and use quite different arguments. This may very well be so. I have been content here to expound Ayer on this point and show that it is not unreasonable to give a soft-determinist account given such psychological phenomena.

5. The phrase is J. L. Austin's, but he denies that all 'cans' are constitutionally iffy. See J. L. Austin, *Philosophical Papers* (Oxford' 1961), chapter 7.

6. J. S. Mill, *System of Logic,* book IV, chapter 2. The relevant sections are reprinted in Paul Edwards and Arthur Pap (eds.), *A Modern Introduction to Philosophy* (New York: 1965), second edition.

Questions on Nielsen

1. The main point of Nielsen's article is to give an account of freedom that is compatible with determinism. Carefully explain this account, and then decide if it is indeed compatible with determinism. Is it compatible with Skinner's science of human behavior, for example?

2. Explain the difference between compulsion and causation made by Nielson. Why is this important in the freedom/determinism controversy?

John Hospers

Psychoanalysis and Free Will

John Hospers is Professor of Philosophy at the University of Southern California and the author of numerous books and articles on philosophy. He ran for President of the United States in 1972 as the nominee of the Libertarian Party.

Perhaps the most obvious conception of freedom is this: an act is free if and only if it is a voluntary act. A response that occurs spontaneously, not as a result of your willing it, such as a reflex action, is not a free act. I do not know that this view is ever held in its pure form, but it is the basis for other ones. As it stands, of course, it is ambiguous: does "voluntary" entail "premeditated? are acts we perform semi-automatically through habit to be called free acts? To what extent is a conscious decision to act required for the act to be classified as voluntary? What of sudden outbursts of feeling? They are hardly premeditated or decided upon, yet they may have their origin in the presence or absence of habit-patterns due to self-discipline which may have been consciously decided upon. Clearly the view needs to be refined.

Now, however we may come to define "voluntary," it is perfectly possible to maintain that all voluntary acts are free acts and vice versa; after all, it is a matter of what meaning we are giving to the word "free" and we can give it this meaning if we choose. But it soon becomes apparent that this is not the meaning which most of us *want* to give it: for there *are* classes of actions which we want to refrain from calling "free" even though they are voluntary (not that we have this denial in mind when we use the word "free"—still, it is significant that we do not use the word in some situations in which the act in question is nevertheless voluntary).

When a man tells a state secret under torture, he does choose voluntarily between telling and enduring more torture; and when he submits to a bandit's command at the point of a gun, he voluntarily chooses to submit rather than to be shot. And still such actions would not generally be called free; it is clear that they are performed under compulsion. Voluntary acts preformed under compulsion would not be called free; and the cruder view is to this extent amended.

For some persons, this is as far as we need to go. Schlick, for example, says that the free-will issue is the scandal of philosophy and nothing but so much wasted ink and paper, because the whole controversy is nothing but an inexcusable confusion between compulsion and universal causality.[1] The free act is the uncompelled act, says Schlick, and controversies about causality and determinism have nothing to do with the case. When one asks whether an act done of necessity is free, the question is ambiguous: if "of necessity" means "by compulsion," then the answer is no; if, on the other hand, "of necessity" is a way of referring to "causal uniformity" in nature—the sense in which we may misleadingly speak of the laws of nature as "necessary" simply because there are no exceptions to them—then the answer is clearly yes; every act is an instance of some causal law (uniformity) or other, but this has nothing to do with its being free in the sense of uncompelled.

For Schlick, this is the end of the matter. Any attempt to discuss the matter further simply betrays a failure to perceive the clarifying distinction that Schlick has made.

Freedom means the opposite of compulsion; a man is free if he does not act under compulsion, and he is compelled or unfree when he is hindered from without in the realization of his natural desires. Hence he is unfree when he is locked up, or chained, or when someone forces him at the point of a gun to do what otherwise he would not do. This is quite clear, and everyone will admit that the everyday or legal notion of the lack of freedom is thus correctly interpreted, and that a man will be considered quite free . . . if no such external compulsion is exerted upon him.[2]

The reading is from John Hospers, "Meaning and Free Will," *Philosophy and Phenomenological Research*, vol. X, no. 3 (March 1950), pp. 307–323. Reprinted with permission.

This all seems clear enough. And yet if we ask whether it ends the matter, whether it states what we "really mean" by "free," many of us will feel qualms. We remember statements about human beings being pawns of their environment, victims of conditions beyond their control, the result of causal influences stemming from parents, etc., and we think, "Still, are we really free?" We do not want to say that the uniformity of nature itself binds us or renders us unfree; yet is there not something in what generations of wise men have said about man being fettered? Is there not something too facile, too sleight-of-hand, in Schlick's cutting of the Gordian knot?

It will be noticed that we have slipped from talking about acts as being free into talking about human beings as free. Both locutions are employed, I would say about 50-50. Sometimes an attempt is made to legislate definitely between the two: Stebbing, for instance, says that one must never call acts free, but only the doers of the acts.[3]

Let us pause over this for a moment. If it is we and not our acts that are to be called free, the most obvious reflection to make is that we are free to do some things and not free to do other things; we are free to lift our hands but not free to lift the moon. We cannot simply call ourselves free or unfree *in toto*; we must say at best that we are free in respect of certain actions only. G. E. Moore states the criterion as follows: we are free to do an act if we can do it *if* we want to; that which we can do if we want to is what we are free to do.[4] Some things certain people are free to do while others are not: most of us are free to move our legs, but paralytics are not; some of us are free to concentrate on philosophical reading matter for three hours at a stretch while others are not. In general, we could relate the two approaches by saying that a *person* is free *in respect of* a given action if he can do it if he wants to, and in this case his *act* is free.

Moore himself, however, has reservations that Schlick has not. He adds that there *is* a sense of "free" which fulfills the criterion he has just set forth; but that there may be *another* sense in which man cannot be said to be free in all the situations in which he could rightly he said to be so in the first sense.

And surely it is not necessary for me to multiply examples of the sort of thing we mean. In practice most of us would not call free many persons who behave voluntarily and even with calculation aforethought, and under no compulsion either of any obvious sort. A metropolitan newspaper headlines an article with the words "Boy Killer Is Doomed Long before He Is Born,"[5] and then goes on to describe how a twelve-year-old boy has just been sentenced to thirty years in Sing Sing for the murder of a girl; his family background includes records of drunkenness, divorce, social maladjustment, epilepsy, and paresis. He early displays a tendency to sadistic activity to hide an underlying masochism and "prove that he's a man"; being coddled by his mother only worsens this tendency, until, spurned by a girl in his attempt on her, he kills her—not simply in a fit of anger, but calculatingly, deliberately. Is he free in respect of his criminal act, or for that matter in most of the acts of his life? Surely to ask this question is to answer it in the negative. Perhaps I have taken an extreme case; but it is only to show the superficiality of the Schlick analysis the more clearly. Though not everyone has criminotic tendencies, everyone has been moulded by influences which in large measure at least determine his present behavior; he is literally the product of these influences, stemming from periods prior to his "years of discretion," giving him a host of character traits that he cannot change now even if he would. So obviously does what a man is depend upon how a man comes to be, that it is small wonder that philosophers and sages have considered man far indeed from being the master of his fate. It is not as if man's will were standing high and serene above the flux of events that have moulded him; it is itself caught up in this flux, itself carried along on the current. An act is free when it is determined by the man's character, say moralists; but when there was nothing the man could do to shape his character, and even the degree of will power available to him in shaping his habits and disciplining himself to overcome the influence of his early environment is a factor over which he has no control, what are we to say of this kind of "freedom?" Is it not rather like the freedom of the machine to stamp labels on cans when it has been devised for just that purpose? Some machines can do so more efficiently than others, but only because they have been better constructed.

It is not my purpose here to establish this thesis in general, but only in one specific respect which has received comparatively little attention, namely, the field referred to by psychiatrists as that of unconscious motivation. In what follows I shall restrict my attention to it because it illustrates as clearly as anything the points I wish to make.

Let me try to summarize very briefly the psychoanalytic doctrine on this point.[6] The conscious life of the human being, including the conscious decisions and volitions, is merely a mouthpiece for **the unconscious**—not directly for the enactment of unconscious drives, but of the compromise between unconscious drives and unconscious reproaches. There is a Big Three behind the scenes which the automaton called the conscious personality carries out: the **id**, an "eternal gimme," presents its wish and demands its immediate satisfaction; the **super-ego** says no to the wish immediately upon presentation, and the unconscious **ego**, the mediator between the two, tries to keep peace by means of compromise.[7]

To go into examples of the functioning of these three "bosses" would be endless; psychoanalytic case books supply hundreds of them. The important point for us to see in the present context is that it is the unconscious that determines what the conscious impulse and the conscious action shall be. Hamlet, for example, had a strong Oedipus wish, which was violently counteracted by super-ego reproaches; these early wishes were vividly revived in an unusual adult situation in which his uncle usurped the coveted position from Hamlet's father and won his mother besides. This situation evoked strong strictures on the part of Hamlet's super-ego, and it was this that was responsible for his notorious delay in killing his uncle. A dozen times Hamlet could have killed Claudius easily; but every time Hamlet "decided" not to: a free choice, moralists would say—but no, listen to super-ego: "What you feel such hatred toward your uncle for, what you are plotting to kill him for, is precisely the crime which you yourself

desire to commit: to kill your father and replace him in the affections of your mother. Your fate and your uncle's are bound up together." This paralyzes Hamlet into inaction. Consciously all he knows is that he is unable to act; this conscious inability he rationalizes, giving a different excuse each time.[8]

We have always been conscious of the fact that we are not masters of our fate in every respect—that there are many things which we cannot do, that nature is more powerful than we are, that we cannot disobey laws without danger of reprisals, etc. Lately we have become more conscious, too, though novelists and dramatists have always been fairly conscious of it, that we are not free with respect to the emotions that we feel—whom we love or hate, what types we admire, and the like. More lately still we have been reminded that there are unconscious motivations for our basic attractions and repulsions, our compulsive actions or inabilities to act. But what is not welcome news is that our very acts of volition, and the entire train of deliberations leading up to them, are but facades for the expression of unconscious wishes, or rather, unconscious compromises and defenses.

A man is faced by a choice: shall he kill another person or not? Moralists would say, here is a free choice—the result of deliberation, an action consciously entered into. And yet, though the agent himself does not know it, and has no awareness of the forces that are at work within him, his choice is already determined for him: his conscious will is only an instrument, a slave, in the hands of a deep unconscious motivation which determines his action. If he has a great deal of what the analyst calls "free-floating guilt," he will not; but if the guilt is such as to demand immediate absorption in the form of self-damaging behavior, this accumulated guilt will have to be discharged in some criminal action. The man himself does not know what the inner clockwork is; he is like the hands on the clock, thinking they move freely over the face of the clock.

A woman has married and divorced several husbands. Now she is faced with a choice for the next marriage: shall she marry Mr. A, or Mr. B, or nobody at all? She may take considerable time to "decide" this question, and her decision may appear as a final triumph of her free will. Let us assume that A is a normal well-adjusted, kind, and generous man, while B is a leech, an impostor, one who will become entangled constantly in quarrels with her. If she belongs to a certain classifiable psychological type, she will inevitably choose B, and she will do so even if her previous husbands have resembled B, so that one would think that she "had learned from experience." Consciously, she will of course "give the matter due consideration," etc., etc. To the psychoanalyst all this is irrelevant chaff in the wind—only a camouflage for the inner workings about which she knows nothing consciously. If she is of a certain kind of masochistic strain, as exhibited in her previous set of symptoms, she *must* choose B: her super-ego, always out to maximize the torment in the situation, seeing what dazzling possibilities for self-damaging behavior are promised by the choice of B, compels her to make the choice she does, and even to conceal the real basis of the choice behind an elaborate facade of rationalizations.

A man is addicted to gambling. In the service of his addiction he loses all his money, spends what belongs to his wife, even sells his property and neglects his children. For a time perhaps he stops; then, inevitably, he takes it up again, although he himself may think he chose to. The man does not know that he is a victim rather than an agent; or, if he sometimes senses that he is in the throes of something-he-knows-not-what, he will have no inkling of its character and will soon relapse into the illusion that he (his conscious self) is freely deciding the course of his own actions. What he does not know, of course, is that he is still taking out on his mother the original lesion to his infantile narcissism, getting back at her for her fancied refusal of his infantile wishes—and this by rejecting everything identified with her, namely education, discipline, logic, common sense, training. At the roulette wheel, almost alone among adult activities, chance—the opposite of all these things—rules supreme; and his addiction represents his continued and emphatic reiteration of his rejection of Mother and all she represents to his unconscious.

This pseudo-aggression of his is of course masochistic in its effects. In the long run he always loses; he can never quit while he is winning. And far from playing in order to win, rather one can say that his losing is a *sine qua non* of his psychic equilibrium (as it was for example with Dostoyevski): guilt demands punishment, and in the ego's "deal" with the super-ego the super-ego has granted satisfaction of infantile wishes in return for the self-damaging conditions obtaining. Winning would upset the neurotic equilibrium.[9]

A man has wash-compulsion. He must be constantly washing his hands—he uses up perhaps 400 towels a day. Asked why he does this, he says, "I need to, my hands are dirty"; and if it is pointed out to him that they are not really dirty, he says "They feel dirty anyway, I feel better when I wash them." So once again he washes them. He "freely decides" every time; he feels that he must wash them, he deliberates for a moment perhaps, but always ends by washing them. What he does not see, of course, is the invisible wires inside him pulling him inevitably to do the thing he does: the infantile id-wish concerns preoccupation with dirt, the super-ego charges him with this, and the terrified ego must respond, "No, I don't like dirt, see how clean I like to be, look how I wash my hands!"

Let us see what further "free acts" the same patient engages in (this is an actual case history): he is taken to a concentration camp, and given the worst of treatment by the Nazi guards. In the camp he no longer chooses to be clean, does not even try to be—on the contrary, his choice is now to wallow in filth as much as he can. All he is aware of now is a disinclination to be clean, and every time he must choose not to be. Behind the scenes, however, another drama is being enacted: the super-ego, perceiving that enough torment is being administered from the outside, can afford to cease pressing its charges in this quarter—the outside world is doing the torturing now, so the super-ego is relieved of the responsibility. Thus the ego is relieved of the agony of constantly making terrified replies in the form of washing to prove that the super-ego is wrong. The defense no longer being needed, the person slides back into what is his natural predilection anyway, for filth. This becomes too much even for the Nazi guards: they take hold of him one day, saying "We'll teach you how to be clean!" drag him into the snow, and pour bucket after bucket of icy water over him until he freezes to death. Such is the end-result of an original id-wish, caught in the machination of a destroying super-ego.

Let us take, finally, a less colorful, more everyday example. A student at a university, possessing wealth, charm, and all that is usually considered essential to popularity, begins to develop the following personality-pattern: although well taught in the graces of social conversation, he always makes a *faux pas* somewhere, and always in the worst possible situation; to his friends he makes cutting remarks which hurt deeply—and always apparently aimed in such a way as to hurt the most: a remark that would not hurt A but would hurt B he invariably makes to B rather than to A, and so on. None of this is conscious. Ordinarily he is considerate of people, but he contrives always (unconsciously) to impose on just those friends who would resent it most, and at just the times when he should know that he should not impose: at 3 o'clock in the morning, without forewarning, he phones a friend in a near-by city demanding to stay at his apartment for the weekend; naturally the friend is offended, but the person himself is not aware that he has provoked the grievance ("common sense" suffers a temporary eclipse when the neurotic pattern sets in, and one's intelligence, far from being of help in such a situation, is used in the interest of the neurosis), and when the friend is cool to him the next time they meet, he wonders why and feels unjustly treated. Aggressive behavior on his part invites resentment and aggression in turn, but all that he consciously sees is others' behavior toward him—and he considers himself the innocent victim of an unjustified "persecution."

Each of these choices is, from the moralist's point of view, free: he chose to phone his friend at 3 A.M.; he chose to make the cutting remark that he did, etc. What he does not know is that an ineradicable masochistic pattern has set in. His unconscious is far more shrewd and clever than is his conscious intellect; it sees with uncanny accuracy just what kind of behavior will damage him most, and unerringly forces him into that behavior. Consciously, the student "doesn't know why he did it"—he gives different "reasons" at different times, but they are all, once again, rationalizations cloaking the unconscious mechanism which propels him willy-nilly into actions that his "common sense" eschews.

The more of this sort of thing you see, the more you can see what the psychoanalyst means when he talks about "the illusion of free-will." And the more of a psychiatrist you become, the more you are overcome with a sense of what an illusion this precious free-will really is. In some kinds of cases most of us can see it already: it takes no psychiatrist to look at the epileptic and sigh with sadness at the thought that soon this person before you will be as one possessed, not the same thoughtful intelligent person you knew. But people are not aware of this in other contexts, for example when they express surprise at how a person whom they have been so good to could treat them so badly. Let us suppose that you help a person financially or morally or in some other way, so that he is in your debt: suppose further that he is one of the many neurotics who unconsciously identify kindness with weakness and aggression with strength, then he will unconsciously take your kindness to him as weakness and use it as the occasion for enacting some aggression against you. He can't help it, he may regret it himself later; still, he will be driven to do it. If we gain a little knowledge of psychiatry, we can look at him with pity, that a person otherwise so worthy should be so unreliable—but we will exercise realism too and be aware that there are some types of people that you cannot be good to; in "free" acts of their conscious volition, they will use your own goodness against you.

Sometimes the persons themselves will become dimly aware that "something behind the scenes" is determining their behavior. The divorcee will sometimes view herself with detachment, as if she were some machine (and indeed the psychoanalyst does call her a "repeating-machine"): "I know I'm caught in a net, that I'll fall in love with this guy and marry him and the whole ridiculous merry-go-round will start all over again."

We talk about free will, and we say, yes, the person is free to do so-and-so if he can do so *if* he wants to—and we forget that his wanting to is itself caught up in the stream of determinism, that unconscious forces drive him into the wanting or not wanting to do the thing in question. The idea of the puppet whose motions are manipulated from behind by invisible wires, or better still, by springs inside, is no mere figure of speech. The analogy is a telling one at almost every point.

And the pity of it is that it all started so early, before we knew what was happening. The personality-structure is inelastic after the age of five, and comparatively so in most cases after the age of three. Whether one acquires a **neurosis** or not is determined by that age—and just as involuntary as if it had been a curse of God. If, for example, a masochistic pattern was set up, under pressure of hyper-narcissism combined with real or fancied infantile deprivation, then the masochistic snowball was on its course downhill long before we or anybody else know what was happening, and long before anyone could do anything about it. To speak of human beings as "puppets" in such a context is no mere metaphor, but a stark rendering of a literal fact: only the psychiatrist knows what puppets people really are; and it is no wonder that the protestations of philosophers that "the act which is the result of a volition, a deliberation, a conscious decision, is free" leave these persons, to speak mildly, somewhat cold.

But, one may object, all the states thus far described have been abnormal, neurotic ones. The well-adjusted (normal) person at least is free.

Leaving aside the question of how clearly and on what grounds one can distinguish the neurotic from the normal, let me use an illustration of a proclivity that everyone would call normal, namely, the decision of a man to support his wife and possibly a family, and consider briefly its genesis.[10]

Every baby comes into the world with a full-fledged case of **megalomania**—interested only in himself, naively assuming that he is the center of the universe and that others are present only to fulfill his wishes, and furious when his own wants are not satisfied immediately no matter for what reason. Gratitude, even for all the time and worry and care expended on him by the mother, is an emotion entirely foreign to the infant, and as he grows older it is inculcated in him only with the greatest difficulty; his natural tendency is to assume that everything that happens to him is due to himself, except for denials and frustrations, which are due to the "cruel, denying" outer world, in particular the mother; and that he owes nothing to anyone, is dependent on no one. This omnipotence-complex, or illusion of non-dependence, has been called the "autarchic fiction." Such a conception of the world is actually fostered in the child by the conduct of adults, who automatically attempt to fulfill the infant's every wish concerning nourishment, sleep, and attention. The child misconceives causality and sees in these wish-fulfillments not the results of maternal kindness and love, but simply the result of his own omnipotence.

This fiction of omnipotence is gradually destroyed by experience, and its destruction is probably the deepest disappointment of the early years of life. First of all, the infant discovers that he is the victim of organic urges and necessities: hunger, defecation, urination. More important, he discovers that the maternal breast, which he has not previously distinguished from his own body (he has not needed to, since it was available when he wanted it), is not a part of himself after all, but of another creature upon whom he is dependent. He is forced to recognize this, e.g., when he wants nourishment and it is at the moment not present; even a small delay is most damaging to the "autarchic fiction." Most painful of all is the experience of weaning, probably the greatest tragedy in every baby's life, when his dependency is most cruelly emphasized; it is a frustrating experience because what he wants is no longer there at all; and if he has been able to some extent to preserve the illusion of non-dependence heretofore, he is not able to do so now—it is plain that the source of his nourishment is not dependent on him, but he on it. The shattering of the autarchic fiction is a great disillusionment to every child, a tremendous blow to his ego which he will, in one way or another, spend the rest of his life trying to repair. How does he do this?

First of all, his reaction to frustration is anger and fury, and he responds by kicking, biting, etc., the only ways he knows. But he is motorically helpless, and these measures are ineffective, and only serve to emphasize his dependence the more. Moreover, against such responses of the child the parental reaction is one of prohibition, generally accompanied by physical force of some kind. Generally the child soon learns that this form of rebellion is profitless, and brings him more harm than good, He wants to respond to frustration with violent aggression, and at the same time learns that he will be punished for such aggression, and that in any case the latter is ineffectual. What face-saving solution does he find? Since he must "face facts," since he must in any case "conform" if he is to have any peace at all, he tries to make it seem as if he himself is the source of the commands and prohibitions: the *external* prohibitive force is *internalized*—and here we have the origin of conscience. By making the prohibitive agency seem to come from within himself, the child can "save face"—as if saying, "The prohibition comes from within me, not from outside, so I'm not subservient to external rule, I'm only obeying rules I've set up myself," thus to some extent saving the autarchic fiction, and at the same time avoiding unpleasant consequences directed against himself by complying with parental commands.

Moreover, the boy[11] has unconsciously never forgiven the mother for his dependence on her in early life, for nourishment and all other things. It has upset his illusion of non-dependence. These feelings have been repressed and are not remembered; but they are acted out in later life in many ways—e.g., in the constant deprecation man has for woman's duties such as cooking and housework of all sorts ("All she does is stay home and get together a few meals, and she calls that work"), and especially in the man's identification with the mother in his sex experiences with women. By identifying with someone one cancels out in effect the person with whom he identifies—

replacing that person, unconsciously denying his existence, and the man, identifying with his early mother, playing the active role in "giving" to his wife as his mother has "given" to him, is in effect the denial of his mother's existence, a fact which is narcissistically embarrassing to his ego because it is chiefly responsible for shattering his autarchic fiction. In supporting his wife, he can unconsciously deny that his mother gave to him, and that he was dependent on her giving. Why is it that the husband plays the provider, and wants his wife to be dependent on no one else, although twenty years before he was nothing but a parasitic baby? This is a face-saving device on his part: he can act out the reasoning "See, I'm not the parasitic baby, on the contrary I'm the provider, the giver." His playing the provider is a constant face-saving device, to deny his early dependence which is so embarrassing to his ego. It is no wonder that men generally dislike to be reminded of their boyhood, when they were dependent on woman.

Thus we have here a perfectly normal adult reaction which is unconsciously motivated. The man "chooses" to support a family—and his choice is as unconsciously motivated as anything could be. (I have described here only the "normal" state of affairs, uncomplicated by the well-nigh infinite number of variations that occur in actual practice.)

Now, what of the notion of responsibility? What happens to it on our analysis?

Let us begin with an example, not a fictitious one. A woman and her two-year-old baby are riding on a train to Montreal in mid-winter. The child is ill. The woman wants badly to get to her destination. She is, unknown to herself, the victim of a neurotic conflict whose nature is irrelevant here except for the fact that it forces her to behave aggressively toward the child, partly to spite her husband whom she despises and who loves the child, but chiefly to ward off super-ego charges of masochistic attachment. Consciously she loves the child, and when she says this she says it sincerely, but she must behave aggressively toward it nevertheless, just as many children love their mothers but are nasty to them most of the time in neurotic pseudo-aggression. The child becomes more ill as the train approaches Montreal; the heating system of the train is not working, and the conductor advises the woman to get off the train at the next town and get the child to a hospital at once. The woman says no, she must get to Montreal. Shortly afterward, as the child's condition worsens, and the mother does all she can to keep it alive, without, however, leaving the train, for she declares that is absolutely necessary that she reach her destination. But before she gets there the child is dead. After that, of course, the mother grieves, blames herself, weeps hysterically, and joins the church to gain surcease from the guilt that constantly overwhelms her when she thinks of how her aggressive behavior has killed her child.

Was she responsible for her deed? In ordinary life, after making a mistake, we say, "Chalk it up to experience." Here we say, "Chalk it up to the neurosis." No, she is not responsible. She could not help it if her neurosis forced her to act this way—she didn't even know what was going on behind the scenes, she merely acted out the part assigned to her. This is far more true than is generally realized: criminal actions in general are not actions for which their agents are responsible; the agents are passive, not active—they are victims of a neurotic conflict. Their very hyper-activity is unconsciously determined.

To say this is, of course, not to say that we should not punish criminals. Clearly, for our own protection, we must remove them from our midst so that they can no longer molest and endanger organized society. And, of course, if we use the word "responsible" in such a way that justly to hold someone responsible for a deed is by definition identical with being justified in punishing him, then we can and do hold people responsible. But this is like the sense of "free" in which free acts are voluntary ones. It does not go deep enough. In a deeper sense we cannot hold the person responsible: we may hold his neurosis responsible, but he is not responsible for his neurosis, particularly since the age at which its onset was inevitable was an age before he could even speak.

The neurosis is responsible—but isn't the neurosis a part of *him*? We have been speaking all the time as if the person and his unconscious were two separate beings; but isn't he one personality, including conscious and unconscious departments together?

I do not wish to deny this. But it hardly helps us here; for what people want when they talk about freedom, and what they hold to when they champion it, is the idea that the *conscious* will is the master of their destiny. "I am the master of my fate, I am the captain of my soul"—and they surely mean their conscious selves, the self that they can recognize and search and introspect. Between an unconscious that willy-nilly determines your actions, and an external force which pushes you, there is little if anything to choose. The unconscious is just *as if* it were an outside force; and indeed, psychiatrists will assert that the inner Hitler can torment you far more than any external Hitler can. Thus the kind of freedom that people want, the only kind they will settle for, is precisely the kind that psychiatry says that they cannot have.

Heretofore it was pretty generally thought that, while we could not rightly blame a person for the color of his eyes or the morality of his parents, or even for what he did at the age of three, or to a large extent what impulses he had and whom he fell in love with, one *could* do so for other of his adult activities, particularly the acts he performed voluntarily and with premeditation. Later this attitude was shaken. Many voluntary acts came to be recognized, at least in some circles, as compelled by the unconscious. Some philosophers recognized this too—Ayer[12] talks about the kleptomaniac being unfree, and about a person being unfree when another person exerts a habitual ascendancy over his personality. But this is as far as he goes. The usual examples, such as the kleptomaniac and the schizophrenic, apparently satisfy most philosophers, and with these exceptions removed, the rest of mankind is permitted to wander in the vast and alluring field of freedom and responsibility. So far, the inroads upon freedom left the vast majority of humanity untouched; they began to hit home when psychiatrists began to realize, though philosophers did not, that the domination of the conscious by the unconscious extended, not merely to a few exceptional individuals, but to all human beings, that the "big three behind the scenes" are not respecters of persons, and dominate us all, even including that **sanctum sanctorum** of freedom, our conscious will. To be sure, the domination in the case of "normal" individuals is somewhat more benevolent than the tyranny and despotism exercised in neurotic cases, and therefore the former have evoked less comment; but the principle remains in all cases the same: the unconscious is the master of every fate and the captain of every soul.

We speak of a machine turning out good products most of the time but every once in a while it turns out a "lemon." We do not, of course, hold the product responsible for this, but the machine, and via the machine, its maker. Is it silly to extend to inanimate objects the idea of responsibility? Of course. But is it any less silly to employ the notion in speaking of human creatures? Are not the two kinds of cases analogous in countless important ways? Occasionally a child turns out badly too, even when his environment and training are the same as that of his brothers and sisters who turn out "all right." He is the "bad penny." His acts of rebellion against parental discipline in adult life (such as the case of the gambler, already cited) are traceable to early experiences of real or fancied denial of infantile wishes. Sometimes the denial has been real, though many denials are absolutely necessary if the child is to grow up to observe the common decencies of civilized life; sometimes, if the child has an unusual quantity of narcissism, every event that occurs is interpreted by him as a denial of his wishes, and nothing a parent could do, even granting every humanly possible wish, would help. In any event, the later neurosis can be attributed to this. Can the person himself be held responsible? Hardly. If he engages in activities which are a menace to society, he must be put into prison, of course, but responsibility is another matter. The time when the events occurred which rendered his neurotic behavior inevitable was a time long before he was capable of thought and decision. As an adult, he is a victim of a world he never made—only this world is inside him.

What about the children who turn out "all right"? All we can say is that "it's just lucky for them" that what happened to their unfortunate brother didn't happen to them; *through no virtue of their own* they are not doomed to the life of unconscious guilt, expiation, conscious depression, terrified ego-gestures for the appeasement of a tyrannical super-ego that he is. The machine turned them out with a minimum of damage. But if the brother cannot be blamed for his evils, neither can they be praised for their good. It will take society a long time to come round to this attitude. We do not blame people for the color of their eyes, but we have not attained the same attitude toward their socially significant activities.

We all agree that machines turn out "lemons", we all agree that nature turns out misfits in the realm of biology—the blind, the crippled, the diseased; but we hesitate to include the realm of the personality, for here, it seems, is the last retreat of our dignity as human beings. Our ego can endure anything but this; this island at least must remain above the encroaching flood. But may not precisely the same analysis be made here also? Nature turns out psychological "lemons", too, in far greater quantities than any other kind; and indeed all of us are "lemons" in some respect or other, the difference being one of degree. Some of us are lucky enough not to have a gambling-neurosis or criminotic tendencies or masochistic mother-attachment or overdimensional repetition-compulsion to make our lives miserable, but most of our actions, those usually considered the most important, are unconsciously dominated just the same. And, if a neurosis may be likened to a curse of God, let those of us, the elect, who are enabled to enjoy a measure of life's happiness without the hell-fire of neurotic guilt, take this, not as our own achievement, but simply for what it is—a gift of God.

Let us, however, quit metaphysics and put the situation schematically in the form of a deductive argument.

1. An occurrence over which we had no control is something we cannot be held responsible for.

2. Events E, occurring during our babyhood, were events over which we had no control.

3. Therefore events E were events which we cannot be held responsible for.

4. But if there is something we cannot be held responsible for, neither can we be held responsible for something that inevitably results from it.

5. Events E have as inevitable consequence Neurosis N, which in turn has an inevitable consequence, Behavior B.

6. Since N is the inevitable consequence of E and B is the inevitable consequence of N, B is the inevitable consequence of E.

7. Hence, not being responsible for E, we cannot be responsible for B.

Notes

1. Moritz Schlick, *The Problems of Ethics*, Chapter VII.

2. Ibid., p. 150.

3. L. Susan Stebbing, *Philosophy and the Physicists*, p. 242.

4. G. E. Moore, *Ethics*, p. 205.

5. *New York Post*, Tuesday, May 18, 1948, p. 4.

6. I am aware that the theory presented below is not accepted by all practicing psychoanalysts. Many non-Freudians would disagree with the conclusions presented below. But I do not believe that this fact affects my argument, as long as the concept of unconscious motivation is accepted. I am aware, too, that much of the language employed in the following descriptions is animistic and metaphorical; but as long as I am presenting a view I would prefer to "go the whole hog" and present it in its strongest possible light. The theory can in any case be made clearest by the use of such language, just as atomic theory can often be made clearest to students with the use of models.

7. This view is very clearly developed in Edmund Bergler, *Divorce Won't Help*, especially Chapter I.

8. See *The Basic Writings of Sigmund Freud*, Modern Library Edition, p. 310. (In *The Interpretation of Dreams*.) Cf. also the essay by Ernest Jones, "A Psycho-analytical Study of Hamlet."

9. See Edmund Bergler's article on the pathological gambler in *Diseases of the Nervous System* (1943). Also "Suppositions about the Mechanism of Criminosis," *Journal of Criminal Psychopathology* (1944) and "Clinical Contributions to the Psychogenesis of Alcohol Addiction," *Quarterly Journal of Studies on Alcohol*, 5: 434 (1944).

10. Edmund Bergler, *The Battle of Conscience*, Chapter I.

11. The girl's development after this point is somewhat different. Society demands more aggressiveness of the adult male, hence there are more super ego strictures on tendencies toward passivity in the male; accordingly his defenses must be stronger.

12. A. J. Ayer, "Freedom and Necessity," *Polemic* (September–October 1946), pp. 40–43.

Questions on Hospers

1. How does unconscious motivation work according to Hospers? Explain it by means of some examples.

2. Is there any sort of freedom or responsibility that is compatible with psychoanalytic theory? How about the kind of freedom that Nielsen describes in the last reading?

3. Critics of psychoanalysis object that it is not really scientific because it is not falsifiable, that is, there is no possible way to show that it is false. (The same criticism is made of Skinner's behaviorism.) Is this a good objection or not? How could Hospers respond?

C. A. Campbell
Contra-Causal Freedom

C. A. Campbell (1897–1974) taught philosophy at the University of Glasgow, and wrote On Selfhood and Godhood *and* In Defense of Free Will.

The reading is from C. A. Campbell, "Is Freewill a Pseudo-Problem?" *Mind*, vol, LX, no. 239, July 1951, pp. 450–464. Reprinted by permission of Oxford University Press.

"Ought" Implies "Can"

The pseudo-problem theorists* usually, and naturally, develop their analysis of moral responsibility by way of contrast with a view which, while it has enjoyed a good deal of philosophic support, I can perhaps best describe as the common view. It will be well to remind ourselves, therefore, of the main features of this view.

[Campbell is referring to soft determinists such as Schlick who think that the freedom-determinism problem is a pseudo problem that can be dissolved by explaining the meaning of the word "free."—Ed.]

So far as the *meaning*, as distinct from the *conditions*, of moral responsibility is concerned, the common view is very simple. If we ask ourselves whether a certain person is morally responsible for a given act (or it may be just "in general"), what we are considering, it would be said, is whether or not that person is a fit subject upon whom to pass moral judgment; whether he can fittingly be deemed morally good or bad, morally praiseworthy or blameworthy. This does not take us any great way: but (*pace* Schlick) so far as it goes it does not seem to me seriously disputable. The really interesting and controversial question is about the *conditions* of moral responsibility, and in particular the question whether freedom of a contra-causal kind is among these conditions.

The answer of the common man to the latter question is that it most certainly *is* among the conditions. Why does he feel so sure about this? Not, I argued earlier, because the common man supposes that causal law exercises "compulsion" in the sense that prescriptive laws do, but simply because he does not see how a person can be deemed morally praiseworthy or blameworthy in respect of an act which he could not help performing. From the stand-point of moral praise and blame, he would say—though not necessarily from other stand-points—it is a matter of indifference whether it is by reason of some external constraint or by reason of his own given nature that the man could not help doing what he did. It is quite enough to make moral praise and blame futile that in either case there were no genuine alternatives, no open possibilities, before the man when he acted. He could not have acted otherwise than he did. And the common man might not unreasonably go on to stress the fact that we all, even if we are linguistic philosophers, do in our actual practice of moral judgment appear to accept the common view. He might insist upon the point alluded to earlier in this paper, that we do all, in passing moral censure, "make allowances" for influences in a man's hereditary nature or environmental circumstances which we regard as having made it more than ordinarily difficult for him to act otherwise than he did: the implication being that if we supposed that the man's heredity and environment made it not merely very *difficult* but actually *impossible* for him to act otherwise than he did, we could not properly assign moral blame to him at all.

Let us put the argument implicit in the common view a little more sharply. The moral "ought" implies "can." If we say that A morally ought to have done X, we imply that in our opinion, he could have done X. But we assign moral blame to a man only for failing to do what we think he morally ought to have done. Hence if we morally blame A for not having done X, we imply that he could have done X even though in fact he did not. In other words, we imply that A could have acted otherwise than he did. And that means that we imply, as a necessary condition of a man's being morally blameworthy, that he enjoyed a freedom of a kind not compatible with unbroken causal continuity. . . .

What then *does* one mean in this class of cases by "A could have acted otherwise"? I submit that the expression is taken in its simple, categorical meaning, without any suppressed "if" clause to qualify it. Or perhaps, in order to keep before us the important truth that it is only as expressions of *will* or *choice* that acts are of moral import, it might be better to say that a condition of A's moral responsibility is that he could have *chosen* otherwise. We saw that there is no real question whether A who told a lie could have acted otherwise *if* he had chosen otherwise. But there is a very real question, at least for any person who approaches the question of moral responsibility at a tolerably advanced level of reflection, about whether A could have *chosen* otherwise. Such a person will doubtless be acquainted with the claims advanced in some quarters that causal law operates universally: or/and with the theories of some philosophies that the universe is throughout the expression of a single supreme principle; or/and with the doctrines of some theologians that the world is created, sustained and governed by an Omniscient and Omnipotent Being. Very understandably such world-views awaken in him doubts about the validity of his first, easy, instinctive assumption that there are genuinely open possibilities before a man at the moment of moral choice. It thus becomes for him a real question whether a man could have chosen otherwise than he actually did, and, in consequence, whether man's moral responsibility is really defensible. For how can a man be morally responsible, he asks himself, if his choices, like all other events in the universe, could not have been otherwise than they in fact were? It is precisely against the background of world-views such as these that for reflective people the problem of moral responsibility normally arises.

Furthermore, to the man who has attained this level of reflexion, it will in *no* class of cases be a sufficient condition of moral responsibility for an act that one could have acted otherwise *if* one had chosen otherwise—not even in these cases where there *was* some possibility of the operation of "external constraint." In these cases he will, indeed, expressly recognize freedom from external constraint as a *necessary condition,* but not as a *sufficient* condition. For he will be aware that, even granted *this* freedom, it is still conceivable that the agent had no freedom to choose otherwise than he did, and he will therefore require that the latter sort of freedom be added if moral responsibility for the act is to be established.

I have been contending that, for persons at a *tolerably advanced level of reflexion,* "A could have acted otherwise," as a condition of A's moral responsibility, means "A could have chosen otherwise." The qualification italicized is of some importance. The unreflective or unsophisticated person, the ordinary "man in the street," who does not know or much care what scientists and theologians and philosophers have said about the world, sees well enough that A is morally responsible only if he could have acted otherwise, but in his intellectual innocence he will, very probably, envisage nothing capable of preventing A from having acted otherwise except some material impediment—like the broken leg in the example above. Accordingly, for the unreflective person, "A could have acted otherwise," as a condition of moral responsibility, *is* apt to mean no more than "A could have acted otherwise *if* he had so chosen."

It would appear, then, that the view now favored by many philosophers, that the freedom required for moral responsibility is merely freedom from external constraint, is a view which they share only with the less reflective type of layman. Yet it should be plain that on a matter of this sort the view of the unreflective person is of little value by comparison with the view of the reflective person. There are some contexts, no doubt, in which lack of sophistication is an asset. But this is not one of them. The question at issue here is as to the kind of impediments which might have prevented a man from acting otherwise than he in fact did: and on this question knowledge and reflection are surely prerequisites of any answer that is worth listening to. It is simply on account of the limitations of his mental vision that the unreflective man interprets the expression "could have acted otherwise," in its context as a condition of moral responsibility, solely in terms of external constraint. He has failed (as yet) to reach the intellectual level at which one takes into account the implications for moral choices of the world-views of science, religion, and philosophy. If on a matter of this complexity the philosopher finds that his analysis accords with the utterances of the uneducated he has, I suggest, better cause for uneasiness than for self-congratulation.

This concludes the main part of what it seems to me necessary to say in answer to the pseudo-problem theorists. My object so far has been to expose the falsity of those innovations (chiefly **Positivist**) in the way of argument and analysis which are supposed by many to have made it impossible any longer to formulate the problem of Free Will in the traditional manner. My contention is that, at least so far as these innovations are concerned, the simple time-honored argument still holds from the nature of the moral ought to the conclusion that moral responsibility implies a contra-causal type of freedom. The attempts to avoid that conclusion by analyzing the proposition "A could have acted otherwise" (acknowledged to be implied in *some* sense in A's moral responsibility) into one or other of certain hypothetical propositions which are compatible with unbroken causal continuity, break down hopelessly when tested against the touchstone of actual moral thinking. It is, I think, not necessary to defend the procedure of testing hypotheses in the ethical field by bringing to bear upon them our actual moral thinking. If there is any other form of test applicable, I should be much interested to learn what it is supposed to be. Certainly "logical analysis" *per se* will not do. That has a function, but a function that can only be ancillary. For what we are seeking to know is the meaning of the expression "could have acted otherwise" not *in the abstract*, but in the context of the question of man's *moral responsibility*. Logical analysis *per se* is impotent to give us this information. It can be of value only in so far as it operates within the orbit of "the moral consciousness." One may admit, with some qualifications, that on a matter of this sort the moral consciousness without logical analysis is blind: but it seems to me to be true without any qualification whatsoever that, on the same problem, logical analysis without the moral consciousness is empty.

Contra-Causal Freedom and Creative Activity

There are times when what seems to a critic the very strength of his case breeds mistrust in the critic's own mind. I confess that in making the criticisms that have preceded I have not been altogether free from uncomfortable feelings of this kind. For the arguments I have criticized, and more particularly the analyses of the conditions of moral responsibility, seem to me to be in many cases quite desperately unplausible. Such a state of affairs ought, I think, to give the critic pause. The thought must at least enter his mind (unless he be a total stranger to modesty) that perhaps, despite his best efforts to be fair, he has after all misrepresented what his opponents are saying. No doubt a similar thought will enter, and perhaps find lodgment in, the minds of many readers.

In this situation there is, however, one course by which the critic may reasonably hope to allay these natural suspicions. He should consider whether there may not be certain predisposing influences at work, extrinsic to the specific arguments, which could have the effect of blinding the proponents of these arguments to their intrinsic demerits. If so, he need not be too much disquieted by the seeming weakness of the case against him. For it is a commonplace that, once in the grip of general prepossessions, even very good philosophers sometimes avail themselves of very bad arguments.

Actually, we can, I think, discern at least two such influences operating powerfully in the case before us. One is sympathy with the general tenets of **Positivism**. . . . Of far wider and more permanent interest, in my judgment, is the second of the "predisposing influences"— the conviction that there just *is* no contra-causal freedom such as is commonly alleged to be a condition of moral responsibility. A natural desire to "save" moral responsibility issues, logically enough, in attempts to formulate its conditions in a manner compatible with unbroken causal continuity. The consequent analyses may be, as I have urged, very unsatisfactory. But there is no doubt that the conviction that motivates the analysis is supported by reasons of great weight: well-known arguments that are the property of no particular school and which most of us learned in our philosophical cradles. A very brief summary of what I take to be the most influential of these arguments will suffice for the comments I wish to make upon them.

A contra-causal freedom, it is argued, such as is implied in the "categorical" interpretation of the proposition "A could have chosen otherwise than he did," posits a breach of causal continuity between a man's character and his conduct. Now apart from the general presumption in favor of the universality of causal law, there are special reasons for disallowing the breach that is here alleged. It is the common assumption of social intercourse that our acquaintances will act "in character"; that their choices will exhibit the "natural" response of their characters to the given situation. And this assumption seems to be amply substantiated, over a wide range of conduct, by the actual success which attends predictions made on this basis. Where there should be, on the contra-causal hypothesis, chaotic variability, there is found in fact a large measure of intelligible continuity. Moreover, what is the alternative to admitting that a person's choices flow from his character? Surely just that the so-called "choice" is not *that person's* choice at all: that, relatively to the person concerned, it is a mere "accident." Now we cannot really believe this. But if it *were* the case, it would certainly not help to establish *moral* freedom, the freedom required for *moral* responsibility. For clearly a man cannot be morally responsible for an act which does not express his own choice but is, on the contrary, attributable simply to chance.

These are clearly considerations worthy of all respect. It is not surprising if they have played a big part in persuading people to respond sympathetically to the view that "Free Will," in its usual contra-causal formulation, is a pseudo-problem. A full answer to them is obviously not practicable in what is little more than an appendix to the body of this paper; but I am hopeful that something can be said, even in a little space, to show that they are very far from being as conclusive against a contra-causal freedom as they are often supposed to be.

To begin with the less troublesome of the two main objections indicated—the objection that the break in causal continuity which free will involves is inconsistent with the predictability of conduct on the basis of the agent's known character. All that is necessary to meet this objection, I suggest, is the frank recognition, which is perfectly open to the Libertarian, that there is a wide area of human conduct, determinable on clear general principles, within which free will does not effectively operate. The most import of these general principles (I have no space to deal here with the others) has often enough been stated by Libertarians. Free will does not operate in these practical situations in which no conflict arises in the agent's mind between what he conceives to be his "duty" and what he feels to be his " desire." It does not operate here because there just is no occasion for it to operate. There is no reason whatever why the agent should here even contemplate choosing any course other than that prescribed by his desire. In all such situations, therefore, he naturally wills in accordance with desire. But his "desire" is simply the specific *ad hoc* expression of that system of conative and emotive dispositions which we call his "character." In all such situations, therefore, whatever may be the case elsewhere, his will is in effect determined by his character as so far formed. Now when we bear in mind that there are an almost immeasurably greater number of situations in a man's life that

conform to *this* pattern than there are situations in which an agent is aware of a conflict between strongest desire and duty, it is apparent that a Libertarianism which accepts the limitation of free will to the *latter* type of situation is not open to the stock objection on the score of "predictability." For there still remains a vast area of human behavior in which prediction on the basis of known character may be expected to succeed: an area which will accommodate without difficulty, I think, all these empirical facts about successful prediction which the critic is apt to suppose fatal to Free Will.

So far as I can see, such a delimitation of the field of effective free will denies to the Libertarian absolutely nothing which matters to him. For it is precisely that small sector of the field of choices which our principle of delimitation still leaves open to free will—the sector in which strongest desire clashes with duty—that is crucial for moral responsibility. It is, I believe, with respect to such situations, and in the last resort to such situations alone, that the agent himself recognizes that moral praise and blame are appropriate. They are appropriate, according as he does or does not "rise to duty" in the face of opposing desires; always granted, that is, that he is free to choose between these courses as genuinely open possibilities. If the reality of freedom be conceded *here*, everything is conceded that the Libertarian has any real interest in securing.

But, of course, the most vital question is, can the reality of freedom be conceded even here? In particular, can the standard objection be met which we stated, that if the person's choice does not, in these situations as elsewhere, flow from his *character*, then it is not *that person's* choice at all.

This is, perhaps, of all the objections to a contra-causal freedom, the one which is generally felt to be the most conclusive. For the assumption upon which it is based, *viz.*, that no intelligible meaning can attach to the claim that an act which is not an expression of the self's *character* may nevertheless be the *self's* act, is apt to be regarded as self-evident. The Libertarian is accordingly charged with being in effect an *In*-determinist, whose "free will," in so far as it does not flow from the agent's character, can only be a matter of "chance." Has the Libertarian—who invariably repudiates this charge and claims to be a *Self*-determinist—any way of showing that, contrary to the assumption of his critics, we *can* meaningfully talk of an act as the self's act even though, in an important sense, it is not an expression of the self's "character"?

I think that he has. I want to suggest that what prevents the critics from finding a meaning in this way of talking is that they are looking for it in the wrong way; or better, perhaps, with the wrong orientation. They are looking for it from the stand-point of the *external observer;* the stand-point proper to, because alone possible for, apprehension of the physical world. Now from the external stand-point we may observe processes of change. But one thing which, by common consent, *cannot* be observed from without is *creative activity.* Yet—and here lies the crux of the whole matter—it is precisely creative activity which we are trying to understand when we are trying to understand what is traditionally designated by "free will." For if there should be an act which is genuinely the self's act and is nevertheless not an expression of its character, such an act, in which the self "transcends" its character as so far formed, would seem to be essentially of the nature of creative activity. It follows that to look for a meaning in "free will" from the external stand-point is absurd. It is to look for it in a way that ensures that it will not be found. Granted that a creative activity of any kind is at least *possible* (and I know of no ground for its a *priori* rejection), there is one way, and one way only, in which we can hope to apprehend it, and that is from the *inner* stand-point of direct participation.

It seems to me therefore, that if the Libertarian's claim to find a meaning in a "free" will which is genuinely the self's will, though not an expression of the self's character, is to be subjected to any test that is worth applying, that test must be undertaken from the inner standpoint. We ought to place ourselves imaginatively at the stand-point of the agent engaged in the typical moral situation in which free will is claimed, and ask ourselves whether from this stand-point the claim in question does or does not have meaning for us. That the appeal must

be to introspection is no doubt unfortunate. But he would be a very doctrinaire critic of introspection who declined to make use of it when in the nature of the case no other means of apprehension is available. Everyone must make the introspective experiment for himself: but I may perhaps venture to report, though at this late stage with extreme brevity, what I at least seem to find when I make the experiment myself.

In the situation of moral conflict, then, I (as agent) have before my mind a course of action X, which I believe to be my duty; and also a course of action Y, incompatible with X, which I feel to be that which I most strongly desire. Y is, as it is sometimes expressed, "in the line of least resistance" for me—the course which I am aware I should take if I let my purely desiring nature operate without hindrance. It is the course towards which I am aware that my *character,* as so far formed, naturally inclines me. Now, as actually engaged in this situation, I find that I cannot help believing that I *can* rise to duty and choose X; the "rising to duty" being effected by what is commonly called "effort of will." And I further find, if I ask myself just what it is I am believing when I believe that I "can" rise to duty, that I cannot help believing that it lies with me here and now, quite absolutely, which of two genuinely open possibilities I adopt; whether, that is, I make the effort of will and choose X, or, on the other hand, let my desiring nature, my character as so far formed, "have its way," and choose Y, the course "in the line of least resistance." These beliefs may, of course, be illusory, but that is not at present in point. For the present argument all that matters is whether beliefs of this sort are in fact discoverable in the moral agent in the situation of "moral temptation." For my own part, I cannot doubt the introspective evidence that they are.

Now here is the vital point. No matter which course, X or Y, I choose in this situation, I cannot doubt, *qua* practical being engaged in it, that my choice is *not* just the expression of my formed character, and yet *is* a choice made by my *self.* For suppose I make the effort and choose X (my "duty"). Since my very purpose in making the "effort" is to enable me to act against the existing "set" of desire, which is the expression of my character as so far formed, I cannot possibly regard the act itself as the expression of my *character*. On the other hand, introspection makes it equally clear that I am certain that it is *I* who choose; that the act is not an "accident," but is genuinely *my* act. Or suppose that I choose Y (the end of "strongest desire"). The course chosen here is, it is true, in conformity with my "character." But since I find myself unable to doubt that I *could* have made the effort and chosen X, I cannot possibly regard the choice of Y as *just* the expression of my character. Yet here again I find that I cannot doubt that the choice is *my* choice, a choice for which *I* am justly to be blamed.

What this amounts to is that I *can* and *do* attach meaning, *qua* moral agent, to an act which is not the self's character and yet is genuinely the self's act. And having no good reason to suppose that other persons have a fundamentally different mental constitution, it seems to me probable that anyone else who undertakes a similar experiment will be obliged to submit a similar report. I conclude, therefore, that the argument against "free will" on the score of its "meaninglessness" must be held to fail. "Free Will" does have meaning; though, because it is of the nature of a creative activity, its meaning is discoverable only in an intuition of the practical consciousness of the participating agent. To the agent making a moral choice in the situation where duty clashes with desire, his "self" is known to him as a creatively active self, a self which declines to be identified with his "character" as so formed. Not, of course, that the self's character—let it be added to obviate misunderstanding—either is, or is supposed by the agent to be, devoid of bearing upon his choices, even in the "sector" in which free will is held to operate. On the contrary, such a bearing is manifest in the empirically verifiable fact that we find it "harder" (as we say) to make the effort of will required to "rise to duty" in proportion to the extent that the "dutiful" course conflicts with the course to which our character as so far formed inclines us. It is only in the polemics of the critics that a "free" will is supposed to be in-

compatible with recognizing the bearing of "character" upon choice.

"But what" (it may be asked) "of the all-important question of the *value* of this 'subjective certainty'? Even if what you say is sound as 'phenomenology,' is there any reason to suppose that the conviction on which you lay so much stress is in fact *true*?" I agree that the question is important; far more important, indeed, than is always realized, for it is not always realized that the only direct evidence there *could* be for a creative activity like "free will" is an intuition of the practical consciousness. But this question falls outside the purview of the present paper. The aim of the paper has not been to offer a constructive defense of free will. It has been to show that the problem as traditionally posed is a real, and not a pseudo, problem. A serious threat to that thesis, it was acknowledged, arises from the apparent difficulty of attaching meaning to an act which is not the expression of the self's character and yet *is* the self's own act. The object of my brief phenomenological analysis was to provide evidence that such an act *does* have meaning for us in the one context in which there is any sense in *expecting* it to have meaning.

My general conclusion is, I fear, very unexciting. It is merely that it is an error to suppose that the "Free Will" problem, when correctly formulated, turns out not to be a "problem" at all. Labouring to reinstate an old problem is dull work enough. But I am disposed to think that the philosophic situation to-day calls for a good deal more dull work of a similar sort.

Questions on Campbell

1. What does "She could have acted otherwise" mean according to Campbell? How does his view of the matter differ from Nielsen's? Why is the difference important?

2. When exactly does a person have contra-causal freedom, the freedom to do otherwise in the categorical sense? Give some examples, if you can.

3. Are there some people who do not have any contra-causal freedom at all? Why do you think that? What would Skinner say?

Richard Taylor

Freedom and Determinism

For biographical information on Taylor, see the reading in chapter 1.

Freedom

To say that it is, in a given instance, up to me what I do, is to say that I am in that instance *free* with respect to what I then do. Thus, I am sometimes free to move my finger this way and that, but not, certainly, to bend it backward or into a knot. But what does this mean?

It means, first, that there is no *obstacle* or *impediment* to my activity. Thus, there is sometimes no obstacle to my moving my finger this way and that, though there are obvious obstacles to my moving it far backward or into a knot. Those things, accordingly, that pose obstacles to my motions limit my freedom. If my hand were strapped in such a way as to permit only a leftward motion of my finger, I would not then be free to move it to the right. If it were encased in a tight cast that permitted no motion, I would not be free to move it at all. Freedom of motion, then, is limited by obstacles.

Further, to say that it is, in a given instance, up to me what I do, means that nothing *constrains* or *forces* me to do one thing rather than another. Constraints are like obstacles, except that while the latter prevent, the former enforce. Thus, if my finger is being forcibly bent to the left—by a machine, for instance, or by another person, or by any force that I cannot overcome—then I am not free to move it this way and that. I cannot, in fact move it at all; I can only watch to see how it is moved, and perhaps vainly resist. Its motions are not up to me, or within my control, but in the control of some other thing or person.

Obstacles and constraints, then, both obviously limit my freedom. To say I am free to perform some action thus means at least that there is no obstacle to my doing it, and that nothing constrains me to do otherwise.

Now if we rest content with this observation, as many have, and construe free activity simply as activity that is unimpeded and unconstrained, there is evidently no inconsistency between affirming both the thesis of determinism and the claim that I am sometimes free. For to say that some action of mine is neither impeded nor constrained does not by itself imply that it is not causally determined. The absence of obstacles and constraints are mere negative conditions, and do not by themselves rule out the presence of positive causes. It might seem, then, that we can say of some of my actions that there are conditions antecedent to their performance so that no other actions were possible, and also that these actions were unobstructed and unconstrained. And to say that would logically entail that such actions were both causally determined, and free.

Soft Determinism

It is this kind of consideration that has led many philosophers to embrace what is sometimes called "soft determinism." All versions of this theory have in common three claims, by means of which, it is naively supposed, a reconciliation is achieved between determinism and freedom. Freedom being, furthermore, a condition of moral responsibility and the only condition that metaphysics seriously questions, it is supposed by the partisans of this view that determinism is perfectly compatible with such responsibility. This, no doubt, accounts for its great appeal and wide acceptance, even by some men of considerable learning.

The three claims of soft determinism are (1) that the thesis of determinism is true, and that accordingly all human behavior, voluntary or other, like the behavior of all other things, arises from antecedent conditions, given which no other behavior is possible—in short, that all

The reading is from Richard Taylor, *Metaphysics*, 3d ed., © 1983, pp. 41–50. Reprinted by permission of Prentice-Hall, Inc., Englewood Cliffs, NJ.

human behavior is caused and determined; (2) that voluntary behavior is nonetheless free to the extent that it is not externally constrained or impeded; and (3) that, in the absence of such obstacles and constraints, the causes of voluntary behavior are certain states, events, or conditions within the agent himself; namely, his own acts of will or volitions, choices, decisions, desires, and so on.

Thus, on this view, I am free, and therefore sometimes responsible for what I do, provided nothing prevents me from acting according to my own choice, desire or volition, or constrains me to act otherwise. There may, to be sure, be other conditions for my responsibility—such as, for example, an understanding of the probable consequences of my behavior, and that sort of thing—but absence of constraint or impediment is, at least, one such condition. And, it is claimed, it is a condition that is compatible with the supposition that my behavior is caused—for it is, by hypothesis, caused by my own inner choices, desires, and volitions.

The Refutation of This

The theory of soft determinism looks good at first—so good that it has for generations been solemnly taught from numberless philosophical chairs and implanted in the minds of students as sound philosophy—but no great acumen is needed to discover that far from solving any problem, it only camouflages it.

My free actions are those unimpeded and unconstrained motions that arise from my own inner desires, choices, and volitions; let us grant this provisionally. But now, whence arise those inner states that determine what my body shall do? Are they within my control or not? Having made my choice or decision and acted upon it, could I have chosen otherwise or not?

Here the determinist, hoping to surrender nothing and yet to avoid the problem implied in that question, bids us not to ask it; the question itself, he announces, is without meaning. For to say that I could have done otherwise, he says, means only that I *would* have done otherwise *if* those inner states that determined my action had been different; if, that is, I had decided or chosen differently. To ask, accordingly, whether I could have chosen or decided differently is only to ask whether, had I decided to decide differently or chosen to choose differently, or willed to will differently, I would have decided or chosen or willed differently. And this, of course, is unintelligible nonsense.

But it is not nonsense to ask whether the causes of my actions—my own inner choices, decisions and desires—are themselves caused. And of course they are, if determinism is true, for on that thesis everything is caused and determined. And if they are, then we cannot avoid concluding that, given the causal conditions of those inner states, I could not have decided, willed, chosen, or desired otherwise than I in fact did, for this is a logical consequence of the very definition of determinism. Of course we can still say that, *if* the causes of those inner states, whatever they were, had been different, then their effects, those inner state themselves, would have been different, and that in this hypothetical sense I could have decided, chosen, willed, or desired differently—but that only pushes our problem back still another step. For we will then want to know whether the causes of those inner states were within my control; and so on, *ad infinitum*. We are, at each step, permitted to say "could have been otherwise" only in a provisional sense—provided, that is, something else had been different—but must then retract it and replace it with "could not have been otherwise" as soon as we discover, as we must at each step, that whatever would have to have been different could not have been different.

Examples

Such is the dialectic of the problem. The easiest way to see the shadowy quality of soft determinism, however, is by means of examples.

Let us suppose that my body is moving in various ways, that these motions are not externally constrained or impeded, and that they are all exactly in accordance with my own desires, choices, or acts of will and what not. When I will that my arm should move in a certain way, I find it moving in that way, unobstructed and unconstrained. When I will to speak, my lips and tongue move, unobstructed and unconstrained, in a manner suitable to the formation of the words I choose to utter. Now given that this is a correct description of my behavior, namely, that it consists of the unconstrained and unimpeded motions of my body in response to my own volitions, then it follows that my behavior is free, on the soft determinist's definition of "free." It follows further that I am responsible for that behavior; or at least, that if I am not, it is not from any lack of freedom on my part.

But if the fulfillment of these conditions renders my behavior free—that is to say, if my behavior satisfies the conditions of free action set forth in the theory of soft determinism—then my behavior will be no less free if we assume further conditions that are perfectly consistent with those already satisfied.

We suppose further, accordingly, that while my behavior is entirely in accordance with my own volitions, and thus "free" in terms of the conception of freedom we are examining, my volitions themselves are caused. To make this graphic, we can suppose that an ingenious physiologist can induce in me any volition he pleases, simply by pushing various buttons on an instrument to which, let us suppose, I am attached by numerous wires. All the volitions I have in that situation are, accordingly, precisely the ones he gives me. By pushing one button, he evokes in me the volition to raise my hand; and my hand, being unimpeded, rises in response to that volition. By pushing another, he induces the volition in me to kick, and my foot, being unimpeded, kicks in response to that volition. We can even suppose that the physiologist puts a rifle in my hands, aims it at some passerby, and then, by pushing the proper button, evokes in me the volition to squeeze my finger against the trigger, whereupon the passer-by falls dead of a bullet wound.

This is the description of a man who is acting in accordance with his inner volitions, a man whose body is unimpeded and unconstrained in its motions, these motions being the effects of those inner states. It is hardly the description of a free and responsible agent. It is the perfect description of a puppet. To render a man your puppet, it is not necessary forcibly to constrain the motions of his limbs, after the fashion that real puppets are moved. A subtler but no less effective means of making a man your puppet would be to gain complete control of his inner states, and ensuring, as the theory of soft determinism does ensure, that his body will move in accordance with them.

The example is somewhat unusual, but it is no worse for that. It is perfectly intelligible, and it does appear to refute the soft determinist's conception of freedom. One might think that, in such a case, the agent should not have allowed himself to be so rigged in the first place, but this is irrelevant; we can suppose that he was not aware that he was, and was hence unaware of the source of those inner states that prompted his bodily motions. The example can, moreover, be modified in perfectly realistic ways, so as to coincide with actual and familiar cases. One can, for instance, be given a compulsive desire for certain drugs, simply by having them administered to him over a course of time. Suppose, then, that I do, with neither my knowledge nor consent, thus become a victim of such a desire and act upon it. Do I act freely, merely by virtue of the fact that I am unimpeded in my quest for drugs? In a sense I do, surely, but I am hardly free with respect to whether or not I shall use drugs. I never chose to have the desire for them inflicted upon me.

Nor does it, of course, matter whether the inner states which allegedly prompt all my "free" activity are evoked in me by another agent or by perfectly impersonal forces. Whether a desire which causes my body to behave in a certain way is inflicted upon me by another person, for instance, or derived from hereditary factors, or indeed from anything at all, matters not the least. In any case, if it is in fact the cause of my bodily behavior, I cannot but act in accordance with it. Wherever it came from, whether from personal or impersonal origins, it was entirely caused or determined, and not within my control. Indeed, if determinism is true, as the theory of soft determinism holds it to be, all those inner states which cause my body to behave in whatever ways it behaves must arise from circumstances that existed before I was born; for the chain of causes and effects is infinite, and none could have been the least different, given those that preceded.

Simple Indeterminism

We might at first now seem warranted in simply denying determinism, and saying that, insofar as they are free, my actions are not caused; or that, if they are caused by my own inner states—my own desires, impulses, choices, volitions, and whatnot—then these, in any case, are not caused. This is a perfectly clear sense in which a man's action, assuming that it was free, could have been otherwise. If it was uncaused, then, even given the conditions under which it occurred and all that preceded, some other act was nonetheless possible, and he did not have to do what he did. Or if his action was the inevitable consequence of his own inner states, and could not have been otherwise given these, we can nevertheless say that these inner states, being uncaused, could have been otherwise, and could thereby have produced different actions.

Only the slightest consideration will show, however, that this simple denial of determinism has not the slightest plausibility. For let us suppose it is true, and that some of my bodily motions—namely, those that I regard as my free acts—are not caused at all or, if caused by my own inner states, that these are not caused. We shall thereby avoid picturing a puppet, to be sure—but only by substituting something even less like a man; for the conception that now emerges is not that of a free man, but of an erratic and jerking phantom, without any rhyme or reason at all.

Suppose that my right arm is free, according to this conception; that is, that its motions are uncaused. It moves this way and that from time to time, but nothing causes these motions. Sometimes it moves forth vigorously, sometimes up, sometimes down, sometimes it just drifts vaguely about—these motions all being wholly free and uncaused. Manifestly I have nothing to do with them at all; they just happen, and neither I nor anyone can ever tell what this arm will be doing next. It might seize a club and lay it on the head of the nearest bystander, no less to my astonishment than his. There will never be any point in asking why these motions occur, or in seeking any explanation of them, for under the condition assumed there is no explanation. They just happen, from no causes at all.

This is no description of free, voluntary, or responsible behavior. Indeed, so far as the motions of my body or its parts are entirely uncaused, such motions cannot even be ascribed to me as my behavior in the first place, since I have nothing to do with them. The behavior of my arm is just the random motion of a foreign object. Behavior that is mine must be behavior that is within my control, but motions that occur from no causes are without the control of anyone. I can have no more to do with, and no more control over, the uncaused motions of my limbs than a gambler has over the motions of an honest roulette wheel. I can only, like him, idly wait to see what happens.

Nor does it improve things to suppose that my bodily motions are caused by my own inner states, so long as we suppose these to be wholly uncaused. The result will be the same as before. My arm, for example, will move this way and that, sometimes up and sometimes down, sometimes vigorously and sometimes just drifting about, always in response to certain inner states, to be sure. But since these are supposed to be wholly uncaused, it follows that I have no control over them and hence none over their effects. If my hand lays a club forcefully on the nearest bystander, we can indeed say that this motion resulted from an inner club-wielding desire of mine; but we must add that I had nothing to do with that desire, and that it arose, to be followed by its inevitable effect, no less to my astonishment than to his. Things like this do, alas, sometimes happen. We are all sometimes seized by compulsive impulses that arise we know not whither, and we do sometimes act upon these. But since they are far from being examples of free, voluntary, and responsible behavior, we need only to learn that behavior was of this sort to conclude that it was not free, voluntary, nor responsible. It was erratic, impulsive, and irresponsible.

Determinism and Simple Indeterminism as Theories

Both determinism and simple **indeterminism** are loaded with difficulties, and no one who has thought much on them can affirm either of them without some embarrassment. Simple indeterminism has nothing whatever to be said for it, except that it appears to remove the grossest difficulties of determinism, only, however, to imply perfect absurdities of its own. Determinism, on the other hand, is at least initially plausible. Men seem to have a natural inclination to believe in it; it is, indeed, almost required for the very exercise of practical intelligence. And beyond this, our experience appears always to confirm it, so long as we are dealing with everyday facts of common experience, as distinguished from the esoteric researches of theoretical physics. But determinism, as applied to human behavior, has implications which few men can casually accept, and they appear to be implications which no modification of the theory can efface.

Both theories, moreover, appear logically irreconcilable to [two apparently self-evident facts of experience]; namely, (1) that my behavior is sometimes the outcome of my deliberation, and (2) that in these and other cases it is sometimes up to me what I do. . . .

I can deliberate only about my own future actions, and then only if I do not already know what I am going to do. If a certain nasal tickle warns me that I am about to sneeze, for instance, then I cannot deliberate whether to sneeze or not; I can only prepare for the impending convulsion. But if determinism is true, then there are always conditions existing antecedently to everything I do, sufficient for my doing just that, and such as to render it inevitable. If I can know what those conditions are and what behavior they are sufficient to produce, then I can in every such case know what I am going to do and cannot then deliberate about it.

By itself this only shows, of course, that I can deliberate only in ignorance of the causal conditions of my behavior; it does not show that such conditions cannot exist. It is odd, however, to suppose that deliberation should be a mere substitute for clear knowledge. . . .

Worse yet, however, it now becomes clear that I cannot deliberate about what I am going to do, if it is even possible for me to find out in advance, whether I do in fact find out in advance or not. I can deliberate only with the view to deciding what to do, to making up my mind; and this is impossible if I believe that it could be inferred what I am going to do, from conditions already existing, even though I have not made that inference myself. If I believe that what I am going to do has been rendered inevitable by conditions already existing, and could be inferred by anyone having the requisite sagacity, then I cannot try to decide whether to do it or not, for there is simply nothing left to decide. I can at best only guess or try to figure it out myself or, all prognostics failing, I can wait and see; but I cannot deliberate. I deliberate in order to *decide* what to do, not to *discover* what it is that I am *going* to do. But if determinism is true, then there are always antecedent conditions sufficient for everything that I do, and this can always be inferred by anyone having the requisite sagacity; that is, by anyone having knowledge of what those conditions are and what behavior they are sufficient to produce.

This suggests what in fact seems quite clear, that determinism cannot be reconciled with our [belief] that it is sometimes up to me what I am going to do. For if it is ever really up to me whether to do this thing or that, then, as we have seen, each alternative course of action must be such that I can do it; not that I can do it in some abstruse or hypothetical sense of "can"; not that I could do it if only something were true that is not true; but in the sense that it is then and there within my power to do it. But this is never so, if determinism is true, for on the very formulation of that theory whatever happens at any time is the only thing that can then happen, given all that precedes it. It is simply a logical consequence of this that whatever I do at any time is the only thing I can then do, given the conditions that precede my doing it. Nor does it help in the least to interpose, among the causal antecedents of my behavior, my own inner states, such as my desires, choices, acts of will, and so on. For even supposing these to be always involved in voluntary behavior—which is highly doubtful in itself—it is a consequence of determinism that these, whatever they are at any time, can never be other than what they then are. Every chain of causes and effects, if determinism is true, is infinite. This is why it is not now up to me whether I shall a moment hence be male or female. The conditions determining my sex have existed through my whole life, and even prior to my life. But if determinism is true, the same holds of anything that I ever am, ever become, or ever do. It matters not whether we are speaking of the most patent facts of my being, such as my sex; or the most subtle, such as my feelings, thoughts, desires, or choices. Nothing could be other than it is, given what was; and while we may indeed say, quite idly, that something—some inner state of mine, for instance—*could* have been different, had only something *else* been different, any consolation of this thought evaporates as soon as we add that whatever would have to have been different could not have been different.

It is even more obvious that our data cannot be reconciled to the theory of simple indeterminism. I can deliberate only about my own actions; this is obvious. But the random, uncaused motion of any body whatever, whether it be a part of my body or not, is no action of mine and nothing that is within my power. I might try to guess what these motions will be, just as I might try to guess how a roulette wheel will behave, but I cannot deliberate about them or try to decide what they shall be, simply because these things are not up to me. Whatever is not caused by anything is not caused by me, and nothing could be more plainly inconsistent with saying that it is nevertheless up to me what it shall be.

The Theory of Agency

The only conception of action that accords with our data is one according to which men—and perhaps some other things too—are sometimes, but of course not always, self-determining beings; that is, beings which are sometimes the causes of their own behavior. In the case of an action that is free, it must be such that it is caused by the agent who performs it, but such that no antecedent conditions were sufficient for his performing just that action. In

the case of an action that is born free and rational, it must be such that the agent who performed it did so for some reason, but this reason cannot have been the cause of it.

Now this conception fits what men take themselves to be; namely, beings who act, or who are agents, rather than things that are merely acted upon, and whose behavior is simply the causal consequence of conditions which they have not wrought. When I believe that I have done something, I do believe that it was I who caused it to be done, I who made something happen, and not merely something within me, such as one of my own subjective states, which is not identical with myself. If I believe that something not identical with myself was the cause of my behavior—some event wholly external to myself, for instance, or even one internal to myself, such as a nerve impulse, volition, or what not—then I cannot regard that behavior as being an act of mine, unless I further believe that I was the cause of that external or internal event. My pulse, for example, is caused and regulated by certain conditions existing within me, and not by myself. I do not, accordingly, regard this activity of my body as my action, and would be no more tempted to do so if I became suddenly conscious within myself of those conditions or impulses that produce it. This is behavior with which I have nothing to do, behavior that is not within my immediate control, behavior that is not only not free activity, but not even the activity of an agent to begin with; it is nothing but a mechanical reflex. Had I never learned that my very life depends on this pulse beat, I would regard it with complete indifference, as something foreign to me, like the oscillations of a clock pendulum that I idly contemplate.

Now this conception of activity, and of an agent who is the cause of it, involves two rather strange metaphysical notions that are never applied elsewhere in nature. The first is that of a *self* or *person*—for example, a man—who is not merely a collection of things or events, but a substance and a self-moving being. For on this view it is a man himself, and not merely some part of him or something within him, that is the cause of his own activity. Now we certainly do not know that a man is anything more than an assemblage of physical things and processes, which act in accordance with those laws that describe the behavior of all other physical things and processes. Even though a man is a living being, of enormous complexity, there is nothing, apart from the requirements of this theory, to suggest that his behavior is so radically different in its origin from that of other physical objects, or that an understanding of it must be sought in some metaphysical realm wholly different from that appropriate to the understanding of nonliving things.

Second, this conception of activity involves an extraordinary conception of causation, according to which an agent, which is a substance and not an event, can nevertheless be the cause of an event. Indeed, if he is a free agent then he can, on this conception, cause an event to occur—namely, some act of his own—without anything else causing him to do so.

. . . The theory of agency avoids the absurdities of simple indeterminism by conceding that human behavior is caused, while at the same time avoiding the difficulties of determinism by denying that every chain of causes and effects is infinite. Some such causal chains, on this view, have beginnings, and they begin with agents themselves. Moreover, if we are to suppose that it is sometimes up to me what I do, and understand this in a sense which is not consistent with determinism, we must suppose that I am an agent or a being who initiates his own actions, sometimes under conditions which do not determine what action I shall perform. Deliberation becomes, on this view, something that is not only possible but quite rational, for it does make sense to deliberate about activity that is truly my own and that depends in its outcome upon me as its author, and not merely upon something . . . that is supposed to be intimately associated with me, such as my thoughts, volitions, choices, or whatnot.

Questions on Taylor

1. What is soft determinism according to Taylor? Why does Taylor find this view unacceptable? Does Nielsen's account of freedom avoid the problem or not?

2. What is simple indeterminism? What is wrong with this view according to Taylor?

3. What criticisms does Taylor make of determinism, as distinguished from soft determinism? How do you think that B. F. Skinner would reply to Taylor's criticisms?

4. Explain Taylor's theory of self-determination, including in your explanation his concept of the self and self-causation. Is this view plausible? Can you think of any problems with it?

Suggested Readings

B. F. Skinner defends his deterministic theory of behaviorism and attacks the traditional view of human freedom in several books. See his *Beyond Freedom and Dignity* (New York: Alfred A. Knopf, 1971), *About Behaviorism* (New York: Alfred A. Knopf, 1974), and his classic *Walden Two* (New York: Macmillan, 1960), which is a story about a utopian society that practices his brand of behaviorism.

Bernard Berofsky, ed., *Free Will and Determinism* (New York: Harper & Row, 1966) is a collection of readings covering determinism, soft determinism (called "reconciliationism"), nondeterminism (called "libertarianism"), action theory, and the problem of the apparent conflict between God's foreknowledge and free will. Another anthology with numerous discussions on various aspects of determinism, freedom, moral responsibility, and punishment is Sidney Hook, ed., *Determinism and Freedom in the Age of Modern Science* (New York: New York University Press, 1958).

Other useful anthologies are Keith Lehrer, ed., *Freedom and Determinism* (New York: Random House, 1966); Gerald Dworkin, ed., *Determinism, Free Will, and Moral Responsibility* (Englewood Cliffs, NJ: Prentice-Hall, 1970; and H. Morris, ed., *Freedom and Responsibility* (Stanford: Stanford University Press, 1966).

Clarence Darrow, Attorney for the Damned, ed. Arthur Weinberg (New York: Simon & Schuster, 1957) has some of Darrow's famous defense speeches including the one in the Loeb and Leopold case where he defends hard determinism.

An interesting imaginary dialogue between a free-willist, determinist, and compatibilist (or soft determinist) is found in Clifford Williams, *Free Will and Determinism: A Dialogue* (Indianapolis: Hackett Publishing Co., 1980).

The terms "soft determinism" and "hard determinism" were coined by William James in his classic essay "The Dilemma of Determinism," in William James, *The Will to Believe and Other Essays in Popular Philosophy* (Cambridge: Harvard University Press, 1979), pp. 114–140. James himself defends a version of indeterminism.

Daniel C. Dennett, *Elbow Room: The Varieties of Free Will Worth Wanting* (Cambridge: The MIT Press, 1985) attempts to solve or dissolve the traditional problem of free will and determinism by defending a version of soft determinism or compatibilism. Peter van Inwagen, *An Essay on Free Will* (Oxford: Clarendon Press, 1983), on the other hand, defends the view that free will and determinism are incompatible.

The Mind-Body Problem

Chapter 5

Introduction

The problem. A traditional Platonic belief that has been adopted by many Christians is that a person is a mind or soul that survives the death of the body. But what is the mind and how is it related to the body? This is the mind-body problem. We will postpone until the next chapter the issue of survival of death, and the related problem of determining what makes a person the same from one time to the next.

Theories about the mind and body. Descartes is usually given credit for raising the mind-body problem in its modern form. His own solution to the problem, customarily called **dualism**, is that the mind and body are two different things or substances having radically different properties. The body is extended in space, has spatial dimensions and location, and is publicly observable, whereas the mind is indivisible, has no spatial dimensions or location, and cannot be publicly observed.

But how do the mind and body interact in perception and volition? How can something immaterial affect something material? Descartes insisted that there is a dualistic interaction between the mind and body (in perception and volition, for example), somehow mediated by the pineal gland. But many philosophers have found this incredible, and tried to give different accounts of the relation between the mind and the body. For example, the German philosopher Leibniz (1646–1716) adopted **parallelism**, the view that the mind and body do not causally interact, but only appear to do so because of a harmony pre-established by God (likened by Leibniz to two clocks set to tick together). The French philosopher Malebranche (1638–1715) held that a physical event in the body is the occasion for God to cause a corresponding mental event. According to this view (called **occasionalism**) a bee stinging a person's toe is the occasion for God to cause a pain in the toe. According to still another dualistic view called **epiphenomenalism**, bodily events cause mental events, as in perception or sensation, but mental events cannot cause bodily events; they are merely a kind of side effect of bodily events, an "epiphenomenon."

These theories are versions of dualism because they all hold that the mind and body are different sorts of things; they disagree only about the interaction of the mind and body. Parallelism and occasionalism hold that no such interaction occurs. Epiphenomenalism says that the interaction is only one way (from the physical to the mental, but not vice versa), while dualistic interactionism (Descartes' view) claims that there is a two-way interaction, both from the mental to the physical (as in volition), and from the physical to the mental (as in sensation and perception).

The main alternative to dualism is **monism**, the view that there is only one sort of thing that exists. One possibility, suggested by Bertrand Russell, is what he called **neutral monism**, the view that the one sort of thing that exists is neither mental nor physical but neutral. This view is similar to the **double-aspect theory** of the

Dutch philosopher Spinoza (1632–1677) that the mind and body are just two different aspects of one substance (God) that is neither mental nor physical.

Instead of saying that what exists is neither mental nor physical, we can say that it is one or the other. If we declare that everything that exists is mental, we have adopted **idealism,** the view that everything that exists is mental, that is, a mind or a mental object or activity.

The other option, **materialism** (or physicalism), is that everything that exists is physical. Many contemporary philosophers have adopted some version of materialism. One theory that has been accepted by philosophers and psychologists is **behaviorism.** This theory takes at least two different forms. The first form, **methodological behaviorism,** is the view that psychologists should study behavior instead of trying to study the mind and its activities by some sort of introspection. It is not clear that this type of behaviorism is incompatible with dualism, however; merely confining one's study to observable behavior is not the same as denying the existence of unobservable private mental objects and activities. The other form of behaviorism, **logical behaviorism,** does seem to conflict with dualism. According to logical behaviorism, our mental language does not refer to private nonphysical things or events, but rather is somehow logically connected to observable behavior. Thus we do not need to suppose that there are mental entities and events to explain our claims about them, for such claims are logically connected to or reducible to claims about behavior, which of course consists of material events. Just what the connection is, however, remains problematic for these theorists. Ryle's view, discussed by D. M. Armstrong in the readings, is that mental states somehow can be reduced to dispositions to behavior, or that mentalistic language is really about dispositions to behavior. The contemporary American philosopher Norman Malcolm thinks that mental language always implies behavior as a criterion. In any event, it is clear that the logical behaviorists reject dualism. Ryle ridicules Descartes' view as "The Ghost in the Machine," and claims that Descartes commits a basic logical mistake, a "category mistake," like thinking that a university is a building in addition to the other college buildings.

Logical behaviorism is no longer in favor with current philosophers. The problem is that the logical connection between mental language and behavior is very hard to make out in some cases. Pains and mental images, for example, do not seem always to correspond to observable behavior. People can refer to the pain in their foot or to a mental image of their mother without necessarily referring to any behavior.

Another materialistic theory is the **identity theory.** One of its leading proponents is the contemporary British philosopher J. J. C. Smart who argues that mental events are identical with brain processes in the same way as lightning flashes are identical with electrical discharges—for example, the pain in Jane's foot is identical with certain brain processes in her head, with certain neuron firings in her brain. A slightly different version of the identity theory is advocated by David M. Armstrong in the readings; according to him, the mind is really the brain.

Like logical behaviorism, the identity theory faces serious difficulties. One objection made by the American philosopher Hilary Putnam and others is that we can imagine a Martian with a body different from ours still having pains or being in mental states, but according to the identity theory the pains or mental states would not be brain processes because we are supposing the Martians don't have brains like ours. Another objection is developed by Thomas Nagel in the readings. We could know everything about a bat's brain and behavior, and still not know what it is like to be a bat. This suggests that the bat's mental states are something different from brain states.

The sort of materialism, or physicalism, that is being currently discussed by many philosophers is either functionalism or eliminative materialism. These views are represented in the readings by Fodor and Churchland, respectively. **Functionalism** is the view that mental events can be defined in terms of what they cause (or what their function is), and this includes both physical events and other mental events. Thus a human being or a Martian or even a computer could have the same mental event, that is, an event that functions causally the same way, even though different physical events occur in their bodies. Mental language cannot be eliminated or simply reduced to physical terms, but this does not mean that there are nonphysical mental substances or events.

Functionalism is often explained in terms of a machine analogy: the relation between the mind and the brain is like the relation between a computer program and a computer. An implication of this is that mental events can occur in many different sorts of things, for example, silicon-based Martian or IBM computers. This consequence of functionalism is attacked by John Searle in his controversial argument about the Chinese room, which is supposed to show that computers cannot really think, and thus that minds are not merely programs.

In view of the problems confronting functionalism, some contemporary philosophers have turned to **eliminative materialism.** This view agrees with functionalism that mental language cannot be reduced to physical language, but then it concludes that mental language should be eliminated because it is defective. Talking about mental events like having pains, desires, and so on is just part of "folk psychology"; actually there aren't any pains, desires, and so on, any more than there are elves and fairies.

René Descartes

The Mind as Distinct from the Body

For biographical information on Descartes, see the reading in chapter 3.

In order to begin this examination, then, I here say, in the first place, that there is a great difference between mind and body, inasmuch as body is by nature always divisible, and the mind is entirely indivisible. For, as a matter of fact, when I consider the mind, that is to say, myself inasmuch as I am only a thinking thing, I cannot distinguish in myself any parts, but apprehend myself to be clearly one and entire; and although the whole mind seems to be united to the whole body, yet if a foot, or an arm, or some other part, is separated from my body, I am aware that nothing has been taken away from my mind. And the faculties of willing, feeling, conceiving, etc. cannot be properly speaking said to be its parts, for it is one and the same mind which employs itself in willing and in feeling and understanding. But it is quite otherwise with corporeal or extended objects, for there is not one of these imaginable by me which my mind cannot easily divide into parts, and which consequently I do not recognise as being divisible; this would be sufficient to teach me that the mind or soul of man is entirely different from the body, if I had not already learned it from other sources.

I further notice that the mind does not receive the impressions from all parts of the body immediately, but only from the brain, or perhaps even from one if its smallest parts, to wit, from that in which the common sense is said to reside, which, whenever it is disposed in the same particular way, conveys the same thing to the mind, although meanwhile the other portions of the body may be differently disposed, as is testified by innumerable experiments which it is unnecessary here to recount.

I notice, also, that the nature of body is such that none of its parts can be moved by another part a little way off which cannot also be moved in the same way by each one of the parts which are between the two, although this more remote part does not act at all. As, for example, in the cord *ABCD* [which is in tension] if we pull the last part *D*, the first part *A* will not be moved in any way differently from what would be the case if one of the intervening parts *B* or *C* were pulled, and the last part *D* were to remain unmoved. And in the same way, when I feel pain in my foot, my knowledge of physics teaches me that this sensation is communicated by means of nerves dispersed through the foot, which, being extended like cords from there to the brain, when they are contracted in the foot, at the same time contract the inmost portions of the brain which is their extremity and place of origin, and then excite a certain movement which nature has established in order to cause the mind to be affected by a sensation of pain represented as existing in the foot. But because these nerves must pass through the tibia, the thigh, the loins, the back and the neck, in order to reach from the leg to the brain, it may happen that although their extremities which are in the foot are not affected, but only certain ones of their intervening parts [which pass by the loins or the neck], this action will excite the same movement in the brain that might have been excited there by a hurt received in the foot, in consequence of which the mind will necessarily feel in the foot the same pain as if it had received a hurt. And the same holds good of all the other perceptions of our senses.

I notice finally that since each of the movements which are in the portion of the brain by which the mind is immediately affected brings about one particular sensation only, we cannot under the circumstances imagine anything more likely than that this movement, amongst all the sensations which it is capable of impressing on it, causes mind to be affected by that one which is best fitted and most generally useful for the conservation of the human body when it is in health. But experience makes us aware that

The reading is from *The Philosophical Works of Descartes*, trans. E. S. Haldane and G. R. T. Ross (New York: Dover Publications, 1955), Sixth Meditation, pp. 196–199. ©Cambridge University Press. Reprinted with the permission of Cambridge University Press.

all the feelings with which nature inspires us are such as I have just spoken of; and there is therefore nothing in them which does not give testimony to the power and goodness of the God [who has produced them]. Thus, for example, when the nerves which are in the feet are violently or more than usually moved, their movement, passing through the medulla of the spine to the inmost parts of the brain, gives a sign to the mind which makes it feel somewhat, to wit, pain, as though in the foot, by which the mind is excited to do its utmost to remove the cause of the evil as dangerous and hurtful to the foot. It is true that God could have constituted the nature of man in such a way that this same movement in the brain would have conveyed something quite different to the mind; for example, it might have produced consciousness of itself either in so far as it is in the brain, or as it is in the foot, or as it is in some other place between the foot and the brain, or it might finally have produced consciousness of anything else whatsoever; but none of all this would have contributed so well to the conservation of the body. Similarly, when we desire to drink, a certain dryness of the throat is produced which moves its nerves, and by their means the internal portions of the brain; and this movement causes in the mind the sensation of thirst, because in this case there is nothing more useful to us than to become aware that we have need to drink for the conservation of our health; and the same holds good in other instances.

From this it is quite clear that, notwithstanding the supreme goodness of God, the nature of man, inasmuch as it is composed of mind and body, cannot be otherwise than sometimes a source of deception. For if there is any cause which excites, not in the foot but in some part of the nerves which are extended between the foot and the brain, or even in the brain itself, the same movement which usually is produced when the foot is detrimentally affected, pain will be experienced as though it were in the foot, and the sense will thus naturally be deceived; for since the same movement in the brain is capable of causing but one sensation in the mind, and this sensation is much more frequently excited by a cause which hurts the foot than by another existing in some other quarter, it is reasonable that it should convey to the mind pain in the foot rather than in any other part of the body. And although the parchedness of the throat does not always proceed, as it usually does, from the fact that drinking is necessary for the health of the body, but sometimes comes from quite a different cause, as is the case with dropsical patients, it is yet much better that it should mislead on this occasion than if, on the other hand, it were always to deceive us when the body is in good health; and so on in similar cases.

Questions on Descartes

1. Why does Descartes think that the mind is distinct from the body? Do you agree? Why or why not?

2. Why is the interaction of the mind and the body a source of deception according to Descartes? Is there any way to be sure that we are not being deceived in perception and sensation? What is it?

Gilbert Ryle
Descartes' Myth

Gilbert Ryle (1900–1976) was Waynflete Professor of Metaphysical Philosophy at Oxford University, and for many years was the editor of the journal Mind.

(1) The Official Doctrine.

There is a doctrine about the nature and place of minds which is so prevalent among theorists and even among laymen that it deserves to be described as the official theory. Most philosophers, psychologists and religious teachers subscribe, with minor reservations, to its main articles and, although they admit certain theoretical difficulties in it, they tend to assume that these can be overcome without serious modifications being made to the architecture of the theory. It will be argued here that the central principles of the doctrine are unsound and conflict with the whole body of what we know about minds when we are not speculating about them.

The official doctrine, which hails chiefly from Descartes, is something like this. With the doubtful exceptions of idiots and infants in arms every human being has both a body and a mind. Some would prefer to say that every human being is both a body and a mind. His body and his mind are ordinarily harnessed together, but after the death of the body his mind may continue to exist and function.

Human bodies are in space and are subject to the mechanical laws which govern all other bodies in space. Bodily processes and states can be inspected by external observers. So a man's bodily life is as much a public affair as are the lives of animals and reptiles and even as the careers of trees, crystals and planets.

But minds are not in space, nor are their operations subject to mechanical laws. The workings of one mind are not witnessable by other observers; its career is private. Only I can take direct cognisance of the states and processes of my own mind. A person therefore lives through two collateral histories, one consisting of what happens in and to his body, the other consisting of what happens in and to his mind. The first is public, the second private. The events in the first history are events in the physical world, those in the second are events in the mental world.

It has been disputed whether a person does or can directly monitor all or only some of the episodes of his own private history; but, according to the official doctrine, of at least some of these episodes he has direct and unchallengeable cognisance. In consciousness, self-consciousness and introspection he is directly and authentically apprised of the present states and operations of his mind. He may have great or small uncertainties about concurrent and adjacent episodes in the physical world, but he can have none about at least part of what is momentarily occupying his mind.

It is customary to express this bifurcation of his two lives and of his two worlds by saying that the things and events which belong to the physical world, including his own body, are external, while the workings of his own mind are internal. This antithesis of outer and inner is of course meant to be construed as a metaphor, since minds, not being in space, could not be described as being spatially inside anything else, or as having things going on spatially inside themselves. But relapses from this good intention are common and theorists are found speculating how stimuli, the physical sources of which are yards or miles outside a person's skin, can generate mental responses inside his skull, or how decisions framed inside his cranium can set going movements of his extremities.

Even when 'inner' and 'outer' are construed as metaphors, the problem how a person's mind and body influence one another is notoriously charged with theoretical difficulties. What the mind wills, the legs, arms and the tongue execute; what affects the ear and the eye has something to do with what the mind perceives; grimaces and smiles betray the mind's moods and bodily castigations lead, it is hoped, to moral improvement. But the actual transactions between the episodes of the private history and those of the public history remain mysterious, since by definition they can belong to neither series. They could not be reported among the happenings described in a person's autobiography of his inner life, but nor could they be reported among those described in some one else's biography of that person's overt career. They can be inspected neither by introspection nor by laboratory experiment. They are theoretical shuttlecocks which are forever being bandied from the physiologist back to the psychologist and from the psychologist back to the physiologist.

Underlying this partly metaphorical representation of the bifurcation of a person's two lives there is a seemingly more profound and philosophical assumption. It is assumed that there are two different kinds of existence or status. What exists or happens may have the status of physical existence, or it may have the status of mental existence. Somewhat as the faces of coins are either heads or tails, or somewhat as living creatures are either male or female, so, it is supposed, some existing is physical existing, other existing is mental existing. It is a necessary feature of what has physical existence that it is in space and time, it is a necessary feature of what has mental existence that it is in time but not in space. What has physical existence is composed of matter, or else is a function of matter; what has mental existence consists of consciousness, or else is a function of consciousness.

There is thus a polar opposition between mind and matter, an opposition which is often brought out as follows. Material objects are situated in a common field, known as 'space', and what happens to one body in one part of space is mechanically connected with what happens to other bodies in other parts of space. But mental happenings occur in insulated fields, known as 'minds', and there is, apart maybe from telepathy, no direct causal connection between what happens in one mind and what happens in another. Only through the medium of the public physical world can the mind of one person make a difference to the mind of another. The mind is its own place and in his inner life each of us lives the life of a ghostly Robinson Crusoe. People can see, hear and jolt one another's bodies, but they are irremediably blind and deaf to the workings of one another's minds and inoperative upon them.

What sort of knowledge can be secured of the workings of a mind? On the one side, according to the official theory, a person has direct knowledge of the best imaginable kind of the workings of his own mind. Mental states and processes are (or are normally) conscious states and processes, and the consciousness which irradiates them can engender no illusions and leaves the door open for no doubts. A person's present thinkings, feelings and willings, his perceivings, rememberings and imaginings are intrinsically 'phosphorescent'; their existence and their nature are inevitably betrayed to their owner. The inner life is a stream of consciousness of such a sort that it would be absurd to suggest that the mind whose life is that stream might be unaware of what is passing down it.

True, the evidence adduced recently by Freud seems to show that there exist channels tributary to this stream, which run hidden from their owner. People are actuated by impulses the existence of which they vigorously disavow; some of their thoughts differ from the thoughts which they acknowledge; and some of the actions which they think they will to perform they do not really will. They are thoroughly gulled by some of their own hypocrisies and they successfully ignore facts about their mental lives which on the official theory ought to be patent to them. Holders of the official theory tend, however, to maintain that anyhow in normal circumstances a person must be directly and authentically seized of the present state and workings of his own mind.

Besides being currently supplied with these alleged immediate data of consciousness, a person is also generally supposed to be able to exercise from time to time a special kind of perception, namely inner perception, or introspection. He can take a (non-optical) 'look' at what is passing in his mind. Not only can he view and scrutinize a flower through his sense of sight and listen to and discriminate the notes of a bell through his sense of hearing; he can also reflectively or introspectively watch, without any bodily organ of sense, the current episodes of his inner life. This self-observation is also commonly supposed to be immune from illusion, confusion or doubt. A mind's reports of its own affairs have a certainty superior to the best that is possessed by its reports of matters in the physical world. Sense-perceptions can, but consciousness and introspection cannot, be mistaken or confused.

On the other side, one person has no direct access of any sort to the events of the inner life of another. He cannot do better than make problematic inferences from the observed behaviour of the other person's body to the states of mind which, by analogy from his own conduct, he supposes to be signalised by that behaviour. Direct access to the workings of a mind is the privilege of that mind itself; in default of such privileged access, the workings of one mind are inevitably occult to everyone else. For the supposed arguments from bodily movements similar to their own to mental workings similar to their own would lack any possibility of observational corroboration. Not unnaturally, therefore, an adherent of the official theory finds it difficult to resist this consequence of his premisses, that he has no good reason to believe that there do exist minds other than his own. Even if he prefers to believe that to other human bodies there are harnessed minds not unlike his own, he cannot claim to be able to discover their individual characteristics, or the particular things that they undergo and do. Absolute solitude is on this showing the ineluctable destiny of the soul. Only our bodies can meet.

As a necessary corollary of this general scheme there is implicitly prescribed a special way of construing our ordinary concepts of mental powers and operations. The verbs, nouns and adjectives, with which in ordinary life we describe the wits, characters and higher-grade performances of the people with whom we have do, are required to be construed as signifying special episodes in their secret histories, or else as signifying tendencies for such episodes to occur. When someone is described as knowing, believing or guessing something, as hoping, dreading, intending or shirking something, as designing this or being amused at that,

these verbs are supposed to denote the occurrence of specific modifications in his (to us) occult stream of consciousness. Only his own privileged access to this stream in direct awareness and introspection could provide authentic testimony that these mental-conduct verbs were correctly or incorrectly applied. The onlooker, be he teacher, critic, biographer or friend, can never assure himself that his comments have any vestige of truth. Yet it was just because we do in fact all know how to make such comments, make them with general correctness and correct them when they turn out to be confused or mistaken, that philosophers found it necessary to construct their theories of the nature and place of minds. Finding mental-conduct concepts being regularly and effectively used, they properly sought to fix their logical geography. But the logical geography officially recommended would entail that there could be no regular or effective use of these mental-conduct concepts in our descriptions of, and prescriptions for, other people's minds.

(2) The Absurdity of the Official Doctrine.

Such in outline is the official theory. I shall often speak of it, with deliberate abusiveness, as 'the dogma of the Ghost in the Machine'. I hope to prove that it is entirely false, and false not in detail but in principle. It is not merely an assemblage of particular mistakes. It is one big mistake and a mistake of a special kind. It is, namely, a category-mistake. It represents the facts of mental life as if they belonged to one logical type or category (or range of types or categories), when they actually belong to another. The dogma is therefore a philosopher's myth. In attempting to explode the myth I shall probably be taken to be denying well-known facts about the mental life of human beings, and my plea that I aim at doing nothing more than rectify the logic of mental-conduct concepts will probably be disallowed as mere subterfuge.

I must first indicate what is meant by the phrase 'Category-mistake'. This I do in a series of illustrations.

A foreigner visiting Oxford or Cambridge for the first time is shown a number of colleges, libraries, playing fields, museums, scientific departments and administrative offices. He then asks 'But where is the University? I have seen where the members of the Colleges live, where the Registrar works, where the scientists experiment and the rest. But I have not yet seen the University in which reside and work the members of your University.' It has then to be explained to him that the University is not another collateral institution, some ulterior counterpart to the colleges, laboratories and offices which he has seen. The University is just the way in which all that he has already seen is organized. When they are seen and when their co-ordination is understood, the University has been seen. His mistake lay in his innocent assumption that it was correct to speak of Christ Church, the Bodleian Library, the Ashmolean Museum *and* the University, to speak, that is, as if 'the University' stood for an extra member of the class of which these other units are members. He was mistakenly allocating the University to the same category as that to which the other institutions belong.

The same mistake would be made by a child witnessing the march-past of a division, who having had pointed out to him such and such battalions, batteries, squadrons, etc., asked when the division was going to appear. He would be supposing that a division was a counterpart to the units already seen, partly similar to them and partly unlike them. He would be shown his mistake by being told that in watching the battalions, batteries, and squadrons marching past he had been watching the division marching past. The march-past was not a parade of battalions, batteries, squadrons *and* a division; it was a parade of the battalions, batteries and squadrons *of* a division.

One more illustration. A foreigner watching his first game of cricket learns what are the functions of the bowlers, the batsmen, the fielders, the umpires and the scorers. He then says 'But there is no one left on the field to contribute the famous element of team-spirit. I see who does the bowling, the batting and the wicket-keeping; but I do not see whose role it is to exercise *'esprit de corps.'* Once more, it would

have to be explained that he was looking for the wrong type of thing. Team-spirit is not another cricketing-operation supplementary to all of the other special tasks. It is, roughly, the keenness with which each of the special tasks is performed, and performing a task keenly is not performing two tasks. Certainly exhibiting team-spirit is not the same thing as bowling or catching, but nor is it a third thing such that we can say the bowler first bowls *and* then exhibits team-spirit or that a fielder is at a given moment *either* catching *or* displaying *esprit de corps.*

These illustrations of category-mistakes have a common feature which must be noticed. The mistakes were made by people who did not know how to wield the concepts *University, division* and *team-spirit.* Their puzzles arose from inability to use certain items in the English vocabulary.

The theoretically interesting category-mistakes are those made by people who are perfectly competent to apply concepts, at least in the situations with which they are familiar, but are still liable in their abstract thinking to allocate those concepts to logical types to which they do not belong. An instance of a mistake of this sort would be the following story. A student of politics has learned the main differences between the British, the French and the American Constitutions, and has learned also the differences and connections between the Cabinet, Parliament, the various Ministries, the Judicature and the Church of England. But he still becomes embarrassed when asked questions about the connections between the Church of England, the Home Office and the British Constitution. For while the Church and the Home Office are institutions, the British Constitution is not another institution in the same sense of that noun. So inter-institutional relations which can be asserted or denied to hold between the Church and the Home Office cannot be asserted or denied to hold between either of them and the British Constitution. 'The British Constitution' is not a term of the same logical type as 'the Home Office' and ' the Church of England'. In a partially similar way, John Doe may be a relative, a friend, an enemy or a stranger to Richard Roe; but he cannot be any of these things to the Average Taxpayer. He knows how to talk sense in certain sorts of discussions about the Average Taxpayer, but he is baffled to say why he could not come across him in the street as he can come across Richard Roe.

It is pertinent to our main subject to notice that, so long as the student of politics continues to think of the British Constitution as a counterpart to the other institutions, he will tend to describe it as a mysteriously occult institution; and so long as John Doe continues to think of the Average Taxpayer as a fellow-citizen, he will tend to think of him as an elusive insubstantial man, a ghost who is everywhere yet nowhere.

My destructive purpose is to show that a family of radical category-mistakes is the source of the double-life theory. The representation of a person as a ghost mysteriously ensconced in a machine derives from this argument. Because, as is true, a person's thinking, feeling and purposive doing cannot be described solely in the idioms of physics, chemistry and physiology, therefore they must be described in counterpart idioms. As the human body is a complex organised unit, so the human mind must be another complex organised unit, though one made of a different sort of stuff and with a different sort of structure. Or, again, as the human body, like any other parcel of matter, is a field of causes and effects, so the mind must be another field of causes and effects, though not (Heaven be praised) mechanical causes and effects.

(3) The Origin of the Category-mistake.

One of the chief intellectual origins of what I have yet to prove to be the Cartesian category-mistake seems to be this. When Galileo showed that his methods of scientific discovery were competent to provide a mechanical theory which should cover every occupant of space, Descartes found in himself two conflicting motives. As a man of scientific genius he could not but endorse the claims of mechanics, yet as a religious and moral man he could not accept, as Hobbes accepted, the discouraging rider to those claims, namely that human nature differs only in degree of complexity from clockwork. The mental could not be just a variety of the mechanical.

He and subsequent philosophers naturally but erroneously availed themselves of the following escape-route. Since mental-conduct words are not to be construed as signifying the occurrence of mechanical processes, they must be construed as signifying the occurrence of non-mechanical processes; since mechanical laws explain movements in space as the effects of other movements in space, other laws must explain some of the non-spatial workings of minds as the effects of other non-spatial workings of minds. The difference between the human behaviours which we describe as intelligent and those which we describe as unintelligent must be a difference in their causation; so, while some movements of human tongues and limbs are the effects of mechanical causes, others must be the effects of non-mechanical causes, i.e. some issue from movements of particles of matter, others from workings of the mind.

The differences between the physical and the mental were thus represented as differences inside the common framework of the categories of 'thing', 'stuff', 'attribute', 'state', 'process', 'change', 'cause' and 'effect'. Minds are things, but different sorts of things from bodies; mental processes are causes and effects, but different sorts of causes and effects from bodily movements. And so on. Somewhat as the foreigner expected the University to be an extra edifice, rather like a college but also considerably different, so the repudiators of mechanism represented minds as extra centres of causal processes, rather like machines but also considerably different from them. Their theory was a para-mechanical hypothesis.

That this assumption was at the heart of the doctrine is shown by the fact that there was from the beginning felt to be a major theoretical difficulty in explaining how minds can influence and be influenced by bodies. How can a mental process, such as willing, cause spatial movements like the movements of the tongue? How can a physical change in the optic nerve have among its effects a mind's perception of a flash of light? This notorious crux by itself shows the logical mould into which Descartes pressed his theory of the mind. It was the selfsame mould into which he and Galileo set their mechanics. Still unwittingly adhering to the grammar of mechanics, he tried to avert disaster by describing minds in what was merely an obverse vocabulary. The workings of minds had to be described by the mere negatives of the specific descriptions given to bodies; they are not in space, they are not motions, they are not modifications of matter, they are not accessible to public observation. Minds are not bits of clockwork, they are just bits of not-clockwork.

As thus represented, minds are not merely ghosts harnessed to machines, they are themselves just spectral machines. Though the human body is an engine, it is not quite an ordinary engine, since some of its workings are governed by another engine inside it—this interior governor-engine being one of a very special sort. It is invisible, inaudible and it has no size or weight. It cannot be taken to bits and the laws it obeys are not those known to ordinary engineers. Nothing is known of how it governs the bodily engine.

A second major crux points the same moral. Since, according to the doctrine, minds belong to the same category as bodies and since bodies are rigidly governed by mechanical laws, it seemed to many theorists to follow that minds must be similarly governed by rigid non-mechanical laws. The physical world is a deterministic system, so the mental world must be a deterministic system. Bodies cannot help the modifications that they undergo, so minds cannot help pursuing the careers fixed for them. *Responsibility, choice, merit* and *demerit* are therefore inapplicable concepts—unless the compromise solution is adopted of saying that the laws governing mental processes, unlike those governing physical processes, have the congenial attribute of being only rather rigid. The problem of the Freedom of the Will was the problem how to reconcile the hypothesis that minds are to be described in terms drawn from the categories of mechanics with the knowledge that higher-grade human conduct is not of a piece with the behaviour of machines.

It is an historical curiosity that it was not noticed that the entire argument was broken-backed. Theorists correctly assumed that any sane man could already recognize the differences between, say, rational and non-rational

utterances or between purposive and automatic behaviour. Else there would have been nothing requiring to be salved from mechanism. Yet the explanation given presupposed that one person could in principle never recognise the difference between the rational and the irrational utterances issuing from other human bodies, since he could never get access to the postulated immaterial causes of some of their utterances. Save for the doubtful exception of himself, he could never tell the difference between a man and a Robot. It would have to be conceded, for example, that for all that we can tell, the inner lives of persons who are classed as idiots or lunatics are as rational as those of anyone else. Perhaps only their overt behaviour is disappointing; that is to say, perhaps 'idiots' are not really idiotic, or 'lunatics' lunatic. Perhaps, too, some of those who are classed as sane are really idiots. According to the theory, external observers could never know how the overt behaviour of others is correlated with their mental powers and processes and so they could never know or even plausibly conjecture whether their applications of mental-conduct concepts to these other people were correct or incorrect. It would then be hazardous or impossible for a man to claim sanity or logical consistency even for himself, since he would be debarred from comparing his own performances with those of others. In short, our characterisations of persons and their performances as intelligent, prudent and virtuous or as stupid, hypocritical and cowardly could never have been made, so the problem of providing a special causal hypothesis to serve as the basis of such diagnoses would never have arisen. The question, 'How do persons differ from machines?' arose just because everyone already knew how to apply mental-conduct concepts before the new causal hypothesis was introduced. This causal hypothesis could not therefore be the source of the criteria used in those applications. Nor, of course, has the causal hypothesis in any degree improved our handling of those criteria. We still distinguish good from bad arithmetic, politic from impolitic conduct and fertile from infertile imaginations in the ways in which Descartes himself distinguished them before and after he speculated how the applicability of these criteria was compatible with the principle of mechanical causation.

He had mistaken the logic of his problem. Instead of asking by what criteria intelligent behaviour is actually distinguished from non-intelligent behaviour, he asked 'Given that the principle of mechanical causation does not tell us the difference, what other causal principle will tell it us?' He realized that the problem was not one of mechanics and assumed that it must therefore be one of some counterpart to mechanics. Not unnaturally psychology is often cast for just that role.

When two terms belong to the same category, it is proper to construct conjunctive propositions embodying them, Thus a purchaser may say that he bought a left-hand glove and a right-hand glove, but not that he bought a left-hand glove, a right-hand glove and a pair of gloves. 'She came home in a flood of tears and a sedan-chair' is a well-known joke based on the absurdity of conjoining terms of different types. It would have been equally ridiculous to construct the disjunction 'She came home either in a flood of tears or else in a sedan-chair'. Now the dogma of the Ghost in the Machine does just this. It maintains that there exist both bodies and minds; that there occur physical processes and mental processes; that there are mechanical causes of corporeal movements and mental causes of corporeal movements. I shall argue that these and other analogous conjunctions are absurd; but, it must be noticed, the argument will not show that either of the illegitimately conjoined propositions is absurd in itself. I am not, for example, denying that there occur mental processes. Doing long division is a mental process and so is making a joke. But I am saying that the phrase 'there occur mental processes' does not mean the same sort of thing as there occur physical processes', and, therefore, that it makes no sense to conjoin or disjoin the two.

If my argument is successful, there will follow some interesting consequences. First, the hallowed contrast between Mind and Matter will be dissipated, but dissipated not by either of the equally hallowed absorptions of Mind by Matter or of Matter by Mind, but in quite a different way. For the seeming contrast of the two will be shown to be as illegitimate as would be the contrast of 'she came home in a flood of tears' and 'she came home in a sedan-chair.' The belief that there is a polar opposition between Mind and Matter is the belief that they are terms of the same logical type.

It will also follow that both Idealism and Materialism are answers to an improper question. The 'reduction' of the material world to mental states and processes, as well as the 'reduction' of mental states and processes to physical states and processes, presuppose the legitimacy of the disjunction 'Either there exist minds or there exist bodies (but not both)'. It would be like saying 'Either she bought a left-hand glove or she bought a pair of gloves (but not both)'.

It is perfectly proper to say, in one logical tone of voice, that there exist minds and to say, in another logical tone of voice, that there exist bodies. But these expressions do not indicate two different species of existence, for 'existence' is not a generic word like 'coloured' or 'sexed'. They indicate two different senses of 'exist', somewhat as 'rising' has different senses in 'the tide is rising', 'hopes are rising', and 'the average age of death is rising'. A man would be thought to be making a poor joke who said that three things are now rising, namely the tide, hopes and the average age of death. It would be just as good or bad a joke to say that there exist prime numbers and Wednesdays and public opinions and navies; or that there exist both minds and bodies. In the succeeding chapters I try to prove that the official theory does rest on a batch of category-mistakes by showing that logically absurd corollaries follow from it. The exhibition of these absurdities will have the constructive effect of bringing out part of the correct logic of mental-conduct concepts.

Questions on Ryle

1. Explain the "dogma of the Ghost in the Machine." Is this a fair account of Descartes' view or not?

2. Ryle claims that this dogma commits a basic conceptual error, a "category mistake." What is this mistake exactly? Does Ryle prove that Descartes actually makes such a mistake or not? How could Descartes reply?

D. M. Armstrong

The Central-State Theory

D. M. Armstrong is Challis Professor of Philosophy at the University of Sydney, Australia. Armstrong is the author of A Materialist Theory of the Mind, Perception and the Physical World, *and* Belief, Truth and Knowledge.

But now we must examine the . . . form of Materialism . . . which identifies mental states with purely physical states of the central nervous system. If the mind is thought of as 'that which has mental states', then we can say that, on this theory, the mind is simply the central nervous system, or, less accurately but more epigrammatically, the mind is simply the brain.

I. Is the Theory Really Paradoxical?

Many philosophers still regard this theory of mind as a very extraordinary one. In 1962, for instance, A. G. N. Flew wrote:

In the face of the powerful and resolute advocacy now offered this admittedly paradoxical view *can no longer be dismissed in such short order.* (Philosophical Review, *Vol. LXXI, 1962, p. 403, my italics*)

At the risk of seeming ungrateful to Professor Flew, it is interesting to notice that, even while conceding that the theory merits serious discussion, he calls it 'admittedly paradoxical'. I think his attitude is shared by many philosophers. Certainly I myself found the theory paradoxical when I first heard it expounded.

But it is important to realize that this opinion that the Central-state theory is paradoxical, is confined almost exclusively to philosophers. They are usually taught as first-year University students that the mind cannot possibly be the brain, and as a result they are inclined to regard the falsity of the Central-state theory as self-evident. But this opinion is not widely shared. Outside philosophy, the Central-state doctrine enjoys wide support.

In the first place, there is evidence from modern idiom. We speak of 'brains', 'brainchild', 'brain-storm', 'racking one's brains' and 'brain-washing', and in each case we are speaking about the mind. If one follows this up, as I have done, by asking people of general education, but no philosophical training, whether they think the mind is the brain or not, many say it is. Some even treat the matter as closed, asking what else it could be. Those who deny that the mind is the brain usually do so for *theological* reasons.

If we then turn to those scientists who are most directly concerned with the problem, viz. the psychologists, we find no tendency to say that the Central-state theory is paradoxical or far-out. D. O. Hebb may be fairly quoted as representative. Now in his *Textbook of Psychology* (Sanders, 1958, p. 3) he writes:

There are two theories of mind, speaking very generally. One is animistic, a theory that the body is inhabited by an entity—the mind or soul—that is quite different from it, having nothing in common with bodily processes. The second theory is physiological or mechanistic, it assumes that mind is a bodily process, an activity of the brain. Modern psychology works with this latter theory only. Both are intellectually respectable (that is, each has support from highly intelligent people, including scientists), and there is certainly no decisive means available of proving one to be right, the other wrong.

These appeals to the authority of the unphilosophic man and the psychologists are, of course, not intended to do anything to settle

The Reading is from D. M. Armstrong, *A Materialist Theory of the Mind* (London: Routledge & Kegan Paul, 1968), pp. 73–90. Reprinted with permission.

the substantive question. They are made only with the hope of moderating philosophical dogmatism. It may be that the unphilosophic man and the psychologists are seriously confused. But it may also be that, as so often in the past, the philosophers have been misled by plausible arguments. The reasonable man ought to regard the question as open.

II. The Theory Measured Against Demands Already Formulated

Getting down to more serious business, let us measure the theory against the various demands that a satisfactory theory of mind must meet as they have emerged in the last four chapters, beginning with the demands that create no difficulty.

(i) It is clear that this theory accounts very simply for the unity of mind and body. The brain is physically inside the body. It is the pilot in the vessel. This fits in remarkably well with ordinary talk about the mind. It is completely natural to speak of the mind as 'in' the body, and to speak of mental processes as 'inner' processes. Now 'in' is primarily a spatial word. The naturalness of this way of speaking is strikingly, and the more strikingly because quite unconsciously, brought out by Hume. For in the course of putting forward a theory of mind according to which it is not in physical space, he says:

Suppose we could see clearly into the breast *of another and observe that succession of perceptions which constitutes his mind or thinking principle . . . (*Treatise, *Bk. I, Pt. IV, Sect. 6, p. 260, ed. Selby-Bigge, my italics)*

Hume's way of talking here, indefensible on his own theory, seems to us *all* to be a natural way of talking, although we might now say 'head', not 'breast'. But a Dualist must say that the mind is not in the body in any gross material sense of the word 'in'. What his own refined sense of the word is, is a mystery.

(ii) Central-state Materialism can provide a simple principle of numerical difference for minds, viz., difference of place . . .

(iii) Central-state Materialism can explain very simply the interaction of mind and body. Brain and body interact, so mind and body interact.

(iv) Central-state Materialism allows us to say that the mind comes into being in a gradual way, and that there is no sharp break between not having a mind and having one. For in the evolution of the species, and in the development of the individual, the brain comes into being in a gradual way. The simplification of our world-picture that results is the especial advantage of Materialist theories (including Behaviourism).

(v) But unlike Behaviourism, a Central-state theory does not deny the existence of inner mental states. On the contrary, it asserts their existence: they are physical states of the brain.

Nevertheless, a Central-state theory seems to face some serious objections. . . .

III. A Further Difficulty Formulated, and an Answer Sketched

. . . [There is] one powerful line of argument that may seem to be a conclusive reason for denying that the mind is the brain. Take the statement 'The mind is the brain'. ('Mental processes are brain-processes' may be substituted if preferred.) Does the statement purport to be a logically necessary truth, or is it simply claimed to be contingently true? Does a defender of the Central-state theory want to assimilate the statement to 'An oculist *is* an eye-doctor' or '7 + 5 *is* 12', on the one hand, or to 'The morning star *is* the evening star' or 'The gene *is* the DNA molecule', on the other?

It is perfectly clear which way the cat must jump here. If there is anything certain in philosophy, it is certain that 'The mind is the brain' is not a logically necessary truth. When Aristotle said that the brain was nothing but an organ for keeping the body cool, he was certainly not guilty of denying a necessary truth. His mistake was an empirical one. So if it is true that the mind is the brain, a model must be found among contingent statements of identity. We must compare the statement to 'The morning star is the evening star' or 'The gene is the DNA molecule', or some other contingent assertion of identity. (The statement 'The gene is the DNA molecule' is not a very exact one from the biological point of view. But it will prove to be a useful example in the development of the argument, and it is accurate enough for our purposes here.)

But if 'The mind is the brain' is a contingent statement, then it follows that it must be possible to give logically independent explanations (or, alternatively, 'ostensive definitions') of the meaning of the two words 'mind' and 'brain'. For consider. 'The morning star is the evening star' is a contingent statement. We can explain the meaning of the phrase 'the morning star' thus: it is the very bright star seen in the sky on certain mornings of the year. We can explain the meaning of the phrase 'the evening star' thus: it is the very bright star seen in the sky on certain evenings of the year. We can give logically independent explanations of the meanings of the two phrases. 'The gene is the DNA molecule' is a contingent statement. We can explain the meaning of the word 'gene' thus: it is that thing or principle within us that is responsible for the transmission of hereditary characteristics, such as colour of eyes. We can explain the meaning of the phrase 'DNA molecule' along the following lines: it is a molecule of a certain very complex chemical constitution which forms the nucleus of the cell. We can give logically independent explanations of the word 'gene' and the phrase 'DNA molecule'.

Now if it is meaningful to say that 'The mind is the brain' it must be possible to treat the words 'mind' and 'brain' in the same way.

The word 'brain' gives no trouble. Clearly it is possible to explain its meaning in a quasi-ostensive way. The problem is posed by the word 'mind'. What verbal explanation or 'ostensive definition' can we give of the meaning of this word without implying a departure from a physicalist view of the world? This seems to be the great problem, or, at any rate, one great problem, faced by a Central-state theory.

The object that we call a 'brain' is called a brain in virtue of certain physical characteristics: it is a certain sort of physical object found inside people's skulls. Yet if we say that this object is also the mind, then, since the word 'mind' does not mean the same as the word 'brain', it seems that the brain can only be the mind in virtue of some *further* characteristic that the brain has. But what can this characteristic be? We seem on the verge of being forced back into an Attribute theory.

Put the problem another way. Central-state Materialism holds that when we are *aware* of our mental states what we are aware of are mere physical states of our brain. But we are certainly not aware of the mental states *as* states of the brain. What then are we aware of mental states as? Are we not aware of them as states of a quite peculiar, mental, sort?

The problem has so daunted one physicalist, Paul Feyerabend, that he has suggested that the materialist ought simply to recognize that his world-view does not allow statements that assert or imply the existence of minds. A true physicalism will simply talk about the operation of the central nervous system, and will write off talk about the mind as an intellectual loss. (See his 'Mental events and the Brain', *The Journal of Philosophy*, Vol. LX, 1963.)

I think that if the situation is as desperate as this it is desperate indeed. It is at least our first duty to see if we can give an explanation of the word 'mind' which will meet the demands that have just been outlined. In order to do this, let us turn to a way of thinking about man that has been popularized by psychology. Psychologists very often present us with the following picture. Man is an object continually acted upon by certain physical stimuli. These stimuli elicit from him certain behaviour, that is to say, a certain physical response. In the causal chain between the stimulus and the response, falls the mind. The mind is that which causally mediates our response to stimuli. Now the Central-state theory wants to say that between the stimulus and the response fall physical processes in the central nervous system, and nothing else at all, not even something 'epiphenomenal'. At the same time the theory cannot mention the central nervous system in its account of the concept of mind. If we now think of the psychologist's picture, the outline of a solution is in our hands. As a first approximation we can say that what we mean when we talk about the mind, or about particular mental processes, is nothing but the effect within a man of certain stimuli, and the cause within a man of certain responses. The intrinsic nature of these effects and causes is not something that is involved in the concept of mind or the particular mental concepts. The concept of a mental state is the concept of that, whatever it may turn out to be, which is brought about in a man by certain stimuli and which in turn brings about certain responses. What it is in its own nature is something for science to discover. Modern science declares that this mediator between stimulus and response is in fact the central nervous system, or more crudely and inaccurately, but more simply, the brain....

V. The Concept of a Mental State

... The concept of a mental state is primarily the concept of *a state of the person apt for bringing about a certain sort of behaviour*. Sacrificing all accuracy for brevity we can say that, although mind is not behaviour, it is the *cause* of behaviour. In the case of some mental states only they are also *states of the person apt for being brought about by a certain sort of stimulus*. But this latter formula is a secondary one.

It will be advisable to dwell rather carefully on this first formula: state of the person apt for bringing about a certain sort of behavior.

In the first place, I attach no special importance to the word 'state'. For instance, it is not meant to rule out 'process' or 'event'. I think that in fact useful distinctions can be made between states, processes and events, and that mental 'items', to use a neutral term, can be variously classified under these quite separate heads. This point will emerge in Part II (cf. in particular, Ch. 7, Sect. I). But in the meanwhile 'state' is not meant to exclude 'process' or 'event'.

In the second place, I call attention to the word 'apt'. Here there are two points to be made: (*a*) By saying only that mental states are states *apt* for bringing about behavior we allow for some mental states being actual occurrences, even although they result in no behaviour. (*b*) The formula is intended to cover more than one sort of relationship between mental state and behaviour. If we consider intentions,

for instance, then they are naturally construed (*pace* Ryle) as causes within our minds that tend to initiate and sustain certain courses of behaviour. But it is most implausible to say that perceptions, for instance, are causes tending to initiate certain courses of behaviour. Suppose I see a magpie on the lawn. It may well be that magpies are things which I can take or leave, and that no impulse to do anything at all is involved in the perception. What must be said about perception (as will be elaborated later) is that it is a matter of acquiring capacities to make systematic physical discriminations within our environment *if we should be so impelled*. (If intentions are like pressures on a door, perceptions are like acquiring a key to the door. You can put the key in your pocket, and never do anything with it.) Other mental states will turn out to stand in still different causal relations to the behaviour which constitutes their 'expression'. In some cases, indeed, it will emerge that certain sorts of mental states can only be described in terms of their *resemblance* to other mental states that stand in causal relations to behaviour. Here the relation to behaviour is very indirect indeed.

A closely connected point is that, in many cases, an account of mental states involves not only their causal relation to behaviour, but their causal relation to other mental states. It may even be that an account of certain mental states will proceed solely in terms of the other mental states they are apt for bringing about. An intention to work out a sum 'in one's head' would be a case in point. The intention is a mental cause apt for bringing about the thoughts that are the successive steps in the calculation. So all that is demanded is that our analysis must *ultimately* reach mental states that are describable in terms of the behaviour they are apt for.

In the third place, the 'bringing about' involved is the 'bringing about' of ordinary, efficient, causality. It is no different in principle from the 'bringing about' involved when the impact of one billiard-ball brings about the motion of another ball. But the mention of Hume's paradigm should not mislead. I do not wish to commit myself for or against a Humean or semi-Humean analysis of the nature of the causal relation. I am simply saying that causality in the mental sphere is no different from causality in the physical sphere.

The further assumptions I will make about the nature of the causal relation in this work will only be two in number. In the first place, I will assume that the cause and its effect are 'distinct existences', so that the existence of the cause does not logically imply the existence of the effect, or *vice versa*. In the second place, I will assume that if a sequence is a causal one, then it is a sequence that falls under some law. The stone causes the glass to break. There may be no law connecting the impact of stones on glass with the breaking of the glass. But in speaking of the sequence as a causal sequence, we imply that there is *some* description of the situation (not necessarily known to us) that falls under a law. These assumptions are not entirely uncontroversial, but at least are relatively modest.

In the fourth place, the word 'behaviour' is ambiguous. We may distinguish between 'physical behaviour', which refers to any merely physical action or passion of the body, and 'behaviour proper', which implies relationship to the mind. 'Behaviour proper' entails 'physical behaviour', but not all 'physical behaviour' is 'behaviour proper', for the latter springs from the mind in a certain particular way. A reflex knee jerk is 'physical behaviour', but it is not 'behaviour proper'. Now if in our formula 'behaviour' were to mean 'behaviour proper', then we would be giving an account of mental concepts in terms of a concept that already presupposes mentality, which would be circular. So it is clear that in our formula 'behaviour' must mean 'physical behaviour'. (And it is clear also that this is going to make our projected account of the mental concepts that much more difficult to carry through.)

It will be seen that our formula 'state of the person apt for bringing about a certain sort of behaviour' is something that must be handled with care. Perhaps it is best conceived of as a slogan or catch-phrase which indicates the general lines along which accounts of the individual mental concepts are to be sought, but does no more than this.

This leads on to a final point to be made about the formula. It should not be regarded as a guide to the producing of *translations* of mental statements. It may well be that it is not possible to translate mental statements into statements that mention nothing but physical happenings, in any but the roughest way. It may be still true, nevertheless, that we can give a satisfactory and complete account of the situations covered by the mental concepts in purely physical and topic-neutral terms.

I think the situation is as follows. We apply certain concepts, the mental concepts, to human beings. That is to say, we attribute mental states to them. Then the question arises whether it is possible to do full justice to the nature of these mental states by means of purely physical or neutral concepts. We therefore try to sketch an account of typical mental states in purely physical or neutral terms. The account might fall indefinitely short of giving translations of mental statements, yet it might still be plausible to say that the account had done justice to the phenomena.

Of course, this does leave us with the question how, lacking the test of translation, we can ever know that we have succeeded in our enterprise. But this is just one instance of the perennial problem of finding a decision-procedure for philosophical problems. I think in fact that all we can do is this: we produce an account of a certain range of phenomena in terms of a favoured set of concepts; we then try to test this account by looking for actual and possible situations falling within this range of phenomena which seem to defy complete description in terms of the favoured concepts. If we can deal successfully with all the difficult cases, we have done all that we can do. But there is unlikely to be any way of *proving* to the general satisfaction that our enterprise has been successful. If there was, philosophy would be easier.

VI. Distinction Between Our View and Behaviourism: the Nature of Dispositions

I turn to a question that may be worrying some readers. Now that I have given an account of the concept of a mental state, does it not appear that I am a Behaviourist in disguise? Admittedly, there is one great divergence from Behaviourism: the mind is not to be identified with behaviour, but only with the inner principle of behaviour. But, in elucidating our formula, there has been talk about tendencies to initiate, and capacities for, behaviour. And are not these perilously close to the Behaviourist's dispositions?

There is some force in this. In talking about dispositions to behave Behaviourism did come quite close to the version of the Central-state theory being defended here, far closer than it came when it talked about behaviour itself. But Behaviourism and the Central-state theory still remain deeply at odds about *the way dispositions are to be conceived.*

Speaking of dispositional properties in *The Concept of Mind* Ryle wrote (p. 43):

To possess a dispositional property is not to be in a particular state, or to undergo a particular change; *it is to be bound or liable to be in a particular state, or to undergo a particular change, when a particular condition is realized. (My italics)*

We might call this the Phenomenalist or Operationalist account of dispositions. A still more striking statement of this view is provided by H. H. Price in his *Thinking and Experience* (Hutchinson, 1953, p. 322), although Price is no Behaviourist. He said:

There is no a priori *necessity for supposing that* all *dispositional properties must have a 'categorical basis'. In particular, there may be mental dispositions which are ultimate . . .*

To this we may oppose what may be called a Realist account of dispositions. According to the Realist view, to speak of an object's having a dispositional property entails that the object is in some non-dispositional state or that it has some property (there exists a 'categorical basis') which is responsible for the object manifesting certain behaviour in certain circumstances, manifestations whose nature makes the dispositional property the particular dispositional property it is. It is true that we may not know anything of the nature of the non-dispositional state. But, the Realist view asserts, in asserting that a certain piece of glass is brittle, for instance, we are *ipso facto* asserting that it is in a certain non-dispositional state which disposes it

to shatter and fly apart in a wide variety of circumstances. Ignorance of the nature of the state does not affect the issue. The Realist view gains some support from ordinary language, where we often seem to identify a disposition and its 'categorical basis'. ('It has been found that brittleness is a certain sort of molecular pattern in the material.')

I will now present an *a priori* argument which purports to prove the truth of the Realist account of dispositions. Let us consider the following case. Suppose that, on a number of occasions, a certain rubber band has the same force, F, applied to it, and that on each occasion it stretches one inch. We can then attribute a disposition to the band. It is disposed to stretch one inch under force F.

Now one essential thing about dispositions is that we can attribute them to objects even at times when the circumstances in which the object manifests its dispositions do not obtain. Suppose, now, that I say of the band that, if it had been subjected to force F at T_1, a time when it was not so subjected, it would have stretched one inch. What warrant have I for my statement? Consider first the answer that a Realist about dispositions will give. He will say that there is every reason to believe that the categorical state of the band which is responsible for its stretching one inch under force F obtains at T_1. Given that it does obtain at T_1, then, as a matter of physical necessity, the band must stretch one inch under force F.

But what answer can the Phenomenalist about dispositions give? For him, a disposition does not entail the existence of a categorical state. The only reason he can give for saying that the band would have stretched one inch under force F at T_1 is that numerically the same band behaved in this way on other occasions. But now we may ask the Phenomenalist 'What is the magic in numerical identity?' A thing can change its properties over a period of time. Why should it not change its dispositional properties? How does the Phenomenalist know what the band's dispositional properties are at T_1? He may reply 'We have every reason to think that the relevant categorical properties of the object are unchanged at T_1, so we have every reason to think that the dispositional properties are unchanged.' But since he has asserted that the connection between 'categorical basis' and dispositional property is not a necessary one, he can only be arguing that there is a *contingent* connection between categorical properties and the fact that the band has that dispositional property at T_1. But how could one ever establish a contingent connection between categorical properties and unfulfilled possibilities? It is not as if one could observe the unfulfilled possibilities independently, in order to see how they are correlated with the categorical properties! It seems that the Phenomenalist about dispositions will be reduced to utter scepticism about dispositions, except on occasions that they are actually manifested.

I think we can imagine the possibility that the band should be acted upon by force F on different occasions, and behave quite differently on these occasions, although there was no relevant difference in the categorical properties of the band on these occasions. That is to say, I think we can imagine that the Principle of Sufficient Reason may be false in the case of the band. But it is only to the extent that we accept the Principle of Sufficient Reason that we can introduce the notion of disposition. It is only to the extent that we relate disposition to 'categorical basis', and difference of disposition to difference of 'categorical basis', that we can speak of dispositions. We must be Realists, not Phenomenalists, about dispositions.

All this is of central importance to the philosophy of mind. Thus, if belief, for instance, is a disposition, then it is entailed that while I believe p my mind is in a certain non-dispositional state, a state which in suitable circumstances gives rise to 'manifestations of belief that p'. The fact that we may not know the concrete nature of this state is irrelevant.

The tremendous difference between this and the 'Phenomenalist' account of disposition emerges when we consider that, on this 'Realist' view of dispositions, we can think of them as *causes* or *causal factors*. On the Phenomenalist view, dispositions cannot be causes. To say the glass breaks because it is brittle is only to say that it breaks because it is the sort of thing that does break easily in the circumstances it is in. But if brittleness can be identified with an actual *state* of the glass, then we can think of it as a cause, or, more vaguely, a causal factor, in the process that brings about breaking. Dispositions are seen to be states that actually *stand behind* their manifestations. It is simply that the states are *identified* in terms of their manifestations in suitable conditions, rather than in terms of their intrinsic nature.

Our argument for a 'Realist' account of dispositions can equally be applied to capacities and powers. They, too, must be conceived of as states of the object that has the capacity or power.

It will now be seen that a Behaviourist must reject this account of mental predicates involving dispositions, capacities or powers. For if he subscribed to it he would be admitting that, in talking about the mind, we were committed to talking about inner states of the person. But to make this admission would be to contradict his Behaviourism. It would contradict the *peripheralistic* or *positivistic* drive that is involved in Behaviourism. Behaviourism concentrates on the case of other minds, and there it substitutes the evidence that we have for the existence of other minds—behaviour—for the mental states themselves. To admit dispositions as states lying behind, and in suitable circumstances giving rise to, behaviour is to contradict the whole programme. If, however, the reader still wishes to call my view a form of Behaviourism, this is no more than a matter of verbal concern. For it remains a 'Behaviourism' that permits the contingent identification of mind and brain.

VII. The Identification of Mind and Brain

Suppose now we accept for argument's sake the view that in talking about mental states we are simply talking about states of the person apt for the bringing about of behaviour of a certain sort. (The detailed working out and defence of this view will in fact occupy the major part of this book—Part Two.) The question then arises 'What in fact is the nature of these inner states? What are these inner causes like?' And here no logical analysis can help us. It is a matter of high-level scientific speculation.

At this point we have one of those exciting turn-arounds where old theories appear in a quite new light. We suddenly get a new view of Dualism . . . not to mention any wilder views that may be proposed. They are not, as we have insisted upon treating them up to this point, accounts of the *concept* of mind at all. Given that the concept of a mental state is the concept of a state of the person apt for bringing about certain sorts of (physical) behaviour, then we should view the different accounts of the mind that have been advanced through the ages as different *scientific* answers to the question of the intrinsic nature of these states.

Take the primitive view that the mind or spirit is breath. Consider the difference between a living man and a corpse. A living man behaves in a quite different, and far more complex, way than any other sort of thing, but a corpse is little different from any other material object. What is the inner principle of the living man's behaviour? One obvious difference is that the living man breathes, the corpse does not. So it is a plausible preliminary hypothesis that the inner principle of man's unique behaviour—his spirit or mind—is breath or air.

Again, it is a meaningful suggestion that the mind is a flame in the body, or a collection of specially smooth and mobile atoms dispersed throughout the members. It is a meaningful suggestion that it is a spiritual substance, or a set of special properties of the body or central nervous system which are not reducible to the physico-chemical properties of matter. Or perhaps, as Central-state Materialism maintains, it is the physico-chemical workings of the central nervous system.

(Some theories, of course, do have to be rejected for conceptual reasons. . . . Behaviourism is unacceptable because, since the mind is the inner principle of behaviour, it cannot *be* behaviour. Any Parallelist theory must be rejected because the essential thing about the mind is that it stands and operates in the causal chain between stimulus and response. But these are unnatural views of the mind, only adopted unwillingly under the stress of great intellectual difficulties.)

At this point we see that the statement 'The gene is the DNA molecule' provides a very good model for many features of the statement 'The mind is the brain'. (I am greatly indebted to Brian Medlin for this very important model.) The concept of the gene, when it was introduced into biology as a result of Mendel's work, was the concept of a factor in the person or animal apt for the production of certain characteristics in that person or animal. The question then arose what in fact the gene was. All sorts of answers were possible. For instance, the gene might have been an immaterial principle which somehow brought it about that my eyes are the colour they are. In fact, however, biologists have concluded that there is sufficient evidence to identify that which is apt for the production of hereditary characteristics as the substance to be found at the centre of cells: deoxyribonucleic acid. This identification is a theoretical one. Nobody has directly observed, or could ever hope to observe in practice, the details of the causal chain from DNA molecule to the colouring of the eye. But the identification is sufficiently certain.

It may now be asserted that, once it be granted that the concept of a mental state is the concept of a state of the person apt for the production of certain sorts of behaviour, the identification of these states with physico-chemical states of the brain is, in the present state of knowledge, nearly as good a bet as the identification of the gene with the DNA molecule.

Questions on Armstrong

1. State and explain the theory of central-state materialism. What "powerful line of argument" seems to give a conclusive reason for rejecting this theory? How does Armstrong reply to this objection? Is his reply convincing or not? Explain your answer.

2. Armstrong admits that his theory is close to behaviorism, at least insofar as mental states are said to be a "state of the person apt for bringing about a certain sort of behaviour," but he claims that his theory is actually different from behaviorism. Just what is the difference supposed to be? Is his view really that much different than behaviorism or not?

Jerry A. Fodor
Functionalism

Jerry A. Fodor is Distinguished Professor of Philosophy at the Graduate School and University Center, City University of New York. His most important books, besides Representations, *are* Psychological Explanation, The Language of Thought, *and* The Modularity of Mind.

The stumbling block for a dualist is the problem of mind/body interaction. If you think, as Descartes did, that minds are immaterial substances, you ought to be worried (as Descartes was) about how there can be mental causes of behavioural effects. Cynicism might suggest that the question how an immaterial substance could contribute to the etiology of physical events is not, after all, much more obscure than the question how material substances could interact causally with one another. But there is this difference: whereas we can produce lots of untendentious examples of the latter kind of interaction, there are no untendentious examples of the former kind. Physical causation we will have to live with; but non-physical causation might be an artifact of the immaterialist contrual of the claim that there are minds.

Viewed this way, the issue is one of **ontological parsimony**. A Cartesian dualist is going to hold that there are species of causal relations over and above physical interactions. He is therefore in need of an argument why mind/body causation should not itself be viewed as an instance of physical interaction. Most philosophers now agree that no such argument has successfully been made. Even philosophers like

Ryle, whose preferred style of anti-Cartesian argument was so very often epistemological, insisted on the force of such considerations: "there was from the beginning felt to be a major theoretical difficulty in explaining how minds can influence and be influenced by bodies. How can a mental process, such as willing, cause spatial movements like movements of the tongue? How can a physical change in the optic nerve have among its effects a mind's perception of a flash of light?" (1949, p. 19).

It is precisely the advantage of materialistic monism that it provides for the subsumption of mind/body interaction as a special case of physical interaction, thereby making problems like the ones that Ryle mentions go away. By the early 1960s, it was becoming clear that there are two quite different strategies for performing this reduction, one corresponding to the program of *logical behaviorism* and the other corresponding to the program of the *central state identity theory*. And it was also becoming clear that each of these strategies has its problems.

The essence of one kind of logical behaviorism is the idea that every truth-valuable ascription of a mental state or process to an organism is semantically equivalent to the ascription of a certain sort of dispositional property to that organism. . . . In particular, in the interesting cases, mental ascriptions were supposed to be semantically equivalent to ascriptions of *behavioral dispositions*. A behavioral disposition is one that an organism has if and only if (iff) it satisfies a certain indefinite (possibly infinite) set of *behavioral hypotheticals* which constitute the *analysis* of the disposition. A behavioral hypothetical is a (possibly counter-factual) statement whose antecedent is couched solely in terms of *stimulus parameters* and whose consequent is couched solely in terms of *response parameters*. Heaven only knows what stimulus and response parameters were supposed to be; but it was an Article of Faith that these notions could, in principle, be made clear. Perhaps stimulus and response parameters are species of physical parameters (parameters that would be acknowledged by an ideally completed physical theory), though not all logical behaviorists would have accepted that identification. In any event, precisely because the ontological impulse of behaviorism was reductionistic, success depended on the possibility of expressing stimulus and response parameters in a vocabulary which contained no mental terms.

What is attractive about logical behaviorism is that the proposed identification of mental properties with dispositional ones provides for a sort of construal of statements that attribute behavioral effects to mental causes—a construal of statements that attribute behavioral effects to mental causes—a construal that is, moreover, conformable to the requirements of materialistic monism. Roughly, mental causation is the manifestation of a behavioral disposition; it's what you get when an organism has such a disposition and the antecedent of a behavioral hypothetical that belongs to the analysis of the disposition happens to be true. It is, no doubt, a travesty to say that for a logical behaviorist "Smith is thirsty" means "if there were water around, Smith would drink it" and "Smith drank because he was thirsty" means "if there were water around Smith would drink it; and there was water around." But it is a travesty that comes close enough for our present purposes. It allows us to see how logical behaviorists proposed to assimilate worrisome etiologies that invoke mental causes to relatively untendentious etiologies like "it broke because it was fragile; it bent because it was pliable," etc.

So, logical behaviorism provides a construal of mental causation, and the glaring question is whether the construal it provides is adequately robust to do the jobs that need doing. In the long run this is the question whether the identification of mental properties with behavioral dispositions yields a notion of mental causation that is rich enough to reconstruct the etiologies propounded by our best psychological theories: the ones that achieve simplicity, explanatory power, and predictive success. However, we needn't wait for the long run, since there are plenty of cases of *pre*-theoretically plausible etiologies for which plausible behavioristic construals are not forthcoming, and these, surely, are straws in the wind.

Here is a quick way of making the point. Suppose "John took aspirin because he had a headache" is true iff conjunction C holds:

> C: John was disposed to produce headache behaviors and being disposed to produce headache behaviors involves satisfying the hypothetical *if there are aspirin around, one takes some,* and there were aspirin around.

So, C gives us a construal of "John took aspirin because he had a headache." But consider that we are also in want of a construal of statements like "John was disposed to produce headache behaviors because he had a headache." Such statements *also* invoke mental causes and, pretheoretically at least, we have no reason to doubt that many of them are true. Yet in these cases it seems unlikely that the putative mental causes can be traded for dispositions; or if they can, the line of analysis we've been pursuing doesn't show us how to do it. We cannot, for example, translate "John had a headache" as "John had a disposition to produce headache behaviors" in these cases, since, patently, "John was disposed to produce headache behaviors because he had a headache" doesn't mean the same as "John was disposed to produce headache behaviors." Yet, "John had a headache" surely means the same in "John took aspirin because he had a headache" and in "John was disposed to produce headache behaviors because he had a headache," so if the behavioristic analysis is wrong for the second case, it must also be wrong for the first.

This is, no doubt, a relatively technical kind of difficulty, but it points in the direction of what is now widely viewed as a hopeless problem for logical behaviorism. Mental causes typically have their overt effects *in virtue of their interactions with one another,* and behaviorism provides no satisfactory analysis of statements that articulate such interactions. Statements that attribute behavioral dispositions to mental causes are of this species, but they are far from exhausting the kind. Consider that having a headache is sufficient to cause a disposition to take aspirin only if it is accompanied by a battery of other mental states: the desire to be rid of the headache; the belief that aspirin exists; the belief that taking aspirin leads to a reduction of headache; the belief that its side effects are not worse than headaches are; the belief that it is not grossly immoral to take aspirin when one has a headache; and so on. Moreover, such beliefs and utilities must be, as it were, *operative;* not only must one *have* them, but some of them must come into play as causal agents contributing to the production of the behavioral effect.

The consequences of this observation are twofold. First, it seems highly unlikely that mental causes can be identified with *behavioral* dispositions, since the antecedents of many putatively behavioral hypotheticals turn out to contain mentalistic vocabulary ineliminably. But, moreover, we shall have to find analyses for etiologies in which interactions among mental states involve possibly quite long and elaborate causal chains; and here we have a fertile source of counterexamples to the generality of *any* kind of dispositional construal of mental ascriptions, behavioral or otherwise. "It occurred to John to move his knight, but then he noticed that that would leave his king in trouble, and since he wanted to avoid check, he thought on balance that he'd better temporize and push a pawn. When, however, he had considered for a while which pawn to push, it all began to look boring and hopeless, and he thought: 'Oh, bother it,' and decided to resign. (Overt behavior finally ensues.)" Surely, the mental life is often like that; such cases occur everywhere where mental *processes* are at issue, and it is, perhaps, the basic problem with behaviorism that it can't reconstruct the notion *mental process.* But these cases seem to be most glaringly the norm in reasoning and problem solving, so it's not surprising that, among psychologists, it has been the cognition theorists who have led the recent antibehaviorist campaign. It seems perfectly obvious that what's needed to construe cognitive processes is precisely what behavior-

ists proposed to do without : causal sequences of mental episodes and a "mental mechanics" to articulate the generalizations that such sequences instantiate. The problem was—and remains—to accommodate these methodological requirements within the ontological framework of materialism.

Which is why the physicalist reading of materialistic monism seemed so very attractive an alternative to the behavioristic version. Suppose we assume that mental particulars (events, states, processes, dispositions, etc.) are identical with physical particulars, and also that the property of being in a certain mental state (such as having a headache or believing that it will rain) is identical with the property of being in a certain physical (e.g. neural) state. Then we have a guaranty that our notion of mental causation will be as robust as our notion of physical causation, the former having turned out to be a special case of the latter. In particular, we will have no difficulty in making sense of the claim that behavioral effects may sometimes be the consequence of elaborate chains of mental causes; or, indeed, that mental causes may interact elaborately *without* eventuating in behavioral effects. If mental processes are, in fact, physical processes, they must enjoy whatever ontological autonomy physical processes are conceded. More than that we surely should not ask for.

This is bracing stuff from the point of view of the psychologist. Endorsing the central state identity theory is tantamount to accepting a Realist interpretation of explanations in which appeal to mental causes figure: If mental particulars are physical particulars, then the singular terms in (true) psychological theories denote. Indeed, they denote precisely the same sorts of things that the singular terms in (true) physical theories do. Moreover, since physicalism is not a semantic thesis, it is immune to many of the kinds of arguments that make trouble for behaviorists. It is, for example, uninteresting from the physicalist's point of view that "John has a headache" doesn't mean the same as "John is in such and such a brain state." The physicalist's claim is not that such sentences are synonymous—that the second provides a linguistically or epistemologically adequate construal of the first—but only that they are rendered true (or false) by the same states of affairs.

I remarked that the identity theory can be held either as a doctrine about mental *particulars* (John's current headache, Bill's fear of cats) or as a doctrine about the nature of mental *properties* (universals like having a pain or being afraid of animals.) These two variants—known as **"token physicalism"** and **"type physicalism"** respectively—differ in both strength and plausibility. For, while the former claims only that all the mental particulars that there happen to be are neurological, the latter makes that claim about all the mental particulars that there *could* be. Token physicalism is thus compatible with the logical—perhaps even the nomological—possibility of unincarnate bearers of mental properties (e.g. angels) and of bearers of mental properties that are incarnate but not in flesh (e.g. machines). Whereas, type physicalism does not recognize such possibilities, since, if the property of having a pain is the same property as that of being in a certain neural state, nothing can have the former property that does not have the latter.

Type physicalism is, on balance, not a plausible doctrine about the nature of mental properties—not even if token physicalism is a plausible doctrine about the nature of mental particulars; not even if token physicalism is a *true* doctrine about the nature of mental particulars. The argument against type physicalism is often made in a way that does it less than justice: "Why shouldn't (e.g.) silicon-based Martians suffer pains? And why shouldn't machines have beliefs? But if it is conceivable that mental properties should have such bearers, then it cannot be that mental properties *are* neural properties, however much the two may prove to be *de facto* coextensive. And neither can it be that they are *physical* properties if what you mean by a physical property is one that can be expressed by a projectible predicate in (say) an ideally completed physics. What silicon-based Martians and IBM machines and you and I are likely to have in common by way of the physical constitution of our nervous systems simply isn't worth discussing." . . .

But that's really not the point. The real point is that, if we want a science of mental phenomena at all, we are required to so identify mental properties that the kinds they subsume are natural from the point of view of psychological theory construction. If, for example, we identify mental properties with neural properties, then we are in effect claiming that domains consisting of creatures with a certain sort of neural organization constitute natural kinds for the psychologist's purposes. (Compare: if we claim that the property of being a fish is the property of living in the water, then we are in effect claiming that a domain consisting of creatures that live in the water constitutes a natural kind for the purposes of the marine biologist. Either that or we are claiming that "is a fish" is not a projectible predicate in marine biology. The essays that follow are neutral on fish, but they do assume the projectibility of properties like those expressed by typical mental predicates.)

Now, there is a level of abstraction at which the generalizations of psychology are most naturally pitched and, as things appear to be turning out, that level of abstraction collapses across the differences between physically quite different kinds of systems. Given the sorts of things we need to say about having pains and believing Ps, it seems to be at best just accidental, and at worst just false, that pains and beliefs are proprietary to creatures like us; if we *wanted* to restrict the domains of our psychological theories to just us, we would have to do so by ad hoc conditions upon their generalizations. Whereas, what does seem to provide a natural domain for psychological theorizing, at least in cognitive psychology, is something like the set of (real and possible) information processing systems. The point being, of course, that there are possible—and, for all we know, real—information processing systems which share our psychology (instantiate its generalizations) but do not share our physical organization.

It would be hard to overemphasize this point, but I shall do my best: Philosophical theories about the nature of mental properties carry empirical commitments about the appropriate domains for psychological generalizations. It is therefore an argument against such a theory if it carves things up in ways that prohibit stating such psychological generalizations as there are to state. And it looks as though type physicalism does carve things up in the wrong ways, assuming that the sort of psychological theories that are now being developed are even close to being true.

This is a state of affairs which cries out for a *relational* treatment of mental properties, one which identifies them in ways that abstract from the physiology of their bearers. Indeed, there is a sense in which behaviorists had the right end of the stick in hand, despite the sorts of objections we reviewed above. Behaviorists, after all, *did* offer a relational construal of mental properties: to have a belief or a pain was to be disposed to exhibit a certain pattern of relations between the responses that one produces and the stimuli that one encounters. So there seemed, ten or fifteen years ago, to be a nasty dilemma facing the materialist program in the philosophy of mind: What central state physicalists seemed to have got right—contra behaviorists—was the ontological autonomy of mental particulars and, of a piece with this, the causal character of mind/body interactions. Whereas, what the behaviorists seemed to have got right—contra the identity theory—was the relational character of mental properties. Functionalism, grounded in the machine analogy, seemed to be able to get both right at once. It was in the cheerful light of that promised synthesis that the now dominant approaches to the philosophy of mind first began to emerge.

It's implicit in the preceding that there is a way of understanding the new functionalism that makes it simply an extension of the logical behaviorist's program. Having a belief (say) was still to be construed as having a relational property, except that, whereas behaviorists had permitted only references to stimuli and responses to appear essentially in specifications of the relata, functionalists allowed reference to *other mental states* as well. A functionalist could thus concede many platitudes that behaviorists are hard put even to construe—as, for example, that it is plausibly a necessary condition for having certain beliefs that one is disposed to draw certain inferences (no belief that P&Q without

a disposition to infer that P and a disposition to infer that Q); that it is plausibly a necessary condition for performing certain acts that one be in certain states of mind (no prevarication without the causal involvement of an intent to deceive); and so forth.

But, in fact, reading functionalism this way—as a liberated form of behaviorism—is more than mildly perverse; for *all* that functionalism and behaviorism have in common is the relational construal of mental properties. If one considers the ontological issues (to say nothing of the epistemological issues), striking differences between the doctrines emerge at once. Unlike behaviorism, functionalism is not a reductionist thesis; it does not envision—even in principle—the elimination of mentalistic concepts from the explanatory apparatus of psychological theories. In consequence, functionalism is compatible with a physicalist (hence Realist) account of mental particulars. It thus tolerates the ascription of causal roles to mental particulars and can take literally theories which represent mental particulars as interacting causally, with whatever degree of complexity, in the course of mental processes. That, as we have seen, was the primary advantage the central state identity theory enjoyed. So it is possible for a functionalist to hold (1) that mental kinds are typically relationally defined; and (2) that the relations that mental particulars exhibit, insofar as they constitute the domains of mental processes, are typically *causal* relations: to stimuli, to responses, and to one another. Of these claims, a logical behaviorist can endorse only the first with an absolutely clear conscience, and a type-physicalist only the second.

So functionalism appeared to capture the best features of the previously available alternatives to dualism while avoiding all the major embarrassments. Viewed from one perspective, it offered behaviorism without reductionism; viewed from another, it offered physicalism without parochialism. The idea that mental particulars are physical, the idea that mental kinds are relational, the idea that mental processes are causal, and the idea that there could, at least in logical principle, be nonbiological bearers of mental properties were all harmonized. And the *seriousness* of the psychologist's undertaking was vindicated by providing for a Realistic interpretation of his theoretical constructs. Bliss!

Questions on Fodor

1. Explain logical behaviorism. According to Fodor, what is the "hopeless problem" that this view faces? Does Armstrong's behavioral account of mental states avoid this problem or not? Explain your answer.

2. Distinguish between token and type physicalism. Explain the objection about the pains of silicon-based Martians and machines.

3. "Functionalism appeared to capture the best features of the previously available alternatives to dualism while avoiding all the major embarrassments." Explain Fodor's reasons for saying this. Do you agree or not? Defend your answer.

John Searle
Can Computers Think?

John Searle is Professor of Philosophy at the University of California, Berkeley. He is the author of Speech Acts, The Philosophy of Language, Expression and Meaning, *and* Intentionality.

In the previous chapter, I provided at least the outlines of a solution to the so-called 'mind-body problem'. Though we do not know in detail how the brain functions, we do know enough to have an idea of the general relationships between brain processes and mental processes. Mental processes are caused by the behaviour of elements of the brain. At the same time, they are realised in the structure that is made up of those elements. I think this answer is consistent with the standard biological approaches to biological phenomena. Indeed, it is a kind of commonsense answer to the question, given what we know about how the world works. However, it is very much a minority point of view. The prevailing view in philosophy, psychology, and artificial intelligence is one which emphasises the analogies between the functioning of the human brain and the functioning of

Reprinted by permission of the publishers from *Minds, Brains and Science* by John Searle, Cambridge, Mass.: Harvard University Press, Copyright © 1984 by John Searle.

digital computers. According to the most extreme version of this view, the brain is just a digital computer and the mind is just a computer program. One could summarise this view—I call it 'strong artificial intelligence', or 'strong AI'—by saying that the mind is to the brain, as the program is to the computer hardware.

This view has the consequence that there is nothing essentially biological about the human mind. The brain just happens to be one of an indefinitely large number of different kinds of hardware computers that could sustain the programs which make up human intelligence. On this view, any physical system whatever that had the right program with the right inputs and outputs would have a mind in exactly the same sense that you and I have minds. So, for example, if you made a computer out of old beer cans powered by windmills; if it had the right program, it would have to have a mind. And the point is not that for all we know it might have thoughts and feelings, but rather that it must have thoughts and feelings, because that is all there is to having thoughts and feelings: implementing the right program.

Most people who hold this view think we have not yet designed programs which are minds. But there is pretty much general agreement among them that it's only a matter of time until computer scientists and workers in artificial intelligence design the appropriate hardware and programs which will be the equivalent of human brains and minds. These will be artificial brains and minds which are in every way the equivalent of human brains and minds.

Many people outside of the field of artificial intelligence are quite amazed to discover that anybody could believe such a view as this. So, before criticising it, let me give you a few examples of the things that people in this field have actually said. Herbert Simon of Carnegie-Mellon University says that we already have machines that can literally think. There is no question of waiting for some future machine, because existing digital computers already have thoughts in exactly the same sense that you and I do. Well, fancy that! Philosophers have been worried for centuries about whether or not a machine could think, and now we discover that they already have such machines at Carnegie-Mellon. Simon's colleague Alan Newell claims that we have now discovered (and notice that Newell says 'discovered' and not 'hypothesised' or 'considered the possibility', but we have *discovered*) that intelligence is just a matter of physical symbol manipulation; it has no essential connection with any specific kind of biological or physical wetware or hardware. Rather, any system whatever that is capable of manipulating physical symbols in the right way is capable of intelligence in the same literal sense as human intelligence of human beings. Both Simon and Newell, to their credit, emphasise that there is nothing metaphorical about these claims; they mean them quite literally. Freeman Dyson is quoted as having said that computers have an advantage over the rest of us when it comes to evolution. Since consciousness is just a matter of formal processes, in computers these formal processes can go on in substances that are much better able to survive in a universe that is cooling off than begins like ourselves made of our wet and messy materials. Marvin Minsky of MIT says that the next generation of computers will be so intelligent that we will 'be lucky if they are willing to keep us around the house as household pets'. My all-time favourite in the literature of exaggerated claims on behalf of the digital computer is from John McCarthy, the inventor of the term 'artificial intelligence'. McCarthy says even 'machines as simple as thermostats can be said to have beliefs'. And indeed, according to him, almost any machine capable of problem-solving can be said to have beliefs. I admire McCarthy's courage. I once asked him:

'What beliefs does your thermostat have?' And he said: 'My thermostat has three beliefs—it's too hot in here, it's too cold in here, and it's just right in here.' As a philosopher, I like all these claims for a simple reason. Unlike most philosophical theses, they are reasonably clear, and they admit of a simple and decisive refutation. It is this refutation that I am going to undertake in this chapter.

The nature of the refutation has nothing whatever to do with any particular stage of computer technology. It is important to emphasise this point because the temptation is always to think that the solution to our problems must wait on some as yet uncreated technological wonder. But in fact, the nature of the refutation is completely independent of any state of technology. It has to do with the very definition of a digital computer, with what a digital computer is.

It is essential to our conception of a digital computer that its operations can be specified purely formally; that is, we specify the steps in the operation of the computer in terms of abstract symbols—sequences of zeroes and ones printed on a tape, for example. A typical computer 'rule' will determine that when a machine is in a certain state and it has a certain symbol on its tape, then it will perform a certain operation such as erasing the symbol or printing another symbol and then enter another state such as moving the tape one square to the left. But the symbols have no meaning; they have no semantic content; they are not about anything. They have to be specified purely in terms of their formal or syntactical structure. The zeroes and ones, for example, are just numerals; they don't even stand for numbers. Indeed, it is this feature of digital computers that makes them so powerful. One and the same type of hardware, if it is appropriately designed, can be used to run an indefinite range of different programs. And one and the same program can be run on an indefinite range of different types of hardwares.

But this feature of programs, that they are defined purely formally or syntactically, is fatal to the view that mental processes and program processes are identical. And the reason can be stated quite simply. There is more to having a mind than having formal or syntactical processes. Our internal mental states, by definition, have certain sorts of contents. If I am thinking about Kansas City or wishing that I had a cold beer to drink or wondering if there will be a fall in interest rates, in each case my mental state has a certain mental content in addition to whatever formal features it might have. That is, even if my thoughts occur to me in strings of symbols, there must be more to the thought than the abstract strings, because strings by themselves can't have any meaning. If my thoughts are to be *about* anything, then the strings must have a *meaning* which makes the thoughts about those things. In a word, the mind has more than a syntax, it has a semantics. The reason that no computer program can ever be a mind is simply that a computer program is only syntactical, and minds are more than syntactical. Minds are semantical, in the sense that they have more than a formal structure, they have a content.

To illustrate this point I have designed a certain thought-experiment. Imagine that a bunch of computer programmers have written a program that will enable a computer to simulate the understanding of Chinese. So, for example, if the computer is given a question in Chinese, it will match the question against its memory, or data base, and produce appropriate answers to the questions in Chinese. Suppose for the sake of argument that the computer's answers are as good as those of a native Chinese speaker. Now then, does the computer, on the basis of this, understand Chinese, does it literally understand Chinese, in the way that Chinese speakers understand Chinese? Well, imagine that you are locked in a room, and in this room are several baskets full of Chinese symbols. Imagine that you (like me) do not understand a word of Chinese, but that you are given a rule book in English for manipulating these Chinese symbols. The rules specify the manipulations of the symbols purely formally, in terms of their syntax, not their semantics. So the rule might say: 'Take a squiggle-squiggle sign out of basket number one and put it next to a squoggle-squoggle sign from basket number two.' Now suppose that some other Chinese symbols are passed into the room, and that you are given further rules for

passing back Chinese symbols out of the room. Suppose that unknown to you the symbols passed into the room are called 'questions' by the people outside the room, and the symbols you pass back out of the room are called 'answers to the questions'. Suppose, furthermore, that the programmers are so good at designing the programs and that you are so good at manipulating the symbols, that very soon your answers are indistinguishable from those of a native Chinese speaker. There you are locked in your room shuffling your Chinese symbols and passing out Chinese symbols in response to incoming Chinese symbols. On the basis of the situation as I have described it, there is no way you could learn any Chinese simply by manipulating these formal symbols.

Now the point of the story is simply this: by virtue of implementing a formal computer program from the point of view of an outside observer, you behave exactly as if you understood Chinese, but all the same you don't understand a word of Chinese. But if going through the appropriate computer program for understanding Chinese is not enough to give *you* an understanding of Chinese, then it is not enough to give *any other digital computer* an understanding of Chinese. And again, the reason for this can be stated quite simply. If you don't understand Chinese, then no other computer could understand Chinese because no digital computer, just by virtue of running a program, has anything that you don't have. All that the computer has, as you have, is a formal program for manipulating uninterpreted Chinese symbols. To repeat, a computer has a syntax, but no semantics. The whole point of the parable of the Chinese room is to remind us of a fact that we knew all along. Understanding a language, or indeed, having mental states at all, involves more than just having a bunch of formal symbols. It involves having an interpretation, or a meaning attached to those symbols. And a digital computer, as defined, cannot have more than just formal symbols because the operation of the computer, as I said earlier, is defined in terms of its ability to implement programs. And these programs are purely formally specifiable—that is, they have no semantic content.

We can see the force of this argument if we

contrast what it is like to be asked and to answer questions in English, and to be asked and to answer questions in some language where we have no knowledge of any of the meanings of the words. Imagine that in the Chinese room you are also given questions in English about such things as your age or your life history, and that you answer these questions. What is the difference between the Chinese case and the English case? Well again, if like me you understand no Chinese and you do understand English, then the difference is obvious. You understand the questions in English because they are expressed in symbols whose meanings are known to you. Similarly, when you give the answers in English you are producing symbols which are meaningful to you. But in the case of the Chinese, you have none of that. In the case of the Chinese, you simply manipulate formal symbols according to a computer program, and you attach no meaning to any of the elements.

Various replies have been suggested to this argument by workers in artificial intelligence and in psychology, as well as philosophy. They all have something in common; they are all inadequate. And there is an obvious reason why they have to be inadequate, since the argument rests on a very simple logical truth, namely, syntax alone is not sufficient for semantics, and digital computers insofar as they are computers have, by definition, a syntax alone.

I want to make this clear by considering a couple of the arguments that are often presented against me.

Some people attempt to answer the Chinese room example by saying that the whole system understands Chinese. The idea here is that though I, the person in the room manipulating the symbols do not understand Chinese, I am just the central processing unit of the computer system. They argue that it is the whole system, including the room, the baskets full of symbols and the ledgers containing the programs and perhaps other items as well, taken as a totality, that understands Chinese. But this is subject to exactly the same objection I made before. There is no way that the system can get from the syntax to the semantics. I, as the central processing unit have no way of figuring out what

any of these symbols means; but then neither does the whole system.

Another common response is to imagine that we put the Chinese understanding program inside a robot. If the robot moved around and interacted causally with the world, wouldn't that be enough to guarantee that it understood Chinese? Once again the inexorability of the semantics-syntax distinction overcomes this manoeuvre. As long as we suppose that the robot has only a computer for a brain then, even though it might behave exactly as if it understood Chinese, it would still have no way of getting from the syntax to the semantics of Chinese. You can see this if you imagine that I am the computer. Inside a room in the robot's skull I shuffle symbols without knowing that some of them come in to me from television cameras attached to the robot's head and others go out to move the robot's arms and legs. As long as all I have is a formal computer program, I have no way of attaching any meaning to any of the symbols. And the fact that the robot is engaged in causal interactions with the outside world won't help me to attach any meaning to the symbols unless I have some way of finding out about that fact. Suppose the robot picks up a hamburger and this triggers the symbol for hamburger to come into the room. As long as all I have is the symbol with no knowledge of its causes or how it got there, I have no way of knowing what it means. The causal interactions between the robot and the rest of the world are irrelevant unless those causal interactions are represented in some mind or other. But there is no way they can be if all that the so-called mind consists of is a set of purely formal, syntactical operations.

It is important to see exactly what is claimed and what is not claimed by my argument. Suppose we ask the question that I mentioned at the beginning: 'Could a machine think?' Well, in one sense, of course, we are all machines. We can construe the stuff inside our heads as a meat machine. And of course, we can all think. So, in one sense of 'machine', namely that sense in which a machine is just a physical system which is capable of performing certain kinds of operations, in that sense, we are all machines, and we can think. So, trivially, there are machines that can think. But that wasn't the question that bothered us. So let's try a different formulation of it. Could an artefact think? Could a man-made machine think? Well, once again, it depends on the kind of artefact. Suppose we designed a machine that was molecule-for-molecule indistinguishable from a human being. Well then, if you can duplicate the causes, you can presumably duplicate the effects. So once again, the answer to that question is, in principle at least, trivially yes. If you could build a machine that had the same structure as a human being, then presumably that machine would be able to think. Indeed, it would be a surrogate human being. Well, let's try again.

The question isn't: 'Can a machine think?' or: 'Can an artefact think?' The question is: 'Can a digital computer think?' But once again we have to be very careful in how we interpret the question. From a mathematical point of view, anything whatever can be described *as if* it were a digital computer. And that's because it can be described as instantiating or implementing a computer program. In an utterly trivial sense, the pen that is on the desk in front of me can be described as a digital computer. It just happens to have a very boring computer program. The program says: 'Stay there.' Now since in this sense, anything whatever is a digital computer, because anything whatever can be described as implementing a computer program, then once again, our question gets a trivial answer. Of course our brains are digital computers, since they implement any number of computer programs. And of course our brains can think. So once again, there is a trivial answer to the question. But that wasn't really the question we were trying to ask. The question we wanted to ask is this: 'Can a digital computer, as defined, think?' That is to say: 'Is instantiating or implementing the right computer program with the right inputs and outputs, sufficient for, or constitutive of, thinking?' And to this question, unlike its predecessors, the answer is clearly 'no'. And it is 'no' for the reason that we have spelled out, namely, the computer program is defined purely syntactically. But thinking is more than just a matter of manipulating meaningless symbols, it involves meaningful se-mantic contents. These semantic contents are what we mean by 'meaning'.

It is important to emphasise again that we are not talking about a particular stage of computer technology. The argument has nothing to do with the forthcoming, amazing advances in computer science. It has nothing to do with the distinction between serial and parallel processes, or with the size of programs, or the speed of computer operations, or with computers that can interact causally with their environment, or even with the invention of robots. Technological progress is always grossly exaggerated, but even subtracting the exaggeration, the development of computers has been quite remarkable, and we can reasonably expect that even more remarkable progress will be made in the future. No doubt we will be much better able to simulate human behaviour on computers than we can at present, and certainly much better than we have been able to in the past. The point I am making is that if we are talking about having mental states, having a mind, all of these simulations are simply irrelevant. It doesn't matter how good the technology is, or how rapid the calculations made by the computer are. If it really is a computer, its operations have to be defined syntactically, whereas consciousness, thoughts, feelings, emotions, and all the rest of it involve more than a syntax. Those features, by definition, the computer is unable to *duplicate* however powerful may be its ability to *simulate*. The key distinction here is between duplication and simulation. And no simulation by itself ever constitutes duplication.

What I have done so far is give a basis to the sense that those citations I began this talk with are really as preposterous as they seem. There is a puzzling question in this discussion though, and that is: 'Why would anybody ever have thought that computers could think or have feelings and emotions and all the rest of it?' After all, we can do computer simulations of any process whatever that can be given a formal description. So, we can do a computer simulation of the flow of money in the British economy, or the pattern of power distribution in the Labour party. We can do computer simulation of rain storms in the home counties, or warehouse fires in East London. Now, in each of these cases, nobody supposes that the computer simulation is actually the real thing; no one supposes that a computer simulation of a storm will leave us all wet, or a computer simulation of a fire is likely to burn the house down. Why on earth would anyone in his right mind suppose a computer simulation of mental processes actually had mental processes? I don't really know the answer to that, since the idea seems to me, to put it frankly, quite crazy from the start. But I can make a couple of speculations.

First of all, where the mind is concerned, a lot of people are still tempted to some sort of behaviourism. They think if a system behaves as if it understood Chinese, then it really must understand Chinese. But we have already refuted this form of behaviourism with the Chinese room argument. Another assumption made by many people is that the mind is not a part of the biological world, it is not a part of the world of nature. The strong artificial intelligence view relies on that in its conception that the mind is purely formal; that somehow or other, it cannot be treated as a concrete product of biological processes like any other biological product. There is in these discussions, in short, a kind of residual dualism. AI partisans believe that the mind is more than a part of the natural biological world; they believe that the mind is purely formally specifiable. The paradox of this is that the AI literature is filled with fulminations against some view called 'dualism', but in fact, the whole thesis of strong AI rests on a kind of dualism. It rests on a rejection of the idea that the mind is just a natural biological phenomenon in the world like any other.

I want to conclude this chapter by putting together the thesis of the last chapter and the thesis of this one. Both of these theses can be stated very simply. And indeed, I am going to state them with perhaps excessive crudeness. But if we put them together I think we get a quite powerful conception of the relations of minds, brains and computers. And the argument has a very simple logical structure, so you can see whether it is valid or invalid. The first premise is:

1. Brains cause minds.

Now, of course, that is really too crude. What we mean by that is that mental processes that we consider to constitute a mind are caused, entirely caused, by processes going on inside the brain. But let's be crude, let's just abbreviate that as three words—brains cause minds. And that is just a fact about how the world works. Now let's write proposition number two:

2. Syntax is not sufficient for semantics.

That proposition is a conceptual truth. It just articulates our distinction between the notion of what is purely formal and what has content. Now, to these two propositions—that brains cause minds and that syntax is not sufficient for semantics—let's add a third and a fourth:

3. Computer programs are entirely defined by their formal, or syntactical, structure.

That proposition, I take it, is true by definition; it is part of what we mean by the notion of a computer program.

4. Minds have mental contents; specifically, they have semantic contents.

And that, I take it, is just an obvious fact about how our minds work. My thoughts, and beliefs, and desires are about something, or they refer to something, or they concern states of affairs in the world; and they do that because their content directs them at these states of affairs in the world. Now, from these four premises, we can draw our first conclusion; and it follows obviously from premises 2, 3 and 4:

CONCLUSION 1. *No computer program by itself is sufficient to give a system a mind. Programs, in short, are not minds, and they are not by themselves sufficient for having minds.*

Now, that is a very powerful conclusion, because it means that the project of trying to create minds solely by designing programs is doomed from the start. And it is important to re-emphasise that this has nothing to do with any particular state of technology or any particular state of the complexity of the program. This is a purely formal, or logical, result from a set of axioms which are agreed to by all (or nearly all) of the disputants concerned. That is, even most of the hardcore enthusiasts for artificial intelligence agree that in fact, as a matter of biology, brain processes cause mental states, and they agree that programs are defined purely formally. But if you put these conclusions together with certain other things that we know, then it follows immediately that the project of strong AI is incapable of fulfillment.

However, once we have got these axioms, let's see what else we can derive. Here is a second conclusion:

CONCLUSION 2. *The way that brain functions cause minds cannot be solely in virtue of running a computer program.*

And this second conclusion follows from conjoining the first premise together with our first conclusion. That is, from the fact that brains cause minds and that programs are not enough to do the job, it follows that the way that brains cause minds can't be solely by running a computer program. Now that also I think is an important result, because it has the consequence that the brain is not, or at least is not just, a digital computer. We saw earlier that anything can trivially be described as if it were a digital computer, and brains are no exception. But the importance of this conclusion is that the computational properties of the brain are simply not enough to explain its functioning to produce mental states. And indeed, that ought to seem a commonsense scientific conclusion to us anyway because all it does is remind us of the fact that brains are biological engines; their biology matters. It is not, as several people in artificial intelligence have claimed, just an irrelevant fact about the mind that it happens to be realised in human brains.

Now, from our first premise, we can also derive a third conclusion:

CONCLUSION 3. *Anything else that caused minds would have to have causal powers at least equivalent to those of the brain.*

And this third conclusion is a trivial consequence of our first premise. It is a bit like saying that if my petrol engine drives my car at seventy-five miles an hour, then any diesel engine that was capable of doing that would have to have a power output at least equivalent to that of my petrol engine. Of course, some other system might cause mental processes using entirely different chemical or biochemical features from those the brain in fact uses. It might turn out that there are beings on other planets, or in other solar systems, that have mental states and use an entirely different biochemistry from ours. Suppose that Martians arrived in earth and we concluded that they had mental states. But suppose that when their heads were opened up, it was discovered that all they had inside was green slime. Well still, the green slime, if it functioned to produce consciousness and all the rest of their mental life, would have to have causal powers equal to those of the human brain. But now, from our first conclusion, that programs are not enough, and our third conclusion, that any other system would have to have causal powers equal to the brain, conclusion four follows immediately:

CONCLUSION 4. *For any artefact that we might build which had mental states equivalent to human mental states, the implementation of a computer program would not by itself be sufficient. Rather the artefact would have to have powers equivalent to the powers of the human brain.*

The upshot of this discussion I believe is to remind us of something that we have known all along: namely, mental states are biological phenomena. Consciousness, intentionality, subjectivity and mental causation are all a part of our biological life history, along with growth, reproduction, the secretion of bile, and digestion.

Questions on Searle

1. What is the view of "strong artificial intelligence?" Carefully explain Searle's alleged refutation of this view, namely his Chinese room argument. Does this argument really provide a conclusive refutation or not? Defend your position.

2. Searle claims that the Chinese room argument refutes behaviorism too. Does it?

3. Searle derives four important conclusions about the mind, the brain, and computers. What are these conclusions? Have they been established to your satisfaction or not? Explain your answer.

Paul M. Churchland

Reductive and Eliminative Materialism

Paul M. Churchland is Professor of Philosophy at the University of California, San Diego. His books include Scientific Realism, The Plasticity of Mind, *and* Matter and Consciousness.

Reductive Materialism (the Identity Theory)

Reductive materialism, more commonly known as *the identity theory,* is the most straightforward of the several materialist theories of mind. Its central claim is simplicity itself: Mental states *are* physical states of the brain. That is, each type of mental state or process is *numerically identical with* (is one and the very same thing as) some type of physical state or process within the brain or central nervous system. At present we do not know enough about the intricate functionings of the brain actually to state the relevant identities, but the identity theory is committed to the idea that brain research will eventually reveal them. . . .

Eliminative Materialism

The identity theory was called into doubt not because the prospects for a materialist account of our mental capacities were thought to be poor, but because it seemed unlikely that the arrival of an adequate materialist theory would bring with it the nice one-to-one match-ups, between the concepts of folk psychology and the concepts of theoretical neuroscience, that intertheoretic reduction requires. The reason

The reading is from Paul M. Churchland, *Matter and Consciousness* (Cambridge: MIT Press, 1984), pp. 26, 43–49. Copyright © by the Massachusetts Institute of Technology. Reprinted with permission.

for that doubt was the great variety of quite different physical systems that could instantiate the required functional organization. *Eliminative materialism* also doubts that the correct neuroscientific account of human capacities will produce a neat reduction of our common-sense framework, but here the doubts arise from a quite different source.

As the eliminative materialists see it, the one-to-one match-ups will not be found, and our common-sense psychological framework will not enjoy an intertheoretic reduction, *because our common-sense psychological framework is a false and radically misleading conception of the causes of human behavior and the nature of cognitive activity.* On this view, folk psychology is not just an incomplete representation of our inner natures; it is an outright *mis*representation of our internal states and activities. Consequently, we cannot expect a truly adequate neurosientific account of our inner lives to provide theoretical categories that match up nicely with the categories of our common-sense framework. Accordingly, we must expect that the older framework will simply be eliminated, rather than be reduced, by a matured neuroscience.

Historical Parallels

As the identity theorist can point to historical cases of successful intertheoretic reduction, so the eliminative materialist can point to historical cases of the outright elimination of the **ontology** of an older theory in favor of the ontology of a new and superior theory. For most of the eighteenth and nineteenth centuries, learned people believed that heat was a subtle *fluid* held in bodies, much in the way water is held in a sponge. A fair body of moderately successful theory described the way this fluid substance—called "caloric"—flowed within a body, or from one body to another, and how it produced thermal expansion, melting, boiling, and so forth. But by the end of the last century it had become abundantly clear that heat was not a substance at all, but just the energy of motion of the trillions of jostling molecules that make up the heated body itself. The new theory—the "corpuscular/kinetic theory of matter and heat"—was much more successful than the old in explaining and predicting the thermal behavior of bodies. And since we were unable to *identify* caloric fluid with kinetic energy (according to the old theory, caloric is a material *substance;* according to the new theory, kinetic energy is a form of *motion*), it was finally agreed that there is *no such thing* as caloric. Caloric was simply eliminated from our accepted ontology.

A second example. It used to be thought that when a piece of wood burns, or a piece of metal rusts, a spiritlike substance called "phlogiston" was being released: briskly, in the former case, slowly in the latter. Once gone, that 'noble' substance left only a base pile of ash or rust. It later came to be appreciated that both processes involve, not the loss of something, but the *gaining* of a substance taken from the atmosphere: oxygen. Phlogiston emerged, not as an incomplete description of what was going on, but as a radical misdescription. Phlogiston was therefore not suitable for reduction to or identification with some notion from within the new oxygen chemistry, and it was simply eliminated from science.

Admittedly, both of these examples concern the elimination of something nonobservable, but our history also includes the elimination of certain widely accepted 'observables'. Before Copernicus' views became available, almost any human who ventured out at night could look up at *the starry sphere of the heavens,* and if he stayed for more than a few minutes he could also see that it *turned,* around an axis through Polaris. What the sphere was made of (crystal?) and what made it turn (the gods?) were theoretical questions that exercised us for over two millennia. But hardly anyone doubted the existence of what everyone could observe with their own eyes. In the end, however, we learned to reinterpret our visual experience of the night sky within a very different conceptual framework, and the turning sphere evaporated.

Witches provide another example. Psychosis is is a fairly common affliction among humans, and in earlier centuries its victims were standardly seen as cases of demonic possession, as instances of Satan's spirit itself, glaring malevolently out at us from behind the victims' eyes. That witches exist was not a matter of any controversy. One would occasionally see them, in any city or hamlet, engaged in incoherent, paranoid, or even murderous behavior. But observable or not, we eventually decided that witches simply do not exist. We concluded that the concept of a witch is an element in a conceptual framework that misrepresents so badly the phenomena to which it was standardly applied that literal application of the notion should be permanently withdrawn. Modern theories of mental dysfunction led to the elimination of witches from our serious ontology.

The concepts of folk psychology—belief, desire, fear, sensation, pain, joy, and so on—await a similar fate, according to the view at issue. And when neuroscience has matured to the point where the poverty of our current conceptions is apparent to everyone, and the superiority of the new framework is established, we shall then be able to set about *re*conceiving our internal states and activities, within a truly adequate conceptual framework at last. Our explanations of one another's behavior will appeal to such things as our neuropharmacological states, the neural activity in specialized anatomical areas, and whatever other states are deemed relevant by the new theory. Our private introspection will also be transformed, and may be profoundly enhanced by reason of the more accurate and penetrating framework it will have to work with—just as the astronomer's perception of the night sky is much enhanced by the detailed knowledge of modern astronomical theory that he or she possesses.

The magnitude of the conceptual revolution here suggested should not be minimized: it would be enormous. And the benefits to humanity might be equally great. If each of us possessed an accurate neuroscientific understanding of (what we now conceive dimly as) the varieties and causes of mental illness, the factors involved in learning, the neural basis of emotions, intelligence, and socialization, then the sum total of human misery might be much reduced. The simple increase in mutual understanding that the new framework made possible could contribute substantially toward a more peaceful and humane society. Of course, there would be dangers as well: increased knowledge means increased power, and power can always be misused.

Arguments for Eliminative Materialism

The arguments for eliminative materialism are diffuse and less than decisive, but they are stronger than is widely supposed. The distinguishing feature of this position is its denial that a smooth intertheoretic reduction is to be expected—even a species-specific reduction —of the framework of folk psychology to the framework of a matured neuroscience. The reason for this denial is the eliminative materialist's conviction that folk psychology is a hopelessly primitive and deeply confused conception of our internal activities. But why this low opinion of our common-sense conceptions?

There are at least three reasons. First, the eliminative materialist will point to the widespread explanatory, predictive, and manipulative failures of folk psychology. So much of what is central and familiar to us remains a complete mystery from within folk psychology. We do not know what *sleep* is, or why we have to have it, despite spending a full third of our lives in that condition. (The answer, "For rest," is mistaken. Even if people are allowed to rest continuously, their need for sleep is undiminished. Apparently, sleep serves some deeper functions, but we do not yet know what they are.) We do not understand how *learning* transforms each of us from a gaping infant to a cunning adult, or how differences in *intelligence* are grounded. We have not the slightest idea how *memory* works, or how we manage to retrieve relevant bits of information instantly from the awesome mass we have stored. We do not know what *mental illness* is, nor how to cure it.

In sum, the most central things about us remain almost entirely mysterious from within folk psychology. And the defects noted cannot be blamed on inadequate time allowed for their correction, for folk psychology has enjoyed no significant changes or advances in well over 2,000 years, despite its manifest failures. Truly successful theories may be expected to reduce, but significantly unsuccessful theories merit no such expectation.

This argument from explanatory poverty has a further aspect. So long as one sticks to normal brains, the poverty of folk psychology is perhaps not strikingly evident. But as soon as one examines the many perplexing behavioral and cognitive deficits suffered by people with *damaged* brains, one's descriptive and explanatory resources start to claw the air. . . . As with other humble theories asked to operate successfully in unexplored extensions of their old domain (for example, Newtonian mechanics in the domain of velocities close to the velocity of light, and the classical gas law in the domain of high pressures or temperatures), the descriptive and explanatory inadequacies of folk psychology become starkly evident.

The second argument tries to draw an inductive lesson from our conceptual history. Our early folk theories of motion were profoundly confused, and were eventually displaced entirely by more sophisticated theories. Our early folk theories of the structure and activity of the heavens were wildly off the mark, and survive only as historical lessons in how wrong we can be. Our folk theories of the nature of fire, and the nature of life, were similarly cockeyed. And one could go on, since the vast majority of our past folk conceptions have been similarly exploded. All except folk psychology, which survives to this day and has only recently begun to feel pressure. But the phenomenon of conscious intelligence is surely a more complex and difficult phenomenon than any of those just listed. So far as accurate understanding is concerned, it would be a *miracle* if we had got *that* one right the very first time, when we fell down so badly on all the others. Folk psychology has survived for so very long, presumably, not because it is basically correct in its representations, but because the phenomena addressed are so surpassingly difficult that any useful handle on them, no matter how feeble, is unlikely to be displaced in a hurry.

A third argument attempts to find an a priori advantage for eliminative materialism over the identity theory and functionalism. It attempts to counter the common intuition that eliminative materialism is distantly possible, perhaps, but is much less probable than either the identity theory or functionalism. The focus again is on whether the concepts of folk psychology will find vindicating match-ups in a matured neuroscience. The eliminativist bets no; the other two bet yes. . . .

The eliminativist will point out that the requirements on a reduction are rather demanding. The new theory must entail a set of principles and embedded concepts that mirrors very closely the specific conceptual structure to be reduced. And the fact is, there are vastly many more ways of being an explanatorily successful neuroscience while *not* mirroring the structure of folk psychology, than there are ways of being an explanatorily successful neuroscience while also *mirroring* the very specific structure of folk psychology. Accordingly, the a priori probability of eliminative materialism is not lower, but substantially *higher* than that of either of its competitors. One's initial intuitions here are simply mistaken.

Granted, this initial a priori advantage could be reduced if there were a very strong presumption in favor of the truth of folk psychology—true theories are better bets to win reduction. But according to the first two arguments, the presumptions on this point should run in precisely the opposite direction.

Arguments against Eliminative Materialism

The initial plausibility of this rather radical view is low for almost everyone, since it denies deeply entrenched assumptions. That is at best a question-begging complaint, of course, since those assumptions are precisely what is at issue. But the following line of thought does attempt to mount a real argument.

Eliminative materialism is false, runs the argument, because one's introspection reveals directly the existence of pains, beliefs, desires, fears, and so forth. Their existence is as obvious as anything could be.

The eliminative materialist will reply that this argument makes the same mistake that an ancient or medieval person would be making if he insisted that he could just see with his own eyes that the heavens form a turning sphere, or that witches exist. The fact is, all observation occurs within some system of concepts, and our observation judgments are only as good as the conceptual framework in which they are expressed. In all three cases—the starry sphere, witches, and the familiar mental states—precisely what is challenged is the integrity of the background conceptual frameworks in which the observation judgements are expressed. To insist on the validity of one's experiences, *traditionally interpreted,* is therefore to beg the very question at issue. For in all three cases, the question is whether we should *reconceive* the nature of some familiar observational domain.

A second criticism attempts to find an incoherence in the eliminative materialist's position. The bald statement of eliminative materialism is that the familiar mental states do not really exist. But that statement is meaningful, runs the argument, only if it is the expression of a certain *belief,* and an *intention* to communicate, and a *knowledge* of the language, and so forth. But if the statement is true, then no such mental states exist, and the statement is therefore a meaningless string of marks or noises, and cannot be true. Evidently, the assumption that eliminative materialism is true entails that it cannot be true.

The hole in this argument is the premise concerning the conditions necessary for a statement to be meaningful. It begs the question. If eliminative materialism is true, then meaningfulness must have some different source. To insist on the 'old' source is to insist on the validity of the very framework at issue. Again, an historical parallel may be helpful here. Consider the medieval theory that being biologically *alive* is a matter of being ensouled by an immaterial *vital spirit.* And consider the following response to someone who has expressed disbelief in that theory.

My learned friend has stated that there is no such thing as vital spirit. But this statement is incoherent. For if it is true, then my friend does not have vital spirit, and must therefore be dead. But if he is dead, then his statement is just a string of noises, devoid of meaning or truth. Evidently, the assumption that antivitalism is true entails that it cannot be true! Q.E.D.

This second argument is now a joke, but the first argument begs the question in exactly the same way.

A final criticism draws a much weaker conclusion, but makes a rather stronger case. Eliminative materialism, it has been said, is making mountains out of molehills. It exaggerates the defects in folk psychology, and underplays its real successes. Perhaps the arrival of a matured neuroscience will require the elimination of the occasional folk-psychological concept, continues the criticism, and a minor adjustment in certain folk-psychological principles may have to be endured. But the large-scale elimination forecast by the eliminative materialist is just an alarmist worry or a romantic enthusiasm.

Perhaps this complaint is correct. And perhaps it is merely complacent. Whichever, it does bring out the important point that we do not confront two simple and mutually exclusive possibilities here: pure reduction versus pure elimination. Rather, these are the end points of a smooth spectrum of possible outcomes, between which there are mixed cases of partial elimination and partial reduction. Only empirical research . . . can tell us where on that spectrum our own case will fall. Perhaps we should speak here, more liberally, of "revisionary materialism", instead of concentrating on the more radical possibility of an across-the-board elimination. Perhaps we should. But it has been my aim in this section to make it at least intelligible to you that our collective conceptual destiny lies substantially toward the revolutionary end of the spectrum.

Questions on Churchland

1. What is the identity theory? How does this theory differ from the central-state theory defended by Armstrong? Why does Churchland reject the identity theory? Does his criticism apply to Armstrong's view too? Is the criticism a good one? Explain.

2. Churchland explains eliminative materialism and discusses the arguments for and against it. Are you persuaded that this theory is superior to the rival theories or not? Defend your position.

Thomas Nagel

What Is It Like to Be a Bat?

Thomas Nagel is Professor of Philosophy at New York University. His most recent book is The View from Nowhere.

Consciousness is what makes the mind-body problem really intractable. Perhaps that is why current discussions of the problem give it little

Thomas Nagel, "What Is It Like to Be a Bat?" *Philosophical Review* 83, No. 4 (Oct. 1974), pp. 435–450. Reprinted with permission of the publisher.

attention or get it obviously wrong. The recent wave of reductionist euphoria has produced several analyses of mental phenomena and mental concepts designed to explain the possibility of some variety of materialism, psychophysical identification, or reduction.[1] But the problems dealt with are those common to this type of reduction and other types, and what makes the mind-body problem unique, and unlike the water-H_2O problem of the Turing machine-IBM machine problem or the lightning-electrical discharge problem or the gene-DNA problem or the oak tree-hydrocarbon problem, is ignored.

Every reductionist has his favorite analogy from modern science. It is most unlikely that any of these unrelated examples of successful reduction will shed light on the relation of mind to brain. But philosophers share the general human weakness for explanations of what is incomprehensible in terms suited for what is familiar and well understood, though entirely different. This has led to the acceptance of implausible accounts of the mental largely because they would permit familiar kinds of reduction. I shall try to explain why the usual examples do not help us to understand the relation between mind and body—why, indeed, we have at present no conception of what an explanation of the physical nature of a mental phenomenon would be. Without consciousness the mind-body problem would be much less interesting. With consciousness it seems hopeless. The most important and characteristic feature of conscious mental phenomena is very poorly understood. Most reductionist theories do not even try to explain it. And careful examination will show that no currently available concept of reduction is applicable to it. Perhaps a new theoretical form can be devised for the purpose, but such a solution, if it exists, lies in the distant intellectual future.

Conscious experience is a widespread phenomenon. It occurs at many levels of animal life, though we cannot be sure of its presence in the simpler organisms, and it is very difficult to say in general what provides evidence of it. (Some extremists have been prepared to deny it even of mammals other than man.) No doubt it occurs in countless forms totally unimaginable to us, on other planets in other solar systems throughout the universe. But no matter how the form may vary, the fact that an organism has conscious experience *at all* means, basically, that there is something it is like to *be* that organism. There may be further implications about the form of the experience; there may even (though I doubt it) be implications about the behavior of the organism. But fundamentally an organism has conscious mental states if and only if there is something that it is like to *be* that organism—something it is like *for* the organism.

We may call this the subjective character of experience. It is not captured by any of the familiar, recently devised reductive analyses of the mental, for all of them are logically compatible with its absence. It is not analyzable in terms of any explanatory system of functional states, or intentional states, since these could be ascribed to robots or automata that behaved like people though they experienced nothing.[2] It is not analyzable in terms of the causal role of experiences in relation to typical human behavior—for similar reasons.[3] I do not deny that conscious mental states and events cause behavior, nor that they may be given functional characterizations. I deny only that this kind of thing exhausts their analysis. Any reductionist program has to be based on an analysis. Any reductionist program has to be based on an analysis of what is to be reduced. If the analysis leaves something out, the problem will be falsely posed. It is useless to base the defense of materialism on any analysis of mental phenomena that fails to deal explicitly with their subjective character. For there is no reason to suppose that a reduction which seems plausible when no attempt is made to account for consciousness can be extended to include consciousness. Without some idea, therefore, of what the subjective character of experience is, we cannot know what is required of physicalist theory.

While an account of the physical basis of mind must explain many things, this appears to be the most difficult. It is impossible to exclude the phenomenological features of experience from a reduction in the same way that one excludes the phenomenal features of an ordinary substance from a physical or chemical reduction of it—namely, by explaining them as effects on the minds of human observers.[4] If physicalism is to be defended, the phenomenological features must themselves be given a physical account. But when we examine their subjective character it seems that such a result is impossible. The reason is that every subjective phenomenon is essentially connected with a single point of view, and it seems inevitable that an objective physical theory will abandon that point of view.

Let me first try to state the issue somewhat more fully than by referring to the relation between the subjective and the objective, or between the **pour soi** and the **en soi.** This is far from easy. Facts about what it is like to be an X are very peculiar, so peculiar that some may be inclined to doubt their reality, or the significance of claims about them. To illustrate the connexion between subjectivity and a point of view, and to make evident the importance of subjective features, it will help to explore the matter in relation to an example that brings out clearly the divergence between the two types of conception, subjective and objective.

I assume we all believe that bats have experience. After all, they are mammals, and there is no more doubt that they have experience than that mice or pigeons or whales have experience. I have chosen bats instead of wasps or flounders because if one travels too far down the phylogenetic tree, people gradually shed their faith that there is experience there at all. Bats, although more closely related to us than those other species, nevertheless present a range of activity and a sensory apparatus so different from ours that the problem I want to pose is exceptionally vivid (though it certainly could be raised with other species). Even without the benefit of philosophical reflection, anyone who has spent some time in an enclosed space with an excited bat knows what it is to encounter a fundamentally *alien* form of life.

I have said that the essence of the belief that bats have experience is that there is something that it is like to be a bat. Now we know that most bats (the microchiroptera, to be precise) perceive the external world primarily by sonar, or echolocation, detecting the reflections, from objects within range, of their own rapid, subtly modulated, high-frequency shrieks. Their brains are designed to correlate the outgoing impulses with the subsequent echoes, and the information thus acquired enables bats to make precise discriminations of distance, size, shape, motion, and texture comparable to those we make by vision. But bat sonar, though clearly a form of perception, is not similar in its operation to any sense that we possess, and there is no reason to suppose that it is subjectively like anything we can experience or imagine. This appears to create difficulties for the notion of what it is like to be a bat. We must consider whether any method will permit us to extrapolate to the inner life of the bat from our own case,[5] and if not, what alternative methods there may be for understanding the notion.

Our own experience provides the basic material for our imagination, whose range is therefore limited. It will not help to try to imagine that one has webbing on one's arms, which enables one to fly around at dusk and dawn catching insects in one's mouth; that one has very poor vision, and perceives the surrounding world by a system of reflected high-frequency sound signals; and that one spends the day hanging upside down by one's feet in an attic. Insofar as I can imagine this (which is not very far), it tells me only what it would be like for *me* to behave as a bat behaves. But that is not the question. I want to know what it is like for a *bat* to be a bat. Yet if I try to imagine this, I am restricted to the resources of my own mind, and those resources are inadequate to the task. I cannot perform it either by imagining additions to my present experience, or by imagining segments gradually subtracted from it, or by imagining some combination of additions, subtractions, and modifications.

To the extent that I could look and behave like a wasp or a bat without changing my fundamental structure, my experiences would not be anything like the experiences of those animals. On the other hand, it is doubtful that any meaning can be attached to the supposition that I should possess the internal neurophysiological constitution of a bat. Even if I could by gradual degrees be transformed into a bat, nothing in my present constitution enables me to imagine what the experiences of such a future stage of myself thus metamorphosed would be like. The best evidence would come from the experiences of bats, if we only knew what they were like.

So if extrapolation from our own case is involved in the idea of what it is like to be a bat, the extrapolation must be incompletable. We cannot form more than a schematic conception of what it *is* like. For example, we may ascribe general *types* of experience on the basis of the animal's structure and behavior. Thus we describe bat sonar as a form of three-dimensional forward perception; we believe that bats feel some versions of pain, fear, hunger, and lust, and that they have other, more familiar types of perception besides sonar. But we believe that these experiences also have in each case a specific subjective character, which it is beyond our ability to conceive. And if there is conscious life elsewhere in the universe, it is likely that some of it will not be describable even in the most general experiential terms available to us.[6] (The problem is not confined to exotic cases, however, for it exists between one person and another. The subjective character of the experience of a person deaf and blind from birth is not accessible to me, for example, nor presumably is mine to him. This does not prevent us each from believing that the other's experience has such a subjective character.)

If anyone is inclined to deny that we can believe in the existence of facts like this whose exact nature we cannot possibly conceive, he should reflect that in contemplating the bats we are in much the same position that intelligent bats or Martians[7] would occupy if they tried to form a conception of what it was like to be us. The structure of their own minds might make it impossible for them to succeed, but we know they would be wrong to conclude that there is not anything precise that it is like to be us: that only certain general types of mental state could be ascribed to us (perhaps perception and appetite would be concepts common to us both; perhaps not). We know they would be wrong to draw such a skeptical conclusion because we know what it is like to be us. And we know that while it includes an enormous amount of variation and complexity, and while we do not possess the vocabulary to describe it adequately, its subjective character is highly specific, and in some respects describable in terms that can be understood only by creatures like us. The fact that we cannot expect ever to accommodate in our language a detailed description of Martian or bat phenomenology should not lead us to dismiss as meaningless the claim that bats and Martians have experiences fully comparable in richness of detail to our own. It would be fine if someone were to develop concepts and a theory that enabled us to think about those things; but such an understanding may be permanently denied to us by the limits of our nature. And to deny the reality or logical significance of what we can never describe or understand is the crudest form of cognitive dissonance.

This brings us to the edge of a topic that requires much more discussion that I can give it here: namely, the relation between facts on the one hand and conceptual schemes or systems of representation on the other. My realism about the subjective domain in all its forms implies a belief in the existence of facts beyond the reach of human concepts. Certainly it is possible for a human being to believe that there are facts which humans never *will* possess the requisite concepts to represent or comprehend. Indeed, it would be foolish to doubt this, given the finiteness of humanity's expectations. After all, there would have been transfinite numbers even if everyone had been wiped out by the Black Death before Cantor discovered them. But one might also believe that there are facts which *could* not ever be represented or comprehended by human beings, even if the species lasted for ever—simply because our structure does not permit us to operate with concepts of the requisite type. This impossibility might even be observed by other beings, but it is not clear that the existence of such beings, or the possibility of their existence, is a precondition of the significance of the hypothesis that there are humanly inaccessible facts. (After all, the nature of beings with access to humanly inaccessible facts is presumably itself a humanly inaccessible fact.) Reflection on what it is like to be a bat seems to lead us, therefore, to the conclusion that there are facts that do not consist in the truth of propositions expressible in a human language. We can be compelled to recognize the existence of such facts without being able to state or comprehend them.

I shall not pursue this subject, however. Its bearing on the topic before us (namely, the mind-body problem) is that it enables us to make a general observation about the subjective character of experience. Whatever may be the status of facts about what it is like to be a human being, or a bat, or a Martian, these appear to be facts that embody a particular point of view.

I am not adverting here to the alleged privacy of experience to its possessor. The point of view in question is not one accessible only to a single individual. Rather it is a *type*. It is often possible to take up a point of view other than one's own, so the comprehension of such facts is not limited to one's own case. There is a sense in which phenomenological facts are perfectly objective: one person can know or say of another what the quality of the other's experience is. They are subjective, however, in the sense that even this objective ascription of experience is possible only for someone sufficiently similar to the object of ascription to be able to adopt his point of view—to understand the ascription in the first person as well as in the third, so to speak. The more different from oneself the other experiencer is, the less success one can expect with this enterprise. In our own case we occupy the relevant point of view, but we will have as much difficulty understanding our own experience properly if we approach it from another point of view as we would if we tried to understand the experience of another species without taking up *its* point of view.[8]

This bears directly on the mind-body problem. For if the facts of experience—facts about what it is like *for* the experiencing organism—are accessible only from one point of view, then it is a mystery how the true character of experiences could be revealed in the physical operation of that organism. The latter is a domain of objective facts *par excellence*—the kind that can be observed and understood from many points of view and by individuals with differing perceptual systems. There are no comparable imaginative obstacles to the acquisition of knowledge about bat neurophysiology by human scientists, and intelligent bats or Martians might learn more about the human brain than we ever will.

This is not by itself an argument against reduction. A Martian scientist with no understanding of visual perception could understand the rainbow, or lightning, or clouds as physical phenomena, though he would never be able to understand the human concepts of rainbow, lightning, or cloud, or the place these things occupy in our phenomenal world. The objective nature of the things picked out by these concepts could be apprehended by him because, although the concepts themselves are connected with a particular point of view and a particular visual phenomenology, the things apprehended from that point of view are not: they are observable from the point of view but external to it; hence they can be comprehended from other points of view also, either by the same organisms or by others. Lightning has an objective character that is not exhausted by its visual appearance, and this can be investigated by a Martian without vision. To be precise, it has a *more* objective character than is revealed in its visual appearance. In speaking of the move from subjective to objective characterization, I wish to remain noncommittal about the existence of an end point, the completely objective intrinsic nature of the thing, which one might or might not be able to reach. It may be more accurate to think of objectivity as a direction in which the understanding can travel. And in understanding a phenomenon like lightning, it is legitimate to go as far away as one can from a strictly human viewpoint.[9]

In the case of experience, on the other hand, the connexion with a particular point of view seems much closer. It is difficult to understand what could be meant by the *objective* character of an experience, apart from the particular point of view from which its subject apprehends it. After all, what would be left of what it was like to be a bat if one removed the viewpoint of the bat? But if experience does not have, in addition to its subjective character, an objective nature that can be apprehended from many different points of view, then how can it be supposed that a Martian investigating my brain might be observing physical processes which were my mental processes (as he might observe physical processes which were bolts of lightning), only from a different point of view? How, for that matter, could a human physiologist observe them from another point of view?[10]

We appear to be faced with a general difficulty about psychophysical reduction. In other areas the process of reduction is a move in the direction of greater objectivity, toward a more accurate view of the real nature of things. This is accomplished by reducing our dependence on individual or species-specific points of view toward the object of investigation. We describe it not in terms of the impressions it makes on our senses, but in terms of its more general effects and of properties detectable by means other than the human senses. The less it depends on a specifically human viewpoint, the more objective is our description. It is possible to follow this path because although the concepts and ideas we employ in thinking about the external world are initially applied from a point of view that involves our perceptual apparatus, they are used by us to refer to things beyond themselves—toward which we *have* the phenomenal point of view. Therefore we can abandon it in favor of another, and still be thinking about the same things.

Experience itself, however, does not seem to fit the pattern. The idea of moving from appearance to reality seems to make no sense here. What is the analogue in this case to pursuing a more objective understanding of the same phenomena by abandoning the initial subjective viewpoint toward them in favour of another that is more objective but concerns the same thing? Certainly it *appears* unlikely that we will get closer to the real nature of human experience by leaving behind the particularity of our human point of view and striving for a description in terms accessible to beings that could not imagine what it was like to be us. If the subjective character in experience is fully comprehensible only from one point of view, then any shift to greater objectivity—that is, less attachment to a specific viewpoint—does not take us nearer to the real nature of the phenomenon: it takes us farther away from it.

In a sense, the seeds of this objection to the reducibility of experience are already detectable in successful cases of reduction; for in discovering sound to be, in reality, a wave phenomenon in air or other media, we leave behind one viewpoint to take up another, and the auditory, human or animal viewpoint that we leave behind remains unreduced. Members of radically different species may both understand the same physical events in objective terms, and this does not require that they understand the phenomenal forms in which those events appear to the senses of members of the other species. Thus it is a condition of their referring to a common reality that their more particular viewpoints are not part of the common reality that they both apprehend. The reduction can succeed only if the species-specific viewpoint is omitted from what is to be reduced.

But while we are right to leave this point of view aside in seeking a fuller understanding of the external world, we cannot ignore it permanently, since it is the essence of the internal world, and not merely a point of view on it. Most of the neobehaviorism of recent philosophical psychology results from the effort to substitute an objective concept of mind for the real thing, in order to have nothing left over which cannot be reduced. If we acknowledge that a physical theory of mind must account for the subjective character of experience, we must admit that no presently available conception gives us a clue how this could be done. The problem is unique. If mental processes are indeed physical processes, then there is something it is like, intrinsically,[11] to undergo certain physical processes. What it is for such a thing to be the case remains a mystery.

What moral should be drawn from these reflections, and what should be done next? It would be a mistake to conclude that physicalism must be false. Nothing is proved by the inadequacy of physicalist hypotheses that assume a faulty objective analysis of mind. It would be truer to say that physicalism is a position we cannot understand because we do not at present have any conception of how it might be true. Perhaps it will be thought unreasonable to require such a conception as a condition of understanding. After all, it might be said, the meaning of physicalism is clear enough: mental states are states of the body; mental events are physical events. We do not know *which* physical states and events they are, but that should not prevent us from understanding the hypothesis. What could be clearer than the words 'is' and 'are'?

But I believe it is precisely this apparent clarity of the word 'is' that is deceptive. Usually, when we are told that X is Y we know *how* it is supposed to be true, but that depends on a conceptual or theoretical background and is not conveyed by the 'is' alone. We know how both 'X' and 'Y' refer, and the kinds of things to which they refer, and we have a rough idea how the two referential paths might converge on a single thing, be it an object, a person, a process, an event or whatever. But when the two terms of the identification are very disparate it may not be so clear how the two referential paths could converge, or what kind of things they might converge on, and a theoretical framework may have to be supplied to enable us to understand this. Without the framework, an air of mysticism surrounds the identification.

This explains the magical flavor of popular presentations of fundamental scientific discoveries, given out as propositions to which one must subscribe without really understanding them. For example, people are now told at an early age that all matter is really energy. But despite the fact that they know what 'is' means, most of them never form a conception of what makes this claim true, because they lack the theoretical background.

At the present time the status of physicalism is similar to that which the hypothesis that matter is energy would have had if uttered by a pre-Socratic philosopher. We do not have the beginnings of a conception of how it might be true. In order to understand the hypothesis that a mental event is a physical event, we require more than an understanding of the word 'is'. The idea of how a mental and a physical term might refer to the same thing is lacking, and the usual analogies with theoretical identification in other fields fail to supply it. They fail because if we construe the reference of mental terms to physical events on the usual model, we either get a reappearance of separate subjective events as the effects through which mental reference to physical events is secured, or else we get a false account of how mental terms refer (for example, a causal behaviourist one).

Strangely enough, we may have evidence for the truth of something we cannot really understand. Suppose a caterpillar is locked in a sterile safe by someone unfamiliar with insect metamorphosis, and weeks later the safe is reopened, revealing a butterfly. If the person knows that the safe has been shut the whole time, he has reason to believe that the butterfly is or was once the caterpillar, without having any idea in what sense this might be so. (One possibility is that the caterpillar contained a tiny winged parasite that devoured it and grew into the butterfly.)

It is conceivable that we are in such a position with regard to physicalism. Donald Davidson has argued that if mental events have physical causes and effects, they must have physical descriptions. He holds that we have reason to believe this even though we do not—and in fact *could* not—have a general psycho-physical theory.[12] His argument applies to intentional mental events, but I think we also have some reason to believe that sensations are physical processes, without being in a position to understand how. Davidson's position is that certain physical events have irreducibly mental properties, and perhaps some view describable in this way is correct. But nothing of which we can now form a conception corresponds to it; nor have we any idea what a theory would be like that enabled us to conceive of it.[13]

Very little work has been done on the basic question (from which mention of the brain can be entirely omitted) whether any sense can be made of experiences' having an objective character at all. Does it make sense, in other words, to ask what my experiences are *really* like, as opposed to how they appear to me? We cannot genuinely understand the hypothesis that their nature is captured in a physical description unless we understand the more fundamental idea that they *have* an objective nature (or that objective processes can have a subjective nature).[14]

I should like to close with a speculative proposal. It may be possible to approach the gap between subjective and objective from another direction. Setting aside temporarily the relation between the mind and the brain, we can pursue a more objective understanding of the mental in its own right. At present we are completely unequipped to think about the subjective character of experience without relying on the imagination—without taking up the point of view of the experiential subject. This should be regarded as a challenge to form new concepts and devise a new method—an objective **phenomenology** not dependent on empathy or the imagination. Though presumably it would not capture everything, its goal would be to describe, at least in part, the subjective character of experiences in a form comprehensible to beings incapable of having those experiences.

We would have to develop such a phenomenology to describe the sonar experiences of bats; but it would also be possible to begin with humans. One might try, for example, to develop concepts that could be used to explain to a person blind from birth what it was like to see. One would reach a blank wall eventually, but it should be possible to devise a method of expressing in objective terms much more than we can at present, and with much greater precision. The loose intermodal analogies—for example, 'Red is like the sound of a trumpet'—which crop up in discussions of this subject are of little use. That should be clear to anyone who has both heard a trumpet and seen red. But structural features of perception might be more accessible to objective description, even though something would be left out. And concepts alternative to those we learn in the first person may enable us to arrive at a kind of understanding even of our own experience which is denied us by the very ease of description and lack of distance that subjective concepts afford.

Apart from its own interest, a phenomenology that is in this sense objective may permit questions about the physical[15] basis of experience to assume a more intelligible form. Aspects of subjective experience that admitted this kind of objective description might be better candidates for objective explanations of a more familiar sort. But whether or not this guess is correct, it seems unlikely that any physical theory of mind can be contemplated until more thought has been given to the general problem of subjective and objective. Otherwise we cannot even pose the mind-body problem without sidestepping it.

Notes

1. Examples are J. J. C. Smart, *Philosophy and Scientific Realism* (London: Routledge & Kegan Paul, 1963); David K. Lewis, 'An Argument for the Identity Theory', *Journal of Philosophy*, LXIII (1966), reprinted with addenda in David M. Rosenthal, *Materialism & the Mind-Body Problem*, (Engelwood Cliffs, N.J.: Prentice-Hall, 1971); Hilary Putnam, 'Psychological Predicates', in *Art, Mind & Religion*, ed. W. H. Capitan and D. D. Merrill (Pittsburgh: University of Pittsburgh, 1967), reprinted in *Materialism*, ed. Rosenthal, as 'The Nature of Mental States'; D. M. Armstrong, *A Materialist Theory of the Mind* (London: Routledge & Kegan Paul, 1968); D. C. Dennett, *Content and Consciousness* (London: Routledge & Kegan Paul, 1969). I have expressed earlier doubts in 'Armstrong on the Mind', *Philosophical Review*, LXXIX (1970), 394–403; a

review of Dennett, *Journal of Philosophy*, LXIX (1972); and chapter 11 above. See also Saul Kripke, 'Naming and Necessity' in *Semanitics of Natural Language*, ed. D. Davidson and G. Harman (Dordrecht: Reidel, 1972), esp. pp. 334–42; and M. T. Thornton. 'Ostensive Terms and Materialism', *The Monist*, LVI (1972), 193–214.

2. Perhaps there could not actually be such robots. Perhaps anything complex enough to behave like a person would have experiences. But that, if true, is a fact which cannot be discovered merely by analyzing the concept of experience.

3. It is not equivalent to that about which we are incorrigible, both because we are not incorrigible about experience and because experience is present in animals lacking language and thought, who have no beliefs at all about their experiences.

4. Cf. Richard Rorty, 'Mind-Body Identity, Privacy, and Categories'. *Review of Metaphysics*, XIX (1965), esp. 37–8.

5. By 'our own case' I do not mean just 'my own case', but rather the mentalistic ideas that we apply unproblematically to ourselves and other human beings.

6. Therefore the analogical form of the English expression 'what it is *like*' is misleading. It does not mean 'what (in our experience) it *resembles*', but rather 'how it is for the subject himself'.

7. Any intelligent extraterrestrial beings totally different from us.

8. It may be easier than I suppose to transcend interspecies barriers with the aid of the imagination. For example, blind people are able to detect objects near them by a form of sonar, using vocal clicks or taps of a cane. Perhaps if one knew what that was like, one could by extension imagine roughly what it was like to possess the much more refined sonar of a bat. The distance between oneself and other persons and other species can fall anywhere on a continuum. Even for other persons the understanding of what it is like to be them is only partial, and when one moves to species very different from oneself, a lesser degree of partial understanding may still be available. The imagination is remarkably flexible. My point, however, is not that we cannot *know* what it is like to be a bat. I am not raising that epistemological problem. My point is rather that even to form a *conception* of what it is like to be a bat (and *a fortiori* to know what it is like to be a bat) one must take up the bat's point of view. Of one can take it up roughly, or partially, then one's conception will also be rough or partial. Or so it seems in our present state of understanding.

9. The problem I am going to raise can therefore be posed even if the distinction between more subjective and more objective descriptions or viewpoints can itself be made only within a larger human point of view. I do not accept this kind of conceptual relativism, but it need not be refuted to make the point that psychophysical reduction cannot be accommodated by the subjective-to-objective model familiar from other cases.

10. The problem is not just that when I look at the *Mona Lisa*, my visual experience has a certain quality, no trace of which is to be found by someone looking into my brain. For even if he did observe there a tiny image of the *Mona Lisa*, he would have no reason to identify it with the experience.

11. The relation would therefore not be a contingent one, like that of a cause and its distinct effect. It would

be necessarily true that a certain physical state felt a certain way. Saul Kripke in *Semantics of Natural Language,* (ed. Davidson and Harman) argues that causal behaviorist and related analyses of the mental fail because they construe, e.g., 'pain' as a merely contingent name of pains. The subjective character of an experience ('its immediate phenomenological quality' Kripke calls it (p.340)) is the essential property left out by such analyses, and the one in virtue of which it is, necessarily, the experience it is. My view is closely related to his. Like Kripke, I find the hypothesis that a certain brain state should *necessarily* have a certain subjective character incomprehensible without further explanation. No such explanation emerges from theories which view the mind-brain relation as contingent, but perhaps there are other alternatives, not yet discovered.

A theory that explained how the mind-brain relation was necessary would still leave us with Kripke's problem of explaining why it nevertheless appears contingent. That difficulty seems to me surmountable, in the following way. We may imagine something by representing it to ourselves either perceptually, sympathetically, or symbolically. I shall not try to say how symbolic imagination works, but part of what happens in the other two cases is this. To imagine something perceptually, we put ourselves in a conscious state resembling the state we would be in if we perceived it. To imagine something sympathetically, we put ourselves in a conscious state resembling the thing itself. (This method can be used only to imagine mental events and states—our own or another's.) When we try to imagine a mental state occurring without its associated brain state, we first sympathetically imagine the occurrence of the mental state: that is, we put ourselves into a state that resembles it mentally. At the same time, we attempt perceptually to imagine the nonoccurrence of the associated physical state, by putting ourselves into another state unconnected with the first: one resembling that which we would be in if we perceived the nonoccurrence of the physical state. Where the imagination of physical features is perceptual and the imagination of mental features is sympathetic, it appears to us that we can imagine any experience occurring without its associated brain state, and vice versa. The relation between them will appear contingent even if it is necessary, because of the independence of the disparate types of imagination.

(**Solipsism**, incidentally, results if one misinterprets sympathetic imagination as if it worked like perceptual imagination: it then seems impossible to imagine any experience that is not one's own.)

12. See 'Mental Events' in *Experience and Theory*, ed. Lawrence Foster and J. W. Swanson (Amherst: University of Massachusetts Press, 1970); though I do not understand the argument against psychophysical laws.

13. Similar remarks apply to my paper 'Physicalism', *Philosophical Review*, LXXIV (1965), 339–56, reprinted with postscript in *Modern Materialism,* ed. John O'Connor (New York: Harcourt Brace Jovanovich, 1969).

14. This question also lies at the heart of the problem of other minds, whose close connection with the mind-body problem is often overlooked. If one understood how subjective experience could have an objective nature, one would understand the existence of subjects other than oneself.

15. I have not defined the term 'physical'. Obviously it does not apply just to what can be described by the concepts of contemporary physics, since we expect further developments. Some may think there is nothing to prevent mental phenomena from eventually being recognized as physical in their own right. But whatever else may be said of the physical, it has to be objective. So if our idea of the physical ever expands to include mental phenomena, it will have to assign them an objective character—whether or not this is done by analyzing them in terms of other phenomena already regarded as physical. It seems to me more likely, however, that mental-physical relations will eventually be expressed in a theory whose fundamental terms cannot be placed clearly in either category.

Questions on Nagel

1. What exactly is the "subjective character of experience?" Can it be described? According to Nagel, why can't it ever be explained by any physicalist theory? Is Nagel right about this? What is your view?

2. Is there any way in which a human could ever understand what it is like to be a bat?

3. Nagel says that "there are facts which humans never *will* possess the requisite concepts to represent or comprehend." Is this true? Why or why not?

Suggested Readings

C. D. Broad, *The Mind and Its Place in Nature* (London: Routledge & Kegan Paul Ltd, 1925) is a classic treatment of the mind-body problem and the standard theories of dualism and materialism, and is a good book to begin with. Broad defends two-way dualistic interactionism.

Baruch Brody, *Beginning Philosophy* (Englewood Cliffs, NJ: Prentice-Hall, 1977), pp. 139–161, covers dualism, behaviorism, and the identity theory. As the title says, the book is intended for beginners.

Anthony Flew, ed., *Body, Mind and Death* (New York: Macmillan, 1964) has both classical and contemporary readings on the mind-body problem. It includes selections from Spinoza and Leibniz and an important paper by U. T. Place on the identity theory.

Jerry A. Fodor, *Psychological Explanation: An Introduction to the Philosophy of Psychology* (New York: Random House, 1968), pp. 121–152, explains functionalism as it relates to computers.

Douglas R. Hofstadter and Daniel C. Dennett, eds., *The Mind's I: Fantasies and Reflections on Self and Soul* (New York: Basic Books, Inc., 1981) is a rather eccentric but fun collection of readings on the mind, computers, selves, and related topics. It includes some pieces by the novelists Jorge Luis Borges and Stanislaw Lem.

John O'Connor, ed., *Modern Materialism: Readings on Mind-Body Identity* (New York: Harcourt, Brace, and World, 1969) concentrates on the identity theory. Another collection of readings on this theory is Clive V. Borst, ed., *The Mind/Brain Identity Theory* (New York: Macmillan, 1970).

Jerome A. Shaffer, *Philosophy of Mind* (Englewood Cliffs, NJ: Prentice-Hall, Inc., 1968) gives a clear discussion of the various theories including dualism, materialism, the identity theory, the double aspect theory, and Strawson's person theory.

J. J. C. Smart, "Sensations and Brain Processes," *Philosophical Review* 68 (1959), pp. 141–156, is a widely reprinted article that gives a definitive statement of the identity theory.

P. F. Strawson, *Individuals* (London: Methuen, 1959) is the classical presentation of Strawson's theory about persons. It is a famous and important book, but hard reading.

Personal Identity and Survival of Death

Chapter 6

Introduction

Personal identity. In chapter 4, C. A. Campbell claimed that one of the necessary conditions of moral responsibility is freedom. If a person is not free when committing a murder, for example, the person is not morally responsible and does not deserve to be punished. But freedom is not the only condition necessary for responsibility. We also assume *personal identity,* that the person we are holding responsible and punishing is one and the same person as the person who committed the crime. We would not hold Jones responsible for a crime that some other person, say Smith, has committed. Jones would be innocent and should not be held responsible or punished.

The assumption of personal identity is also made when people talk about survival of death. Most people who believe in such a survival believe that it is they who survive as the same person and not somebody else. Furthermore, rewards and punishments in a next life would not make sense if the survivors did not retain their identity. Otherwise, the reward or punishment would not be deserved.

The problem of personal identity. How do we establish that a person is the same? This is an important question to answer if we want to establish moral responsibility and justify punishment, or if we believe in personal survival of death. A commonsense answer suggested by Locke in the first reading is that memory is the basis for personal identity. If a person remembers doing things in the past, then that person is the subject of the memories. Unfortunately, this plausible solution to the problem has difficulties. One obvious objection is that a person may lose every memory and still be the same person with amnesia. Locke's counter-intuitive reply to this is that we have the same human being but not the same person. His theory results in even more puzzling cases. To use Locke's own example, if we suppose that a prince's memories enter into a cobbler's body, then the cobbler is now a prince. And what if the prince's memories exist along with the cobbler's? Then we would have two persons with only one body.

Another standard answer is to say that we establish personal identity by looking at the body—if it is the same body, then it is the same person. But what if the body changes or is transformed into a completely different body and yet has the same memories? Surely we would agree with Locke that this is the same person with a different body. Or consider the plight of philosopher Daniel Dennett in the story "Where Am I?" in our readings. His brain is put in a vat and controls his body by remote control. Unfortunately his body is buried alive, but he survives as a brain in a vat. Clearly we do not want to identify Dennett with his dead body; after all, he is still conscious as a disembodied brain in the vat. But we should not conclude that Dennett is the same as his brain, for it turns out that there is a computer program that duplicates the brain's control, and this suggests that Dennett is neither his body nor his brain, but could be identified as a computer program. If so, then at the end of the story Dennett has divided into two persons with the same personality.

Puzzle cases such as those described by Dennett in his fascinating story may lead us to question the very idea of personal identity. In our second reading for the chapter, Hume presents a famous attack on this idea. According to Hume, our ordinary notion of personal identity is based on a confusion between numerical identity, where one thing remains the same unchanged thing throughout time, and similarity, where different things that resemble each other are connected. An examination of our mind shows that there is a diverse collection of thoughts and ideas that resemble each other but are not one and the same thing, but because of the resemblances we mistakenly think that there is an unchanging self that remains the same throughout time. Hume concludes that numerical personal identity is a fiction.

Thus far we have been assuming that personal identity is all or nothing—we are either the same person or we are not. But Derek Parfit suggests an alternative to this simple view of personal identity that he calls the "complex view." According to the complex view, personal identity is a matter of degree that is determined by complex factors such as the number of memory connections to a past life, continuity of character traits, and so on. Parfit argues that this complex view, if true, would have important consequences for moral responsibility and punishment.

Survival of death. The belief in personal survival of death is not only a basic religious belief, it is also an essential part of Hick's solution to the problem of evil, as we saw in chapter 2.

But how are we to conceive of this survival? The traditional Platonic view, which has been adopted by some philosophers (for example, H. H. Price—see the suggested readings), is that a person survives death as a disembodied soul or spirit. This assumes, of course, a dualistic view of humans, that there is both a soul and a body, and neither can be reduced to the other. But this view has serious difficulties, some of which are discussed by Peter Geach in the readings. One problem concerns personal identity: How could a disembodied spirit be the same person as the embodied person who died? Don't we need bodily continuity in order to retain personal identity? Those who accept Locke's view could reply that memory is all that is needed; if the disembodied spirit has the same memories as the embodied person who died, then it is the same person. But there are further difficulties. How do we distinguish between these souls or spirits if they do not have bodies? How do we know if there are two or one? Is it possible for one soul to have two persons' memories, or should we say that each different memory makes for a different person? Another conceptual difficulty involves seeing and feeling. Geach thinks that it would not make sense to say that a disembodied spirit sees or feels.

Another conception of survival, found in Hinduism and Buddhism, is **reincarnation**. A person dies and is then reborn or reincarnated in a new body—a human body or possibly the body of an animal. But the problem of establishing personal identity crops up again. How do we know that the reborn person is the same as the one who died? If there are no memories or mental continuity, and no bodily continuity either, then we would have to admit, it seems, that it is not the same person. At least this is how Geach attacks this view. The Buddhist, however, would be untroubled by this objection since according to the Buddha's anatman (no-self) doctrine, there is no permanent self in the first place. Thus, according to Buddhism, a person is not numerically the same person from one time to the next, but is only similar. The Buddhist view is not much different from Hume's account of personal identity.

A third conception of survival is the Christian doctrine of **resurrection**. This doctrine is understood in different ways. In the readings John Hick suggests that we imagine our bodies are replicated or exactly duplicated on some other planet after we have died. He thinks that if there is mental continuity—memories of the former life, similar thoughts, desires, and so on—the replica will be counted as the same person as the original person who died.

Peter Geach, however, would not accept the replica theory. According to him, mere mental continuity is not enough to guarantee personal identity; there has to be bodily continuity as well. Geach thinks that our only hope for survival is bodily resurrection of the sort described by St. Paul, in which our dead bodies are brought to life again by God.

John Locke

The Idea of Personal Identity

For biographical information on Locke, see the reading in chapter 3.

. . . I presume it is not the idea of a thinking or rational being alone that makes the *idea of a man* in most people's sense: but of a body, so and so

The reading is from John Locke, *An Essay Concerning Human Understanding*, ed. Alexander Cambell Fraser (New York: Dover Publications, 1959), pp. 448–461.

shaped, joined to it: and if that be the idea of a man, the same successive body not shifted all at once, must, as well as the same immaterial spirit, go to the making of the same man.

This being premised, to find wherein personal identity consists, we must consider what *person* stands for;—which, I think, is a thinking intelligent being, that has reason and reflection, and can consider itself as itself, the same thinking thing, in different times and places; which it does only by that consciousness which is inseparable from thinking, and, as it seems to me, essential to it: it being impossible for any one to perceive without *perceiving* that he does perceive. When we see, hear, smell, taste, feel, meditate, or will anything, we know that we do so. Thus it is always as to our present sensations and perceptions: and by this every one is to himself that which he calls *self*:—it not being considered, in this case, whether the same self be continued in the same or divers substances. For, since consciousness always accompanies thinking, and it is that which makes every one to be what he calls self, and thereby distinguishes himself from all other thinking things, in this alone consists personal identity, i.e. the sameness of a rational being: and as far as this consciousness can be extended backwards to any past action or thought, so far reaches the identity of that person, it is the same self now it was then; and it is by the same self with this present one that now reflects on it, that that action was done.

10. But it is further inquired, whether it be the same identical substance. This few would think they had reason to doubt of, if these perceptions, with their consciousness, always remained present in the mind, whereby the same thinking thing would be always consciously present, and, as would be thought, evidently the same to itself. But that which seems to make the difficulty is this, that this consciousness being interrupted always by forgetfulness, there being no moment of our lives wherein we have the whole train of all our past actions before our eyes in one view, but even the best memories losing the sight of one part whilst they are viewing another; and we sometimes, and that the greatest part of our lives, not reflecting on our past selves, being intent on our present thoughts, and in sound sleep having no thoughts at all, or at least none with that consciousness which remarks our waking thoughts—I say, in all these cases, our consciousness being interrupted, and we losing the sight of our past selves, doubts are raised whether we are the same thinking thing, i.e. the same *substance* or no. Which, however reasonable or unreasonable, concerns not *personal* identity at all. The question being what makes the same person; and not whether it be the same identical substance, which always thinks in the same person, which, in this case, matters not at all: different substances, by the same consciousness (where they do partake in it) being united into one person, as well as different bodies by the same life are united into one animal, whose identity is preserved in that change of substances by the unity of one continued life. For, it being the same consciousness that makes a man be himself to himself, personal identity depends on that only, whether it be annexed solely to one individual substance, or can be continued in a succession of several substances. For as far as any intelligent being *can* repeat the idea of any past action with the same consciousness it had of it at first, and with the same consciousness it has of any present action; so far it is the same personal self. For it is by the consciousness it has of its present thoughts and actions, that it is *self to itself* now, and so will be the same self, as far as the same consciousness can extend to actions past or to come; and would be by distance of time, or change of substance, no more two persons, than a man be two men by wearing other clothes to-day than he did yesterday, with a long or a short sleep between: the same consciousness uniting those distant actions into the same person, whatever substances contributed to their production.

11. That this is so, we have some kind of evidence in our very bodies, all whose particles, whilst vitally united to this same thinking conscious self, so that *we feel* when they are touched, and are affected by, and conscious of good or harm that happens to them, are a part of ourselves; i.e. of our thinking conscious self. Thus, the limbs of his body are to every one a part of himself; he sympathizes and is concerned for them. Cut off a hand, and thereby separate it from that consciousness he had of its heat, cold, and other affections, and it is then no longer a part of that which is himself, any more than the remotest part of matter. Thus we see the *substance* whereof personal self consisted at one time may be varied at another, without the change of personal identity; there being no question about the same person, though the limbs which but now were a part of it, be cut off....

And thus may we be able, without any difficulty, to conceive the same person at the resurrection, though in a body not exactly in make or parts the same which he had here,—the same consciousness going along with the soul that inhabits it. But yet the soul alone, in the change of bodies, would scarce to any one but to him that makes the soul the man, be enough to make the same man. For should the soul of a prince, carrying with it the consciousness of the prince's past life, enter and inform the body of a cobbler, as soon as deserted by his own soul, every one sees he would be the same *person* with the prince, accountable only for the prince's actions: but who would say it was the same *man?* The body too goes to the making the man, and would, I guess, to everybody determine the man in this case, wherein the soul, with all its princely thoughts about it, would not make another man: but he would be the same cobbler to every one besides himself. I know that, in the ordinary way of speaking, the same person, and the same man, stand for one and the same thing. And indeed every one will always have a liberty to speak as he pleases, and to apply what articulate sounds to what ideas he thinks fit, and change them as often as he pleases. But yet, when we will inquire what makes the same *spirit, man,* or *person,* we must fix the ideas of spirit, man, or person in our minds; and having resolved with ourselves what we mean by them, it will not be hard to determine, in either of them, or the like, when it is the same, and when not.

But though the same immaterial substance or soul does not alone, wherever it be, and in whatsoever state, make the same *man*; yet it is plain, consciousness, as far as ever it can be extended—should it be to ages past—unites existences and actions very remote in time into the same *person*, as well as it does the existences and actions of the immediately preceding moment: so that whatever has the consciousness of present and past actions, is the same person to whom they both belong. Had I the same consciousness that I saw the ark and Noah's flood, as that I saw an overflowing of the Thames last winter, or as that I write now, I could no more doubt that I who write this now, that saw the Thames overflowed last winter, and that viewed the flood at the general deluge, was the same *self,*—place that self in what *substance* you please—than that I who write this am the same *myself* now whilst I write (whether I consist of all the same substance, material or immaterial, or no) that I was yesterday. For as to this point of being the same self, it matters not whether this present self be made up of the same or other substances—I being as much concerned, and as justly accountable for any action that was done a thousand years since, appropriated to me now by this self-consciousness, as I am for what I did the last moment. . . .

But yet possibly it will still be objected,—Suppose I wholly lose the memory of some parts of my life, beyond a possibility of retrieving them, so that perhaps I shall never be conscious of them again; yet am I not the same person that did those actions, had those thoughts that I once was conscious of, though I have now forgot them? To which I answer, that we must here take notice what the word *I* is applied to; which, in this case, is the *man* only. And the same man being presumed to be the same person, I is easily here supposed to stand also for the same person. But if it be possible for the same man to have distinct incommunicable consciousness at different times, it is past doubt the same man would at different times make different persons; which, we see, is the sense of mankind in the solemnest declaration of their opinions, human laws not punishing the mad man for the sober man's actions, nor the sober man for what the mad man did,—thereby making them two persons: which is somewhat explained by our way of speaking in English when we say such an one is 'not himself,' or is 'beside-himself'; in which phrases it is insinuated, as if those who now, or at least first used them, thought that self was changed; the self-same person was no longer in that man.

12. But yet it is hard to conceive that Socrates, the same individual man, should be two persons. To help us a little in this, we must consider what is meant by Socrates, or the same individual *man.*

First, it must be either the same individual, immaterial, thinking substance; in short, the same numerical soul, and nothing else.

Secondly, or the same animal, without any regard to an immaterial soul.

Thirdly, or the same immaterial spirit united to the same animal.

Now, take which of these suppositions you please, it is impossible to make personal identity to consist in anything but consciousness; or reach any further than that does.

Questions on Locke

1. How does Locke define the word "person"?

Given this definition, could a nonhuman being be a person, and could a human being not be a person? Give some examples.

2. What is the basis of personal identity according to Locke? Could a person with amnesia be the same person according to Locke? How does Locke deal with this problem? Is his answer acceptable or not? Explain.

3. Locke suggests that if the memories of a prince should enter the body of a cobbler, the cobbler would be the same person as the prince (but not the same man, since it is not the prince's body). Is this possible?

David Hume
Of Personal Identity

For biographical information on Hume, see the reading in chapter 1.

There are some philosophers, who imagine we are every moment intimately conscious of what we call our SELF; that we feel its existence and its continuance in existence; and are certain, beyond the evidence of a demonstration, both of its perfect identity and simplicity. The strongest sensation, the most violent passion, say they, instead of distracting us from this view, only fix it the more intensely, and make us consider their influence on *self* either by their pain or pleasure. To attempt a farther proof of this were to weaken its evidence; since no proof can be deriv'd from any fact, of which we are so intimately conscious; nor is there any thing, of which we can be certain, if we doubt of this.

Unluckily all these positive assertions are contrary to that very experience, which is pleaded for them, nor have we any idea of *self*, after the manner it is here explain'd. For from what impression cou'd this idea be deriv'd? This question 'tis impossible to answer without a manifest contradiction and absurdity; and yet 'tis a question, which must necessarily be answer'd, if we wou'd have the idea of self pass for clear and intelligible. It must be some one

impression, that gives rise to every real idea. But self or person is not any one impression, but that to which our several impressions and ideas are suppos'd to have a reference. If any impression gives rise to the idea of self, that impression must continue invariably the same, thro' the whole course of our lives; since self is suppos'd to exist after that manner. But there is no impression constant and invariable. Pain and pleasure, grief and joy, passions and sensations succeed each other, and never all exist at the same time. It cannot, therefore, be from any of these impressions, or from any other, that the idea of a self is deriv'd; and consequently there is no such idea.

But farther, what must become of all our particular perceptions upon this hypothesis? All these are different, and distinguishable, and separable from each other, and may be separately consider'd, and may exist separately, and have no need of any thing to support their existence. After what manner, therefore, do they belong to self; and how are they connected with it? For my part, when I enter most intimately into what I call *myself*, I always stumble on some particular perception or other, of heat or cold, light or shade, love or hatred, pain or pleasure. I never can catch *myself* at any time without a perception, and never can observe any thing but the perception. When my perceptions are remov'd for any time, as by sound sleep; so long am I insensible of *myself*, and may truly be said not to exist. And were all my perceptions remov'd by death, and cou'd I neither think, nor feel, nor see, nor love, nor hate after the dissolution of my body, I shou'd be entirely annihilated, nor do I conceive what is farther requisite to make me a perfect non-entity. If any one

The reading is from David Hume, *A Treatise of Human Nature*, ed. L. A. Selby Bigge (Oxford: Clarendon Press, 1988), pp. 251–260.

upon serious and unprejudic'd reflexion, thinks he has a different notion of *himself*, I must confess I can reason no longer with him. All I can allow him is, that he may be in the right as well as I , and that we are essentially different in this particular. He may, perhaps, perceive something simple and continu'd, which he calls *himself*; tho' I am certain there is no such principle in me.

But setting aside some metaphysicians of this kind, I may venture to affirm of the rest of mankind, that they are nothing but a bundle or collection of different perceptions, which succeed each other with an inconceivable rapidity, and are in a perpetual flux and movement. Our eyes cannot turn in their sockets without varying our perceptions. Our thought is still more variable than our sight; and all our other senses and faculties contribute to this change; nor is there any single power of the soul, which remains unalterably the same, perhaps for one moment. The mind is a kind of theatre, where several perceptions successively make their appearance; pass, re-pass, glide away, and mingle in an infinite variety of postures and situations. There is properly no *simplicity* in it at one time, nor *identity* in different; whatever natural propension we may have to imagine that simplicity and identity. The comparison of the theatre must not mislead us. They are the successive perceptions only, that constitute the mind; nor have we the most distant notion of the place, where these scenes are represented, or of the materials, of which it is compos'd.

What then gives us so great a propension to ascribe an identity to these successive perceptions, and to suppose ourselves possessed of an invariable and uninterrupted existence thro' the whole course of our lives? . . . We have a distinct idea of an object, that remains invariable and uninterrupted thro' a suppos'd variation of time; and this idea we call that of *identity* or *sameness*. We have also a distinct idea of several different objects existing in succession, and connected together by a close relation; and this to an accurate view affords as perfect a notion of *diversity*, as if there was no manner of relation among the objects. But tho' these two ideas of identity, and a succession of related objects be in themselves perfectly distinct, and even con-

trary, yet 'tis certain, that in our common way of thinking they are generally confounded with each other. That action of the imagination, by which we consider the uninterrupted and invariable object, and that by which we reflect on the succession of related objects, are almost the same to the feeling, nor is there much more effort of thought requir'd in the latter case than in the former. The relation facilitates the transition of the mind from one object to another, and renders its passage as smooth as if it contemplated one continu'd object. This resemblance is the cause of the confusion and mistake, and makes us substitute the notion of identity, instead of that of related objects. However at one instant we may consider the related succession as variable or interrupted, we are sure the next to ascribe to it a perfect identity, and regard it as invariable and uninterrupted. Our propensity to this mistake is so great from the resemblance above-mention'd, that we fall into it before we are aware; and tho' we incessantly correct ourselves by reflexion, and return to a more accurate method of thinking, yet we cannot long sustain our philosophy, or take off this bias from the imagination. Our last resource is to yield to it, and boldly assert that these different related objects are in effect the same, however interrupted and variable. In order to justify to ourselves this absurdity, we often feign some new and unintelligible principle, that connects the objects together, and prevents their interruption or variation. Thus we feign the continu'd existence of the perceptions of our senses, to remove the interruption; and run into the notion of a *soul,* and *self,* and *substance,* to disguise the variation. But we may farther observe, that where we do not give rise to such a fiction, our propension to confound identity with relation is so great, that we are apt to imagine something unknown and mysterious, connecting the parts, beside their relation; and this I take to be the case with regard to the identity we ascribe to plants and vegetables. And even when this does not take place, we still feel a propensity to confound these ideas, tho' we are not able fully to satisfy ourselves in that particular, nor find any thing invariable and uninterrupted to justify our notion of identity.

Thus the controversy concerning identity is

not merely a dispute of words. For when we attribute identity, in an improper sense, to variable or interrupted objects, our mistake is not confin'd to the expression, but is commonly attended with a fiction, either of something invariable and uninterrupted, or of something mysterious and inexplicable, or at least with a propensity to such fictions. What will suffice to prove this hypothesis to the satisfaction of every fair enquirer, is to shew from daily experience and observation, that the objects, which are variable or interrupted, and yet are suppos'd to continue the same, are such only as consist of a succession of parts, connected together by resemblance, contiguity, or causation. For as such a succession answers evidently to our notion of diversity, it can only be by mistake we ascribe to it an identity; and as the relation of parts, which leads us into this mistake, is really nothing but a quality, which produces an association of ideas, and an easy transition of the imagination from one to another, it can only be from the resemblance, which this act of the mind bears to that, by which we contemplate one continu'd object, that the error arises. Our chief business, then, must be to prove, that all objects, to which we ascribe identity, without observing their invariableness and uninterruptedness, are such as consist of a succession of related objects . . . . A ship, of which a considerable part has been chang'd by frequent reparations, is still consider'd as the same; nor does the difference of the materials hinder us from ascribing an identity to it. The common end, in which the parts conspire, is the same under all their variations, and affords an easy transition of the imagination from one situation of the body to another.

But this is still more remarkable, when we add a *sympathy* of parts to their *common end*, and suppose that they bear to each other, the reciprocal relation of cause and effect in all their actions and operations. This is the case with all animals and vegetables; where not only the several parts have a reference to some general purpose, but also a mutual dependance on, and connexion with each other. The effect of so strong a relation is, that tho' every one must allow, that in a very few years both vegetables and animals endure a *total* change, yet we still attribute identity to them, while their form, size, and substance

are entirely alter'd. An oak, that grows from a small plant to a large tree, is still the same oak; tho' there be not one particle of matter, or figure of its parts the same. An infant becomes a man, and is sometimes fat, sometimes lean, without any change in his identity.

We may also consider the two following phenomena, which are remarkable in their kind. The first is, that tho' we commonly be able to distinguish pretty exactly betwixt numerical and specific identity, yet it sometimes happens, that we confound them, and in our thinking and reasoning employ the one for the other. Thus a man, who hears a noise, that is frequently interrupted and renew'd, says, it is still the same noise; tho' 'tis evident the sounds have only a specific identity or resemblance, and there is nothing numerically the same, but the cause, which produc'd them. In like manner it may be said without breach of the propriety of language, that such a church, which was formerly of brick, fell to ruin, and that the parish rebuilt the same church of free-stone, and according to modern architecture. Here neither the form nor materials are the same, nor is there any thing common to the two objects, but their relation to the inhabitants of the parish; and yet this alone is sufficient to make us denominate them the same. But we must observe, that in these cases the first object is in a manner annihilated before the second comes into existence; by which means, we are never presented in any one point of time with the idea of difference and multiplicity; and for that reason are less scrupulous in calling them the same.

Secondly, We may remark, that tho' in a succession of related objects, it be in a manner requisite, that the change of parts be not sudden nor entire, in order to preserve the identity, yet where the objects are in their nature changeable and inconstant, we admit of a more sudden transition, than wou'd otherwise be consistent with that relation. Thus as the nature of a river consists in the motion and change of parts; tho' in less than four and twenty hours these be totally alter'd; this hinders not the river from continuing the same during several ages. What is natural and essential to any thing is, in a manner, expected; and what is expected makes less impression, and appears of less moment, than what is unusual and extraordinary. A considerable change of the former kind seems really less to the imagination, then the most trivial alteration of the latter; and by breaking less the continuity of the thought, has less influence in destroying the identity.

We now proceed to explain the nature of *personal identity,* which has become so great a question in philosophy, especially of late years in *England,* where all the abstruser sciences are study'd with a peculiar ardour and application. And here 'tis evident, the same method of reasoning must be continu'd, which has so successfully explain'd the identity of plants, and animals, and ships, and houses, and of all the compounded and changeable productions either of art or nature. The identity, which we ascribe to the mind of man, is only a fictitious one, and of a like kind with that which we ascribe to vegetables and animal bodies. It cannot, therefore, have a different origin, but must proceed from a like operation of the imagination upon like objects.

But lest this argument shou'd not convince the reader; tho' in my opinion perfectly decisive; let him weigh the following reasoning, which is still closer and more immediate. 'Tis evident, that the identity, which we attribute to the human mind, however perfect we may imagine it to be, is not able to run the several different perceptions into one, and make them lose their characters of distinction and difference, which are essential to them. 'Tis still true, that every distinct perception, which enters into the composition of the mind, is a distinct existence, and is different, and distinguishable, and separable from every other perception, either contemporary or successive. But, as notwithstanding this distinction and separability, we suppose the whole train of perceptions to be united by identity, a question naturally arises concerning this relation of identity; whether it be something that really binds our several perceptions together, or only associates their ideas in the imagination. That is, in other words, whether in pronouncing concerning the identity of a person,

we observe some real bond among his perceptions, or only feel one among the ideas we form of them. This question we might easily decide, if we wou'd recollect what has been already prov'd at large, that the understanding never observes any real connexion among objects, and that even the union of cause and effect, when strictly examin'd, resolves itself into a customary association of ideas. For from thence it evidently follows, that identity is nothing really belonging to these different perceptions, and uniting them together; but is merely a quality, which we attribute to them, because of the union of their ideas in the imagination, when we reflect upon them. Now the only qualities, which can give ideas an union in the imagination, are these three relations above-mention'd. These are the uniting principles in the ideal world, and without them every distinct object is separable by the mind, and may be separately consider'd, and appears not to have any more connexion with any other object, than if disjoin'd by the greatest difference and remoteness. 'Tis, therefore, on some of these three relations of resemblance, contiguity and causation, that identity depends; and as the very essence of these relations consists in their producing an easy transition of ideas; it follows, that our notions of personal identity, proceed entirely from the smooth and uninterrupted progress of the thought along a train of connected ideas, according to the principles above-explain'd.

Questions on Hume

1. According to Hume, why don't we have any real idea of the self? Do you think Hume right about this or not?

2. What is the mind according to Hume? Do you agree? Why or why not?

3. Explain Hume's account of identity, including personal identity. Do you think his account of the matter is correct or not?

4. Suppose that we grant that Hume's view of personal identity is correct. What would be the consequences for moral responsibility and punishment?

Derek Parfit

Later Selves and Moral Principles

Derek Parfit is a fellow at All Souls College, Oxford University, and the author of Reasons and Persons.

I shall first sketch different views about the nature of personal identity, then suggest that the views support different moral claims.*

I

Most of us seem to have certain beliefs about our own identity. We seem for instance to believe that, whatever happens, any future person must be either us, or someone else.

These beliefs are like those that some of us have about a simpler fact. Most of us now think that to be a person, as opposed to a mere animal, is just to have certain more specific properties, such as rationality. These are matters of degree. So we might say that the fact of personhood is just the fact of having certain other properties, which are had to different degrees.

There is a different view. Some of us believe that personhood is a further, deep, fact, and cannot hold to different degrees.

This second view may be confused with some trivial claims. Personhood is, in a sense, a further fact. And there is a sense in which all persons are equally persons.

Let us first show how these claims may be trivial. We can use a different example. There is a sense in which all our relatives are equally our relatives. We can use the phrase 'related to' so that what it means has no degrees; on this use, parents and remote cousins are as much rela-

Published with the permission of the publisher, McGill-Queen's University Press, from their *Philosophy and Personal Relations* edited by Montefiore (Routledge, 1973).

*[The footnotes have been eliminated.—Ed.]

tives. It is obvious, though, that kinship has degrees. This is shown in the phrase 'closely related to': remote cousins are, as relatives, less close. I shall summarize such remarks in the following way. On the above use, the fact of being someone's relative has in its *logic* no degrees. But in its *nature*—in what it involves—it does have degrees. So the fact's logic hides its nature. Hence the triviality of the claim that all our relatives are equally our relatives. (The last few sentences may be wrongly worded, but I hope that the example suggests what I mean.)

To return to the claims about personhood. These were: that it is a further fact, and that all persons are equally persons. As claims about the fact's logic, these are trivial. Certain people think the claims profound. They believe them to be true of the fact's nature.

The difference here can be shown in many ways. Take the question, 'When precisely does an embryo become a person?' If we merely make the claims about the fact's logic, we shall not believe that this question must have a precise answer. Certain people do believe this. They believe that any embryo must either be, or not be, a complete person. Their view goes beyond the 'logical claims'. It concerns the nature of personhood.

We can now return to the main argument. About the facts of both personhood and personal identity, there are two views. According to ther first, these facts have a special nature. They are further facts, independent of certain more specific facts; and in every case they must either hold completely, or completely fail to hold. According to the second view, these facts are not of this nature. They consist in the holding of the more specific facts; and they are matters of degree.

Let us name such opposing views. I shall call the first kind 'Simple' and the second 'Complex'.

Such views may affect our moral principles, in the following way. If we change from a Simple to a Complex View, we acquire two beliefs: we decide that a certain fact is in its nature less deep, and that it sometimes holds to reduced degrees. These beliefs may have two effects: the first belief may weaken certain principles, and the second give the principles a new scope.

Take the views about personhood. An ancient principle gives to the welfare of people absolute precedence over that of mere animals. If the difference between people and mere animals is in its nature less deep, this principle can be more plausibly denied. And if embryos are not people, and become them only by degrees, the principle forbidding murder can be more plausibly given less scope.

I have not defended these claims. They are meant to parallel what I shall defend in the case of the two views about personal identity.

II

We must first sketch these views. It will help to revive a comparison. What is involved in the survival of a nation are just certain continuities, such as those of a people and a political system. When there is a weakening of these continuities, as there was, say, in the Norman Conquest, it may be unclear whether a nation survives. But there is here no problem. And the reason is that the survival of a nation just involves these continuities. Once we know how the continuities were weakened, we need not ask, as a question about an independent fact, 'Did a nation cease to exist?' There is nothing left to know.

We can add the following remarks. Though identity has no degrees, these continuities are matters of degree. So the identity of nations over time is only in its logic 'all-or-nothing'; in its nature it has degrees.

The identity of people over time is, according to the 'Complex View', comparable. It consists in bodily and psychological continuity. These, too, are matters of degree. So we can add the comparable remark. The identity of people over time is only in its logic 'all-or-nothing'; in its nature it has degrees.

How do the continuities of bodies and minds have degrees? We can first dismiss bodies, since they are morally trivial. Let us next call 'direct' the psychological relations which hold between: the memory of an experience and this experience, the intention to perform some later action and this action, and different expressions of some lasting character-trait. We can now name two general features of a person's life. One, 'connectedness', is the holding, over time, of

particular 'direct' relations. The other, 'continuity', is the holding of a chain of such relations. If, say, I cannot now remember some earlier day, there are no 'connections of memory' between me now and myself on that day. But there may be 'continuity of memory'. This there is if, on every day between, I remembered the previous day.

Of these two general relations, I define 'continuous with' so that, in its logic, it has no degrees. It is like 'related to' in the use on which all our relatives are equally our relatives. But 'connectedness' has degrees. Between different parts of a person's life, the connections of memory, character, and intention are—in strength and number—more or less. ('Connected to' is like 'closely related to'; different relatives can be more or less close.)

We can now restate the Complex View. What is important in personal identity are the two relations we have just sketched. One of these, continuity, is in its logic all-or-nothing. But it just involves connectedness, which clearly has degrees. In its nature, therefore, continuity holds to different degrees. So the fact of personal identity also, in its nature, has degrees.

To turn to the Simple View. Here the fact is believed to be, in its nature, all-or-nothing. This it can only be if it does not just consist in (bodily and) psychological continuity—if it is, in its nature, a further fact. To suggest why: These continuities hold, over time, to different degrees. This is true in actual cases, but is most clearly true in some imaginary cases. We can imagine cases where the continuities between each of us and a future person hold to every possible degree. Suppose we think, in imagining these cases, 'Such a future person must be either, and quite simply, *me*, or *someone else*'. (Suppose we think, 'Whatever happens, any future experience must be either *wholly* mine, or *not* mine *at all*'.) If the continuities can hold to every degree, but the fact of our identity must hold completely or not at all, then this fact cannot consist in these continuities. It must be a further, independent, fact.

It is worth repeating that the Simple View is about the nature of personal identity, not its logic. This is shown by the reactions most of us have to various so-called 'problem cases'. These reactions also show that even if, on the surface, we reject the Simple View, at a deeper level we assume it to be true.

We can add this—rough—test of our assumptions. Nations are in many ways unlike people; for example, they are not organisms. But if we take the Complex View, we shall accept this particular comparison: the survival of a person, like that of a nation, is a matter of degree. If instead we reject this comparison, we take the Simple View.

One last preliminary. We can use 'I', and the other pronouns, so that they cover only the part of our lives to which, when speaking, we have the strongest psychological connections. We assign the rest of our lives to what we call our 'other selves'. When, for instance, we have undergone any marked change in character, or conviction, or style of life, we might say, 'It was not *I* who did that, but an earlier self'.

Such talk can become natural. To quote three passages:

Our dread of a future in which we must forego the sight of faces, the sound of voices, that we love, friends from whom we derive today our keenest joys, this dread, far from being dissipated, is intensified, if to the grief of such a privation we reflect that there will be added what seems to us now in anticipation an even more cruel grief: not to feel it as a grief at all—to remain indifferent: for if that should occur, our self would then have changed. It would be in a real sense the death of ourself, a death followed, it is true, by a resurrection, but in a different self, the life, the love of which are beyond the reach of those elements of the existing self that are doomed to die. . . .

It is not because other people are dead that our affection for them grows faint, it is because we ourself are dying. Albertine had no cause to rebuke her friend. The man who was usurping his name had merely inherited it. . . . My new self, while it grew up in the shadow of the old, had often heard the other speak of Albertine; through that other self . . . it thought that it knew her, it found her attractive . . . but this was merely an affection at second hand.

Nadya had written in her letter: 'When you return. . . .' But that was the whole horror: that there would be no return. . . . A new, unfamiliar person would walk in bearing the name of her husband, and she would see that the man, her beloved, for whom she had shut herself up to wait for fourteen years, no longer existed. . . .

Whether we are inclined to use such talk will depend upon our view about the nature of personal identity. If we take the Simple View, we shall not be so inclined, for we shall think it deeply true that all the parts of a person's life are as much parts of his life. If we take the Complex View, we shall be less impressed by this truth. It will seem like the truth that all the parts of a nation's history are as much parts of its history. Because this latter truth is superficial, we at times subdivide such a history into that of a series of successive nations, such as Anglo-Saxon, Medieval, or Post-Imperial England. The connections between these, though similar in kind, differ in degree. If we take the Complex View, we may also redescribe a person's life as the history of a series of successive selves. And the connections between these we shall also claim to be similar in kind, different in degree.

III

We can now turn to our question. Do the different views tend to support different moral claims?

I have space to consider only three subjects: desert, commitment, and distributive justice. And I am forced to oversimplify, and to distort. So it may help to start with some general remarks.

My suggestions are of this form: 'The Complex View supports certain claims.' By 'supports' I mean both 'makes more plausible' and 'helps to explain'. My suggestions thus mean: 'If the true view is the Complex, not the Simple, View, certain claims are more plausible. We may therefore be, on the Complex View, more inclined to make these claims.'

I shall be discussing two kinds of case: those in which the psychological connections are as strong as they ever are, and those in which they are markedly weak. I choose these kinds of case for the following reason. If we change from the Simple to the Complex View, we believe (I shall claim) that our identity is in its nature less deep, and that it sometimes holds to reduced degrees. The first of these beliefs covers every case, even those where there are the strongest connections. But the second of the two beliefs only covers cases where there are weak connections. So the two kinds of case provide separate testing-grounds for the two beliefs.

Let us start with the cases of weak connection. And our first principle can be that we deserve to be punished for certain crimes.

We can suppose that, between some convict now and himself when he committed some crime, there are only weak psychological connections. (This will usually be when conviction takes place after many years.) We can imply the weakness of these connections by calling the convict, not the criminal, but his later self.

Two grounds for detaining him would be unaffected. Whether a convict should be either reformed, or preventively detained, turns upon his present state, not his relation to the criminal. A third ground, deterrence, turns upon a different question. Do potential criminals care about their later selves? Do they care, for instance, if they do not expect to be caught for many years? If they do, then detaining their later selves could perhaps deter.

Would it be deserved? Locke thought that if we forget our crimes we deserve no punishment. Geach considers this view 'morally repugnant'. Mere loss of memory does seem to be insufficient. Changes of character would appear to be more relevant. The subject is, though, extremely difficult. Claims about desert can be plausibly supported with a great variety of arguments. According to some of these loss of memory would be important. And according to most the nature and cause of any change in character would need to be known.

I have no space to consider these details, but I shall make one suggestion. This appeals to the following assumption. When some morally important fact holds to a lesser degree, it can be more plausibly claimed to have less importance—even, in extreme cases, none.

I shall not here defend this assumption. I shall only say that most of us apply the assumption to many kinds of principle. Take, for example, the two principles that we have special duties to help our relatives, or friends. On the assumption, we might claim that we have less of a special duty to help our less close relatives, or friends, and, to those who are very distant, none at all.

My suggestion is this. If the assumption is acceptable, and the Complex View correct, it becomes more plausible to make the following claim: when the connections between convicts and their past criminal selves are less, they deserve less punishment; if they are very weak, they perhaps deserve none. This claim extends the idea of 'diminished responsibility'. It does not appeal to mental illness, but instead treats a later self like a sane accomplice. Just as a man's deserts correspond to the degree of his complicity with some criminal, so his deserts, now, for some past crime correspond to the degree of connectedness between himself now and himself when committing that crime.

If we add the further assumption that psychological connections are, in general, weaker over longer periods, the claim provides a ground for Statutes of Limitations. (They of course have other grounds.)

IV

We can next consider promises. There are here two identities involved. The first is that of the person who, once, made a promise. Let us suppose that between this person now and himself then there are only weak connections. Would this wipe away his commitment? Does a later self start with a clean slate?

On the assumption that I gave, the Complex View supports the answer, 'yes'. Certain people think that only short-term promises carry moral weight. This belief becomes more plausible on the Complex View.

The second relevant identity is that of the person who received the promise. There is here an asymmetry. The possible effect of the Complex View could be deliberately blocked. We could ask for promises of this form: 'I shall help you, and all your later selves.' If the promises that I *receive* take this form, they cannot be plausibly held to be later undermined by any change in *my* character, or by any other weakening, over the rest of *my* life, in connectedness.

The asymmetry is this: similar forms cannot so obviously stay binding on the *maker* of a promise. I might say, 'I, and all my later selves, shall help you'. But it is plausible to reply that I can only bind my present self. This is plausible because it is like the claim that I can only bind myself. No one, though, denies that I can promise you that I shall help someone else. So I can clearly promise you that I shall help your later selves.

Such a promise may indeed seem especially binding. Suppose that you change faster than I do. I may then regard myself as committed, not to you, but to your earlier self. I may therefore think that you cannot waive my commitment (It would be like a commitment, to someone now dead, to help his children. We cannot be released from such commitments.)

Such a case would be rare. But an example may help the argument. Let us take a nineteenth-century Russian who, in several years, should inherit vast estates. Because he has socialist ideals, he intends, now, to give the land to the peasants. But he knows that in time his ideals may fade. To guard against this possibility, he does two things. He first signs a legal document, which will automatically give away the land, and which can only be revoked with his wife's consent. He then says to his wife, 'If I ever change my mind, and ask you to revoke the document, promise me that you will not consent'. He might add, 'I regard my ideals as essential to me. If I lose these ideals, I want you to think that *I* cease to exist. I want you to regard your husband, then, not as me, the man who asks you for this promise, but only as his later self. Promise me that you would not do what he asks.'

This plea seems understandable. And if his wife made this promise, and he later asked her to revoke the document, she might well regard herself as in no way released from her commitment. It might seem to her as if she has obligations to two different people. She might think that to do what her husband now asks would be to betray the young man whom she loved and married. And she might regard what her husband now says as unable to acquit her of disloyalty to this young man—of disloyalty to her husband's earlier self.

Such an example may seem not to require the distinction between successive selves. Suppose that I ask you to promise me never to give me cigarettes, even if I beg you for them. You

might think, that I cannot, in begging you, simply release you from this commitment. And to think this you need not deny that it is I to whom you are committed.

This seems correct. But the reason is that addiction clouds judgment. Similar examples might involve extreme stress or pain, or (as with Odysseus, tied to the mast) extraordinary temptation. When, though, nothing clouds a person's judgment, most of us believe that the person to whom we are committed can always release us. He can always, if in sound mind, waive our commitment. We believe this whatever the commitment may be. So (on this view) the content of commitment cannot stop its being waived.

To return to the Russian couple. The man's ideals fade, and he asks his wife to revoke the document. Though she promised him to refuse, he declares that he now releases her from this commitment. We have sketched two ways in which she might think that she is not released. She might, first, take her husband's change of mind as proof that he cannot now make considered judgments. But we can suppose that she has no such thought. We can also suppose that she shares our view about commitment. If so, she will only believe that her husband is unable to release her if she thinks that it is, in some sense, not *he* to whom she is committed. We have sketched such a sense. She may regard the young man's loss of his ideals as involving his replacement by a later self.

The example is of a quite general possibility. We may regard some events within a person's life as, in certain ways, like birth or death. Not in all ways, for beyond these events the person has earlier or later selves. But it may be only one out of the series of selves which is the object of some of our emotions, and to which we apply some of our principles.

The young Russian socialist regards his ideals as essential to his present self. He asks his wife to promise to this present self not to act against these ideals. And, on his way of thinking, she can never be released from her commitment. For the self to whom she is committed would, in trying to release her, cease to exist.

The way of thinking may seem to be within

our range of choice. We can indeed choose when to *speak* of a new self, just as we can choose when to speak of the end of Medieval England. But the way of speaking would express beliefs. And the wife in our example cannot choose her beliefs. That the young man whom she loved and married has, in a sense, ceased to exist, that her middle-aged and cynical husband is at most the later self of this young man—these claims may seem to her to express more of the truth than the simple claim, 'but they are the same person'. Just as we can give a more accurate description if we divide the history of Russia into that of the Empire and of the Soviet Union, so

it may be more accurate to divide her husband's life into that of two successive selves.

Questions on Parfit

1. Distinguish between the Simple View and the Complex View. Would it be accurate to say that Locke holds the Simple View and Hume the Complex View? Explain your answer. Which of these views do you think is more correct? Why?

2. What are the implications for moral responsibility, punishment, and promises if the Complex View is true? What, for example, should the Russian wife do if the Complex View is true? What should she do if the Simple View is true?

Daniel C. Dennett

Where Am I?

Daniel C. Dennett is Professor of Philosophy at Tufts University. In addition to his well-known book Brainstorms, *he is the author of* Elbow Room: The Varieties of Free Will Worth Wanting.

Now that I've won my suit under the Freedom of Information Act, I am at liberty to reveal for the first time a curious episode in my life that may be of interest not only to those engaged in research in the philosophy of mind, artificial intelligence and neuroscience but also to the general public.

Several years ago I was approached by Pentagon officials who asked me to volunteer for a highly dangerous and secret mission. In collaboration with NASA and Howard Hughes, the Department of Defense was spending billions to develop a Supersonic Tunneling Underground Device, or STUD. It was supposed to tunnel

The reading is from Daniel C. Dennett, *Brainstorms* (Bradford Books, 1978), pp. 310–323. Copyright © 1978 by Bradford Books, published by MIT Press. Reprinted with permission.

through the earth's core at great speed and deliver a specially designed atomic warhead "right up the Red's missile silos," as one of the Pentagon brass put it.

The problem was that in an early test they had succeeded in lodging a warhead about a mile deep under Tulsa, Oklahoma, and they wanted me to retrieve it for them. "Why me?" I asked. Well, the mission involved some pioneering applications of current brain research, and they had heard of my interest in brains and of course my Faustian curiosity and great courage and so forth. . . . Well, how could I refuse? The difficulty that brought the Pentagon to my door was that the device I'd been asked to recover was fiercely radioactive, in a new way. According to monitoring instruments, something about the nature of the device and its complex interactions with pockets of material deep in the earth had produced radiation that could cause severe abnormalities in certain tissues of the brain. No way had been found to shield the brain from these deadly rays, which were apparently harmless to other tissues and organs of the body. So it had been decided that the person sent to recover the device should *leave his brain behind.* It would be kept in a safe place where it could execute its normal control functions by elaborate radio links. Would I submit to a surgical procedure that would completely remove my brain, which would then be placed in a life-support system at the Manned Spacecraft Center in Houston? Each input and output pathway, as it was severed, would be restored by a pair of microminiaturized radio transceivers, one attached precisely to the brain, the other to the nerve stumps in the empty cranium. No information would be lost, all the connectivity would be preserved. At first I was a bit reluctant. Would it really work? The Houston brain surgeons encouraged me. "Think of it," they said, "as a mere *stretching* of the nerves. If your brain were just moved over an *inch* in your skull, that would not alter or impair your mind. We're simply going to make the nerves indefinitely elastic by splicing radio links into them."

I was shown around the life-support lab in Houston and saw the sparkling new vat in which my brain would be placed, were I to agree. I met the large and brilliant support team of neurologists, hematologists, biophysicists, and electrical engineers, and after several days of discussions and demonstrations, I agreed to give it a try. I was subjected to an enormous array of blood tests, brain scans, experiments, interviews, and the like. They took down my autobiography at great length, recorded tedious lists of my beliefs, hopes, fears and tastes. They even listed my favorite stereo recordings and gave me a crash session of psychoanalysis.

The day for surgery arrived at last and of course I was anesthetized and remember nothing of the operation itself. When I came out of anesthesia, I opened my eyes, looked around, and asked the inevitable, the traditional, the lamentably hackneyed post-operative question: "Where am I?" The nurse smiled down at me. "You're in Houston," she said, and I reflected that this still had a good chance of being the truth one way or another. She handed me a mirror. Sure enough, there were the tiny antennae poling up through their titanium ports cemented into my skull.

"I gather the operation was a success," I said, "I want to go see my brain." They led me (I was a bit dizzy and unsteady) down a long corridor and into the life-support lab. A cheer went up from the assembled support team, and I responded with what I hoped was a jaunty salute. Still feeling lightheaded, I was helped over to the life-support vat. I peered through the glass.

There, floating in what looked like ginger-ale, was undeniably a human brain, though it was almost covered with printed circuit chips, plastic tubules, electrodes, and other paraphernalia. "Is that mine?" I asked. "Hit the output transmitter switch there on the side of the vat and see for yourself," the project director replied. I moved the switch to OFF, and immediately slumped, groggy and nauseated, into the arms of the technicians, one of whom kindly restored the switch to its ON position. While I recovered my equilibrium and composure, I thought to myself: "Well, here I am, sitting on a folding chair, staring through a piece of plate glass at my own brain. . . . But wait," I said to myself, "shouldn't I have thought, 'Here I am, suspended in a bubbling fluid, being stared at by my own eyes'?" I tried to think this latter thought. I tried to project it into the tank, offering it hopefully to my brain, but I failed to carry off the exercise with any conviction. I tried again. "Here am *I*, Daniel Dennett, suspended in a bubbling fluid, being stared at by my own eyes." No, it just didn't work. Most puzzling and confusing. Being a philosopher of firm physicalist conviction, I believed unswervingly that the tokening of my thoughts was occurring somewhere in my brain: yet, when I thought "Here I am," where the thought occurred to me was *here*, outside the vat, where I, Dennett, was standing staring at my brain.

I tried and tried to think myself into the vat, but to no avail. I tried to build up to the task by doing mental exercises. I thought to myself, "The sun is shining *over there*," five times in rapid succession, each time mentally ostending a different place: in order, the sun-lit corner of the lab, the visible front lawn of the hospital, Houston, Mars, and Jupiter. I found I had little difficulty in getting my "there's" to hop all over the celestial map with their proper references. I could loft a "there" in an instant through the farthest reaches of space, and then aim the next "there" with pinpoint accuracy at the upper left quadrant of a freckle on my arm. Why was I having such trouble with "here"? "Here in Houston" worked well enough, and so did "here in the lab," and even "here in this part of the lab," but "here in the vat" always seemed merely an unmeant mental mouthing. I tried closing my eyes while thinking it. This seemed to help, but still I couldn't manage to pull it off, except perhaps for a fleeting instant. I couldn't be sure. The discovery that I couldn't be sure was also unsettling. How did I know *where* I meant by "here" when I thought "here"? Could I *think* I meant one place when in fact I meant another? I didn't see how that could be admitted without untying the few bonds of intimacy between a person and his own mental life that had survived the onslaught of the brain scientists and philosophers, the physicalists and behaviorists. Perhaps I was incorrigible about where I *meant* when I said "here." But in my present circumstances it seemed that either I was doomed by sheer force of mental habit to thinking systematically false indexical thoughts, or where a person is (and hence where his thoughts are tokened for purposes of semantic analysis) is not necessarily where his brain, the physical seat of his soul, resides. Nagged by confusion, I attempted to orient myself by falling back on a favorite philosopher's ploy. I began naming things.

"Yorick," I said aloud to my brain, "you are my brain. The rest of my body, seated in this chair, I dub 'Hamlet.'" So here we all are: Yorick's my brain, Hamlet's my body, and I am Dennett. *Now*, where am I? And when I think "where am I?" where's that thought tokened? Is it tokened in my brain, lounging about in the vat, or right here between my ears where it *seems* to be tokened? Or nowhere? Its *temporal* coordinates give me no trouble; must it not have spatial coordinates as well? I began making a list of the alternatives.

(1) *Where Hamlet goes, there goes Dennett.* This principle was easily refuted by appeal to the familiar brain transplant thought-experiments so enjoyed by philosophers. If Tom and Dick switch brains, Tom is the fellow with Dick's former body—just ask him; he'll claim to be Tom, and tell you the most intimate details of Tom's autobiography. It was clear enough, then, that my current body and I could part company, but not likely that I could be separated from my brain. The rule of thumb that emerged so plainly from the thought experiments was that in a brain-transplant operation, one wanted to be the *donor*, not the recipient. Better to call

such an operation a *body*-transplant, in fact. So perhaps the truth was,

(2) *Where Yorick goes, there goes Dennett.* This was not at all appealing, however. How could I be in the vat and not about to go anywhere, when I was so obviously outside the vat looking in and beginning to make guilty plans to return to my room for a substantial lunch? This begged the question I realized, but it still seemed to be getting at something important. Casting about for some support for my intuition, I hit upon a legalistic sort of argument that might have appealed to Locke.

Suppose, I argued to myself, I were now to fly to California, rob a bank, and be apprehended. In which state would I be tried: In California, where the robbery took place, or in Texas, where the brains of the outfit were located? Would I be a California felon with an out-of-state brain, or a Texas felon remotely controlling an accomplice of sorts in California? It seemed possible that I might beat such a rap just on the undecidability of that jurisdictional question, though perhaps it would be deemed an inter-state, and hence Federal, offense. In any event, suppose I were convicted. Was it likely that California would be satisfied to throw Hamlet into the brig, knowing that Yorick was living the good life and luxuriously taking the waters in Texas? Would Texas incarcerate Yorick, leaving Hamlet free to take the next boat to Rio? This alternative appealed to me. Barring capital punishment or other cruel and unusual punishment, the state would be obliged to maintain the life-support system for Yorick though they might move him from Houston to Leavenworth, and aside from the unpleasantness of the opprobrium, I, for one, would not mind at all and would consider myself a free man under those circumstances. If the state has an interest in forcibly relocating persons in institutions, it would fail to relocate me in any institution by locating Yorick there. If this were true, it suggested a third alternative.

(3) *Dennett is wherever he thinks he is.* Generalized, the claim was as follows: At any given time a person has a *point of view*, and the location of the point of view (which is determined internally by the content of the point of view) is also the location of the person.

Such a proposition is not without its perplexities, but to me it seemed a step in the right direction. The only trouble was that it seemed to place one in a heads-I-win/tails-you-lose situation of unlikely infallibility as regards location. Hadn't I myself often been wrong about where I was, and at least as often uncertain? Couldn't one get lost? Of course, but getting lost *geographically* is not the only way one might get lost. If one were lost in the woods one could attempt to reassure oneself with the consolation that at least one knew where one was: one was right *here* in the familiar surroundings of one's own body. Perhaps in this case one would not have drawn one's attention to much to be thankful for. Still, there were worse plights imaginable, and I wasn't sure I wasn't in such a plight right now.

Point of view clearly had something to do with personal location, but it was itself an unclear notion. It was obvious that the the content of one's point of view was not the same as or determined by the content of one's beliefs or thoughts. For example, what should we say about the point of view of the Cinerama viewer who shrieks and twists in his seat as the roller-coaster footage overcomes his psychic distancing? Has he forgotten that he is safely seated in the theater? Here I was inclined to say that the person is experiencing an illusory shift in point of view. In other cases, my inclination to call such shifts illusory was less strong. The workers in laboratories and plants who handle dangerous materials by operating feedback-controlled mechanical arms and hands undergo a shift in point of view that is crisper and more pronounced than anything Cinerama can provoke. They can feel the heft and slipperiness of the containers they manipulate with their metal fingers. They know perfectly well where they are and are not fooled into false beliefs by the experience, yet it is as if they were inside the isolation chamber they are peering into. With mental effort, they can manage to shift their point of view back and forth, rather like making a transparent Neckar cube or an Escher drawing change orientation before one's eyes. It does seem extravagant to suppose that in performing this bit of mental gymnastics, they are transporting *themselves* back and forth.

Still their example gave me hope. If I was in fact in the vat in spite of my intuitions, I might be able to train myself to adopt that point of view even as a matter of habit. I should dwell on images of myself comfortably floating in my vat, beaming volitions to that familiar body *out there*. I reflected that the ease or difficulty of this task was presumably independent of the truth about the location of one's brain. Had I been practicing before the operation, I might now be finding it second nature. You might now yourself try such a *tromp l'oeil*. Imagine you have written an inflammatory letter which has been published in the *Times*, the result of which is that the Government has chosen to impound your brain for a probationary period of three years in its Dangerous Brain Clinic in Bethesda, Maryland. Your body of course is allowed freedom to earn a salary and thus to continue its function of laying up income to be taxed. At this moment, however, your body is seated in an auditorium listening to a peculiar account by Daniel Dennett of his own similar experience. Try it. Think yourself to Bethesda, and then hark back longingly to your body, far away, and yet *seeming* so near. It is only with long-distance restraint (yours? the Government's?) that you can control your impulse to get those hands clapping in polite applause before navigating the old body to the rest room and a well-deserved glass of evening sherry in the lounge. The task of imagination is certainly difficult, but if you achieve your goal the results might be consoling.

Anyway, there I was in Houston, lost in thought as one might say, but not for long. My speculations were soon interrupted by the Houston doctors, who wished to test out my new prosthetic nervous system before sending me off on my hazardous mission. As I mentioned before, I was a bit dizzy at first, and not suprprisingly, although I soon habituated myself to my new circumstances (which were, after all, well nigh indistinguishable from my old circumstances). My accommodation was not perfect, however, and to this day I continue to be plagued by minor coordination difficulties. The speed of light is fast, but finite, and as my brain and body move farther and farther apart, the delicate interaction of my feedback systems is thrown into disarray by the time lags. Just as one is rendered close to speechless by a delayed or echoic hearing of one's speaking voice so, for instance, I am virtually unable to track a moving object with my eyes whenever my brain and my body are more than a few miles apart. In most matters my impairment is scarcely detectable, though I can no longer hit a slow curve ball with the authority of yore. There are some compensations of course. Though liquor tastes as good as ever, and warms my gullet while corroding my liver, I can drink it in any quantity I please, without becoming the slightest bit inebriated, a curiosity some of my close friends may have noticed (though I occasionally have *feigned* inebriation, so as not to draw attention to my unusual circumstances). For similar reasons, I take aspirin orally for a sprained wrist, but if the pain persists I ask Houston to administer codeine to me *in vitro*. In times of illness the phone bill can be staggering.

But to return to my adventure. At length, both the doctors and I were satisfied that I was ready to undertake my subterranean mission. And so I left my brain in Houston and headed by helicopter for Tulsa. Well, in any case, that's the way it seemed to me. That's how I would put it, just off the top of my head as it were. On the trip I reflected further about my earlier anxieties and decided that my first post-operative speculations had been tinged with panic. The matter was not nearly as strange or metaphysical as I had been supposing. Where was I? In two places, clearly: both inside the vat and outside it. Just as one can stand with one foot in Connecticut and the other in Rhode Island, I was in two places at once. I had become one of those scattered individuals we used to hear so much about. The more I considered this answer, the more obviously true it appeared. But, strange to say, the more true it appeared, the less important the question to which it could be the true answer seemed. A sad, but not unprecedented, fate for a philosophical question to suffer. This answer did not completely satisfy me, of course. There lingered some question to which I should have liked an answer, which was neither "Where are all my various and sundry parts?" nor "What is my current point of view?" Or at least there seemed to be such a question. For it did seem undeniable that in some sense *I* and not merely *most of me* was descending into the earth under Tulsa in search of an atomic warhead.

When I found the warhead, I was certainly glad I had left my brain behind, for the pointer on the specially built Geiger counter I had brought with me was off the dial. I called Houston on my ordinary radio and told the operation control center of my position and my progress. In return, they gave me instructions for dismantling the vehicle, based upon my on-site observations. I had set to work with my cutting torch when all of a sudden a terrible thing happened. I went stone deaf. At first I thought it was only my radio earphones that had broken, but when I tapped on my helmet, I heard nothing. Apparently the auditory transceivers had gone on the fritz. I could no longer hear Houston or my own voice, but I could speak, so I started telling them what had happened. In mid-sentence, I knew something else had gone wrong. My vocal apparatus had become paralyzed. Then my right hand went limp—another transceiver had gone. I was truly in deep trouble. But worse was to follow. After a few more minutes, I went blind. I cursed my luck, and then I cursed the scientists who had led me into this grave peril. There I was, deaf, dumb, and blind, in a radioactive hole more than a mile under Tulsa. Then the last of my cerebral radio links broke, and suddenly I was faced with a new and even more shocking problem: whereas an instant before I had been buried alive in Oklahoma, now I was disembodied in Houston. My recognition of my new status was not immediate. It took me several very anxious minutes before it dawned on me that my poor body lay several hundred miles away, with heart pulsing and lungs respiring, but otherwise as dead as the body of any heart transplant donor, its skull packed with useless, broken electronic gear. The shift in perspective I had earlier found well nigh impossible now seemed quite natural. Though I could think myself back into my body in the tunnel under Tulsa, it took some effort to sustain the illusion. For surely it was an illusion to suppose I was still in Oklahoma: I had lost all contact with that body.

It occurred to me then, with one of those rushes of revelation of which we should be suspicious, that I had stumbled upon an impressive demonstration of the immateriality of the soul based upon physicalist principles and premises. For as the last radio signal between Tulsa and Houston died away, had I not changed location from Tulsa to Houston at the speed of light? And had I not accomplished this without any increase in mass? What moved from A to B at such speed was surely myself, or at any rate my soul or mind—the massless center of my being and home of my consciousness. My *point of view* had lagged somewhat behind, but I had already noted the indirect bearing of point of view on personal location. I could not see how a physicalist philosopher could quarrel with this except by taking the dire and counter-intuitive route of banishing all talk of persons. Yet the notion of personhood was so well entrenched in everyone's world view, or so it seemed to me, that any denial would be as curiously unconvincing, as systematically disingenuous, as the Cartesian negation, "non sum."

The joy of philosophic discovery thus tided me over some very bad minutes or perhaps hours as the helplessness and hopelessness of my situation became more apparent to me. Waves of panic and even nausea swept over me, made all the more horrible by the absence of their normal body-dependent phenomenology. No adrenalin rush of tingles in the arms, no pounding hart, no premonitory salivation. I did feel a dread sinking feeling in my bowels at one point, and this tricked me momentarily into the false hope that I was undergoing a reversal of the process that landed me in this fix—a gradual undisembodiment. But the isolation and uniqueness of that twinge soon convinced me that it was simply the first of a plague of phantom body hallucinations that I, like any other amputee, would be all too likely to suffer.

My mood then was chaotic. On the one hand, I was fired up with elation of my philosophic discovery and was wracking my brain (one of the few familiar things I could still do), trying to figure out how to communicate my discovery to the journals; while on the other, I was bitter, lonely, and filled with dread and uncertainty. Fortunately, this did not last long, for my technical support team sedated me into a dreamless sleep from which I awoke, hearing with magnificent fidelity the familiar opening strains of my favorite Brahms piano trio. So that was why they had wanted a list of my favorite recordings! It did not take me long to realize that I was hearing the music without ears. The output from the stereo stylus was being fed through some fancy rectification circuitry directly into my auditory nerve. I was mainlining Brahms, an unforgettable experience for any stereo buff. At the end of the record it did not surprise me to hear the reassuring voice of the project director speaking into a microphone that was now my prosthetic ear. He confirmed my analysis of what had gone wrong and assured me that steps were being taken to re-embody me. He did not elaborate, and after a few more recordings, I found myself drifting off to sleep. My sleep lasted, I later learned, for the better part of a year, and when I awoke, it was to find myself restored to my senses. When I looked into the mirror, though, I was a bit startled to see an unfamiliar face. Bearded and a bit heavier, bearing no doubt a family resemblance to my former face, and with the same look of spritely intelligence and resolute character, but definitely a new face. Further self-explorations of an intimate nature left me no doubt that this was a new body and the project director confirmed my conclusions. He did not volunteer any information on the past history of my new body and I decided (wisely, I think in retrospect) not to pry. As many philosophers unfamiliar with my ordeal have more recently speculated, the acquisition of a new body leaves one's *person* intact. And after a period of adjustment to a new voice, new muscular strengths and weaknesses, and so forth, one's *personality* is by and large also preserved. More dramatic changes in personality have been routinely observed in people who have undergone extensive plastic surgery, to say nothing of sex change operations, and I think no one contests the survival of the person in such cases. In any event I soon accomodated to my new body, to the point of being unable to recover any of its novelties to my consciousness or even memory. The view in the mirror soon became utterly familiar. That view, by the way, still revealed antennae, and so I was not surprised to learn that my brain had not been moved from its haven in the life-support lab.

I decided that good old Yorick deserved a visit. I and my new body, whom we might as well call Fortinbras, strode into the familiar lab to another round of applause from the technicians, who were of course congratulating themselves, not me. Once more I stood before the vat and contemplated poor Yorick, and on a whim I once again cavalierly flicked off the output transmitter switch. Imagine my surprise when nothing unusual happened. No fainting spell, no nausea, no noticeable change. A technician hurried to restore the switch to ON, but still I felt nothing. I demanded an explanation, which the project director hastened to provide. It seems that before they had even operated on the first occasion, they had constructed a computer duplicate of my brain, reproducing both the complete information processing structure and the computational speed of my brain in a giant computer program. After the operation, but before they had dared to send me off on my mission to Oklahoma, they had run this computer system and Yorick side by side. The incoming signals from Hamlet were sent simultaneously to Yorick's transceivers and to the computer's array of inputs. And the outputs from Yorick were not only beamed back to Hamlet, my body; they were recorded and checked against the simultaneous output of the computer program, which was called "Hubert" for reasons obscure to me. Over days and even weeks, the outputs were identical and synchronous, which of course did not *prove* that they had succeeded in copying the brain's functional structure, but the empirical support was greatly encouraging.

Hubert's input, and hence activity, had been kept parallel with Yorick's during my disembodied days. And now, to demonstrate this, they had actually thrown the master switch that put Hubert for the first time in on-line control of my body—not Hamlet, of course but Fortinbras. (Hamlet, I learned, had never been recovered from its underground tomb and could be assumed by this time to have largely returned to the dust. At the head of my grave still lay the magnificent bulk of the abandoned device, with the word STUD emblazoned on its side in large letters—a circumstance which may provide archeologists of the next century with a curious insight into the burial rites of their ancestors.)

The laboratory technicians now showed me the master switch, which had two positions, labeled *B*, for Brain (they didn't know my brain's name was Yorick) and *H*, for Hubert. The switch did indeed point to *H*, and they explained to me that if I wished, I could switch it back to *B*. With my heart in my mouth (and my brain in its vat), I did this. Nothing happened. A click, that was all. To test their claim, and with the master switch now set at *B*, I hit Yorick's output transmitter switch on the vat and sure enough, I begin to faint. Once the output switch was turned back on and I had recovered my wits, so to speak, I continued to play with the master switch, flipping it back and forth. I found that, with the exception of the transitional click, I could detect no trace of a difference. I could switch in mid-utterance, and the sentence I had begun speaking under the control of Yorick was finished without a pause or hitch of any kind under the control of Hubert. I had a spare brain, a prosthetic device which might some day stand me in very good stead, were some mishap to befall Yorick. Or alternatively, I could keep Yorick as a spare and use Hubert. It didn't seem to make any difference which I chose, for the wear and tear and fatigue on my body did not have any debilitating effect on either brain, whether or not it was actually causing the motions of my body, or merely spilling its output into thin air.

The one truly unsettling aspect of this new development was the prospect, which was not long in dawning on me, of someone detaching the spare—Hubert or Yorick, as the case might be—from Fortinbras and hitching it to yet another body—some Johnny-come-lately Rosencrantz or Guildenstern. Then (if not before) there would be *two* people, that much was clear. One would be me, and the other would be a sort of super-twin brother. If there were two bodies, one under the control of Hubert and the other being controlled by Yorick, then which would the world recognize as the true Dennett? And whatever the rest of the world decided, which one would be *me*? Would I be the

Yorick-brained one, in virtue of Yorick's causal priority and former intimate relationship with the original Dennett body, Hamlet? That seemed a bit legalistic, a bit too redolent of the arbitrariness of consanguinity and legal possession, to be convincing at the metaphysical level. For, suppose that before the arrival of the second body on the scene, I had been keeping Yorick as the spare for years, and letting Hubert's output drive my body—that is, Fortinbras—all that time. The Hubert-Fortinbras couple would seem then by squatter's rights (to combat one legal intuition with another) to be the true Dennett and the lawful inheritor of everything that was Dennett's. This was an interesting question, certainly, but not nearly so pressing as another question that bothered me. My strongest intuition was that in such an eventuality *I* would survive so long as *either* brain-body couple remained intact, but I had mixed emotions about whether I should want both to survive.

I discussed my worries with the technicians and the project director. The prospect of two Dennetts was abhorrent to me, I explained, largely for social reasons. I didn't want to be my own rival for the affections of my wife, nor did I like the prospect of the two Dennetts sharing my modest professor's salary. Still more vertiginous and distasteful, though, was the idea of knowing *that much* about another person, while he had the very same goods on me. How could we ever face each other? My colleagues in the lab argued that I was ignoring the bright side of the matter. Weren't there many things I wanted to do but, being only one person, had been unable to do? Now one Dennett could stay at home and be the professor and family man, while the other could strike out on a life of travel and adventure—missing the family of course, but happy in the knowledge that the other Dennett was keeping the home fires burning. I could be faithful and adulterous at the same time. I could even cuckold myself—to say nothing of other more lurid possibilities my colleagues were all too ready to force upon my overtaxed imagination. But my ordeal in Oklahoma (or was it Houston?) had made me less adventurous, and I shrank from this opportunity that was being offered (though of course I was never quite sure it was being offered to *me* in the first place).

There was another prospect even more disagreeable—that the spare, Hubert or Yorick as the case might be, would be detached from any input from Fortinbras and just left detached. Then, as in the other case, there would be two Dennetts, or at least two claimants to my name and possessions, one embodied in Fortinbras, and the other sadly, miserably disembodied. Both selfishness and altruism bade me take steps to prevent this from happening. So I asked that measures be taken to ensure that no one could ever tamper with the transceiver connections or the master switch without my (our? no, *my*) knowledge and consent. Since I had no desire to spend my life guarding the equipment in Houston, it was mutually decided that all the electronic connections in the lab would be carefully locked: both those that controlled the life-support system for Yorick and those that controlled the power supply for Hubert would be guarded with fail-safe devices, and I would take the only master switch, outfitted for radio remote control, with me wherever I went. I carry it strapped around my waist and—wait a moment—*here it is*. Every few months I reconnoiter the situation by switching channels. I do this only in the presence of friends of course, for if the other channel were, heaven forbid, either dead or otherwise occupied, there would have to be somebody who had my interests at heart to switch it back, to bring me back from the void. For while I could feel, see, hear, and otherwise sense whatever befell my body, subsequent to such a switch, I'd be unable to control it. By the way, the two positions on the switch are intentionally unmarked, so I never have the fanciest idea whether I am switching from Hubert to Yorick or *vice versa*. (Some of you may think that in this case I really don't know *who* I am, let alone where I am. But such reflections no longer make much of a dent on my essential Dennettness, on my own sense of who I am. If it is true that in one sense I don't know who I am then that's another one of your philosophical truths of underwhelming significance.)

In any case, every time I've flipped the switch so far, nothing has happened. *So let's give it a try. . . .*

"THANK GOD! I THOUGHT YOU'D NEVER FLIP THAT SWITCH! You can't imagine how horrible it's been these last two weeks—but now you know, it's your turn in purgatory. How I've longed for this moment! You see, about two weeks ago—excuse me, ladies and gentlemen, but I've got to explain this to my . . . um, brother, I guess you could say, but he's just told you the facts, so you'll understand—about two weeks ago our two brains drifted just a bit out of synch. I don't know whether *my* brain is now Hubert or Yorick, any more than you do, but in any case, the two brains drifted apart, and of course once the process started, it snowballed, for I was in a slightly different receptive state for the input we both received, a difference that was soon magnified. In no time at all the illusion that I was in control of my body—our body—was completely dissipated. There was nothing I could do—no way to call you. YOU DIDN'T EVEN KNOW I EXISTED! It's been like being carried around in a cage, or better, like being possessed—hearing my own voice say things I didn't mean to say, watching in frustration as my own hands performed deeds I hadn't intended. You'd scratch our itches, but not the way I would have, and you kept me awake, with your tossing and turning. I've been totally exhausted, on the verge of a nervous breakdown, carried around helplessly by your frantic round of activities, sustained only by the knowledge that some day you'd throw the switch.

"Now it's your turn, but at least you'll have the comfort of knowing *I* know you're in there. Like an expectant mother, I'm eating—or at any rate tasting, smelling, seeing—for *two* now, and I'll try to make it easy for you. Don't worry. Just as soon as this colloquium is over, you and I will fly to Houston, and we'll see what can be done to get one of us another body. You can have a female body—your body could be any color you like. But let's think it over. I tell you what—to be fair, if we both want this body, I promise I'll let the project director flip a coin to settle which of us gets to keep it and which then gets to choose a new body. That should guarantee justice, shouldn't it? In any case, I'll take care of you, I promise. These people are my witnesses.

"Ladies and gentlemen, this talk we have just heard is not exactly the talk *I* would have given, but I assure you that everything he said was perfectly true. And now if you'll excuse me, I think I'd—we'd better sit down."

Questions on Dennett

1. At the start of the story, after the initial operation, where is the hero Daniel Dennett? Is he where his brain is (in the vat) or is he where his body is (outside the vat) or somewhere else?

2. Does Daniel survive the death of his body? Why or why not?

3. Who is he after he loses his body? Is he a new person with a new body and a new brain, or the same person with a different body and a different brain (Hubert, the computer program), or are there now two Daniel Dennetts, one with the organic brain and with a computer program?

John Hick

The Resurrection of the Person

For biographical information on Hick, see the reading in chapter 2.

1. The Idea of Resurrection

'I believe', says the Apostles' Creed, 'in the resurrection of the body and the life everlasting.' The resurrection of the body, or of the flesh, has been given a variety of meanings in different ages and different theological circles; but we are not at present concerned with the history of the concept.[1] We are concerned with the meaning that can be given to it today in terms of our contemporary scientific and philosophical understanding.

The prevailing view of man among both contemporary scientists and western philosophers is that he is an indissoluble psycho-physical unity. The only self of which we know is the empirical self, the walking, talking, acting, sleeping individual who lives, it may be, for some sixty to eighty years and then dies. Mental events and mental characteristics are analysed into the modes of behaviour and behavioural dispositions of this empirical self. The human being is described as an organism capable of acting in the high-level ways which we characterize as intelligent, resentful, humorous, calculating and the like. The concept of mind or soul is thus not that of a 'ghost in the machine' but of the more flexible and sophisticated ways in which human beings behave and have it in them to behave. On this view there is no room for the notion of soul in distinction from body; and if there is no soul in distinction from body there can be no question of the soul surviving the death of the body.

Against this background of thought the specifically christian and jewish belief in the resurrection of the body, in contrast to the hellenic idea of the survival of a disembodied soul, might be expected to have attracted more attention than it has. For it is consonant with the conception of man as an indissoluble psycho-physical unity and yet it also offers the possibility of an empirical meaning for the idea of life after death.

St. Paul is the chief biblical expositor of the idea of the resurrection of the body. His basic conception, as I understand it, is this. When someone has died he is, apart from any special divine action, extinct. A human being is by nature mortal and subject to annihilation at death. But in fact God, by an act of sovereign power, either sometimes or always resurrects or reconstitutes or recreates him—not however as the identical physical organism that he was before death, but as a *soma pneumatikon* ('spiritual body') embodying the dispositional characteristics and memory traces of the deceased physical organism, and inhabiting an environment with which the *soma pneumatikon* is continuous as our present bodies are continuous with our present world. We are not concerned here with the difficult exegetical question of how precisely Paul thought of the resurrection body but with the conceptual question as to how, if at all, we can intelligibly think of it today.

2. The 'Replica' Theory

I wish to suggest that we can think of it as the divine creation in another space of an exact psycho-physical 'replica' of the deceased person.

The first point requiring clarification is the idea of spaces in the plural.[2] In this context the possibility of two spaces is the possibility of two sets of extended objects such that each member of each set is spatially related to each other member of the same set but not spatially related to any member of the other set. Thus everything in the space in which I am is at a certain distance and in a certain direction from me, and vice versa; but if there is a second space, nothing in it is at any distance or in any direction from where I now am. In other words, from my point of view the other space is nowhere and therefore does not exist. But if there *is* a second space, unobservable by me, the objects in it are entirely real to an observer within that space, and our own world is to him nowhere—not at any distance nor in any direction—so that from his point of view it does not exist. Now it is logically possible for there to be any number of worlds, each in its own space, these worlds being all observed by the universal consciousness of God but only one of them being observed by an embodied being who is part of one of these worlds. And the idea of bodily resurrection requires (or probably requires) that there be at least two such worlds, and that when an individual dies in our present world in space number one he is either immediately or after a lapse of time re-created in a world in space number two.[3]

In order to develop this idea more fully I shall present a series of three cases, which I claim to be logically possible of fulfilment.

We begin with the idea of someone suddenly ceasing to exist at a certain place in this world and the next instant coming into existence at another place which is not contiguous with the first. He has not moved from A to B by making a path through the intervening space but has disappeared at A and reappeared at B. For example, at some learned gathering in London one of the company suddenly and inexplicably disappears and the next moment an exact 'replica' of him suddenly and inexplicably appears at some comparable meeting in New York. The person who appears in New York is exactly similar, as to both bodily and mental characteristics, to the person who disappears in London. There is continuity of memory, complete similarity and bodily features, including fingerprints, hair and eye coloration and stomach contents, and also of beliefs, habits, and mental propensities. In fact there is everything that would lead us to identify the one who appeared with the one who disappeared, except continuous occupancy of space.

It is I think clear that this is a logically possible sequence of events. It is of course factually impossible: that is to say, so long as matter function in accordance with the 'laws' which it has

exhibited hitherto, such things will not happen. But nevertheless we can imagine changes in the behaviour of matter which would allow it to happen, and we can ask what effect this would have upon our concept of personal identity. Would we say that the one who appears in New York is the same person as the one who disappeared in London? This would presumably be a matter for decision, and perhaps indeed for a legal decision affecting such matters as marriage, property, debts, and other social rights and obligations. I believe that the only reasonable and generally acceptable decision would be to acknowledge identity. The man himself would be conscious of being the same person, and I suggest that his fellow human beings would feel obliged to recognize him as being the one whom he claims to be. We may suppose, for example, that a deputation of the colleagues of the man who disappeared fly to New York to interview the 'replica' of him which is reported there, and find that he is in all respects but one exactly as though he had travelled from London to New York by conventional means. The only difference is that he describes how, as he was listening to Dr Z reading a paper, on blinking his eyes he suddenly found himself sitting in a different room listening to a different paper by an american scholar. He asks his colleagues how the meeting had gone after he had ceased to be there, and what they had made of his disappearance, and so on. He clearly thinks of himself as the one who was present with them at their meeting in London. He is presently reunited with his wife, who is quite certain that he is her husband; and with his children, who are quite certain that he is their father. And so on. I suggest that faced with all these circumstances those who know him would soon, if not immediately, find themselves thinking of him and treating him as the individual who had so inexplicably disappeared from the meeting in London; and that society would accord legal recognition of his identity. We should be extending our normal use of 'same person' in a way which the postulated facts would both demand and justify if we said that the person who appears in New York is the same person as the one who disappeared in London. The factors inclining us to identify them would, I suggest, far outweigh the factors disinclining us to do so. The personal, social, and conceptual cost of refusing to make this extension would so greatly exceed the cost of making it that we should have no reasonable alternative but to extend our concept of 'the same person' to cover this strange new case.

This imaginary case, bizarre though it is, establishes an important conceptual bridgehead for the further claim that a post-mortem 'replica' of Mr X in another space would likewise count as the same person as the this-world Mr X before his death. However, let me strengthen this bridgehead at two points before venturing upon it.

The cyberneticist, Norbert Wiener, has graphically emphasized the non-dependence of human bodily identity through time upon the identity of the physical matter momentarily composing the body. He points out that the living human body is not a static entity but a pattern of change: 'The individuality of the body is that of a flame rather than that of a stone, of a form rather than of a bit of substance.'[4] The pattern of the body can be regarded as a message that is in principle capable of being coded, transmitted, and then translated back into its original form, as sight and sound patterns may be transmitted by radio and translated back into sound and picture. Hence 'there is no absolute distinction between the types of transmission which we can use for sending a telegram from country to country and the types of transmission which at least are theoretically possible for transmitting a living organism such as a human being.'[5] Strictly, one should not speak, as Wiener does here, of a living organism or body being transmitted; for it would not be the body itself but its coded form that is transmitted. At other times, however, Wiener is more precise. It is, he says, possible to contemplate transmitting 'the whole pattern of the human body, of the human brain with its memories and cross connections, so that a hypothetical receiving instrument could re-embody these messages in appropriate matter, capable of continuing the processes already in the body and the mind, and of maintaining the integrity needed for this continuation by a process of homeostasis'.[6] Accordingly Wiener concludes that the telegraphing of the pattern of a man from one place to another

is theoretically possible even though it remains at the present time technically impossible.[7] And it does indeed seem natural in discussing this theoretical possibility to speak of the bodily individual who is constituted at the end of the process as being the same person as the one who was 'encoded' at the beginning. He is not composed of numerically the same parcel of matter; and yet it is more appropriate to describe him as the same person than as a different person because the matter of which he is composed embodies exactly the same 'information'. Similarly, the rendering of Beethoven's ninth symphony which reaches my ears from the radio loudspeaker does not consist of numerically the same vibrations that reached the microphone in the concert hall; those vibrations have not travelled on through another three hundred miles to me. And yet it is more appropriate to say that I am hearing this rendering of the ninth symphony than that I am hearing something else.

The kind of transmission which Wiener envisages differs of course from my case number one in that I have postulated no machinery for coding and decoding, and no procession of radio impulses proceeding from London to New York and requiring a certain elapse of time for their journey. It differs even more radically from the notion of resurrection as 'replication' in another space, since *ex hypothesi* in this case no physical connection between the two spaces, as by radio impulses, is possible. But if we abstract from all questions of practical logistics, Wiener's contribution to the present argument is his insistence that psycho-physical individuality does not depend upon the numerical identity of the ultimate physical constituents of the body but upon the pattern or 'code' which is exemplified. So long as the same 'code' operates, different parcels of matter can be used, and those parcels can be in different places.[8]

The second strengthening of the bridgehead concerns the term 'replica' which, it will be observed, I have used in quotes. The quotes are intended to mark a difference between the normal concept of a replica and the more specialized concept in use here. The paradigm sense of 'replica' is that in which there is an original object, such as a statue, of which a more or less exact copy is then made. It is logically possible (though not of course necessary) for the original and the replica to exist simultaneously; and also for there to be any number of replicas of the same original. In contrast to this, in the case of the disappearance in London and reappearance in New York it is not logically possible for the original and the 'replica' to exist simultaneously or for there to be more than one 'replica' of the same original. If a putative 'replica' did exist simultaneously with its original it would not be a 'replica' but a replica; and if there were more than one they would not be 'replicas' but replicas. For 'replica' is the name that I am proposing for the second entity in the following case. A living person ceases to exist at a certain location, and a being exactly similar to him in all respects subsequently comes into existence at another location. And I have argued so far that it would be a correct decision, causing far less linguistic and conceptual disruption than the contrary one, to regard the 'replica' as the same person as the original.

Let us now move on to a second imaginary case, a step nearer to the idea of resurrection. Let us suppose that the event in London is not a sudden and inexplicable disappearance, and indeed not a disappearance at all, but a sudden death. Only, at the moment when the individual dies a 'replica' of him as he was at the moment before his death, and complete with memory up to that instant, comes into existence in New York. Even with the corpse on our hands it would still, I suggest, be an extension of 'same person' required and warranted by the postulated facts to say that the one who died has been miraculously re-created in New York. The case would, to be sure, be even odder than the previous one because of the existence of the dead body in London contemporaneously with the living person in New York. And yet, striking though the oddness undoubtedly is, it does not amount to a logical impossibility. Once again we must imagine some of the deceased's colleagues going to New York to interview the person who has suddenly appeared there. He would perfectly remember them and their meeting, be interested in what had happened, and be as amazed and dumbfounded about it as anyone else; and he would perhaps be worried about the possible legal complications if he should re-

turn to London to claim his property; and so on. Once again, I believe, they would soon find themselves thinking of him and treating him as the same person as the dead Londoner. Once again the factors inclining us to say that the one who died and the one who appeared are the same person would far outweigh the factors inclining us to say that they are different people. Once again we should have to extend our usage of 'same person' to cover the new case.

However, rather than pause longer over this second picture let us proceed to the idea of 'replication' in another space, which I suggest can give content to the notion of resurrection. For at this point the problem of personal identity shifts its focus from second- and third-person criteria to first-person criteria. It is no longer a question of how we in this world could know that the 'replica' Mr X is the same person as the now deceased Mr X, but of how the 'replica' Mr X himself could know this. And since this raises new problems it will be well to move directly to this case and the issues which it involves.

The picture that we have to consider is one in which Mr X dies and his 'replica', complete with memory, etc., appears, not in America, but as a resurrection 'replica' in a different world altogether, a resurrection world inhabited by resurrected 'replicas'—this world occupying its own space distinct from the space with which we are familiar. It is, I think, manifestly an intelligible hypothesis that after my death I shall continue to exist as a consciousness and shall remember both having died and some at least of my states of consciousness both before and after death. Suppose then that I exist, not as a disembodied consciousness but as a psycho-physical being, a psycho-physical being exactly like the being that I was before death, though existing now in a different space. I have the experience of waking up from unconsciousness, as I have on other occasions woken up from sleep; and I am no more inclined in the one case than in the others to doubt my own identity as an individual persisting through time. I realize, either immediately or presently, that I have died, both because I can remember being on my death-bed and because my environment is now different and is populated by people some of whom I know to have died. Evidences of this kind could mount up to the point at which they are quite as strong as the evidence which, in the previous two pictures, convinces the individual in question that he has been miraculously translated to New York. Resurrected persons would be individually no more in doubt about their own identity than we are now, and would presumably be able to identify one another in the same kinds of ways and with a like degree of assurance as we do now.

3. Identity from World to World

But if it be granted that resurrected persons might be able to arrive at a rationally founded conviction that their existence is *post-mortem*, how could they know that the world in which they find themselves is in a different space from that of their pre-mortem life? How could such a person know that he is not in a number-two type situation in which he has died and has been re-created somewhere else in the same physical universe— except that the 'replica' is situated, not in New York, but on a planet of some other star?

It is no doubt conceivable that the space of the resurrection world should have properties which are manifestly incompatible with its being a region of physical space as we know it. But on the other hand, it is not of the essence of the notion of a resurrection world that its space should have different properties from those of physical space. And supposing it not to have different properties it is not evident that a resurrected individual could learn from any direct observations that he was not on a planet of some sun at so great a distance from our own sun that the stellar scenery visible from it does not correlate with that which we now see. And indeed, it is not essential to the conception of resurrection which I am presenting that God's re-creation of us should in fact take place in another space rather than elsewhere in this space. There are however probable arguments in favour of the plural space hypothesis. The main ground that a resurrected person would have for believing that he is in another space would be his belief that case-one and case-two type events would be incompatible with the 'laws' of the space in which he was before death. Thus although such

'replication' is logically conceivable within our space we have good reason to believe that it does not in fact occur. But on the other hand we have no experience to indicate that 'replication' does not (or does) occur as between different spaces; and we should I think therefore be strongly, and reasonably, inclined to opt for the latter hypothesis.

I have already acknowledged that there can be no scope for our normal second-person and third-persons criteria of personal identity in the case of 'replication' in another space, except as between persons in that space. For the notion of life in a resurrection world that is spatially unrelated to this world is not simply an extrapolation of the conditions of our present existence. The resurrection world is not just further away from Europe than, say, America is but is not at any distance, great or small. Consequently it is impossible to travel from the one to the other. Thus the ways in which we come to judge that our vanished or our deceased colleague has been re-created in New York cease to be available when the question shifts to his re-creation in another space. Nevertheless we can still ask this question: Suppose we believe, on whatever grounds (say, revelation), that such 'replicas' do indeed come into existence as indicated in the hypothesis, how could we best describe the situation? Should we say that 'replica' Mr X is the same person as Mr X, or that he is a different person, or that it is uncertain whether he is the same or a different person? We are supposing it to be the case that after my death someone comes into existence in another space who is physically and psychologically indistinguishable from me, and who thus has all the memories that I have had up to the moment of death plus, as time goes on, further post-mortem memories. To believe that this happens would be to believe that we are faced with a new situation which may well require us to adjust some of the concepts with which we have hitherto operated. But this is a familiar enough kind of requirement. Indeed, the growth of the scientific understanding of the universe has involved a continuous evolution of our concepts, as well as occasional theoretical revolutions made possible by the formation of new concepts—and all this in response to the demands of the facts. If we were not willing to face the possibility of conceptual development and change we should, as a race, have remained at the level of primitive savages. Thus if the universe—in the sense of the range of possible objects of human consciousness—turned out to be more extensive and more complex than our present science assumes, we should I hope be more likely to enlarge our system of concepts than to close our minds to the facts.

What reconceptualization, then, would be appropriate given the phenomena outlined in our hypothesis?

I suggest that if we knew it to be a 'law of nature' that re-creation or 'replication' occurs in another space, we should be obliged to modify our concept of 'same person' to permit us to say that the 'replica' Mr X in space two is the same person as the former Mr X in space one. For such an extension of use involves far less arbitrariness and paradox than would be generated by saying either that they are not the same person or that it is uncertain whether they are the same person. They have everything in common that they could possibly have, given that they exist successively in different spaces. They are physically alike in every particular; psychologically alike in every particular; and the Mr X stream of consciousness, memory, emotion and volition continues in 'replica' Mr X where it left off at the death of earthly Mr X. In these circumstances it would, I submit, be wantonly paradoxical to rule that they are not the same person and that the space-two 'replica' ought not to think of himself as the person whose past he remembers and whom he is conscious of being.

Terence Penelhum has discussed this concept of resurrection and suggests that although the identification of resurrection-world Mr X with the former earthly Mr X is permissible it is not mandatory. He argues that in my cases number two and number three (and probably number one also) it would be a matter for decision as to whether or not to make the identification. The general principle on which he is working is that there can only be an automatic and unquestionable indentification when there is bodily continuity. As soon as this is lost, identity becomes a matter for decision, with arguments arising both for and against. He concludes that although 'the identification of the former and the later persons in each of the three pictures is not absurd', yet 'in situations like these it is a matter of decision whether to say that physical tests of identity reveal personal identity or very close similarity. We can, reasonably, decide for identity, but we do not have to. And this seems to leave the description of the future life in a state of chronic ambiguity.'[9] In response to this I would agree, and have indeed already acknowledged, that these are cases for decision. Indeed, I would say that *all* cases other than ordinary straightforward everyday identity require a decision. Even physical identity, as such, is no guarantee against the need for decisions, as is shown by such imaginary cases as that of the prince whose consciousness, memory, and personality is transferred into the body of a cobbler, and vice versa.[10] Thus all cases outside the ordinary require linguistic legislation. My contention is not that the identification of resurrection-world Mr X with the former this-world Mr X is entirely unproblematic, but that the decision to identify is much more reasonable, and is liable to create far fewer problems, than would be the decision to regard them as different people.

Notes

1. On this, see chapter 9, section 4.

2. The conceivability of plural spaces is argued by Anthony Quinton in an important article to which I should like to draw the reader's attention: 'Spaces and Times', in *Philosophy*, April 1962.

3. See below, pp. 284–5.

4. Norbert Wiener, *The Human Use of Human Beings*, p. 91.

5. ibid.

6. ibid., p. 86.

7. ibid., p. 92.

8. For a discussion of Norbert Wiener's ideas in this connection, see David L. Mouton, 'Physicalism and Immortality', in *Religious Studies*, March 1972.

9. *Survival and Disembodied Existence*, pp. 100–1.

10. Locke's *Essay concerning Human Understanding*, book II, ch. 27, para. 15.

Questions on Hick

1. According to Hick, how should we understand the Christian doctrine of resurrection?

2. Hick discusses an imaginary example of a person disappearing in London and an exact replica body appearing in New York. Is the New York replica the same person as the one who disappeared in London? Explain your answer.

3. Hick also considers the possibility of transmitting a person to a different place. Suppose, then, that Jane's body is transmitted to explore Mars (using a transporter machine like the one in the Star Trek television series)

but that a replica body is retained on Earth, just in case Jane dies while exploring. Is the replica on Earth the same person as Jane who is exploring on Mars? Suppose that Jane does die on Mars. Is the replica body *now* Jane even though it was not Jane before death? What is Hick's view?

Peter Geach

Immortality

Peter Geach is a British philosopher and the author of God and the Soul, *from which our reading is taken, and* Mental Acts: Their Content and Their Objects.

When *philosophers* talk of life after death, what they mostly have in mind is a doctrine that may be called Platonic—it is found in its essentials in the *Phaedo*. It may be briefly stated thus: Each man's make-up includes a wholly immaterial thing, his mind and soul. It is the mind that sees and hears and feels and thinks and chooses—in a word, is conscious. The mind is the person; the body is extrinsic to the person, like a suit of clothes. Though body and mind affect one another, the mind's existence is quite independent of the body's; and there is thus no reason why the mind should not go on being conscious indefinitely after the death of the body, and even if it never again has with any body that sort of connection which it now has.

This Platonic doctrine has a strong appeal, and there are plausible arguments in its favor. It appears a clearly intelligible supposition that I should go on after death having the same sorts of experience as I now have, even if I then have no body at all. For although these experiences are connected with processes in the body— sight, for example, with processes in the eyes,

optic nerves, and brain—nevertheless there is no necessity of thought about the connection—it is easy to conceive of someone who has no eyes having the experience called sight. He would be having the same experience as I who have eyes do, and I know what sort of experience that is because I have the experience.

Let us now examine these arguments. When a word can be used to stand for a private experience, like the words "seeing" or "pain," it is certainly tempting to suppose that the giving these words a meaning is itself a private experience— indeed that they get their meaning just from the experiences they stand for. But this is really nonsense: if a sentence I hear or utter contains the word "pain," do I help myself to grasp its sense by giving myself a pain? Might not this be, on the contrary, rather distracting?...Our concepts of seeing, hearing, pain, anger, etc., apply in the first instance to human beings; we willingly extend them (say) to cats, dogs, and horses, but we rightly feel uncomfortable about extending them to very alien creatures and speaking of a slug's hearing or an angry ant. Do we know at all what it would be to apply such concepts to an immaterial being? I think not.

One may indeed be tempted to evade difficulties by saying: "An immaterial spirit is angry or in pain if it feels *the same way* as I do when I am angry or in pain." But,...if there is a difficulty in passing from "I am in pain" or "Smith is in pain" to "an immaterial spirit is in pain," there is equally a difficulty in passing from "Smith feels the same way as I do" to "an immaterial spirit feels the same way as I do."

In fact, the question is, whether a private experience does suffice, as is here supposed, to give a meaning to a psychological verb like "to see." I am not trying to throw doubt on there

The reading is from Peter Geach, *God and the Soul* (London: Routledge & Kegan Paul, Ltd., 1969). Reprinted with permission.

being private experiences; of course men have thoughts they do not utter and pains they do not show; of course I may see something without any behavior to show I see it; nor do I mean to emasculate these propositions with neo-behaviorist dialectics. But it is not a question of whether seeing is (sometimes) a private experience, but whether one can attach meaning to the verb "to see" by a private uncheckable performance; and this is what I maintain one cannot do to any word at all.

One way to show that a word's being given a meaning cannot be a private uncheckable performance is the following: We can take a man's word for it that a linguistic expression has given him some private experience—e.g. has revived a painful memory, evoked a visual image, or given him a thrill in the pit of the stomach. But we cannot take his word for it that he attached a sense to the expression, even if we accept his *bona fides*; for later events may convince us that in fact he attached no sense to the expression. Attaching sense to an expression is thus not to be identified with any private experience that accompanies the expression; and I have argued this, not by attacking the idea of private experiences, but by contrasting the attaching of sense to an expression with some typical private experiences that may be connected with the expression.

We give words a sense—whether they are psychological words like "seeing" and "pain," or other words—by getting into a way of using them; and though a man can invent for himself a way of using a word, it must be a way that other people *could* follow—otherwise we are back to the idea of conferring meaning by a private uncheckable performance. Well, how do we eventually use such words as "see," "hear," "feel," when we have got into the way of using them? We do not exercise these concepts only so as to pick our cases of seeing and the rest in our separate worlds of sense-experience; on the contrary, these concepts are used in association with a host of other concepts relating, e.g., to the physical characteristics of what is seen and the behavior of those who do see. In saying this I am not putting forward a theory, but just reminding you of very familiar features in the everyday use of the verb "to see" and related expressions; our ordinary talk about seeing would cease to be intelligible if there were cut out of it such expressions as "I can't see, it's too far off," "I caught his eye," "Don't look round," etc. Do not let the bogy of behaviorism scare you off observing these features; I am not asking you to believe that "to see" is itself a word for a kind of behavior. But the concept of seeing can be maintained only because it has threads of connection with these other non-psychological concepts; break enough threads, and the concept of seeing collapses.

We can now see the sort of difficulties that arise if we try to apply concepts like *seeing* and *feeling* to disembodied spirits. Let me give an actual case of a psychological concept's collapsing when its connections were broken. Certain hysterics claimed to have a magnetic sense; it was discovered, however, that their claim to be having magnetic sensations did not go with the actual presence of a magnet in their environment, but only with their belief that a magnet was present. Psychologists did not now take the line: We may take the patients' word for it that they have peculiar sensations—only the term "magnetic sensations" has proved inappropriate, as having been based on a wrong causal hypothesis. On the contrary, patients' reports of magnetic sensations were thenceforward written off as being among the odd things that hysterical patients sometimes say. Now far fewer of the ordinary connections of a sensation-concept were broken here than would be broken if we tried to apply a sensation-concept like seeing to a disembodied spirit.

If we conclude that the ascription of sensations and feelings to a disembodied spirit does not make sense, it does not obviously follow, as you might think, that we must deny the possibility of disembodied spirits altogether. Aquinas for example was convinced that there are disembodied spirits but ones that cannot see or hear or feel pain or fear or anger; he allowed them no mental operations except those of thought and will. Damned spirits would suffer from frustration of their evil will, but not from aches and pains or foul odors or the like. It would take me too far to discuss whether his reasons for thinking this were good; I want to show what follows from this view. In our human life thinking and choosing are intricately bound up with a play of sensations and mental images and emotions; if after a lifetime of thinking and choosing in this human way there is left only a disembodied mind whose thought is wholly nonsensuous and whose rational choices are unaccompanied by any human feelings—can we still say there remains the same person? Surely not: such a soul is not the person who died but a mere remnant of him. And this is just what Aquinas says (in his commentary on I Corinthians 15): *anima mea non est ego,* my soul is not I; and if only souls are saved, *I* am not saved, nor is any man. If some time after Peter Geach's death there is again a man identifiable as Peter Geach, then Peter Geach again, or still, lives: otherwise not.

Though a surviving mental remnant of a person, preserving some sort of physical continuity with the man you knew, would not be Peter Geach, this does not show that such a measure of survival is not possible; but its possibility does raise serious difficulties; even if such dehumanized thinking and willing is really conceivable at all. For *whose* thinking would this be? Could we tell whether *one* or *many* disembodied spirits thought the thoughts in question? We touch here on the old problem: what constitutes there being two disembodied minds (at the same time, that is)? Well, what constitutes there being two pennies? It may happen that one penny is bent and corroded while another is in mint condition; but such differences cannot be what make the two pennies to be two—the two pennies could not have these varied fortunes if they were not already distinct. In the same way, differences of memories or of aims could not constitute the difference between two disembodied minds, but could only supervene upon a difference already existing. What does constitute the difference between two disembodied human minds? If we could find no ground of differentiation, then not only would that which survived be a mere remnant of a person—there would not even be a surviving individuality.

Could we say that souls are different because in the first instance they were souls of different bodies, and then remain different on that account when they are no longer embodied? I do not think this solution would do at all if differentiation by reference to different bodies were merely retrospective. It might be otherwise if we held, with Aquinas, that the relation to a body was not merely retrospective—that each disembodied human soul permanently retained a capacity for reunion to such a body as would reconstitute a man identifiable with the man who died. This might satisfactorily account for the individuation of disembodied human souls; they would differ by being fitted for reunion to different bodies; but it would entail that the possibility of disembodied human souls stood or fell with the *possibility* of a dead man's living again as a man.

Some Scholastics held that just as two pennies or two cats differ by being different bits of matter, so human souls differ by containing different "spiritual matter." Aquinas regarded this idea as self-contradictory; it is at any rate much too obscure to count as establishing a possibility of distinct disembodied souls. Now this recourse to "spiritual matter" might well strike us merely as the filling of a conceptual lacuna with a nonsensical piece of jargon. But it is not only Scholastic philosophers who assimilate mental processes to physical ones, only thinking of mental processes as taking place in an *immaterial* medium; and many people think it easy to conceive of distinct disembodied souls because they are illegitimately ascribing to souls a sort of differentiation—say, by existing *side by side*—that can be significantly ascribed only to bodies. The same goes for people who talk about souls as being "fused" or "merged" in a Great Soul; they are imagining some such change in the world of souls as occurs to a drop of water falling into a pool or to a small lump of wax that is rubbed into a big one. Now if only people *talked* about "spiritual matter," instead of just thinking in terms of it unawares, their muddle could be more easily detected and treated.

To sum up what I have said so far: The possibility of life after death for Peter Geach appears to stand or fall with the possibility of there being once again a man identifiable as Peter Geach. The existence of a disembodied soul would not be a survival of the person Peter Geach; and even in such a truncated form, individual existence seems to require at least a persistent possibility of the soul's again entering into the make-up of a man who is identifiably Peter Geach.

This suggests a form of belief in survival that seems to have become quite popular of late in the West—at any rate as a half-belief—namely the belief in reincarnation. Could it in fact have a clear sense to say that a baby born in Oxford this year is Hitler living again?

How could it be shown that the Oxford baby was Hitler? Presumably by memories and similarities of character. I maintain that no amount of such evidence would make it reasonable to identify the baby as Hitler. Similarities of character are of themselves obviously insufficient. As regards memories: If on growing up the Oxford baby reveals knowledge of what we should ordinarily say only Hitler can have known, does this establish a presumption that the child is Hitler? Not at all. In normal circumstances we know when to say "only he can have known that"; when queer things start happening, we have no right to stick to our ordinary assumptions as to what can be known. And suppose that for some time the child "is" Hitler by our criteria, and later on "is" Goering? or might not several children simultaneously satisfy the criteria for "being" Hitler?

These are not merely captious theoretical objections. Spirit-mediums, we are told, will in trance convincingly enact the part of various people: sometimes of fictitious characters, like Martians, or Red Indians ignorant of Red Indian languages, or the departed "spirits" of Johnny Walker and John Jamieson; there are even stories of mediums' giving convincing "messages" from people who were alive and normally conscious at the time of the "message." Now a medium giving messages from the dead is not said to be the dead man, but rather to be controlled by his spirit. What then can show whether the Oxford child "is" Hitler or is merely "controlled" by Hitler's spirit? For all these reasons the appearance that there might be good evidence for reincarnation dissolves on a closer view.

Nor do I see, for that matter, how the mental phenomena of mediumship could ever make it reasonable to believe that a human soul survived and communicated. For someone to carry on in a dramatic way quite out of his normal character is a common hysterical symptom; so if a medium does this in a trance, it is no evidence of anything except an abnormal condition of the medium's own mind. As for the medium's telling us things that "only the dead can have known," I repeat that in these queer cases we have no right to stick to our ordinary assumptions about what can be known. Moreover, as I said, there are cases, as well-authenticated as any, in which the medium convincingly enacted the part of X and told things that "Only X could have known" when X was in fact alive and normally conscious, so that his soul was certainly not trying to communicate by way of the medium! Even if we accept all the queer stories of spirit-messages, the result is only to open up a vast field of queer possibilities—not in the least to force us to say that mediums were possessed by such-and-such souls. This was argued by Bradley long ago in his essay "The Evidences of Spiritualism," and he has never been answered.

How could a living man be rightly identifiable with a man who previously died? Let us first consider our normal criteria of personal identity. When we say an old man is the same person as the baby born seventy years before, we believe that the old man has material continuity with the baby. Of course this is not a criterion in the sense of being what we judge identity by; for the old man will not have been watched for seventy years continuously, even by rota! But something we regarded as disproving the material continuity (e.g. absence of a birthmark, different fingerprints) would disprove personal identity. Further, we believe that material continuity establishes a one-one relation: one baby grows up into one old man, and one old man has grown out of one baby. (Otherwise there would have to be at some stage a drastic change, a fusion or fission, which we should regard as destroying personal identity.) Moreover, the baby-body never coexists with the aged body, but develops into it.

Now it seems to me that we cannot rightly identify a man living "again" with a man who died unless *material* conditions of identity are fulfilled. There must be some one-one relation of material continuity between the old body and the new. I am not saying that the new body need be even in part materially *identical* with the old; this, unlike material continuity, is not required for personal identity, for the old man need not have kept even a grain of matter from the baby of seventy years ago.

We must here notice an important fallacy. I was indicating just now that I favor Aquinas's doctrine that two coexisting souls differ by being related to two different bodies and that two coexisting human bodies, like two pennies or two cats, differ by being different bits of matter. Well, if it is difference of matter that makes two bodies different, it may seem to follow that a body can maintain its identity only if at least some identifiable matter remains in it all the time; otherwise it is no more the same body than the wine in a cask that is continuously emptied and refilled is the same wine. But just this is the fallacy: it does not follow, if difference in a certain respect at a certain time suffices to show non-identity, that sameness in that respect over a period of time is necessary to identity. Thus, Sir John Cutler's famous pair of stockings were the same pair all the time, although they started as silk and by much mending ended as worsted; people have found it hard to see this, because if at a given time there is a silk pair and also a worsted pair then there are two pairs. Again, it is clear that the same man may be in Birmingham at noon and in Oxford at 7 p.m., even though a man in Birmingham and a man in Oxford at a given time must be two different men. Once formulated, the fallacy is obvious, but it might be deceptive if not formulated.

"Why worry even about material continuity? Would not mental continuity be both necessary and sufficient?" Necessary, but not sufficient. Imagine a new "Tichborne" trial. The claimant knows all the things he ought to know, and talks convincingly to the long-lost heir's friends. But medical evidence about scars and old fractures and so on indicates that he cannot be the man; moreover, the long-lost heir's corpse is decisively identified at an exhumation. Such a case would bewilder us, particularly if the claimant's *bona fides* were manifest. (He might, for example, voluntarily take a lie-detecting test.) But we should certainly not allow the evidence of mental connections with the long-lost heir to settle the matter in the claimant's favor: the claimant cannot be the long-lost heir, whose body we know lies buried in Australia, and if he honestly thinks he is then we must try to cure him of a delusion.

"But if I went on being conscious, why should I worry which body I have?" To use the repeated "I" prejudges the issue; a fairer way of putting the point would be: If there is going to be a consciousness that includes ostensible memories of my life, why should I worry about which body the consciousness goes with? When we put it that way, it is quite easy to imagine circumstances in which one would worry— particularly if the ostensible memories of my life were to be produced by processes that can produce entirely spurious memories.

If, however, memory is not enough for personal identity; if a man's living again does involve some bodily as well as mental continuity with the man who lived formerly; then we might fairly call his new bodily life a resurrection. So the upshot of our whole argument is that unless a man comes to life again by resurrection, he does not live again after death. At best some mental remnant of him would survive death; and I should hold that the possibility even of such survival involves at least a permanent *capacity* for renewed human life; if reincarnation is excluded, this means: a capacity for resurrection. It may be hard to believe in the resurrection of the body: but Aquinas argued in his commentary on I Corinthians 15, which I have already cited, that it is much harder to believe in an immortal but permanently disembodied human soul; for that would mean believing that a soul, whose very identity depends on the capacity for reunion with one human body rather than another, will continue to exist for ever with this capacity unrealized.

Speaking of the resurrection, St. Paul used the simile of a seed that is planted and grows into an ear of corn, to show the relation between the corpse and the body that rises again from the dead. This simile fits in well enough with our discussion. In this life, the bodily aspect of personal identity requires a one-one relationship and material continuity; one baby body grows into one old man's body by a continuous process. Now similarly there is one-one relationship between the buried seed and the ear that grows out of it; one seed grows into one ear, one ear comes from one seed; and the ear of corn is materially continuous with the seed but need not have any material identity with it.

There is of course no philosophical reason to expect that from a human corpse there will arise at some future date a new human body, continuous in some way with the corpse; and in some particular cases there appear strong empirical objections. But apart from the *possibility* of resurrection, it seems to me a mere illusion to have any hope for life after death. I am of the mind of Judas Maccabeus: if there is no resurrection, it is superfluous and vain to pray for the dead.

The traditional faith of Christianity, inherited from Judaism, is that at the end of this age Messiah will come and men rise from their graves to die no more. That faith is not going to be shaken by inquiries about bodies burned to ashes or eaten by beasts; those who might well suffer just such death in martyrdom were those who were most confident of a glorious reward in the resurrection. One who shares that hope will hardly wish to take out an occultistic or philosophical insurance policy, to guarantee some sort of survival as an annuity, in case God's promise of resurrection should fail.

Questions on Geach

1. What difficulties does Geach raise for the view that a person survives death as a disembodied soul? Do these difficulties make for a decisive refutation of this view or not? Why or why not?

2. Geach also reflects the doctrine of reincarnation. What are his arguments? Are they sound or not? Defend your answer.

3. How does Geach understand the doctrine of resurrection? Compare his view with that of Hick in the previous reading. Which account seems more plausible to you? Why?

Suggested Readings

C. J. Ducasse, *A Critical Examination of the Belief in Life After Death* (Springfield, IL: Charles C. Thomas, 1961) discusses arguments for survival, and concludes that it is possible. See also his *Nature, Mind, and Death* (LaSalle, IL: Open Court, 1951).

Anthony Flew, *A New Approach to Psychical Research* (London: Watts, 1953) critically examines the appeal to psychical research to support belief in survival, that is, the appeal to reports from mediums who allegedly communicate with the dead, apparitions, memories from former lives, and so on.

Corliss Lamont, *The Illusion of Immortality* (New York: G. P. Putnam's Sons, 1935) attacks belief in survival of death.

Derek Parfit, "Personal Identity," *Philosophical Review*, LXXX, I (Jan. 1971), pp. 3–27, is an important article that carefully presents Parfit's controversial view of personal identity. His most complete discussion of personal identity is found in Part Three of his book *Reasons and Persons* (Oxford: Clarendon Press, 1984).

John Perry, ed., *Personal Identity* (Berkeley: University of California Press, 1975) would be a good place to start for classical and contemporary readings on personal identity. This anthology includes classical statements by Locke, Butler, and Reid; and contemporary discussions by Quinton, Grice, Shoemaker, and of course, Perry himself.

Terence Penelhum, *Survival and Disembodied Existence* (London: Routledge & Kegan Paul, 1970) critically examines various conceptions of disembodied survival of death.

H. H. Price, "Survival and the Idea of 'Another World'," in John Hick, *Classical and Contemporary Readings in the Philosophy of Religion,* 2d ed. (Englewood Cliffs, NJ: Prentice-Hall, 1970) suggests that we can imagine a disembodied survival of death as involving a dream world where we communicate with other spirits by means of mental telepathy. This conception of survival is attacked by both Hick and Geach. Price gives a more complete presentation of his view in *Personal Identity and Survival* (London: Society for Psychical Research, 1958).

Amelie Oksenberg Rorty, ed., *The Identities of Persons* (Berkeley: University of California Press, 1976) is a very good collection of readings on personal identity by important contemporary authors such as Lewis, Parfit, Shoemaker, Wiggins, Dennett, Williams, and Perry. This book has a complete bibliography on the topic.

Bertrand Russell, "Do We Survive Death?" in Bertrand Russell, *Why I Am Not a Christian* (London: George Allen and Unwin, 1957), pp. 88–93, argues against belief in survival—this belief is based on the questionable theory of an immaterial soul or on emotions unsupported by reason.

The Basis
for Morality

Chapter 7

INTRODUCTION

THE EUTHYPHRO
Plato

THE MORAL LAW AND THE LAW OF GOD
Peter Geach

MORALITY WITHOUT GOD
John Arthur

THE CHALLENGE OF CULTURAL RELATIVISM
James Rachels

SCIENCE AND ETHICS
Bertrand Russell

THE OBJECTIVITY OF MORAL JUDGMENTS
A. C. Ewing

SUGGESTED READINGS

Introduction

What is the basis of morality?   Morality is concerned with values, with what is right or wrong, and what is good or bad. Deciding questions about values is obviously very important, both theoretically and practically. But how do we do this? What is the basis of morality? In this chapter we consider some of the standard philosophical answers to this question.

The sort of inquiry we are making here is usually said to belong to the area of philosophy called *metaethics,* the study of the nature of moral values and how they are justified. Are they based on God's commands? Are statements about values based on subjective emotions or are they objective? Are values relative to the society in which one lives? Are there universal values found in all societies? These are some of the metaethical questions we will discuss in this chapter.

Metaethics is about morality, about the meaning of moral terms like "right" and "good" and about the way moral judgments such as "Abortion is wrong" are justified. Normative ethics itself, by contrast, is concerned with the actual making of moral judgments. It tries to answer questions like these: Which experiences are good and which are bad? Which actions are good and which are bad? What is a just society? Contemporary applied ethics is also very concerned with practical moral problems like abortion, euthanasia, capital punishment, discrimination, world hunger, and nuclear war. None of these moral problems are covered in this text (although they are included in my *Contemporary Moral Problems,* 2d ed., West Publishing Co., 1988). We will confine our attention to metaethical theories (this chapter) and normative ethical theories (next chapter).

The divine command theory.   In its simplest form, the popular divine command theory says that an act is right if God commands it, and wrong if God forbids it. (Some people might classify this as an ethical theory about what is right, but it seems to be about the basis or foundation of morality, and for that reason it will be treated as one of the metaethical theories.)

In our readings John Arthur raises a number of objections to the theory. To begin with, how do we know that God exists? This is of course a serious problem, as we saw in chapter 1. Even assuming that we know that God exists, or at least have faith that God exists, which God of which religion should we worship—the God of Christianity, Islam, or Judaism (to name the world's major monotheistic religions)? How do we know what God's commands are? If we say that God's commands are found in the Bible and not the Koran, we still need to interpret these commands. Does the commandment "Thou shalt not kill" require us to be absolute pacifists, or are there exceptions such as capital punishment and just wars? Even supposing all these problems have been dealt with, the stubborn critic might still ask "But why should I obey God's commands at all?"

The most famous objection, however, comes from Plato in his dialogue *Euthyphro*. The original dialogue is about piety or holiness: Euthyphro tries to define piety in terms of what is loved by the gods, but Socrates asks a famous question that Euthyphro is unable to answer: Is something holy because it is loved by the gods, or loved by the gods because it is holy? This question is easily reformulated to challenge the divine command theory: Is an act right because God commands it, or does God command it because it is right? It seems that no satisfactory reply can be given. If an act is right just because God commands it, then its being right is arbitrary and any act, even a wicked one like killing your only beloved son (as in the Bible story about Abraham and Isaac), could become right by virtue of God's commanding it. On the other hand, if God commands an act because it is right, there must be an independent standard of rightness that God is following. But in that case we do not need to know God's commands to find out what is right; we can consult the independent standard, at least in principle.

Many philosophers have thought that Plato's objection is conclusive, but in our second reading for the chapter Peter Geach claims that it is a sophistry that he has "completely refuted" by advancing the principle that "we must not do evil that good may come" as one of God's commands.

Cultural relativism. Another view of moral values can be found in the writings of sociologists and anthropologists. They are struck by the fact that different societies seem to have different moral codes. The Eskimos, for example, practice infanticide (for female babies) and leave old people in the snow to die; in our society these practices would be considered wrong. These social scientists are not content to point out factual differences in the moral codes of different societies; they think that this establishes the truth of cultural relativism, the view that there are no universal values and that the moral code of a society determines what is right or wrong.

In our readings, James Rachels asserts that the argument used by the cultural relativists is invalid; the conclusion that there are no universal values does not follow from the premise that different societies have different values. Furthermore, the premise itself is false. Rachels thinks that all societies share certain values, for example, they all value their young and prohibit murder. Finally, cultural relativism has absurd consequences: we could no longer criticize other societies as being morally inferior, say an anti-Semitic society; we would have to decide if an action is right or wrong by consulting the standards of our society, even if these standards are unjust, for example, racist or sexist; and we would have to abandon the notion of moral progress.

Subjectivism. The simplest form of *subjectivism*, as A. C. Ewing says in the readings, can be put in the formula "This is right" means "I approve of it." Ewing does a good job of refuting this view, by presenting six absurd consequences of the formula that seem to indicate that it cannot be true.

But this simple view seems to be a position that no respectable philosopher ever held. Bertrand Russell's explanation of the theory is more plausible. He claims that questions about values cannot be settled by science, and that disagreements about values are not disagreements about some matter of objective fact. They are disagreements about taste that cannot be objectively resolved any more than we can convince someone who hates oysters that they are good. This sounds more plausible, and it is not clear that Ewing has shown that there are objective ways of settling serious moral disputes, for example, about whether abortion is wrong or not. Such disputes seem to involve disagreements about basic moral values, and as such they have proven to be resistant to easy resolution. Perhaps such disagreements are an inevitable feature of the pluralistic society in which we live.

Plato
The Euthyphro

Plato (427–347 B.C.), along with his student Aristotle, dominates Western philosophy; indeed Western philosophy has been said to be a series of footnotes to Plato, since he discussed most of its important questions in his more than thirty dialogues.

SOCRATES: Then tell me, what do you say the holy is? And what is the unholy?

EUTHYPHRO: Well, I say that the holy is what I am doing now, prosecuting murder and temple theft and everything of the sort, whether father or mother or anyone else is guilty of it. And not prosecuting is unholy. Now, Socrates, examine the proof I give you that this is a dictate of divine law. I have offered it before to other people to show that it is established right not to let off someone guilty of impiety,

no matter who he happens to be. For these same people worship Zeus as the best and most righteous of the gods. They agree that he put his own father in bonds for unjustly swallowing his children; yes, and that that father had in his turn castrated his father for similar reasons. Yet me they are angry at for indicting my father for his injustice. So they contradict themselves; they say one thing about the gods and another about me.

SOCRATES: I wonder if this is why I am being prosecuted, Euthyphro, because when anyone says such things about the gods, I somehow find it difficult to accept? Perhaps this is why people claim I transgress. But as it is, if even you who know such things so well accept them, people like me must apparently concede. What indeed are we to say, we who ourselves agree that we know nothing of them. But in the name of Zeus, the God of Friendship, tell me: do you truly believe that these things happened so?

EUTHYPHRO: Yes, and things still more wonderful than these, Socrates, things the multitude does not know.

SOCRATES: Do you believe there is really war among the gods, and terrible enmities and battles, and other sorts of things our poets

The reading is from *The Dialogues of Plato*, vol. 1, trans. R. E. Allen (New Haven: Yale University Press, 1984), pp. 45–52. Copyright © 1984 by Yale University. Reprinted with permission.

tell, which embellish other things sacred to us through the work of our capable painters, but especially the robe covered with embroidery that is carried to the Acropolis at the Great Panathenaea? Are we, Euthyphro, to say those things are so?

EUTHYPHRO: Not only those, Socrates. As I just said, I shall explain many other things about religion to you if you wish, and you may rest assured that what you hear will amaze you.

SOCRATES: I should not be surprised. But explain them another time at your leisure; right now, try to answer more clearly the question I just asked. For, my friend, you did not sufficiently teach me before, when I asked you what the holy is; you said that the thing you are doing now is holy, prosecuting your father for murder.

EUTHYPHRO: Yes, and I told the truth, Socrates.

SOCRATES: Perhaps. But, Euthyphro, are there not many other things you say are holy too?

EUTHYPHRO: Of course there are.

SOCRATES: Do you recall that I did not ask you to teach me about some one or two of the many things which are holy, but about that characteristic itself by which all holy things are holy? For you agreed, I think, that it is by one character that unholy things are unholy and holy things holy. Or do you not recall?

EUTHYPHRO: I do.

SOCRATES: Then teach me what this very character is, so that I may look to it and use it as a standard by which, should those things which you or someone else may do be of that sort, I may affirm them to be holy, but should they not be of that sort, deny it.

EUTHYPHRO: Well if you wish it so, Socrates, I shall tell you.

SOCRATES: I do indeed wish it.

First Definition: The Holy, What Is Loved by the Gods (6e–8b)

EUTHYPHRO: Then what is dear to the gods is holy, and what is not dear to them is unholy.

SOCRATES: Excellent, Euthyphro. You have now answered as I asked. Whether correctly, I do not yet know—but clearly you will now go on to teach me in addition that what you say is true.

EUTHYPHRO: Of course.

SOCRATES: Come then, let us examine what it is we are saying. The thing and the person dear to the gods is holy; the thing and the person hateful to the gods is unholy; and the holy is not the same as the unholy, but its utter opposite. Is that what we are saying?

EUTHYPHRO: It is.

SOCRATES: Yes, and it appears to be well said?

EUTHYPHRO: I think so, Socrates.

SOCRATES: Now, Euthyphro, we also said, did we not, that the gods quarrel and disagree with one another and that there is enmity among them?

EUTHYPHRO: We did.

SOCRATES: But what is that disagreement which causes enmity and anger about, my friend? Look at it this way: If you and I disagreed about a question of number, about which of two sums is greater, would our disagreement cause us to become angry with each other and make us enemies? Or would we take to counting in a case like that, and quickly settle our dispute?

EUTHYPHRO: Of course we would.

SOCRATES: So too, if we disagreed about a question of the larger or smaller, we would take to measurement and put an end to our disagreement quickly?

EUTHYPHRO: True.

SOCRATES: And go to the balance, I imagine, to settle a dispute about heavier and lighter?

EUTHYPHRO: Certainly.

SOCRATES: But what sort of thing would make us enemies, angry at each other, if we disagree about it and are unable to arrive at a decision? Perhaps you cannot say offhand, but I suggest you consider whether it would not be the just and unjust, beautiful and ugly, good and evil. Are not these the things, when we disagree about them and cannot reach a satisfactory decision, concerning which we on occasion become enemies—you, and I, and all other men?

EUTHYPHRO: Yes, Socrates. This kind of disagreement has its source there.

SOCRATES: What about the gods, Euthyphro? If

they were to disagree, would they not disagree for the same reasons?

EUTHYPHRO: Necessarily.

SOCRATES: Then by your account, my noble friend, different gods must believe that different things are just—and beautiful and ugly, good and evil. For surely they would not quarrel unless they disagreed on this. True?

EUTHYPHRO: You are right.

SOCRATES: Now, what each of them believes to be beautiful and good and just they also love, and the opposites of those things they hate?

EUTHYPHRO;   Of course.

SOCRATES: Yes, but the same things, you say, are thought by some gods to be just and by others unjust. Those are the things concerning which disagreement causes them to quarrel and make war on one another. True?

EUTHYPHRO: Yes.

SOCRATES: Then the same things, it seems, are both hated by the gods and loved by the gods, and would be both dear to the gods and hateful to the gods.

EUTHYPHRO: It seems so.

SOCRATES: Then by this account, Euthyphro, the same things would be both holy and unholy.

EUTHYPHRO: I suppose so.

SOCRATES: Then you have not answered my question, my friend. I did not ask you what same thing happens to be both holy and unholy; yet what is dear to the gods is hateful to the gods, it seems. And so, Euthyphro, it would not be surprising if what you are now doing in punishing your father were dear to Zeus, but hateful to Cronos and Uranus, and loved by Hephaestus, but hateful to Hera, and if any of the other gods disagree about it, the same will be true of them too.

First Interlude (8b–9c)

EUTHYPHRO: But Socrates, surely none of the gods disagree about this, that he who kills another man unjustly should answer for it.

SOCRATES: Really, Euthyphro? Have you ever heard it argued among *men* that he who kills unjustly or does anything else unjustly should not answer for it?

EUTHYPHRO: Why, people never stop arguing things like that, especially in the law courts. They do a host of wrongs and then say and do everything to get off.

SOCRATES: Yes, but do they admit the wrong, Euthyphro, and admitting it, nevertheless claim they should not answer for it?

EUTHYPHRO: No, they certainly do not do that.

SOCRATES: Then they do not do and say everything: for they do not, I think, dare to contend or debate the point that if they in fact did wrong they should not answer for it. Rather, I think, they deny they did wrong. Well?

EUTHYPHRO: True.

SOCRATES: So they do not contend that those who do wrong should not answer for it, but rather, perhaps, about who it is that did the wrong, and what he did, and when.

EUTHYPHRO: True.

SOCRATES: Now is it not also the same with the gods, if as your account has it, they quarrel about what is just and unjust, and some claim that others do wrong and some deny it? Presumably no one, god or man, would dare to claim that he who does a wrong should not answer for it.

EUTHYPHRO: Yes, on the whole what you say is true, Socrates.

SOCRATES: But I imagine that those who disagree—both men and gods, if indeed the gods do disagree—disagree about particular things which have been done. They differ over given actions, some claiming they were done justly and others unjustly. True?

EUTHYPHRO: Certainly.

SOCRATES: Come now, my friend, teach me and make me wiser. Where is your proof that all gods believe that a man has been unjustly killed who was hired as a laborer, became a murderer, was bound by the master of the dead slave, and died of his bonds before the man who bound him could learn from the religious advisers what to do? Where is your proof that it is right for a son to indict and prosecute his father for murder in behalf of a man like that? Come, try to show me clearly that all the gods genuinely believe this action right. If you succeed, I shall praise you for your wisdom and never stop.

EUTHYPHRO: Well, I can certainly do it, Socrates, but it is perhaps not a small task.

SOCRATES: I see. You think I am harder to teach than the judges, for you will certainly make it clear to them that actions such as your father's are wrong, and that all the gods hate them.

EUTHYPHRO: Very clear indeed, Socrates, if they listen to what I say.

Second Definition: The Holy, What Is Loved by All the Gods (9c–11b)

SOCRATES: They will listen, if you seem to speak well. But here is something that occurred to me while you were talking. I asked myself, "If Euthyphro were to teach me beyond any question that all the gods believe a death of this sort wrong, what more have I learned from Euthyphro about what the holy and the unholy are? The death, it seems, would be hateful to the gods, but what is holy and what is proved just now not to be marked off by this, for what was hateful to the gods proved dear to the gods as well." So I let you off on that point, Euthyphro: if you wish, let all the gods believe your father's action wrong and let all of them hate it. But is this the correction we are now to make in your account, that what *all* the gods hate is unholy, and what *all* the gods love is holy, but what some love and some hate is neither or both? Do you mean for us now to mark off the holy and the unholy in that way?

EUTHYPHRO: What is to prevent it, Socrates?

SOCRATES: Nothing, at least as far as I am concerned, Euthyphro. But, examine your account to see whether if you assume this, you will most easily teach me what you promised.

EUTHYPHRO: But I would certainly say that the holy is what all the gods love, and that the opposite, what all the gods hate, is unholy.

SOCRATES: Well, Euthyphro, should we examine this in turn to see if it is true? Or should we let it go, accept it from ourselves or anyone else without more ado, and agree that a thing is so if only someone says it is? Or should we examine what a person means when he says something?

EUTHYPHRO: Of course. I believe, though, that this time what I say is true.

SOCRATES: Perhaps we shall learn better, my friend. For consider: is the holy loved by the gods because it is holy? Or is it holy because it is loved by the gods?

EUTHYPHRO: I do not know what you mean, Socrates.

SOCRATES: Then I will try to put it more clearly. We speak of carrying and being carried, of leading and being led, of seeing and being seen. And you understand in such cases, do you not, that they differ from each other, and how they differ?

EUTHYPHRO: I think I do.

SOCRATES: Now, is there such a thing as being loved, and is it different from loving?

EUTHYPHRO: Of course.

SOCRATES: Then tell me: if a thing is being carried, is it being carried because of the carrying, or for some other reason?

EUTHYPHRO: No, for that reason.

SOCRATES: And if a thing is being led, it is being led because of the leading? And if being seen, being seen because of the seeing?

EUTHYPHRO: Certainly.

SOCRATES: Then it is not because a thing is being seen that the seeing exists; on the contrary, it is because of the seeing that it is being seen. Nor is it because a thing is being led that the leading exists; it is because of the leading that it is being led. Nor is it because a thing is being carried that the carrying exists; it is because of the carrying that it is being carried. Is what I mean quite clear, Euthyphro? I mean this: if something comes to be or something is affected, it is not because it is a thing which is coming to be that the process of coming to be exists, but, because of the process of coming to be, it is a thing which is coming to be; and it is not because it is affected that the affecting exists, but because of the affecting, the thing is affected. Do you agree?

EUTHYPHRO: Yes.

SOCRATES: Now, what is being loved is either a thing coming to be something or a something affected by something.

EUTHYPHRO: Of course.

SOCRATES: And so it is as true here as it was before: it is not because a thing is being loved that there is loving by those who love it; it is because of the loving that it is being loved.

EUTHYPHRO: Necessarily.

SOCRATES: Then what are we to say about the holy, Euthyphro? Is it loved by all the gods, as your account has it?

EUTHYPHRO: Yes.

SOCRATES: Because it is holy? Or for some other reason?

EUTHYPHRO: No, for that reason.

SOCRATES: Then it is loved because it is holy, not holy because it is loved?

EUTHYPHRO: It seems so.

SOCRATES: Moreover, what is loved and dear to the gods is loved because of their loving.

EUTHYPHRO: Of course.

SOCRATES: Then what is dear to the gods is not [the same as] holy, Euthyphro, nor is the holy [the same as] dear to the gods, as you claim: the two are different.

EUTHYPHRO: But why, Socrates?

SOCRATES: Because we agreed that the holy is loved because it is holy, not holy because it is loved.

EUTHYPHRO: Yes.

SOCRATES: But what is dear to the gods is, because it is loved by the gods, dear to the gods by reason of this same loving; it is not loved because it is dear to the gods.

EUTHYPHRO: True.

SOCRATES: But if in fact what is dear to the gods and the holy were the same, my friend, then, if the holy were loved because it is holy, what is dear to the gods would be loved because it is dear to the gods; but if what is dear to the gods were dear to the gods because the gods love it, the holy would be holy because it is loved. But as it is, you see, the opposite is true, and the two are completely different. For the one (what is dear to the gods) is of the sort to be loved *because* it is loved; the other (the holy), because it is of the sort to be loved, *therefore* is loved. It would seem, Euthyphro, that when you asked what the holy is, you did not mean to make its nature and reality clear to me; you mentioned a mere affection of it—the holy has been so affected as to be loved by all the gods. But what it really is, you have not yet said. So if you please, Euthyphro, do not conceal things from me: start again from the beginning and tell me what sort of thing the holy is. We will not quarrel over whether it is loved by the gods, or whether it is affected in other ways. Tell me in earnest: what is the holy and unholy?

EUTHYPHRO: But, Socrates, I do not know how to tell you what I mean. Somehow everything I propose goes round in circles on us and will not stand still.

Questions on Plato

1. Carefully explain why each of Euthyphro's attempts to define piety is defective.

2. In Genesis 22 of the Bible we find the story of God's testing of Abraham's faith by commanding him to kill his only son Isaac. God says to Abraham, "Take now thy son, thine only son Isaac, whom you lovest, and get thee into the land of Moriah; and offer him there for a burnt offering upon one of the mountains I will tell thee of." Let us assume that this really is God's command to Abraham. Should he obey or not? Explain and defend your answer.

Peter Geach

The Moral Law and the Law of God

For biographical information on Geach, see the reading in chapter 6.

In modern ethical treatises we find hardly any mention of God; and the idea that if there really is a God, his commandments might be morally relevant is wont to be dismissed by a short and simple argument that is generally regarded as irrefutable. 'If what God commands *is not* right, then the fact of his commanding it is no moral reason for obedience, though it may in that case be dangerous to disobey. And if what God commands *is* right, even so it is not God's commanding it that makes it right; on the contrary, God as a moral being would command only what was right apart from his commanding it. So God has no essential place in the foundations of morals.'

The use of this argument is not confined to a recent or narrowly local school of philosophers; it was used by the British Idealists when they dominated British philosophy, and, as we shall see, it was used much earlier than that. Nor is its use confined to people who do not believe in God; on the occasion when I attacked the argument, my chief opponents were not atheists but professing Christians. This is not surprising; for the argument was used by Christians of an earlier generation, the Cambridge Platonists, as a stick to beat that dreadful man Hobbes with. (I shall have more to say about Hobbes later on.) And they in turn got the argument from Plato's *Euthyphro*.

Let me summarize that dialogue. Euthyphro and Socrates are discussing the trial in which Euthyphro's father had tied up a peasant who killed another peasant in a drunken brawl, notified the authorities, thrown the prisoner into a ditch, and put the matter out of his mind; meanwhile the prisoner died of hunger and cold. Euthyphro (Mr. Right-mind, as Bunyan might have called him) feared lest the gods might punish him if he sat at meat with a man who had done such a deed, unless he set matters right by prosecuting the offender. He must have known that this would be an ineffectual gesture; the old-fashioned Homeric idea that Zeus will punish men for callous insolence to the poor was not going to impress the Athenian court.

Socrates (that is, I presume, Plato) finds it outrageous that a man prosecutes his own father over the death of a no-good peasant (he reiterates this term *'thēs'* to rub it in how little the man's death mattered) and he tries to dissuade Euthyphro by tricky arguments, in a style much admired and imitated by modern moral philosophers. Euthyphro is easily tied in knots by asking him whether pious deeds are pious because they please the gods, or please the gods because they are pious deeds; whether men ever disagree except about moral matters, for which there is no decision procedure like arithmetical calculation or physical measurements; and so on. But Mr. Right-mind is not convinced; again and again he cuts himself loose from these dialectical knots with the assertion that it doesn't matter who was the murderer and what relation he was to the prosecutor and whether the victim was a peasant, but only whether a man was foully done to death in a way that all the gods must hate. The dialogue ends with Euthyphro telling Socrates he has no more time for discussion and going off on his legal business.

Was this, as the received view represents, a victory for Socrates? Or was it a victory for simple piety over sophistical tricks? Euthyphro admittedly had one weak point: he believed in many gods who were sometimes at variance with one another and so might command different things. But this is irrelevant for our purposes; for Euthyphro's unswerving fidelity to the divine law would be no less objectionable to modern moral philosophers if he had believed in one God. The main issue is whether a man's moral code ought to be influenced in this way by beliefs about Divine commands.

The reading is from Peter Geach, *God and the Soul* (London: Routledge & Kegan Paul Ltd., 1969), pp. 117–129. Reprinted with permission.

In the first place, I want to reject a view—which some Christians have at least approached—that all our appraisals of good and bad logically depend on knowledge of God. To get a clear and indisputable example I shall take a bad sort of act. For there is a logical asymmetry between good and bad acts: an act is good only if everything about it is good, but may be bad if *anything* about it is bad; so it might be risky to say we knew an act to be good *sans phrase,* rather than to have some good features. But there is no such risk in saying that we know certain kinds of act to be bad. Lying, for example, is bad, and we all know this; giving a man the lie is a deadly insult the world over.

If a philosopher says he doubts whether there is anything objectionable in the practice of lying, he is not to be heard. Perhaps he is not sincere in what he says; perhaps his understanding is debauched by wickedness; perhaps, as often happens to philosophers, he has been deluded by a fallacious argument into denying what he really knows to be the case. Anyhow, it does not lie in his mouth to say that here I am abandoning argument for abuse; there is something logically incongruous, to use Newman's phrase, if we take the word of a Professor of Lying that he does not lie. Let me emphasize that I am not saying a sane and honest man must think one should *never* lie; but I say that, even if he thinks lying is sometimes a necessary evil, a sane and honest man must think it an evil.

Now it is logically impossible that our knowledge that lying is bad should depend on revelation. For obviously a revelation from a deity whose 'goodness' did not include any objection to lying would be worthless; and indeed, so far from getting our knowledge that lying is bad from revelation, we may use this knowledge to test alleged revelations. Xenophanes rejected traditional Greek religious beliefs because the gods were represented as liars and cheats; and (if Browning could be trusted) it would be a fatal objection to the claims of the Druses' Messiah Hakim that he commanded his followers to lie about their religion under persecution. It is not that it would be too dreadful to believe in mendacious deities; a revelation destroys its own credibility if it is admitted to come from deities or from a prophet who may lie. We know

lying to be bad before needing to examine any alleged revelation. Sir Arnold Lunn has jeered at unbelievers for esteeming truthfulness apart from any supernatural hopes or fears, and has quoted with approval a remark of Belloc that one can't be loyal to an abstraction like truth; a pagan Greek would have retorted that Lunn and Belloc were *akolastoi,* incorrigibly wicked, if they could not see directly the badness of lying.

The knowledge of God is thus *not* prerequisite to our having *any* moral knowledge. I shall argue however that we do need it in order to see that we must not do evil that good may come, and that this principle actually follows from a certain conception of God. If I can make this out, the sophistry from which I started will have been completely refuted; for accepting or rejecting this principle makes an enormous difference to one's moral code.

I must first clear up an ambiguity in the phase 'doing evil that good may come'. We cannot ask whether e.g. Caesar's death was a good or bad *thing to happen;* there are *various* titles under which it may be called good or bad. One might very well say e.g. that a violent death was a bad *thing to happen to a living organism* but a good *thing to happen to a man who claimed divine worship,* and this would again leave it open whether doing Caesar to death was a good or bad *thing to do* for Brutus and the rest. Now when I speak of 'not doing evil that good may come', what I mean is that certain sorts of act are such *bad things to do* that they must never be done to secure any good or avoid any evil. For A to kill a man or cut off his arm is not necessarily a *bad thing to do,* though it is necessarily bad that such a thing should happen to a living organism. Only by a fallacy of equivocation can people argue that if you accept the principle of not doing evil that good may come, then you must be against capital punishment and surgical operations.

Suppose that A and B are agreed that adultery is a bad sort of behaviour, but that A accepts the principle of not doing evil that good may come, whereas B rejects it. Then in A's moral deliberations adultery is simply out: as Aristotle said, there can be no deliberating when and how and with whom to commit it.... For B, on the other hand, the *prima facie* objection to adultery is defeasible, and in some circumstances he may decide: Here and how adultery is the best thing. Similarly, Sir David Ross holds that the objection to punishing the innocent, viz. that then we are not 'respecting the rights of those who have respected the rights of others', is only a *prima facie* objection; in the general interest it may have to be over-ruled, 'that the whole nation perish not'—a Scripture quotation that we may hope Sir David made without remembering who was speciously justifying whose judicial murder.

It is psychologically possible to hold the principle of not doing evil that good may come independently of any belief in Divine com-mandments: I have already cited the example of Aristotle on adultery. We have to see whether this is also logically consistent.

We must first settle what sort of answer is relevant if a man asks 'Why shouldn't I commit adultery?'; only then can we see what reason against, if any, is decisive. One obviously rele-vant sort of reply to a question 'Why shouldn't I?' is an appeal to something the questioner wants, and cannot get if he does so-and-so. I maintain that only such a reply is relevant and rational. In post-Kantian moral theory another sort of reply has been offered as relevant—an appeal not to an agent's Inclinations but to his Sense of Duty. Now indeed you can so train a man that 'You *must* not', said in a peculiar man-ner, strikes him as a sufficient answer to 'Why shouldn't I?'; he may feel a peculiar awe at hear-ing this from others, or even on saying it him-self; it may even be part of the training to make him think he *must* not ask why he *must* not. (Cf. Lewis Carroll's juvenile poem 'My Fairy'.) The result of such training is what people like Sir David Ross call 'apprehending obligation'. When I speak of the Sense of Duty (in capitals) I shall always be referring to this notion.

Now, as we know, a totalitarian regime can make a man 'apprehend' all sorts of things as his 'obligations', if Providence does not specially protect him. But on the Sense of Duty theory a man so trained is admirable if he does what he thinks he *must* do, regardless of the nature and quality of his acts; for is he not acting from the highest of motives, the Sense of Duty? If a young Nazi machine-guns a column of refugees

till he bleeds to death, instead of retiring for medical treatment, is not his Sense of Duty something to fill us with awe?

To myself, it seems clear that although '*You mustn't*' said in this peculiar way may psycholog-ically work as a final answer to 'Why shouldn't I?', it is no rational answer at all. This Sense of Duty, as Bradley said (*Appearance and Reality,* c. 25) 'is empty self-will and self-assurance, which swollen with private sentiment or chance de-sire, wears the mask of goodness. And hence that which professes itself moral would be the same as mere badness, if it did not differ, even for the worse, by the addition of hypocrisy. We may note here that our country, the chosen home of Moral Philosophy, has the reputation abroad of being the chief home of hypocrisy and cant.'

Let us forget about the Sense of Duty, for I think it can be shown that an action's being a good or bad thing for a human being to do is of itself a fact calculated to touch an agent's incli-nations. I shall here appropriate the powerful arguments, in the spirit of Aristotle, recently developed by Mrs. Philippa Foot. Moral virtues, she argues, are habits of action and avoidance; and they are such as a man cannot rationally choose to go without, any more than he can ra-tionally choose to be blind, paralytic, or stupid; to choose to lack a virtue would be to choose a maimed life, ill-adapted to this difficult and dangerous world. But if you opt for virtue, you opt for being the sort of man who *needs* to act virtuously (just as if you choose to take up smok-ing you opt to be the kind of man who *needs* to smoke); moreover, you cannot decide at the outset to act virtuously only when it is not too awkward or dangerous or unpleasant—that is deciding not to have the habit of virtue at all. If, for example, you opt for courage, you may per-ish through facing danger a coward would have shirked; but our world is such that it is not even safe not to be brave—as Horace said, death pursues after cowards too. And if you opt for chastity, then you opt to become the sort of per-son who *needs* to be chaste; and then for you, as Aristotle said, there can be no deliberating when and with whom to commit adultery; adul-tery is out.

But somebody might very well admit that

not only is there something bad about certain acts, but also it is desirable to become the sort of person who needs to act in the contrary way; and yet *not* admit that such acts are to be avoided in all circumstances and at any price. To be sure, a virtuous person cannot be ready in advance to do such acts; and if he does do them they will damage his virtuous habits and perhaps irreparably wreck his hard-won integrity of soul. But at this point someone may protest 'Are you the only person to be considered? Suppose the price of your precious integrity is a most fearful disaster! Haven't you got a hand to burn for your country (or mankind) and your friends?". This sort of appeal has not, I think, been adequately answered on Aristotelian lines, either by Aristotle or by Mrs. Foot.

It is just at this point, I think, that the law of God becomes relevant. I shall not argue as to the truth of the theological propositions I shall use in the following discussion; my aim in this essay is to show that *if* a man accepts them he may rationally have quite a different code from someone who does not. And the propositions I shall use all belong to natural theology; in Hobbes's language, I am considering only 'the Kingdom of God by Nature'.

If God and man are voluntary agents, it is reasonable to believe that God will not only direct men to his own ends willy-nilly like the irrational creatures, but will govern them by command and counsel. The question is then whether God has given laws to man which forbid whole classes of actions, as human laws do. There appear strong reasons for doubting whether God's commands could be like this.

Laws have to be framed in broad general terms because the foresight of legislation is limited, and because the laws would be unmanageably complicated if the legislators even tried to bring in all the contingencies they could themselves foresee; nor can there be somebody always at every man's elbow to give him commands suiting the particular contingency. But God is subject to none of these human limitations; so is it not a grossly anthropomorphic view of God to imagine him legislating in general terms because hard cases make bad law?

It is not a question, I reply, of God's knowledge and power, but of man's. Man's reason can readily discern that certain practices, like lying, infanticide, and adultery, are generally undesirable, even to the point that it is generally desirable that men should not *think* of resorting to them. But what man is competent judge in his own cause, to make exception in a particular case? Even apart from bias, our knowledge of the present relevant circumstances is grossly fallible; still more, our foresight of the future. Some men, like Dr. Buchman's disciples, have claimed to have Divine guidance in all conjunctures of life; but such claims are open to doubt, and certainly most men are not thus favored. So unless the rational knowledge that these practices are *generally undesirable* is itself a promulgation of the Divine law *absolutely forbidding* such practices, God has left most men without any promulgation of commands to them on these matters at all; which, on the theological premises I am assuming, is absurd.

The rational recognition that a practice is generally undesirable and that it is best for people on the whole not even to think of resorting to it is thus *in fact* a promulgation to a man of the Divine law forbidding the practice, even if he does not realize that this is a promulgation of the Divine law, even if he does not believe there is a God.

This is not a paradox. You have had a city's parking regulation promulgated to you by a No Parking notice, even if you are under the illusion that you may ignore the notice and think it has been put up by a neighbour who dislikes cars. And similarly anyone who can see the general objectionableness of lying and adultery has had God's law against such actions promulgated to him, even if he does not recognize it as God's law.

This means that the Divine law is in some instances promulgated to all men of sound understanding. No man can sincerely plead ignorance that lying, for example, is generally objectionable. I am *not* saying that a sane and honest man must see that lying is *absolutely excluded;* but he must have some knowledge of the *general objectionableness* of lying, and this is in fact a promulgation to him of the Divine law against lying. And he can advance from this knowledge to recognition of the Divine law as such, by a purely rational process.

To make this point clearer, let us consider a modern ethical philosopher who says 'I do on the whole object to lying, but this is just a practical attitude I take up—it is quite wrong to call it "knowledge"'. I do *not* say of him what I should of a man who professed to have no special objection to lying: that he is just a vicious fellow, or a fool talking at random, who deserves no answer. What I do say is that his very protest shows that he does possess the sort of knowledge which is in fact God's promulgation of a law to him. His erroneous philosophy will not allow him to call it knowledge; but that does not prevent it from *being* knowledge—philosophers in fact know many things that their own theories would preclude them from knowing. And since he has this knowledge, he has had God's law against lying promulgated to him, even if he does not believe in God.

Thus, whatever a man may think, his rational knowledge that it is a bad way of life for a man to be a liar or an adulterer is in fact a promulgation to him of the Divine law; and he is able to infer that it is such a promulgation if he rightly considers the matter. As Hobbes said:

These dictates of reason men use to call by the name of laws, but improperly: for they are but conclusions or theorems concerning what conduceth to the conservation and defense of themselves: whereas law, properly, is the word of him that by right hath command over others. But yet if we consider the same theorems as delivered in the word of God that by right commandeth over all things, then are they properly called laws.

There is a current malicious interpretation of Hobbes on which 'the word of God' would mean whatever the sovereign chooses to decree to be canonical Scripture. High-minded people are prepared to talk about Hobbes with reckless disregard of the truth: the late Lord Lindsay, in his Preface to the Everyman *Leviathan,* perpetrated a horrid mangling of Hobbes' text, giving the false text an air of authenticity by the use of antique spelling.[1] But what Hobbes himself says elsewhere is: 'God declareth his laws by the dictates of natural reason.' As an historical footnote I add that a very similar line of reasoning is to be found in Berkeley's youthful sermon on Passive Obedience. The debt Berkeley owes

to Hobbes is quite obvious: but no doubt a clergyman could hardly cite such an authority explicitly without destroying the edifying effect of his discourse.

But what if somebody asks 'Why should I obey God's Law?' This is really an insane question. For Prometheus to defy Zeus made sense because Zeus had not made Prometheus and had only limited power over him. A defiance of an Almighty God is insane: it is like trying to cheat a man to whom your whole business is mortgaged and who you know is well aware of your attempts to cheat him, or again, as the prophet said, it is as if a stick tried to beat, or an axe to cut, the very hand that was wielding it. Nebuchadnezzar had it forced on his attention that only by God's favour did his wits hold together from one end of a blasphemous sentence to another—and so he saw that there was nothing for him but to bless and glorify the King of Heaven, who is able to abase those who walk in pride. To quote Hobbes again 'God is King, though the nations be angry: and he that sitteth upon the cherubim, though the earth be moved. Whether men will or no they must be subject always to the Divine power. By denying the existence or Providence of God, men may shake off their ease, but not their yoke.'

This reasoning will not convince everybody; people may still *say* that it makes sense, given that there is a God, to defy him; but this is so only because, as Prichard said, you can no more make a man think than you can make a horse drink. A moral philosopher once said to me: 'I don't think I am morally obliged to obey God unless God is good: and surely it is a synthetic proposition that God is good.' I naturally asked him how he understood the proposition that God is good; he replied 'Well, I have no considered view how it should be analyzed; but provisionally I'd say it meant something like this: God is the sort of God whom I'd choose to be God if it were up to me to make the choice.' I fear he has never understood why I found the answer funny.

I shall be told by such philosophers that since I am saying not: It is your supreme moral duty to obey God, but simply: It is insane to set about defying an Almighty God, my attitude is plain power-worship. So it is: but it is worship of the Supreme power, and as such is wholly different from, and does not carry with it, a cringing attitude towards earthly powers. An earthly potentate does not compete with God, even unsuccessfully: he may threaten all manner of afflictions, but only from God's hands can any affliction actually come upon us. If we fully realize this, we shall have such fear of God as destroys all earthly fear: 'I will show you whom you shall fear', said Jesus Christ to his disciples.

'But now you are letting your view of the facts distort your values.' I am not sure whether this piece of claptrap is meant as moral reprobation or as a logical objection; either way, there is nothing in it. Civilized men know that sexual intercourse is liable to result in childbearing; they naturally have quite different sexual morals, one way or another, from savages who do not know this. And they are logically justified in evaluating sexual intercourse differently; for they have a different view of what sort of act it is. Now for those who believe in Almighty God, a man's every act is an act either of obeying or of ignoring or of defying that God; so naturally and logically they have quite different standards from unbelievers—they take a different view as to what people are in fact doing.

'But suppose circumstances are such that observance of one Divine law, say the law against lying, involves breach of some other absolute Divine prohibition?'—If God is rational, he does not command the impossible; if God governs all events by his Providence, he can see to it that circumstances in which a man is inculpably faced by a choice between forbidden acts do not occur. Of course such circumstances (with the clause 'and there is no way out' written into their description) are consistently describable; but God's Providence could ensure that they do not in fact arise. Contrary to what unbelievers often say, belief in the existence of God does make a difference to what one expects to happen.

Let us then return to our friend, Euthyphro. Euthyphro regarded his father's act of leaving a poor man to die forgotten in a ditch as not just *prima facie* objectionable, but as something *forbidden* by the gods who live for

ever; and he was horribly afraid for himself if he went on living with the offender as if nothing had happened. He did well to be afraid, the fear of God is the beginning of wisdom. To be sure, it is not all of wisdom.

The fear of God of which I have spoken is such fear as restrains even the wish to disobey him; not merely servile fear, which restrains the outward act, but leaves behind the wish 'If only I could do it and get away with it!' And, as is proper in a paper of this kind, I have confined myself to what Hobbes called the Kingdom of God by Nature. It is no part of our merely natural knowledge of God that we can boldly call God our Father and serve him in filial love: we are his children, if we are, purely by his free gift of the Spirit of adoption, and not by birthright: and the fear of God for his power irresistible is at least the *beginning* of wisdom—without it there is only pitiable folly. I agree, indeed, with Hobbes that gratitude for God's benefits would not be a sufficient ground for unreserved obedience if it were severed from fear of God's irresistible power.

That fear is an ultimate suasion. We cannot balance against our obedience to God some good to be gained, or evil to be avoided, by disobedience. For such good or evil could in fact come to us only in the order of God's Providence; we cannot secure good or avoid evil, either for ourselves or for others, in God's despite and by disobedience. And neither reason nor revelation warrants the idea that God is at all likely to be lenient with those who presumptuously disobey his law because of the way they have worked out the respective consequence of obedience and disobedience. Eleazer the scribe (2 Maccabees 6), with only Sheol to look forward to when he died, chose rather to go there by martyrdom—*praemitti se velle in infernum*—than to break God's law. 'Yet should I not escape the hand of the Almighty, neither alive nor dead.'

The wicked can for the moment use God's creation in defiance of God's commandments. But this is a sort of miracle or mystery; as St. Paul said, God has made the creature subject to vanity against its will. It is reasonable to expect, if the world's whole *raison d'être* is to effect God's good pleasure, that the very natural agents and operations of the world should be such as to frustrate and enrage and torment those who set their wills against God's. If things are not at present like this, that is only a gratuitous mercy, on whose continuance the sinner has no reason to count. 'The world shall fight with him against the unwise. . . . Yea, a mighty wind shall stand up against them, and like a storm shall blow them away.'

Notes

1. p. xvi of Everyman edition. Lindsay's version confounds Law and Right of Nature; which Hobbes emphatically distinguishes in the very passage (c. 14 *ad init.*) that Lindsay claims to be quoting!

Questions on Geach

1. What argument is used to show that God's commands are not the foundation of morality? This is not so easy, but see if you can figure out what Geach's reply to this argument is. Is his reply, as you understand it, successful? Has he really refuted the famous objection in the Euthyphro?

2. How does Geach conceive of God's laws? Do you agree that they are not like human laws that forbid whole classes of action? Why or why not? Can you have God's laws given to you and not recognize them as such? Defend your answer.

3. "But why should I obey God's law in the first place?" How does Geach answer this objection? Do you think he has a good answer?

John Arthur
Morality Without God

John Arthur teaches philosophy at Tennessee State University.

The issue which I address in this paper is the nature of the connection, if any, between morality and religion. I will argue that although there are a variety of ways the two could be connected, in fact morality is independent of religion, both logically and psychologically. First, however, it will be necessary to say something about the subjects: just what are we referring to when we speak of morality and of religion?

A useful way to approach the first question—the nature of morality—is to ask what it would mean for a society to exist without a moral code. What would such a society look like? How would people think? And behave? The most obvious thing to say is that its mem-

bers would never feel any moral responsibilities or any guilt. Words like duty, rights, fairness, and justice would never be used, except in the legal sense. Feelings such as that I ought to remember my parents' anniversary, that he has a moral responsibility to help care for his children after the divorce, that she has a right to equal pay for equal work, and that discrimination on the basis of race is unfair would be absent in such a society. In short, people would have no tendency to evaluate or criticize the behavior of others, nor to feel remorse about their own behavior. Children would not be taught to be ashamed when they steal or hurt others, nor would they be allowed to complain when others treat them badly.

Such a society lacks a moral code. What, then, of religion? Is it possible that a society such as the one I have described would have religious beliefs? It seems clear that it is possible. Suppose every day these same people file into their place of worship to pay homage to God (they may believe in many gods or in one all-powerful creator of heaven and earth). Often they can be heard praying to God for help in dealing with their problems and thanking Him for their good fortune. Whenever a disaster befalls them, the people assume that God is angry with them; when things go well they believe He

John Arthur, "Morality Without God," in *Morality and Moral Controversies*, John Arthur—Editor, 2/E, © 1986, pp. 10–15. Reprinted by permission of Prentice-Hall, Inc., Englewood Cliffs, NJ.

is pleased. Frequently they give sacrifices to God, usually in the form of money spent to build beautiful temples and churches.

To have a moral code, then, is to tend to evaluate (perhaps without even expressing it) the behavior of others and to feel guilt at certain actions when we perform them. Religion, on the other hand, involves beliefs in supernatural power(s) that created and perhaps also control nature, along with the tendency to worship and pray to those supernatural forces or beings. The two—religion and morality—are thus very different. One involves our attitudes toward various forms of behavior (lying and killing, for example), typically expressed using the notions of rules, rights, and obligations. The other, religion, typically involves a different set of activities (prayer, worship) together with beliefs about the supernatural.

We come, then, to the central question: What is the connection, if any, between a society's moral code and its religious beliefs? Many people have felt that there must be a link of some sort between religious beliefs and morality. But is that so? What sort of connection might there be? In what follows I distinguish various ways in which one might claim that religion is necessary for a moral code to function in society. I argue, however, that such connections are not necessary, and indeed that often religion is detrimental to society's attempt to encourage moral conduct among its members.

One possible role which religion might play in morality relates to motives people have. Can people be expected to behave in any sort of decent way towards one another without religious faith? Religion, it is often said, is necessary so that people will DO right. Why might somebody think that? Often, we know, doing what is right has costs: you don't cheat on the test, so you flunk the course; you return the lost billfold, so you don't get the contents. Religion can provide motivation to do the right thing. God rewards those who follow His commands by providing for them a place in heaven and by insuring that they prosper and are happy on earth. He also punishes with damnation those who disobey. Other people emphasize less selfish ways in which religious motives may encour-

age people to act rightly. God is the creator of the universe and has ordained that His plan should be followed. How better to live one's life than to participate in this divinely ordained plan? Only by living a moral life, it is said, can people live in harmony with the larger, divinely created order.

But how are we to assess the relative strength of these various motives for acting morally, some of which are religious, others not? How important is the fear of hell or the desire to live as God wishes in motivating people? Think about the last time you were tempted to do something you knew to be wrong. Surely your decision not to do so (if that was your decision) was made for a variety of reasons: "What if I get caught? What if somebody sees me—what will he or she think? How will I feel afterwards? Will I regret it?" Or maybe the thought of cheating just doesn't occur to you. You were raised to be an honest person, and that's what you want to be—period. There are thus many motives for doing the right thing which have nothing whatsoever to do with religion. Most of us in fact do worry about getting caught, about being blamed and looked down on by others. We also may do what is right just for that reason, because it's our duty, or because we don't want to hurt others. So to say that we need religion to act morally is mistaken; indeed it seems to me that most of us, when it really gets down to it, don't give much of a thought to religion when making moral decisions. All those other reasons are the ones which we tend to consider, or else we just don't consider cheating and stealing at all. So far, then, there seems to be no reason to suppose that people can't be moral yet irreligious at the same time.

Another oft-heard argument that religion is necessary for people to do the right questions whether people would know how to do the right thing without the guidance of religion. In other words, however much people may *want* to do the right thing, it is only with the help of God that true moral understanding can be achieved. People's own intellect is simply inadequate to this task; we must consult revelation for help.

Again, however, this argument fails. Just consider what we would need to know in order for religion to provide moral guidance. First we must be sure that there is a God. And then there's the question of which of the many religions is true. How can anybody be sure his or her religion is the right one? After all, if you have been born in China or India or Iran your religious views would almost certainly not have been the ones you now hold. And even if we can somehow convince ourselves that the Judeo-Christian God is the real one, we still need to find out just what it is He wants us to do. Revelation comes in at least two forms, according to theists, and not even Christians agree which form is real. Some hold that God tells us what he wants by providing us with His words: the Ten Commandments are an example. Many even believe, as Billy Graham once said, that the entire *Bible* was written by God using 39 secretaries. Others doubt that every word of the *Bible* is literally true, believing instead that it is merely an historical account of the *events* in history whereby God revealed Himself. So on this view revelation is not understood as statements made by God but, instead, as His intervening into historical events, such as leading His people from Egypt, testing Job, and sending His son as an example of the ideal life. But if we are to use revelation as a guide we must know what is to count as revelation—words given us by God, events, or both? Supposing that we could somehow solve all those puzzles, the problems of relying on revelation are still not over. Even if we can agree on who God is and on how and when He reveals Himself, we still must interpret that revelation. Some feel that the *Bible* justifies various forms of killing, including war and capital punishment, on the basis of such statements as "An eye for an eye." Others, emphasizing such sayings as "Judge not lest ye be judged" and "Thou shalt not kill," believe the *Bible* demands absolute pacifism. How are we to know which interpretation is correct?

Far from providing a short-cut to moral understanding, looking to revelation for guidance just creates more questions and problems. It is much simpler to address problems such as abortion, capital punishment, and war directly than to seek answers in revelation. In fact, not only is religion unnecessary to provide moral understanding, it is actually a hindrance. (My own hunch is that often those who are most likely to appeal to Scripture as justification for their moral beliefs are really just rationalizing positions they already believe.)

Far from religion being necessary to people to do the right thing, it often gets in the way. People do not need the motivation of religion; they for the most part are not motivated by religion as much as by other factors; and religion is of no help in discovering what our moral obligations are. But others give a different reason for claiming morality depends on religion. They think religion, and especially God, is necessary for morality because without God there could BE no right or wrong. The idea was expressed by Bishop R. C. Mortimer: "God made us and all the world. Because of that He has an absolute claim on our obedience. . . . From [this] it follows that a thing is not right simply because we think it is. . . . It is right because God commands it."[1]

What Mortimer has in mind can best be seen by comparing moral rules with legal ones. Legal statutes, we know, are created by legislatures. So if there had been no law passed requiring that people limit the speed they travel then there would be no such legal obligation. Without the commands of the legislature statutes simply would not exist. The view defended by Mortimer, often called the divine command theory, is that God has the same relation to moral law as the legislature does to statutes. Without God's commands there would be no moral rules.

Another tenet of the divine command theory, besides the belief that God is the author of morality, is that only the divine command theory is able to explain the objective difference between right and wrong. This point was forcefully argued by F. C. Copleston in a 1948 British Broadcasting Corporation radio debate with Bertrand Russell.

RUSSELL: But aren't you now saying in effect "I mean by God whatever is good or the sum total of what is good—the system of what is good, and, therefore, when a young man loves anything that is good he is loving God." Is that what you're saying, because if so, it wants a bit of arguing.

COPLESTON: I don't say, of course, that God is the sum total or system of what is good... but I do think that all goodness reflects God in some way and proceeds from Him, so that in a sense the man who loves what is truly good, loves God even if he doesn't avert to God. But still I agree that the validity of such an interpretation of man's conduct depends on the recognition of God's existence, obviously.... Let's take a look at the Commandant of the [Nazi] concentration camp at Belsen. That appears to you as undesirable and evil and to me too. To Adolph Hitler we suppose it appeared as something good and desirable. I suppose you'd have to admit that for Hitler it was good and for you it is evil.

RUSSELL: No, I shouldn't go so far as that. I mean, I think people can make mistakes in that as they can in other things. If you have jaundice you see things yellow that are not yellow. You're making a mistake.

COPLESTON: Yes, one can make mistakes, but can you make a mistake if it's simply a question of reference to a feeling or emotion? Surely Hitler would be the only possible judge of what appealed to his emotions.

RUSSELL: ...you can say various things about that; among others, that if that sort of thing makes that sort of appeal to Hitler's emotions, then Hitler makes quite a different appeal to my emotions.

COPLESTON: Granted. But there's no objective criterion outside feeling then for condemning the conduct of the Commandant of Belsen, in your view.... The human being's idea of the content of the moral law depends certainly to a large extent on education and environment, and a man has to use his reason in assessing the validity of the actual moral ideas of his social group. But the possibility of criticizing the accepted moral code presupposes that there is an objective standard, that there is an ideal moral order, which imposes itself.... It implies the existence of a real foundation of God.[2]

God, according to Copleston, is able to provide the basis for the distinction, which we all know to exist, between right and wrong. With-

out that obligation we would have no real reason for condemning the behavior of anybody, even Nazis. Morality would be little more than an expression of personal feeling.

Before assessing the divine command theory, let's first consider this last point. Is it really true that only the commands of God can provide an objective basis for moral judgements? Certainly many philosophers... have felt that morality rests on its own, perfectly sound footing; to prejudge those efforts or others which may be made in the future as unsuccessful seems mistaken. And, second, if it were true that there is no nonreligious basis for claiming moral objectivity, then perhaps that means there simply is no such basis. Why suppose that there *must* be such a foundation?

What of the divine command theory itself? Is it reasonable, even though we need not do so, to equate something's being right with its being commanded by God? Certainly the expressions "is commanded by God" and "is morally required" do not *mean* the same thing; atheists and agnostics use moral words without understanding them to make any reference to God. And while it is of course true that God (or any other moral being for that matter) would tend to want others to do the right thing, this hardly shows that being right and being commanded by God are the same thing. Parents want their children to do the right thing, too, but that doesn't mean they, or anybody else, can make a thing right just by commanding it!

I think that, in fact, theists themselves if they thought about it would reject the divine command theory. One reason is because of what it implies. Suppose we grant (just for the sake of argument) that the divine command theory is correct. Notice what we have now said: Actions are right just because they are commanded by God. And the same, of course, can be said about those deeds which we believe are wrong. If God hadn't commanded us not to do them, they would not be wrong. (Recall the comparison made with the commands of the legislature, which would not be a law except for the legislature having passed a statute.)

But now notice this. Since God is all-powerful, and since right is determined solely by His commands, is it not possible that He might change the rules and make what we now think of as wrong into right? It would seem that according to the divine command theory it is possible that tomorrow God will decree that virtues such as kindness and courage have become vices while actions which show cruelty and cowardice are the right actions. Rather than it being right for people to help each other out and prevent innocent people from suffering unnecessarily, it would be right to create as much pain among innocent children as we possibly can! To adopt the divine command theory commits its advocate to the seemingly absurd position that even the greatest atrocities might be not only acceptable but morally required if God were to command them.

Plato made a similar point in the dialogue *Euthyphro*. Socrates is asking Euthyphro what it is that makes the virtue of holiness a virtue, just as we have been asking what makes kindness and courage virtues. Euthyphro has suggested that holiness is just whatever all the gods love.

SOCRATES: Well, then, Euthyphro, what do we say about holiness? Is it not loved by all the gods, according to your definition?

EUTHYPHRO: Yes.

SOCRATES: Because it is holy, or for some other reason?

EUTHYPHRO: No, because it is holy.

SOCRATES: Then it is loved by the gods because it is holy: it is not holy because it is loved by them?

EUTHYPHRO: It seems so.

SOCRATES: . . . Then holiness is not what is pleasing to the gods, and what is pleasing to the gods is not holy as you say, Euthyphro. They are different things.

EUTHYPHRO: And why, Socrates?

SOCRATES: Because we are agreed that the gods love holiness because it is holy; and that it is not holy because they love it.[3]

Having claimed that virtues are what is loved by the gods why does Euthyphro so readily agree that the gods love holiness *because* it's holy? One possibility is that he is assuming whenever the gods love something they do so with good reason, not just arbitrarily. If something is pleasing to gods, there must be a reason. To deny this and say that it is simply the gods' love which makes holiness a virtue would mean that the gods have no basis for their opinions, that they are arbitrary. Or to put it another way, if we say that it is simply God's loving something that makes it right, then what sense does it make to say God wants us to do right? All that could mean is that God wants us to do what He wants us to do. He would have no reason for wanting it. Similarly "God is good" would mean little more than "God does what He pleases." Religious people who find this an unacceptable consequence will reject the divine command theory.

But doesn't this now raise another problem? If God approves kindness because it is a virtue, then it seems that God discovers morality rather than inventing it. And haven't we then suggested a limitation on God's power, since He now, being a good God, must love kindness and command us not to be cruel? What is left of God's omnipotence?

But why should such a limitation on God be unacceptable for the theist? Because there is nothing God cannot do? But is it true to say God can do absolutely anything? Can He, for example, destroy Himself? Can God make a rock so heavy that He cannot lift it? Or create a universe which was never created by Him? Many have thought that God's inability to do these sorts of things does not constitute a genuine limitation on His power because these are things which cannot logically be done. Thomas Aquinas, for example, wrote that, "whatever implies contradiction does not come within the scope of divine omnipotence, because it cannot have the aspect of possibility. Hence it is more appropriate to say that such things cannot be done than that God cannot do them."[4] Many theists reject the view that there is nothing which God cannot do.

But how, then, ought we to understand God's relationship to morality if we reject the divine command theory? Can religious people consistently maintain their faith in God the Creator and yet deny that what is right is right because He commands it? I think the answer to this is "yes." First, note that there is still a sense in which God could change morality (assuming, of course, there is a God). Whatever moral code we decide is best (most justified), that choice will in part depend on such factors as how we reason, what we desire and need, and the circumstances in which we find ourselves. Presumably, however, God could have constructed us or our environment very differently, so that we didn't care about freedom, weren't curious about nature, and weren't influenced by others' suffering. Or perhaps our natural environment could be altered so that it is less hostile to our needs and desires. If He had created either nature or us that way, then it seems likely that the most justified moral code might be different in important ways from the one it is now rational for us to support. In that sense, then, morality depends on God whether or not one supports the divine command theory.

In fact, it seems to me that it makes little difference for ethical questions whether a person is religious. The atheist will treat human nature simply as a given, a fact of nature, while the theist may regard it as the product of divine intention. But in any case the right thing to do is to follow the best moral code, the one that is most justified. Instead of relying on revelation to discover morality, religious and nonreligious people alike can inquire into which system is best.

In sum, I have argued first that religion is neither necessary nor useful in providing moral motivation or guidance. My objections to the claim that without God there would be no morality are somewhat more complex. First, it is wrong to say that only if God's will is at its base can morality be objective. The idea of the best moral code—the one fully rational persons would support—may prove to provide sound means to evaluate one's own code as well as those of other societies. Furthermore, the divine command theory should not be accepted

even by those who are religious. This is because it implies what clearly seems absurd, namely that God might tomorrow change the moral rules and make performing the most extreme acts of cruelty an obligation we all should meet. And, finally, I discussed how the theist and atheist might hope to find common ground about the sorts of moral rules to teach our children and how we should evaluate each other's behavior. Far from helping resolve moral disputes, religion does little more than sow confusion. Morality does not need religion and religion does not need morality.

Notes

1. R. C. Mortimer, *Christian Ethics* (London: Hutchinson's University Library, 1950) pp. 7–8.
2. This debate was broadcast on the Third Program of the British Broadcasting Corporation in 1948.
3. Plato, *Euthyphro* tr. H. N. Fowler (Cambridge Mass.: Harvard University Press, 1947).
4. Thomas Aquinas, *Summa Theologica,* Part I, Q. 25, Art. 3.

Questions on Arthur

1. According to Arthur, why don't we need religion to act morally?

2. Why don't we need religion in order to know what is right on Arthur's view? Do you think this is correct? How do you think Geach would respond to this?

3. Arthur concludes that religion doesn't need morality and that morality doesn't need religion. Why is this? Has he shown that religion and morality are completely separate? Again, what would Geach say about this?

4. People sometimes say that morality is "based" on religion. Is there any sense in which this is true?

James Rachels
The Challenge of Cultural Relativism

James Rachels is University Professor of Philosophy at the University of Alabama at Birmingham. He has written articles on world hunger, reverse discrimination, the treatment of animals, and other topics in ethics, and he is the author of The Elements of Moral Philosophy *(from which our reading is taken).*

> Morality differs in every society, and is a convenient term for socially approved habits.
>
> Ruth Benedict, *Patterns of Culture* (1934)

How Different Cultures Have Different Moral Codes

Darius, a king of ancient Persia, was intrigued by the variety of cultures he encountered in his travels. He had found, for example, that the Callatians (a tribe of Indians) customarily ate the bodies of their dead fathers. The Greeks, of course, did not do that—the Greeks practiced cremation and regarded the funeral pyre as the natural and fitting way to dispose of the dead. Darius thought that a sophisticated understanding of the world must include an appreciation of such differences between cultures. One day, to teach this lesson, he summoned some Greeks who happened to be present at his court and asked them what they would take to eat the bodies of their dead fathers. They were shocked, as Darius knew they would be, and replied that no amount of money could persuade them to do such a thing. Then Darius called in some Callatians, and while the Greeks listened asked them what they would take to burn their dead fathers' bodies. The Callatians were horrified and told Darius not even to mention such a dreadful thing.

This story, recounted by Herodotus in his *History,* illustrates a recurring theme in the literature of social science: different cultures have different moral codes. What is thought right within one group may be utterly abhorrent to the members of another group, and vice versa. Should we eat the bodies of the dead or burn them? If you were a Greek, one answer would seem obviously correct; but if you were a Callatian, the opposite would seem equally certain.

It is easy to give additional examples of the same kind. Consider the Eskimos. They are a remote and inaccessible people. Numbering only about 25,000, they live in small, isolated settlements scattered mostly along the northern fringes of North America and Greenland. Until the beginning of this century, the outside world knew little about them. Then explorers began to bring back strange tales.

Eskimo customs turned out to be very different from our own. The men often had more than one wife, and they would share their wives with guests, lending them for the night as a sign of hospitality. Moreover, within a community, a dominant male might demand—and get—regular sexual access to other men's wives. The women, however, were free to break these arrangements simply by leaving their husbands and taking up with new partners—free, that is, so long as their former husbands chose not to make trouble. All in all, the Eskimo practice was a volatile scheme that bore little resemblance to what we call marriage.

But it was not only their marriage and sexual practices that were different. The Eskimos also seemed to have less regard for human life. Infanticide, for example, was common. Knud Rasmussen, one of the most famous early explorers, reported that he met one woman who had borne twenty children but had killed ten of them at birth. Female babies, he found, were especially liable to be destroyed, and this was permitted simply at the parents' discretion, with no social stigma attached to it. Old people also, when they became too feeble to contribute to the family, were left out in the snow to die. So there seemed to be, in this society, remarkably little respect for life.

To the general public, these were disturbing revelations. Our own way of living seems so natural and right that for many of us it is hard to conceive of others living so differently. And when we do hear of such things, we tend immediately to categorize those other peoples as "backward" or "primitive." But to anthropologists and sociologists, there was nothing particularly surprising about the Eskimos. Since the time of Herodotus, enlightened observers have been accustomed to the idea that conceptions of right and wrong differ from culture to culture. If we assume that *our* ideas of right and wrong will be shared by all peoples at all times, we are merely naive.

Cultural Relativism

To many thinkers, this observation— "Different cultures have different moral codes"—has seemed to be the key to understanding morality. The idea of universal truth in ethics, they say, is a myth. The customs of different societies are all that exist. These customs cannot be said to be "correct" or "incorrect," for that implies we have an independent standard of right and wrong by which they may be judged. But there is no such independent standard; every standard is culture-bound. The great pioneering sociologist William Graham Sumner, writing in 1906, put the point like this:

The "right" way is the way which the ancestors used and which has been handed down. The tradition is its own warrant. It is not held subject to verification by experience. The notion of right is in the folkways. It is not outside of them, of independent origin, and brought to test them. In the folkways, whatever is, is right. This is because they are traditional, and therefore contain in themselves the authority of the ancestral ghosts. When we come to the folkways we are at the end of our analysis.

This line of thought has probably persuaded more people to be skeptical about ethics than any other single thing. *Cultural Relativism*, as it has been called, challenges our ordinary belief in the objectivity and universality of moral truth. It says, in effect, that there is no such thing as universal truth in ethics; there are only the various cultural codes, and nothing more.

Moreover, our own code has no special status; it is merely one among many.

As we shall see, this basic idea is really a compound of several different thoughts. It is important to separate the various elements of the theory because, on analysis, some parts of the theory turn out to be correct, whereas others seem to be mistaken. As a beginning, we may distinguish the following claims, all of which have been made by cultural relativists:

1. Different societies have different moral codes.
2. There is no objective standard that can be used to judge one societal code better than another.
3. The moral code of our own society has no special status; it is merely one among many.
4. There is no "universal truth" in ethics— that is, there are no moral truths that hold for all peoples at all times.
5. The moral code of a society determines what is right within that society; that is, if the moral code of a society says that a certain action is right, then that action *is* right, at least within that society.
6. It is mere arrogance for us to try to judge the conduct of other peoples. We should adopt an attitude of tolerance toward the practices of other cultures.

Although it may seem that these six propositions go naturally together, they are independent of one another, in the sense that some of them might be true even if others are false. In what follows, we will try to identify what is correct in Cultural Relativism, but we will also be concerned to expose what is mistaken about it.

The Cultural Differences Argument

Cultural Relativism is a theory about the nature of morality. At first blush it seems quite plausible. However, like all such theories, it may be evaluated by subjecting it to rational analysis; and when we analyze Cultural Relativism we find that it is not so plausible as it first appears to be.

The first thing we need to notice is that at the heart of Cultural Relativism there is a certain *form of argument*. The strategy used by cultural relativists is to argue from facts about the differences between cultural outlooks to a conclusion about the status of morality. Thus we are invited to accept this reasoning:

1. The Greeks believed it was wrong to eat the dead, whereas the Callatians believed it was right to eat the dead.
2. Therefore, eating the dead is neither objectively right nor objectively wrong. It is merely a matter of opinion, which varies from culture to culture.

Or, alternatively:

1. The Eskimos see nothing wrong with infanticide, whereas Americans believe infanticide is immoral.
2. Therefore, infanticide is neither objectively right nor objectively wrong. It is merely a matter of opinion, which varies from culture to culture.

Clearly, these arguments are variations of one fundamental idea. They are both special cases of a more general argument, which says:

1. Different cultures have different moral codes.
2. Therefore, there is no objective "truth" in morality. Right and wrong are only matters of opinion, and opinions vary from culture to culture.

We may call this the *Cultural Differences Argument*. To many people, it is very persuasive. But from a logical point of view, is it a *sound* argument?

It is not sound. The trouble is that the conclusion does not really follow from the premise—that is, even if the premise is true, the conclusion still might be false. The premise concerns what people *believe*: in some societies, people believe one thing; in other societies, people believe differently. The conclusion, however, concerns *what really is the case*. The trouble is that this sort of conclusion does not follow logically from this sort of premise.

Consider again the example of the Greeks and Callatians. The Greeks believed it was wrong to eat the dead; the Callatians believed it was right. Does it follow, *from the mere fact that they disagreed,* that there is no objective truth in the matter? No, it does not follow; for it *could* be that the practice was objectively right (or wrong) and that one or the other of them was simply mistaken.

To make the point clearer, consider a very different matter. In some societies, people believe the earth is flat. In other societies, such as our own, people believe the earth is (roughly) spherical. Does it follow, *from the mere fact that they disagree,* that there is no "objective truth" in geography? Of course not; we would never draw such a conclusion because we realize that, in their beliefs about the world, the members of some societies might simply be wrong. There is no reason to think that if the world is round everyone must know it. Similarly, there is no reason to think that if there is moral truth everyone must know it. The fundamental mistake in the Cultural Differences Argument is that it attempts to derive a substantive conclusion about a subject (morality) from the mere fact that people disagree about it.

It is important to understand the nature of the point that is being made here. We are *not* saying (not yet, anyway) that the conclusion of the argument is false. Insofar as anything being said here is concerned, it is still an open question whether the conclusion is true. We *are* making a purely logical point and saying that the conclusion does not *follow from* the premise. This is important, because in order to determine whether the conclusion is true, we need arguments in its support. Cultural Relativism proposes this argument, but unfortunately the argument turns out to be fallacious. So it proves nothing.

The Consequences of Taking Cultural Relativism Seriously

Even if the Cultural Differences Argument is invalid, Cultural Relativism might still be true. What would it be like if it were true?

In the passage quoted above, William Graham Sumner summarizes the essence of Cultural Relativism. He says that there is no measure of right and wrong other than the standards of one's society: "The notion of right is in the folkways. It is not outside of them, of independent origin, and brought to test them. In the folkways, whatever is, is right."

Suppose we took this seriously. What would be some of the consequences?

1. *We could no longer say that the customs of other societies are morally inferior to our own.* This, of course, is one of the main points stressed by Cultural Relativism. We would have to stop condemning other societies merely because they are "different." So long as we concentrate on certain examples, such as the funerary practices of the Greeks and Callatians, this may seem to be a sophisticated, enlightened attitude.

However, we would also be stopped from criticizing other, less benign practices. Suppose a society waged war on its neighbors for the purpose of taking slaves. Or suppose a society was violently anti-Semitic and its leaders set out to destroy the Jews. Cultural Relativism would preclude us from saying that either of these practices was wrong. We would not even be able to say that a society tolerant of Jews is *better* than the anti-Semitic society, for that would imply some sort of transcultural standard of comparison. The failure to condemn these practices does not seem "enlightened"; on the contrary, slavery and anti-Semitism seem wrong *wherever* they occur. Nevertheless, if we took Cultural Relativism seriously, we would have to admit that these social practices also are immune from criticism.

2. *We could decide whether actions are right or wrong just by consulting the standards of our society.* Cultural Relativism suggests a simple test for determining what is right and what is wrong: all one has to do is ask whether the action is in accordance with the code of one's society. Suppose a resident of South Africa is wondering whether his country's policy of *apartheid*—rigid racial segregation—is morally correct. All he has to do is ask whether this policy conforms to his society's moral code. If it does, there is nothing to worry about, at least from a moral point of view.

This implication of Cultural Relativism is disturbing because few of us think that our soci-

ety's code is perfect—we can think of ways it might be improved. Yet Cultural Relativism would not only forbid us from criticizing the codes of *other* societies; it would stop us from criticizing our *own*. After all, if right and wrong are relative to culture, this must be true for our own culture just as much as for others.

3. *The idea of moral progress is called into doubt.* Usually, we think that at least some changes in our society have been for the better. (Some, of course, may have been changes for the worse.) Consider this example: Throughout most of Western history the place of women in society was very narrowly circumscribed. They could not own property; they could not vote or hold political office; with a few exceptions, they were not permitted to have paying jobs; and generally they were under the almost absolute control of their husbands. Recently much of this has changed, and most people think of it as progress.

If Cultural Relativism is correct, can we legitimately think of this as progress? Progress means replacing a way of doing things with a *better* way. But by what standard do we judge the new ways as better? If the old ways were in accordance with the social standards of their time, then Cultural Relativism would say it is a mistake to judge them by the standards of a different time. Eighteenth-century society was, in effect, a different society from the one we have now. To say that we have made progress implies a judgment that present-day society is better, and that is just the sort of transcultural judgment that, according to Cultural Relativism, is impermissible.

Our idea of social *reform* will also have to be reconsidered. A reformer such as Martin Luther King, Jr., seeks to change his society for the better. Within the constraints imposed by Cultural Relativism, there is one way this might be done. If a society is not living up to its own ideals, the reformer may be regarded as acting for the best: the ideals of the society are the standard by which we judge his or her proposals as worthwhile. But the "reformer" may not challenge the ideals themselves, for those ideals are by definition correct. According to Cultural Relativism, then, the idea of social reform makes sense only in this very limited way.

These three consequences of Cultural Relativism have led many thinkers to reject it as implausible on its face. It does make sense, they say, to condemn some practices, such as slavery and anti-Semitism, wherever they occur. It makes sense to think that our own society has made some moral progress, while admitting that it is still imperfect and in need of reform. Because Cultural Relativism says that these judgments make no sense, the argument goes, it cannot be right.

Why There is Less Disagreement Than It Seems

The original impetus for Cultural Relativism comes from the observation that cultures differ dramatically in their views of right and wrong. But just how much do they differ? It is true that there are differences. However, it is easy to overestimate the extent of those differences. Often, when we examine what *seems* to be a dramatic difference, we find that the cultures do not differ nearly as much as it appears.

Consider a culture in which people believe it is wrong to eat cows. This may even be a poor culture, in which there is not enough food; still, the cows are not to be touched. Such a society would *appear* to have values very different from our own. But does it? We have not yet asked why these people will not eat cows. Suppose it is because they believe that after death the souls of humans inhabit the bodies of animals, especially cows, so that a cow may be someone's grandmother. Now do we want to say that their values are different from ours? No; the difference lies elsewhere. The difference is in our belief systems, not in our values. We agree that we shouldn't eat Grandma; we simply disagree about whether the cow *is* (or could be) Grandma.

The general point is this. Many factors work together to produce the customs of a society. The society's values are only one of them. Other matters, such as the religious and factual beliefs held by its members and the physical circumstances in which they must live, are also important. We cannot conclude, then, merely because customs differ, that there is a disagreement about *values*. The difference in customs may be attributable to some other aspect of social life. Thus there may be less disagreement about values than there appears to be.

Consider the Eskimos again. They often kill perfectly normal infants, especially girls. We do not approve of this at all; a parent who did this in our society would be locked up. Thus there appears to be a great difference in the values of our two cultures. But suppose we ask *why* the Eskimos do this. The explanation is not that they have less affection for their children or less respect for human life. An Eskimo family will always protect its babies if conditions permit. But they live in a harsh environment, where food is often in short supply. A fundamental postulate of Eskimo thought is: "Life is hard, and the margin of safety small." A family may want to nourish its babies but be unable to do so.

As in many "primitive" societies, Eskimo mothers will nurse their infants over a much longer period of time than mothers in our culture. The child will take nourishment from its mother's breast for four years, perhaps even longer. So even in the best of times there are limits to the number of infants that one mother can sustain. Moreover, the Eskimos are a nomadic people—unable to farm, they must move about in search of food. Infants must be carried, and a mother can carry only one baby in her parka as she travels and goes about her outdoor work. Other family members can help, but this is not always possible.

Infant girls are more readily disposed of because, first, in this society the males are the primary food providers—they are the hunters, according to the traditional division of labor—and it is obviously important to maintain a sufficient number of food gatherers. But there is an important second reason as well. Because the hunters suffer a high casualty rate, the adult men who die prematurely far outnumber the women who die early. Thus if male and female infants survived in equal numbers, the female adult population would greatly outnumber the male adult population. Examining the available statistics, one writer concluded that "were it not for female infanticide . . . there would be approximately one-and-a-half times as many females in the average Eskimo local group as there are food-producing males."

So among the Eskimos, infanticide does not signal a fundamentally different attitude toward children. Instead, it is a recognition that drastic measures are sometimes needed to ensure the family's survival. Even then, however, killing the baby is not the first option considered. Adoption is common; childless couples are especially happy to take a more fertile couple's "surplus." Killing is only the last resort. I emphasize this in order to show that the raw data of the anthropologists can be misleading; it can make the differences in values between cultures appear greater than they are. The Eskimos' values are not all that different from our values. It is only that life forces upon them choices that we do not have to make.

How All Cultures Have Some Values in Common

It should not be surprising that, despite appearances, the Eskimos are protective of their children. How could it be otherwise? How could a group survive that did *not* value its young? This suggests a certain argument, one which shows that all cultural groups must be protective of their infants:

1. Human infants are helpless and cannot survive if they are not given extensive care for a period of years.
2. Therefore, if a group did not care for its young, the young would not survive, and the older members of the group would not be replaced. After a while the group would die out.
3. Therefore, any cultural group that continues to exist must care for its young. Infants that are *not* cared for must be the exception rather than the rule.

Similar reasoning shows that other values must be more or less universal. Imagine what it would be like for a society to place no value at all on truth telling. When one person spoke to another, there would be no presumption at all that he was telling the truth—for he could just as easily be speaking falsely. Within that society, there would be no reason to pay attention to what anyone says. (I ask you what time it is, and you say "Four o'clock." But there is no presumption that you are speaking truly; you could just as easily have said the first thing that came into your head. So I have no reason to pay attention to your answer—in fact, there was no point in my asking you in the first place!) Communication would then be extremely difficult, if not impossible. And because complex societies cannot exist without regular communication among their members, society would become impossible. It follows that in any complex society there *must* be a presumption in favor of truthfulness. There may of course be exceptions to this rule: there may be situations in which it is thought to be permissible to lie. Nevertheless, these will be exceptions to a rule that *is* in force in the society.

Let me give one further example of the same type. Could a society exist in which there was no prohibition on murder? What would this be like? Suppose people were free to kill other people at will, and no one thought there was anything wrong with it. In such a "society," no one could feel secure. Everyone would have to be constantly on guard. People who wanted to survive would have to avoid other people as much as possible. This would inevitably result in individuals trying to become as self-sufficient as possible—after all, associating with others would be dangerous. Society on any large scale would collapse. Of course, people might band together in smaller groups with others that they *could* trust not to harm them. But notice what this means: they would be forming smaller societies that *did* acknowledge a rule against murder. The prohibition of murder, then, is a necessary feature of all societies.

There is a general theoretical point here, namely, that *there are some moral rules that all societies will have in common, because those rules are necessary for society to exist*. The rules against lying and murder are two examples. And in fact, we do find these rules in force in all viable cultures. Cultures may differ in what they regard as legitimate exceptions to the rules, but this disagreement exists against a background of agreement on the larger issues. Therefore, it is a mistake to overestimate the amount of difference between cultures. Not *every* moral rule can vary from society to society.

What Can Be Learned from Cultural Relativism

At the outset, I said that we were going to identify both what is right and what is wrong in Cultural Relativism. Thus far I have mentioned only its mistakes: I have said that it rests on an invalid argument, that it has consequences that make it implausible on its face, and that the extent of cultural disagreement is far less than it implies. This all adds up to a pretty thorough repudiation of the theory. Nevertheless, it is still a very appealing idea, and the reader may have the feeling that all this is a little unfair. The theory *must* have something going for it, or else why has it been so influential? In fact, I think there *is* something right about Cultural Relativism, and now I want to say what that is. There are two lessons we should learn from the theory, even if we ultimately reject it.

1. Cultural Relativism warns us, quite rightly, about the danger of assuming that all our preferences are based on some absolute rational standard. They are not. Many (but not all) of our practices are merely peculiar to our society, and it is easy to lose sight of that fact. In reminding us of it, the theory does a service.

Funerary practices are one example. The Callatians, according to Herodotus, were "men who eat their fathers"—a shocking idea, to us at least. But eating the flesh of the dead could be understood as a sign of respect. It could be taken as a symbolic act that says: We wish this person's spirit to dwell within us. Perhaps this was the understanding of the Callatians. On such a way of thinking, burying the dead could be seen as an act of rejection, and burning the corpse as positively scornful. If this is hard to imagine, then we may need to have our imaginations stretched. Of course we may feel a visceral repugnance at the idea of eating human flesh in any circumstances. But what of it? This repugnance may be, as the relativists say, only a matter of what is customary in our particular society.

There are many other matters that we tend to think of in terms of objective right and wrong, but that are really nothing more than social conventions. Should women cover their breasts? A publicly exposed breast is scandalous in our society, whereas in other cultures it is unremarkable. Objectively speaking, it is neither right nor wrong—there is no objective reason why either custom is better. Cultural Relativism begins with the valuable insight that many of our practices are like this—they are only cultural products. Then it goes wrong by concluding that, because *some* practices are like this, *all* must be.

2. The second lesson has to do with keeping an open mind. In the course of growing up, each of us has acquired some strong feelings: we have learned to think of some types of conduct as acceptable, and others we have learned to regard as simply unacceptable. Occasionally, we may find those feelings challenged. We may encounter someone who claims that our feelings are mistaken. For example, we may have been taught that homosexuality is immoral, and we may feel quite uncomfortable around gay people and see them as alien and "different." Now someone suggests that this may be a mere prejudice; that there is nothing evil about homosexuality; that gay people are just people, like anyone else, who happen, through no choice of their own, to be attracted to others of the same sex. But because we feel so strongly about the matter, we may find it hard to take this seriously. Even after we listen to the arguments, we may still have the unshakable feeling that homosexuals *must*, somehow, be an unsavory lot.

Cultural Relativism, by stressing that our moral views can reflect the prejudices of our society, provides an antidote for this kind of dogmatism. When he tells the story of the Greeks and Callatians, Herodotus adds:

For if anyone, no matter who, were given the opportunity of choosing from amongst all the nations of the world the set of beliefs which he thought best, he would inevitably, after careful consideration of their relative merits, choose that of his own country. Everyone without exception believes his own native customs, and the religion he was brought up in, to be the best.

Realizing this can result in our having more open minds. We can come to understand that our feelings are not necessarily perceptions of the truth—they may be nothing more than the result of cultural conditioning. Thus when we hear it suggested that some element of our social code is *not* really the best and we find ourselves instinctively resisting the suggestion, we might stop and remember this. Then we may be more open to discovering the truth, whatever that might be.

We can understand the appeal of Cultural Relativism, then, even though the theory has serious shortcomings. It is an attractive theory because it is based on a genuine insight—that many of the practices and attitudes we think so natural are really only cultural products. Moreover, keeping this insight firmly in view is im-

portant if we want to avoid arrogance and have open minds. These are important points, not to be taken lightly. But we can accept these points without going on to accept the whole theory.

Questions on Rachels

1. What is cultural relativism? What is the cultural differences argument on which it is based? How does Rachels attack this argument? Does he show that it is unsound?

2. What other criticisms of cultural relativism does he make? Are these good criticisms or not? Do you think that Rachels is making any assumptions about moral values? What are they?

3. Do you agree that certain values are universal? Why or why not?

Bertrand Russell

Science and Ethics

For biographical information on Russell, see the reading in chapter 3.

Questions as to "values"—that is to say, as to what is good or bad on its own account, independently of its effects—lie outside the domain of science, as the defenders of religion emphatically assert. I think that in this they are right, but I draw the further conclusion, which they do not draw, that questions as to "values" lie wholly outside the domain of knowledge. That is to say, when we assert that this or that has "value," we are giving expression to our own emotions, not to a fact which would still be true if our personal feelings were different. To make

The reading is from Bertrand Russell, *Religion and Science* (New York: Oxford University Press, [1935] 1961), ch. 9, pp. 230–243. Reprinted by permission of Oxford University Press.

this clear, we must try to analyze the conception of the Good.

It is obvious, to begin with, that the whole idea of good and bad has some connection with *desire. Prima facie,* anything that we all desire is "good," and anything that we all dread is "bad." If we all agreed in our desires, the matter could be left there, but unfortunately our desires conflict. If I say "what I want is good," my neighbor will say "No, what *I* want." Ethics is an attempt—though not, I think, a successful one—to escape from this subjectivity. I shall naturally try to show, in my dispute with my neighbor, that my desires have some quality which makes them more worthy of respect than his. If I want to preserve a right of way, I shall appeal to the landless inhabitants of the district; but he, on his side, will appeal to the landowners. I shall say: "What use is the beauty of the countryside if no one sees it?" He will retort: "What beauty will be left if trippers are allowed to spread devastation?" Each tries to enlist allies by showing that his own desires harmonize with those of other people. When this is obviously impossible, as in the case of a burglar, the man is condemned by public opinion, and his ethical status is that of a sinner.

Ethics is thus closely related to politics: it is an attempt to bring the collective desires of a group to bear upon individuals; or, conversely, it is an attempt by an individual to cause his desires to become those of his group. This latter is, of course, only possible if his desires are not too obviously opposed to the general interest: the burglar will hardly attempt to persuade people that he is doing them good, though plutocrats make similar attempts, and often succeed. When our desires are for things which all can enjoy in common, it seems not unreasonable to hope that others may concur; thus the philosopher who values Truth, Goodness and Beauty seems, to himself, to be not merely expressing his own desires, but pointing the way to the welfare of all mankind. Unlike the burglar, he is able to believe that his desires are for something that has value in an impersonal sense.

Ethics is an attempt to give universal, and not merely personal, importance to certain of our desires. I say "certain" of our desires, because in regard to some of them this is obviously impossible, as we saw in the case of the burglar. The man who makes money on the Stock Exchange by means of some secret knowledge does not wish others to be equally well informed: Truth (in so far as he values it) is for him a private possession, not the general human good that it is for the philosopher. The philosopher may, it is true, sink to the level of the stock-jobber, as when he claims priority for a discovery. But this is a lapse: in his purely philosophic capacity, he wants only to enjoy the contemplation of Truth, in doing which he in no way interferes with others who wish to do likewise.

To seem to give universal importance to our desires—which is the business of ethics—may be attempted from two points of view, that of the legislator, and that of the preacher. Let us take the legislator first.

I will assume, for the sake of argument, that the legislator is personally disinterested. That is to say, when he recognizes one of his desires as being concerned only with his own welfare, he does not let it influence him in framing the laws; for example, his code is not designed to in-crease his personal fortune. But he has other desires which seem to him impersonal. He may believe in an ordered hierarchy from king to peasant, or from mine-owner to black indentured laborer. He may believe that women should be submissive to men. He may hold that the spread of knowledge in the lower classes is dangerous. And so on and so on. He will then, if he can, so construct his code that conduct promoting the ends which he values shall, as far as possible, be in accordance with individual self-interest; and he will establish a system of moral instruction which will, where it succeeds, make men feel wicked if they pursue other purposes than his.[1] Thus "virtue" will come to be in fact, though not in subjective estimation, subservience to the desires of the legislator, in so far as he himself considers these desires worthy to be universalized.

The standpoint and method of the preacher are necessarily somewhat different, because he does not control the machinery of the State, and therefore cannot produce an artificial harmony between his desires and those of others. His only method is to try to rouse in others the same desires that he feels himself, and for this purpose his appeal must be to the emotions. Thus Ruskin caused people to like Gothic architecture, not by argument, but by the moving effect of rhythmical prose. *Uncle Tom's Cabin* helped to make people think slavery an evil by causing them to imagine themselves as slaves. Every attempt to persuade people that something is good (or bad) in itself, and not merely in its effects, depends upon the art of rousing feelings, not upon an appeal to evidence. In every case the preacher's skill consists in creating in others emotions similar to his own—or dissimilar, if he is a hypocrite. I am not saying this as a criticism of the preacher, but as an analysis of the essential character of his activity.

When a man says "this is good in itself," he *seems* to be making a statement, just as much as if he said "this is square" or "this is sweet." I believe this to be a mistake. I think that what the man really means is: "I wish everybody to desire this," or rather "Would that everybody desired this." If what he says is interpreted as a statement, it is merely an affirmation of his own personal wish; if, on the other hand, it is interpreted in a general way, it states nothing, but merely desires something. The wish, as an occurrence, is personal, but what it desires is universal. It is, I think, this curious interlocking of the particular and the universal which has caused so much confusion in ethics.

The matter may perhaps become clearer by contrasting an ethical sentence with one which makes a statement. If I say "all Chinese are Buddhists," I can be refuted by the production of a Chinese Christian or Mohammedan. If I say "I believe that all Chinese are Buddhists," I cannot be refuted by any evidence from China, but only by evidence that I do not believe what I say; for what I am asserting is only something about my own state of mind. If, now, a philosopher says "Beauty is good," I may interpret him as meaning either "Would that everybody loved the beautiful" (which corresponds too "all Chinese are Buddhists") or "I wish that everybody loved the beautiful" (which corresponds to "I believe that all Chinese are Buddhists"). The first of these makes no assertion, but expresses a wish; since it affirms nothing, it is logically impossible that there should be evidence for or against it, or for it to possess either truth or falsehood. The second sentence, instead of being merely optative, does make a statement, but it is one about the philosopher's state of mind, and it could only be refuted by evidence that he does not have the wish that he says he has. This second sentence does not belong to ethics, but to psychology or biography. The first sentence, which does belong to ethics, expresses a desire for something, but asserts nothing.

Ethics, if the above analysis is correct, contains no statements, whether true or false, but consists of desires of a certain general kind, namely such as are concerned with the desires of mankind in general—and of gods, angels, and devils, if they exist. Science can discuss the causes of desires, and the means for realizing them, but it cannot contain any genuinely ethical sentences, because it is concerned with what is true or false.

The theory which I have been advocating is a form of the doctrine which is called the "subjectivity" of values. This doctrine consists in maintaining that, if two men differ about values, there is not a disagreement as to any kind of truth, but a difference of taste. If one man says "oysters are good" and another says "*I* think they are bad," we recognize that there is nothing to argue about. The theory in question holds that all differences as to values are of this sort, although we do not naturally think them so when we are dealing with matters that seem to us more exalted than oysters. The chief ground for adopting this view is the complete impossibility of finding any arguments to prove that this or that has intrinsic value. If we all agreed, we might hold that we know values by intuition. We cannot *prove*, to a color-blind man, that grass is green and not red. But there are various ways of proving to him that he lacks a power of discrimination which most men possess, whereas in the case of values there are no such ways, and disagreements are much more frequent than in the case of colors. Since no way can be even imagined for deciding a difference as to values, the conclusion is forced upon us that the difference is one of tastes, not one as to any objective truth.

The consequences of this doctrine are considerable. In the first place, there can be no such thing as "sin" in any absolute sense; what one man calls "sin" another may call "virtue," and though they may dislike each other on account of this difference, neither can convict the other of intellectual error. Punishment cannot be justified on the ground that the criminal is "wicked," but only on the ground that he has behaved in a way which others wish to discourage. Hell, as a place of punishment for sinners, becomes quite irrational.

In the second place, it is impossible to uphold the way of speaking about values which is common among those who believe in Cosmic Purpose. Their argument is that certain things which have been evolved are "good" and therefore the world must have had a purpose which was ethically admirable. In the language of subjective values, this argument becomes: "Some things in the world are to our liking, and therefore they must have been created by a Being with our tastes, Whom, therefore, we also like, and Who, consequently, is good." Now it seems fairly evident that, if creatures having likes and dislikes were to exist at all, they were pretty sure to like *some* things in their environment, since otherwise they would find life intolerable. Our values have been evolved along with the rest of our constitution, and nothing as to any original purpose can be inferred from the fact that they are what they are.

Those who believe in "objective" values often contend that the view which I have been advocating has immoral consequences. This seems to me to be due to faulty reasoning. There are, as has already been said, certain ethical consequences of the doctrine of subjective values, of which the most important is the rejection of vindictive punishment and the notion of "sin." But the more general consequences which are feared, such as the decay of all sense of moral obligation, are not to be logically deduced. Moral obligation, if it is to influence conduct, must consist not merely of a belief, but of a desire. The desire, I may be told, is the desire to be "good" in a sense which I no longer allow. But when we analyze the desire to be "good" it generally resolves itself into a desire to be approved, or, alternatively, to act so as to bring about certain general consequences which we desire. We have wishes which are not purely personal, and, if we had not, no amount of ethical teaching would influence our conduct except through fear of disapproval. The sort of life that most of us admire is one which is guided by large impersonal desires; now such desires can, no doubt, be encouraged by example, education, and knowledge, but they can hardly be created by the mere abstract belief that they are good, nor discouraged by an analysis of what is meant by the word "good."

When we contemplate the human race, we may desire that it should be happy, or healthy, or intelligent, or warlike, and so on. Any one of these desires, if it is strong, will produce its own morality; but if we have no such general desires, our conduct, whatever our ethic may be, will only serve social purposes in so far as self-interest and the interests of society are in harmony. It is the business of wise institutions to create such harmony as far as possible, and for the rest, whatever may be our theoretical definition of value, we must depend upon the existence of impersonal desires. When you meet a man with whom you have a fundamental ethical disagreement—for example, if you think that all men count equally, while he selects a class as alone important—you will find yourself no better able to cope with him if you believe in objective values than if you did not. In either case, you can only influence his conduct through influencing his desires: if you succeed in that, his ethic will change, and if not, not.

Some people feel that if a general desire, say for the happiness of mankind, has not the sanction of absolute good, it is in some way irrational. This is due to a lingering belief in objective values. A desire cannot, in itself, be either rational or irrational. It may conflict with other desires, and therefore lead to unhappiness; it may rouse opposition in others, and therefore be incapable of gratification. But it cannot be considered "irrational" merely because no reason can be given for feeling it. We may desire A because it is a means to B, but in the end, when we have done with mere means, we must come to something which we desire for no reason, but not on that account "irrationally." All systems of ethics embody the desires of those who advocate them, but this fact is concealed in a mist of words. Our desires are, in fact, more general and less purely selfish than many moralists imagine; if it were not so, no theory of ethics would make moral improvement possible. It is, in fact, not by ethical theory, but by the cultivation of large and generous desires through intelligence, happiness, and freedom from fear, that men can be brought to act more than they do at present in a manner that is consistent with the general happiness of mankind. Whatever our definition of the "Good," and whether we believe it to be subjective or objective, those who do not desire the happiness of mankind will not endeavor to further it, while those who desire it will do what they can to bring it about.

I conclude that, while it is true that science cannot decide questions of value, that is because they cannot be intellectually decided at all, and lie outside the realm of truth and falsehood. Whatever knowledge is attainable, must be attained by scientific methods; and what science cannot discover, mankind cannot know.

Notes

1. Compare the following advice by a contemporary of Aristotle (Chinese, not Greek): "A ruler should not listen to those who believe in people having opinions of their own and in the importance of the individual. Such teachings cause men to withdraw to quiet places and hide away in caves or on mountains, there to rail at the prevailing government, sneer at those in authority, belittle the importance of rank and emoluments, and despise all who hold official posts." Waley, *The Way and its Power,* p. 37.

Questions on Russell

1. According to Russell, why do questions about values lie outside the domain of science and even

of knowledge? Do you think he is right about this or not? Explain.

2. Russell claims that when we say "This is good," we mean "I wish everybody to desire this" or "Would that everybody desired this." Do you think this analysis is correct? See if you can show that it is false.

3. Explain Russell's account of ethical disagreements and apply it to some issue, for example, the disagreement about abortion or mercy killing. Does the account work for the example or not? Explain.

A. C. Ewing

The Objectivity of Moral Judgements

A. C. Ewing (1899–1974) taught philosophy at Cambridge University. He was the author of many books including The Morality of Punishment, Idealism: A Critical Survey, The Definition of Good *(from which the reading is taken),* The Fundamental Questions of Philosophy, *and* Non-Linguistic Philosophy.

The simplest form of the subjectivist view is that according to which ethical judgements, though genuine judgements, assert only that the person who makes the judgement has or tends to have certain feelings. "This is good' or "right" on such a view becomes "I have [or tend to have] an emotion of approval on considering this." A number of incredibly paradoxical consequences would follow from the adoption of this view. Firstly, the judgements could not be false unless the person judging had made a mistake about his own psychology. Secondly, two different people would never mean the same

The reading is from A. C. Ewing, *The Definition of Good* (New York: Macmillan, 1947).

thing when they made such a judgement, since each would mean "This is approved by *me*." Indeed the same person would never mean the same by it on two different occasions, because each time he would mean "I *now* feel [or tend to feel] approval of this."

Thirdly, if I judge something to be good and you judge it to be bad, our judgements would never be logically incompatible with each other. It is not a sufficient reply to point out that they can still be incompatible with each other in some different sense, for example in the sense that they express attitudes which are in conflict with each other or lead to incompatible policies. For we do not see merely that A's judgement "This is good" and B's judgement "This is bad" (in the corresponding sense of the word) lead to or express incompatible policies like A's judgement "I desire to further X" and B's judgement "I desire to oppose X." We see that the two judgements logically contradict each other so that it is logically impossible that they could both be true. No doubt, since "good" and "bad" can each be used in different senses, "this is bad" may not always contradict "this is good," because, for example, "good" may mean "**instrumentally good**" and "bad" may mean "**intrinsically bad**"; but at any rate they sometimes do so, and on the view under discussion they could, when asserted by different people, never do so. Fourthly, no argument or rational discussion, nor indeed any citation of empirical facts, could be in any degree relevant to supporting or casting doubt on any ethical judgement unless it could be directed to showing that the person who makes the judgement has made a mistake about his own feelings or tendencies to have feelings. It is true that argument or fresh knowledge about the circumstances and likely consequences of an act might lead me to have different feelings about it and so judge it right while I had judged it wrong before, or vice versa; but it would not in any way indicate that my previous judgement was false.[1] The judgements would be different; but since they referred only to my feelings at different times they would not contradict each other any more than "I was ill on January 1" contradicts "I was well on February 1." Yet it is clear that argument can really cast doubt on propositions in ethics.

Fifthly, I could not, while asserting an ethical belief, conceive that I might possibly be wrong in this belief and yet be certain that I now feel (or tend to feel) disapproval. Since it is quite clear that I can conceive this in some cases at least, this argument provides another *reductio ad absurdum* of the theory. To think that an ethical belief now expressed by me may possibly be wrong is not the same as thinking that I may come in the future to have different feelings, for I think that the present judgement may be wrong and not a future one. To put the objection in another way, it would follow from the theory that to say "If I feel approval of A, A is always right [good]" is to utter a tautology. But it is not, it is a piece of gross conceit, if made in any ordinary context. Even if it were true that, if I feel approval of A, I shall always at the time judge A to be right (good), this is quite a different statement. I need not always be certain that my judgements are correct (unless judgement is so defined as to cover only cases of *knowledge*).

Sixthly, it would follow from the theory under discussion that, when I judge that Hitler was bad or acted wrongly, I am not really talking about Hitler at all but about my own psychology.

To me the consequences that I have mentioned are all quite incredible and constitute a fully sufficient *reductio ad absurdum* of the theory from which they are deduced. They hold whether it is applied both to "good" and to "right" or only to one of them.

Let us now examine the case against the objectivity of ethical judgements. If it is conclusive we shall have to be subjectivists in the sense that we shall have to admit the impossibility of making any true or at least any justified ethical judgements, even if we do not admit that ethical judgements are of such a nature that they could not conceivably be true at all or true of anything but the mental state or dispositions of the speaker.

One argument is based on the striking differences in ethical views between people. But the differences between the views of savages and those of modern scientists about eclipses, or between the views of different politicians as to the causes and likely effects of contemporary events, are as great as the differences between the views of savages and of Christians, or the views of democrats and of Nazis, as to ethics. Are we to conclude from this that the scientists are no more right than the savages or that the political events about which the disputes turn have not objectively any causes or effects? If we do not draw this conclusion here, why draw the corresponding conclusion about ethics? There are also various ways of explaining the differences of view that exist without casting doubt on the objectivity of ethics. In the first place, acts which bear the same name may be very different acts in different states of society, because the circumstances and the psychology of the people concerned are very different. So it might be the case that, for example, slavery or polygamy was right, as the course which involved least evil, in certain more primitive societies and wrong in ours. This is quite compatible with the objectivity of ethical judgements. The proposition that slavery was right in ancient Egypt would not contradict the proposition that it was wrong in the United States in 1850 A.D. Both we and the ancient Egyptians may be right in our ethical judgements. Let us, however, take cases where one party is wrong. Now it is important to note that differences in ethical beliefs are often due to differences of opinion as to matters of fact. If A and B differ as to the likely consequences of an action, they may well differ as to whether the action is right or wrong, and this is perhaps the most fertile source of disputes as to what is right. But it is not an ethical difference at all; it is a difference such as arises between rival scientific predictions based on inductive evidence. Differences or apparent differences of opinion of these two kinds obviously constitute no possible argument against the objectivity of ethics.

But there are also genuine ethical differences—that is, differences as to our judgements not of fact but of value. These may sometimes be explained by differences in people's experience of life. If I never experience A, I cannot realize the intrinsic goodness of A and may therefore wrongly subordinate it to something less good. And we must remember that what is intrinsically good is not a physical thing or a physical act, but the experience or state of mind associated with it . . . .

Or the judgement that something is good or bad on the whole may have been due to concentrating attention on one side of it while ignoring or underestimating the other sides, as, for instance, militarists concentrate their attention on the unselfish heroism which war brings out in men and forget or underestimate war's evils. Lesser degrees of such onesidedness it is impossible to avoid, and yet they may detrimentally influence ethical judgements. To decide what is right in a particular case is often a difficult matter of balancing the good or evil likely to be produced by one proposed act against that likely to be produced by others. For, even if we do not hold the view that the rightness of an act depends solely on its consequences, we cannot in any case deny that such balancing of the consequences should play the predominant part in at least many ethical decisions. Perhaps, if we foresaw all the consequences clearly as they would be in their factual character and could keep our attention fixed equally on them all, we should always be in agreement as to the degree in which they were good or evil as compared with the consequences of other possible acts. But, apart from the difficulty of estimating what the consequences of an act will be, it is practically impossible in cases which are at all complex to keep our attention sufficiently fixed at the same time on all the foreseeable consequences likely to be seriously relevant for good or evil, and so we are likely through lack of attention to underestimate the value or disvalue of some as compared to that of others.

The lack of attention I have mentioned is in some degree inevitable, but it is greatly enhanced by the influence of desire and prejudice. It is a commonplace that ethical mistakes are often due to non-intellectual factors. Whether these act only through affecting the attention or whether they can lead to mistaken valuations even in the presence of full attention to the object valued we need not discuss. Their influence is certainly not confined to ethical mistakes; we may note the different conclusions as to the factual consequences of a policy which members of different political parties may draw from the same evidence. There is in any case a large class of errors for which some form of "psychoanalysis" (I do not say necessarily the Freudian) is required rather than argument, and another (probably much larger) of which it can be said only that the person in question fell into error because he did not steadfastly will to seek the truth and therefore did not fix his attention on points which displeased him. The convictions of some people as to the objectivity of ethics appear to have been shaken by the fact that enthusiastic Nazis seem to have believed that it was their duty to do things which we are convinced are completely wrong, such as illtreating the Jews; but is there any reason to think that these Nazis really wanted to arrive at the truth regarding the question whether it was right or wrong to send Jews to concentration camps? If not, we need not be so surprised that they did not attain the truth which they did not seek.

So it may well be the case that all differences in people's judgements whether certain actions are right or wrong or certain things good or bad are due to factors other than an irreducible difference in ethical intuition. But, even if they should not be, we must remember that ethical intuition, like our other capacities, is presumably a developing factor and therefore may be capable of error. But in any case we have said enough to show that great differences of opinion as to ethics are quite compatible with the objectivity of ethical judgements.

Differences between philosophers about the general theory of ethics are remarkably great; but experience shows that very wide philosophical differences are quite compatible with striking agreement as regards the kind of action judged right or wrong, just as radical differences between philosophers in their theory of perception and of physical objects are quite compatible with complete agreement in ordinary life as to what particular physical objects are in a particular place at a particular time. The differences between philosophers are differences not mainly as to their ethical judgements in concrete ethical situations, but as to the general theory explaining these. We may add that the differences between different peoples and different civilizations as to concrete ethical judgements are commonly exaggerated. David Livingstone says that nowhere had he need to teach the African savages [sic] at any rate the ethical, as opposed to the religious, portion of the Decalogue. But there is of course a great inconsistency (not only among savages [sic]) in confining to a limited group rules which demand universal extension. . . .

Probably the principal reason which makes people inclined to deny the objectivity of ethics is the fact that in ethical argument we are very soon brought to a point where we have to fall back on intuition, so that disputants are placed in a situation where there are just two conflicting intuitions between which there seem to be no means of deciding. However, it is not only ethics but all reasoning which presupposes intuition. I cannot argue A, ∴ B, ∴ C, without seeing that A entails B and B entails C, and this must either be seen immediately or require a further argument. If it is seen immediately, it is a case of intuition;[2] if it has to be established by a further argument, this means that another term, D, must be interpolated between A and B such that A entails D and D entails B, and similarly with B and C, but then the same question arises about A entailing D, so that sooner or later we must come to something which we see intuitively to be true, as the process of interpolation cannot go on *ad infinitum*. We cannot therefore, whatever we do, get rid of intuition if we are to have any valid inference at all. It may, however, be said that in subjects other than ethics people at any rate agree in their intuitions. But outside mathematics or formal logic this is by no means universally true. There is frequent disagreement about matters of fact as to what has happened or will happen or concerning the causes of something, and when we have exhausted the arguments on a given point in these matters there still remains a difference between the ways in which these arguments are regarded by the disputants. In any science where you cannot prove your conclusions but only make them more or less probable there will be different estimates as to the balance of probability. As in ethics you have to balance different values against each other in order to decide what you ought to do, so here you have to balance different probable arguments, and in order to do this you must rely at some point or other on an estimate of their strength which cannot itself be further justified by mediate reasoning. Yet, when everything has been said in the way of argument, people may not all agree. Some will attribute more weight to one consideration, others to another, as they do in ethical questions about what is the right action in a given case. Our decision as to which of two probable arguments is the stronger may be influenced by other arguments in turn; but in order to deal with the situation rationally we must also estimate the weight of these other arguments, so that in the last resort it is a matter of insight into their nature which cannot be settled by other arguments *ad infinitum*. Just as in a demonstrative argument you must see intuitively how each step follows from the preceding one, so in the case of a probable argument you must rely on estimates of the degree of probability given by the argument as compared to that given by arguments on the other side, and these estimates, unless the degree of probability can be mathematically calculated, must either be themselves intuitive or be deduced from other estimates which are intuitive. I do not wish to maintain that reasoning in these matters is altogether analogous to that which occurs in dealing with ethical questions, but at any rate it is the case here that, as in ethics, we are often confronted with a situation in which we either see or do not see, and cannot logically prove, that what we seem to see is true. Yet we cannot surely therefore conclude that the scientific or historical propositions under discussion are really only propositions about the state of mind of the people who assert them, or that they are neither true nor false, or that we have no justification whatever for believing any of them!

We must therefore have intuition, and in a subject where infallibility is not attainable intuitions will sometimes disagree. Some philosophers indeed prefer not to call them intuitions when they are wrong, but then the problem will be to distinguish real from ostensible intuitions, since people certainly sometimes think they see intuitively what is not true. Now Earl Russell says: "Since no way can be even imagined for deciding a difference as to values, the conclusion is forced upon us that the difference is one of tastes, not one as to any objective truth";[3] but what I have said shows that we can imagine plenty of ways. I have indicated that errors as to judgements of value may arise (a) from lack of the requisite experience, (b) from intellectual confusions of some sort, (c) from failure to attend adequately to certain aspects of the situation or of the consequences, or (d) from psychological causes such as those with which the psychoanalyst deals. Therefore to remove errors we may (a) supply the lacking experience, or failing this, if possible, describe it in a way which will make its nature clear to the other party; we may (b) dispel intellectual confusions by making adequate distinctions or exposing actual fallacies such as make a person think he has seen that A is C when he has really only seen that A is B and mistakenly identified B with C; we may (c) suggest the direction of attention to the neglected points, or we may (d) use psychological methods. And we shall, if we are wise, also look out to see whether we ourselves have tripped up in any of these ways. Further, even when inference cannot completely prove or disprove, we may use it to confirm or cast doubt on ostensible intuition. The large class of errors which result mainly from an unwillingness really to seek for the truth can hardly be used as

an argument against objectivity, since they are due to the moral fault of the persons who are in error and could have been removed if the latter had tried. In these cases the trouble is not that there are no means of deciding but that the means are not used.

The methods I have suggested will not always be successful, but then is there any sphere in which human efforts always do succeed? Even the methodology of physical science cannot lay down rules which will guarantee that any scientist can make discoveries or show him in detail in advance how to prove to others the truth of the discoveries when made. I am not claiming that it is possible in practice to remove all ethical differences, but how do we know that it could not be done if there were a will on each side to listen to what the other had to say and an intelligence to discern the best methods to adopt in order to facilitate a decision? A person cannot be brought into agreement even with the established truths of science if he will not listen to what the scientist says, and there is no reason to think even with ethical intuition that there are not describable processes by which any cause of error can on principle be removed. I insert the words "on principle" simply because it will still often be the case that none of the disputants thinks of the right way of removing the error or that the person in error will not or cannot take it, as also occurs in disputes about questions of fact outside ethics.

Where the intuitive belief is due to non-intellectual factors of a kind which vitiate it, there seem to be two possibilities of cure. First, the person concerned may lose all tendency to hold the intuitive conviction when its alleged cause is clearly pointed out to him. The alleged cause is then in his case probably at least an essential part of the real cause. If, on the other hand, the intuitive belief remains unimpaired, and the man does not react to the causal explanation in a way which suggests that it has really touched a sore point, this is presumptive evidence that the explanation is mistaken. But, secondly, the cure from a false belief due to non-intellectual factors is more likely to arise because the man has been induced to approach the subject in a new spirit than merely because the true causation of the belief has been suggested to him. After all it is impossible to prove even to an unprejudiced person that such a causal theory as to the origin of a person's belief is really correct. How to induce a person to make such a new approach is a question not of logical argument but of practical psychology.

We must not think of intuition as something quite by itself, uninfluenced by inference; it is helped by inference but sees beyond what could be proved by inference. And, when intuitive ethical views differ, use may be made of inference to support one or other of the clashing views, especially by showing that it fits well into a coherent ethical system. This will not settle the question absolutely conclusively, but it can help toward settlement. Perhaps as the result of the inference one of the parties to the dispute may realize that he does not see by intuition what he claimed to see, but something rather different. It would thus be a great mistake to say that, when two men disagree on an ethical question, there is nothing to be done about it or that there is no scope in ethics for inference. No argument is available which could prove the subjectivity or fallaciousness of all ethics without establishing a similar conclusion about all other branches of study except mathematics and formal logic.

Notes

1. I am therefore quite unmoved by the elaborate discussion by C. L. Stevenson in *Ethics and Language* as to how argument can be relevant to ethical disagreements on a subjectivist view. It does not show it to be relevant in the sense in which we really see it to be relevant, but in some other sense. The book is no doubt a very able exposition of subjectivism for those who are already convinced, but it does not, as far as I can see, bring any real argument for it or avoid any of the objections that I have mentioned against it.

2. This proposition is not convertible: I include under "intuition" cases where some mediation is required but insight goes beyond anything that could be strictly proved by the mediation.

3. [See the previous reading by Russell.—Ed.]

Questions on Ewing

1. What is the simplest form of the subjectivist view? Summarize Ewing's reductio ad absurdum of this view. Is this the view that Russell holds in the previous reading? Explain.

2. Ewing distinguishes between disagreements about facts and disagreements about values. How is this distinction drawn? Are there any cases where this distinction is not clear? What about the anti-abortionist who says that fetuses are persons, and the pro-choice person who says that fetuses are not persons? Is this a factual dispute or one about values?

3. Toward the end of his article, Ewing quotes Russell's view about moral differences, and then tries to show how such differences could be resolved. Would the methods he suggests work in a real case? Try to apply them to the euthanasia debate where some people believe that defective infants should be quickly and painlessly killed, say by a lethal injection, and others insist that this is wrong.

Suggested Readings

J. L. Mackie, *Ethics* (New York: Penguin Books, 1977) presents subjectivism and tries to meet objections to it.

Gilbert Harman, *The Nature of Morality: An Introduction to Ethics* (New York: Oxford University Press, 1977) defends a sophisticated version of ethical relativism.

P. Helm, ed., *Divine Commands and Morality* (New York: Oxford University Press, 1981) is a useful anthology on the divine command theory.

John Ladd, ed., *Ethical Relativism* (Belmont, CA: Wadsworth Publishing Co., 1973) is a good collection of readings on ethical relativism.

Philip Quinn, *Divine Commands and Moral Requirements* (Oxford: Clarendon Press, 1978) gives a sophisticated defense of a version of the divine command theory using all the technical tools of modern logic. Some of this is too advanced for the beginning reader, but portions are interesting, particularly chapter 1 in which Quinn replies to the objection that the theory is incompatible with human freedom.

Social scientist Edward Westermarck, in his *Ethical Relativity* (London: Routledge & Kegan Paul, 1932), gives a clear statement of the sort of cultural relativism that Rachels attacks.

James Rachels, in his highly recommended *The Elements of Moral Philosophy* (New York: Random House, 1986), gives a clear discussion of different types of subjectivism in chapter 3. Chapter 4 of this book has a helpful treatment of the divine command theory and the appeal to natural law.

C. L. Stevenson, *Ethics and Language* (New Haven: Yale University Press, 1944) develops a subtle type of subjectivism known as emotivism. The book is fairly difficult reading.

Paul W. Taylor, *Principles of Ethics: An Introduction* (Belmont, CA: Wadsworth Publishing Co., 1975) gives a very clear discussion of ethical relativism in chapter 2.

What Should I Do?

Chapter 8

Introduction

Chapter 8

Normative ethical theories.   In this chapter, we turn to normative ethical theories, which try to tell us how to act and what sort of person we should be. It is customary to distinguish between normative theories of conduct that tell us how to act, theories of character that tell us what makes a person good, and theories of value that tell us what is good in itself or as a means to something else. Our primary concern is with theories about the right and good character and not with theories of the good, but it should be noted that philosophers often combine the different sorts of theory. Aristotle, for example, says that happiness is the highest practical good, but contrary to popular opinion, he denies that happiness is pleasure. Instead he argues that happiness consists of virtuous activity, where this includes both moral and intellectual activities. Thus Aristotle combines a theory of value with a theory of virtue that tells us what sort of character we should have, what sort of life we should lead, and how we should act.

John Stuart Mill agrees with Aristotle that happiness is the supreme good, but unlike Aristotle, Mill accepts the popular view that happiness is pleasure and the absence of pain. Thus Mill accepts *hedonism,* the theory of value that says only pleasure is intrinsically good. Of course Mill also advocates utilitarianism, the normative theory that the rightness of an action is determined by its consequences. Utilitarianism is a theory of the right that requires some theory about the good, since rightness is determined by good consequences, but the theory by itself leaves open just what theory of the good is adopted. Thus the British philosopher G. E. Moore (1873–1958) accepted a version of utilitarianism called ideal utilitarianism in which beauty and other things besides pleasure are recognized as good.

Despite their differences, these normative theories have certain features in common. None of them appeals to God's commands; they try to establish what is right independent of religious belief. They are universal theories that are supposed to apply to everyone, not just to the members of some particular society or group. None of the theories accepts cultural relativism. Last, they are objective theories in that they do not make emotions or subjective feelings or opinions the basis for judgments about rightness or wrongness; these theories appeal instead to reason.

Ethical egoism.   Ethical egoism is not usually favored by philosophers, but it is still an important theory because of its popular appeal and the fact that it is used to defend non-welfare capitalism (for example, by the novelist Ayn Rand and some conservative economists). *Universal ethical egoism* can be defined as the theory that everyone ought to act in his or her own self-interest. As Paul Taylor points out in the reading, we must be careful to distinguish this theory from at least three other views. *Psychological egoism* is the view that everyone in fact acts in their own self-interest, that everyone always acts selfishly, as distinguished from saying that everyone *ought* to act this way. Taylor is mainly concerned with demonstrating the internal inconsistency of universal ethical egoism and not with showing that psychological egoism is false. Another type of ethical egoism is *personal egoism,* the view that individuals should promote their own interest without taking any position on how others should act. As such this does not qualify as a normative theory because it is not universal; it does not tell us how everyone should act. Third, there is what Taylor calls *individual egoism.* This theory is best expressed in the first-person: "I should promote my self-interest, and everyone else should also promote my self-interest rather than their own self-interest." The trouble with this implausible view is that no reason is given why I, the individual egoist, should receive such special treatment.

Utilitarianism. It is safe to say that utilitarianism in some form or other has been the most popular and widely discussed of the normative ethical theories. The theory was originally formulated by the British philosopher Jeremy Bentham (1748–1832). Bentham's version is that we should act to produce pleasure, but it does not matter what sort of pleasure is produced; the pig's pleasure in eating is just as important as Socrates' pleasure in doing philosophy. Mill, by contrast, thinks that Socrates' pleasure is more valuable than the pig's because the person who has experienced both sorts of pleasure would, Mill thinks, prefer the pleasure of Socrates over that of the pig. Mill's official statement of the theory is that it accepts the "greatest happiness principle," which says that actions are right insofar as they tend to promote happiness, where happiness includes both pleasure and the absence of pain.

One very important advantage that utilitarianism offers is a way of resolving moral conflicts, at least in principle. On a subjectivist theory, it is impossible to resolve a basic moral conflict since the conflict involves a basic difference in taste, and there is no disputing about taste. But with a utilitarian theory, we can resolve such basic differences because we can try to calculate the net happiness that an act or practice will produce, counting everyone equally. If the act produces a greater net balance of happiness than the alternative or alternatives, it is the right thing to do. If people disagree, and insist that the act is wrong, we can reply that they are just mistaken—the act is right, and objectively so.

Like most other theories in philosophy, utilitarianism has its problems. One is the problem of proof: How can the principle of utility or the greatest happiness principle be proven? Mill offers a famous argument—that the only proof that can be given that something is desirable is that it is desired, and since happiness is desired, it must, therefore, be desirable. Commentators have spent a great deal of time and energy either attacking or defending this argument.

The standard objection to utilitarianism is that it results in injustice. Various examples are used to show this. Suppose that a number of lives can be saved if we execute an innocent person (use your imagination to fill in the details). Utilitarianism seems to require us to do this even though it is unjust. Paul Taylor discusses this sort of objection in the readings and tries to reply to it from a utilitarian point of view. His reply is that injustice will not turn out to have the best consequences over the long run, and hence utilitarianism will not result in injustice after all, at least not in the long run.

Kant's theory.   No treatment of normative theories would be complete without Kant's theory. It is difficult to read, and even harder to summarize. Kant begins with a discussion of the good. Contrary to popular opinion and to hedonistic utilitarians like Mill, Kant does not think that pleasure and happiness are good without qualification (to use his phrase). If these things are found in an evil person they are not good. The only thing that is good without qualification, according to Kant, is "the good will."

The good will involves the intention to do what is right, or to do one's duty. Kant then turns to the notion of duty. He believes that we can discover our duty, the "moral law," simply by using our reason. What we discover is that the moral law must be a universal law of conduct applying to everyone without exception. According to Kant, this moral law takes the form of a "categorical imperative." The categorical imperative is formulated in different ways, but one of the main formulations in the readings is this: "I ought never to act except in such a way that I can also will that my maxim should become a universal law." Perhaps the best way to understand this rule is to apply it to particular actions, for example, making a false promise. As Kant says, we would not want to have making false promises a universal law that everyone follows. Thus this action is wrong.

In the readings, Onora O'Neill applies Kantain principles to famine problems. The particular principle she uses is not the one just quoted but another version of the categorical imperative that has the rather grand title of the Formula of the End in Itself. This principle says that we should treat people as ends rather than as mere means. O'Neill clearly explains what this principle means, how it is related to other Kantian principles, and how it applies to the important social problem of famine relief in comparison with utilitarian ethics.

Aristotle

Happiness and the Good Life

Aristotle (384–322 B.C.) was the foremost student of Plato. Recognized as one of the greatest philosophers, he made important contributions to all areas of philosophy including the formulation of traditional logic.

Book I*

1

Every art and every inquiry, and similarly every action and pursuit, is thought to aim at some good; and for this reason the good has rightly been declared to be that at which all things aim. But a certain difference is found among ends; some are activities, others are products apart from the activities that produce them. Where there are ends apart from the actions, it is the nature of the products to be better than the activities. Now, as there are many actions, arts, and sciences, their ends also are many; the end of the medical art is health, that of ship building a vessel, that of strategy victory, that of economics wealth. But where such arts fall under a single capacity—as bridlemaking and the other arts concerned with the equipment of horses fall under the art of riding, and this and every military action under strategy, in the same way other arts fall under yet others—in all of these the ends of the master arts are to be preferred to all the subordinate ends; for it is for the sake of the former that the latter are pursued. It makes no difference whether the activities themselves are the ends of the actions, or something else apart from the activities, as in the case of the sciences just mentioned.

Books I: 1–5, 7–9, 13; II: 1, 6, 7, 9; and X: 7, 8 from *Ethica Nicomachea* translated by W. D. Ross in *The Oxford Translation of Aristotle*, vol. 9 (Oxford: Oxford University Press, [1925] 1944). Reprinted by permission of Oxford University Press.

*[The footnotes have been eliminated.—Ed.]

2

If, then, there is some end of the things we do, which we desire for its own sake (everything else being desired for the sake of this), and if we do not choose everything for the sake of something else (for at that rate the process would go on to infinity, so that our desire would be empty and vain), clearly this must be the good and the chief good. Will not the knowledge of it, then, have a great influence on life? Shall we not, like archers who have a mark to aim at, be more likely to hit upon what is right? If so, we must try, in outline at least to determine what it is, and of which of the sciences or capacities it is the object. It would seem to belong to the most authoritative art and that which is most truly the master art. And politics appears to be of this nature; for it is this that ordains which of the sciences should be studied in a state, and which each class of citizens should learn and up to what point they should learn them; and we see even the most highly esteemed of capacities to fall under this, e. g. strategy, economics, rhetoric; now, since politics uses the rest of the sciences, and since, again, it legislates as to what we are to do and what we are to abstain from, the end of this science must include those of the others, so that this end must be the good for man. For even if the end is the same for a single man and for a state, that of the state seems at all events something greater and more complete whether to attain or to preserve; though it is worth while to attain the end merely for one man, it is finer and more godlike to attain it for a nation or for city-states. These, then, are the ends at which our inquiry aims, since it is political science, in one sense of that term.

3

Our discussion will be adequate if it has as much clearness as the subject-matter admits of, for precision is not to be sought for alike in all discussions, any more than in all the products of the crafts. Now fine and just actions, which political science investigates, admit of much variety and fluctuation of opinion, so that they may be thought to exist only by convention, and not by nature. And goods also give rise to a similar fluctuation because they bring harm to many people; for before now men have been undone by reason of their wealth, and others by reason of their courage. We must be content, then, in speaking of such subjects and with such premises to indicate the truth roughly and in outline, and in speaking about things which are only for the most part true and with premises of the same kind to reach conclusions that are no better. In the same spirit, therefore, should each type of statement be received; for it is the mark of an educated man to look for precision in each class of things just so far as the nature of the subject admits; it is evidently equally foolish to accept probable reasoning from a mathematician and to demand from a rhetorician scientific proofs.

Now each man judges well the things he knows, and of these he is a good judge. And so the man who has been educated in a subject is a good judge of that subject, and the man who has received an all-round education is a good judge in general. Hence a young man is not a proper hearer of lectures on political science; for he is inexperienced in the actions that occur in life, but its discussions start from these and are about these; and, further, since he tends to follow his passions, his study will be vain and unprofitable, because the end aimed at is not knowledge but action. And it makes no difference whether he is young in years or youthful in character; the defect does not depend on time, but on his living, and pursuing each successive object, as passion directs. For to such persons, as to the incontinent, knowledge brings no profit; but to those who desire and act in accordance with a rational principle knowledge about such matters will be of great benefit.

These remarks about the student, the sort of treatment to be expected, and the purpose of the inquiry, may be taken as our preface.

4

Let us resume our inquiry and state, in view of the fact that all knowledge and every pursuit aims at some good, what it is that we say political science aims at and what is the highest of all goods achievable by action. Verbally there is very general agreement; for both the general run of men and people of superior refinement say that it is happiness, and identify living well and doing well with being happy; but with regard to what happiness is they differ, and the many do not give the same account as the wise. For the former think it is some plain and obvious thing, like pleasure, wealth, or honour; they differ, however, from one another—and often even the same man identifies it with different things, with health when he is ill, with wealth when he is poor; but, conscious of their ignorance, they admire those who proclaim some great ideal that is above their comprehension. Now some thought that apart from these many goods there is another which is self-subsistent and causes the goodness of all these as well. To examine all the opinions that have been held were perhaps somewhat fruitless; enough to examine those that are most prevalent or that seem to be arguable . . . .

5

Let us, however, resume our discussion from the point at which we digressed. To judge from the lives that men lead, most men, and men of the most vulgar type, seem (not without some ground) to identify the good, or happiness, with pleasure; which is the reason why they love the life of enjoyment. For there are, we may say, three prominent types of life—that just mentioned, the political, and thirdly the contemplative life. Now the mass of mankind are evidently quite slavish in their tastes, preferring a life suitable to beasts, but they get some ground for their view from the fact that many of those in high places share the tastes of Sardanapallus. A consideration of the prominent types of life shows that people of superior refinement and of active disposition identify happiness with honour; for this is, roughly speaking, the end of the political life. But it seems too superficial to be what we are looking for, since it is thought to depend on those who bestow honour rather than on him who receives it, but the good we divine to be something proper to a man and not easily taken from him. Further, men seem to pursue honour in order that they may be assured of their goodness; at least it is by men of practical wisdom that they seek to be honoured, and among those who know them, and on the ground of their virtue; clearly, then, according to them, at any rate, virtue is better. And perhaps one might even suppose this to be, rather than honour, the end of the political life. But even this appears somewhat incomplete; for possession of virtue seems actually compatible with being asleep, or with life-long inactivity, and, further, with the greatest sufferings and misfortunes; but a man who was living so no one would call happy, unless he were maintaining a thesis at all costs. But enough of this; for the subject has been sufficiently treated even in the current discussions. Third comes the contemplative life, which we shall consider later.

The life of money-making is one undertaken under compulsion, and wealth is evidently not the good we are seeking; for it is merely useful and for the sake of something else. And so one might rather take the aforenamed objects to be ends; for they are loved for themselves. But it is evident that not even these are ends; yet many arguments have been thrown away in support of them. . . .

7

Let us again return to the good we are seeking, and ask what it can be. It seems different in different actions and arts; it is different in medicine, in strategy, and in the other arts likewise. What then is the good of each? Surely that for whose sake everything else is done. In medicine this is health, in strategy victory, in architecture a house, in any other sphere something else, and in every action and pursuit the end; for it is for the sake of this that all men do whatever else they do. Therefore, if there is an end for all that we do, this will be the good achievable by action, and if there are more than one, these will be the goods achievable by action.

So the argument has by a different course reached the same point; but we must try to state this even more clearly. Since there are evidently more than one end, and we choose some of these (e. g. wealth, flutes, and in general instruments) for the sake of something else, clearly not all ends are final ends; but the chief good is evidently something final. Therefore, if there is only one final end, this will be what we are seeking, and if there are more than one, the most

final of these will be what we are seeking. Now we call that which is in itself worthy of pursuit more final than that which is worthy of pursuit for the sake of something else, and that which is never desirable for the sake of something else more final than the things that are desirable both in themselves and for the sake of that other thing, and therefore we call final without qualification that which is always desirable in itself and never for the sake of something else.

Now such a thing happiness, above all else, is held to be; for this we choose always for itself and never for the sake of something else, but honour, pleasure, reason, and every virtue we choose indeed for themselves (for if nothing resulted from them we should still choose each of them), but we choose them also for the sake of happiness, judging that by means of them we shall be happy. Happiness, on the other hand, no one chooses for the sake of these, nor, in general, for anything other than itself.

From the point of view of self-sufficiency the same result seems to follow; for the final good is thought to be self-sufficient. Now by self-sufficient we do not mean that which is sufficient for a man by himself, for one who lives a solitary life, but also for parents, children, wife, and in general for his friends and fellow citizens, since man is born for citizenship. But some limit must be set to this; for if we extend our requirement to ancestors and descendants and friends' friends we are in for an infinite series. Let us examine this question, however, on another occasion; the self-sufficient we now define as that which when isolated makes life desirable and lacking in nothing; and such we think happiness to be; and further we think it most desirable of all things, without being counted as one good thing among others—if it were so counted it would clearly be made more desirable by the addition of even the least of goods; for that which is added becomes an excess of goods, and of goods the greater is always more desirable. Happiness, then, is something final and self-sufficient, and is the end of action.

Presumably, however, to say that happiness is the chief good seems a platitude, and a clearer account of what it is is still desired. This might perhaps be given, if we could first ascertain the function of man. For just as for a fluteplayer, a sculptor, or any artist, and, in general, for all things that have a function or activity, the good and the 'well' is thought to reside in the function, so would it seem to be for man, if he has a function. Have the carpenter, then, and the tanner certain functions or activities, and has man none? Is he born without a function? Or as eye, hand, foot, and in general each of the parts evidently has a function, may one lay it down that man similarly has a function apart from all these? What then can this be? Life seems to be common even to plants, but we are seeking what is peculiar to man. Let us exclude, therefore, the life of nutrition and growth. Next there would be a life of perception, but *it* also seems to be common even to the horse, the ox, and every animal. There remains, then, an active life of the element that has a rational principle; of this, one part has such a principle in the sense of being obedient to one, the other in the sense of possessing one and exercising thought. And, as 'life of the rational element' also has two meanings, we must state that life in the sense of activity is what we mean; for this seems to be the more proper sense of the term. Now if the function of man is an activity of soul which follows or implies a rational principle, and if we say 'a so-and-so' and 'a good so-and-so' have a function which is the same in kind, e. g. a lyre-player and a good lyre-player, and so without qualification in all cases, eminence in respect of goodness being added to the name of the function (for the function of a lyre-player is to play the lyre, and that of a good lyre-player is to do so well): if this is the case, [and we state the function of man to be a certain kind of life, and this to be an activity or actions of the soul implying a rational principle, and the function of a good man to be the good and noble performance of these, and if any action is well performed when it is performed in accordance with the appropriate excellence: if this is the case,] human good turns out to be activity of soul in accordance with virtue, and if there are more than one virtue, in accordance with the best and most complete.

But we must add 'in a complete life'. For one swallow does not make a summer, nor does one day; and so too one day, or a short time, does not make a man blessed and happy.

Let this serve as an outline of the good; for we must presumably first sketch it roughly, and then later fill in the details. But it would seem that any one is capable of carrying on and articulating what has once been well outlined, and that time is a good discoverer or partner in such a work; to which facts the advances of the arts are due; for any one can add what is lacking. And we must also remember what has been said before, and not look for precision in all things alike, but in each class of things such precision as accords with the subject-matter, and so much as is appropriate to the inquiry. For a carpenter and a geometer investigate the right angle in different ways; the former does so in so far as the right angle is useful for his work, while the latter inquires what it is or what sort of thing it is; for he is a spectator of the truth. We must act in the same way, then, in all other matters as well, that our main task may not be subordinated to minor questions. Nor must we demand the cause in all matters alike; it is enough in some cases that the *fact* be well established, as in the case of the first principles; the fact is the primary thing or first principle. Now of first principles we see some by induction, some by perception, some by a certain habituation, and others too in other ways. But each set of principles we must try to investigate in the natural way, and we must take pains to state them definitely, since they have a great influence on what follows. For the beginning is thought to be more than half of the whole, and many of the questions we ask are cleared up by it.

8

We must consider it, however, in the light not only of our conclusion and our premises, but also of what is commonly said about it; for with a true view all the data harmonize, but with a false one the facts soon clash. Now goods have been divided into three classes, and some are described as external, others as relating to soul or to body; we call those that relate to soul most properly and truly goods, and psychical actions and activities we class as relating to soul. Therefore our account must be sound, at least according to this view, which is an old one and agreed on by philosophers. It is correct also in that we identify the end with certain actions and activities; for thus it falls among goods of the soul and not among external goods. Another belief which harmonizes with our account is that the happy man lives well and does well; for we have practically defined happiness as a sort of good life and good action. The characteristics that are looked for in happiness seem also, all of them, to belong to what we have defined happiness as being. For some identify happiness with virtue, some with practical wisdom, others with a kind of philosophic wisdom, others with these, or one of these, accompanied by pleasure or not without pleasure; while others include also external prosperity. Now some of these views have been held by many men and men of old, others by a few eminent persons; and it is not probable that either of these should be entirely mistaken, but rather that they should be right in at least some one respect or even in most respects.

With those who identify happiness with virtue or some one virtue our account is in harmony; for to virtue belongs virtuous activity. But it makes, perhaps, no small difference whether we place the chief good in possession or in use, in state of mind or in activity. For the state of mind may exist without producing any good result, as in a man who is asleep or in some other way quite inactive, but the activity cannot; for one who has the activity will of necessity be acting, and acting well. And as in the Olympic Games it is not the most beautiful and the strongest that are crowned but those who compete (for it is some of these that are victorious), so those who act win, and rightly win, the noble and good things in life.

Their life is also in itself pleasant. For pleasure is a state of *soul*, and to each man that which he is said to be a lover of is pleasant; e. g. not only is a horse pleasant to the lover of horses, and a spectacle to the lover of sights, but also in the same way just acts are pleasant to the lover of justice and in general virtuous acts to the lover of virtue. Now for most men their pleasures are in conflict with one another because

these are not by nature pleasant, but the lovers of what is noble find pleasant the things that are by nature pleasant; and virtuous actions are such, so that these are pleasant for such men as well as in their own nature. Their life, therefore, has no further need of pleasure as a sort of adventitious charm, but has its pleasure in itself. For, besides what we have said, the man who does not rejoice in noble actions is not even good; since no one would call a man just who did not enjoy acting justly, nor any man liberal who did not enjoy liberal actions; and similarly in all other cases. If this is so, virtuous actions must be in themselves pleasant. But they are also *good* and *noble,* and have each of these attributes in the highest degree, since the good man judges well about these attributes; his judgement is such as we have described. Happiness then is the best, noblest, and most pleasant thing in the world, and these attributes are not severed as in the inscription at Delos—

Most noble is that which is justest, and best is health;
But pleasantest is it to win what we love.

For all these properties belong to the best activities; and these, or one—the best—of these, we identify with happiness.

Yet evidently, as we said, it needs the external goods as well; for it is impossible, or not easy, to do noble acts without the proper equipment. In many actions we use friends and riches and political power as instruments; and there are some things the lack of which takes the lustre from happiness, as good birth, goodly children, beauty; for the man who is very ugly in appearance or ill-born or solitary and childless is not very likely to be happy, and perhaps a man would be still less likely if he had thoroughly bad children or friends or had lost good children or friends by death. As we said, then, happiness seems to need this sort of prosperity in addition; for which reason some identify happiness with good fortune, though others identify it with virtue.

9

For this reason also the question is asked, whether happiness is to be acquired by learning or by habituation or some other sort of training, or comes in virtue of some divine providence or again by chance. Now if there is *any* gift of the gods to men, it is reasonable that happiness should be god-given, and most surely god-given of all human things inasmuch as it is the best. But this question would perhaps be more appropriate to another inquiry; happiness seems, however, even if it is not god-sent but comes as a result of virtue and some process of learning or training, to be among the most god-like things; for that which is the prize and end of virtue seems to be the best thing in the world, and something godlike and blessed.

It will also on this view be very generally shared; for all who are not maimed as regards their potentiality for virtue may win it by a certain kind of study and care. But if it is better to be happy thus than by chance, it is reasonable that the facts should be so, since everything that depends on the action of nature is by nature as good as it can be, and similarly everything that depends on art or any rational cause, and especially if it depends on the best of all causes. To entrust to chance what is greatest and most noble would be a very defective arrangment.

The answer to the question we are asking is plain also from the definition of happiness; for it has been said to be a virtuous activity of soul, of a certain kind. Of the remaining goods, some must necessarily pre-exist as conditions of happiness, and others are naturally co-operative and useful as instruments. And this will be found to agree with what we said at the outset; for we stated the end of political science to the best end, and political science spends most of its pains on making the citizens to be of a certain character, viz. good and capable of noble acts.

It is natural, then, that we call neither ox nor horse nor any other of the animals happy; for none of them is capable of sharing in such activity. For this reason also a boy is not happy; for he is not yet capable of such acts, owing to his age; and boys who are called happy are being congratulated by reason of the hopes we have for them. For there is required, as we said, not only complete virtue but also a complete life, since many changes occur in life, and all manner of chances, and the most prosperous may

fall into great misfortunes in old age, as is told of Priam in the Trojan Cycle; and one who has experienced such chances and has ended wretchedly no one calls happy. . . .

13

Since happiness is an activity of soul in accordance with perfect virtue, we must consider the nature of virtue; for perhaps we shall thus see better the nature of happiness. . . .

Book II
1

Virtue, then, being of two kinds, intellectual and moral, intellectual virtue in the main owes both its birth and its growth to teaching (for which reason it requires experience and time), while moral virtue comes about as a result of habit. . . . From this it is also plain that none of the moral virtues arises in us by nature; for nothing that exists by nature can form a habit contrary to its nature. For instance the stone which by nature moves downwards cannot be habituated to move upwards, not even if one tries to train it by throwing it up ten thousand times; nor can fire be habituated to move downwards, nor can anything else that by nature behaves in one way be trained to behave in another. Neither by nature, then, nor contrary to nature do the virtues arise in us; rather we are adapted by nature to receive them, and are made perfect by habit. . . .

6

We must, however, not only describe virtue as a state of character, but also say what sort of state it is. We may remark, then, that every virtue or excellence both brings into good condition the thing of which it is the excellence and makes the work of that thing be done well; e. g. the excellence of the eye makes both the eye and its work good; for it is by the excellence of the eye that we see well. Similarly the excellence of the horse makes a horse both good in itself and good at running and at carrying its rider and at awaiting the attack of the enemy. Therefore, if this is true in every case, the virtue of man also will be the state of character which makes a man good and which makes him do his own work well.

How this is to happen we have stated already, but it will be made plain also by the following consideration of the specific nature of virtue. In everything that is continuous and divisible it is possible to take more, less, or an equal amount, and that either in terms of the thing itself or relatively to us; and the equal is an intermediate between excess and defect. By the intermediate in the object I mean that which is equidistant from each of the extremes, which is one and the same for all men; by the intermediate relatively to us that which is neither too much nor too little—and this is not one, nor the same for all. For instance, if ten is many and two is few, six is the intermediate, taken in terms of the object; for it exceeds and is exceeded by an equal amount; this is intermediate according to arithmetical proportion. But the intermediate relatively to us is not to be taken so; if ten pounds are too much for a particular person to eat and two too little, it does not follow that the trainer will order six pounds; for this also is perhaps too much for the person who is to take it, or too little—too little for Milo, too much for the beginner in athletic exercises. The same is true of running and wrestling. Thus a master of any art avoids excess and defect, but seeks the intermediate and chooses this—the intermediate not in the object but relatively to us.

If it is thus, then, that every art does its work well—by looking to the intermediate and judging its works by this standard (so that we often say of good works of art that it is not possible either to take away or to add anything, implying that excess and defect destroy the goodness of works of art, while the mean preserves it; and good artists, as we say, look to this in their work), and if, further, virtue is more exact and better than any art, as nature also is, then virtue must have the quality of aiming at the intermediate. I mean moral virtue; for it is this that is concerned with passions and actions, and in these there is excess, defect, and the intermediate. For instance, both fear and confidence and appetite and anger and pity and in general pleasure and pain may be felt both too much and too little, and in both cases not well; but to feel them at the right times, with reference to the right objects, towards the right people, with the right motive, and in the right way, is what is both intermediate and best, and this is characteristic of virtue. Similarly with regard to actions also there is excess, defect, and the intermediate. Now virtue is concerned with passions and actions, in which excess is a form of failure, and so is defect, while the intermediate is praised and is a form of success; and being praised and being successful are both characteristics of virtue. Therefore virtue is a kind of mean, since, as we have seen, it aims at what is intermediate.

Again, it is possible to fail in many ways (for evil belongs to the class of the unlimited, as the Pythagoreans conjectured, and good to that of the limited), while to succeed is possible only in one way (for which reason also one is easy and the other difficult—to miss the mark easy, to hit it difficult); for these reasons also, then, excess and defect are characteristic of vice, and the mean of virtue;

For men are good in but one way, but bad in many.

Virtue, then, is a state of character concerned with choice, lying in a mean, i. e. the mean relative to us, this being determined by a rational principle, and by that principle by which the man of practical wisdom would determine it. Now it is a mean between two vices, that which depends on excess and that which depends on defect; and again it is a mean because the vices respectively fall short of or exceed what is right in both passions and actions, while virtue both finds and chooses that which is intermediate. Hence in respect of its substance and the definition which states its essence virtue is a mean, with regard to what is best and right an extreme.

But not every action nor every passion admits of a mean; for some have names that already imply badness, e. g. spite, shamelessness, envy, and in the case of actions adultery, theft, murder; for all of these and suchlike things imply by their names that they are themselves bad, and not the excesses or deficiencies of them. It is not possible, then, ever to be right with regard to them; one must always be wrong.

Nor does goodness or badness with regard to such things depend on committing adultery with the right woman, at the right time, and in the right way, but simply to do any of them is to go wrong. It would be equally absurd, then, to expect that in unjust, cowardly, and voluptuous action there should be a mean, an excess, and a deficiency; for at that rate there would be a mean of excess and of deficiency, an excess of excess, and a deficiency of deficiency. But as there is no excess and deficiency of temperance and courage because what is intermediate is in a sense an extreme, so too of the actions we have mentioned there is no mean nor any excess and deficiency, but however they are done they are wrong; for in general there is neither a mean of excess and deficiency, nor excess and deficiency of a mean.

7

We must, however, not only make this general statement, but also apply it to the individual facts. For among statements about conduct those which are general apply more widely, but those which are particular are more genuine, since conduct has to do with individual cases, and our statements must harmonize with the facts in these cases. We may take these cases from our table. With regard to feelings of fear and confidence courage is the mean; of the people who exceed, he who exceeds in fearlessness has no name (many of the states have no name), while the man who exceeds in confidence is rash, and he who exceeds in fear and falls short in confidence is a coward. With regard to pleasures and pains—not all of them, and not so much with regard to the pains—the mean is temperance, the excess self-indulgence. Persons deficient with regard to the pleasures are not often found; hence such persons also have received no name. But let us call them 'insensible'.

With regard to giving and taking of money the mean is liberality, the excess and the defect prodigality and meanness. In these actions people exceed and fall short in contrary ways; the prodigal exceeds in spending and falls short in taking, while the mean man exceeds in taking and falls short in spending. (At present we are

giving a mere outline or summary, and are satisfied with this; later these states will be more exactly determined.) With regard to money there are also other dispositions—a mean, magnificence (for the magnificent man differs from the liberal man; the former deals with large sums, the latter with small ones), and excess, tastelessness, and vulgarity, and a deficiency, niggardliness; these differ from the states opposed to liberality. . . .

9

That moral virtue is a mean, then, and in what sense it is so, and that it is a mean between two vices, the one involving excess, the other deficiency, and that it is such because its character is to aim at what is intermediate in passions and in actions, has been sufficiently stated. Hence also it is no easy task to be good. For in everything it is no easy task to find the middle, e. g. to find the middle of a circle is not for every one but for him who knows; so, too, any one can get angry—that is easy—or give or spend money; but to do this to the right person, to the right extent, at the right time, with the right motive, and in the right way, *that* is not for every one, nor is it easy; wherefore goodness is both rare and laudable and noble. . . .

Book III
7

If happiness is activity in accordance with virtue, it is reasonable that it should be in accordance with the highest virtue; and this will be that of the best thing in us. Whether it be reason or something else that is this element which is thought to be our natural ruler and guide and to take thought of things noble and divine, whether it be itself also divine or only the most divine element in us, the activity of this in accordance with its proper virtue will be perfect happiness. That this activity is comtemplative we have already said.

Now this would seem to be in agreement both with what we said before and with the truth. For, firstly, this activity is the best (since not only is reason the best thing in us, but the objects of reason are the best of knowable objects); and, secondly, it is the most continuous, since we can contemplate truth more continuously than we can do anything. And we think happiness has pleasure mingled with it, but the activity of philosophic wisdom is admittedly the pleasantest of virtuous activities; at all events the pursuit of it is thought to offer pleasures marvellous for their purity and their enduringness, and it is to be expected that those who know will pass their time more pleasantly than those who inquire. And the self-sufficiency that is spoken of must belong most to the contemplative activity. For while a philosopher, as well as a just man or one possessing any other virtue, needs the necessaries of life, when they are sufficiently equipped with things of that sort the just man needs people towards whom and with whom he shall act justly, and the temperate man, the brave man, and each of the others is in the same case, but the philosopher, even when by himself, can contemplate truth, and the better the wiser he is; he can perhaps do so better if he has fellow-workers, but still he is the most self-sufficient. And this activity alone would seem to be loved for its own sake; for nothing arises from it apart from the contemplating, while from practical activities we gain more or less apart from the action. And happiness is thought to depend on leisure; for we are busy that we may have leisure, and make war that we may live in peace. Now the activity of the practical virtues is exhibited in political or military affairs, but the actions concerned with these seem to be unleisurely. Warlike actions are completely so (for no one chooses to be at war, or provokes war, for the sake of being at war; any one would seem absolutely murderous if he were to make enemies of his friends in order to bring about battle and slaughter); but the action of the statesman is also unleisurely, and—apart from the political action itself—aims at despotic power and honours, or at all events happiness, for him and his fellow citizens—a happiness different from political action, and evidently sought as being different. So if among virtuous actions political and military actions are distinguished by nobility and greatness, and these are unleisurely and aim at an end and are not desirable for their own sake, but the activity of reason, which is contemplative, seems both

to be superior in serious worth and to aim at no end beyond itself, and to have its pleasure proper to itself (and this augments the activity), and the self-sufficiency, leisureliness, unweariedness (so far as this is possible for man), and all the other attributes ascribed to the supremely happy man are evidently those connected with this activity, it follows that this will be the complete happiness of man, if it be allowed a complete term of life (for none of the attributes of happiness is *in*complete).

But such a life would be too high for man; for it is not in so far as he is man that he will live so, but in so far as something divine is present in him; and by so much as this is superior to our composite nature is its activity superior to that which is the exercise of the other kind of virtue. If reason is divine, then in comparison with man, the life according to it is divine in comparison with human life. But we must not follow those who advise us, being men, to think of human things, and, being mortal, of mortal things, but must, so far as we can, make ourselves immortal, and strain every nerve to live in accordance with the best thing in us; for even if it be small in bulk, much more does it in power and worth surpass everything. This would seem, too, to be each man himself, since it is the authoritative and better part of him. It would be strange, then, if he were to choose not the life of his self but that of something else. And what we said before will apply now; that which is proper to each thing is by nature best and most pleasant for each thing; for man, therefore, the life according to reason is best and pleasantest, since reason more than anything else *is* man. This life therefore is also the happiest.

8

But in a secondary degree the life in accordance with the other kind of virtue is happy; for the activities in accordance with this befit our human estate. Just and brave acts, and other virtuous acts, we do in relation to each other, observing our respective duties with regard to contracts and services and all manner of actions and with regard to passions; and all of these seem to be typically human. Some of them seem even to arise from the body, and virtue of character to be in many ways bound up with the passions. Practical wisdom, too, is linked to virtue of character, and this to practical wisdom, since the principles of practical wisdom are in accordance with the moral virtues and rightness in morals is in accordance with practical wisdom. Being connected with the passions also, the moral virtues must belong to our composite nature; and the virtues of our composite nature are human; so, therefore, are the life and the happiness which correspond to these. The excellence of the reason is a thing apart; we must be content to say this much about it, for to describe it precisely is a task greater than our purpose requires. It would seem, however, also to need external equipment but little, or less than moral virtue does. Grant that both need the necessaries, and do so equally, even if the statesman's work is the more concerned with the body and things of that sort; for there will be little difference there; but in what they need for the exercise of their activities there will be much difference. The liberal man will need money for the doing of his liberal deeds, and the just man too will need it for the returning of services (for wishes are hard to discern, and even people who are not just pretend to wish to act justly); and the brave man will need power if he is to accomplish any of the acts that correspond to his virtue, and the temperate man will need opportunity; for how else is either he or any of the others to be recognized? It is debated, too, whether the will or the deed is more essential to virtue, which is assumed to involve both; it is surely clear that its perfection involves both; but for deeds many things are needed, and more, the greater and nobler the deeds are. But the man who is contemplating the truth needs no such thing, at least with a view to the exercise of his activity; indeed they are, one may say, even hindrances, at all events to his contemplation; but in so far as he is a man and lives with a number of people, he chooses to do virtuous acts; he will therefore need such aids to living a human life.

But that perfect happiness is a contemplative activity will appear from the following consideration as well. We assume the gods to be above all other beings blessed and happy; but what sort of actions must we assign to them?

Acts of justice? Will not the gods seem absurd if they make contracts and return deposits, and so on? Acts of a brave man, then, confronting dangers and running risks because it is noble to do so? Or liberal acts? To whom will they give? It will be strange if they are really to have money or anything of the kind. And what would their temperate acts be? Is not such praise tasteless, since they have no bad appetites? If we were to run through them all, the circumstances of action would be found trivial and unworthy of gods. Still, every one supposes that they *live* and therefore that they are active; we cannot suppose them to sleep like Endymion. Now if you take away from a living being action, and still more production, what is left but contemplation? Therefore the activity of God, which surpasses all others in blessedness, must be contemplative; and of human activities, therefore, that which is most akin to this must be most of the nature of happiness.

This is indicated, too, by the fact that the other animals have no share in happiness, being completely deprived of such activity. For while the whole life of the gods is blessed, and that of men too in so far as some likeness of such activity belongs to them, none of the other animals is happy, since they in no way share in contemplation. Happiness extends, then, just so far as contemplation does, and those to whom contemplation more fully belongs are more truly happy, not as a mere concomitant but in virtue of the contemplation; for this is in itself precious. Happiness, therefore, must be some form of contemplation.

But, being a man, one will also need external prosperity; for our nature is not self-sufficient for the purpose of contemplation, but our body also must be healthy and must have food and other attention. Still, we must not think that the man who is to be happy will need many things or great things, merely because he cannot be supremely happy without external goods; for self-sufficiency and action do not involve excess, and we can do noble acts without ruling earth and sea; for even with moderate advantages one can act virtuously (this is manifest enough; for private persons are thought to do worthy acts no less than despots—indeed even more); and it is enough that we should have so much as that; for the life of the man who is active in accordance with virtue will be happy. Solon, too, was perhaps sketching well the happy man when he described him as moderately furnished with externals but as having done (as Solon thought) the noblest acts, and lived temperately; for one can with but moderate possessions do what one ought. Anaxagoras also seems to have supposed the happy man not to be rich nor a despot, when he said that he would not be surprised if the happy man were to seem to most people a strange person; for they judge by externals, since these are all they perceive. The opinions of the wise seem, then, to harmonize with our arguments. But while even such things carry some conviction, the truth in practical matters is discerned from the facts of life; for these are the decisive factor. We must therefore survey what we have already said, bringing it to the test of the facts of life, and if it harmonizes with the facts we must accept it, but if it clashes with them we must suppose it to be mere theory. Now he who exercises his reason and cultivates it seems to be both in the best state of mind and most dear to the gods. For if the gods have any

care for human affairs, as they are thought to have, it would be reasonable both that they should delight in that which was best and most akin to them (i. e. reason) and that they should reward those who love and honour this most, as caring for the things that are dear to them and acting both rightly and nobly. And that all these attributes belong most of all to the philosopher is manifest. He, therefore, is the dearest to the gods. And he who is that will presumably be also the happiest; so that in this way too the philosopher will more than any other be happy.

Questions on Aristotle

1. What is happiness according to Aristotle? How is it related to virtue?

2. How does Aristotle understand virtue? Give some examples.

3. Is it possible for everyone in our society to be happy, as Aristotle explains it? Why or why not?

4. Aristotle claims that the philosopher will be happier than anyone else. Why is this? Do you agree? Why or why not?

Paul Taylor
Ethical Egoism

Paul Taylor is Professor of Philosophy at Brooklyn College, City University of New York. In addition to his well-known textbook, Principles of Ethics: An Introduction, *from which we have two readings in this chapter, Taylor is the author of* Normative Discourse.

At the beginning of this chapter, the distinction between psychological egoism and ethical egoism was made as follows. Psychological egoism

is intended to be a factual, explanatory account of human motivation, stating a universal empirical truth about man's nature. Ethical egoism, on the other hand, is intended as a normative theory which sets up an ultimate standard or principle for determining right and wrong conduct. Psychological egoism means to tell us why people act the way they do, while ethical egoism attempts to tell us how people ought to act. The question now is, What reasons are there for accepting, or rejecting, the principle of ethical egoism as a guide to conduct?

One proposed argument for accepting the principle has already been examined. This states (1) that psychological egoism is true, and (2) that ethical egoism provides the only normative principle which it is psychologically possible for people to comply with. Since the purpose of accepting a normative principle is to guide people's conduct, once psychological egoism is accepted, ethical egoism must be accepted, too. For if psychological egoism is true, each person's actions can only be motivated by what he believes will promote his self-interest. What actually *will* promote his self-interest must then become the sole basis for judging conduct. No other principle could function as a norm for human conduct because every individual, being egoistically motivated, would be unable to use a nonegoistic principle in deciding how to act.

Some reasons for questioning the truth of psychological egoism have been brought out in the preceding section of this chapter, and its final acceptance or rejection is left open. Whatever one's views on psychological egoism might be, however, the normative principle of ethical egoism must still be considered on its own merits. For some ethical egoists do not believe that their theory presupposes the acceptance of psychological egoism. Furthermore, they do not appeal to psychological egoism in support of their theory since they think psychological egoism actually gives a false account of human motivation. These ethical egoists hold that a person *can* be altruistically motivated to perform actions which he himself correctly believes to be contrary to his own self-interest. Nevertheless, these ethical egoists continue, no action is *right* unless it does further the individual's well-being. So let us now inquire into the grounds for accepting—or rejecting—ethical egoism independently of any stand we might take regarding the truth or falsity of psychological egoism.

When the ethical egoist is asked why everyone ought to act so as to promote his own self-interest, there are two sorts of reply he might make. First, he can simply assert that this is an ultimate principle of normative ethics. Or secondly, he might argue that this principle, if consistently followed by everyone, would have better results than some other guiding norm. Putting aside the first reply for the moment, let us look at the second.

The claim that everyone's following one principle would have *better* results than everyone's following another principle presupposes a standard of goodness or value by which some results are judged superior to others. If this

standard were anything but the fulfillment of everyone's self-interest to the greatest possible extent, it would seem that the position is not (universal) ethical egoism. Yet the fulfillment of everyone's self-interest in this argument constitutes an *end* to which the practice of each person following the rule "Do what will most promote my own interests" is taken as a *means*. Now suppose there were another, more effective means for bringing about this same end. For example, suppose that everyone's following the rule "Do what will most promote the interests of all people affected by my action" would actually tend to result in the fulfillment of everyone's self-interest to a greater extent than would result from everyone's complying with "Do what will most promote my own interests." In that case, the egoist would have to admit that it is our duty to follow the first rule. But that rule, as we shall see in the next chapter, is a principle of utilitarianism, not of egoism. To justify his own theory, the egoist would have to show that the universal following of the rule of self-interest will in fact more effectively promote everyone's self-interest than will the universal practice of utilitarianism. Whether this can indeed be shown is left to the reader's judgment, after consideration of utilitarianism in the next chapter.

However, most ethical egoists have supported their theory in the first way mentioned above. They have held each person's promotion of his own self-interest to be the supreme norm or ultimate principle of ethics, not merely a means to some further end. A famous example of this position is to be found in the philosophy of Thomas Hobbes. In his work, *Leviathan* (1651), Hobbes begins by distinguishing between two conditions of human life, which he calls "the state of nature" and "the Commonwealth." The state of nature is the human condition (as we may imagine it to be, even if it never occurred in actual history or in prehistorical times) where there is no legal or political system governing the relations among men. People in the state of nature do not recognize anyone as having authority over them. Their conduct is not regulated by laws, nor are they organized into a civil community with an established government to make and enforce laws and set policies binding on everyone. In such a social condition, it is impossible to break the law since there is none to break. We might then inquire, What about moral laws? Even if a group of people have no legal system or form of government, they might still have a set of moral rules which they acknowledge as binding upon them and which they back up by sanctions. But Hobbes denies this. The state of nature, in his view, is neither a legal nor a moral community. It is impossible in the state of nature to do anything morally wrong, since a "wrong" act means one that violates a moral rule, and no such precepts are binding upon men in that state.

Nevertheless, in the state of nature there is a standard of value. Meaning can be given to the words "good" and "bad," and the meaning Hobbes gives to them may be considered a form of ethical (or valuational) egoism. *"Good and evil,"* Hobbes says, "are names that signify our appetites and aversions." That is, good is what we like or desire; evil is what we dislike or wish to avoid. "In the condition of mere nature," he asserts, "private appetite is the measure of good and evil." Thus a person's only directive for right conduct is what will bring about the things *he* wants and prevent those he does not want. Furthermore, a person can do no wrong or injustice to others in the pursuit of his self-interest, because in the state of nature, Hobbes says, "the notions of right and wrong, justice and injustice, have there no place." Therefore Hobbes's position can be considered a form of ethical egoism.

It is true that Hobbes speaks of "laws of nature" as guiding men's conduct in the state of nature. One such law, for example, is *"to seek peace, and follow it."* Another is *"by all means we can, to defend ourselves."* But these laws of nature, as Hobbes views them, are not moral rules. They are simply maxims of prudence and carry with them no moral obligations toward others. That is, they are rules which an intelligent man will see he ought to follow if he is to pursue his self-interest successfully, but the interests of others can make no claim on him. The only reason he has to consider the welfare of others is to avoid their hostility, since this might lead them to try to frustrate his own interests. Thus the clever man in the state of nature will

see that it is to his benefit to protect himself from others. This might require that he join with someone else, if necessary, for mutual protection from the hostile action of a third person. But joining with others and cooperating with them is never an end in itself; nor is there a moral duty on one person's part to protect or further the interests of others.

Once a civil society is formed, however, a new condition of human life arises, one in which persons are members of a Commonwealth. It is only in this condition of life, according to Hobbes, that the concept of obligation is applicable. But even here the obligation is not other-regarding or altruistic (that is, an obligation grounded on the claims which the interests of others make upon us). It is and remains a self-regarding obligation. The obligation, binding upon everyone in the Commonwealth, is simply to obey the law set up by the Sovereign, who is given the authority to punish violators. The purpose of the law is to maintain the security of each person by protecting him from the harm others might do him. Hence the obligation to obey the law is grounded on self-interest and is binding only so long as the Sovereign makes sure that others will obey. For unless the ruler does so, one individual's obedience will not be a means for the protection of his own interests. Thus each person has good reason to obey the law only when others do likewise. Furthermore, each person is motivated to comply with the law by fear of punishment and not by a sense of duty toward others nor by a desire to further the common good. These considerations make clear that Hobbes's view of man in civil society is essentially as egoistic as his view of man in the state of nature. Indeed, an element of psychological egoism is introduced in this account of the basis of moral obligation. At one point Hobbes says, "Of the voluntary acts of every man, the object is some *good to himself,*"—a clear statement of the principle of psychological egoism. Hobbes makes this statement in explaining why a person would voluntarily renounce the condition of having no obligation to obey law and accept such an obligation (thereby creating the necessary conditions for the social contract or covenant and, with it, the Commonwealth). Hobbes thus gives self-interest as the motive for a person's deciding to join a moral and legal community where his conduct can be judged to be right or wrong. Whether or not his psychological egoism is accepted, Hobbes's ethical egoism does provide a systematic account of how the principle of self-interest can function as the ultimate ground of right conduct, not only in a "state of nature" where there are no moral rules, but also in a rule-governed community of moral agents.

What objections might be raised against the theory of universal ethical egoism, and what replies might be given to those objections? The most frequent criticism of universal ethical egoism is that it must be false because it contains an *internal inconsistency*. The argument goes as follows. The universal ethical egoist says that each person should promote his own self-interest. There will be many situations, however, in which a conflict of interest occurs between the egoist and others. In such situations, if others pursue their ends the egoist himself will be hindered or prevented from pursuing his own, and vice versa. Yet according to his theory, an action ought to be done whenever it furthers the interests of the agent, *whoever that agent may be.* It follows that in all cases of conflict of interest between the egoist himself and others, the principle of universal ethical egoism entails contradictory ought-statements. For it entails that another person ought to do a certain action (because it would promote his interests) and at the same time it entails that he ought not to, since his doing it would interfere with the egoist's pursuit of his own interests. Similarly, if the egoist's action would benefit him, then according to his theory he ought to do it. However, in a situation where his action conflicts with another's self-interest, that other would *correctly* judge that the action ought not to be done. Thus the two contradictory judgments: "The egoist ought to do the act" and "The egoist ought not to do the act" would both be true of the same action. It follows, therefore, that universal ethical egoism is internally inconsistent.

The egoist's reply to this argument is that, according to his theory, he need not *assert* that others ought to pursue their interests when doing so conflicts with the promotion of his own. He can simply keep quiet about the matter. Indeed, if he is to further his interests in the most effective way possible he should publicly urge others to be altruistic, since by following his counsel they will not interfere with him but, on the contrary, will help him attain his goals. If, then, he is true to the egoist principle that he ought to do everything that will most effectively further his own ends, he will not advocate publicly that everyone be an ethical egoist. Instead, he will declare that all persons should be altruists—at least with regard to the way they treat him!

It has seemed to the critics of egoism, however, that this reply does not get rid of the inconsistency. They point out that it follows from the theory of universal egoism that *each and every person* ought to think in the way described above. Thus everyone ought to urge others to be altruistic as a means to promoting his self-interest. And since each person's pursuit of self-interest requires that he not become altruistic himself, the theory implies that no one should be an altruist. Hence, every individual ought to do something (namely, promote his own self-interest by getting others to be altruistic) and at the same time ought to prevent another from doing what that other ought to do (namely, getting others to be altruistic without becoming altruistic himself).

The logical consequence of universal ethical egoism thus appears to be that everyone should do a certain sort of thing while actually it is impossible that everyone do it successfully. If one person succeeds in doing it (that is, succeeds in getting another to be altruistic while remaining egoistic himself), someone else must fail to do it (if he happens to be the person whom the other has successfully made altruistic). Ethical egoism need not be *advocated* universally for this internal inconsistency to arise. It is an inconsistency that arises from everyone's *practicing* ethical egoism by *not* advocating that everyone become an ethical egoist.

It should be noted that these considerations apply to what we have called "universal ethical egoism." The other two forms of ethical egoism, which were designated by the terms "individual" and "personal," can escape the foregoing difficulties, since neither claims that every person should promote his own self-interest. The "individual" ethical egoist holds that *he* should promote his self-interest and that all others should also promote his, the ethical egoist's, self-interest. There is nothing internally inconsistent with everyone's putting this principle into practice. The "personal" ethical egoist, on the other hand, asserts that *he* should promote his own self-interest and simply has nothing to say, one way or the other, concerning what anyone else ought to do. Here also, no contradiction is involved in what the personal ethical egoist claims ought to be done.

Can we accept, then, either of these forms of ethical egoism as a justifiable normative system? That there remain certain problems which each of them has to face becomes clear from the following reflections.

Consider, first, the position of the individual ethical egoist. He says that his interests ought to be furthered not only by his own actions but also by those of everyone else. One implication of his view is that his wishes, desires, and needs have a right to be fulfilled even at the cost of frustrating the wants of others. His ultimate principle, in other words, entails an inequality of rights among persons. We can then formulate a challenge which will reasonably be addressed to the egoist by all others: "Why should your self-interest count more than anyone else's? On what grounds do your wants and needs make a higher claim to fulfillment than those of anyone else? Unless you can show that you merit special consideration, there is no reason why others owe you a duty (namely, to further your interests) which you do not owe to them. And your theory itself offers no basis for your claim to special consideration, since anyone else can propose the same ultimate principle on his own behalf and thus endow his interests with a higher claim to fulfillment than yours. Your theory provides no *reasons* why you should be given unique treatment." It is difficult to see how the egoist could reply to this challenge. As long as others knew that it was contrary to their interests to accept his principle, they would need to be shown why they

should accept it before they could have a reason to do the actions it required of them. But the only way the individual egoist could justify others' accepting his principle would be by pointing out some *characteristic* of himself that made him deserving of special consideration. If he were to do this, however, the possession of the given characteristic would be the supreme principle of his system, not the principle of egoism itself. He would then have to admit that if anyone else were found to have the attribute in question, that person's interest would have a claim to fulfillment equal to his own. And this would be giving up individual ethical egoism.

Let us look, next, at the position of personal ethical egoism. The personal egoist escapes the foregoing criticism since he does not claim that others ought to promote his self-interest. He simply says that he ought to do those actions that will most benefit him, and makes no ought-statements about anyone else's actions (not even the statement that they ought not to interfere with or frustrate him in the pursuit of his interests). It is important to realize that the principle of personal ethical egoism does not provide any basis for judging the rightness or wrongness of the conduct of any individual other than the egoist himself. Once we see clearly that personal ethical egoism has this implication, we see how it is possible to raise the following objection to it. (It is an objection, be it noted, which cannot be raised against the theories of universal or individual ethical egoism.)

How can personal ethical egoism be considered a normative ethical system at all? Since it tells only one person in the world what *he* ought and ought not to do but remains completely silent about the actions of everyone else, it turns out to be nothing more than a private policy of action adopted by one person with regard to himself alone. It is a policy by which he can guide his own conduct, but it cannot serve to guide anyone else's. Consequently it does not qualify as a moral principle. Even if everyone were to accept the principle, it would leave all but one person completely in the dark about what they morally ought or ought not to do. It may indeed be *consistent* for someone to adopt the principle for himself and use it as a policy governing his own actions. But such a personal policy cannot provide others with moral reasons for or against doing anything they please.

This argument assumes that an ethical system must give an account of *moral* reasons for action and that a *moral* reason for action cannot be merely a personal policy adopted by one individual as a guide to his own conduct alone. If a statement about the properties or consequences of an action constitutes a moral reason for (or against) the action, then it must be a reason for *anyone's* performing (or refraining from) that kind of conduct, whenever *anyone* is in a situation in which doing and refraining from an action of the given kind are alternatives

open to him. Whether this view of a moral reason for action is itself acceptable is an issue that requires further inquiry into normative ethical systems.

Questions on Taylor

1. The main objection that Taylor makes against universal ethical egoism is that it is inconsistent. What is this inconsistency? Does the egoist have any way of avoiding it without giving up the universal form of ethical egoism? Explain your answer.

2. Taylor discusses two other forms of ethical egoism. What are they, and what is wrong with them according to Taylor? Do you agree that they are unacceptable theories? Why or why not?

John Stuart Mill
Utilitarianism

John Stuart Mill (1806–1873) was one of the most important and influential British empiricist philosophers. His main books are A System of Logic, Utilitarianism, *from which the reading is taken, and* On Liberty.

The creed which accepts as the foundation of morals, Utility, or the Greatest Happiness Principle, holds that actions are right in proportion as they tend to promote happiness, wrong as they tend to produce the reverse of happiness. By happiness is intended pleasure, and the absence of pain; by unhappiness, pain, and the privation of pleasure. To give a clear view of the moral standard set up by the theory, much more requries to be said; in particular, what things it includes in the ideas of pain and pleasure; and to what extent this is left an open question. But these supplementary explanations do

not affect the theory of life on which this theory of morality is grounded—namely, that pleasure, and freedom from pain, are the only things desirable as ends; and that all desirable things (which are as numerous in the utilitarian as in any other scheme) are desirable either for the pleasure inherent in themselves, or as means to the promotion of pleasure and the prevention of pain.

Now, such a theory of life excites in many minds, and among them in some of the most estimable in feeling and purpose, inveterate dislike. To suppose that life has (as they express it) no higher end than pleasure—no better and nobler object of desire and pursuit—they designate as utterly mean and grovelling; as a doctrine worthy only of swine, to whom the followers of Epicurus were, at a very early period, contemptuously likened; and modern holders of the doctrine are occasionally made the subject of equally polite comparisons by its German, French, and English assailants.

When thus attacked, the Epicureans have always answered, that it is not they, but their accusers, who represent human nature in a degrading light; since the accusation supposes human beings to be capable of no pleasures except those of which swine are capable. If this

---

The reading is from Mill's *Utilitarianism,* chapters II and IV.

supposition were true, the charge could not be gainsaid, but would then be no longer an imputation; for if the sources of pleasure were precisely the same to human beings and to swine, the rule of life which is good enough for the one would be good enough for the other. The comparison of the Epicurean life to that of beasts is felt as degrading, precisely because a beast's pleasures do not satisfy a human being's conceptions of happiness. Human beings have faculties more elevated than the animal appetites, and when once made conscious of them, do not regard anything as happiness which does not include their gratification. I do not, indeed, consider the Epicureans to have been by any means faultless in drawing out their scheme of consequences from the utilitarian principle. To do this in any sufficient manner, many Stoic, as well as Christian elements require to be included. But there is no known Epicurean theory of life which does not assign to the pleasures of the intellect, of the feelings and imagination, and of the moral sentiments, a much higher value as pleasures than to those of mere sensation. It must be admitted, however, that utilitarian writers in general have placed the superiority of mental over bodily pleasures chiefly in the greater permanency, safety, uncostliness, &c., of the former—that is, in their circumstantial advantages rather than in their intrinsic nature. And on all these points utilitarians have fully proved their case; but they might have taken the other, and, as it may be called, higher ground, with entire consistency. It is quite compatible with the principle of utility to recognise the fact, that some *kinds* of pleasure are more desirable and more valuable than others. It would be absurd that while, in estimating all other things, quality is considered as well as quantity, the estimation of pleasures should be supposed to depend on quantity alone.

If I am asked, what I mean by difference of quality in pleasures, or what makes one pleasure more valuable than another, merely as a pleasure, except its being greater in amount, there is but one possible answer. Of two pleasures, if there be one to which all or almost all who have experience of both give a decided preference, irrespective of any feeling of moral obligation to prefer it, that is the more desir-

able pleasure. If one of the two is, by those who are competently acquainted with both, placed so far above the other that they prefer it, even though knowing it to be attended with a greater amount of discontent, and would not resign it for any quantity of the other pleasure which their nature is capable of, we are justified in ascribing to the preferred enjoyment a superiority in quality, so far outweighing quantity as to render it, in comparison, of small account.

Now it is an unquestionable fact that those who are equally acquainted with, and equally capable of appreciating and enjoying, both, do give a most marked preference to the manner of existence which employs their higher faculties. Few human creatures would consent to be changed into any of the lower animals, for a promise of the fullest allowance of a beast's pleasures; no intelligent human being would consent to be a fool, no instructed person would be an ignoramus, no person of feeling and conscience would be selfish and base, even though they should be persuaded that the fool, the dunce, or the rascal is better satisfied with his lot than they are with theirs. They would not resign what they possess more than he, for the most complete satisfaction of all the desires which they have in common with him. If they ever fancy they would, it is only in cases of unhappiness so extreme, that to escape from it they would exchange their lot for almost any other, however undesirable in their own eyes. A being of higher faculties requires more to make him happy, is capable probably of more acute suffering, and is certainly accessible to it at more points, than one of an inferior type; but in spite of these liabilities, he can never really wish to sink into what he feels to be a lower grade of existence. We may give what explanation we please of this unwillingness; we may attribute it to pride, a name which is given indiscriminately to some of the most and to some of the least estimable feelings of which mankind are capable; we may refer it to the love of liberty and personal independence, an appeal to which was with the Stoics one of the most effective means for the inculcation of it; to the love of power, or to the love of excitement, both of which do really enter into and contribute to it: but its most appropriate appellation is a sense of dignity, which all human beings possess in one form or other, and in some, though by no means in exact, proportion to their higher faculties, and which is so essential a part of the happiness of those in whom it is strong, that nothing which conflicts with it could be, otherwise than momentarily, an object of desire to them. Whoever supposes that this preference takes place at a sacrifice of happiness—that the superior being, in anything like equal circumstances, is not happier than the inferior—confounds the two very different ideas, of happiness, and content. It is indisputable that the being whose capacities of enjoyment are low, has the greatest chance of having them fully satisified; and a highly-endowed being will always feel that any happiness which he can look for, as the world is constituted, is imperfect. But he can learn to bear its imperfections, if they are at all bearable; and they will not make him envy the being who is indeed unconscious of the imperfections, but only because he feels not at all the good which those imperfections qualify. It is better to be a human being dissatisfied than a pig satisfied; better to be Socrates dissatisfied than a fool satisfied. And if the fool, or the pig, is of a different opinion, it is because they only know their own side of the question. The other party to the comparison knows both sides.

It may be objected, that many who are capable of the higher pleasures, occasionally, under the influence of temptation, postpone them to the lower. But this is quite compatible with a full appreciation of the intrinsic superiority of the higher. Men often, from infirmity of character, make their election for the nearer good, though they know it to be the less valuable; and this no less when the choice is between two bodily pleasures, than when it is between bodily and mental. They pursue sensual indulgences to the injury of health, though perfectly aware that health is the greater good. It may be further objected, that many who begin with youthful enthusiasm for everything noble, as they advance in years sink into indolence and selfishness. But I do not believe that those who undergo this very common change, voluntarily choose the lower description of pleasures in preference to the higher. I believe that before they devote themselves exclusively to the one, they have al-ready become incapable of the other. Capacity for the nobler feelings is in most natures a very tender plant, easily killed, not only by hostile influences, but by mere want of sustenance; and in the majority of young persons it speedily dies away if the occupations to which their position in life has devoted them, and the society into which it has thrown them, are not favourable to keeping that higher capacity in exercise. Men lose their high aspirations as they lose their intellectual tastes, because they have not time or opportunity for indulging them; and they addict themselves to inferior pleasures, not because they deliberately prefer them, but because they are either the only ones to which they have access, or the only ones which they are any longer capable of enjoying. It may be questioned whether any one who has remained equally susceptible to both classes of pleasures, ever knowingly and calmly preferred the lower; though many, in all ages, have broken down in an ineffectual attempt to combine both.

From this verdict of the only competent judges, I apprehend there can be no appeal. On a question which is the best worth having of two pleasures, or which of two modes of existence is the most grateful to the feelings, apart from its moral attributes and from its consequences, the judgement of those who are qualified by knowledge of both, or, if they differ, that of the majority among them, must be admitted as final. And there needs be the less hesitation to accept this judgment respecting the quality of pleasures, since there is no other tribunal to be referred to even on the question of quantity. What means are there of determining which is the acutest of two pains, or the intensest of two pleasurable sensations, except the general suffrage of those who are familiar with both? Neither pains nor pleasures are homogeneous, and pain is always heterogeneous with pleasure. What is there to decide whether a particular pleasure is worth purchasing at the cost of a particular pain, except the feelings and judgment of the experienced? When, therefore, those feeling and judgment declare the pleasures derived from the higher faculties to be preferable *in kind*, apart from the question of intensity, to those of which the animal nature, disjoined from the higher faculties, is susceptible, they are entitled on this subject to the same regard. . . .

I must again repeat, what the assailants of utilitarianism seldom have the justice to acknowledge, that the happiness which forms the utilitarian standard of what is right in conduct, is not the agent's own happiness, but that of all concerned. As between his own happiness and that of others, utilitarianism requires him to be as strictly impartial as a disinterested and benevolent spectator. In the golden rule of Jesus of Nazareth, we read the complete spirit of the ethics of utility. To do as one would be done by, and to love one's neighbour as oneself, constitute the ideal perfection of utilitarian morality. As the means of making the nearest approach to this ideal, utility would enjoin, first, that laws and social arrangements should place the happiness, or (as speaking practically it may be called) the interest, of every individual, as nearly as possible in harmony with the interest of the whole; and secondly, that education and opinion, which have so vast a power over human character, should so use that power as to establish in the mind of every individual an indissoluble association between his own happiness and the good of the whole; especially between his own happiness and the practice of such modes of conduct, negative and positive, as regard for the universal happiness prescribes: so that not only he may be unable to conceive the possibility of happiness to himself, consistently with conduct opposed to the general good, but also that a direct impulse to promote the general good may be in every individual one of the habitual motives of action, and the sentiments connected therewith may fill a large and prominent place in every human being's sentient existence. If the impugners of the utilitarian morality represented it to their own minds in this its true character, I know not what recommendation possessed by any other morality they could possibly affirm to be wanting to it: what more beautiful or more exalted developments of human nature any other ethical system can be supposed to foster, or what springs of action, not accessible to the utilitarian, such systems rely on for giving effect to their mandates.

The objectors to utilitarianism cannot always be charged with representing it in a discreditable light. On the contrary, those among them who entertain anything like a just idea of its disinterested character, sometimes find fault with its standard as being too high for humanity. They say it is exacting too much to require that people shall always act from the inducement of promoting the general interests of society. But this is to mistake the very meaning of a standard of morals, and to confound the rule of action with the motive of it. It is the business of ethics to tell us what are our duties, or by what test we may know them; but no system of ethics requires that the sole motive of all we do shall be a feeling of duty; on the contrary, ninety-nine hundredths of all our actions are done from other motives, and rightly so done, if the rule of duty does not condemn them. It is the more unjust to utilitarianism that this particular misapprehension should be made a ground of objection to it, inasmuch as utilitarian moralists have gone beyond almost all others in affirming that the motive has nothing to do with the morality of the action, though much with the worth of the agent. He who saves a fellow creature from drowning does what is morally right, whether his motive be duty, or the hope of being paid for his trouble: he who betrays the friend that trusts him, is guilty of a crime, even if his object be to serve another friend to whom he is under greater obligations. But to speak only of actions done from the motive of duty, and in direct obedience to principle: it is a misapprehension of the utilitarian mode of thought, to conceive it as implying that people should fix their minds upon so wide a generality as the world, or society at large. The great majority of good actions are intended, not for the benefit of the world, but for that of individuals, of which the good of the world is made up; and the thoughts of the most virtuous man need not on these occasions travel beyond the particular persons concerned, except so far as is necessary to assure himself that in benefiting them he is not violating the rights—that is, the legitimate and authorized expectations—of any one else. The mulitiplication of happiness is, according to the utilitarian ethics, the object of virtue: the occasions on which any person (except one in a thousand) has it in his power to do this on an extended scale, in other words, to be a public benefactor, are but exceptional; and on these occasions alone is he called on to consider public utility; in every other case, private utility, the interest or happiness of some few persons, is all he has to attend to. Those alone the influence of whose actions extends to society in general, need concern themselves habitually about so large an object. In the case of abstinences indeed—of things which people forbear to do, from moral considerations, though the consequences in the particular case might be beneficial—it would be unworthy of an intelligent agent not to be consciously aware that the action is of a class which, if practised generally, would be generally injurious, and that this is the ground of the obligation to abstain from it. The amount of regard for the public interest implied in this recognition, is no greater than is demanded by every system of morals; for they all enjoin to abstain from whatever is manifestly pernicious to society. . . .

Again, Utility is often summarily stigmatized as an immoral doctrine by giving it the name of Expediency, and taking advantage of the popular use of that term to contrast it with Principle. But the Expedient, in the sense in which it is opposed to the Right, generally means that which is expedient for the particular interest of the agent himself; as when a minister sacrifices the interest of his country to keep himself in place. When it means anything better than this, it means that which is expedient for some immediate object, some temporary purpose, but which violates a rule whose observance is expedient in a much higher degree. The Expedient, in this sense, instead of being the same thing with the useful, is a branch of the hurtful. Thus, it would often be expedient, for the purpose of getting over some momentary embarrassment, or attaining some object immediately useful to ourselves or others, to tell a lie. But inasmuch as the cultivation in ourselves of a sensitive feeling on the subject of veracity, is one of the most useful, and the enfeeblement of that feeling one of the most hurtful, things to which our conduct can be instrumental; and inasmuch as any, even unintentional, deviation from truth, does that much towards weakening the trustworthiness of human assertion, which is not

only the principal support of all present social well-being, but the insufficiency of which does more than any one thing that can be named to keep back civilization, virtue, everything on which human happiness on the largest scale depends; we feel that the violation, for a present advantage, of a rule of such transcendant expediency, is not expedient, and that he who, for the sake of a convenience to himself or to some other individual, does what depends on him to deprive mankind of the good, and inflict upon them the evil, involved in the greater or less reliance which they can place in each other's word, acts the part of one of their worst enemies. Yet that even this rule, sacred as it is, admits of possible exceptions, is acknowledged by all moralists; the chief of which is when the withholding of some fact (as of information from a malefactor, or of bad news from a person dangerously ill) would preserve some one (especially a person other than oneself) from great and unmerited evil, and when the withholding can only be effected by denial. But in order that the exception may not extend itself beyond the need, and may have the least possible effect in weakening reliance on veracity, it ought to be recognised, and, if possible, its limits defined; and if the principle of utility is good for anything, it must be good for weighing these conflicting utilities against one another, and marking out the region within which one or the other preponderates.

Again, defenders of utility often find themselves called upon to reply to such objections as this—that there is not time, previous to action, for calculating and weighing the effects of any line of conduct on the general happiness. This is exactly as if any one were to say that it is impossible to guide our conduct by Christianity, because there is not time, on every occasion on which anything has to be done, to read through the Old and New Testaments. The answer to the objection is, that there has been ample time, namely, the whole past duration of the human species. During all that time mankind have been learning by experience the tendencies of actions; on which experience all the prudence, as well as all the morality of life, is dependent. People talk as if the commencement of this course of experience had hitherto been put off, and as if, at the moment when some man feels tempted to meddle with the property or life of another, he had to begin considering for the first time whether murder and theft are injurious to human happiness. Even then I do not think that he would find the question very puzzling; but, at all events, the matter is now done to his hand. It is truly a whimsical supposition that if mankind were agreed in considering utility to be the test of morality, they would remain without any agreement as to what *is* useful, and would take no measures for having their notions on the subject taught to the young, and enforced by law and opinion. There is no difficulty in proving any ethical standard whatever to work ill, if we suppose universal idiocy to be conjoined with it; but on any hypothesis short of that, mankind must by this time have acquired positive beliefs as to the effects of some actions on their happiness; and the beliefs which have thus come down are the rules of morality for the multitude, and for the philosopher until he has succeeded in finding better. That philosophers might easily do this, even now, on many subjects; that the received code of ethics is by no means of divine right; and that mankind have still much to learn as to the effects of actions on the general happiness, I admit, or rather, earnestly maintain. The corollaries from the principle of utility, like the precepts of every practical art, admit of indefinite improvement, and, in a progressive state of the human mind, their improvement is perpetually going on. But to consider the rules of morality as improvable, is one thing; to pass over the intermediate generalizations entirely, and endeavour to test each individual action directly by the first principle, is another. It is a strange notion that the acknowledgment of a first principle is inconsistent with the admission of secondary ones. To inform a traveller respecting the place of his ultimate destination, is not to forbid the use of landmarks and direction-posts on the way. The proposition that happiness is the end and aim of morality, does not mean that no road ought to be laid down to that goal, or that persons going thither should not be advised to take one direction rather than another. Men really ought to leave off talking a kind of nonsense on this subject, which they would neither talk nor listen to

on other matters of practical concernment. Nobody argues that the art of navigation is not founded on astronomy, because sailors cannot wait to calculate the Nautical Almanack. Being rational creatures, they go to sea with it ready calculated; and all rational creatures go out upon the sea of life with their minds made up on the common questions of right and wrong, as well as on many of the far more difficult questions of wise and foolish. And this, as long as foresight is a human quality, it is to be presumed they will continue to do. Whatever we adopt as the fundamental principle of morality, we require subordinate principles to apply it by: the impossibility of doing without them, being common to all systems, can afford no argument against any one in particular: but gravely to argue as if no such secondary principles could be had, and as if mankind had remained till now, and always must remain, without drawing any general conclusions from the experience of human life, is as high a pitch, I think, as absurdity has ever reached in philosophical controversy.

The remainder of the stock arguments against utilitarianism mostly consist in laying to its charge the common infirmities of human nature, and the general difficulties which embarrass conscientious persons in shaping their course through life. We are told that an utilitarian will be apt to make his own particular case an exception to moral rules, and, when under temptation, will see an utility in the breach of a rule, greater than he will see in its observance. But is utility the only creed which is able to furnish us with excuses for evil doing, and means of cheating our own conscience? They are afforded in abundance by all doctrines which recognise as a fact in morals the existence of conflicting considerations; which all doctrines do, that have been believed by sane persons. It is not the fault of any creed, but of the complicated nature of human affairs, that rules of conduct cannot be so framed as to require no exceptions, and that hardly any kind of action can safely be laid down as either always obligatory or always condemnable. There is no ethical creed which does not temper the rigidity of its laws, by giving a certain latitude, under the moral responsibility of the agent, for accommodation to peculiarities of circumstances; and under every creed, at the opening thus made, self-deception and dishonest casuistry get in. There exists no moral system under which there do not arise unequivocal cases of conflicting obligation. These are the real difficulties, the knotty points both in the theory of ethics, and in the conscientious guidance of personal conduct. They are overcome practically with greater or with less success according to the intellect and virtue of the individual; but it can hardly be pretended that any one will be the less qualified for dealing with them, from possessing an ultimate standard to which conflicting rights and duties can be referred. If utility is the ultimate source of moral obligations, utility may be invoked to decide between them when their demands are incompatible. Though the application of the standard may be difficult, it is better than none at all: while in other systems, the moral laws all claiming independent authority, there is no common umpire entitled to interfere between them; their claims to precedence one over another rest on little better than sophistry, and unless determined, as they generally are, by the unacknowledged influence of considerations of utility, afford a free scope for the action of personal desires and partialities. We must remember that only in these cases of conflict between secondary principles is it requisite that first principles should be appealed to. There is no case of moral obligation in which some secondary principle is not involved; and if only one, there can seldom be any real doubt which one it is, in the mind of any person by whom the principle itself is recognised.

Of What Sort of Proof the Principle of Utility Is Susceptible

It has already been remarked, that questions of ultimate ends do not admit of proof, in the ordinary acceptation of the term. To be incapable of proof by reasoning is common to all first principles; to the first premises of our knowledge, as well as to those of our conduct. But the former, being matter of fact, may be the subject of a direct appeal to the faculties which judge of fact—namely, our senses, and our internal consciousness. Can an appeal be made to the same faculties on questions of practical ends? Or by what other faculty is cognizance taken of them?

Questions about ends are, in other words, questions what things are desirable. The utilitarian doctrine is, that happiness is desirable, and the only thing desirable, as an end; all other things being only desirable as means to that end. What ought to be required of this doctrine—what conditions is it requisite that the doctrine should fulfil—to make good its claim to be believed?

The only proof capable of being given that an object is visible, is that people actually see it. The only proof that a sound is audible, is that people hear it: and so of the other sources of our experience. In like manner, I apprehend, the sole evidence it is possible to produce that anything is desirable, is that people do actually desire it. If the end which the utilitarian doctrine proposes to itself were not, in theory and in practice, acknowledged to be an end, nothing could ever convince any person that it was so. No reason can be given why the general happiness is desirable, except that each person, so far as he believes it to be attainable, desires his own happiness. This, however, being a fact, we have not only all the proof which the case admits of, but all which it is possible to require, that happiness is a good: that each person's happiness is a good to that person, and the general happiness, therefore, a good to the aggregate of all persons. Happiness has made out its title as *one* of the ends of conduct, and consequently one of the criteria of morality.

But it has not, by this alone, proved itself to be the sole criterion. To do that, it would seem, by the same rule, necessary to show, not only that people desire happiness, but that they never desire anything else. Now it is palpable that they do desire things which, in common language, are decidedly distinguished from happiness. They desire, for example, virtue, and the absence of vice, no less really than pleasure and the absence of pain. The desire of virtue is not as universal, but it is as authentic a fact, as the desire of happiness. And hence the opponents of the utilitarian standard deem that they have a right to infer that there are other ends of human action besides happiness, and that happiness is not the standard of approbation and disapprobation.

But does the utilitarian doctrine deny that people desire virtue, or maintain that virtue is not a thing to be desired? The very reverse. It maintains not only that virtue is to be desired, but that it is to be desired disinterestedly, for itself. Whatever may be the opinion of utilitarian moralists as to the original conditions by which virtue is made virtue; however they may believe (as they do) that actions and dispositions are only virtuous because they promote another end than virtue; yet this being granted, and it having been decided, from considerations of this description, what *is* virtuous, they not only place virtue at the very head of the things which are good as means to the ultimate end, but they also recognise as a psychological fact the possibility of its being, to the individual, a good in itself, without looking to any end beyond it; and hold, that the mind is not in a right state, not in a state conformable to Utility, not in the state most conducive to the general happiness, unless it does love virtue in this manner—as a thing desirable in itself, even although, in the individual instance, it should not produce those other desirable consequences which it tends to produce, and on account of which it is held to be virtue. This opinion is not, in the smallest degree, a departure from the Happiness principle. The ingredients of happiness are very various, and each of them is desirable in itself, and not merely when considered as swelling an aggregate. The principle of utility does not mean that any given pleasure, as music, for instance, or any given exemption from pain, as for example health, are to be looked upon as means to a collective something termed happiness, and to be desired on that account. They are desired and desirable in and for themselves; besides being means, they are a part of the end. Virtue, according to the utilitarian doctrine, is not naturally and originally part of the end, but it is capable of becoming so; and in those who love it disinterestedly it has become so, and is desired and cherished, not as a means to happiness, but as a part of their happiness.

To illustrate this farther, we may remember that virtue is not the only thing, originally a

means, and which if it were not a means to anything else, would be and remain indifferent, but which by association with what it is a means to, comes to be desired for itself, and that too with the utmost intensity. What, for example, shall we say of the love of money? There is nothing originally more desirable about money than about any heap of glittering pebbles. Its worth is solely that of the things which it will buy; the desires for other things than itself, which it is a means of gratifying. Yet the love of money is not only one of the strongest moving forces of human life, but money is, in many cases, desired in and for itself; the desire to possess it is often stronger than the desire to use it, and goes on increasing when all the desires which point to ends beyond it, to be compassed by it, are falling off. It may be then said truly, that money is desired not for the sake of an end, but as part of the end. From being a means to happiness, it has come to be itself a principal ingredient of the individual's conception of happiness. The same may be said of the majority of the great objects of human life—power, for example, or fame; except that to each of these there is a certain amount of immediate pleasure annexed, which has at least the semblance of being naturally inherent in them; a thing which cannot be said of money. Still, however, the strongest natural attraction, both of power and of fame, is the immense aid they give to the attainment of our other wishes; and it is the strong association thus generated between them and all our objects of desire, which gives to the direct desire of them the intensity it often assumes, so as in some characters to surpass in strength all other desires. In these cases the means have become a part of the end, and a more important part of it than any of the things which they are means to. What was once desired as an instrument for the attainment of happiness, has come to be desired for its own sake. In being desired for its own sake it is, however, desired as *part* of happiness. The person is made, or thinks he would be made, happy by its mere possession; and is made unhappy by failure to obtain it. The desire of it is not a different thing from the desire of happiness, any more than the love of music, or the desire of health. They are included in happiness. They are some of the elements of which the desire of happiness is made up. Happiness is not an abstract idea, but a concrete whole; and these are some of its parts. And the utilitarian standard sanctions and approves their being so. Life would be a poor thing, very ill provided with sources of happiness, if there were not this provision of nature, by which things originally indifferent, but conducive to, or otherwise associated with, the satisfaction of our primitive desires, become in themselves sources of pleasure more valuable than the primitive pleasures, both in permanency, in the space of human existence that they are capable of covering, and even in intensity.

Virtue, according to the utilitarian conception, is a good of this description. There was no original desire of it, or motive to it, save its conduciveness to pleasure, and especially to protection from pain. But through the association thus formed, it may be felt a good in itself, and desired as such with as great intensity as any other good; and with this difference between it and the love of money, of power, or of fame, that all of these may, and often do, render the individual noxious to the other members of the society to which he belongs, whereas there is nothing which makes him so much a blessing to them as the cultivation of the disinterested love of virtue. And consequently, the utilitarian standard, while it tolerates and approves those other acquired desires, up to the point beyond which they would be more injurious to the general happiness than promotive of it, enjoins and requires the cultivation of the love of virtue up to the greatest strength possible, as being above all things important to the general happiness.

It results from the preceding considerations, that there is in reality nothing desired except happiness. Whatever is desired otherwise than as a means to some end beyond itself, and ultimately to happiness, is desired as itself a part of happiness, and is not desired for itself until it has become so. Those who desire virtue for its own sake, desire it either because the consciousness of it is a pleasure, or because the consciousness of being without it is a pain, or for both reasons united; as in truth the pleasure and pain seldom exist separately, but almost always together, the same person feeling pleasure in the degree of virtue attained, and pain in not having attained more. If one of these gave him no pleasure, and the other no pain, he would not love or desire virtue, or would desire it only for the other benefits which it might produce to himself or to persons whom he cared for.

We have now, then, an answer to the question, of what sort of proof the principle of utility is susceptible. If the opinion which I have now stated is psychologically true—if human nature is so constituted as to desire nothing which is not either a part of happiness or a means of happiness, we can have no other proof, and we require no other, that these are the only things desirable. If so, happiness is the sole end of human action, and the promotion of it the test by which to judge of all human conduct; from whence it necessarily follows that it must be the criterion of morality, since a part is included in the whole.

And now to decide whether this is really so; whether mankind do desire nothing for itself but that which is a pleasure to them, or of which the absence is a pain; we have evidently arrived at a question of fact and experience, dependent, like all similar questions, upon evidence. It can only be determined by practised self-consciousness and self-observation, assisted by observation of others. I believe that these sources of evidence, impartially consulted, will declare that desiring a thing and finding it pleasant, aversion to it and thinking of it as painful, are phenomena entirely inseparable, or rather two parts of the same phenomenon; in strictness of language, two different modes of naming the same psychological fact: that to think of an object as desirable (unless for the sake of its consequences), and to think of it as pleasant, are one and the same thing; and that to desire anything, except in proportion as the idea of it is pleasant, is a physical and metaphysical impossibility.

So obvious does this appear to me, that I expect it will hardly be disputed: and the objection made will be, not that desire can possibly be directed to anything ultimately except pleasure and exemption from pain, but that the will is a different thing from desire; that a person of confirmed virtue, or any other person whose purposes are fixed, carries out his purposes without any thought of the pleasure he has in contemplating them, or expects to derive from their fulfilment; and persists in acting on them, even though these pleasures are much diminished, by changes in his character or decay of his passive sensibilities, or are outweighed by the pains which the pursuit of the purposes may bring upon him. All this I fully admit, and have stated it elsewhere, as positively and emphatically as any one. Will, the active phenomenon, is a different thing from desire, the state of passive sensibility, and though originally an offshoot from it, may in time take root and detach itself from the parent stock; so much so, that in the case of an habitual purpose, instead of willing the thing because we desire it, we often desire it only because we will it. This, however, is but an instance of that familiar fact, the power of habit, and is nowise confined to the case of virtuous actions. Many indifferent things, which men originally did from a motive of some sort, they continue to do from habit. Sometimes this is done unconsciously, the consciousness coming only after the action: at other times with conscious volition, but volition which has became habitual, and is put into operation by the force of habit, in opposition perhaps to the deliberate preference, as often happens with those who have contracted habits of vicious or hurtful indulgence. Third and last comes the case in which the habitual act of will in the individual instance is not in contradiction to the general intention prevailing at other times, but in fulfilment of it; as in the case of the person of confirmed virtue, and of all who pursue deliberately and consistently any determinate end. The distinction between will and desire thus understood, is an authentic and highly important psychological fact; but the fact consists solely in this—that will, like all other parts of our constitution, is amenable to habit, and that we may will from habit what we no longer desire for itself, or desire only because we will it. It is not the less true that will, in the beginning, is entirely produced by desire; including in that term the repelling influence of pain as well as the attractive one of pleasure. Let us take into consideration, no longer the person who has a confirmed will to do right, but him in whom that virtuous will is still feeble, conquerable by temptation, and not to be fully relied on; by what means can it be strengthened? How can the will to be virtuous, where it does not exist in sufficient force, be implanted or awakened? Only by making the person *desire* virtue—by making him think of it in a pleasurable light, or of its absence in a painful one. It is by associating the doing right with pleasure, or the doing wrong with pain, or by eliciting and impressing and bringing home to the person's experience the pleasure naturally involved in the one or the pain in the other, that it is possible to call forth that will to be virtuous, which, when confirmed, acts without any thought of either pleasure or pain. Will is the child of desire, and passes out of the dominion of its parent only to come under that of habit. That which is the result of habit affords no presumption of being intrinsically good; and there would be no reason for wishing that the purpose of virtue should become independent of pleasure and pain, were it not that the influence of the pleasurable and painful associations which prompt to virtue is not sufficiently to be depended on for unerring constancy of action until it has acquired the support of habit. Both in feeling and in conduct, habit is the only thing which imparts certainty; and it is because of the importance to others of being able to rely absolutely on one's feelings and conduct, and to oneself of being able to rely on one's own, that the will to do right ought to be cultivated into this habitual independence. In other words, this state of the will is a means to good, not intrinsically a good; and does not contradict the doctrine that nothing is a good to human beings but in so far as it is either itself pleasurable, or a means of attaining pleasure or averting pain.

But if this doctrine be true, the principle of utility is proved. Whether it is so or not, must now be left to the consideration of the thoughtful reader.

Questions on Mill

1. How does Mill respond to the objection that

Epicureanism (or hedonism) is a "doctrine only worthy of swine?" Is this a good reply or not? Explain.

2. How does Mill distinguish between the "higher pleasures" and the "lower pleasures?" Why does Mill think that the higher pleasures are superior in quality to the lower ones? Is his argument circular? What about the person who prefers the lower pleasures over the higher?

3. "In the golden rule of Jesus of Nazareth, we read the complete spirit of the ethics of utility." Is this true or not? Explain your answer.

4. Carefully explain Mill's so-called proof of the principle of utility. Many commentators have thought that this proof is defective. Do you agree? If so, what exactly is the mistake? Is there any way to reconstruct the proof so that it is free of error? How?

Paul Taylor

A Problem for Utilitarianism

For biographical information on Taylor, see his earlier reading in this chapter.

Utility and Justice

Some contemporary philosophers claim that, whether or not **act- and rule-utilitarianism** are compatible with each other, *neither* theory is acceptable as a normative ethical system. In the present section the reasoning behind this rejection of both forms of utilitarianism is examined. Afterwards, in the last section of the chapter,

From *Principles of Ethics: An Introduction* by Paul W. Taylor © 1975 by Dickenson Publishing Company, Inc. Reprinted by permission of Wadsworth, Inc.

we shall consider a philosophical defense of utilitarianism.

The objection raised against both forms of utilitarian ethics is that *the principle of utility does not provide a sufficient ground for the obligations of justice.* Since the idea of justice is a fundamental moral concept, no normative ethical system can be considered adequate that does not show the basis for our duty to be just. The argument starts with a careful examination of the ultimate norm of utilitarian ethics, the principle of utility itself. Exactly what is utility? It has been described in the words, "the maximizing of intrinsic value and the minimizing of intrinsic disvalue." What, precisely, does this mean?

It will be helpful in answering this question to think of measurable units of intrinsic value and disvalue. We shall accordingly speak of units of happiness and unhappiness, giving plus and minus signs to happiness and unhappiness, respectively. This will enable us to see the difficulty more clearly, although no particular view of what is to be taken as the measurement of a unit of happiness or unhappiness will be presupposed. We all know in general what it means to be very happy, quite happy, not especially happy, rather unhappy, and extremely unhappy. Thus the idea of degrees of happiness corresponds to something in our experience. We also know what it means to be happy for a brief moment, or for a day, and we use such phrases as "It was a happy two-week vacation," "I was not very happy during my early teens," and "He has led an unhappy life." There is some basis, therefore, in our everyday concept of happiness (and also of pleasure) for giving meaning to the idea of quantities or amounts of happiness, even though we do not ordinarily measure these quantities in arithmetical terms.

What, then does the utilitarian mean by maximizing intrinsic value and minimizing intrinsic disvalue? There are three variables or factors that must be introduced in order to make this idea clear. First, it means to bring about, in the case of *one* person, the greatest balance of value over disvalue. Thus if one act or rule yields $+1000$ units of happiness and -500 units of unhappiness for a given person, while another act or rule yields $+700$ units and

−100 units for that person, then, all other factors being equal, the second alternative is better than the first, since the balance of the second (+600) is greater than the balance of the first (+500). Similarly, to "minimize disvalue" would mean that an act or rule which yielded +100 and −300 for a given person would be better than one that yielded +500 and −1000 for the same person, other things being equal (even though more happiness is produced by the second than by the first).

The second factor is that the happiness and unhappiness of *all persons* affected must be considered. Thus if four persons, A, B, C, and D, each experiences some difference of happiness or unhappiness in his life as a consequence of the act or rule but no difference occurs in the lives of anyone else, then the calculation of maximum value and minimum disvalue must include the balance of pluses and minuses occurring in the experience of every one of the four persons. Suppose in one case the balance is +300 for A, +200 for A, −300 for C, and −400 for D. And suppose the alternative yields +200 for A, +100 for B, −400 for C, and +500 for D. Then if someone were to claim that the first is better than the second because D's happiness or unhappiness does not count (D, for example, might be a slave while A, B, and C are free men), this conclusion would not be acceptable to utilitarians. For them, the second alternative is better than the first because the second yields a higher total balance than the first when *all* persons are considered.

The third factor in the utilitarian calculus has been tacitly assumed in the foregoing discussion of the second factor. This is the principle that, in calculating the units of happiness or unhappiness for different persons, the same criteria for measuring quantity are used. If totals of +500 and −200 represent sums of happiness and unhappiness in the experience of A and +300 and −400 represent sums of happiness and unhappiness in the experience of B, then one unit of plus (or minus) for A must be equal to one unit of plus (or minus) for B. No differences between A and B are to be considered as grounds for assigning a different weight to one or the other other's happiness or unhappiness. When utilitarians assert that everyone's happiness is to count *equally,* they mean that, in calculating consequences, it is irrelevant *whose* happiness or unhappiness is affected by the act or rule. This may be called the principle of the equality of worth of every person as a person. (It does not mean, of course, that everyone is just as morally good or bad as everyone else!)

Now when these three factors are used in calculating utility, it is still possible for some persons to be unfairly or unjustly treated. For the greatest total balance of pluses over minuses may be brought about in a given society by actions or rules which discriminate against certain persons on irrelevant grounds. Although a greater quantity of happiness and a lesser amount of unhappiness are produced, they are distributed unjustly among the persons affected. To illustrate this possibility, consider two societies, one of which distributes different amounts of happiness to people on the basis of their race or religion, the other dispensing them on the basis of people's different needs, abilities, and merits, where "merits" are determined by contributions to the common good or general happiness. In the first society, people belonging to one race or religion are favored in educational opportunities, comfortable housing, and high-paying jobs, while people of another race or religion are disfavored. Race and religion function in that society as grounds for discrimination. In the second society, on the other hand, race or religion do not matter as far as education, housing and jobs are concerned. All that counts are such things as, Does the individual have a need for special treatment, a need which, if overlooked, would unfairly handicap him in matters of education, housing, or jobs? (For example, a blind person might be given special schooling and a special job, so that his blindness will not mean that he has less of a chance for happiness in life than others.) Or, has the individual, through fair and open competition, proven himself qualified for a high-paying job? Or, does he have exceptional abilities—such as musical genius or mathematical brilliance—which deserve the society's recognition, so that advanced education and scholarships are made available to him? Here race and religion do not function as grounds for discrimination, since they are not considered in determining the proper distribution of happiness and unhappiness throughout the population.

The problem of utility and justice arises when it is seen that, in the two societies described above, it is possible for the first to produce a greater total net balance of happiness over unhappiness than the second. Thus suppose the first society can force the members of the disfavored race or religion to work long hours for little or no pay, so that they produce much more and use up much less of what is produced than they would without such coercion. Then, even if the calculation of utility includes the unhappiness of the disadvantaged, the total balance of happiness over unhappiness could be greater than that resulting from the second society's system of production and consumption. A utilitarian, it seems, would have to say in that case that the first society was morally better than the second, since its policies and rules yielded a higher net utility. Yet the first society, if not simply and self-evidently unjust, would at least be considered (even by utilitarians) to be less just than the second. Hence, utility and justice are incompatible when applied to certain types of societies under certain conditions.

Such conflicts between utility and justice can occur because, as far as utility alone is concerned, it is always morally right to increase one person's happiness at the expense of another's, if the total net balance of pluses over minuses is greater than would be the case were the two persons treated equally. It would seem, in contrast to this, that justice requires that no individual serve as a mere instrument or means to someone else's happiness. (If a person freely consents to sacrifice his happiness for the sake of another, he is not, of course, being used merely as a means to someone else's ends.) On this point the opposition between justice and utility appears to be fundamental.

It should be noted in this connection that utility not only permits but actually requires one individual's being made unhappy if doing so adds to a group's happiness, *however small an increase in happiness might be experienced by each of its members,* as long as the total amount of happiness to the group outweighs the unhappiness of the individual in question. Thus suppose an in-

nocent man is made a scapegoat for the guilt of others and accordingly suffers punishment. If he experiences, say -100 units of unhappiness and if there are 101 persons who, in victimizing him, gain $+1$ unit of happiness each (perhaps in relief at seeing another blamed for their own wrongdoing), then the principle of utility *requires* that the scapegoat be punished. This is not because the scapegoat's unhappiness is being ignored or is being assigned less intrinsic worth than the happiness of others. Each unit of unhappiness (-1) experienced by the scapegoat is equal in "weight" to a unit of happiness ($+1$) of someone in the group. It just happens that in the given situation the total quantity of the group's happiness is greater than that of the scapegoat's unhappiness. Consequently the principle of utility, when applied to this situation, entails that the scapegoat be made to suffer.

It is in this way that the idea of justice seems to present a major philosophical difficulty for all forms of utilitarianism. How might utilitarians reply to this criticism? They would begin by pointing out that, when we leave abstract speculations about theoretical possibilities behind and face the actual world around us, we find that any conflict between justice and utility is highly unlikely. The apparent plausibility of the cases given above, they would say, depends on their being abstracted from the real processes of historical and social development. They hold that when these processes are fully taken into account, it becomes clear that injustice inevitably yields great disutility.

In support of this claim, utilitarians ask us to consider how the principle of utility would apply to situations of social conflict, where one person's (or group's) interests can be furthered only if another person's (or group's) interests are frustrated. For this is where the concepts of justice and injustice are applicable. Now with regard to such situations, the principle of utility requires social rules which enable people to resolve their disagreements and live in harmony with one another. To live in harmony means, not that no social conflicts occur, but that whenever they do occur, there is a set of rules everyone can appeal to as a fair way to resolve them. Such rules will (a) take everyone's interests into account, (b) give equal consideration to the interests of each person, and (c) enable all parties to a dispute to decide issues on grounds freely acceptable by all. For it is only when everyone can appeal to such a system of conflict-resolving rules that the society as a whole can achieve its maximum happiness and minimum unhappiness.

This can be seen by referring to the condition of anyone who does *not* accept a set of conflict-resolving rules as fair. Such a person will simply consider himself to be under social coercion with respect to those rules. That is, he will conform to the rules only because he is forced to by society. If his interests are frustrated by their operation, he will believe he has legitimate moral complaints against the rest of society, and will then think any action necessary to right the wrongs carried out in the name of the rules to be justified. The greater the number of such disaffected persons, the deeper will be the state of social disharmony. It is obvious that very little happiness can be realized in such a society.

At this point the following objection might be raised. To make sure that social conflict will not get out of hand, let those who accept the rules establish a power structure which will ensure their domination over those who reject them. In this way, although some (the powerless) may suffer, those in power can maximize their happiness. To this the utilitarian replies, History has shown us that no such power structure can last for long; even while it does last, the effort spent by the "ins" on maintaining domination over the "outs" makes it impossible for the "ins" to obtain much happiness in life. A social system of this kind is constantly liable to break down. The need to preserve their position of power drives the "ins" to ever greater measures of surveillance and repression. The society as a whole becomes a closed system in which the freedom of all individuals is diminished. Accompanying this curtailment of human freedom is a dwindling in the very conception of man and his creative powers. Inevitably, there develops an intolerance of diversity in thought, in speech, in styles of life. A narrow conformity of taste, ideas, and outward behavior becomes the main concern of everyone.

What kind of "happiness" is this? What amount of intrinsic value does such a narrow way of life really make possible for people, even people who have the power to advance their interests at the expense of others?

The upshot of the argument is now apparent: Given a clearheaded view of the world as it is and a realistic understanding of man's nature, it becomes more and more evident that injustice will never have, in the long run, greater utility than justice. Even if the two principles of justice and utility can logically be seperated in the abstract and even if they can be shown to yield contradictory results in hypothetical cases, it does not follow that the fundamental idea of utilitarianism must be given up. For it remains the case that, when we are dealing with the actual practices of people in their social and historical settings, to maximize happiness and minimize unhappiness requires an open, freely given commitment on the part of *everyone* to comply with the rules for settling conflicts among them. Anyone who is coerced into following the rules when he, in good conscience, cannot accept them as being fair to everyone (and consequently to himself) will not consider himself morally obligated to abide by them. Since he will either feel unjustly treated himself or see himself as a participant in the unfair treatment of others, society stands condemned in his judgment. From his point of view, he will have good reason to do what he can to change or abolish the rules. He will join with anyone else who rejects them as unfair, in an effort to overcome his powerlessness. Thus injustice becomes, in actual practice, a source of great social disutility. If society's reaction to the challenge of its dissidents is only a stronger attempt to impose its rules by force, this response will, sooner or later, bring about a situation in which no one really benefits. Not only is it profoundly true that "might does not make right," it is equally true that might cannot create the maximum balance of human happiness over human misery, when the lives of everyone are taken into account.

Whether this argument provides a successful rebuttal to the criticism of utilitarianism when viewed in the light of justice is a matter for the reader's own reflection.

Despite the difficulties raised in connection with the relation between justice and utility, it is appropriate to end the present chapter with a general defense of this ethical theory which a great many philosophers have found attractive. Utilitarianism is the only theory, its proponents claim, that makes good sense when we ask ourselves, What, after all, is the whole point of morality, *including* the rules of justice? Even if the rules of justice cannot be derived from utility taken strictly as a happiness maximizing principle, nevertheless there would be no point (that is, no intelligible purpose) in having moral norms guide people's conduct unless they contributed ultimately to human happiness. For the rules of morality, including those of justice, restrict individuals' actions. These limitations need to be justified, and it is only by appealing to the principle of utility that, in the last analysis, they *can* be justified. Why is this so? The utilitarians' answer to this question, which is aimed at showing the rationality of utilitarian ethics as a whole, may be summed up as follows.

The first step in their reasoning is offered in support of the proposition: No limitation on human freedom is justified unless it serves a good purpose.

Questions on Taylor

1. Explain the objection Taylor raises against utilitarianism using your own examples.

2. How does Taylor defend utilitarianism against this objection? Is his defense successful or not? Explain your position.

3. Another way to respond to Taylor's objection is to supplement utilitarianism with a principle of justice. Try to formulate an acceptable principle of justice.

Immanuel Kant

The Categorical Imperative

Immanuel Kant (1726–1806), a German philosopher, was one of the most important philosophers of all time; he made important contributions in epistemology, metaphysics, and ethics. He wrote numerous books, but the most important ones are Critique of Pure Reason, Prolegomena to All Future Metaphysics, The Foundations of the Metaphysics of Morals *(from which the reading is taken),* Critique of Practical Reason, *and* Critique of Judgment.

The reading is from *The Moral Law: Kant's Groundwork of the Metaphysic of Morals,* trans. H. J. Paton (New York: Barnes & Noble, Inc., 1948), pp. 59–68. Permission granted by Barnes & Noble, Totowa, N.J.

The Good Will*

It is impossible to conceive anything at all in the world, or even out of it, which can be taken as good without qualification, except a *good will*. Intelligence, wit, judgement, and any other *talents* of the mind we may care to name, or courage, resolution, and constancy of purpose, as qualities of *temperament*, are without doubt good and desirable in many respects; but they can also be extremely bad and hurtful when the will is not good which has to make use of these gifts of nature, and which for this reason has the term '*character*' applied to its peculiar quality. It is exactly the same with *gifts of fortune*. Power, wealth, honour, even health and that complete well-being and contentment with one's state which goes by the name of '*happiness*', produce boldness, and as a consequence often overboldness as well, unless a good will is present by which their influence on the mind—and so too the whole principle of action—may be cor-

---

[The footnotes have been eliminated.—Ed.]

rected and adjusted to universal ends; not to mention that a rational and impartial spectator can never feel approval in contemplating the uninterrupted prosperity of a being graced by no touch of a pure and good will, and that consequently a good will seems to constitute the indispensable condition of our very worthiness to be happy.

Some qualities are even helpful to this good will itself and can make its task very much easier. They have none the less no inner unconditioned worth, but rather presuppose a good will which sets a limit to the esteem in which they are rightly held and does not permit us to regard them as absolutely good. Moderation in affections and passions, self-control, and sober reflexion are not only good in many respects: they may even seem to constitute part of the *inner* worth of a person. Yet they are far from being properly described as good without qualification (however unconditionally they have been commended by the ancients). For without the principles of a good will they may become exceedingly bad; and the very coolness of a scoundrel makes him, not merely more dangerous, but also immediately more abominable in our eyes than we should have taken him to be without it.

The Good Will and Its Results

A good will is not good because of what it effects or accomplishes—because of its fitness for attaining some proposed end; it is good through its willing alone—that is, good in itself. Considered in itself it is to be esteemed beyond comparison as far higher than anything it could ever bring about merely in order to favour some inclination or, if you like, the sum total of inclinations. Even if, by some special disfavour of destiny or by the niggardly endowment of step-motherly nature, this will is entirely lacking in power to carry out its intentions; if by its utmost effort it still accomplished nothing, and only good will is left (not, admittedly, as a mere wish, but as the straining of every means so far as they are in our control); even then it would still shine like a jewel for its own sake as something which has its full value in itself. Its usefulness or fruitfulness can neither add to, nor sub-

tract from, this value. Its usefulness would be merely, as it were, the setting which enables us to handle it better in our ordinary dealings or to attract the attention of those not yet sufficiently expert, but not to commend it to experts or to determine its value. . . .

The Good Will and Duty

We have now to elucidate the concept of a will estimable in itself and good apart from any further end. This concept, which is already present in a sound natural understanding and requires not so much to be taught as merely to be clarified, always holds the highest place in estimating the total worth of our actions and constitutes the condition of all the rest. We will therefore take up the concept of *duty,* which includes that of a good will, exposed, however, to certain subjective limitations and obstacles. These, so far from hiding a good will or disguising it, rather bring it out by contrast and make it shine forth more brightly.

The Motive of Duty

I will here pass over all actions already recognized as contrary to duty, however useful they may be with a view to this or that end; for about these the question does not even arise whether they have been done *for the sake of duty* inasmuch as they are directly opposed to it. I will also set aside actions which in fact accord with duty, yet for which men have *no immediate inclination,* but perform them because impelled to do so by some other inclination. For there it is easy to decide whether the action which accords with duty has been done *from duty* or from some purpose of self-interest. This distinction is far more difficult to perceive when the action accords with duty and the subject has in addition an *immediate* inclination to the action. For example, it certainly accords with duty that a grocer should not overcharge his inexperienced customer; and where there is much competition a sensible shopkeeper refrains from so doing and keeps to a fixed and general price for everybody so that a child can buy from him just as well as anyone else. Thus people are served *honestly;* but this is not nearly enough to justify us in believing that the shopkeeper has acted in this way from duty or from principles of fair dealing; his interest required him to do so. We cannot assume him to have in addition an immediate inclination towards his customers, leading him, as it were out of love, to give no man preference over another in the matter of price. Thus the action was done neither from duty nor from immediate inclination, but solely from purposes of self-interest.

On the other hand, to preserve one's life is a duty, and besides this every one has also an immediate inclination to do so. But on account of this the often anxious precautions taken by the greater part of mankind for this purpose have no inner worth, and the maxim of their action is without moral content. They do protect their lives *in conformity with duty,* but not *from the motive of duty.* When on the contrary, disappointments and hopeless misery have quite taken away the taste for life; when a wretched man, strong in soul and more angered at his fate than faint-hearted or cast down, longs for death and still preserves his life without loving it—not from inclination or fear but from duty; then indeed his maxim has a moral content.

To help others where one can is a duty, and besides this there are many spirits of so sympathetic a temper that, without any further motive of vanity or self-interest, they find an inner pleasure in spreading happiness around them and can take delight in the contentment of others as their own work. Yet I maintain that in such a case an action of this kind, however right and however amiable it may be, has still no genuinely moral worth. It stands on the same footing as other inclinations—for example, the inclination for honour, which if fortunate enough to hit on something beneficial and right and consequently honourable, deserves praise and encouragement, but not esteem; for its maxim lacks moral content, namely, the performance of such actions, not from inclination, but *from duty.* Suppose then that the mind of this friend of man were overclouded by sorrows of his own which extinguished all sympathy with the fate of others, but that he still had power to help those in distress, though no longer stirred by the need of others because sufficiently occupied with his own; and suppose that, when no

longer moved by any inclination, he tears himself out of this deadly insensibility and does the action without any inclination for the sake of duty alone; then for the first time his action has its genuine moral worth. Still further: if nature had implanted little sympathy in this or that man's heart; if (being in other respects an honest fellow) he were cold in temperament and indifferent to the sufferings of others—perhaps because, being endowed with the special gift of patience and robust endurance in his own sufferings, he assumed the like in others or even demanded it; if such a man (who would in truth not be the worst product of nature) were not exactly fashioned by her to be a philanthropist, would he not still find in himself a source from which he might draw a worth far higher than any that a good-natured temperament can have? Assuredly he would. It is precisely in this that the worth of character begins to show—a moral worth and beyond all comparison the highest—namely, that he does good, not from inclination, but from duty.

To assure one's own happiness is a duty (at least indirectly); for discontent with one's state, in a press of cares and amidst unsatisfied wants, might easily become a great *temptation to the transgression of duty.* But here also, apart from regard to duty, all men have already of themselves the strongest and deepest inclination towards happiness, because precisely in this Idea of happiness all inclinations are combined into a sum total. The prescription for happiness is, however, often so constituted as greatly to interfere with some inclinations, and yet men cannot form under the name of 'happiness' any determinate and assured conception of the satisfaction of all inclinations as a sum. Hence it is not to be wondered at that a single inclination which is determinate as to what it promises and as to the time of its satisfaction may outweigh a wavering Idea; and that a man, for example, a sufferer from gout, may choose to enjoy what he fancies and put up with what he can—on the ground that on balance he has here at least not killed the enjoyment of the present moment because of some possibly groundless expectations of the good fortune supposed to attach to soundness of health. But in this case also, when the universal inclination towards happiness has failed to determine his will, when good health, at least for him, has not entered into his calculations as so necessary, what remains over, here as in other cases, is a law—the law of furthering his happiness, not from inclination, but from duty; and in this for the first time his conduct has a real moral worth.

It is doubtless in this sense that we should understand too the passages from Scripture in which we are commanded to love our neighbor and even our enemy. For love out of inclination cannot be commanded; but kindness done from duty—although no inclination impels us, and even although natural and unconquerable disclination stands in our way—is *practical*, and not *pathological*, love, residing in the will and not in the propensions of feeling, in principles of action and not of melting compassion; and it is this practical love alone which can be an object of command. . . .

The Categorical Imperative

But what kind of law can this be the thought of which, even without regard to the results expected from it, has to determine the will if this is to be called good absolutely and without qualification? Since I have robbed the will of every inducement that might arise for it as a consequence of obeying any particular law, nothing is left but the conformity of actions to universal law as such, and this alone must serve the will as its principle. That is to say, I ought never to act except in such a way *that I can also will that my maxim should become a universal law.* Here bare conformity to universal law as such (without having as its base any law prescribing particular actions) is what serves the will as its principle, and must so serve it if duty is not to be everywhere an empty delusion and a chimerical concept. The ordinary reason of mankind also agrees with this completely in its practical judgements and always has the aforesaid principle before its eyes.

Take this question, for example. May I not, when I am hard pressed, make a promise with the intention of not keeping it? Here I readily distinguish the two senses which the question can have—Is it prudent, or is it right, to make a false promise? The first no doubt can often be the case. I do indeed see that it is not enough for me to extricate myself from present embarrassment by this subterfuge: I have to consider whether from this lie there may not subsequently accrue to me much greater inconvenience than that from which I now escape, and also—since, with all my supposed *astuteness,* to foresee the consequences is not so easy that I can be sure there is no chance, once confidence in me is lost, of this proving far more disadvantageous than all the ills I now think to avoid— whether it may not be a *more prudent* action to proceed here on a general maxim and make it my habit not to give a promise except with the intention of keeping it. Yet it becomes clear to me at once that such a maxim is always founded solely on fear of consequences. To tell the truth for the sake of duty is something entirely different from doing so out of concern for inconvenient results; for in the first case the concept of the action already contains in itself a law for me, while in the second case I have first of all to look around elsewhere in order to see what effects may be bound up with it for me. When I deviate from the principle of duty, this is quite certainly bad; but if I desert my prudential maxim, this can often be greatly to my advantage, though it is admittedly safer to stick to it. Suppose I seek, however, to learn in the quickest way and yet unerringly how to solve the problem 'Does a lying promise accord with duty?' I have then to ask myself 'Should I really be content that my maxim (the maxim of getting out of a difficulty by a false promise) should hold as a universal law (one valid both for myself and others)? And could I really say to myself that every one may make a false promise if he finds himself in a difficulty from which he can extricate himself in no other way?' I then become aware at once that I can indeed will to lie, but I can by no means will a universal law of lying; for by such a law there could properly be no promises at all, since it would be futile to profess a will for future action to others who would not believe my profession or who, if they did so over-hastily, would pay me back in like coin; and consequently my maxim, as soon as it was made a universal law, would be bound to annul itself.

Thus I need no far-reaching ingenuity to find out what I have to do in order to possess a good will. Inexperienced in the course of world affairs and incapable of being prepared for all the chances that happen in it, I ask myself only 'Can you also will that your maxim should become a universal law?' Where you cannot, it is to be rejected, and that not because of a prospective loss to you or even to others, but because it cannot fit as a principle into a possible enactment of universal law. For such an enactment reason compels my immediate reverence, into whose grounds (which the philosopher may investigate) I have as yet no *insight,* although I do at least understand this much: reverence is the assessment of a worth which far outweighs all the worth of what is commended by inclination, and the necessity for me to act out of *pure* reverence for the practical law is what constitutes duty, to which every other motive must give way because it is the condition of a will good *in itself,* whose value is above all else.

Questions on Kant

1. According to Kant, why is the good will the only thing in the world that is good without qualification? Do you agree or not? Defend your answer.

2. Explain the distinction between acting in conformity with duty and acting from the motive of duty. Does Kant's view on this make any sense to you? Explain.

3. State and explain the categorical imperative. Can you think of any cases in which the application of the categorical imperative might result in immoral or unjust actions? Think, for example, about how a Nazi might use it.

Onora O'Neill

Kantian Approaches to Some Famine Problems

Onora O'Neill is Professor of Philosophy at the University of Essex. She is the author of Acting on Principle.

§22 A Simplified Account of Kant's Ethics

Kant's moral theory has acquired the reputation of being forbiddingly difficult to understand and, once understood, excessively demanding in its requirements. I don't believe that this reputation has been wholly earned, and I am going to try to undermine it. In §§23–26 I shall try to reduce some of the difficulties, and in §§27–30 I shall try to show the implications of a Kantian moral theory for ac-

From *Matters of Life and Death: New Introductory Essays in Moral Philosophy* edited by T. Regan. Copyright © 1980 by Random House, Inc. Reprinted by permission of the publisher.

tion toward those who do or may suffer famine. Finally, I shall compare Kantian and utilitarian approaches and assess their strengths and weaknesses.

The main method by which I propose to avoid some of the difficulties of Kant's moral theory is by explaining only one part of the theory. This does not seem to me to be an irresponsible approach in this case. One of the things that makes Kant's moral theory hard to understand is that he gives a number of different versions of the principle that he calls the Supreme Principle of Morality, and these different versions don't look at all like one another. They also don't look at all like the utilitarians' Greatest Happiness Principle. But the Kantian principle is supposed to play a similar role in arguments about what to do.

Kant calls his supreme Principle the *Categorical Imperative:* its various versions also have sonorous names. One is called the Formula of Universal Law; another is the Formula of the Kingdom of Ends. The one on which I shall concentrate is known as the *Formula of the End in Itself.* To understand why Kant thinks that these picturesquely named principles are equivalent to one another takes quite a lot of close and detailed analysis of Kant's philosophy. I shall avoid this and concentrate on showing the implications of this version of the Categorical Imperative.

§23 The Formula of the End in Itself

Kant states the Formula of the End in Itself as follows:

Act in such a way that you always treat humanity, whether in your own person or in the person of any other, never simply as a means but always at the same time as an end.[1]

To understand this we need to know what it is to treat a person as a means or as an end. According to Kant, each of our acts reflects one or more *maxims*. The maxim of the act is the principle on which one sees oneself as acting. A maxim expresses a person's policy, or if he or she has no settled policy, the principle underlying the particular intention or decision on which he or she acts. Thus, a person who decides "This year I'll give 10 percent of my income to famine relief" has as a maxim the principle of tithing his or her income for famine relief. In practice, the difference between intentions and maxims is of little importance, for given any intention, we can formulate the corresponding maxim by deleting references to particular times, places, and persons. In what follows I shall take the terms 'maxim' and 'intention' as equivalent.

Whenever we act intentionally, we have at least one maxim and can, if we reflect, state what it is. (There is of course room for self-deception here—"I'm only keeping the wolf from the door" we may claim as we wolf down enough to keep ourselves overweight, or, more to the point, enough to feed someone else who hasn't enough food.)

When we want to work out whether an act we propose to do is right or wrong, according to Kant, we should look at our maxims and not at how much misery or happiness the act is likely to produce, and whether it does better at increasing happiness than other available acts. We just have to check that the act we have in mind will not use anyone as a mere means, and,

if possible, that it will treat other persons as ends in themselves.

§24 Using Persons as Mere Means

To use someone as a *mere means* is to involve them in a scheme of action *to which they could not in principle consent*. Kant does not say that there is anything wrong about using someone as a means. Evidently we have to do so in any cooperative scheme of action. If I cash a check I use the teller as a means, without whom I could not lay my hands on the cash; the teller in turn uses me as a means to earn his or her living. But in this case, each party consents to her or his part in the transaction. Kant would say that though they use one another as means, they do not use one another as *mere* means. Each person assumes that the other has maxims of his or her own and is not just a thing or a prop to be manipulated.

But there are other situations where one person uses another in a way to which the other could not in principle consent. For example, one person may make a promise to another with every intention of breaking it. If the promise is accepted, then the person to whom it was given must be ignorant of what the promisor's intention (maxim) really is. If one knew that the promisor did not intend to do what he or she was promising, one would, after all, not accept or rely on the promise. It would be as though there had been no promise made. Successful false promising depends on deceiving the person to whom the promise is made about what one's real maxim is. And since the person who is deceived doesn't know that real maxim, he or she can't in principle consent to his or her part in the proposed scheme of action. The person who is deceived, is, as it were, a prop or a tool—a mere means—in the false promisor's scheme. A person who promises falsely treats the acceptor of the promise as a prop or a thing and not as a person. In Kant's view, it is this that makes false promising wrong.

One standard way of using others as mere means is by deceiving them. By getting someone involved in a business scheme or a criminal activity on false pretenses, or by giving a misleading account of what one is about, or by making a false promise or a fraudulent contract, one involves another in something to which he or she in principle cannot consent, since the scheme requires that he or she doesn't know what is going on. Another standard way of using others as mere means is by coercing them. If a rich or powerful person threatens a debtor with bankruptcy unless he or she joins in some scheme, then the creditor's intention is to coerce; and the debtor, if coerced, cannot consent to his or her part in the creditor's scheme. To make the example more specific: If a moneylender in an Indian village threatens not to renew a vital loan unless he is given the debtor's land, then he uses the debtor as a mere means. He coerces the debtor, who cannot truly consent to this "offer he can't refuse." (Of course the outward form of such transactions may look like ordinary commercial dealings, but we know very well that some offers and demands couched in that form are coercive.)

In Kant's view, acts that are done on maxims that require deception or coercion of others, and so cannot have the consent of those others (for consent precludes both deception and coercion), are wrong. When we act on such maxims, we treat others as mere means, as things rather than as ends in themselves. If we act on such maxims, our acts are not only wrong but unjust; such acts wrong the particular others who are deceived or coerced.

§25 Treating Persons as Ends in Themselves

Duties of justice are, in Kant's view (as in many others'), the most important of our duties. When we fail in these duties, we have used some other or others as mere means. But there are also cases where, though we do not use others as mere means, still we fail to use them as ends in themselves in the fullest possible way. To treat someone as an end in him or herself requires in the first place that one not use him or her as mere means, that one respect each as a rational person with his or her own maxims. But beyond that, one may also seek to foster others' plans and maxims by sharing some of their ends. To act beneficently is to seek others' happiness, therefore to intend to achieve some of the things that those others aim at with their maxims. If I want to make others happy, I will adopt maxims that not merely do not manipulate them but that foster some of their plans and activities. Beneficent acts try to achieve what others want. However, we cannot seek everything that others want; their wants are too numerous and diverse, and, of course, sometimes incompatible. It follows that beneficence has to be selective.

There is then quite a sharp distinction between the requirements of justice and beneficence in Kantian ethics. Justice requires that we act on *no* maxims that use others as mere means. Beneficence requires that we act on *some* maxims that foster others' ends, though it is a matter for judgment and discretion which of their ends we foster. Some maxims no doubt ought not to be fostered because it would be unjust to do so. Kantians are not committed to working interminably through a list of happiness-producing and misery-reducing acts; but there are some acts whose obligatoriness utilitarians may need to debate as they try to compare total outcomes of different choices, to which Kantians are stringently bound. Kantians will claim that they have done nothing wrong if none of their acts is unjust, and that their duty is complete if in addition their life plans have in the circumstances been reasonably beneficent.

In making sure that they meet all the demands of justice, Kantians do not try to compare all available acts and see which has the best effects. They consider only the proposals for action that occur to them and check that these proposals use no other as mere means. If they do not, the act is permissible; if omitting the act would use another as mere means, the act is obligatory. Kant's theory has less scope than utilitarianism. Kantians do not claim to discover whether acts whose maxims they don't know fully are just. They may be reluctant to judge others' acts or policies that cannot be regarded as the maxim of any person or institution. They cannot rank acts in order of merit. Yet, the theory offers more precision than utilitarianism when data are scarce. One can usually tell whether one's act would use others as mere means, even when its impact on human happiness is thoroughly obscure.

§26 Kantian Deliberations on Famine Problems

The theory I have just sketched may seem to have little to say about famine problems. For it is a theory that forbids us to use others as mere means but does not require us to direct our benevolence first to those who suffer most. A conscientious Kantian, it seems, has only to avoid being unjust to those who suffer famine and can then be beneficent to those nearer home. He or she would not be obliged to help the starving, even if no others were equally distressed.

Kant's moral theory does make less massive demands on moral agents than utilitarian moral theory. On the other hand, it is somewhat clearer just what the more stringent demands are, and they are not negligible. We have here a contrast between a theory that makes massive but often undeterminate demands and a theory that makes fewer but less unambiguous demands and leaves other questions, in particular the allocation of beneficence, unresolved. We have also a contrast between a theory whose scope is comprehensive and one that is applicable only to persons acting intentionally and to those institutions that adopt policies, and so maxims. Kantian ethics is silent about the moral status of unintentional action; utilitarians seek to assess all consequences regardless of the intentions that led to them.

§27 Kantian Duties of Justice in Times of Famine

In famine situations, Kantian moral theory requires unambiguously that we do no injustice. We should not act on any maxim that uses another as mere means, so we should neither deceive nor coerce others. Such a requirement can become quite exacting when the means of life are scarce, when persons can more easily be coerced, and when the advantage of gaining more than what is justly due to one is great. I shall give a list of acts that on Kantian principles it would be unjust to do, but that one might be strongly tempted to do in famine conditions.

I will begin with a list of acts that one might be tempted to do as a member of a famine-stricken population. First, where there is a rationing scheme, one ought not to cheat and seek to get more than one's share—any scheme of cheating will use someone as mere means. Nor may one take advantage of others' desperation to profiteer or divert goods onto the black market or to accumulate a fortune out of others' misfortunes. Transactions that are outwardly sales and purchases can be coercive when one party is desperate. All the forms of corruption that deceive or put pressure on others are also wrong: hoarding unallocated food, diverting relief supplies for private use, corruptly using one's influence to others' disadvantage. Such requirements are far from trivial and frequently violated in hard times. In severe famines, refraining from coercing and deceiving may risk one's own life and require the greatest courage.

Second, justice requires that in famine situations one still try to fulfill one's duties to particular others. For example, even in times of famine, a person has duties to try to provide for dependents. These duties may, tragically, be unfulfillable. If they are, Kantian ethical theory would not judge wrong the acts of a person who had done her or his best. There have no doubt been times in human history where there was nothing to be done except abandon the weak and old or to leave children to fend for themselves as best they might. But providing the supporter of dependents acts on maxims of attempting to meet their claims, he or she uses no others as mere means to his or her own survival and is not unjust. A conscientious attempt to meet the particular obligations one has undertaken may also require of one many further maxims of self-restraint and of endeavor—for example, it may require a conscientious attempt to avoid having (further) children; it may require contributing one's time and effort to programs of economic development. Where there is no other means to fulfill particular obligations, Kantian principles may require a generation of sacrifice. They will not, however, require one to seek to maximize the happiness of later generations but only to establish the modest security and prosperity needed for meeting present obligations.

The obligations of those who live with or near famine are undoubtedly stringent and exacting; for those who live further off it is rather harder to see what a Kantian moral theory demands. Might it not, for example, be permissible to do nothing at all about those suffering famine? Might one not ensure that one does nothing unjust to the victims of famine by adopting no maxims whatsoever that mention them? To do so would, at the least, require one to refrain from certain deceptive and coercive practices frequently employed during the European exploration and economic penetration of the now underdeveloped world and still not unknown. For example, it would be unjust to "purchase" valuable lands and resources from persons who don't understand commercial transactions or exclusive property rights or mineral rights, so do not understand that their acceptance of trinkets destroys their traditional economic pattern and way of life. The old adage "trade follows the flag" reminds us to how great an extent the economic penetration of the less-developed countries involved elements of coercion and deception, so was on Kantian principles unjust (regardless of whether or not the net effect has benefited the citizens of those countries).

Few persons in the developed world today find themselves faced with the possibility of adopting on a grand scale maxims of deceiving or coercing persons living in poverty. But at least some people find that their jobs require them to make decisions about investment and aid policies that enormously affect the lives of those nearest to famine. What does a commitment to Kantian moral theory demand of such persons?

It has become common in writings in ethics and social policy to distinguish between one's *personal responsibilities* and one's *role responsibilities*. So a person may say, "As an individual I sympathize, but in my official capacity I can do nothing"; or we may excuse persons' acts of coercion because they are acting in some particular capacity—e.g., as a soldier or a jailer. On the other hand, this distinction isn't made or accepted by everyone. At the Nuremberg trials of war criminals, the defense "I was only doing my job" was disallowed, at least for those whose command position meant that they had some discretion in what they did. Kantians generally would play down any distinction between a person's own responsibilities and his or her role responsibilities. They would not deny that in any capacity one is accountable for certain things for which as a private person one is not accountable. For example, the treasurer of an organization is accountable to the board and has to present periodic reports and to keep specified records. But if she fails to do one of these things for which she is held accountable she will be held responsible for that failure—it will be imputable to her as an individual. When we take on positions, we *add* to our responsibilities those that the job requires; but we do not lose those that are already required of us. Our social role or job gives us, on Kant's view, no license to use others as mere means; even business executives and aid officials and social revolutionaries will act unjustly, so wrongly, if they deceive or coerce—however benevolent their motives.

If persons are responsible for all their acts, it follows that it would be unjust for aid officials to coerce persons into accepting sterilization, wrong for them to use coercive power to achieve political advantages (such as military bases) or commercial advantages (such as trade agreements that will harm the other country). It would be wrong for the executives of large corporations to extort too high a price for continued operation employment and normal trading. Where a less-developed country is pushed to exempt a multinational corporation from tax laws, or to construct out of its meager tax revenues the infrastructure of roads, harbors, or airports (not to mention executive mansions) that the corporation—but perhaps not the country—needs, then one suspects that some coercion has been involved.

The problem with such judgments—and it is an immense problem—is that it is hard to identify coercion and deception in complicated institutional settings. It is not hard to understand what is coercive about one person threatening another with serious injury if he won't comply with the first person's suggestion. But it is not at all easy to tell where the outward forms of political and commercial negotiation—which often involve an element of threat—have become coercive. I can't here explore this fascinating question. But I think it is at least fairly clear that the preservation of the outward forms of negotiation, bargaining, and voluntary consent do *not* demonstrate that there is no coercion, especially when one party is vastly more powerful or the other in dire need. Just as our judiciary has a long tradition of voiding contracts and agreements on grounds of duress or incompetence of one of the parties, so one can imagine a tribunal of an analogous sort rejecting at least some treaties and agreements as coercive, despite the fact that they were negotiated between "sovereign" powers or their representatives. In particular, where such agreements were negotiated with some of the cruder deceptions and coercion of the early days of European economic expansion or the subtler coercions and deceptions of contemporary superpowers, it seems doubtful that the justice of the agreement could be sustained.

Justice, of course, is not everything, even for Kantians. But its demands are ones that they can reasonably strive to fulfill. They may have some uncertain moments—for example, does advocating cheap raw materials mean advocating an international trade system in which the less developed will continue to suffer the pressures of the developed world—or is it a benevolent policy that will maximize world trade and benefit all parties, while doing no one an injustice? But for Kantians, the important moral choices are above all those in which one acts directly, not those in which one decides which patterns of actions to encourage in others or in those institutions that one can influence. And such moral decisions include decisions about the benevolent acts that one will or will not do.

§28 Kantian Duties of Beneficence in Times of Famine

The grounds of duties of beneficence are that such acts not merely don't use others as mere means but are acts that develop or promote others' ends and that, in particular, foster others' capacities to pursue ends, to be autonomous beings.

Clearly there are many opportunities for beneficence. But one area in which the *primary* task of developing others' capacity to pursue their own ends is particularly needed is in the parts of the world where extreme poverty and hunger leave people unable to pursue *any* of their other ends. Beneficence directed at putting people in a position to pursue whatever ends they may have has, for Kant, a stronger claim on us than beneficence directed at sharing ends with those who are already in a position to pursue varieties of ends. It would be nice if I bought a tennis racquet to play with my friend who is tennis mad and never has enough partners; but it is more important to make people able to plan their own lives to a minimal extent. It is nice to walk a second mile with someone who requests one's company; better to share a cloak with someone who may otherwise be too cold to make any journey. Though these suggestions are not a detailed set of instructions for the allocation of beneficence by Kantians, they show that relief of famine must stand very high among duties of beneficence.

§29 The Limits of Kantian Ethics: Intentions and Results

Kantian ethics differs from utilitarian ethics both in its scope and in the precision with which it guides action. Every action, whether of a person or of an agency, can be assessed by utilitarian methods, provided only that information is available about all the consequences of the act. The theory has unlimited scope, but, owing to lack of data, often lacks precision. Kantian ethics has a more restricted scope. Since it assesses actions by looking at the maxims of agents, it can only assess intentional acts. This means that it is most at home in assessing individuals' acts; but it can be extended to assess acts of agencies that (like corporations and governments and student unions) have decision-making procedures. It can do nothing to assess patterns of action that reflect no intention or policy, hence it cannot assess the acts of groups lacking decision-making procedures, such as the student movement, the women's movement, or the consumer movement.

It may seem a great limitation of Kantian ethics that it concentrates on intentions to the neglect of results. It might seem that all conscientious Kantians have to do is to make sure that they never intend to use others as mere means, and that they sometimes intend to foster others' ends. And, as we all know, good intentions sometimes lead to bad results, and correspondingly, bad intentions sometimes do no harm, or even produce good. If Hardin is right, the good intentions of those who feed the starving lead to dreadful results in the long run. If some traditional arguments in favor of capitalism are right, the greed and selfishness of the profit motive have produced unparalleled prosperity for many.

But such discrepancies between intentions and results are the exception and not the rule. For we cannot just *claim* that our intentions are good and do what we will. Our intentions reflect what we expect the immediate results of our action to be. Nobody credits the "intentions" of a couple who practice neither celibacy nor contraception but still insist "we never meant to have (more) children." Conception is likely (and known to be likely) in such cases. Where people's expressed intentions ignore the normal and predictable results of what they do, we infer that (if they are not amazingly ignorant) their words do not express their true intentions. The Formula of the End in Itself applies to the intentions on which one acts—not to some prettified version that one may avow. Provided this intention—the agent's real intention—uses no other as mere means, he or she does nothing unjust. If some of his or her intentions foster others' ends, then he or she is sometimes beneficent. It is therefore possible for people to test their proposals by Kantian arguments even when they lack the comprehensive causal knowledge that utilitarianism requires. Conscientious Kantians can work out whether they will be doing wrong by some act even though they know that their foresight is limited and that they may cause some harm or fail to cause some benefit. But they will not cause harms that they can foresee without this being reflected in their intentions.

V. Respect for Life: A Comparison of Kantian and Utilitarian Views

§30 Utilitarianism and Respect for Life

From the differing implications that Kantian and utilitarian moral theories have for our ac-tions towards those who do or may suffer famine, we can discover two sharply contrasting views of the value of human life. Utilitarians value happiness and the absence or reduction of misery. As a utilitarian one ought (if conscientious) to devote one's life to achieving the best possible balance of happiness over misery. If one's life plan remains in doubt, this will be because the means to this end are often unclear. But whenever the causal tendency of acts is clear, utilitarians will be able to discern the acts they should successively do in order to improve the world's balance of happiness over unhappiness.

This task is not one for the faint-hearted. First, it is dauntingly long, indeed interminable. Second, it may at times require the sacrifice of happiness, and even of lives, for the sake of a greater happiness. Such sacrifice may be morally required not only when the person whose happiness or even whose life is at stake volunteers to make the sacrifice. It may be necessary to sacrifice some lives for the sake of others. As our control over the means of ending and preserving human life has increased, analogous dilemmas have arisen in many areas for utilitarians. Should life be preserved at the cost of pain when modern medicine makes this possible? Should life be preserved without hope of consciousness? Should triage policies, because they may maximize the number of survivors, be used to determine who should be left to starve? Should population growth be fostered wherever it will increase the total of human happiness—or on some views so long as average happiness is not reduced? All these questions can be fitted into utilitarian frameworks and answered *if* we have the relevant information. And sometimes the answer will be that human happiness demands the sacrifice of lives, including the sacrifice of unwilling lives. Further, for most utilitarians, it makes no difference if the unwilling sacrifices involve acts of injustice to those whose lives are to be lost. It might, for example, prove necessary for maximal happiness that some persons have their allotted rations, or their hard-earned income, diverted for others' benefit. Or it might turn out that some generations must sacrifice comforts or liberties and even lives to rear "the fabric of felicity" for their successors. Utilitarians do not deny these possibilities, though the imprecision of our knowledge of consequences often blurs the implications of the theory. If we peer through the blur, we see that the utilitarian view is that lives may indeed be sacrificed for the sake of a greater good even when the persons are not willing. There is nothing wrong with using another as a mere means provided that the end for which the person is so used is a happier result than could have been achieved any other way, taking into account the misery the means have caused. In utilitarian thought, persons are not ends in themselves. Their special moral status derives from their being means to the production of happiness. Human life has therefore a high though derivative value, and one life may be taken for the sake of greater happiness in other lives, or for ending of misery in that life. Nor is there any deep difference between ending a life for the sake of others' happiness by not helping (e.g., by triaging) and doing so by harming. Because the distinction between justice and beneficence is not sharply made within utilitarianism, it is not possible to say that triaging is a matter of not benefiting, while other interventions are a matter of injustice.

Utilitarian moral theory has then a rather paradoxical view of the value of human life. Living, conscious humans are (along with other sentient beings) necessary for the existence of everything utilitarians value. But is not their being alive but the state of their consciousness that is of value. Hence, the best results may require certain lives to be lost—by whatever means—for the sake of the total happiness and absence of misery that can be produced.

§31 Kant and Respect for Persons

Kantians reach different conclusions about human life. Human life is valuable because humans (and conceivably other beings, e.g., angels or apes) are the bearers of rational life. Humans are able to choose and to plan. This capacity and its exercise are of such value that they ought not to be sacrificed for anything of lesser value. Therefore, no one rational or autonomous creature should be treated as mere means for the enjoyment or even the happiness of another. We may in Kant's view justifiably—even nobly—risk or sacrifice our lives for others. For in doing so we follow our own maxim and nobody uses us as mere means. But no others may use either our lives or our bodies for a scheme that they have either coerced or deceived us into joining. For in doing so they would fail to treat us as rational beings; they would use us as mere means and not as ends in ourselves.

It is conceivable that a society of Kantians, all of whom took pains to use no other as mere means, would end up with less happiness or with fewer persons alive than would some societies of complying utilitarians. For since the Kantians would be strictly bound only to justice, they might without wrongdoing be quite selective in their beneficence and fail to maximize either survival rates or happiness, or even to achieve as much of either as a strenuous group of utilitarians, who somehow make the right calculations. On the other hand, nobody will have been made an instrument of others' survival or happiness in the society of complying Kantians.

§32 Is Famine a Moral Problem After All?

Utilitarian and Kantian moral theories are not the only possible ones. There is no space here to examine further possibilities, but one basic criticism of our enterprise cannot be avoided. It is this: Many people would hold that no *moral* theory is appropriate for considering famine. These critics would assert that famine can be averted only by economic changes and that these can be produced only by political action, whether of a reforming or a revolutionary sort. They would point to China, where control over famine that was widespread and endemic has been achieved not by acting on a moral theory but by enormous social and political changes. They would hold that the theories relevant for controlling famine are political and social theories, and many would see Marxist theories of social change as particularly important.

Theories of political and social change and of economic development are vital in choosing *how* to lessen famine, and they may show us what is possible and what impossible in particular circumstances. Even so, these theories do not eliminate moral questions. We still have to decide (and the Chinese leaders had to decide) about any possible or proposed social or political change, whether the results it seeks and the means it uses are morally acceptable. Revolutions have costs as well as benefits, and some of these may be morally unacceptable. Some ways of ending famine may cost far more in human lives and misery than other ways. Choices between different policies are, of course, social and political choices; but they are also unavoidably moral choices. In making them we must rely on some moral theory or other, however vague or imprecise our understanding of the theory. So it is worth our while to make sure that the moral theory on which we do rely is not deficient in ways that can be avoided by care and reflection.

Notes

1. I. Kant, *Groundwork of the Metaphysic of Morals,* tr. H. H. Paton, New York, Harper Torchbooks, 1964, p. 96.

Questions on O'Neill

1. Explain the Formula of the End in Itself using your own examples, not O'Neill's.

2. How does O'Neill apply Kant's theory to famine problems? Do you see any difficulties? What are they?

3. O'Neill ends with a comparison of the Kantian and utilitarian views. What is O'Neill's preference? Why?

Suggested Readings

Frederick Copleston, *A History of Philosophy* (Baltimore: Newman Press, 1946), I, chapter 31, gives a clear account of Aristotle's ethics including his theory of virtue.

Alasdair MacIntyre, *After Virtue: A Study in Moral Theory* 2d ed. (Notre Dame, IN: University of Notre Dame Press, 1984), is an important and widely discussed book that defends the old-fashioned tradition of the virtues.

Ayn Rand's defense of ethical egoism can be found in *The Virtue of Selfishness* (New York: Signet, 1964).

David P. Gauthier, ed., *Morality and Rational Self-Interest* (Englewood Cliffs, NJ: Prentice-Hall, 1970) is a collection of readings on psychological egoism and ethical egoism. Another useful anthology on these theories is Ronald D. Milo, ed., *Egoism and Altruism)* Belmont, CA: Wadsworth Publishing Co., Inc., 1973).

For the egoistic view of Thomas Hobbes, see his *Leviathan,* Parts I and II, ed. Herbert W. Schneider (Indianapolis: The Bobbs-Merrill Co., 1958).

Joseph Butler gives a famous critique of psychological egoism in his "Sermons Preached at the Rolls Chapel." The most important of these are found in *Five Sermons,* ed. Stuart M. Brown, Jr. (Indianapolis: The Bobbs-Merrill Co., 1950).

Jeremy Bentham, *An Introduction to the Principles of Morals and Legislation,* new ed. (Oxford: Oxford University Press, 1832) is, along with Mill's *Utilitarianism,* the classical statement of utilitarianism.

J. J. Smart and Bernard Williams, *Utilitarianism: For and Against* (Cambridge: Cambridge University Press, 1973) is an interesting debate by two contemporary philosophers. Smart is for utilitarianism and Williams is against it.

David Lyons, *Forms and Limits of Utilitarianism*) Oxford: Clarendon Press, 1965) gives a complete discussion of different types of utilitarianism.

Joel Feinberg and Henry West, eds., *Moral Philosophy: Classical Text and Contemporary Problems* (Belmont, CA: Dickenson Publishing Co., 1977) is a valuable collection of readings covering the most important topics in ethics including the classical theories of Aristotle, Kant, Mill, Bentham, and others, and contemporary problems such as euthanasia and adultery.

Robert Paul Wolff, ed., *Kant: Foundations of the Metaphysics of Morals, with Critical Essays* (Indianapolis: The Bobbs-Merrill Co., 1969) has a complete translation of the Foundations and nine critical essays. A good commentary on Kant's moral philosophy is H. J. Paton, *The Categorical Imperative: A Study in Kant's Moral Philosophy* (New York: Harper & Row, 1967).

William Frankena, *Ethics,* 2d ed. (Englewood Cliffs, NJ: Prentice-Hall, Inc., 1973) gives a clear presentation of the standard theories in both ethics and metaethics for introductory students. Frankena's own theory combines a utilitarian principle of beneficence with a principle of justice; thus it is a "mixed theory."

Glossary

Ad hoc hypothesis An ad hoc hypothesis is one created for a specific purpose that is unjustified. In the reading, Nagel claims that hypotheses about God are ad hoc, for example, the hypothesis that God created the universe. This hypothesis, he thinks, is not supported by science and is unnecessary.

Agnosticism This term means "lack of knowledge." It is the view that one does not know or lacks knowledge, as distinguished from "gnosticism" or "having knowledge." This word was coined by Thomas Huxley to characterize his view that there is insufficient evidence to know if God exists or not; as a result, he did not know whether God exists or not.

A priori and a posteriori "A priori" means "that which comes before," and "a posteriori" means "that which comes after." Statements are said to be a priori if they can be known to be true or false before having any experiences, or independent of experiences. Standard examples would be truths of definition such as "A triangle has three sides" and truths of mathematics like "Two plus three equals five." Statements are said to be a posteriori if they are known to be true or false after having experiences. Examples would be statements made in the empirical sciences like astronomy, physics, and chemistry, for example, "A gas expands when heated" or "Water boils at 100 degrees Centigrade." There is a secondary usage in which arguments are a priori or a posteriori depending on whether their premises are a priori or a posteriori. Thus the ontological argument is classified as a priori, while the cosmological argument, the teleological argument, and the argument from religious experience are classified as a posteriori arguments.

Argument In logic an argument is a series of statements where one of the statements, the conclusion of the argument, is supposed to be justified by the other statements, the premises. Conclusions are often indicated by certain words such as "therefore," "thus," and "hence." Premises are sometimes indicated by words such as "since" and "because." It is sometimes difficult to tell which statements are the premises and which is the conclusion. One technique is to identify the conclusion first and then try to see which statements are used to justify it. Sometimes arguments are stated incompletely with missing premises. For example, the famous argument of Descartes, "Cogito, ergo sum" or "I think, therefore I am" has a missing premise, namely "If I think, then I am."

Argument from design See Teleological Argument.

Atheism Atheism is the view that the creator God that is omnipotent, omniscient, and omnibenevolent does not exist. Given this definition, pantheism and deism are forms of atheism, and so is Buddhism (as Nagel says), since the Buddha's anatman (no self) doctrine is a denial of the existence of permanent unchanging selves, and this includes the theistic God as well as the immortal soul.

Nagel classifies the view that it is meaningless to talk about God as a form of atheism, but it seems better to classify this as a different view, noncognitivism, since strictly speaking, this view does not say that "God exists" is false (as the atheist says) but that this statement is meaningless.

In the narrow sense, atheism means the view that God does not exist, but in the broad sense, it means any view that leads to the rejection of theism, including noncognitivism and other views such as Marxism and Fʀeud's psychoanalytic theory.

Augustinian theodicy Augustinian theodicy is St. Augustine's attempt to give a rational explanation of why God allows evil to exist. The main answer is that evil is not something positive but only a privation or lack of goodness. Evil is thus nothing for God to be responsible for, strictly speaking. But in his writings, Augustine gives other answers too: there is evil as punishment for sin, and evil as resulting from the actions of free agents—humans, Satan, and other demons.

Begging the question This is a fallacy of reasoning where one assumes in a premise the conclusion one is trying to establish. A standard example is this argument: "The Bible says that God exists, and the Bible is the Word of God; therefore, God exists." (The second premise assumes that God exists, and this is the conclusion that is supposed to be established.)

Behaviorism Behaviorism is a school of psychology advocated by B. F. Skinner that studies observable behavior and not inner mental states or events. *Methodological behaviorism* is the view that psychologists should confine their study to observable behavior and should not try to study mental events and states using a method of introspection. *Logical behaviorism* is the philosophical view that mental terms such as "pain" can be defined in behavioral terms referring to overt behavior or dispositions to behavior; thus "pain" means "wincing, moaning, and other such behavior or dispositions to such behavior."

Buddhism Buddhism is the philosophy and religion founded by Gautama the Buddha (or the Enlightened One) who lived in northern India around 563 to 483 B.C. His teachings are usually summed up in the Four Noble Truths, which are in the form of a doctor's diagnosis of a patient: (1) the problem is that life is suffering, (2) the cause of suffering is craving or desire, (3) the cure is the cessation of craving or desire (or nirvana), and (4) the prescription is the Eightfold Path, which involves right views, right aspiration, right speech, right conduct, right livelihood, right effort, right mindfulness, and right contemplation.

Categorical imperative In Kant's philosophy, the categorical imperative is an overriding moral command or law for all rational beings that has no exceptions, and is contrasted with hypothetical impera-

tives. Kant states the categorical imperative in several different ways, but the two most important formulations are (1) act so that the rule or maxim under which your act falls can be universalized, that is, followed by everyone, and (2) treat everyone as an end and never as a means only or, in other words, treat everyone as having intrinsic worth or value, and not as having merely instrumental value as a means to some end.

Compatibilist thesis See Hard determinism.

Conclusion See Argument.

Contingent truth and necessary truth In logic a statement is a contingent truth if it can be denied without contradiction, for example, "It is raining today." By contrast, a necessary truth is one that cannot be denied without contradiction, for example, "It is either raining or not raining today." It is a matter of debate whether the statement "God exists" is a contingent or necessary truth—Anselm seems to think it is a necessary truth, but Nagel would deny this and insist that it is only a contingent truth, if it is true at all.

Contra-causal freedom This is a phrase coined by C. A. Campbell to refer to the sort of freedom required for moral responsibility. According to Campbell, people have contra-causal freedom when they "could have done otherwise," where this phrase is understood in a categorical sense rather than a hypothetical sense. It means that people could have done what they didn't do, or could have not done what they did do. It does not mean that they "could have done otherwise" only if they had willed otherwise; this hypothetical interpretation makes freedom into a mere lack of external compulsion. Campbell insists that the sort of freedom he has in mind requires a break in the causal chain—it is contra-causal in the sense of opposing causes, specifically desires that ordinarily cause one to act.

Contradiction In logic a contradiction is a statement that is false because of its logical form, for example, "It is raining, and it is not raining" or false because of the meanings of terms, for example, "Squares are round." Kant calls the latter statement a contradiction in terms.

Copernican theory This is the theory of the solar system advanced by Copernicus (1473–1543). According to his theory the earth is spherical rather than flat, and it is in uniform motion around the sun, the sun being at the center of the solar system. This theory is an opposition to the Ptolemaic system (accepted at that time), which had the earth as the fixed center of the universe surrounded by eight spherical shells. Copernicus' theory was strongly opposed by the Church because it did not put the earth, and thus human beings, at the center of the universe.

Cosmological argument   A cosmological argument is one about the origin or creation of the universe, and specifically, an argument claiming that God is the creator or cause of the universe. The term was originally used by Kant to refer to arguments that begin with the fact that there is a universe and try to prove that God is its explanation. As Kant used the term all five of St. Aquinas' ways of proving God's existence would be cosmological arguments. But most commentators agree that only the first three ways are formulations of the cosmological argument, and the last way is a version of the argument from design.

Deductive argument and inductive argument   In logic a deductive argument is one that claims to establish conclusively the truth of its conclusion, while an inductive argument does not claim to do this, but only claims to establish that its conclusion is true with some degree of probability. Another way of drawing the distinction is to say that a deductive argument claims that it is a contradiction to deny the truth of the conclusion given the truth of its premises, while an inductive argument does not claim this, but only that the premises give some degree of evidence for the truth of the conclusion.

Deism   Deism is the belief that God created the universe, but after the creation, God does not meddle in the affairs of the universe by answering prayers or violating the laws of nature by working miracles. It is unnecessary to suppose that God is omnibenevolent, omniscient, or omnipotent. The existence of God is invoked to explain the existence of the universe, but not to support belief in miracles. Historically, one of the most famous advocates of this view was the French philosopher Voltaire (1694–1778) whose most famous work was his novel *Candide,* in which he ridiculed Leibniz' belief that this is the best of all the possible worlds that God could have created (this was Leibniz' solution to the problem of evil).

Denotation   In logic the denotation of a word is what it refers to; for example, the name "Ronald Reagan" refers to the man who was President of the United States in 1988. Some words do not have a de-

notation, for example, the phrase "the present king of France."

Determinism   Determinism is the view that every event in the universe is caused by physical conditions or events that are a sufficient condition for the occurrence of the event. The opposite of determinism is *indeterminism,* the view that some events are not so caused, for example, God's creation of the universe from nothing, or an action resulting from the operation of the free will that is not itself caused to act. Determinism is not to be confused with *predestination,* the belief that God has chosen certain individuals for salvation or not.

Double-aspect theory   In the philosophy of Spinoza (1632–1677) there is only one infinite substance (God) that has an infinite number of attributes, two of which are mind and matter. Mind and matter are not themselves substances but are two different attributes or aspects of the one infinite substance.

Dualism   Dualism is the view that there are two different sorts of things that exist, material substances and mental substances or minds and ideas, and neither is reducible to the other. The opposite of dualism is *monism,* the theory that there is only one sort of thing that exists—something that is either mental or material or neutral (that is, neither mental nor material). The last view is called *neutral monism.* Dualists have different views about the relation between the mental and the material: *parallelism* is the view that they do not causally interact; *occasionalism* says that a material event is the occasion for God to cause a mental event; and *epiphenomenalism* holds that material events cause mental events, but not vice versa.

Efficient cause   In the philosophy of the Greek philosopher Aristotle (384–322 B.C.), the efficient cause of something is that which produces change or existence. To use Aristotle's own example, the father is the efficient cause of the child. Aristotle distinguishes three other causes—the material cause (that from which something is made, for example, the bronze of the statue), the formal cause (the shape or form into which something is changed, for example, a statue), and the final cause (the purpose for which something is done or the end aimed at, for example, a representation of Zeus.)

Ego   See Psychoanalytic theory.

Eliminative materialism   See Materialism.

Empiricist   An empiricist is one who accepts empiricism, the theory in epistemology that knowledge about the world, or knowledge of matters of fact, can be gained only from sensory observation. It denies that there are any innate ideas, ideas that we have independent of any experience. Empiricism is contrasted with *rationalism*, the view that knowledge about the world can be gained by the "natural light" of reasoning independent of experience. Locke is usually classified as an empiricist (although other empiricists are critical of many of his assumptions), and Descartes and Leibniz are held to be rationalists.

En soi   See Pour soi.

Epiphenomenalism   See Dualism.

Equivocation   In logic an equivocation is a fallacy of reasoning that occurs when one uses a word in more than one sense. For example, the following argument equivocates on the world "mad": "Joe was mad at his wife last night; mad people should be put in insane asylums; so Joe should be put in an insane asylum." A more controversial example is the argument used by conservatives to attack abortion: "A zygote is human; something human has a right to life; so the zygote has a right to life." Critics claim that the argument equivocates on the word "human"; in the first premise it means "genetically human" and in the second phrase it means "morally a person," or person in the sense of a being with rights.

Fideism   See Theism.

Functionalism   This is the view that mental states and events can be defined in terms of their functions, that is, their causal relations to each other and to physical events. Different physical systems could be functionally equivalent and thus have the same mental states and events. For example, silicon-based Martians or computers or human beings all could have pains or thoughts as they are functionally defined.

Hard determinism   This theory holds that determinism is true and applies to human actions or behavior (see Determinism) and that determinism is incompatible with human freedom, moral responsibility, and retributive punishment (punishment done for the sake of justice rather than for benefits to the individual or society). Sometimes those who hold this view are called *incompatibilists* because they accept the *incompatibilist thesis* that it is logically impossible for humans to be free or engage in free actions if determinism is true. Hard determinism is usually contrasted with *soft determinism,* the view that even though determinism is true when applied to human actions, it is compatible with some kind of freedom or some meaning of the word "free," for example, "free" as "not compelled" or "caused by volition" or "self-caused." Thus soft determinists, or compatibilists, accept the *compatibilist thesis* that it is logically possible for humans to be free or engage in free actions even if determinism is true.

Hedonism   Hedonism is a theory of value that says that pleasure, and only pleasure, is intrinsically good, and only pain is intrinsically bad. Other things may be good as a means to pleasure (instrumentally good). One of the classical versions of the theory is found in the writings of the Greek philosopher Epicurus (341–270 B.C.)—hence the theory is sometimes called Epicureanism. Epicurus emphasized the attainment of long-lasting pleasures such as those found in friendship and conversation, and the avoidance of pain by prudence and discipline. Hedonism was accepted by the utilitarians Bentham and Mill.

Id   See Psychoanalytic theory.

Idealism   Idealism is a metaphysical theory that says everything that exists is mental—either a mind or an idea—and denies that matter exists. Idealism is usually contrasted with materialism, the belief that everything that exists is physical.

Ideal utilitarianism   This ia a non-hedonistic form of utilitarianism that accepts other things besides pleasure as being good. In the version adopted by G. E. Moore, knowledge and beauty are considered to be intrinsically good, and some pleasant states of mind can be intrinsically bad.

Identity theory   This theory of mind holds that mental states and events are just brain states and events and nothing else, where this identity is an empirical matter and not one of logical necessity. Another way of putting it is to say that mental terms refer to the same thing as neurophysiological terms, that "pain" refers to the same thing as "such-and-such neuron firings in the brain," just as "lightning" and "electrical discharge" refer to the same thing.

Incompatibilist thesis   See Hard determinism.

Indeterminism   See Determinism.

Intrinsic versus instrumental good   Something is intrinsically good if it is good considered in and of itself, apart from any consequences. For example, hedonists believe that pleasure is intrinsically good. Something is instrumentally good if it is a means to something intrinsically good. For example, money may be used to obtain pleasure.

Invalid argument   See Valid argument.

Irenaean theodicy   This is the explanation of why God allows evil given by St. Irenaeus (about 130–202). Like St. Augustine, St. Irenaeus sees moral evil as resulting from free actions; natural evil is part of God's plan to perfect human character. In order for the plan to work, there has to be life after death, and every human being must eventually attain heaven.

Logical behaviorism   See Behaviorism.

Logical impossibility   A logical impossibility is a statement or state of affairs that involves a contradiction, for example, the statement "Something is both round and square" or the state of affairs of some object being both round and square. By contrast, a logical possibility is a statement or state of affairs that does not involve any contradiction.

Logical necessity   A logical necessity is a statement or state of affairs the denial of which involves a contradiction, for example, the statement "A circle is round" or a circle's being round.

Materialism   This is the view that everything that exists, every object or event, is a material object or event. This view is also called *physicalism* by contemporary philosophers (although sometimes the word "physicalism" is used to mean something not equivalent to materialism—that everything can be explained by the physical sciences). *Token physicalism* is the view that each particular mental state or event is a particular physical state or event, but it leaves open the possibility that different conscious beings, say silicon-based Martians and human beings, could have different physical states or events, for example, when they feel a pain. *Type physicalism* is the version of physicalism that holds that a kind of mental state or event is a certain kind of physical event. So a Martian and a human being could both have a pain only if the same kind of physical event occurs in both. These materialistic theories are reductionist in that they try to reduce mental states or events to physical ones. *Eliminative materialism* does not do this, but claims that the terms of ordinary psychological talk are part of a folk psychology that should be abandoned; these mentalistic terms do not refer to enti-

ties that are helpful or necessary in scientifically explaining behavior.

Megalomania   This term refers to infantile feelings of omnipotence that are usually restrained in later life.

Metaphysically certain   This is a technical term introduced by Feldman. As he explains it, a belief is metaphysically certain if we have no reason to doubt it. According to Feldman, it is what Descartes called an "absolutely certain" belief. Feldman contrasts this with a "practically certain" belief that we might have reason to doubt, but that is justified well enough for practical purposes. For example, we can be practically certain that our food is not poisoned, but not metaphysically certain. An example Feldman gives of a metaphysically certain belief is people's belief that they exist.

Methodological behaviorism   See Behaviorism.

Monism   See Dualism.

Necessary and sufficient conditions   A necessary condition for some thing or event is one without which the thing or event would not exist or occur. For example, the presence of oxygen is a necessary condition for human life. By contrast, a sufficient condition for something is one that guarantees the occurrence or presence of that thing or event. For instance, prolonged absence of oxygen is a sufficient condition for human death.

Necessary truth   See Contingent truth.

Neurosis   See Psychoanalytic theory.

Neutral monism   See Dualism.

Noncognitivism   This is the view that a statement or type of statement that is not verifiable or falsifiable does not make cognitive sense or does not have any truth value; it is neither true nor false. For example, in our readings Flew takes a noncognitivist position on the statement "God exists." A. J. Ayer (a contemporary English philosopher) and other philosophers in the logical positivist school of philosophy took a similar view of statements in ethics and metaphysics; such statements are factually meaningless because they are neither true by definition nor capable of empirical verification by making sensory observations.

Nondeterminism This is the view that humans are free and can engage in free actions that are not caused by antecedent physical events or conditions. Thus nondeterminists agree with hard determinists that determinism and freedom are incompatible (they both accept the incompatibilist thesis), but they deny that determinism is true for human actions.

Non sequitur This term refers to a fallacy of reasoning in which the conclusion is irrelevant to the premises, and the argument does not even appear to be valid. An example is the ad hominem fallacy where one attacks a person rather than the person's statements.

Occasionalism See Dualism.

Omnibenevolent To say that God is omnibenevolent, as traditional theists do, means that God is perfectly good both in action and in character; God always does the morally right thing, and God has all the virtues in the greatest possible degree and no vices. The traditional problem with this, as we see in chapter 2, is that God's goodness and omnipotence seem to be incompatible with the existence of evil in the world (and with the existence of eternal suffering in hell too.)

Omnipotent This term, which means "all-powerful," is one of God's attributes according to theism. As such it must be carefully explained to avoid contradictions. As theist philosophers interpret it, God's omnipotence does not allow God to do anything that conflicts with God's other attributes. For instance, God cannot do something wicked or stupid. Furthermore, God cannot do anything that is logically impossible or that involves a contradiction, for example, create a stone too heavy for God to lift or get up and sit down at the same time. Whether or not God can create something from nothing or create God's own self is controversial.

Omniscient Meaning "all knowing," this term is usually used to refer to one of God's attributes. At the very least we can say that God's omniscience means that God knows every truth and every falsehood. One problem that arises is that God's knowledge of what humans will do, called God's foreknowledge, seems to conflict with human freedom. If God knows everything we will do before we do it, then it seems that we cannot do otherwise, and do not have genuine freedom.

Ontological argument An ontological argument is an argument about God's existence. Kant is credited with calling Anselm's argument (or arguments) the "ontological argument," and most commentators follow his terminology.

Ontological parsimony This phrase means roughly "having as few beings as possible." There is an implicit reference to Ockham's razor, the principle that "entities are not to be multiplied beyond necessity." This principle is usually attributed to William of Ockham (1285–1349), although the standard formulation quoted here is not actually found in his writings.

Ontology Ontology is the philosophical study of existence or being or of the basic sorts of things that exist.

Pantheism Pantheism is the belief that God is Nature or the totality of everything that exists, that is, the whole universe. The Dutch metaphysician and pantheist Spinoza (1632–1677) held that God is the one all-inclusive substance. It follows that God could not be the creator of the universe in the way that this is usually understood (that is, as an "outside" or transcendent cause), since God *is* the universe.

Parallelism See Dualism.

Phenomenology This school of philosophy, founded by the German philosopher Edmund Husserl (1859–1938), tries to describe phenomena given in consciousness without any presuppositions and independent of external objects or events.

Positivism This term coined by the French philosopher Auguste Comte (1798–1857) refers to any philosophical theory (including his own) that rejects metaphysics as idle speculation. For Comte intellectual history has three stages: (1) a theological stage where events are explained by referring to the supernatural, (2) a metaphysical stage in which events are believed to result from fundamental energies or things, and (3) a positive stage where events are explained by using the method of science, that is, by making observations, formulating hypotheses, and conducting experiments. More recently, logical positivism is a school of philosophy that holds that metaphysical statements are nonsense because they are neither definitions nor subject to verification, and ethical statements are merely expressions of emotion that are neither true nor false.

Positivist A positivist is one who accepts some form of positivism. See Positivism.

Pour soi   In the philosophy of the French philosopher Jean-Paul Sartre (1905–1980) there are two types of being, *pour-soi* ("for-itself") and *en-soi* ("in-itself"). Being-for-itself is conscious or thinking existence, the sort of existence that human beings have, while being-in-itself is unconscious or unthinking existence, the sort of existence that objects like rocks have.

Premise   See Argument.

Principle of indeterminancy   This principle formulated by the German physicist Werner Heisenberg (1901–) states that it is impossible to determine both the position and the velocity of a subatomic particle such as an electron. The effect of this principle is to turn the laws of physics into statements of probabilities rather than certainties. The principle is usually called Heisenberg's Uncertainty Principle.

Principle of sufficient reason   This principle, originally stated by the German philosopher and mathematician Gottfried Wilhelm Leibniz (1646–1716), says that for every fact there must be a reason why it is and why it is so rather than otherwise. Leibniz used this principle to prove some rather interesting things, for example, that the world could not have begun at a moment in time.

Process theology   This term refers to a theory about God influenced by the English philosopher A. N. Whitehead (1861–1947) that emphasizes the processes of the universe. As Hick explains it, this theory holds that God is not unlimited in power and can influence the processes or ongoing events in the universe but cannot stop them or totally change them. God cannot, for example, violate the basic laws of the universe.

Psychoanalytic theory   This theory, founded and named by the Austrian psychiatrist Sigmund Freud (1856–1939), posits the existence of *the unconscious,* an active collection of various desires, thoughts, prohibitions, and so on, of which a person is not ordinarily aware, but that is an important influence on a person's behavior. Freud postulated the existence of the unconscious after he observed that the physical symptoms of hysterical patients sometimes disappeared after they remembered certain traumatic episodes. He used hypnosis and later free association and the analysis of dreams (interpreted as wish fulfillments) to study the unconscious. In the most developed statement of the theory Freud divided the unconscious into three parts: the *id,* the mass of instinctive drives for sex, food, and other things, ruled by the pleasure principle; the *superego,* the internalized prohibitions of parents that oppose the id drives, thus creating an ongoing unconscious conflict; and the partly conscious *ego* that mediates the id-superego conflicts and deals with the external world. *Neurosis* results from unresolved unconscious conflicts between the id and the superego, and it produces mental disorders such as anxiety, depression, and hysteria.

Rationalist   See Empiricist.

Reductio ad absurdum   This Latin term for "reduction to absurdity" refers to an argument that attempts to show that a given statement is false because it implies an absurd consequence. For example, consider this argument: If God did not exist, then the universe would not exist. But it is absurd to say that the universe does not exist. So it is false that God does not exist—God does exist.

Reincarnation   This term refers to rebirth in a different body. In Hinduism it is believed that the soul transmigrates to another body, so that the reborn person is the same person as the one who died. In Buddhism the existence of a permanent soul or self is denied; the reborn person may be similar to the one who died but is not numerically the same.

Resurrection   This word means "arising from death." In Christianity it is believed that Jesus rose from death to live forty days, after which he ascended into heaven. Jesus' resurrection is considered a guarantee that all dead humans will be in turn brought back to life on judgment day. This general resurrection is understood in different ways. According to St. Paul the dead will be resurrected with a "spiritual body" or a glorified body that is changed so that it is no longer mortal.

Sanctum sanctorum   "The most holy place."

Scepticism   This is the view that knowledge is not possible, where knowledge implies certainty. In the broad sense, it is the view that we cannot be certain about any belief, that we know nothing at all. In the narrow sense, it is applied to various areas that are doubtful; thus there is scepticism about God's existence, about the existence of external objects, about causality, and so on.

Sense-data (the singular is "sense-datum"). This technical term was introduced by the English philosopher G. E. Moore and adopted by Bertrand Russell and other twentieth-century philosophers. As Moore defined the term, "sense-data" refers to the direct objects of perception such as colors, shapes, pains, and after-images, and not to the physical objects that help cause us to have perceptual experiences. According to Moore, in perception we are only indirectly aware of physical objects; what we are directly aware of are sense-data. As we can see in the reading by Russell, the sense-data theory leads to scepticism about the existence and nature of external objects.

Solipsism Solipsism is the view that I am the only thing that independently exists, and that everything else exists merely as an object of my consciousness. There are no other persons or minds that exist besides me.

Sound argument A sound argument is a deductive argument that is valid and has true premises.

Stultitiam "Something foolish or absurd."

Subsistent entity In the philosophy of the Austrian philosopher Alexius von Meinong (1853–1928), a subsistent entity is one that has a mode of being different from ordinary existence in space and time. Subsistent existence was supposed to be possessed by numbers and universals (where universals are qualities that can be possessed by individuals, for example, the property of redness.)

Substance This term has more than one sense, but in the philosophy of the Greek philosopher Aristotle (384–322 B.C.) a thing is a substance if it can have attributes. Thus the color red is not a substance in this sense, but something red is a substance. Another definition is that a thing is a substance if it has an independent existence. For example, Aristotle said that a particular human being is a substance, while Spinoza thought that only God is a substance.

Superego See Psychoanalytic theory.

Tautology A tautology is a statement that is always true because of the logical form of the statement or the meaning of terms. Examples are "It is raining, or it is not raining" and "Circles are round."

Teleological argument A teleological argument is one that tries to show that God exists by appealing to design in the sense of goal or purpose in nature. Such an argument is also called an argument from design.

Theism Theism is the belief that a creator God who is omnipotent omniscient, and omnibenevolent can be known to exist by reasoning or experience. Theism is distinguished from fideism, the view that belief in God can be based on faith alone.

Token physicalism See Materialism.

Type physicalism See Materialism.

The Unconscious See Psychoanalytic theory.

Utilitarian This term refers to people who hold utilitarianism, a standard theory in ethics that uses the principle of utility to determine whether an act is morally right or wrong. This principle is formulated in different ways, but a standard version is this: Everyone ought to act so as to bring about the greatest good for the greatest number. Utilitarians do not agree about what is good or bad. Some of them, called hedonists, think that only pleasure is intrinsically good (good in itself), and that only pain is intrinsically bad. For example, the classic utilitarians Jeremy Bentham (1748–1832) and John Stuart Mill (1806–1873) were hedonistic utilitarians. Other utilitarians believe that satisfaction of one's desires is what is good and not having them satisfied is bad. They are called preference utilitarians.

Valid and invalid deductive argument In logic, a valid deductive argument is one in which the conclusion follows from the premises. It is logically impossible for the premises to be true and the conclusion false. Saying that the premises are true and the conclusion false involves a contradiction. An invalid deductive argument is one that is not valid, where the conclusion does not follow from the premises, and it is logically possible for the premises to be true and the conclusion false. Of course this is a technical use of the terms "valid" and "invalid" that should not be confused with ordinary language where "valid" is sometimes used to mean "true" and "invalid" used to mean "false." In logic premises and conclusions are true or false, but arguments are not; deductive arguments are said to be valid or invalid, but not true or false.

Index

and morality, 273
of nature, 142
Lehrer, Keith, 92
Leibniz, Gottfried
Wilhelm, 116, 117, 172
Leopold, Nathan, 133
Leviathan (Hobbes), 310
Libertarianism, 41, 160–61
Life after death
characteristics of, 249
and dualism, 221
and Geach, 221, 222
and Hick, 221
and memory, 221
and personal identity, 220
and Plato, 249
and Price, 221
purposes of, 64
and senses, 221
Limitation of independent
variety principle, of
Keynes, 126
Locke, John, 93–94, 110, 220,
232
Lodge, Oliver, 139
Loeb, Richard, 133
Logic, x, xi–xii
Logical behaviorism, 173, 192,
193. *See also* Behaviorism
Logical necessities, 67
Lower pleasures, 315–17. *See
also* Pleasure
Lunn, Arnold, 266

McCarthy, John, 198
Machine analogy, 174
Mackie, J. L., 61
Malcolm, Norman, 173
Malebranche, Nicolas de, 172
Materialism. *See also* Central-
state materialism;
Eliminative materialism
and atheism, 40–41
defined, 173
and experience, 215
and Feyerabend, 186
and functionalism, 196
and mental states, 213, 214
and objectivism, 213,
216*n*.15
Matter
and Berkeley, 115–16, 117
and body, 253
defined, 115, 116
and Leibniz, 116, 117

and mind, 115–16, 178, 183
and physical existence, 178
Matters of fact, 117, 118, 119
Means, using persons as, 333–
34, 335, 337–38, 339
Mediums, 252
Megalomania, defined, 152
Memory, 220, 221, 224, 253
Mental continuity,
defined, 222
Mental existence, 178, 182.
See also Existence
Mental states
and behavior, 187, 188, 209
and behaviorism, 193
and brain, 204, 215*n*.11
and causation, 193
characteristics of, 199, 203
and Davidson, 214
defined, 187, 190, 191
and disposition, 193, 194
and functionalism, 196
interactions of, 193, 194
and Kripke, 215*n*.11
and Malcolm, 173
and materialism, 213, 214
and Ryle, 173
Metaethics, defined, 258. *See
also* Morality
Metaphysically certain, 93
Metaphysics, defined, x
Methodological behaviorism,
defined, 173. *See also*
Behaviorism
Mill, John Stuart
and behavior, 146
and character, 145
and determinism, 141, 142
and freedom, 146
and happiness, 296
and necessity, 142
and utilitarianism, 297
Mind
and behavior, 187
and Berkeley, 115–16
and body, 175, 177–78, 183,
249
and brain, 184, 185, 186,
187, 191, 195, 197,
202, 203, 208–9
and causation, 203
characteristics of, 172, 175,
177, 181, 182, 183,
186, 191
as computer program, 197,

199, 200, 202–3
and consciousness, 249
and deception, 176
defined, 184, 186–87
and Descartes, 192
and disposition, 190
as ghost in the
machine, 182–83
and habit, 123
and Hume, 185, 187
and ideas, 111
and matter, 115–16, 178,
183
and objectivism, 213
and personal identity, 228,
235–42
and Ryle, 192
and semantics, 199, 200,
202
and syntax, 199, 200, 202
Mind-body problem, 172,
173. *See also* Descartes,
René
Minsky, Marvin, 198
Monism, 172, 192, 194
Moore, G. E., 148, 296
Moral evil, 52, 53, 60–61, 62.
See also Evil
Morality. *See also* Ethics
and atheism, 41–42
and behavior, 141, 145
and chance, 160
characteristics of, 83, 258,
267
and contra-causal
freedom, 158
and cultural relativism, 278–
79, 280, 282–83
defined, 272
and determinism, 141
and Foot, 267
and freedom, 141, 158
and God, 265, 266, 267,
273, 275–76
and Kant, 38, 298
and laws, 273
and Mortimer, 273
and motivation, 272
and religion, 271, 272–73,
276
and responsibility, 157–58,
159, 160
and soft determinism, 141,
156
and truth, 278, 279